THE PRINCIPLES OF ROMAN LAW

AND

THEIR RELATION TO MODERN LAW

BY

WILLIAM L. BURDICK
Professor of Law and Dean Emeritus
University of Kansas

THE LAWBOOK EXCHANGE, LTD.
Clark, New Jersey

ISBN 9781584772538 (hardcover)
ISBN 9781616192556 (paperback)

Lawbook Exchange edition 2004, 2012

The quality of this reprint is equivalent to the quality of the original work.

THE LAWBOOK EXCHANGE, LTD.
33 Terminal Avenue
Clark, New Jersey 07066-1321

Please see our website for a selection of our other publications and fine facsimile reprints of classic works of legal history:
www.lawbookexchange.com

Library of Congress Cataloging-in-Publication Data

Burdick, William L. (William Livesey), 1860-1946.
    The principles of Roman law and their relation to modern law/by William L. Burdick.
      p. cm.
    Originally published: Rochester, N.Y. : Lawyers Co-operative Pub. Co., c1938.
    Includes bibliographical references and index.
    ISBN 1-58477-253-0 (cloth: alk. paper)
      1. Roman law. 2. Common law. 3. Civil law—United States. I. Title.

KJA 160 .B87 2002
340.5'4—dc21   2002025946

Printed in the United States of America on acid-free paper

THE PRINCIPLES OF ROMAN LAW

AND

THEIR RELATION TO MODERN LAW

BY

WILLIAM L. BURDICK
Professor of Law and Dean Emeritus
University of Kansas

THE LAWYERS CO-OPERATIVE PUBLISHING CO
ROCHESTER, NEW YORK

Copyright 1938
by
WILLIAM L. BURDICK

AFFECTIONATELY DEDICATED

TO

MY COLLEAGUES

AND

STUDENTS PAST AND PRESENT

OF THE

KANSAS UNIVERSITY LAW SCHOOL

PREFACE

This book is an attempt to show the relation of Roman Law principles to modern law, including the present day Civil Law, the English Common Law, and the law of our American states. It is intended not only for lawyers and law students, but also for all who may be interested in the story of the development of law. It seeks to emphasize the fact that Roman Law is not dead, not a mere matter of ancient legal history, but is still alive and even yet influences and molds law in all parts of the world.

Years ago in conversation with the distinguished James Bryce, then Professor of Roman Law at Oxford, the writer expressed his admiration of that eminent scholar's ability as a teacher. Professor Bryce, with the modesty that always characterized him, replied: "I hesitate to profess being a 'teacher' of such a vast subject as Roman Law. I am only trying to teach it, or rather a part of it." The writer never forgot those words in his subsequent efforts for more than twenty years to impart instruction in that field, and he fully realizes that all that can be attempted in a work like the present volume is to deal with the elementary principles of Roman Law. He hopes, however, that the book will be of interest to his readers, refreshing the memory of some, supplementing the information of others, and calling the attention of students of our own law to the importance of Roman Law as a great source of legal learning. For that law is the parent of the present law of most of continental Europe, of the Latin countries of the western hemisphere, and of the modern codes of Turkey, China, and

Japan. It is also the too often unappreciated and even rejected cornerstone of many legal doctrines in our own law.

The principles of Roman Law herein set forth are all taken, at first hand, from the authoritative Latin texts, including the Institutes, Digest, Codex, and Novels of the Corpus Juris Civilis, the Institutes of Gaius, the Sententiae of Paulus, the writings of Cicero, and of various other jurists and authors who preceded Justinian. In furtherance of the effort to show the influence of Roman Law upon our own law, the English and American reports have been searched for references to this system of jurisprudence, and many cases discovered in this search are cited herein in connection with the text.

WM. L. BURDICK

The University of Kansas,
December, 1938.

TABLE OF CONTENTS

CHAPTER
I. THE WORLD WIDE EXTENSION OF ROMAN LAW 1
II. THE CIVIL LAW IN THE UNITED STATES AND CANADA 35
III. THE INFLUENCE OF ROMAN LAW UPON ENGLISH LAW 56
IV. OUTLINES OF ROMAN LAW HISTORY 87
From the Founding of the City to the Beginning of the Empire.
V. OUTLINES OF ROMAN LAW HISTORY, *Continued* 119
The Empire to the Death of Justinian.
VI. THE CORPUS JURIS CIVILIS 155
VII. THE LAW OF PERSONS.
A. Introduction 180
B. Status of Persons 183
VIII. THE LAW OF PERSONS, *Continued* 212
Marriage; Husband and Wife; Divorce.
IX. THE LAW OF PERSONS, *Continued*.
A. Parent and Child 241
B. Guardian and Ward 262
X. ARTIFICIAL PERSONS OR CORPORATIONS 274
XI. THE LAW OF PROPERTY 298
Introduction, Divisions of Property.

CHAPTER

XII. THE LAW OF PROPERTY, *Continued* 324
   The Acquisition of Property.

XIII. THE LAW OF PROPERTY, *Continued* 354
   Jura in Re Aliena.

XIV. THE LAW OF OBLIGATIONS 386
   General Principles.

XV. THE LAW OF OBLIGATIONS, *Continued* ... 410
   Causa; Culpa; Joint Obligations.

XVI. THE LAW OF OBLIGATIONS, *Continued* ... 431
   Contracts.

XVII. THE LAW OF OBLIGATIONS, *Continued* ... 462
   Innominate Real Contracts; Pacts; Quasi-Contracts.

XVIII. THE LAW OF OBLIGATIONS, *Continued* ... 485
   Delicts and Quasi Delicts.

XIX. THE LAW OF OBLIGATIONS, *Continued* 515
   Dissolution.

XX. THE LAW OF SUCCESSION 546
   Intestate Succession.

XXI. THE LAW OF SUCCESSION, *Continued* ... 577
   Testamentary Succession.

XXII. THE LAW OF ACTIONS 626

XXIII. THE LAW OF PUBLIC WRONGS 676

TABLE OF CASES CITED

References are to pages.

A.

Abbott v. Godfroy's Heirs (Mich.) 46
Adams v. Norris (U. S.) 587
Aguilar v. Lazaro (Philippine) 217
Aldrich v. Hunter (Mass.) 340
Allen v. Moss (Mo.) 44
Altuna v. Ortiz (P. R.) 230
American Ins. Co. v. Canter (U. S.) 50
Amy v. Smith (Ky.) 201
Antelope, The (U. S.) 186
Arias v. Registrar (P. R.) 230
Arnott v. Kansas Pac. Ry. Co. (Kan.) 318
Arnott v. Ry. Co. (Kan.) 340
Atty. Gen. v. Moore (Eng.) 336
Axtmayer, Ex parte (P. R.) 52

B.

Ball v. Bender (La.) 428
Banks v. Haskee (Md.) 377
Bardes v. Herman (N. Y.) 181
Barlin v. Ramirez (Philippine) 321
Barnard v. Adams (U. S.) 335
Barnett v. Barnett (N. M.) 49
Barrow v. Landry (La.) 364
Bates v. Brown (U. S.) 575
Baxter v. Mohr (N. Y.) 210
Beall v. Beall (Ga.) 245
Beard v. Poydras (La.) 15, 40, 42
Beauregard v. Piernas (La.) 268
Bechervaise v. Lewis (Eng.) 7
Bellows v. Sackett (N. Y.) 369
Benedicto v. de la Rama (Philippine) 15, 52
Bennett, Re (Cal.) 212
Bigelow v. Porto Rico Planters Co. (P. R.) 413
Bird v. Montgomery (Mo.) 44
Birthwhistle v. Vardill (Eng.) 246
Bosler v. Kuhn (Pa.) 377
Boucier v. Lanux (La.) 42
Boyd v. Conklin (Mich.) 366
Bradhurst v. Columbian Ins. Co. (N. Y.) 452

Brawn v. Lyford (Me.) 410
Bray v. Miles (Ind.) 252
Breidenstein v. Bertram (Mo.) 245
Brian v. Bonvillain (La.) 273
Bright v. Boyd (Fed.) 340, 475
Bringloe v. Morrice (Eng.) 439
Brown v. Gerald (Me.) 181
Brush v. Beecher (Mich.) 377
Bryant v. Bryant (N. C.) 196
Buchanan v. Kennard (Mo.) 295
Bulkley v. Honold (U. S.) 446

C.

Cahoon v. Miers (Md.) 338, 380
Caldwell v. Hall (Miss.) 318, 434
Campbell v. Lambert & Co. (La.) 410
Campbell's Appeal (Conn.) 567
Canal Appraisers v. People (N. Y.) 39, 51
Carroll v. Carroll (Tex.) 45
Carroll v. Waters (La.) 417
Carter v. Crawley (Eng.) 575
Cartwright v. Cartwright (Tex.) 188, 356, 384
Casalla v. Enage (Philippine) 230
Casey v. Cavaroc (U. S.) 380
Cater v. N. W. Teleph. Co. (Minn.) 362
C. B. Sanford, The (Fed.) 657, 674
Charlotte v. Chouteau (Mo.) 194
Chavez, Re (Fed.) 49
Chavez v. McKnight (N. M.) 49
Chenot v. Lefevre (Ill.) 529
Cheshire v. Burlington (Conn.) 212
Childress v. Waddingham (Mo.) 44
Christy v. Casanane (La.) 449
Church of Jesus Christ v. U. S. (U. S.) 295
Clark v. Clark (N. H.) 252
Clarkson v. Hatton (Mo.) 252
Coates v. Hughes (Pa.) 7
Coffey, Re (Cal.) 211
Coffin v. United States (U. S.) 692
Coggs v. Bernard (Eng.) 55, 434, 439, 458
Colburn v. Harvey (Wis.) 46
Coles v. Perry (Tex.) 45, 382
Colt v. McMechen (N. Y.) 482
Columbian Ins. Co. v. Ashby (U. S.) 452
Columbus, etc., Ry. v. Gaffney (Ohio) 475
Com. v. Shaver (Pa.) 210
Copley v. Flint (La.) 447

TABLE OF CASES CITED xiii

Corvallis, etc., R. Co. v. Benson (Or.) 181
Cottin v. Cottin (La.) 42
County of St. Clair v. Livingston (U. S.) 339
Cowan v. Stamps (Miss.) 194
Crane v. Reeder (Mich.) 46
Crespin v. United States (U. S.) 697
Crockett v. Madison (La.) 574
Culbreath v. Culbreath (Ga.) 475
Cumberland Glass Mfg. Co. v. DeWitt (U. S.) 544
Currie v. Assurance Society (Va.) 4
Curry, Re (Cal.) 575
Cutter v. Waddingham (Mo.) 40, 44, 575

D.

Dalton v. Angus (Eng.) 355
Danielson v. Roberts (Or.) 336
Danielson v. Wilson (Ill.) 212
Darling v. Wilson (N. H.) 338
Davis v. Baugh (Tenn.) 591
Davis v. Carey (Pa.) 210
Davis v. Shaw (La.) 439
Decoster v. Wing (Me.) 575
De Lovio v. Boit (Fed.) 76, 674
Delpit v. Young (La.) 41
Derepas v. Shallus (La.) 273
Diamond v. Harris (Tex.) 45
Dockum v. Robinson (N. H.) 588
Dorvin v. Wiltz (La.) 544
Douglass v. Ritchie (Mo.) 195
Dred Scott Case (U. S.) 194
Duclaud v. Rousseau (La.) 383
Duncan v. Crook (Mo.) 273
Duncan v. Magette (Tex.) 181
Dunham v. Williams (N. Y.) 51
Dunscomb v. Dunscomb (N. Y.) 267
Dupre's Succession (La.) 251

E.

Eagan v. Call (Pa.) 446
Ebreo v. Sichon (Philippine) 15, 17, 52
Eckford v. Knox (Tex.) 251, 252
Ector v. Grant (Ga.) 567
Eddy v. Livingston (Mo.) 458
Edwards v. Turner (La.) 514
Effinger v. Lewis (Pa.) 377
Eglauch v. Labadie (Canada) 383
Eingartner v. Ill. Steel Co. (Wis.) 530
Ellerson v. Westcott (N. Y.) 609
Ellis v. Craig (N. Y.) 406, 519

xiv   TABLE OF CASES CITED

Entick v. Carrington (Eng.) 490
Export v. Meason (Pa.) 212

F.

Fable v. Brown (S. C.) 7
False v. Triche (La.) 323
Farkas v. Towns (Ga.) 365
Ferguson v. Ray (Or.) 336
Ferris v. Public Administrator (N. Y.) 216
Fisk v. Fisk (La.) 384
Fleckner v. Bank of U. S. (U. S.) 42
Fordyce v. Woman's Christian Nat. Library Ass'n (Ark.) 295
Fortier, Re (La.) 273
Fosdick v. Green (Ohio) 434
Fowler v. Smith (Cal.) 47, 48
Fox, Re (N. Y.) 578
Friendly v. Olcott (Or.) 201
Frost-Johnson Lumber Co. v. Salling's Heirs (La.) 372, 373

G.

Gaines v. Chew (U. S.) 625
Gaines v. Hennen (U. S.) 243
Garcia v. Del Rosario (Philippine) 220
Gayle v. Cunningham (S. C.)   6
Geer v. Connecticut (U. S.) 334
Gibbs v. Usher (Fed.) 436
Gillham v. Madison Co. R. Co. (Ill.) 365
Gilman v. Illinois, etc., Tel. Co. (U. S.) 54, 379
Girard v. New Orleans (La.) 322
Gray v. Holmes (Kan.) 252
Gray v. McWilliams (Cal.) 365
Great Northern Railway v. Johnson (Fed.) 228
Green v. Biddle (U. S.) 338
Griggs v. Austin (Mass.) 12
Grove, Re (Eng.) 246
Groves v. Sentell (U. S.) 41
Guerin's Heirs v. Bagneries (La.) 42
Guerra v. Porto Rico Treasurer (P. R.) 413
Guess v. Lubbock (Tex.) 188, 194
Gurley v. New Orleans (La.) 461

H.

Hall v. Hall (Ala.) 194
Hanes v. Shapiro (N. C.) 458
Hardison v. Reel (N. C.) 410
Harmon v. Harmon (Cal.) 234
Harper v. Terry (La.) 484
Harrison v. Boring (Tex.) 354
Hart v. Hoss (La.) 244

Harvey v. Walters (Eng.) 369
Hayes v. Berwick (La.) 42
Head v. Head (Ga.) 234
Hecht v. Batcheller (Mass.) 402
Hellwig v. West (La.) 230
Henslee v. Boyd (Tex.) 354
Hernandez v. Hermanos (P. R.) 337
Hertzog v. Hertzog (Pa.) 475
Hockaday v. Lynn (Mo.) 252
Hodges v. Hodges (N. M.) 234
Hodges v. U. S. (U. S.) 186
Holliday v. West (Cal.) 48
Houghton v. Dickinson (Mass.) 245
Hubbard v. Hubbard (N. Y.) 587
Huie v. Bailey (La.) 410
Humphrys v. Polak (Eng.) 252
Huthmacher v. Harris (Pa.) 336
Hutson v. Jordan (U. S.) 673, 674
Hyderabad, The (Fed.) 335

I.

Ingersoll v. Sergeant (Pa.) 377
Inglis v. Trustees (U. S.) 295
Insurance Co. v. Dunham (U. S.) 70

J.

Jackson v. Phillips (Mass.) 295
Jeffries v. East Land Co. (U. S.) 339
Jenkins v. Tom (Va.) 196
Jennison v. Warmack (La.) 3
Johnson v. Reynolds (Kan.) 417, 440
Jones, Re (Cal.) 246
Jones v. Steamship Cortes (Cal.) 673
Jones v. Wootten (Del.) 195

K.

Kaskaskia v. McClure (Ill.) 11
Kauffman v. Griesemer (Pa.) 364
Keegan v. Geraghty (Ill.) 252
Kelsey v. Hardy (N. H.) 575
Ker v. Cauden (Philippine) 15, 52
Kirby, Re (S. D.) 211
Kirby-Carpenter Co. v. Burnett (Fed.) 410
Klumpert v. Vrieland (Iowa) 295
Knoop v. Blaffer (La.) 514
Knowlton v. Moore (U. S.) 576
Kraft v. Egan (Md.) 377
Krant v. Crawford (Iowa) 339
Kunemann's Succession (La.) 574

TABLE OF CASES CITED

L.

Lamphere, Matter of (Mich.)	46
Lander, Re (N. Y.)	575
Lane v. Cotton (Eng.)	5, 7, 58
Langdeau v. Hanes (U. S.)	47
Larkin v. U. S. (Fed.)	300
Larned v. Renshaw (Mo.)	273
Laumier v. Francis (Mo.)	354
Lavella v. Strobel (Ill.)	46
Lee v. Sprague (Mo.)	195
Leitensdorfer v. Webb (N. M.)	17, 49, 206
Lerma v. Mamaril (Philippine)	217
Lickbarrow v. Mason (Eng.)	77
Livermore v. White (Me.)	335, 336
Livingston v. McDonald (Iowa)	4, 7
Livingston v. Story (U. S.)	4, 41, 42, 383
Logan v. Herbert (La.)	353
Longwith v. Butler (Ill.)	54, 379
Lorman v. Benson (Mich.)	46
Lovell v. Cragin (U. S.)	514
Lovell v. Stroble (Ill.)	46
Lumpkin v. Mills (Ga.)	4, 54
Lyon v. Crego (Mich.)	567

M.

McCall v. Irion (La.)	353
McCann v. Telephone Co. (Kan.)	362
McClurg v. Brenton (Iowa)	490
McCormick v. Kansas City, etc., R. Co. (Mo.)	364
McCreery v. Davis (S. C.)	234
McDonough's Executors v. Murdoch (U. S.)	625
McEmery v. Pargoud (La.)	321
McKinney v. Abbott (Tex.)	575
McLaughlin v. Waite (N. Y.)	336
McLean v. McLean (Kan.)	246
McNair v. Lott (Mo.)	383
McSorley v. Faulkner (N. Y.)	475
Macurty v. Bagnieres (La.)	446
Maddock v. Riggs (Kan.)	458
Magoun v. Bank (U. S.)	578
Magoun v. Illinois Trust & Savings Bank (U. S.)	576
Marguerite v. Chouteau (Mo.)	196
Markover v. Krauss (Ind.)	252
Marquise E. Portes v. Hurlbut (N. J.)	383
Martin v. Jett (La.)	364
Mathurin v. Livaudais (La.)	620
May v. Rumney (Mich.)	46
Mayor of City of Albany v. Sikes (Ga.)	4, 7

TABLE OF CASES CITED

Mazone v. Caze (La.) 348
Means v. Robinson (Tex.) 272
Merrit v. Johnson (N. Y.) 339, 340
Mexican Central Ry. Co. v. Marshall (Fed.) 45
Michoud v. Girod (U. S.) 41
Millard v. McMullin (N. Y.) 377
Miller v. Fox (Tenn.) 524
Miller v. Miller (N. Y.) 51, 245
Miller v. Pennington (Ill.) 245
Miller v. Schloss (N. Y.) 475
Mills v. Wyman (Mass.) 410
Minor v. Hoppersett (U. S.) 201
Mirkil v. Morgan (Pa.) 364
Missouri Pac. Ry. Co. v. Goodholm (Kan.) 524
Mitchel v. United States (U. S.) 50
Mitchell v. Merrill (Ind.) 520
Mitchell v. Tuckers (Mo.) 44, 352
Mogadara v. Holt (Eng.) 305
Monget v. Tessier (La.) 273
Montgomery v. Evans (Ga.) 458
Monton v. Noble (La.) 410
Moore v. Davey (N. M.) 49
Moore v. Shaw (Cal.) 47
Morales v. Registrar (P. R.) 52
Morgan v. Livingston (La.) 339
Morgan v. Yarborough (La.) 220
Morgan R. R. & S. S. Co., Re (La.) 325
Morrison v. Estate of Sessions (Mich.) 251
Morton Trust Co. v. American Salt Co. (Fed.) 322
Moses v. Macferlan (Eng.) 475
Moussier v. Zunts (La.) 322, 382
Mouton v. Noble (La.) 413, 424
Mubry v. Norton (N. Y.) 339
Municipality v. Cotton Press (La.) 339
Munro v. Munro (Eng.) 246
Murphy v. Murphy (Iowa) 246
Mussina v. Alling (La.) 4

N.

Nakdimen v. Atkinson Improv. Co. (Ark.) 377
National Bank of Com. v. Sullivan (La.) 322
Neal v. Farmer (Ga.) 195
Neale v. Sealey (N. Y.) 369
Nebraska v. Iowa (U. S.) 339
Nellis v. Munson (N. Y.) 312
New England Mut. Mar. Ins. Co. v. Dunham (U. S.) 674
New Orleans v. Bank (La.) 514
New Orleans v. Camp (La.) 41

xviii TABLE OF CASES CITED

Nigro, Re (Cal.) 567
Nininger v. Norwood (Ala.) 366
Nott v. Hill (Eng.) 447

O.

Oakland v. Oakland Water Front Co. (Cal.) 181
Orleans Navigation Co. v. Mayor of New Orleans (La.) 425
Ortega v. Lara (U. S.) 52
Osborn v. Nicholson (U. S.) 444
Owings v. Hull (U. S.) 41

P.

P. v. Cullen (N. Y.) 234
Panaud v. Jones (Cal.) 17, 47, 49
Parsons v. Bedford (U. S.) 41
Parsons v. Moses (Iowa) 475
Pattison v. Hull (N. Y.) 520
Paul v. Carter (N. C.) 567
Pavesich v. New England Life Ins. Co. (Ga.) 502
Payne v. Gardner (N. Y.) 434
Pearson v. Pearson (Cal.) 192
Peck v. Herrington (Ill.) 365
Peirce v. Goddard (Mass.) 338
Pelloat's Succession (La.) 574
Penniman v. French (Mass.) 314, 322
People v. Ruggles (N. Y.) 181
Perrillat v. Puech (La.) 514
Pettus v. Dawson (Tex.) 242
Pick v. Pick (Neb.) 234
Pickersgill v. Brown (La.) 383
Pittsburgh, etc., R. Co. v. Ferrell (Ind.) 514
Planters' Bank v. George (La.) 42
Police Jury v. Hampton (La.) 476
Ponce v. Roman Cath. Apostolic Church (U. S.) 52
Portis v. Hill (Tex.) 623
Power v. Hafley (Ky.) 252
Prescott v. Carr (N. H.) 575
President of Kaskaskia v. McClure (Ill.) 46
Prince v. Hazleton (N. Y.) 587
Pringle v. McPherson (S. C.) 212
Pulcifer v. Page (Me.) 338, 340
Pullman's Palace Car Co. v. Central Transp. Co. (Fed.) 210

R.

Race v. Oldridge (Ill.) 212
Race v. Ward (Eng.) 355
Raffles v. Wichelhaus (Eng.) 402
Rahilly v. Wilson (Fed.) 318, 434
Ralli v. Troop (U. S.) 335

TABLE OF CASES CITED xix

Rann v. Hughes (Eng.) 410
Reinders v. Koppelmann (Mo.) 252
Reynolds v. Swayne (La.) 42
Richardson v. Futrell (Miss.) 458
Riddick v. Walsh (Mo.) 15, 44
Riggs v. Palmer (N. Y.) 609
Robinson v. Ruprecht (Ill.) 245
Rockingham v. Mount Holly (Vt.) 245
Rolli v. Troop (U. S.) 121
Ross v. Ross (Mass.) 251
Rountree v. Pursell (Ind.) 575

S.

St. L. Ry. Co. v. Mo. Ry. Co. (Mo.) 339
Samuels v. Brownlee (La.) 384
Sanguinetti v. Pock (Cal.) 364
Santiago v. Water Co. (Cal.) 47
Scott v. Ward (Cal.) 15, 47
Seguin v. Maverick (Tex.) 45
Sharp v. Fly (Tenn.) 525
Sharpe v. Sharpe (Mo.) 234
Sheffield v. Lovering (Mass.) 575
Silsbury v. McCoon (N. Y.) 342
Singerland v. Morse (N. Y.) 520
Smith, Re (Kan.) 211
Smith v. Braun (La.) 220
Smith v. Madison (Mo.) 44
Smith v. Rentz (N. Y.) 51
Smith v. St. Louis Public Schools (Mo.) 339
Smith v. Smith (La.) 573
Smith v. Smith (Tex.) 45
Snedeker v. Waring (N. Y.) 121, 132
Southern R. Co. v. Lewis (Ala.) 364
Sparke v. Denne (Eng.) 322
Spigener v. Cooner (S. C.) 335
Standard Oil Co. v. Codina Arenas (Philippine) 413
Star, The (U. S.) 206
State v. Alston (Tenn.) 576
State v. Clark (Kan.) 210
State v. Greer (Mo.) 273
State v. Guthrie (Me.) 490
State v. Mason (Or.) 210
State v. Snure (Minn.) 514
State v. Van Waggoner (N. J.) 196
Stead v. Presidente (Ill.) 46
Stevenson v. Sullivant (U. S.) 242, 245
Stewart v. Harper (La.) 544
Strausse v. Sheriff (La.) 384

XX   TABLE OF CASES CITED

Strong v. Eakin (N. M.) 49
Strong v. White (Conn.) 322
Succession of Richmond (La.) 479
Succession of Justus (La.) 573
Succession of McCan (La.) 625
Succession of Meunier (La.) 620
Suzanna, Ex parte (Fed.) 228
Swetland v. Curtiss Airports Corporation (Fed.) 74, 175

T.

Taylor v. Wooten (La.) 410
Thickstun v. Howard (Ind.) 482
Thomas v. Osborn (U. S.) 674
Thomasson v. State (Ind.) 201
Thompson v. Duncan (Tex.) 304
Thompson v. Riggs (U. S.) 434
Thorne, Matter of (N. Y.) 251
Thurston v. Hancock (Mass.) 366
Tisdale v. Harris (Mass.) 300
Totel v. Bonnefoy (Ill.) 365
Townsend v. Jemison (U. S.) 344
Tyler v. Heidorn (N. Y.) 377

U.

United States v. City of Santa Fe (U. S.) 17
United States v. Dorr (Philippine) 52
United States v. Fox (U. S.) 578
United States v. Midway Northern Oil Co. (Fed.) 340
United States v. Rice (U. S.) 206
United States v. Wonson (Fed.) 675

V.

Van Giesen v. Bridgeford (N. Y.) 51
Van Rensselaer v. Hays (N. Y.) 377
Venus, The (U. S.) 206
Vidol v. Commagere (La.) 252
Villegracia v. Vlibare (Philippine) 413
Viterbo v. Friedlander (U. S.) 444
Von Schmidt v. Huntington (Cal.) 47

W.

Wall v. Pfanschmidt (Ill.) 575
Walworth's Estate, Re (Vt.) 252
Waring v. Mason (N. Y.) 446
Warner v. Beers (N. Y.) 274, 281
Warren v. Chambers (Ark.) 339
Weeks v. Hackett (Me.) 336
Wells v. Lane (N. Y.) 192
Wemple v. Nabors Oil & Gas Co. (La.) 304

Wentz v. Chicago, etc., R. Co. (Mo.) 212
Westbrook v. Mitchell (Tex.) 187
Wetherbee v. Green (Mich.) 342
Wheeler v. Insurance Co. (U. S.) 38, 379
Whitaker v. Hawley (Kan.) 43
White v. Clements (Ga.) 201, 202
White v. Gay's Ex'rs (Tex.) 15
White v. Sheriff (La.) 353
White v. White (Eng.) 295
Wickham v. Hawker (Eng.) 355
Wiggins v. City of Chicago (Ill.) 514
Williams v. Conger (U. S.) 460
Wilson, Ex parte (U. S.) 210
Winter v. Landphere (Iowa) 338
Woodman v. Fulton (Miss.) 530
Woodward v. Squires (Iowa) 514
Woodward's Appeal (Conn.) 241, 251
Wright's Adm'r v. Thomas (Mo.) 44
Wylly v. Collins (Ga.) 226

Z.

Ziegler, Matter of (N. Y.) 251, 253

PRINCIPLES OF ROMAN LAW

CHAPTER I

THE WORLD WIDE EXTENSION OF ROMAN LAW

The Roman Empire as a political organization passed away centuries ago, but Roman jurisprudence through its influence still remains a world power. In its modernized form Roman Law has become the law of more than three-fourths of the civilized globe, and Gibbon's words written in the eighteenth century,[1] "the laws of Justinian still command the respect or obedience of independent nations," are even more significant today than then.

Prominent among the outstanding causes that have made Roman Law dominant are its equity and its universal adaptability. It is the later Roman Law of which this is said, the law developed by the Roman judges, or praetors, and known as the jus gentium or the praetorian law in distinction from the more ancient law known as the jus civile. The latter was quite a different law and was restricted entirely to Roman citizens.

As Rome expanded, her genius for government be-

---

1. Decline and Fall of the Roman Empire, Ch. 44.

came more and more manifest. In time, she became great, and, later, colossal. As a world power history has yet to see her equal. Her ability to govern races and peoples of every type, greatly differing from each other in character and civilization, was marvelous. It is far from the truth to say that her government was merely a despotic military power. She ruled, indeed, with an iron hand where it was necessary, but Rome was also an adept in the art of diplomacy. The secret of her governmental power was not that her armies conquered the world, for other great conquerors before and since have done that, but for centuries she held together her conquered peoples. They did not, as in the case of Alexander, pass from her control upon the death of her great military commanders, but she organized and long retained under one central power many subdued races.

To understand Rome's greatness we must look beyond her warlike spirit and her great military leaders. Alexander and Hannibal were probably greater soldiers than Caesar and Scipio. It was Rome's genius for statesmanship, political organization, world wide law that made her great. The mind of the typical Roman of the intelligent class was what may be called the legal mind. It was logical, practical, just. It was free from misapplied sentiment. When in time, the Roman became a cosmopolitan, he also became the most scientific law giver the world has known, sensible, equitable, tolerant, broad-minded.

It is, perhaps, in the universality of its application, that the genius of the Roman Law is best appreciated. The customary laws of most peoples are restricted to themselves and, hence, *local*. Hebrew Law, for example, was for the Hebrews, and not for the gentiles. Early English Law was for the English, an insular

[Roman Law]

and isolated people. The early law of Rome, the jus civile, was likewise the law of the Romans alone, the citizen dwellers of the city of Rome; but the later Roman Law, the old law as shaped and moulded by the jus gentium, became the law for the entire Roman Empire and was developed for the needs of a world.

The ancient law of Rome, the jus civile, furnished, however, the term, "the Civil Law," that is used in modern times to designate the system of law of those countries which base their jurisprudence upon the Roman Law. In this sense the term is used in contradistinction to "English Law."[2] In our English Law the word "civil" is used in a special sense, in contrast with the words "military" and "criminal," as "civil law," or "civil jurisdiction" in distinction from "military law," "criminal law," or "criminal jurisdiction." In the Roman or Latin sense, however, civil law (jus civile) is the entire system of law, including all its branches, that a people or a state (civitas) establishes for itself.[3] It is a nation's own peculiar law in distinction from the law of nature (jus naturale), or from the law or customs of mankind in general (jus gentium) in connection with their mutual relations.[4]

The fairness or equity of Roman Law is also another cause of its enduring influence. In England, two systems of jurisprudence, namely, law and equity, grew up side by side, and separate courts presided over by separate judges were, in time, organized. The most notable thing, in fact, in the history of our law during the past century has been the gradual merger or coalescing of these two systems. In the Roman Law, however, there is no discrimination between "law"

2. Jennison v. Warmack, 5 La. 493.
3. Dig. 1, 1, 9.
4. Dig. 1, 1, 1, 4.

and "equity,"[5] because, in theory, it is all equity.[6] The phrase "Ex bono et aequo," "right and fair," was often upon the lips of Roman praetors as they developed the jus gentium which eventually became the prevailing law. The Digest of Justinian defines law (jus) as "the art of what is right and fair" (ars boni et aequi, Dig. 1, 1, 1, pr.); and the Institutes (I. 1, 1) define justice (justitia) as "the constant and perpetual desire to render every one his due." The elements of fairness, good faith, and morality are much more discernible in the later Roman Law than in the English Common Law. As Judge Dillon said,[7] "The Civil Law is often of great service to the inquirer after principles of natural justice and right." The Roman or Civil Law has also been designated as the law of *justice* or of right in contrast with the Common Law of England as the law of force.[8]

Blackstone defined municipal law, meaning by that term the laws of a state or nation, to be "a rule of civil conduct prescribed by the supreme power in a state commanding what is right and prohibiting what is wrong."[9] Mr. Justice Roane of the Court of Appeals of Virginia, however, has said:[10] "It is evident that this definition of municipal law is by far too limited and narrow. I would rather adopt the definition of Justinian, that civil or municipal law, is 'quod quisque populus sibi constituit,'[11] bounded only in this country,

5. Baldwin, J., in Livingston v. Story, 11 Pet. (U. S.) 351, 393. See, also, Livingston v. Story, 9 Pet. (U. S.) 632, 637; Mussina v. Alling, 11 La. Ann. 568, 572.
6. This refers, of course, to the jus gentium. It took 500 years for the jus gentium to replace the jus civile. "The Roman Law is the source of many of our principles of Equity."—Lumpkin v. Mills, 4 Ga. 343.
7. Livingston v. McDonald, 21 Iowa 160.
8. See e. g. Mayor of City of Albany v. Sikes, 94 Ga. 30, 20 S. E. 257.
9. Com., Introduction.
10. Currie v. Assurance Society, 4 Hening & Munford (Va.) 315.
11. "The law which any people establishes for itself" (Inst. 1, 2, 1).

in relation to legislative acts, by the constitutions of the general and state governments, and limited also by considerations of justice."

Many are the tributes spontaneously paid by jurists and scholars to the genius of the Roman Law. Especially do they praise its broad, equitable principles and recognize the great influence that Roman Law has had upon modern jurisprudence and civilization.

Sir John Holt, chief-justice of the King's Bench, and one of the wisest and most just of English jurists, said,[12] in the seventeenth century:

"Inasmuch as the laws of all nations are doubtless raised out of the ruins of the Civil Law, as all governments are sprung out of the ruins of the Roman Empire, it must be owned that the principles of our law are borrowed from the Civil Law, therefore grounded upon the same reason in many things."

Sir William Jones, lawyer, judge, Orientalist, noted for his vast erudition, writing in the eighteenth century, said: "The Digest of Justinian is a most valuable mine of judicial knowledge. It gives law at this day to the greatest part of Europe, and though few English lawyers dare make such an acknowledgment, it is the true source of nearly all our English laws that are not of feudal origin."[13]

The same authority says again: "In questions of rational law, no cause can be assigned why we should not shorten our own labor, by resorting occasionally to the wisdom of ancient jurists, many of whom were the most ingenious and sagacious of men. What is good sense in one age, must be good sense, all circumstances remaining, in another; and pure unsophisticated reason is the same in Italy and in England, in the mind of a Papinian and of a Blackstone." [14]

12. Lane v. Cotton, 12 Mod. 482.
13. See his life by Lord Teignmouth, p. 308, 4th ed.
14. Works, Vol. 6, p. 604.

Chancellor Kent, in his Commentaries, writes as follows:[15]

"The whole body of the Civil Law will excite never failing curiosity, and receive the homage of scholars, as a singular monument of wisdom. It fills such a large space in the eye of human reason; it regulates so many interests of man as a social and civilized being; it embodies so much thought, reflection, experience, and labor; it leads us so far into the recesses of antiquity, and it has stood so long 'against the waves and weathers of time,' that it is impossible, while engaged in the contemplation of the system, not to be struck with some portion of the awe and veneration which are felt in the midst of the solitude of a majestic ruin."

Kent also says:[16] "Upon subjects relating to private rights and personal contracts, and the duties which flow from them, there is no system of law in which principles are investigated with more good sense, or declared or enforced with more accurate and impartial justice."

Again, it is said:[17] "The Civil Law, as a system of jurisprudence, framed by wise men and approved by the experience of ages, must in every country and in every age, furnish principles which modified and applied as circumstances may require, will greatly contribute to the real interests and welfare of society."

"From the sixteenth century to the present day," writes a distinguished German jurist,[18] "Roman jurisprudence has dominated all juristic thought in Germany. . . . The road to proficiency in legal science lies through a study of the ancient jurists. As an

---
15. Comm. Vol. 1, 548; 14th ed.
16. Comm. Vol. 1, 547; 14th ed.
17. Gayle v. Cunningham, 5 S. C. Eq. 124, 133; 1 Fonblanque Eq., 255.
18. Sohm, Inst. of Rom. Law, Trans. by Ledlie, 3d ed., pp. 2, 13.

instrument of legal education the Corpus Juris is irreplaceable."

"When we remember," says Emory Washburn,[19] "what an exhaustless fountain the Civil Law has been, to which the nations of modern Europe have resorted from time to time, to supply the wants which their higher and broader civilization has developed, its importance as a liberal study, can hardly fail to be appreciated. . . . To the student of the Common Law, who wishes to master it as a liberal science, a knowledge, to a certain extent, at least, of the Civil Law, may be regarded as well nigh indispensable."[20]

Roman Law is not binding, of course, upon our courts as authority, yet it may be referred to "in order to illustrate and explain our common law,"[21] for, as Judge Dillon has said,[22] "It embodies the accumulated wisdom and experience of the refined and cultivated Roman people for over a thousand years." And Chief Justice Telgham, of Pennsylvania, long ago observed that while "the lawyers and people of England have always shown a jealousy both of the principles and the practice of the Civil Law, by degrees in cases where the Civil Law is clearly right, jealousy gives way to good sense and justice."[23]

Roman, or Civil, Law, in its modernized form, and modified, with varying degrees of extent, by local customary law and statutes, is the basis of the law today of Italy, France, Spain, Portugal, Switzerland, Belgium, Holland, Germany, Jugo-Slavia, Czechoslovakia, the Balkan States, Greece, the Scandinavian

19. Professor in Harvard Law School, author of Washburn on Real Property.
20. Am. Law Reg., Vol. 12, p. 673, 680.
21. Fable v. Brown, 11 S. C. Eq. 378, 390; Lane v. Cotton, 12 Mod. 482; Bechervaise v. Lewis, 7 C. P. 372.
22. Livingston v. McDonald, 21 Iowa 160, 168; quoted in Mayor, etc. v. Sikes, 94 Ga. 30, 20 S. E. 257.
23. Coates v. Hughes, 3 Binney (Pa.) 498, 507.

countries (although the Scandinavian countries have less Roman Law than the other European states), Turkey, Egypt, Abyssinia, Mauritius, the South African Colonies, Ceylon, Sumatra, Java, the Philippines, China, and Japan. In the western hemisphere the Civil Law obtains in Quebec, Louisiana, Mexico, all the countries of Central and South America, the West Indies, including Cuba and Porto Rico.

Roman Law in its modern form has thus been diffused over a large part of the world. The former law of Russia, prior to the present socialist government, consisted of Slavonic customs modified and influenced by Roman Law. So much of its law was taken from France and Germany that it could be described, says Bryce,[24] "as being Roman 'at the second remove.'" In Persia, Western Turkestan, Afghanistan, and northern Africa Mohammedan Law prevails, and in India the law of to-day consists of Hindu, Mohammedan, and English Law. Our own English Law is confined to England, Wales, Ireland, the United States (excepting Louisiana), Canada (excepting Quebec), Australia, New Zealand, Liberia in Africa, and to some English colonies on the East African coast. Scotland, in the reign of James V, in the sixteenth century, "received" the Civil Law from France, but since its union with England its law has been increasingly influenced by the English Common Law. However, by an express article of the Treaty of Union, judges of Scotland's Court of Sessions must be learned in Roman Law.[25]

Roman Law is a codified law. Its fundamental principles have been collected into one body, systematized, topically arranged, reduced to writing, and promulgated by legislative authority. In other words, its

---

24. "The Extension of Roman and English Law Throughout the World," p. 101.

25. Mackenzie, Rom. Law, p. 47 (7th ed.).

principles and doctrines are to be found in the codes and not in judicial decisions as in English Law jurisdictions. Modern Civil Law countries have likewise codified their laws, each country having its own codes. These codes are based upon Roman Law, yet they differ in details owing to the influence of long established local customs and other causes. In their codification of law Roman and modern Civil Law are in sharp contrast to English and American Law. While many of our Common Law principles have been enacted into statutes and thus with other statutes have become a part of our "written" law, yet much of our law remains unwritten, although in England and in many of our American states some special branches of law have been codified. Conspicuously is this true of our statutory or codified Civil Procedure, many states being called, in this particular, "code states" in distinction from a few states which still follow an unwritten or, as often loosely called, "Common Law" procedure. Codification of Civil Procedure was inaugurated in the state of New York, in 1848, and this code has since been substantially copied by many other states. Some states have also codified their substantive law of crimes, no act being punishable as a crime, in such jurisdictions, unless the act is forbidden by some statute. Various states have also a Code of Criminal Procedure. Moreover, through the efforts of the National Conference of Commissioners of Uniform Laws, whose work is to prepare model acts, particularly in connection with Commercial Law, and to submit these acts to all the states for legislative adoption, a number of other legal topics has been codified in many states. Outstanding among these are the Negotiable Instruments Act which has been adopted by all the states, and the Uniform Sales Act which has been made law in more than thirty states. In addition to these special matters, efforts have been made, in some states, to codify the substantive law, either in whole or in part. Thus, California, in 1872, enacted a series of codes, including a Civil Code which contains many elementary principles of law, and some other states, namely, Delaware, Georgia, Idaho, Iowa, Maryland, Mississippi, Montana, New Mexico, North Dakota, Ohio, South Dakota, Tennessee, Virginia, and West Virginia have incorporated into what is locally called "the Code" various matters of substantive law. None of these codes, however, is as complete as the codes of Civil Law countries, and in their interpretation and application the courts do not hesitate to invoke the aid of unwritten, or Common Law, principles.

Outside of these exceptions there has been little disposition in this country to undertake any general codification of the law.

Turning to the Civil Law countries, the oldest of the modern codes is the French Civil Code which owes its existence to the genius of Napoleon. Prior to the adoption of this code in 1804, France had no general law for the country at large, since the law of one part of France varied from the law of another part. After the fall of the Roman power in ancient Gaul and Spain the country was overrun by Germanic tribes. The northern part of Gaul was held by the Franks, a part of the south was invaded by the Burgundians and other tribes, while the Goths occupied another portion of the south and also Spain. The Franks had very little contact previously with Roman Law, and they brought with them into northern Gaul, or France, their own tribal customs. The result was that in the course of time northern France became known as the land of "the unwritten law," or of "the law of customs." In the progress of the years the different kinds of law or of "customs" in this part of France became almost intolerable. Even in Voltaire's day the "customs" were so many that he said that in traveling through

France one changes law oftener than he changes horses.

The law of customs took its particular name from its locality, as, for example, "the Custom of Paris," "the Custom of Orleans," "the Custom of Normandy."

Due, however, to the prominence of the city of Paris, its laws, or "the Custom of Paris," became, in time, the standard for the greater part of the French people. Also after the revival of legal learning in Italy, in the middle of the eleventh century, the renewed study of Roman Law extended to Paris, and that city became one of the European centers of Roman law education. The "Custom of Paris" became, therefore, more and more patterned upon the Roman Law. Famous law schools were also established in other parts of France, and the names of Cujas and Doneau who flourished in the sixteenth century, of Domat in the seventeenth, and of Pothier in the eighteenth are among the most celebrated of all the great Roman law jurists of the past four hundred years. Pothier was a professor of law at Orleans. He wrote a great work on Roman Law,[26] and also wrote, among other things, a Commentary on the Custom of Paris and Orleans. This latter work, likewise, is substantially Roman Law, and it is the work that was largely drawn upon in the preparation of the French Civil Code. The laws known as the "Custom of Paris" were made the laws also for the French colonial possessions in this continent, that is, for Louisiana and Quebec.

It was not until the promulgation of the Code Napoleon that a uniform law was established for the whole of France.[27] There had been attempts to codify the law before Napoleon's time but they were fruitless. However, in the year 1800, Napoleon applied himself

[26]. Pandects of Justinian digested into New Order, 3 vols. (1748-1752).
[27]. Kaskaskia v. McClure, 167 Ill. 23.

to the task. In this great work he was an imitator of Justinian.[28] He appointed a commission to prepare a civil code, and the first draft was completed in four months. This was submitted to eminent French jurists for their criticisms. As a result, a second draft was made which was finally adopted by legislative action, and it became the law of France on March 21, 1804. This code consists of both customary and Roman law, the Roman element being taken largely from the writings of Pothier and Domat.

Napoleon frequently presided over the commission which drew up this code and literally astonished those present by the soundness of his views. Napoleon was educated only at a military school, but he was the son of a lawyer and he had also a considerable knowledge of Justinian's Digest. During the deliberations of the commission he cited the Digest so frequently that the jurists present asked one another, "Where did the First Consul get his knowledge of Roman Law."[29]

When this code was first promulgated it was called "The French Civil Code" (Le Code Civil des Français), but in 1807, after Napoleon became emperor, the title "Code Napoleon" was given to it.[30] Years later, in his days of exile, Napoleon said:[31] "My true glory is not in having won forty battles; Waterloo will blot out the memory of those victories. But nothing can blot out my civil code. That will live eternally."

The French Civil Code contains 2,281 sections, many of them only a line or two in length. After more than a century, the number of articles remains the same, although they have been amended and modified from time to time by new legislation.

28. Chief Justice Parker, in Griggs v. Austin, 3 Pick. (Mass.) 20.
29. Wells, "Things Not Generally Known," p. 105.
30. It has been known as "The Civil Code," since the establishment of the Republic, in 1870.
31. De Montholon, Récit de la Captivité de l'Empereur Napoleon," p. 401.

Besides the Civil Code[32] there are seven other French codes, the eight codes comprising the whole body of French law. The seven other codes are the Code of Civil Procedure, 1806; the Commercial Code, 1807; the Penal Code, 1810; the Code of Criminal Procedure, 1808; Le Code Forestier; and two Codes de Justice Militaire, 1857.

The present civil code of Spain dates from 1889. For centuries Spain was a Roman province and under the immediate influence of Roman Law. In the fifth century of the present era the country was invaded and conquered by the Goths, or rather, by that branch of the Goths known as the Visigoths, or the Western Goths. Euric, or Evaric, was the king of this people from 466 to 484, and during his reign he ordered the Visigothic laws to be compiled. This compilation, known as the Laws of Euric, was based upon the traditional and customary laws of the Gothic tribes. However, when Euric was succeeded by his son, Alaric II, that king determined upon a compilation of laws for his Roman subjects. Alaric II may well be called the Justinian of the West. In fact he preceded Justinian in the attempt to compile the Roman Law, using for his material the writings of the great Roman jurists and also the Theodosian Code, published by the order of the Emperor Theodosius II, in 438. Alaric's compilation was published in the year 506,[33] twenty-seven years before the Digest of Justinian was given to the world.[34] It is variously known as Lex Romana Visigothorum, Breviarium Alarici, and Breviarium Amiani, the last name being derived from Amianus, the secretary and chief minister of Alaric.

32. The Civil Code is divided into three books or parts, treating respectively of Persons, Property and Ownership, and the Ways of Acquiring Property.
33. Alaric was slain in battle, in 507, by Clovis, king of the Franks.
34. 533 A. D.

The people of Spain lived under the laws of Euric and of Alaric for nearly two hundred years. About 690 A. D., a new and general code of laws was published, known originally as the Forum Judicum, or the Liber Judicum. In the thirteenth century the Spanish name Fuero Juzgo was applied to it, and it is now generally known as the Visigothic Code. This is a remarkable piece of work, especially so when we consider the semi-barbarous source from which it sprung. Following the analogy of Roman Law publications, it is divided into "books," "titles," and "chapters." It was originally written in ecclesiastical Latin,[35] and its material was taken from Gothic, Roman, and Ecclesiastical Law, and from Royal Edicts. Many of its principles and rules exhibit the highest ideals of justice and integrity, while others set forth amazing bigotry and intolerance. This code, however, had a great influence in preserving a uniformity of law for many centuries throughout Spain and Southern France, and some of its laws still survive in the modern code of Spain.

The Moorish invasion of 711 A. D. marked the beginning of the downfall of the Visigothic Kingdom. For nearly eight successive centuries the Christians and the Moslems fought for the possession of the Spanish peninsula. Not till 1492 did Granada, the last stronghold of the Moors, come into the hands of the Spaniards.

For five hundred years after the Arabs invaded Spain there was very little development of general law for the country as a whole. There was, in fact, great confusion in the law. Each city or district, or petty kingdom, enforced its own laws or customs as best it could.

The Laws of Castile were compiled in a work known

---

[35]. A valuable English translation of the Visigothic Code was made by Scott, Boston Book Co., 1910.

as the Fuero Viejo late in the tenth century, and in the middle of the thirteenth century, about 1255, Alfonso X, surnamed "The Wise," King of Leon and Castile, promulgated a code of laws known as the Fuero Real or Fuero de las Leyes. This was a compilation in four "books," of the laws of the Castilian monarchy, and was largely based upon Roman Law.

A few years later (1263), in the reign of the same king, the most pretentious and voluminous legal work up to that time appearing in Spain, the Libro de las Leyes, was published. It was virtually a digest of Roman Law, intended for scholars, yet contained practically all the important laws found in former codes. This famous work was later known as the Partidas, or Las Siete Partidas (The Seven Parts),[36] the popular name given to it, in 1347, by Alfonso XI who at that time also gave it the authority of law. The Partidas contains 182 titles and 2479 sections. They were extended to the Spanish colonies, in 1530, by Charles I, and are still authoritative as fundamental law in many modern Civil Law countries that were formerly under Spanish rule.[37] Even in some of our American states that were originally Spanish territory, the Partidas may yet be cited in support of the early local law.[38] There is also a work known as the Laws of Toro which was promulgated by the Cortes of Toledo in 1502.[39] This work consists of eighty-three laws, and was compiled to supplement and amend the existing laws of the time. The Laws of Toro were later included in the Nueva Recopilacion, and also in

---

36. Each part, or "book," being designated, in order, with the seven letters of Alfonso's name.

37. See Benedicto v. de la Rama, 3 Philippines, 34, 40; Ker v. Cauden, 6 Philippines, 732, 738.

38. See, for example, Scott v. Ward, 13 Cal. 458, 473; Riddick v. Walsh, 15 Mo. 519, 536; White v. Gay's Ex'rs, 1 Tex. 384, 388, 389; Beard v. Poydras, 4 Mart. (La.) 348.

39. Cited in Ebreo v. Sichon, 4 Phil. 705, 706.

the Novissima. La Nueva Recopilacion, (The New Compilation) of the Laws of Spain appeared in the reign of Philip II, in the year 1567. The object of this "New Compilation" was to collect, arrange, and to bring down to date the mass of statutory law that had accumulated, and to harmonize the same with the principles of the existing code. It consists of nine "books" divided into two hundred and fourteen titles. The Partidas and the Nueva Recopilacion together made up the body of the general Spanish Law.

After the discovery of America, in 1492, Spain became the ruler of the seas and was the most powerful nation in Europe. Her colonies were spread over all parts of the world. In 1661, there was made by order of Philip IV a compilation of colonial law, known as the Recopilacion de las Indias. A second edition of this work appeared in 1681, in the reign of Charles II. It was a collection of laws derived from different Spanish sovereigns, and was an elaborate and systematic code for the government of the Spanish-American provinces. The term "Indias" is derived from the fact that the Spanish colonies were under the control of the Council of the Indias, the popular name "Indias" being applied to the Spanish foreign possessions in general. The plan of the Recopilacion de las Indias is similar to that of the Nueva Recopilacion, being divided into nine books, covering two hundred and eighteen titles. This special compilation of colonial law was supplemental to the general law of Spain, consequently the Partidas, the Nueva Recopilacion, and the Recopilacion de las Indias unitedly formed the basis, and may yet be said to be the foundation, of the laws of the South American independent republics. The Recopilacion of the Indias is also cited by the courts of this country in connection with matters arising in states that were once a part of Spanish territory, particularly in questions relating to Spanish and Mexican land grants.[40]

In the year 1805, the general laws of Spain were again compiled, the result being known as the Novissima Recopilacion.[41] It was published in five volumes, a sixth supplementary volume being added in 1829. The entire work is practically a second edition of the Nueva Recopilacion, certain obsolete and repealed laws being omitted and new laws added. It is divided into twelve parts, or "books," comprising three hundred and forty titles.

The present Spanish Civil Code was promulgated by royal decree in 1889. It is yet in force, so far as its general principles of law are concerned, in Cuba, Porto Rico, and the Philippines, despite the recent changes in the government of those former Spanish colonies. This code resembles the Civil Code of France very closely, article after article being substantially the same.[42] Both codes are the result of over twenty centuries of Roman Law evolution since the days of the Twelve Tables, for "the French and the Spanish civil law are derived from the same source, the Roman Law,"[43] although, of course, these modern forms of Roman Law differ in many respects from the parent stock.[44]

In addition to the Civil Code, Spain has several other special codes; namely, the Criminal Code; the Codes of Civil and Criminal Procedure; the Commercial Code; and the Military Code.

Based upon the Civil Code of either France or Spain, the following countries have enacted their own civil codes: Belgium, 1804; Austria, 1811; Hayti,

40. See United States v. City of Santa Fe, 165 U. S. 675.
41. Cited in Ebreo v. Sichon, 4 Philippines, 705, 707.
42. See "Napoleon Centenary and Its Significance," by C. S. Lobingier, Am. Bar Ass'n Journal, Aug. 1921.
43. Leitensdorfer v. Webb, 1 N. M. 34.
44. Panaud v. Jones, 1 Cal. 488, 501.

1825; Greece, 1835; Holland, 1838; Bolivia, 1852; Peru, 1855; Chile, 1855; Italy, 1865; Portugal, 1867; Argentine, 1871; Nicaragua, 1871; Guatemala, 1877; Honduras, 1880; Mexico, 1884; Ecuador, 1887; Costa Rica, 1888; Salvador, 1889; Paraguay, 1889; Colombia, 1893; Uruguay, 1895; Venezuela, 1896; Switzerland, 1912; and Brazil, 1917.

That Italy, the birthplace of Roman Law, should have taken its modern Civil Code from the Code of France may require some explanation. Even in the dark days following the barbaric invasions the Roman Law never lost its influence over Italy. In the eleventh century there were schools of Roman Law in Ravenna and in Lombardy. In the following century Irenerius established the famous Law School of Bologna, and there were other schools of law in other Italian cities. In the thirteenth century Bologna had over ten thousand students who came from all the countries of Europe, including many from England.

The modern codes began with the French Code of 1804, as already stated, and the codes of the various Italian kingdoms, prior to the unification of the country in 1861, were greatly influenced by the French codes. When Victor Emmanuel II became king, the Civil Code of Sardinia, his former kingdom, was adopted in 1865 for the whole of Italy, and a Code of Civil Procedure was also adopted that same year. Italy's first Code of Criminal Procedure, likewise of 1865, also came from Sardinia, and this was substantially the French Criminal Procedure Code of 1808. The original Penal Code of Italy appeared soon after the beginning of Victor Emmanuel's reign, but in 1890 a new Penal Code was adopted, and in 1912, the Criminal Procedure Code of 1865 was replaced by a code which soon became famous. In fact, the Penal Code of 1890 and the Criminal Procedure Code of 1912 caused Italy to be regarded by many European legal scholars as the leader in scientific criminology. They were used as models by later code makers in a number of other Civil Law countries. When, however, the present Fascist government came into power, these codes were not deemed to be in accord with the views of the new regime. Consequently, on July 1, 1931, the present Penal Code and the Code of Criminal Procedure became Italy's law, resulting in radical changes in the former law.

The German Civil Code which became effective on January 1, 1900 was the result of the most thorough and painstaking effort to prepare a system of laws for a nation that history has recorded. The several commissions that worked upon it devoted over twenty years to the task.

Medieval Germany, after the division of the Empire of Charlemagne, had no general law. Different cities, districts, principalities, and states had their own unwritten customs, and there were many turbulent years during which no system of law was known, save the law of the feudal lord over his vassal.

The restoration of the Holy Roman Empire by Otto the Great (962), whereby kings elected by the German nation became also kings of Italy and emperors, and thus were entitled to wear the triple crown, and the revival of Roman Law learning in Italy in the eleventh century, had great influence in bringing about a change. German students were attracted to the Italian schools, and brought back to their own country new ideas concerning law. German schools were also organized where both the Roman and Canon Law were taught. German princes and rulers were not long in discovering that Roman Law was better adapted to their needs.

In the reign of Maximilian I, in 1495, a judicial body was created, known as the Court of the Imperial Chamber. It consisted of a president and sixteen assessors and had original jurisdiction between princes of the Empire and appellate jurisdiction for persons of lower rank. The law regulating the practice before this court provided that it should judge in accordance with "the common law of the Empire," and also in accordance with such statutes and customs of the German principalities and courts when the same were duly proved by proper evidence. The "common law of the Empire," the Germano-Roman or "Holy Roman Empire," was the Roman Law as developed and taught in the Italian schools. This law was thus made binding upon the new German court except in such instances as local statutes and customs were proved to the contrary. Proof, however, of such customs was often difficult and seldom offered, and the result was that from the date of 1495 the Roman Law was said to be "received" in Germany, and in the succeeding century the German customary law was more and more displaced and in time practically disappeared. In the seventeenth and eighteenth centuries, however, a reaction set in against the dominance of the Roman Law, owing to the growing weakness of the Empire after the Reformation, the increasing strength of the many loosely confederated states and principalities, and the desire of some of them to have their own independent laws. In consequence, a number of codes of local laws appeared, although all of them, as far as general principles were concerned, were influenced by Roman Law. The best known of these codes was the Prussian Code, or Landrecht, of 1794.

In 1874, three years after the late German Empire was organized at the close of the Franco-Prussian war, a commission was appointed to prepare a code of civil law for the whole country. At this time, according to the Imperial office of Justice, there was great confusion in the private law of the different parts of the Empire. A third of the population in the center of Germany had the Roman Law, as received in 1495, supplemented with many local laws. Prussia, containing about half of the entire population, was still using its Code of 1794. In the Rhine provinces nearly seven millions of the inhabitants followed the Code Napoleon of 1804. Saxony employed its Code of 1863, and Schleswig-Holstein observed the Danish Code of 1683.

The commission appointed in 1874 worked upon the project for thirteen years and then submitted its report to the Bundesrat in 1887. It was made the subject of very heated debate. Some said it contained too much Roman Law. Others objected to it because it favored the capitalists at the expense of the laboring class. Still others insisted that it was the work of theorists and did not sufficiently recognize the needs of commerce, agriculture, and manufacturing. So great was the opposition that a new commission was appointed in 1890. Their report was made in 1895, but still it did not find sufficient support, and a third revision was made. Finally, in 1896, it was submitted to the Reichstag. This legislative body referred the report to a special committee which held over fifty meetings for its consideration, and then, after this committee reported, another long debate ensued. At last, however, it was enacted into law, August 18, 1896, and went into effect on January 1, 1900.

The German Civil Code (Das Bürgerliches Gesetzbuch für das Deutsche Reich) as thus enacted consists of an Introductory Act, followed by Five Books, divided into Sections, Titles, and Paragraphs.[45] The First Book treats of General Principles, the Second of Obligations, the Third of Property or "Things," the Fourth of Family Law, the Fifth of Inheritance. The whole work contains 2385 paragraphs

---

45. An excellent English translation made by a Chinese legal scholar, Chung Hui Wang, was published in London, in 1907.

or what we would call sections. Its sources are Roman Law, the Code Napoleon, the 1883 Swiss Code on Obligations, the Prussian Code of 1794, and various codes of other German states. Professor Maitland said that it is "the most carefully considered statement of a nation's laws that the world has ever seen."[46]

But long before the German Civil Code became effective at the beginning of the present century much work had been done in preparing other codes. It was in 1867 that the initial step in the modern unification of Germany was taken by organizing the North German Confederation. In 1870, this Confederation adopted a Criminal Code which, in 1871, after the formation of the German Empire, at the close of the Franco-Prussian War, became the Criminal Code for the Empire. In 1877, a Code of Criminal Procedure appeared, and in 1879 a Code of Civil Procedure became effective. In 1897, a Commercial Code was adopted, and in that same year the Codes of Civil and of Criminal Procedure were revised. Another revision of these two codes was made in 1924. The Imperial Criminal Code of 1871 continued to be the criminal law of Germany until the new Nazi Criminal Code, which went into effect September 1, 1935.

The great Civil Code of Germany upon which so many years of labor were spent and which finally became effective in 1900 has received some amendments from time to time, but it still remains substantially the same and is still studied in the German universities. However, in 1934, Chancellor Hitler instructed the German Law Academy to prepare codes more in accord with the views of the present government. The Criminal Code has been prepared and enacted into law, and only time will reveal whether the greatest civil code of Europe will also be replaced.

---

46. "Political Theories in the Middle Ages," p. 17.

It is insisted by Nazi writers that the present Civil Code contains too much Roman Law, and Roman Law they assert is not Aryan law, but is a system of law produced by a people in whom was mingled the blood of many races. Germany's law, it is declared, can be created only by Nordic-Aryan men.

It is in Russia, however, that the most radical departure from long developed legal standards has been made that has ever taken place in history.

Previous to the Revolution of 1917, the Law of Russia had received many contributions from Roman Law, Bryce, as already said, stating that it might be described as being Roman "at the second remove."

The history of Russia covers a period of over a thousand years, its earliest law being derived from Scandinavian, Slavic, and Mongolian customs. The eastern, or the Greek, Church was established in Russia in the tenth century, the titular head of that church being the Patriarch of Constantinople. From close proximity to and contact with the Eastern Roman Empire, Russia undoubtedly was influenced in the course of time by Roman Law from that source.

The first collection of Russian Laws was the Code of Yaroslaff, which was compiled in the eleventh century. This consisted for the most part of Scandinavian law or customs. Later codes were the Code of Ivan III, in 1497; the Code of Ivan IV, or Ivan the Terrible, in 1550; and the Code of Alexis, in 1650. In the Code of Ivan III many Scandinavian laws were retained, some of which, as wager of battle and wergeld, are also found in early English law. The Code of Ivan IV, or Ivan the Terrible, was based upon that of Ivan III, his grandfather. It was Ivan IV who first assumed the title "Czar," or "Tsar," the Slavonic form of the Roman "Caesar." The Code of Alexis was characterized by many cruel and despotic punishments.

For example, any one who used tobacco should suffer the penalty of having his nose cut off.

Peter the Great reigned from 1689 to 1725. He was an extensive traveler, had many advisers at his court from western Europe, and was ambitious to model the laws of Russia after the laws of those countries. From England he brought back the law of primogeniture but was unable to make this law acceptable to his people. However, he did introduce and put into effect many reforms in the Russian legal system. He also built the city of St. Petersburg, now called Leningrad, and made it the imperial capital in place of the ancient city of Moscow.

Catherine II, or Catherine the Great, was empress from 1762 to 1796. She was a native German princess, well versed in the literature of France, and endeavored to introduce a code of laws for Russia on the model of Montesquieu's L'Esprit des Lois. Although she failed in this attempt, yet she did succeed in making a great codification of the laws of Russia which work bore the impress of her own views. In 1830, another code entitled "A Complete Collection of the Laws of the Russian Empire" was made by the Emperor Nicholas I. This code, particularly in contract law and property rights, was based upon the Code Napoleon, and in 1864 the judicial system of Russia was patterned after the courts of France.

Since the Revolution of 1917 all this has been overthrown. There is in Russia, today, no system of law like unto that of any other country. All former laws have been swept away, and the present government has substituted various codes and regulations based upon communistic doctrines. "Law," as understood by legal scholars generally, is regarded as an evil. As said by a Russian socialist writer: "Every enlightened proletariat knows . . . that religion is opium for the people. But the law manifests itself as an even more poisonous narcotic for the same people."⁴⁷

Russia has promulgated several codes during the past few years, the Civil Code of 1923, the Code of Civil Procedure, and several other codes upon other subjects. The Civil Code is not, however, a law code as we understand the term, but rather a digest of socialistic doctrines, including the status of workmen, the hours of labor, and other economic matters. It contains various decrees relating to the courts, also certain directions concerning contracts and partnerships.

Turning to the new republic of Turkey another surprise is experienced, but a surprise of a different character. Since the Turkish revolution of 1919 a new nation has come into being. The sultanate has been abolished and a republic has been proclaimed, although its president is clothed with dictatorial powers. The capital has been transferred from Constantinople to Angora in Asia Minor. The state religion, Mohammedanism, has been disestablished, the fez prohibited, and polygamy forbidden. No more drastic changes could be made by any nation. Turkey has turned its face to the light, with a determination to establish its government upon the tested standards of Europe. The former Ottoman Empire based both its religious and civil law upon the Koran. This was in accord with the thought of the Mohammedan world, church and state being inseparable in the teachings of its founder. The Koran of Mohammed contains not only religious doctrines, but also laws for the administration of government and for the regulation of individuals in their family and business relations. It is a sort of code of spiritual and secular law combined.

In 1923, a commission was appointed to consider the matter of adopting a new system of private law. The

---

47. Goichbarg, "Fundamentals of Private Law," op. cit. p. 7.

civil codes of Europe, particularly those of France, Germany, and Switzerland, doubtless because some of the leading jurists in Turkey had studied in those countries, were carefully examined.

The French Code was regarded as not sufficiently modern. The German Code was thought to be too technical. The Swiss Code of 1912 was adopted as being "the most recent, the most perfect, and the most democratic."[48] The Swiss Code was adopted in toto without change. In addition to the Civil Code, a new Penal Code following substantially the Italian Penal Code of 1890 has been promulgated, also a Commercial Code based upon the commercial codes of Germany, France, Italy, and Japan. The courts of the country have likewise been newly organized, being modeled largely after the French plan. Truly has Professor Hudson of Harvard said:[49] "It is a fresh indication of the strength of the Roman Law system that Turkey should be making this new draft upon it." It may be further said that it is also an added proof that the law of Rome still dominates the world. For it seems more like a romantic tale than a historical fact that Turkey, in order to take its place among the modern progressive nations should be adopting the law promulgated from the very city that the Turks conquered nearly five hundred years ago. It was at Constantinople that Justinian enacted into law the Institutes, the Digest, and the Code, and here for nearly a thousand years, until its capture by the Turks in 1453, the principles of the Roman Law survived in the Greek commentaries of the Byzantine period. Then Mohammedan Law, a system of law based partly upon the Koran, supplanted the Roman Law, to abdicate, however, after the lapse

48. From the preface to the French translation of the Turkish Civil Code by Rizzo, Constantinople, 1926.

49. "Law Reforms in Turkey," Am. Bar Association Journal, January 1927.

of centuries, in favor of a modern descendant of the law that had been displaced. A law school has also been recently established at Angora for instruction in the Civil Law.

Mohammedan Law has been called one of the three great legal systems of the world. It has regulated the affairs of many millions of men since the days of Mohammed who died nearly thirteen hundred years ago. Mohammed was almost a contemporary of Justinian. The latter died in 565, and Mohammed was born some four or five years later, dying in 632. Within a dozen years after Mohammed's death, his followers conquered Syria, Phoenicia, Palestine, and Egypt. Northern Africa soon after fell into their hands, and, in 711, the Moors invaded Spain, and destroyed the kingdom of the Ostrogoths. In 732, a century after Mohammed's death, their ambition to overrun Western Europe was crushed by Charles Martel, in the decisive battle of Tours, in France, and they reached no further north. However, at this time the Mohammedan power extended from the Gulf of Arabia and the Indus to the Mediterranean, and from Egypt across northern Africa to southern France, embracing also the Balearic Isles as well as Sardinia and Corsica.

Moreover, for more than seven hundred years after these conquests, and prior to the fall of Constantinople in 1453, the Mohammedans were constantly striving to extend their sway over the world. They even invaded India several times between the eleventh and fifteenth centuries.

But a large part of the vast territory acquired by the Mohammedans was at the time under Roman Law. They conquered "countries in which schools of Roman Law, Roman Law courts, and magistrates and officials imbued with Roman Law existed."[50] There would, therefore, seem to be no doubt that in such countries

---

50. Amos, Roman Civil Law, p. 415.

the law of the conquerors was greatly influenced by the prevailing Roman Law. The notion that Mohammedan Law is all found in the Koran is erroneous. The Koran is, indeed, made the basis of that law, civil as well as religious, but while in matters of religion the Koran, the written law, is the only law, yet in civil affairs Mohammedans recognize an unwritten law also. In addition to the precepts of the Koran, which are very scanty with reference to strictly private law, commentaries on the Koran and the opinions of men learned in the law are accepted as authoritative upon questions relating to secular matters. In fact, the greater part of the Mohammedan civil law has been developed from such sources outside the Koran. "If Aristotle," says Professor Amos,[51] "supplied the Arabians with their logic, it was Basil, Leo, and their Greek commentators who supplied them with their law." Many principles of law recognized by the Mohammedans, and not found in the Koran, show conclusively, it would seem, that they were adopted from the Roman Law. For example, Mohammedan Law divides things into movable and immovable; it deals with usufruct and servitudes; it has the same general rules governing sales as the Roman Law;[52] in the law of wills and intestate succession there are many likenesses to the law of Rome; and in contract law, in general, there are found in both Roman and Mohammedan Law common principles regulating letting and hiring, partnership, loan, deposit, mandate, pledge, and mortgage.[53] Indeed, there is so much similarity in many respects in the law of both systems that Professor Amos was led to say: "If, as Emanuel Deutsch said and seemed to establish, the Mohammedan religion is nothing but Hebraism adapted to Arabian

---

51. Roman Civil Law, p. 409.
52. Colquhoun, A Summary of the Roman Civil Law, p. 1660.
53. See Amos, Roman Civil Law, p. 406, et seq.

soil, it seems also true that Mohammedan Law is nothing but the Roman Law of the Eastern Empire adapted to the political conditions of the Arab dominions."

Even a part of our own present day insular possessions came long ago under the sway of Mohammedan Law, which made its way from India to Java, thence to Sumatra and the Malay Peninsula, and finally to certain parts of the Philippines, particularly Mindanao and Sulu. It is still recognized there in some matters, the marriage law for example, by the native population, although it is being gradually displaced by the present Spanish and American law.

Coming to China, an even more amazing change in legal ideas is found than in Turkey. Such, at least, was the writer's opinion after a recent sojourn there for the express purpose of studying its courts and legal system. The modern judicial history of China began in 1910 when the first National Assembly met at Peking. The old courts of China were whatever each provincial administration desired for itself, the governors of provinces having, under the emperor, supreme judicial authority as well as executive. Such tribunals as they set up were entirely under their own control, each local mandarin, under the governor, being both civil administrator and judge. Instead of resorting to the courts, the people usually settled their civil disputes in family councils or submitted them to the headmen of their particular occupational group.

However, since the inauguration of the Republic, a modern system of courts has been organized and several modern codes have been promulgated, beginning with the Provisional Criminal Code of 1912. Soon after the revolution the Chinese Law Codification Commission began its work assisted by French and Japanese legal scholars. When the present government was set up in 1928 and made Nanking the capital, the work of the Commission was divided among special commissioners, and the preparation of a civil, a commercial, a land, and a labor code was assigned to separate experts. The original Commission completed the revision of the Provisional Criminal Code in 1919, and a Code of Criminal Procedure was prepared in 1921. After much delay and many re-draftings, China's Civil Code was issued in 1931. In connection with these codifications the old Chinese laws were carefully examined, local customs and usages considered, and, most of all, European continental law, or the Civil Law, was freely drawn upon. No English adviser, however, assisted in the work and practically no English law was borrowed.

China's modern Civil Code consists of five "books," or divisions, dealing, respectively, with (I) General Principles; (II) Obligations; (III) Property Rights; (IV) Family Law; and (V) Succession, including Wills and Inheritance. It has been prepared with great ability and is largely based upon French law. It is literally new law for China, being quite different from the old law, although some parts of the old Household law have been retained.

Finally in our survey we reach Japan, that great country which only in comparatively recent times has taken its place among the leading nations of the world. Its sweeping law reforms, including an entire change in legal system and an adoption of European Civil Law codes, afford a striking illustration of the yet dominant world-wide influence of the laws that came from the Roman people.

Japanese law was formerly native or customary law, moulded largely upon the legal theories of China. It was about fifty years ago that Japan, in a great forward movement, determined to place itself in line with the ideas of Western civilization. A commission was appointed to revise the laws of the Empire, with the assistance of European jurists. The first draft of a civil code was based upon the French Civil Code, but upon further consideration another committee was appointed which prepared an entirely new draft which was substantially identical with the first draft, or first project of the German Civil Code, the code that was presented to the Bundesrat in 1887. This draft, as previously stated, was rejected in Germany because it was alleged to have been drawn up by "the Romanists" and to contain too much Roman Law. To the Japanese committee, however, the first draft of the German code seemed to be quite satisfactory, and the work of the committee was adopted. Japan thus established for its civil code what many jurists regarded as the most scientific exposition of legal principles that up to the time had appeared. The first three books of the code relate to general principles of the law, to property rights, and to obligations. These books are based almost entirely upon the first draft of the German code. In family law and in the law of succession, treated in books four and five of the Japanese Code, the former customary law of Japan is largely followed although this native law has been considerably changed to meet modern conditions. For the most part, says Professor Kenzo Takayanagi, of the Imperial University of Tokyo, "the Japanese Civil Code reflects not so much the national life of Japan as it does that of the Roman people or of some modern European nation."[54] Roman Law is studied in the law schools of Japan for two reasons, Professor Takayanagi says, "one, because Japan's system of private law is largely based upon that system, the other, because the study of the historical development of the Roman Law is a valuable training in giving any student of law an insight into the historical life of law in general."

54. "Legal Education in Japan," Am. Law School Review, December, 1927.

Thus from all around the world come encomiums upon the Roman Law. This in itself should especially impress students of history and students of law with the scientific character and lasting value of that law. Not only has it survived in countries that were once a part of the Roman Empire, but in many other lands it has been adopted as the wisest and most practical system of law known.

The words of Chancellor Kent our own great early jurist, chief justice of the Supreme Court of New York, Chancellor of New York, professor of law in Columbia college, a man whose legal learning was greater than that of Blackstone, are as true today as when he wrote them a century ago:

"The history of the venerable system of the civil law is peculiarly interesting. It was created and gradually matured on the banks of the Tiber, by the successive wisdom of Roman statesmen, magistrates, and sages; and after governing the greatest people in the ancient world for the space of thirteen or fourteen centuries, and undergoing extraordinary vicissitudes after the fall of the western empire, it was revived, admired, and studied in modern Europe, on account of the variety and excellence of its general principles. It is now taught and obeyed, not only in France, Spain, Germany, Holland, and Scotland, but in the islands of the Indian Ocean, and on the banks of the Mississippi and the St. Lawrence. So true, it seems, are the words of D'Aguesseau, that 'the grand destinies of Rome are not yet accomplished; she reigns throughout the world by her reason, after having ceased to reign by her authority.' "[55]

And James Bryce, who for over twenty years was Regius professor of Roman Law at Oxford, said in his valedictory address at that University:

"In the Roman Law one may find something of value

---

55. Com. 14th Ed. Vol. 1, p. 515.

upon almost every principle and general legal doctrine with which a jurist has to deal. The legal conceptions set forth are those upon which all subsequent law has been based; and nearly all of them find their place in our own system, which they have largely contributed to mould. . . . No rules could better conform to the three canons of good law, that it should be definite, self-consistent, and delicately adapted to the practical needs of society. No study can be better fitted to put a fine edge upon the mind, or to form in it the habit of clear logical thinking. . . .

"The learner will make quite as rapid progress with English Law if he has begun with Roman as if he proceeds to break his teeth from the first upon the hard nuts of our own system. Twenty-one years ago I ventured to say this here and I venture now to repeat it with fuller confidence. Two men of equal ability and diligence start together after taking their B. A. degree. One gives a year to Roman Law and the two next to English. The other devotes to English the whole three years. At the end of the three years the first will know as much English Law as the second. He may not have covered so much ground or got on his tongue the names of so many cases, but he will know what he does know—nor will it be much less in quantity—more thoroughly and rationally. The explanation is twofold. In learning Roman Law, one learns the elements of law in general, and therefore of English Law also, these elements being more easily learnt from Roman sources than they could be in the form they have taken among ourselves. And, secondly, in learning Roman Law one obtains a means of testing one's comprehension of the real meaning of English terms and the nature and compass of English rules, which deepens and strengthens the learner's hold upon his knowledge. The main difficulty which besets students till they have had a good deal of actual

practice is to turn into the concrete the rules they have learnt in the abstract, or as a Roman says, Leges scire non est verba earum tenere sed vim atque potestatem.
. . . "The Roman Law is indeed still world-wide, for it represents the whilom unity of civilized mankind. There is not a problem of jurisprudence which it does not touch; there is scarcely a corner of political science on which its light has not fallen. . . .

"To no scholars ought the early history of the Roman Law to be at once so easily comprehensible and so instructive as to us in England, because the history of our own law is full of beautiful analogies therewith. So no jurists are better able to estimate the value of Roman doctrines on many principles of contractual law, because our system has developed independently, and illustrates the Roman equally where it differs and where it agrees. We in England cannot pretend to rival the work which the great Germans of this century, men like Savigny and Vangerow, Ihering and Windscheid and Mommsen, have done for the investigation and exposition of Roman jurisprudence and legal history. But our detached position ought to give us a perspective and a freshness of critical insight, perhaps even a means of comprehending things by reading our own experience into them, which continental scholars sometimes lack; and of that experience, we may trust, due use will some day be made. For I cannot doubt, looking not only to the progress of the study in England, but to its rapid and solid growth in the Universities of America, that the study of the Roman Law, once so nearly extinct among us, is now destined to shine with a steady light for generations to come."

[Roman Law]

CHAPTER II

THE CIVIL LAW IN THE UNITED STATES AND CANADA

Our next inquiry deals with a question nearer home; namely, what, if any, has been, or is, the connection of the Civil Law, the modern descendant of the Roman Law, with the law of our own country, and also with the law of the adjoining Dominion of Canada?

With the exception of the state of Louisiana, the system of jurisprudence that now prevails in our American states is that which has been derived from the Common Law of England. An important factor in the survival of the English Common Law in America was the fact that Blackstone's Commentaries, published in 1766 in England and followed by an American edition in 1771, became a sort of gospel upon the law for all American judges, lawyers, and law students. No other law book ever occupied an equal place in the respect and veneration of thousands of law readers on this side of the Atlantic. The book enjoyed a much greater popularity in America than it did in England. Its great influence in the Colonies was largely due to the time of its appearance, the psychologic moment, so to speak, most favorable to its reception. It was the eve of the Revolution, the period just preceding the Declaration of Independence. Every public leader was intensely interested in English constitutional law, and hundreds of promising young men in the Colonies were eager to study law. The great grievance against the mother country was that she was depriving the Colonists of their legal rights as Englishmen, and, consequently, English precedents and English law were so often cited in the public addresses of that era that Edmund Burke, the great English statesman, declared that in America everybody was a lawyer.

The publication of Blackstone's Commentaries was an event in the legal history of this country. Every lawyer possessed a copy, and every judge cited it as an authority. It was made the basis of legal study, and for several generations, the chief requirement for admission to the bar was an ability to pass a satisfactory examination upon Blackstone's Commentaries. Down to the close of the nineteenth century it was usually the first law book placed in the hands of American law students,[1] and it maintained for nearly a hundred and fifty years a reputation that was regarded as almost of absolute verity. A quotation from Blackstone was received in practically every court of the land as the last word, the final authority, in every dispute concerning the common law. To question its accuracy was legal heresy.

Yet Blackstone's reputation as a legal writer rests more on the clearness, dignity, and beauty of his style than upon his great learning. While he was highly respected by English legal scholars yet he was not regarded by them as an unquestioned authority. Horne Took, one of his contemporaries, and a distinguished writer, describes Blackstone's Commentaries as "a good, gentleman's law-book, clear but not deep." Similar views were expressed by Mackintosh, Fox, and Lord Eldon. Jeremy Bentham criticized him very severely. He attended Blackstone's lectures at Oxford, and writes thus of him:

"I attended with two collegiates of my acquaintance. They both took notes, which I attempted to do, but could not continue it, as my thoughts were occupied in

---

1. In 1803, Tucker's Edition of Blackstone, with an added commentary on the Constitution of the United States, became the recognized textbook of American law.

reflecting on what I heard. I immediately detected his fallacy respecting natural rights. Blackstone was a formal, precise, and affected lecturer—just what you would expect from the character of his writings; cold, reserved, and wary—exhibiting a frigid pride. But his lectures were popular, though the subject did not then excite a wide-spreading interest, and his attendants were not more than from thirty to fifty."[2]

Blackstone was, in fact, an ultra conservative. Bentham calls him "a determined and persevering enemy of reform, although his writings were not wholly without merit."[3] He was much prejudiced against the growing system of equity jurisprudence. "With all his various learning," says Holdsworth,[4] "he was not familiar with the existing literature of equity, so that his knowledge of the principles of equity was scanty." Both the Common Law and equity were being rapidly developed in England at this time, and Mansfield was doing a great work in striving to reform existing conditions by engrafting equitable principles upon the Common Law and endeavoring to reduce it to a more satisfactory system.

With these liberal movements among the lawyers of England, the United States, says a writer in The Solicitors' Journal, of London,[5] would have no part. "They took their law from 'Blackstone,' and from him they imbibed an intense legal conservatism which has shaped American jurisprudence ever since."

Had there been in the American Colonies a good work on French or Civil Law in place of Blackstone's book, it is more than probable that the Civil Law would have been established in America. Both of the politi-

2. Works of Bentham (Edinburgh, 1843), Vol. 10, p. 45.
3. Vol. 1, 227, 239.
4. "Blackstone's Treatment of Equity," Harvard Law Review, Nov., 1929.
5. The Solicitors' Journal and Weekly Reporter, London, July, 1924; reprinted in The Irish Law Times, Aug. 2, 1924.

cal parties of the day, the Federalists and the Democrats[6] were intensely anti-English and decidedly pro-French. Alexander Hamilton, the master mind of the new Republic, was planning the preparation of a code of laws based upon Roman-French law when his early and most regrettable death deprived his country of his priceless and incomparable services.

Nevertheless, some parts of the territory that now is included within the United States were settled by France and Spain, and in connection with such settlements the Civil Law found lodgment in this country. In this way the Civil Law came to Louisiana where it still remains the basis of that state's system of jurisprudence.[7] In a number of localities, however, where the Civil Law was originally introduced, it was displaced later by the English Common Law owing to large accessions of population from other parts of the country where that system of law prevailed.

LOUISIANA: In 1682, the French explorer LaSalle descended the Mississippi river to its mouth, being the first white man to make the trip. To a vast tract of land extending northward and westward in the Mississippi valley the name Louisiana was given in honor of the King of France, Louis XIV. The boundaries of this region were very indefinite. Theoretically they stretched northward in unknown distance from the Gulf of Mexico and westward, according to some claimants, to the shores of the Pacific Ocean.

The first settlement in this territory was made by the French at Biloxi, now located in the State of Mississippi. In 1712, the French king granted by charter the entire commercial rights of the whole district of Louisiana to Anthony Crozat, a prominent French merchant. This charter provided that the laws, edicts and ordinances of Paris, that is, "The

6. Originally known as Republicans.
7. Wheeler v. Insurance Co., 101 U. S. 439, 443.

Custom of Paris," should be extended to "Louisiana." New Orleans was founded in 1717.

In 1762, France by a secret treaty ceded to Spain all of Louisiana "west of the Mississippi," together with the city of New Orleans and the island on which it stood. A few years later, in 1768, General (or Count) Alexander O'Reilly,[8] a Spaniard of Irish descent, was appointed Spanish governor of the district. Thirty-five years later (in 1803) Spain restored "Louisiana" to France (Nov. 30, 1803), and twenty days later (Dec. 20) France ceded the territory to the United States.

The following year (1804) the Territory of Orleans, having about the same boundaries as the present state of Louisiana, was organized by Congress. The rest of the great district comprised in "the Louisiana purchase" was designated as "the District of Louisiana." A year later (1805) the name "District of Louisiana" was changed to "the Territory of Louisiana," and in 1812 the name was again changed to "the Territory of Missouri" when, in that same year, the Territory of Orleans was admitted to the Union as the State of Louisiana.

The "Custom of Paris" which was made the law of Louisiana in 1712 prevailed there till the country was ceded to Spain in 1762. "Count O'Reilly, the new Spanish governor acting in the name of the Spanish king, abolished, by proclamation," said Chancellor Walworth of New York,[9] "not only the previous form of government of the colony, but the whole code of the French law, the Custom of Paris, which had theretofore existed, and substituted the Spanish law in their stead."

However, whether Spanish law did supplant the former French law has been much disputed. O'Reilly

---

8. Pronounced O-ré-li.
9. The Canal Appraisers v. The People, 17 Wend. (N. Y.) 571, 588.

upon assuming his duties issued two proclamations, the first establishing the new Spanish colonial government, the second providing instructions as to procedure in the institutions of suits, both civil and criminal, and in the pronouncing of judgments. He proclaimed that procedure should be, in general, in conformity with an abstract (made by himself and his legal adviser) of "the statutes of the Recopilacion de Castile et des Indias," owing to the lack of advocates in the country and the people's scant knowledge of Spanish laws. It seems that there were no lawyers, no men learned in the law, in the colony at this time, and that the judges of the courts were Spanish army officers. The law of Spain was theoretically the law but as a matter of fact the customs of the people were those of France. President Jefferson, years later, after the Louisiana Purchase in 1803, insisted that French law still remained, so far as the civil rights of the inhabitants were concerned. He said:[10] "Probably the Spanish authorities found in the progress of their administration that the difference between the French and Spanish Codes, taken both from the same Roman original, would not justify disturbing the popular mind by a formal suppression of the one and substitution of the other."

The generally prevailing opinions of the courts located in this area have been, however, to the effect that the Spanish law superseded the French. In 1816, the supreme court of Louisiana decided that the Spanish law was introduced into the province of Louisiana by the Spanish authorities, shortly after O'Reilly's proclamation issued in 1769.[11]

In 1805, the territorial legislature of Orleans adopted the English Common Law procedure in crim-

---

10. The Batture Case, 2 State Papers, Public Lands, 1.
11. Beard v. Poydras, 4 Mart. (La.) 367; Cutter v. Waddingham, 22 Mo. 206, 251.

inal cases. In 1806, a commission was appointed to prepare a civil code. This commission possessed a copy of the first project or draft of the Code Napoleon, no copy of the final draft of that code, as adopted, in France, in 1804, being, it is said, in the country.[12] Using this first draft of the French Code as a basis, the commissioners adapted and modified it in various places in order to make it adaptable to local conditions in the new Territory, and in 1808 the work was adopted by the legislature. It was revised in 1825, and a third time in 1870. As thus revised it constitutes the present Civil Code of Louisiana.

While it is true that many of the provisions of the Louisiana code are derived from the Code Napoleon where often identical language may be found,[13] yet the Supreme Court of that state has said that the Code was adopted in the English language, by a legislative body composed mainly of English-speaking members, and that it is probable they had no intention to adopt the theories of French commentators on the Code Napoleon.[14]

It is evident that the state of Louisiana occupies an entirely different position with reference to the Civil Law than it would if it were an independent republic, and had Civil Law neighbors as so many continental European states have. Louisiana has both her state and federal courts as all states have, and has her contacts with the laws of other states where the Common Law prevails. Her law has necessarily, therefore, been influenced by the prevailing laws of the other parts of the country. A hundred years ago, Mr. Justice McLean, in the case of Parsons v. Bedford, said[15]

12. City of New Orleans v. Camp, 105 La. 288.
13. For example, see Groves v. Sentell, 153 U. S. 465, 477.
14. Delpit v. Young, 51 La. Ann. 923.
15. Parsons v. Bedford, 3 Pet. (U. S.) 432 (1830). See further as to the Civil Law in Louisiana, Livingston v. Story, 9 Pet. (U. S.) 661; Owings v. Hull, 9 Pet. (U. S.) 625; Michoud v. Girod, 4 How. (U. S.)

that the people of Louisiana "have a system peculiar to themselves, adopted by their statutes, which embodies much of the Civil Law, some of the principles of the Common Law, and, in a few instances, the statutory provisions of other States. This system may be called the Civil Law of Louisiana, and is peculiar to that state."

Henry P. Dart, of Louisiana, has also said,[16] in speaking of the revision in 1825 of the first Code, or Digest of 1808: "The report of the commissioners shows that they took the Digest of 1808 as a basis and rearranged the matter, struck out old articles and incorporated new ones, the result being that for the first time the Civil Code took on that physical resemblance to the Code Napoleon which further strengthened the tradition that it is substantially the same. Comparison will show that, while the resemblances are in fundamental principles of Civil Law, the results of our own jurisprudence are incorporated, arising from the interpretation of all the old and new laws, and from the experience of the colony and Territory. Other differences are the product of original thought of which the most signal example is Livingston's creation of our 'Law of Obligation,' which merges the Common Law and Civil Law in a way which would shock the sensibilities of a French jurist."

In the matter of pleading and procedure, says Judge Howe,[17] Louisiana has substantially the practice which prevailed in the time of Justinian. As to criminal law,

503; Livingston v. Story, 11 Pet. 351, 393; Fleckner v. Bank of U. S., 8 Wheat. (U. S.) 444; Hayes v. Berwick, 2 Mart. (O. S.) 138; Boucier v. Lanux, 3 Mart. (O. S.) 581; Beard v. Poydros, 4 Mart. (O. S.) 367; Cottin v. Cottin, 5 Mart. (O. S.) 93; Reynolds v. Swayne, 13 La. 193.

16. "The Sources of the Civil Code of Louisiana," and introduction to "Saunder's Lectures on the Civil Code." New Orleans, 1925, p. XXXVI.

17. Studies in the Civil Law, 2d ed., p. 139. See, also, Planters' Bank v. George, 6 Mart. (O. S.) 674; Guerin's Heirs v. Bagneries, 18 La. 590.

says that same author,[18] it was felt that it would not be proper to continue the Spanish methods, and early Statutes were passed, which are still practically in force, with a few amendments, providing that the Common Law of England should be the basis of law in criminal cases.

KANSAS: The territory embraced within the present state of Kansas, with the exception of its extreme southwestern portion which belonged to Mexico till 1848, was a part of the tract known as "Louisiana" which was bought by this country from the French in 1803. Theoretically, therefore, the first law of the domain that now comprises the State of Kansas was the Civil Law.[19] The Civil Law never gained a foothold, however, in this territory since it was never settled by the French or Spanish. Coronado's exploring party of Spaniards visited this region in 1541, crossing from the south to the north, and in 1719, a French party, under Dutisne, also visited here. However, it was not organized as a territory till 1854, and its civilized population was made up almost entirely of immigrants from English Common Law states who brought the common law of their own states with them.

MISSOURI: The present state of Missouri was also a part of the "Louisiana purchase." After the admission of the state of Louisiana (1812), all the rest of the purchase was called the Territory of Missouri. There were already several French settlements in the area of the present State of Missouri when the purchase of 1803 was made. St Genevieve, the oldest town, was founded in 1755, and St. Louis was founded in 1764.

According to the supreme court of Missouri, French law was supplanted in the territory by the Spanish law, as already mentioned in connection with Louisi-

18. Ib., p. 138.
19. See argument of counsel in Whitaker v. Hawley, 25 Kan. 471.

ana.[20] The English Common Law was introduced into Missouri in 1816, but before that time the Spanish law prevailed in all the country west of the Mississippi ceded by France to the United States by the treaty of 1803.[21]

In 1846, an action of ejectment was brought, in Missouri, involving title to a tract of land, based upon an oral contract made in 1815, prior to the introduction of the Common Law. By this contract one party gave to another a right to select for his own certain land out of a tract owned by the first party. It was held that the selection being made the title had passed since, under the Spanish law prevailing in 1815, a deed was not necessary to convey land. It could be conveyed by parol.[22] Again, in Missouri, in 1855, it was held, in connection with another action in ejectment wherein title turned upon the law governing marriages in 1777, that the Spanish law prevailing at said time controlled.[23] In this case, the court said:

"The Roman Law must be looked to as the original of the Spanish law upon this subject, although, of course, it has been greatly changed in the long lapse of years, by usage and by the written laws of the Spanish sovereigns."

TEXAS: The state now known as Texas was originally settled by the Spanish early in the eighteenth century, and was called by them the province of the New Philippines. Between the French of Louisiana and the Spanish there were many disputes concerning

---

20. Cutter v. Waddingham, 22 Mo. 206. See, also, Childress v. Waddingham, 16 Mo. 24, 43; Wright's Adm'r v. Thomas, 4 Mo. 260; Bird v. Montgomery, 6 Mo. 510; Smith v. Madison, 67 Mo. 694.

21. Riddick v. Walsh, 15 Mo. 536; Mitchell v. Tuckers, 10 Mo. 260; Bird v. Montgomery, 6 Mo. 510.

22. Mitchell v. Tuckers, 10 Mo. 260.

23. Cutter v. Waddingham, 22 Mo. 206. See also, Allen v. Moss, 27 Mo. 354.

the boundary lines between the two provinces, which in fact were never settled by them.

Later, Texas became a part of the Spanish province of Mexico. In 1822, Mexico became independent of Spain, and in 1835, Texas gained her independence of Mexico, becoming an American State in 1845. It is obvious from these facts that the Spanish law was the original law of Texas.[24] In fact, it remained the law until 1840 when the congress of the Texan republic adopted the Common Law of England as the groundwork of its jurisprudence. From that time, the courts of Texas, as said by the supreme court of that state, "cannot ignore the Common Law, and apply conflicting principles of the Civil Law, though the latter seem more equitable."[25] However, in a proper case, the Texas courts will take judicial notice of the laws common to both Mexico and Texas prior to the separation.[26] In a case involving the validity of marriage, for example, a Texas marriage having been contracted before the introduction of the Common Law, the rights and obligations flowing from it were held to depend on the principles of Spanish jurisprudence.[27]

The supreme court of Texas also said, in 1859, that the adoption of the substantive Common Law did not include the pleadings and practice either of the courts of law or chancery, as known in the remedial jurisprudence of Common Law countries. Such rules of practice are not of any obligatory force, in Texas, as matter of absolute principle, unless they have received legislative affirmation.[28]

THE NORTHWEST TERRITORY: The French explorers who founded Canada pushed westward to the present

---

24. Mexican Central Ry. Co. v. Marshall, 91 Fed. 933; Carroll v. Carroll, 20 Tex. 731; Coleo v. Perry, 7 Tex. 109, 146.
25. Diamond v. Harris, 33 Tex. 634.
26. Mexican Central Ry. Co. v. Marshall, 91 Fed. 933.
27. Smith v. Smith, 1 Tex. 621.
28. Seguin v. Maverick, 24 Tex. 526.

sites of Detroit and Mackinac, and also to the region of the upper Mississippi. They established trading posts along the way and carried French law with them. Thus the Custom of Paris, as the old French law was called, was introduced within the present areas of the states of Michigan, Wisconsin and Minnesota.

It was in 1763 that France ceded to Great Britain the district known in this country as the Northwest Territory, or the land northwest of the Ohio river. In 1783, the territory was ceded by Great Britain to the United States, although its actual possession was not delivered till July, 1796. However, in 1787, four years after the cession, the famous Act of Congress, known as the Ordinance for the Government of the Northwest Territory, was passed. This act was designed for the whole territory, including Ohio, Indiana, Illinois, and Michigan.[29] Prior, therefore, to the taking effect of the Ordinance of 1787, the territory was governed in civil matters by the French law including the Custom of Paris as modified by royal edicts.[30] The Ordinance of 1787 recognized this fact,[31] and the French laws as well as the English and Canadian laws were expressly repealed by the Territorial legislature of Michigan, in 1810.[32]

Previous to 1776, the Northwest Territory was also claimed by Virginia as a part of her chartered limits. Prior, however, to the war of the Revolution numerous settlements had been formed in the district now comprising the states of Indiana and Illinois, consisting

---

29. May v. Rumney, 1 Mich. 1, 4; Abbott v. Godfroy's Heirs, 1 Mich. 178, 181.

30. Crane v. Reeder, 21 Mich. 24, 61; Lorman v. Benson, 8 Mich. 18; Lovell v. Strobel, 89 Ill. 370; President of Kaskaskia v. McClure, 167 Ill. 23; Colburn v. Harvey, 18 Wis. 156; Stead v. Presidente, 243 Ill. 239.

31. Section 2; Lavella v. Strobel, 89 Ill. 370, 380.

32. 1 Terr. Laws 900; Lorman v. Benson, 8 Mich. 18, 24; Crane v. Reader, 21 Mich. 24, 61; Matter of Lamphere, 61 Mich. 105, 108.

principally of French inhabitants from Canada who held the lands they occupied under French and English grants. When Virginia, in 1783, ceded the territory to the United States, the rights of the French settlers in these lands were expressly confirmed.[33]

CALIFORNIA: Throughout the Pacific coast region of the present area of the United States, the Spanish made settlements, or rather established agricultural missions, at an early day. More than twenty such missions were planted, the oldest being that at San Diego, in 1769. Later, when Mexico became independent of Spain in 1822, all this previous Spanish territory was claimed by Mexico, and in the succeeding years many Mexican and other settlers of Spanish descent took up their homes in this region, carrying with them Mexican and Spanish law. At the close of the Mexican war, in 1848, a large part of this vast tract of land was, under the terms of the treaty of Guadalupe-Hidalgo, ceded by Mexico to the United States, and from this territory were later carved the states of California, Nevada, Utah, Arizona, and New Mexico. That Mexican law, which was derived from Spanish law, formerly prevailed in the district now comprising the state of California has been recognized by the courts of that state.[34] The discovery of gold in California, in 1848, caused an unprecedented influx of population from other parts of the United States. Within a few months, "the emigration from older states exceeded five times the original population of the country,"[35] and in another year it had reached about one hundred thousand. These new comers brought their own customs and local laws with them. The case was without

33. Langdeau v. Hanes, 21 Wall. (U. S.) 521, 526.
34. Von Schmidt v. Huntington, 1 Cal. 55; Panaud v. Jones, 1 Cal. 488; Fowler v. Smith, 2 Cal. 39, 47; Scott v. Ward, 13 Cal. 458, 470. And see Moore v. Shaw, 17 Cal. 119; City of Santiago v. Water Co., 77 Cal. Dec. 766.
35. Fowler v. Smith, 2 Cal. 39, 47.

parallel in history. It was not merely the passing of a country from one sovereignty to another, with the retention, as is customary in such cases, of its former laws, but it was a change in sovereignty coupled with such a vast incursion of settlers from many sections of the new sovereignty, a new population overwhelmingly greater than the old, that the laws of the new settlers necessarily superseded, almost at once, the original law, which "was that of the Roman Law," says the supreme court of California,[36] "modified by Spanish and Mexican legislation." "The laws of Mexico, written in a different language, and founded on a different system of jurisprudence, were to the new comers a sealed book. Justice was administered by American judges, without regard to Mexican law."[37]

The first session of the California territorial legislature adopted the Common Law of England as the basis of legal principles, and, on April 22, 1850, another act was passed repealing all laws previously in force, but providing "that no right acquired, contracts made, or suits pending shall be affected thereby." For many years afterwards, and even yet occasionally, land titles originating by Spanish and Mexican grants have required the attention of the courts.

NEW MEXICO: New Mexico, as already stated, was a part of the territory embraced in the treaty of Guadalupe-Hidalgo made at the end of the war with Mexico. This region was visited by the Spaniards, as early, it is believed, as 1536. It was colonized in 1582, Santa Fe being, next to St. Augustine, the oldest town in the United States. At the time of its cession by Mexico, New Mexico had become a state in the Mexican republic. It was made an American territory in 1850, and a state in 1911. When it became a part of the

---

36. Fowler v. Smith, supra; Holliday v. West, 6 Cal. 519.
37. Fowler v. Smith, 2 Cal. 39, 47.

United States, the Civil Law as it existed in Spain and Mexico was its law,[38] and that law has been repeatedly recognized in the decisions of the supreme court of the territory and of the state.[39]

It is sometimes said that Spanish and Mexican law is not Roman or Civil Law but consists of its own system of law.[40] It is quite true that Spanish and Mexican law has, in the course of time, become modified and changed, and differs in many respects from Roman Law, nevertheless, as said by the supreme court of New Mexico, "Spanish and French Civil Law are derived from the same source, the Roman Civil Law." [41]

FLORIDA: Florida was purchased by the United States from Spain in 1819. The territory had long been an area of colonization for both the Spanish and the French. In fact, St. Augustine, permanently settled by the Spanish in 1565, is the oldest settlement in the United States. Pensacola was settled by the French in 1696. Three years after the purchase, or in 1822, a territorial government was established, it being provided by such act that the laws in force in the territory, at the commencement of the act, and not inconsistent with it, should remain in force until altered or repealed by the legislature.[42] It was in 1829, ten years after the purchase that the territorial legislature adopted the Common Law of England.[43] Florida became a state in 1845.

In taking possession of Florida pursuant to the treaty of 1819, this country followed the procedure

38. In re Chavez, 149 Fed. 73, 75; Moore v. Davey, 1 N. M. 303, 305.
39. Chavez v. McKnight, 1 N. M. 153; Barnett v. Barnett, 9 N. M. 205, 213; Strong v. Eakin, 11 N. M. 113, 114.
40. Judge Bennett in Panaud v. Jones, 1 Cal. 488, 501.
41. Leitensdorfer v. Webb, 1 N. M. 34.
42. Sec. 13, Act of March 30, 1822.
43. Rev. Gen. Sts. of Florida, 1920, Sec. 71.

usually recognized in all similar transactions. In fact, it is a fundamental principle, under the law of nations, that the inhabitants, citizens, or subjects of a conquered or ceded country, territory, or province, retain all the rights of property, not taken away by the conqueror or by the terms of the treaty, and remain under their former laws until they are changed. In 1821, Congress enacted that the government of Florida should be vested in such person as the President might appoint. The governor thus appointed, announced by proclamation, in the same year, that all laws in existence at the time of the cession of Florida by Spain should continue in force till altered by the local legislature. Therefore, till that time, the Civil Law was in force in Florida,[44] for as Chief Justice Marshall said,[45] "no laws could then have been in force but those enacted by the Spanish government."

NEW YORK: Even the land where now stands our country's greatest city was at one time under the Civil Law. It was an Englishman, Henry Hudson, who discovered Manhattan Island, but he was in the employ at the time of the East India Company of Holland, and was sailing a Dutch ship. He explored the bay and then sailed up the great river named after him. This was in 1609. Five years later, in 1614, Manhattan Island was settled by the Dutch who named the town New Amsterdam. They held it for fifty years before under England's claim of right of discovery it was forcibly taken from them in a time of peace by the English under the Duke of York, in 1664, and the name of the colony changed to New York. However, the Roman Dutch Law which was brought to the colony by the original settlers from Holland, in 1614, re-

---

44. See Mitchel v. United States, 9 Pet. (U. S.) 711.
45. American Ins. Co. v. Canter, 1 Pet. (U. S.) 544.

[Roman Law]

mained a part of the law of the colony after the capitulation of Governor Stuyvesant,[46] and on several occasions that law has been recognized by the courts of New York,[47] particularly in matters dealing with property rights derived from Dutch colonial sources.

In the case of Dunham v. Williams,[48] for example, a deed describing a piece of land as bounded "on a highway," carried prima facie, it was said, the title of the grantee to the center of the road. This presumption may be repelled, however, if the roadbed in question belonged to another. The road in the case cited was proven to be an old Dutch road, laid out before the "capitulation" to the English in 1664. This caused the court to hold that the boundary in the deed in question carried title only to the roadside, since by the rule of the Civil Law, which prevailed in all the colonial provinces of the Dutch, the title to all roadbeds was in the government. It is interesting further to recall that when the Dutch were forced to give up to the English the settlement of New Amsterdam, they obtained from them a pledge that the Dutch colonists should remain in the enjoyment of their own laws concerning inheritances, and that all contracts made before the day of surrender, Aug. 27, 1664, should be construed according to the Civil Law of Holland.[49]

In the matter of the disposition of property by will, the Roman Dutch Law of Holland left abdiing traces. Long after the first English occupation the practice of making a will by oral declaration before a notary,

46. Chancellor Walworth in the Canal Appraisers v. The People, 17 Wend. (N. Y.) 584; Van Giesen v. Bridgeford, 83 N. Y. 348.

47. The Canal Appraisers v. The People, 17 Wend. (N. Y.) 571; Dunham v. Williams, 37 N. Y. 251; Miller v. Miller, 91 N. Y. 315; Smith v. Rentz, 131 N. Y. 169.

48. Dunham v. Williams, 37 N. Y. 251, 253.

49. Dunham v. Williams, supra.

or by leaving with him a sealed instrument, was commonly observed.[50]

PHILIPPINES AND PORTO RICO: By the terms of the Treaty of Paris, at the close of the Spanish American War in 1899, the islands of the Philippine archipelago and Porto Rico became a part of the territory of the United States. We have previously alluded to the Civil Code of Spain promulgated in 1889. That code was, that same year, extended by royal decree to the islands of Porto Rico, and the Philippines.[51]

The status of the Philippines after becoming our insular possessions corresponded to that of Florida during the early period of the American sovereignty,[52] and the Supreme Court of the United States has said that it will take judicial notice of the Spanish law existing in those islands.[53]

The Civil Code of Spain is still the basic law in the Philippines, although it has been amended in a number of matters by legislation.[54] In Porto Rico, the code was revised in 1902,[55] and again in 1930. In the Philippine reports, begun in 1901, authoritative compilations of Spanish law, such as the Partidas[56] and the Novissima,[57] are frequently cited.

CANADA: In the Dominion of Canada, the Civil Law is the legal system of the province of Quebec. Jacques Cartier, a French navigator, sailed up the St. Lawrence River in 1535, and the first settlements in the country were made by the French under Cartier, in 1541, near

50. Fernow, Calendar of Wills, p. IV; Reinsch, English Common Law in American colonies, University of Wisconsin Bulletin, Oct., 1899.
51. Also to Cuba.
52. United States v. Dorr, 2 Phil. 269, 276; affirmed, 195 U. S. 138.
53. Ponce v. Roman Cath. Apostolic Church, 210 U. S. 296.
54. See Development of Law in the Philippines, Iowa Law Review, XVI, 464 (1931), by former Governor Gilmore.
55. Morales v. Registrar, 16 P. R. 109, 114; Ex parte Axtmayer, 19 P. R. 378; Ortega v. Lara, 202 U. S. 339.
56. Benedicto v. de la Rima, 3 Phil. 34, 40; Ker v. Couden, 6 Phil. 735.
57. Ebreo v. Sichon, 4 Phil. 705, 707.

the present city of Quebec. The French also settled near Montreal the following year. Canada, or New France as it was first called, was a vast territory, indefinite in extent. Over this great domain the laws of France and the Custom of Paris were theoretically extended.[58]

The City of Quebec was founded in 1608, and was made the capital of the royal colony in 1663. With the exception of a brief period in its early history, the country remained under French control till Quebec was captured by the English forces under General Wolfe, in 1759. Four years later the entire territory was transferred to England.

The other provinces of Canada were later settled by the English, and for that reason the Common Law of England became established in them. The district now known as the province of Quebec retained, however, the law of its early settlers, the French. In criminal matters, English law was introduced into the province by the Statute of 14 Geo. III, ch. 83 (1774), but private law was left undisturbed. In 1866, a civil code for the province of Quebec was adopted, and this code follows in part the French model.

Mr. Justice Riddel of the Appellate Court of Ontario, speaking before the American Bar Association upon the Canadian courts, said at the close of his address:[59]

"Now, I do not know that I should say anything more about our law with the exception, perhaps, of that of the province of Quebec. There the common law is not the Common Law of England; it is not the common law of New York state, or the common law of any of your states, except, perhaps, Louisiana. It is the Civil Law, based upon the old Roman Law, based upon the French law; and let no man despise

---

58. Howe, Studies in the Civil Law, 2d Ed., p. 134.
59. In 1910.

that law; let no man sneer at French-Canadian law unless he is prepared to maintain and prove that Coke was a greater lawyer than Tribonian, and Lord Mansfield than Pothier. The Roman Law, which was the law of the ancient Roman, and which, if ever there be a universal law, will be the basis of that universal law, which is the basis of the law of Scotland, the basis of the law of France, which is the basis of the law of Germany—Let no man despise that law unless indeed he happens to be like us, a Common Law lawyer. Then, of course, he has a right to consider that absurd which differs from his own Common Law, 'the perfection of human reason.' "

That the Civil Law was introduced into various parts of this country by the early Spanish, French, and Dutch settlers, and that it continues to be the prevailing law, even at the present time, in the state of Louisiana and in our insular possessions, is, however, only a small part of the story concerning the existence of the Civil Law in these United States. One must consider the influence of the Civil Law in general upon our law. For more than a century American law has been gradually and imperceptibly moulded by Civil Law doctrines. The English feudal law has been changed by such doctrines in every one of our states. Our law of inheritance is based upon the principles of the law of Justinian. The Civil Law is the source of our law upon the subject of mortgages,[60] and it is also the parent of very many of our principles of Equity.[61] Amid the recorded dicta of the English Chancery judges "we often," says Maine,[62] "find entire texts from the Corpus Juris Civilis imbedded with their terms unaltered, though their origin is never acknowledged."

60. Gilman v. Illinois, etc. Tel. Co., 91 U. S. 603, 615; Longwith v. Butler, 8 Ill. 32, 36.
61. Lumpkin v. Mills, 4 Ga. 343, 344.
62. Ancient Law, Pollock ed., 42.

The Civil Law is also the springhead of much of our law of bailments,[63] guardian and ward, wills, contracts, easements, corporations, admiralty, and other special topics. In addition to all this, many of our statutes that have modified or completely changed our Common Law have but merely incorporated Civil Law principles.

It should, in contemplation of these facts, be apparent that the Civil Law is a subject of special value to all Americans who are interested not only in the history of our law but also in a better understanding of its doctrines. When we further reflect that the Civil Law is the law of this entire hemisphere south of the United States, it becomes evident that our commercial interests in connection with trade with Mexico, Central and South America will find it more and more a matter of practical importance to have some knowledge of that law.

63. See Coggs v. Bernard, 2 Ld. Raym. 909; Jones on Bailments, 125 et seq.

CHAPTER III

THE INFLUENCE OF ROMAN LAW UPON ENGLISH LAW

To what extent, if any, has Roman Law influenced the early law of England and, thereby, by derivation, the law of our own country? Various answers have been made to this question, the character of the replies depending, in some instances, upon the prejudices or the sympathies of the different writers. Some have vigorously asserted that English law is not at all indebted to Roman Law, while others have insisted that to a very great extent English law has been influenced and moulded by the principles of the law of Rome.

The fact that many principles of English law are similar to or identical with principles found in Roman (or Civil) Law, does not convince all writers that the English law in such instances was borrowed or copied from the Roman Law, since, it is asserted, such likenesses may be merely accidental analogies originating from entirely independent sources. The great conservatism of some English writers, also pride in the alleged indigenous laws of their own country, and prejudice, perhaps, against foreign influence, have, in all probability, affected some of their conclusions upon this subject.

Blackstone in his first lecture as Vinerian professor at Oxford,[1] published later as an introduction to his Commentaries,[2] speaks with courteous diplomacy of the Civil Law, but emphasizes the greater importance

1. Oct., 1758.
2. Comm. Introduc., Sec. 1.

of the Common Law of England, and attributes the continued teaching, in his day, of the Civil Law in the English universities to the influence of "the popish clergy." He also ascribes the revival of the study of the Civil Law to the long ago exploded story that the Civil Law had become obsolete and forgotten upon the Continent when an accidental finding of a copy of the Digest of Justinian, at Amalfi, in 1135, again brought it into vogue all over the west of Europe.[3] Blackstone's views were influenced, doubtless, by his political and ecclesiastical environment. Due to the fact that the law of the Church of Rome (the Canon Law) was drawn largely from Civil Law sources, there grew up in English Protestant circles a conviction, or at least a fixed impression, that the Civil Law, in which the clergy of Rome were more or less versed, was, in some occult or insidious way, being used to propagate popish doctrines. The very term "Roman" Law seemed to connect it with the Church of Rome, and probably many zealous adherents of the English Church believed they were prompting a righteous cause by discouraging the spread, or even the retention, of Civil Law doctrines.

William Wirt Howe, in lecturing many years ago to the students of Yale University, said in connection with Blackstone's prejudices in favor of the Common Law of England and against the Civil Law of Rome:

"No doubt there were some Oxford dons who enjoyed this treatment of the subject, and when they went to dinner that day, drank confusion in their crusty port to the Pope, the Pretender, and the Civil Law; but they perhaps forgot that the classical jurists who made the Civil Law never heard of any pope, but were merely poor pagans looking for that justice which

3. "The romantic fable of the capture of an unique copy (of the Digest) at the siege of Amalfi, in 1135, has long been disproved." P. & M. Hist. of Eng. Law, 2d ed., I, 23.

is the uniform and enduring endeavor to render to every man that which is his due."[4]

However, other English writers have been more emphatic than Blackstone in denying indebtedness on the part of English Law to Roman Law. William Stubbs, professor of history at one time at Oxford, also a bishop in the Church of England, and author of "The Constitutional History of England," said that "England has inherited no portion of the Roman legislation, except in the form of scientific or professional axioms, introduced at a late period, and through the ecclesiastical or scholastic or international university studies. Her Common Law is, to a far greater extent than is commonly recognized, based on usages anterior to the influx of feudality,—that is, on strictly primitive custom."

On the other hand, Lord Holt, at one time England's chief justice, said: "It must be owned that the principles of our law are borrowed from the Civil Law."[5] Sir William Jones likewise said: "Though few English lawyers dare make the acknowledgment, the Civil Law is the source of nearly all our English laws that are not of feudal origin."

And Welsby, another English writer, in speaking of Lord Mansfield, says:

"The Civil Law—that splendid monument of human wisdom was to him a well-filled storehouse of reasoning, from which a ready supply of principles and of rules might always be drawn, to guide him in the decision of cases unprovided for by our own jurisprudence. There are very few departments of our own law on which some light may not be thrown by it in the way of analogical illustration, and with respect to very many, as he has frequently had occasion to show, it is of more direct application, being in fact the

4. Howe, Studies in The Civil Law, 2d Ed., 112.
5. Lane v. Cotton, 12 Mod. 482.

source from which they have been either partially or entirely deduced."

In the same manner, Lord Campbell, one of Mansfield's successors, has written of him: "Lord Mansfield had only to consider what was just, expedient, and sanctioned by the experience of nations further advanced in the science of jurisprudence. His plan seems to have been, to avail himself, as often as opportunity admitted, of his ample stores of knowledge acquired from his study of the Roman Civil Law, not only in doing justice to the parties litigating before him, but in settling with precision and upon sound principles a general rule, afterwards to be quoted and recognized as governing all similar cases."

And Holdsworth, in his History of English Law, says:[6]

"It would not be true to say that English law owes nothing to Roman Law. At different periods in English history the development of our law has been materially helped by its contact with Roman Law. In the age of Bracton, Roman Law taught the fathers of the Common Law the way to construct an intelligent legal system. In the sixteenth century it helped to make English law sufficient for the needs of a modern state. In the eighteenth century it helped Lord Mansfield to found our modern system of mercantile law. We have received Roman Law, but we have received it in small homeopathic doses, at different periods, and as and when required."

By "the contact of English law," says Holdsworth, "with Roman Law." What this contact has been is shown by the history of England.

It is altogether probable that the Roman or Civil Law would have been the system of jurisprudence in the land we now call England if the Teutonic invaders

---

6. Vol. 4, 292, 293.

had not reached it shores and possessed themselves of the country.

In the earliest times of which we have knowledge Britain was inhabited by a branch of the Celtic race, which people likewise inhabited parts of western Europe. Presumably the first dwellers in Britain came over from ancient Gaul, the Gallia of Caesar.

Caesar invaded Britain in 54 B. C., and for 500 years thereafter Rome exercised dominion over the island. It was not till 455 A. D. that Rome, in order to defend Italy from the Germans, withdrew her forces from Britain.

"Roman Law," says Mommsen, "made rapid strides in Britain during the second and third centuries A. D., as is attested by the writings of the Roman jurists Javolenus and Ulpian, who discussed cases arising in Britain."[7] Moreover, an illustrious galaxy of Roman judges honored Britain with their presence. York was the seat for three years of the two highest Roman tribunals, with Papinian, the prince of Roman jurisconsults, as chief justice, and the famous Ulpian and Paulus as associate justices,[8]—a wonderfully able and brilliant court. "It was," says Sherman, "as if the United States Supreme Court were to hold sessions in Alaska."[9]

In the middle of the fifth century, about 449 A. D., certain Teutonic tribes, the Saxons, the Angles, and the Jutes, dwelling on the North Sea and the Baltic, invaded the country, and for a century these Barbarians carried on their wars of conquest against the Britains. They drove the Britains from the more fertile parts of the country and established their own

---

7. Mommsen, Provinces of the Roman Empire (Dickson's translation) Vol. 1, Ch. 5, p. 194.
8. Walton, Introduction to Roman Law, p. 140.
9. Sherman, The Romanization of English Law, Yale Law Journal, Feb. 1914.

settlements therein. The towns built by the Romans were destroyed, and large tracts of land were left barren and desolate. Gradually the various groups of the Teutonic conquerors separated into seven or eight different states, each having its own chief. Bitter rivalries and contests continued, however, between these states until about the year 827, when Egbert, King of Wessex, became the ruler of the entire country which received the name of Angelcyn, or Angleland, a term derived from the Angles. From this name the modern name England was in turn derived.

Whether the Romans left any influence upon the early English law of this Anglo-Saxon period is disputed by the investigators. Coote [10] and Finlayson [11] are of the opinion that the Teutonic invaders adopted the Roman Law they found existing in the country and consequently derived most of their law from the Romans who had for a long time preceded them. Seebohm,[12] a German writer, is of the opinion that the origin of the land law of England is to be found in a blending of Roman and South German law. Holdsworth [13] is of the opinion that the Roman Law exerted only a small influence upon the laws of the Anglo-Saxons.

In 596, the Roman prior Augustine was sent, as a missionary, to Britain by Pope Gregory I. From the earliest days of its existence in Britain the influence of the Church upon British law must be considered. Whatever legal learning the ecclesiastics had was in the Roman Law. Augustine was the founder of the religious See of Canterbury, which still retains the leadership of the English Church. Under the teach-

---

10. "Romans in Britain;" also "Angle-Saxon Law."
11. Introduction to Reeve's Hist. of Eng. Law.
12. "Village Community."
13. Hist. of Eng. Law, II, 3, 4, 75, 86, 105.

ings of Augustine and his colleagues the pagan Anglo-Saxons embraced Christianity.

Among the converts of Augustine was Ethelbert, King of Kent. He married Bertha of Paris, a French princess. About 600 A. D., he compiled the laws of his Kingdom, "according to the example of the Romans,"[14] says Bede,[15] the historian, writing about 735. This code of Ethelbert as preserved contains only ninety brief sections, originally written in Anglo-Saxon, and deals with punishments for various wrongs.[16] There is nothing in these laws themselves which show any Roman influence, but it is pertinent to note that they were the first code of laws ever written in England, that Ethelbert was the first of the Anglo-Saxon kings to be converted to Christianity, that he was in close touch with the Continent where Roman Law influence predominated, that he married a French wife, that Augustine who was sent from Rome had great influence at his court, and that Ethelbert's code was promulgated on "St. Augustine's Day."[17] Is it reasonable or unreasonable to suppose that no Roman Law at all through ecclesiastical sources influenced the laws of Ethelbert's Kingdom?

About 700 A. D., a hundred years after the appearance of the code of Ethelbert, the first law book of Wessex was compiled by order of King Ina.[18] This code of Ina consisted of seventy-six sections, in the form of "dooms" or penal judgments.

In about 827 the seven or eight states or petty kingdoms, called in English history, "the Heptarchy," became united under Egbert, King of Wessex. About 871, Alfred, of illustrious and revered memory, be-

14. "Juxta exempla Romanorum."
15. Hist. Ecc., 2, 5.
16. Thorpe, Ancient Laws and Institutes of England, p. 1.
17. Jenks, Short Hist. of Eng. Law, Boston, 1912, p. 4.
18. Thorpe, 20.

came king. He drove out the Danish invaders, and by reason of the heroic efforts he put forth to establish law and order in his dominions, also on account of his literary attainments, English historians have acclaimed him "the Great." He reigned till about 901. He was a sincere law giver and promulgated a code known as "The Laws of King Alfred."[19] Into this collection of laws Alfred himself states [20] he gathered such laws of Ina and of Ethelbert as seemed good to him, while those that seemed not good he rejected. "The Laws of King Alfred," about 125 sections in all, are not of such a character that comparisons may be made with Roman Law principles, yet Alfred was greatly interested in, and encouraged, the learning of the Continent. He also made a visit to Rome. It is, therefore, entirely within the range of probabilities that, at least, some Roman Law doctrines influenced the views of the king and his advisers. As has been well said by a special investigator [21] of this period of English law, "The possible elements" (of English law up to this time) "have been: (1) British or Celtic, (2) Roman, (3) Teutonic. Fourthly, it is probable that some institutions of South German tribes, who had come more under Roman influence than their North German brethren, had influence on at least the English land system."

In 1016, the wars that for many years had been going on with the Danes resulted in the Danish conquest of the island, and Canute established there the Danish sovereignty which continued till 1042. During the reign of Canute, from 1016 to 1035, he established several monasteries and made a pilgrimage to Rome. Denmark and Norway were also under his sway, and

---

19. Thorpe, 20.
20. Thorpe, 27.
21. Scrutton, "The influence of the Roman Law on the Law of England, London, 1885, p. 6.

whatever influence he exerted upon the laws of his day was, doubtless, derived largely from Roman sources. Canute married Emma, the widow of Ethelred II, the former King of the Anglo-Saxons. Upon the death of Canute in 1035, his sons Hardicanute and Harold, who were also sons of Emma, shared the Kingdom of England, but Harold's death in 1040, left Hardicanute the sole ruler. He, however, died in 1042, and Edward, the son of Emma by her former husband, Ethelred II, an Anglo-Saxon, became king. This Edward by reason of his piety is known in English history as Edward the Confessor. Previous to the death of Canute, Edward had been living in exile in Normandy, and had been brought up in the court of his cousin, the Norman duke. It is obvious, therefore, that Edward was the product of Norman ideas and Norman influences. Upon the beginning of his reign, Norman French became the language of the English court, and Edward's Norman friends were appointed to various important offices of both State and Church. William, the Norman Duke, was also a visitor at Edward's court. The Normanizing of England may be truly said to have begun with Edward the Confessor's reign.[22]

In 1066, Edward died without issue. He was succeeded by his wife's brother, Harold. The claim of Harold was disputed by William, Duke of Normandy, and the Norman leader landed in Sussex with an army of sixty thousand men. In the battle of Hastings that followed, Oct. 14, 1066, Harold, the last of the Anglo-Saxon kings, after a long and stubborn combat was defeated and killed, William becoming the master of England.

The reign of William was an epoch in English history. He developed a feudal system of land tenure founded on a personal allegiance to the king on the part of each tenant of the land. The term feud (or

22. Johnson, The Normans in Europe, Ch. 10 and 12.

fee) meant a grant of land by a monarchical lord to his follower on certain conditions. In the feudal law of the Continent, the term "feud" seems to have been equivalent to the Roman "beneficium," that is, a beneficial grant of land to be held merely at the owner's pleasure. During the closing years of the disintegration of the Roman Empire feudalism appeared, and long before William of Normandy was born it was the prevailing land system of Italy, Germany, and France.[23] That it had its origin in Roman sources there can be no doubt. Even Stubbs admits that feudalism was partly of Roman origin, as it was also partly of German, "a compound of archaic barbarian usage with Roman Law." In other words, the idea of the feud, the use of the land, came from Roman law; the idea of the personal allegiance to the lord of the land came from German sources.

One of the most significant things in connection with the question of the influence of Roman Law upon English law during this period is the fact that William's prime minister and chief adviser was Lanfranc, the distinguished Italian scholar. He was the adviser of William in Normandy, and later became his chief minister in England. In 1070, William appointed him Archbishop of Canterbury. He was learned in the law as well as in theology, having studied Roman Law at Pavia, his birthplace in Italy. He is said to have been a lawyer of world-wide fame. "He knew Lombard law and Roman Law and Canon Law; when he was Archbishop the decreta and canones were ever in his mouth."[24] The very fact that such a celebrated Civil Law scholar was the chief adviser of the king is in itself sufficient to cause one to believe that many principles of Roman Law must have been injected into English law at this period.

23. See Kent's Comm., 14th ed., pp. 488 et seq.
24. P. & M., Hist. of Eng. Law, I, 77.

There was, however, another channel through which some Roman Law flowed into English courts, and that was the Ecclesiastical court. In the Anglo-Saxon period secular and ecclesiastical matters were heard and adjudged in the same court, but in the time of William they became separated, and the Ecclesiastical courts, being entirely in the hands of the Church, administered the Canon Law of the Continent. This body of law while differing in many details from the Roman Civil Law, yet was permeated with many principles of that law, the procedure being almost entirely derived from Roman Law. The Ecclesiastical courts, by virtue of their authority in matters pertaining to the health of souls, asserted their right of jurisdiction over many things, both civil and criminal, including questions of legitimacy, marriage, divorce, wills, debts due the Church, offenses against Church law (such as perjury, bigamy, defamation, adultery), and, in general, all matters in which an ecclesiastic was interested. As time went on, the business of the Ecclesiastical courts increased, and for centuries they maintained their jurisdiction over matrimonial and testamentary causes. It was not until the middle of the nineteenth century that the English Ecclesiastical courts were confined to matters of church discipline. That considerable Roman Law was received in England through the long existence of these courts there would appear to be no question. Hale, writing over two hundred and fifty years ago said in connection with the Ecclesiastical courts: "Where the Canon Law is silent, the Civil Law is taken in as a director." [25]

The Norman Conquest of England took place at a time when a great revival of legal learning was beginning to sweep over Europe. In Lombardy, a law school had been established at the university of Pavia,

---

25. Hale, Com. Law, 28.

[Roman Law]

and soon after the famous law school of Bologna arose. The new culture of Roman Law studies was carried to France. In the year 1038, Conrad II, the King of Germany who had been crowned as emperor by the pope at Rome, in 1027, ordained that Roman Law should be once more the territorial law of the city of Rome.[26] The law school at the university of Bologna attracted to it great crowds of students who came from all parts of Europe, as many as ten thousand studying there, it is said,[27] at one period of its history.

About the year 1143, in the reign of Stephen, Vacarius, a learned teacher of Roman Law, was induced by Theobald, the Archbishop of Canterbury, to leave the law school at Bologna, and to found a school of law at the university of Oxford. Vacarius thus became the first professor of law in England, and Oxford university from that day to this has been the chief seat of Roman Law learning in England. Oxford's degree of "bachelor of civil law" carries with it, says Scrutton,[28] honors in its law school, and the degree of "Doctor of Civil Law" is the most honorable degree the university confers.

While at Oxford, Vacarius published an abbreviation of the Digest and Code of Justinian, "for use of students," so he declared, "too poor to buy copies of the originals." For this reason, law students at Oxford were for a long time called "Pauperistae." [29]

The new teachings of Vacarius aroused the opposition of King Stephen who disliked Theobald. The king forbade Vacarius to teach and also prohibited the retention by students of a Roman Law book. This

26. P. & M., Hist. Eng. Law, I, p. 23.
27. Ortolan, Hist. Rom. Law, Cutler's ed., p. 422.
28. Influence of Roman Law on Law of Eng., 68.
29. See Ortolan, Hist. Rom. Law, p. 615; Colquhoun, Rom. Law, p. 144.

opposition soon ceased, however, and the prohibitions were soon removed either by Stephen or his successors.[30]

King Stephen died in 1154, being succeeded by Henry II, the first of the Plantagenet dynasty. He was born in France. He married Eleanor, Duchess of Guienne who had previously been Queen of France, having been divorced by Louis VII. When Henry II invaded England in 1153, in his contest against Stephen for the English throne, he was the master, as Duke of Normandy, of nearly half of the territory of France. It should be obvious, therefore, that all his views and inclinations in matters legal and judicial were those of the country from which he came.

The reign of Henry II (1154–1189) is conspicuous for its legal reforms, especially in his organization of the courts and in matters of procedure. Hale says[31] of him: "He raised the municipal laws of the Kingdom to a greater perfection, and a more orderly and regular administration, than before." Previously the English courts were purely local, consisting of "the county courts, the hundred courts, and the courts baron."[32] The administration of justice in these courts was very irregular and very unsatisfactory. The local judges were freeholders of the county and were not learned in the law. This resulted in a great variety and confusion of laws. Henry II centralized the courts in the authority of the king. He commissioned and sent out into the various counties judges to try all cases, civil and criminal, specified in their commission. This was the beginning of a regular system of judicature, and was caused, says Finlayson,[33] by the influence of Roman Law. "If we try to sum up in a few

30. Hunter, Rom. Law, p. 109.
31. Hist. Com. Law, c. 7, p. 120.
32. Ib.
33. Preface to Reeve's Hist. of Com. Law.

words," say Pollock and Maitland,[34] "the results of Henry's reign which are to be the most durable and the most fruitful, we may say that the whole of English law is centralized and unified by the institution of a permanent court of professional judges, by the frequent mission of itinerant judges throughout the land, by the introduction of the 'inquest' or 'recognition' and the 'original writ' as normal parts of the machinery of justice."

The "recognition" referred to was the commencement of our modern jury system. Formerly jurors were the witnesses summoned by a party to a suit to testify to their belief in the oath of compurgation of the suitor. The "recognition" (from recognoscere, to declare) is a declaration of the truth sworn to by "twelve free and lawful men of the neighborhood," summoned by a public officer, and given in answer to a question of fact propounded by the officer.[35] The use of recognitors antedates the reign of Henry II, since they were previously used to determine the truth of any question under investigation by some public official. It was, however, in the use of such recognitors (sworn declarants of truth) in legal trials, both civil and criminal, that procedure in the days of Henry II is distinguished. The great feature that more than anything else, perhaps, makes this reign an era in our law, says Finlayson,[36] is the importance given to procedure, and, above all, to an intelligent and rational system of trial by selected and sworn jurors, "precisely upon the principle of the Roman Law." And a greater authority says:[37] "The English jury has been so highly prized by Englishmen, so often copied by foreigners, that its origin has been sought in many dif-

34. Hist. of Eng. Law, I, 138.
35. Glanville, XIII, 3, 19, 33.
36. Preface to Reeve's Hist. of Com. Law.
37. P. & M., Hist. of Eng. Law, I, 140.

ferent directions. At the present day, however, there can be little doubt as to the quarter to which we ought to look. We must look to the Frankish inquisitio, the prerogative rights of the Frankish Kings. Not to the ordinary procedure of the Frankish courts; that, like the procedure of our own ancient communal courts, knows but such antique modes of proof as the ordeal and the oath with oath-helpers. But the Frankish King has in some measure placed himself outside the formalism of the old folk-law, his court can administer an equity which tempers the rigor of the law and makes short cuts to the truth. In particular, imitating, it may be, the procedure of the Roman fiscus, he assumes to himself the privilege of ascertaining and maintaining his own rights by means of an inquest. He orders that a group of men, the best and most trustworthy men of a district, be sworn to declare what rights he has or ought to have in their district. . . . On the whole we may say that, but for the conquest of England, this procedure would have perished and long ago have become a matter for the antiquary. Such is now the prevailing opinion, and it has triumphed in this country over the natural disinclination of Englishmen to admit that this 'palladium of our liberties' is in its origin not English but Frankish, not popular but royal. It is certain that of the inquest of office or of the jury of trial the Anglo-Saxon dooms give us no hint, certain also that by no slow process of evolution did the doomsman or the oath-helper become a recognitor."

During the reign of Henry II there appeared, sometime between 1180 and 1190, the earliest book on the Laws of England, entitled "A Treatise on the Laws and Customs of the Kingdom of England" (Tractatus de Legibus et Consuetudinibus Regni Angliae). It is generally believed to be the work of Ranulph de Glanville who was chief justiciar of the king. It is more of a manual of procedure and practice than a treatise on substantive law, but it is evident that its author was acquainted with Roman and Canon Law.[38] The introduction of his book is modelled upon the preface to the Institutes of Justinian, and in various places throughout the volume he compares the existing English law with the Roman or Canon Law. In his treatment of contracts [39] he follows the order of the Roman writers and borrows many of their terms. Glanville's book was originally written in Latin, but an English translation appeared in 1812.[40]

Between the years, probably, of 1250 and 1258, in the reign of Henry III, Bracton, (otherwise written Bratton or Bretton) a justice of the court of King's Bench, wrote his great treatise on "The Laws and Customs of England." It was pre-eminently the most important law book that England had thus far produced. Bracton has often been called "the father of the English Common Law," and "the Blackstone of the 13th century." His work, written in Latin, is divided into five parts or "books," [41] and in its general form or arrangement it seems more like a Roman than an English law book.[42] Its contents also show great familiarity with Roman Law, from whose sources a part of the text was obviously drawn. Sir Henry Maine says [43] that "it is one of the most hopeless enigmas in the history of jurisprudence that an English writer of the time of Henry III should have been able to put off on his countrymen as a compendium

38. P. & M., Hist. of Eng. Law, I, 165.
39. Book X.
40. Beames, London, 1812. There is an American edition, 1900, with an introduction by Prof. Beale. Glanville's work existed only in manuscript until 1554 when it was printed in Latin.
41. Books I and II are divided into chapters and paragraphs; the remaining three books are divided into treatises on procedure.
42. It follows the order of the Institutes of Justinian as to the law of (1) Persons; (2) Things; and (3) Actions.
43. Ancient Law, Ch. 4.

of pure English Law, a treatise of which the entire form and a third of its contents were directly borrowed from the Corpus Juris." Other writers, however, insist that Bracton did not impose Roman Law, as such, upon his countrymen, but that the law he cited, although largely Roman in its origin, was also, in fact, English Law.[44]

Prof. Maitland says that Maine's statement is "stupendous exaggeration," since the amount of matter that Bracton "directly" borrowed from the Corpus Juris is not a thirtieth part of his book.[45] Possibly the difference in opinion of these two eminent legal scholars is explained by the use of the word "directly," since there is an "indirect" borrowing as well as a "direct."

The discovery by Professor Vinogradoff of "Bracton's note book," among the piles of manuscript of the British Museum, shows, however, that Bracton based a part of his work upon actually decided English cases. This note book "contains some two thousand cases over against some of which marginal notes have been written, apparently in Bracton's hand." [46]

Much of the Roman Law material used by Bracton was obtained from the Roman Law texts of Azo, a distinguished professor of law in the university of Bologna. He wrote a summary (Summa) of the Code of Justinian, and also a Summa of the Institutes. Azo's work was well known upon the Continent, and that Bracton was well acquainted with it is manifest both from the form and substance of his English treatise. In addition to his use of Azo, Bracton directly cites

---

44. Spence, I, 124; Güterbock, Bracton and his Relation to the Roman Law.

45. Introduction to "Bracton and Azo," a publication of the Selden Society, London, 1895.

46. P. & M., I, 207. This material has been edited and published by Professor Maitland, under the title of "Bracton's Note Book," 3 Vols., 1887.

a number of times both the Digest and the Codex of the Corpus Juris.

There are three other books that belong to the latter part of the 13th century, all of them being written probably, in the reign of Edward I. They are Thornton's Abridgment or "Summa;" "Fleta;" and "Britton." A fourth book, known as the Mirror of Justices, is also placed by many in this period. The "Summa" or Abridgment of Thornton was an abridgment of Bracton's work prepared by Gilbert Thornton, chief justice of the King's bench. This book is no longer in existence. "Fleta," written about 1292, is of unknown authorship, but is believed to have been written by some judge while a prisoner in the Fleet, one of the jails of London. It is written in Latin, and is entitled "A Commentary on the Laws of England." It is a comparatively small book, taking most of its text in an abridged form from Bracton, and adding some new material drawn from Roman Law sources. Somewhere about 1300 the work known as "Britton" appeared. Some are of the opinion that the name "Britton" was merely another form of the name "Bracton," and that "Britton," written in French,[47] was intended to be a popular abridgment of the larger work of Bracton which was written in Latin and not accessible to many judges and lawyers. Others, however, believe that Britton was the name of an individual distinct from Bracton. Sir Edward Coke thought he was John de Breton, bishop of Hereford. Most scholars, however, identify him as John de Breton or John de Bretaign, a justice of the time of Edward I. The work is divided into six "books" and is prefaced by the king's proclamation that it is the law of the realm, analagous to the royal authority given by Justinian to the Institutes.

The book known as "The Mirror of Justices," writ-

---

47. The "French" of the 13th Century.

ten as generally believed, in the time of Edward I, was formerly by some scholars believed to be the most ancient of all English law books, since it purports to treat of the laws of King Alfred. The general consensus of scholars at the present time, however, is that the work is of no value, being written merely for the purpose of discrediting the justices of King Edward's reign. It is called by experts competent to speak, "apocryphal," [48] "an invention," [49] and declared to be "full of fables and falsehoods, and worthless as an authority." [50]

The 12th and 13th centuries have been called the "Roman epoch of English legal history." [51] The writings of this period both lay and professional show that the spirit of Roman Law prevailed almost everywhere. The courts cited it with approval [52] and it was taught in the schools of learning, beginning with the lectures of Vacarius at Oxford in 1143. There is also a tradition that in the following century the son of the great Accursius of Bologna was brought to England by Edward I for the purpose of teaching Roman Law at the same university.[53] During all this period Roman Law authorities "were habitually cited in the common law courts, and relied upon by legal writers, not as illustrative and secondary testimonies as at present, but as primary and as practically conclusive." [54] It is also said by a very conservative writer upon the history of English law [55] that, during this period of the twelfth and thirteenth centuries, the Civil and Canon Law

48. Palgrave, Proofs, 113.
49. Stephen, Hist., Crim. Law, I, 52.
50. P. & M., II, 478.
51. Güterbock, Bracton and his Relation to the Roman Law (Coxe, Eng. Transl.), p. 16.
52. Selden, c. 8, p. 1, et seq.
53. Swetland v. Curtiss Airports Corporation, 41 Fed. Rep. (2d series) 929.
54. Amos, Roman Civil Law, p. 450.
55. Holdsworth, II, 109.

were perhaps the most important of all the external influences which have shaped the English law. And another English writer [56] has said that as an antidote to the teaching of Vacarius at Oxford, the professors of the Common Law were settled "in the Inns of Court, between the palace of Westminster and the cathedral. Soon the cleric, sheltered beneath the coif which concealed his tonsure, was pleading and judging causes in the new royal courts of the Common Law. But we may be sure, even if we had no evidence, that he did not entirely forget the law which he had learned at Oxford or Cambridge,[57] that when the customs of the realm, faithfully searched, gave no answer to a new problem, he fell back on the Digest and the Code."

In the 14th Century, after the times of Edward I, a reaction against Roman Law set in, and its influence upon English Law began to decline. There was no succeeding period that was visibly marked with additional Roman Law principles, and there were sporadic cases of open opposition to the reception of Roman Law doctrines in certain matters, but the Roman Law already incorporated within or adopted by English law still remained.

In a previous paragraph reference was made to the influence of the Roman Law upon the Ecclesiastical Law of England. However, in another branch of our law the moulding influence of Roman Law was, perhaps, even more marked. This was the Maritime Law, or the law administered in the courts of admiralty. Maritime Law is the law of the sea, the law relating to such matters as contracts for the building, equipping and repairing of ships; contracts of freightage; the carriage of passengers by sea; the duties and rights of seamen, also of the owners of vessels; bills

---

56. Jenks, A Short Hist. of Eng. Law, Boston, 1912, p. 20.
57. The study of Roman Law was introduced in the University of Cambridge in the thirteenth century.

of lading; insurance; bottomry and respondentia bonds; general average; salvage; marine torts; crimes committed on the high seas; and matters connected with harbors and navigation in general. In medieval times the law governing these things was the law of "big business," since in those days the important commercial interests were connected with the transportation of merchandise by sea.

Maritime or admiralty law is not a part of the Common Law of England. It grew up from the customs of merchants in towns and cities bordering on the Mediterranean and the Atlantic. It is founded on the broadest principles of equity and justice, deriving, however, much of its completeness and its system of procedure from the Roman Law.[58] It is Roman Law as found in the customs and usages of merchants (the Law Merchant, or Lex Mercatoria), in various codes of maritime law, and in the decisions of various judges. The best known of the codes are Consolato del Mare; the Laws of Oleron, the Laws of Wisbuy; and Ordonnance de la Marine of Louis XIV.[59]

The most important, perhaps, of these codes is the Laws of Oleron. It was introduced into England in 1150. It contains the customary laws of the sea in force in the island of Oleron, on the western coast of France near La Rochelle. It was published under the patronage of Eleanor, duchess of Guienne (Aquitaine). She became the wife of Henry II of England, and the mother of Richard I, "Coeur de Lion."

The Law Merchant of England was greatly improved and extended by Lord Mansfield, who was Lord Chief Justice of the King's Bench for thirty-two years (1756–1788). He was a Scotchman, learned in Roman

---

[58]. DeLovic v. Boit, 7 Fed. Cas. No. 3,776; Insurance Co. v. Dunham, 11 Wall. (U. S.) 1, 23.

[59]. These last three codes may be found in the appendix of 30 Fed. Cas., p. 1171 et seq.

Law, and his great ability enabled him to mould and influence in the interests of justice and equity many principles now accepted as English Law which, however, involved many questions unsettled by prior decisions.[60] Mansfield was accused by his enemies of introducing into English Law principles unknown to its courts. "The Roman code, the law of nations, and the opinions of foreign civilians are your perpetual theme," said one of the letters of "Junius."[61] Mansfield, however, to-day, looms in history as one of the greatest jurists England ever had. "Truly," said Mr. Justice Buller, "Lord Mansfield may be said to be the founder of the Commercial Law of England."[62]

It was, however, the rise and development of the court of Chancery that had more influence in shaping English and American Law by Roman Law principles than any other cause. For a long time in the history of the English Law, especially in the days following the Conquest, the rulers, the clergy, the courts, and the writers were friendly to, and inclined toward, Continental influences. Without question or thought of "foreign" influence such principles of Roman Law as naturally and helpfully served to expand and perfect the somewhat limited and imperfect character of native English Law were gladly "received." It is true that in later times, after political and racial lines had become more distinct, and particularly after religious differences had separated the peoples, matters that were associated with things either "foreign" or "Roman" were opposed by the English. Moreover, the natural and characteristic conservative attitude of the English would cause them to resist changes or innovations in established principles of law. An illustration of this tendency is found as early as 1236. The

60. Campbell, Lives of the Chief Justices, II, 438, 439.
61. Campbell, II, 437.
62. Lickbarrow v. Mason, 2 T. R. 63, 73 (1787).

incident in question was connected with the passage of the Statute of Merton.[63] The English clergy had demanded that the Roman Law of legitimacy per subsequens matrimonium be adopted in England. The barons, however, curtly refused to adopt such a law. Coke says concerning this incident: "All the bishops instanted the lords that they would consent that all such as were born afore matrimony should be legitimate, as well as they that be born *within* matrimony, as to the succession of inheritance, forsomuch as the Church accepteth such for legitimate. And all the earls and barons with one voice answered that they would not change the laws of the realm which hitherto have been used and approved."[64]

The law book known as Fleta was written, as already stated, near the close of the 13th century, and for the next two hundred and fifty years, or until about the middle of the 16th century no important works on the laws of England appeared. However, during this period there was established a tribunal, separate from the courts of law, in which the spirit and the principles of Roman Law were constantly invoked and applied. This was the English Court of Chancery which in time became the most distinguished court of the realm and whose system of jurisprudence has during the past hundred years moulded and shaped to an incalculable degree our present day laws both unwritten and statutory. The institution of the Court of Chancery as a separate court is usually said to date from the middle of the 14th century when King Edward III ordered that all judicial matters that were of Grace, should be referred to and disposed of by the Chancellor, or by the Keeper of the Privy Seal. This decree of the king was, however,

---

63. From the monastery of Merton, in county of Surrey, seven miles from London.

64. Coke, II Inst. ch. 9.

but confirmatory of a general practice that had already been in existence for many years.[65]

A "Keeper of the King's conscience," as he was called, was appointed from very early times. From the time of William I to the time of Henry VIII, this official was always a high dignitary of the Church. He ranked next to the king, and was virtually the king's prime minister. There were many instances where the remedies afforded by the courts of law were wholly inadequate to meet the requirements of justice, and appeals to the Keeper of the King's conscience increased in number. He, in his judicial capacity as Chancellor, applied to the matter presented by a petitioner the principles of fairness, honesty, and good conscience, just as the ancient Roman praetor applied aequitas to aliens who had no right to resort to the law courts reserved exclusively for Roman citizens. "In fact, the equity administered by the early English chancellors, and the jurisdiction of their court, were confessedly borrowed from the aequitas and judicial powers of the Roman magistrates; and the one cannot be fully understood without some knowledge of the other."[66] The chancellor, being an ecclesiastic and versed in the Roman Law, never hesitated to draw from it such principles as would enable him to deal fairly and conscientiously (ex aequo et bono) with the case submitted to him. Owing to the formal rigidity and ultra conservatism of the Common Law the judges of those courts often found it impossible to furnish remedies to many who invoked their aid. On the other hand, the broad, general principles of the Roman Law enabled the successive chancellors to find therein remedies to meet in many matters the needs of those who had no remedy at Common Law. Not without opposition, however, did the Court of Chancery maintain its

---

65. Pomeroy, Eq. Juris., 3d ed., § 34.
66. Pomeroy, Eq. Juris., 3d ed., § 2.

jurisdiction. The Common Law courts were very jealous of the growing influence and popularity of their great rival, and a struggle often bitter was carried on between them for over two hundred years. Each at times refused to recognize the authority of the other. The lawyers trained in the Inns of Court had little respect for the Chancery practitioners who were educated in the Civil Law taught in the universities of Oxford and Cambridge.[67]

The Court of Chancery finally triumphed, however, in the reign of James I when the king upheld the contention of Lord Chancellor Ellesmere against Lord Chief Justice Coke that Chancery could by injunction prevent the enforcement of a judgment obtained in a Common Law court.[68] In the years that have since ensued the principles of equity as they have become more widely understood have been adopted in many courts of law since they have been found more just and practical than the rules of Common Law. Equitable theories and principles have also been incorporated in many modern statutes. Consequently, by such means Roman Law has, indirectly, had a great influence in moulding our law of the present time. A notable piece of evidence of this shaping process is found in a remarkable letter written a hundred years ago by our own Chancellor Kent, of New York, the author of Kent's Commentaries. He said in speaking of his work upon the bench: "I made much use of the Civil Law, and as the judges (Livingston excepted) knew nothing of French or Civil Law, I had immense advantage over them. I could generally put my brethren to rout and carry my point by mysterious want of French and Civil Law. The judges were republicans[69] and very

67. See Bryce, Studies, etc., p. 861.
68. Blackstone, III, 54; Jenks, Hist. Eng. Law, 166.
69. That is, the early Republican party as distinguished from the Federalists.

kindly disposed to everything that was French, and this enabled me, without exciting any alarm or jealousy, to make free use of such authorities, and thereby enrich our commercial law." [70]

After the book known as "Fleta," no other work of note dealing with English law appeared till Littleton's famous treatise "On Tenures," about 1470. Sir Thomas Littleton (1420–1481) studied in the Inner Temple. In 1455 he rode the circuit as a judge of assize, and in 1466 he was appointed a judge of the court of Common Pleas. His great work "On Tenures," written in law French, is the basic authority on the medieval land law of England. There is no Roman Law in Littleton for he was dealing with our feudal law which had nothing in common with the allodial land law of the Romans.[71]

However, about 1557, Sir William Staunford (1509–1558), a judge of Common Pleas, wrote his work on "The Pleas of the Crown." It was the first book that presented a general and connected account of the English criminal law. It was written in "law French," and cites Bracton many times, even quoting his words. In fact Staunford says in his preface that Bracton and Britton are cited by him in order to show what the Common Law was before being changed by succeeding statutes.

In about 1605, Dr. John Cowell (1554–1611), an instructor of Civil Law at the University of Cambridge, wrote, in Latin, a book entitled "The Institutes of English Law," "arranged and digested upon the method and order of the imperial institutes." He assorts and assembles the texts of Bracton, Britton, and Fleta

---

70. From a letter by Chancellor Kent, in 1828, to a correspondent in Tennessee, published in the Green Bag, Boston, 1897, Vol. 9, pp. 206–211.

71. Littleton, however, refers to the Civil Law. In 123a, he says that the doctrine partus sequitur ventrem of the Civil Law is not the law of England.

according to the order of the treatment of corresponding topics in the Institutes of Justinian. The avowed object of his book was to show the practical identity of the English and the Roman Law.

Also in the works of Sir Henry Spelman (1562–1641), the well-known antiquarian, which were written probably in the early part of the 17th century although not published till long after his death, are found these words: "A great part of our Common Law is derived from the Civil, which Bracton also, above three hundred years ago, well understanding not only cited the Digests and Books of Civil Law in many places for warrant of our Common Law, but in handling our law pursued the method, phrases, and matter of Justinian's Institutes. I think the foundation of our laws were laid by our German ancestors, but were built upon and polished by material taken from the Canon and Civil laws. . . . When and how these several parts were brought into our Common Law is neither easily nor definitely to be expressed. . . . Those no doubt of the Canon Law by the prevalency of the clergy in their several ages. . . . Those of the Civil Law by such of our revered judges and sages of ancient time, as for justice and knowledge's sake sought instruction therein when they found no rule at home to guide the judgment by. For I suppose they in those days judged may things ex aequo et bono and that their judgments after (as Responsa Prudentium among the Romans) became precedents of law unto posterity." [72]

A contemporary of Spelman was Sir Edward Coke who was born in 1552 and died in 1633. He was Attorney-general of England from 1594 to 1606, Chief Justice of the Common Pleas from 1606 to 1613, and Lord Chief Justice of King's Bench from 1613 to 1616.

---

72. "On the Law Terms," last chapter, pp. 99, 101; Scrutton, "Rom. Law and Law of Eng.," 128.

During the latter part of his life he wrote his great work known as "The Institutes," a term taken from the Roman Law writers although Coke was bitterly opposed to the Civil Law and to the Court of Chancery. Of English law he says:[73] "Our common laws are aptly and properly called the laws of England, because they are appropriated to this Kingdom of England . . . and have no dependency upon any foreign law whatever, no, not upon the Civil or Canon law other than in cases allowed by the Laws of England." Also in his preface to his Second Institute he says: "Upon the text of the Civil Law there be so many glosses and interpretations, and again upon those so many commentaries, and all these written by doctors of equal degree and authority, and therein so many diversities of opinion as they do rather increase than resolve doubts and uncertainties, and the professors of that noble science say that it is like a sea of waves. . . . Their glosses and commentaries are written by doctors, which be advocates, and so in a manner private interpretations; our expositions or commentaries . . . are the resolutions of judges in courts of justice in judicial courses of proceedings . . . and therefore . . . produce certainty, the mother and nurse of repose and quietness, and are not like to waves of the sea."

The first part of Coke's celebrated work, or "the First Institute" is a commentary upon Littleton's Tenures, otherwise known as "Coke on Littleton." The "Second Institute" deals with various ancient English statutes; the "Third" (published in 1644 after Coke's death) with Crimes; and the "Fourth" with the jurisdiction of courts. Despite his evident contempt for Roman Law, he nevertheless refers from time to time to its principles, and frequently cites Bracton as an authority, unconscious, doubtless, that he was there-

---

73. II Inst. 98.

by citing Roman Law, Coke's own knowledge of the Civil Law being very slight. Coke lived at a period when the antagonism between the Courts of Common Law and the Court of Chancery was very bitter, and we should not expect to find him friendly to a system of law that was highly approved by those who did business in the latter court.

There were, however, two other great names in the legal literature of this same period which more than offset the unfriendliness which Coke manifested to the Civil Law. They are Francis Bacon (1561-1626) and John Selden (1584-1654). Bacon, one of the most illustrious of England's great names, became Lord Chancellor in 1618. He was great both as a jurist and as a philosopher. Lord Campbell says of him: "His mind was thoroughly familiar with the principles of jurisprudence." . . . "No one ever sat in Westminster Hall with a finer judicial understanding." [74] He was a profound student of Roman Law, and he urged Queen Elizabeth to codify English law, holding up to her the illustrious example of Justinian who codified Roman laws "from infinite volumes and much repugnancy into one competent and uniform corps of laws." [75]

John Selden was celebrated both as a lawyer and a statesman. He was one of the greatest legal scholars that England or any other country ever produced. The Selden Society of England, famous for its publications on English law, was named in honor of him. He was profoundly versed in history, languages, and antiquities as well as in law. He was a voluminous writer on many subjects. In 1635 he published his Mare Clausum. Among his other important legal works are Dissertatio ad Fletam (1647), or "A Com-

---

74. Lives of the Lord Chancellors, Vol. 2, Chaps. 5, 6.
75. Bacon's Maxims of the Law; Great Jurists of the World Cont. Leg. Hist. Series, Boston, 1914, Vol. 2, pp. 144 et seq.

mentary on English Law," and his work on "The Law of Nature and of Nations" (1640). His writings show a profound knowledge of not only Roman Law but also of International Law.

In the year 1609 was born Mathew Hale who died in 1676. He is justly remembered in history as one of the greatest and wisest judges that ever sat upon the English bench. He was educated at Oxford and at Lincoln's Inn. In 1653 he was appointed by Oliver Cromwell judge of the common bench. Upon the restoration of Charles II he was appointed baron of the exchequer (1660), and Lord Chief Justice in 1671. He was the author of two celebrated works, "The History of the Common Law" and "Pleas of the Crown," both being regarded as of high authority. In his "History of the Common Law," Hale, while contending that "neither the Canon Law nor the Civil Law have any obligation as laws within the kingdom" save to the extent that they have "been received and admitted by us," yet acknowledges the influence of the Civil Law in various courts of England other than the courts of Common Law.

Seventy-four years after the death of Sir Mathew Hale, or in the year 1753, William Blackstone, a young man thirty years old, began his lectures on English Law at Oxford University. It is a notable fact that he was the first lecturer on "English Law" in the history of that renowned seat of learning, Civil or Roman Law having been the only law previously taught at either Oxford or Cambridge. The influence upon the laws of this country of Blackstone's great work, "Commentaries on the Laws of England," compiled from his university lectures, has been already noted, likewise Blackstone's conservative attitude as to the independence of the Common Law in relation to the Civil Law. He follows Hale in saying that the Civil Law has no authority of itself in the courts of England except to the extent of its actual reception or adoption by them, yet like Hale he recognizes the fact that in particular courts the principles of the Civil Law have been largely adopted, and that "the rules of the Roman Law either left in England in the days of Papinian, or imported by Vacarius and his followers" constitute a part of the original sources of English law. He frequently cites Bracton, and admits that many principles of Roman Law have been by that author and by others who followed him incorporated in the laws of England.

Such, then, from the earliest beginnings of English law to the time of the separation of the American colonies from the motherland, is a brief summary of the principal historical points of contact on the part of the law of England and the law of ancient Rome. What was said, therefore, over sixty years ago by Emory Washburn, professor at the Harvard school of law, and author of a great treatise on the law of Real Property, is also true to-day, namely, that "to the student of the Common Law who wishes to master it as a liberal science, a knowledge, to a certain extent, at least, of the Civil Law, may be regarded as well nigh indispensable. And if this be true of England, it must be still more so of our own country, whose juridical notions, if not her laws themselves, are in a measure the outgrowth of every civilization and form of government which are found in the old world." [76]

[76]. "The Relation of the Civil to the Common Law," American Law Register, Nov., 1873.

CHAPTER IV

OUTLINES OF ROMAN LAW HISTORY

A. From the Founding of the City to the Beginning of the Empire

The political history of Rome and the development of Roman Law are inseparably linked. Consequently in discussing Roman Law it is important to bear in mind the age or period of Roman history with which any particular legal doctrine or question is connected. The laws of all countries and of all peoples, even including the fanciful immutability of the laws of the ancient Medes and Persians, change from century to century and even from generation to generation owing to the changes in the character and needs of the people. The law of our own country at the present time is not the law of the colonial days, and the law of modern England is quite different from English law in the time of Coke.

The evolution of Roman Law continued for a long period, much longer than the period thus far of our English law. From the founding of Rome to the death of Justinian there were more than thirteen centuries. During this time Rome experienced many changes in government. She passed from a little kingdom to a republic, and from a great republic to a world empire. Each age influenced and left its impress upon her laws. In connection with the different periods of Roman history it is customary to speak of the "old law," or the "jus civile;" praetorian law, or the jus gentium; and the imperial law. We also distinguish between the law of the early and the later empire.

The importance of associating the political history of a people with its laws was recognized by Gaius, the Roman jurist, one of the great authorities upon the law. In the very first book of the Digest of Justinian,[1] occurs an extract from the writings of Gaius, taken from his Commentary upon the Law of the Twelve Tables. In writing for the instruction of those of his own day, he said: "Being about to take up an interpretation of our ancient statutes, I have thought it essential that the law of the Roman people should be traced from the foundation of the city, not because I wish to write verbose commentaries, but because in all matters I perceive a thing is complete only when all its parts are assembled, and surely the most important part of anything is its beginning." What was thus helpful for a better understanding of the law of the Roman people at the time when Gaius wrote, likewise when his words were quoted in the Digest, over three hundred and fifty years later, is even more helpful at the present time. Accordingly, an outline of the more important matters in Roman history bearing upon the development of Roman Law is attempted in this and in the succeeding chapter. This outline is necessarily brief and somewhat fragmentary, owing to its immediate objective.

For our present purpose it will be convenient to divide the political and legal history of Rome into four general periods which we may designate as follows:

I. From the Founding of the city to the Twelve Tables, or from 753 B. C. to 450 B. C., a period of three hundred years. This covers the time of the kings, from 753 to 510 B. C. and also the first sixty years of the republic.

II. From the Twelve Tables to the institution of the praetorship in 366 B. C., a period of eighty-six years.

III. From the institution of the praetorship to the

1. Dig. 1, 2, 1.

conquest of the world, or to the beginning of the Empire, from 366 B. C. to 31 B. C., a period of three hundred thirty-five years.

IV. From the Empire to the Death of Justinian or from 31 B. C. to 565 A. D., a period of nearly six hundred years.

These four periods may approximately be further differentiated as follows:

I. The period of the Quiritary Law.
II. The period of the Jus Civile.
III. The period of the Jus Gentium.
IV. The period of Imperial Law.

I. FROM THE FOUNDING OF THE CITY TO THE TWELVE TABLES

About 753 B. C., the Ramnes (Romani) made a settlement around the Palatine Hill, one of the "Seven Hills" of Rome, and fortified it for a stronghold. All accounts, however, of the beginning of Rome are but traditions, and purely mythical are many reported incidents of the entire regal period. The usually assigned dates of the Kings of Rome are only approximations, and that Romulus, the legendary founder of Rome, was its first king is not history but fable. He was compelled, it is said, to wage war with various surrounding tribes in order to establish his city, and appointed a group of men, known as "the senate," or body of elders, to advise and co-operate with him in the government.

Romulus was succeeded by Numa Pompilius, known as the Lawgiver. His long reign, from about 715 to 673 B. C., was one of great tranquillity, marked with peace and progress, and often cited among the traditions of the Romans as an era of happiness and prosperity. He is said to have been the author of many laws, and to have been guided in wisdom by the nymph

Egeria, particularly in matters of religion and worship. Under the inspiration of this prophetic divinity, Numa established the Roman religion, and appointed pontiffs, augurs, flamens, and vestals. Even Cicero speaks of certain laws of Numa as having come down to his time.

The reign of Tullus Hostilius (673–641 B. C.) followed that of Numa. He is often called the Warrier by reason of the many wars waged by him. He was succeeded by Ancus Marcius (641–616 B. C.), a grandson of Numa. It was during the period usually designated as his reign that the plebeians became organized as a political group. Ancus, it is said, waged wars against the Latin towns, founded Ostia, and built the famous pons sublicius.

The fifth king of Rome was Tarquinius Priscus (616–578 B. C.), the Builder. After the death of Ancus Marcius he was successful in his efforts to get himself elected king in opposition to the son of Ancus. The Roman kingship was not an inheritable but an elective office, a life tenure. Tarquin's political scheming was in face of the fact that Ancus had made him his trusted friend, and had appointed him guardian of his sons. Yet Tarquin carried on successful wars against the surrounding tribes. He built the temple of Jupiter on the Capitoline hill, also the great sewers of Rome, likewise the Circus Maximus. He was finally assassinated, however, by the sons of Ancus.

There are many legends connected with Servius Tullius, the next king (578?534 B. C.), who is said to have reigned for forty-four years. He is reputed to have been a son of Ocrisia, a female slave of Tanaquil, the wife of Tarquinius Priscus, but was accepted by Tarquin as his own son and succeeded him as leader of the Roman state. He showed great qualities of statesmanship. He rebuilt the walls of Rome; reorganized the government; reformed the method of voting; and introduced the census. He also formed a league between Rome and the towns of Latium. The changes which he inaugurated are often cited as the Constitution of Servius Tullius. He organized two assemblies of the people, known as the comitia centuriata and the comita tributa. He gave his daughter Tullia in marriage to Tarquinius Superbus, the son of Tarquinius Priscus. Ambitious for the throne, his own daughter and her husband murdered the king.

Tarquinius Superbus (534–510 B. C.) was king for twenty-four years. His reign was not popular. He received his title, the Proud, from his haughty and despotic character. He caused those senators who favored the reforms of Servius to be put to death. He carried on several successful campaigns, erected a number of public buildings, and planted several colonies. The oldest compilation of laws, according to tradition, date from the time of Superbus, the Jus Papirianum, a body of laws enacted during the days of the kings. They are, therefore, also called Leges Regiae, and were said to have been collected by Sextus Papirius who lived in the time of Superbus.

According to the Digest, the people of Rome, during the period of the Kingdom, passed such laws as were from time to time suggested to them by the kings. "All these statutes," says the Digest,[2] "are preserved in writing in the book of Sextus Papirius who lived in the times of Superbus, and was one of the prominent men. That book is called the Papirian civil law, not because Papirius composed it himself, but because he reduced into a single body of law the statutes which had been passed in an unsystematic way."[3]

2. Dig. 1, 2, 2, 2.
3. This passage is taken from the writings of Pomponius who lived

The Digest further says that after the Kingdom passed away all these laws went out of use. Livy, however, says [4] that the laws of the Twelve Tables and the extant Leges Regiae were collected as far as possible, after the destruction of the city by the Gauls, and continued to be the basis of the law.

With the termination of the reign of Superbus, the Romans abolished the Kingdom as a form of government. The violation of Lucretia by Sextus, the son of Superbus, brought the exasperations of the people to a climax. Under the leadership of Junius Brutus the people deposed the King and drove him from the city. He later attempted to regain the throne, but was decisively defeated in the battle of Lake Regillus. Meanwhile the people had already organized a republic and instead of a king they chose two consuls. These consuls were not elected for life as was the king, but were chosen annually.

During the time of the Kings, a time that is usually designated as the prehistoric period of Rome, the clan, or the gens, was the social unit upon which the political organization was built. A gens consisted of a group of households that claimed descent from some common ancestor. When the state became somewhat enlarged, "the tradition is that Romulus divided the citizens into thirty parts, which he called curiae," [5] or wards. It is generally accepted as historic that Rome was founded first by the Ramnes, and that two other groups or tribes later settled on the Tiber with them, the Tities and Luceres. It is further believed that each of these tribes was divided into ten curiae, or wards, thus accounting for the thirty wards, or curiae, of the early days. Romulus is further said to have organized

in the second century of the present era. It is doubtful if any fragments of these early laws remain.

4. Livy 2, 1.
5. Dig. 1, 2, 2, 2.

a senate, or group of elders, of a hundred men, being selected from the various clans, or gentes. Later, he increased the number to three hundred, the additional two hundred being taken, it is supposed, from the two other tribes. It was these old settlers or tribe groups, divided into many clans, that formed the fathers, the patres, or the original patricians of Rome. For centuries their descendants comprised the aristocratic party. Between this party and the plebeians, a later developed political group, there was bitter rivalry. The history of the first five hundred years of Rome is largely a history of the struggles of the masses of the people, the plebeians, to gain political equality.

Another fact which had an influence upon Roman jurisprudence was the division of the people into the freeborn (freemen), the unfree, and slaves. Freemen and slaves existed from the earliest times. A large part of the population known as "clients" was a later addition. As Rome extended her government over other towns, the people of the conquered and absorbed territory was not admitted into the membership of the Roman State. They were not "freemen" and they were not slaves. They were known as clientes, adherents, because many of the Roman patricians, shrewd and ambitious as they were, took large groups of them under the patronage of their households and clans. Although they were not "free" in the sense that they had the legal rights of Roman freemen, yet they were treated as free members of the household. They were not members of the clan to which they were attached, but were known as a "clanless" people. They formed the beginning of that class which later developed into the plebs, or "the common people."

As we have seen, the regal period was contemporaneous with the beginning of the clan period. The clan or gens was the unit. Individual ownership of land was unknown. All titles vested in the gens. Even the very house and garden of the individual belonged to the clan. It was an early form of communism. Even movables in the early days were not owned by the person, but were owned by the clan. In later days, but long before it was true of immovables, movable things became subject to individual ownership. In time, private ownership of town land, that is, the house and its ground within the city, was recognized, but it was yet a much later period before one could obtain the personal ownership of farm or arable land.

In the first days of Rome, the people, says Pomponius in the Digest,[6] lived without any fixed law at all, everything being regulated by the direct control of the kings. However, in time, the assembly created by Romulus, the comitia curiata, exercised legislative functions. This assembly was presided over by the king, and seems to have had supreme legislative and judicial powers. In the time of Servius Tullius, two other assemblies were created, the comitia centuriata and the comitia tributa; the former, the assembly of the hundreds, the latter an assembly of the people by tribes. The comitia centuriata was the great assembly, the assembly in which the popular will was voiced during the Republic. The people were divided into 194 "centuries" or "hundreds." The old curiate assembly had been based upon descent, an aristocracy of birth. The assembly of the centuries was based upon property, each century theoretically representing a certain amount of rateable property in land. Under the old régime, the comitia curiata, only the patricians had political rights. All others were excluded both from public office and also from membership in the comitia. This applied to all plebeians no matter how wealthy they may have become. However, under the plan of the comitia centuriata, plebeians as

6. Dig. 1, 2, 2, 1.

well as patricians were included, each voting in his own "hundred" or "century."

The main purpose of the plan was to organize the fighting strength of Rome. It was a military classification of the people, based, however, upon an aristocracy of wealth. According to Livy and Dionysius,[7] there were besides the knights (the equites or cavalry), five classes of citizens. The knights were exempt from property qualifications. Then all citizens who possessed land to the value of a hundred thousand pounds of copper were placed in the first class; those who possessed seventy-five thousand, in the second class; fifty thousand pounds, in the third class; twenty-five thousand, in the fourth; twelve thousand five hundred[8] pounds, in the fifth class. Persons who had even less comprised a sixth class, according to Dionysius, while Livy says they were not classified at all. The knights were divided into eighteen centuries, and the first class into eighty centuries. All the remaining classes were divided into ninety-six centuries. The comitia voted by centuries, of which it will be observed the wealthier classes constituted a majority. This political organization required the plebeians to share the burdens of military service, yet left the voting power with the patricians, as the wealthy classes continued to be called. The comitia centuriata became the machinery of Rome's government. It elected the consuls, enacted laws, declared war, and was the final court of appeal. The comitia centuriata superseded the comitia curiata, which latter assembly was, afterwards, invoked only in cases of certain religious functions and ancient legal customs, particularly to give sanction, in certain cases, to wills and to matters of adoption.

The comitia tributa, also said to have been organ-

---

7. Liv. 1, 43; Dionys. 4, 16.

8. So says Dionysius. Livy says eleven thousand pounds.

ized in the time of Servius Tullius, was a division of the people into tribes. According to Mommsen, it was a land division rather than a division based upon population.

Originally this assembly was composed of both patricians and plebeians. Eventually it became the legislative body of the plebeians alone.[9]

As already stated, when the Roman people drove out their kings and abolished the Kingdom they established a Republic, electing annually two administrative officers, possessing also magisterial powers. These officials were called consuls. Not only did this period mark a fundamental change in the form of government, but it was also the beginning of a new theory of legal rights. Under the kings, one had to be a member of a curia, a quiris as he was called, a patrician, and his legal rights were those recognized by the patrician assembly, the comitia curiata, or the rights given him by the "quiritary law," as it has been called. With the advent of the Republic, the old quiritary law was a thing of the past. Men no longer claimed their legal rights as "quirites," but as "cives," citizens. From this time on, the Law of Rome is the citizen's law, the jus civile, the term citizen including both patrician and plebeian. No longer do we think of the gens, the clan, as the legal unit, but the individual citizen. While a plebeian could be a citizen, yet we are not to think of him as enjoying equal privileges with a patrician. There was a law of caste that separated these two classes for many years. Marriage between the two classes was not legal. Only patricians were eligible to public office, the senate being composed entirely of patricians. Many other advantages were accorded them. Indeed, as we shall see, the history of Roman Law for over two hundred years yet

---

9. This assembly later elected the tribunes of the people.

to come is an incessant conflict between patrician and plebeian.

Upon the expulsion of the Tarquins, the Romans, according to the continually repeated statement, established a republic. The new government was, however, practically a monarchy, "the one life-King being simply replaced by two year-Kings, who called themselves consuls (colleagues)."[10]

The two consuls were elected annually by the comitia centuriata. Connected with the earliest days of the Republic are the famous **Valerian laws**, named from Publius Valerius who is said to have been a consul in 508 B. C. The object of these laws was to establish the Republic upon a legal foundation. "The first of these laws threatened with the curse of the gods anyone who, without the consent of the people, should dare to assume the highest magistracy."[11] Another provided that in criminal trials where the life of a citizen was at stake, the sentence of the consul should be subject to an appeal to the comitia centuriata. This law of appeal has been called the Roman Habeas Corpus Act.[12]

In the immediate succeeding years the economic condition of the common people was deplorable. Owing to their service in the army during the periods of war they were unable to till their fields and became hopelessly involved in debt. Being promised that, if they would still further serve in the war against the Sabines, laws would be passed to relieve their distress, they complied. However, upon their victorious return to Rome the promise was not kept, and great throngs of them marched from the city and took up their abode on the Sacred Mount (Mons Sacer) intending never to return. This momentous event in Roman history is

---
10. T. Mommsen, Hist. of Rome, Bk. 2, Ch. 1.
11. W. Ihne, Hist. of Rome, Bk. 2, Ch. 1 (V. 1).
12. Ib.

[Roman Law]—7

known as the first secession of the plebs. A peace, however, was effected by the patricians agreeing that the plebs should have magistrates of their own. Such was the origin of the tribunes of the plebs.[13] They were not judicial magistrates, only counsellors and defenders of the rights of the people, but they were declared by law to be consecrated and inviolable (sacrosancti), and whoever attacked them or hindered them in the exercise of their functions, including a veto power over any command of the patrician authorities, might be killed by anyone without fear of punishment.[14] Originally the tribunes were two in number, but, in 471 B. C. they were increased to five.[15] Besides the two tribunes, as originally created, two plebeian aediles were also created who were assistants to the tribunes. These aediles had also minor magisterial functions in the imposing of fines in certain breaches of the peace. In 471 B. C. a law was passed (Lex Publilia) providing that the tribunes and aediles of the plebs should be elected by the plebeians themselves in the assembly of the tribes (comitia tributa) instead of in the comitia centuriata.[16]

The strife between the two classes at Rome, the plebs and the patricians, did not, however, long abate. There were, in reality, two entirely different peoples in Rome, and they had practically nothing in common. There was also a dual system of laws, those passed by the senate (senatus consulta) for the patricians, and those passed by the plebs in their comitia for themselves (plebiscita). Neither class regarded the laws of the other. This condition created great uncertainty as to the "law," the patricians insisting that the law as preserved by them should be the law for the en-

---

13. Horton, Hist. of the Romans, Ch. 3.
14. Ihne, Hist. of Rome, Bk. 2, Ch. 2, and Bk. 6, Ch. 8.
15. In 457 B. C. they were increased to ten.
16. In the comitia tributa the people voted per capita.

tire people. Finally, in 462 B. C., the tribune Terentilius proposed a law for the election of five plebeian commissioners who should prepare a law defining and limiting the powers and duties of the consuls, and also should reduce to writing the entire body of the laws so that there might be one law for the entire body of citizens. This proposal was bitterly opposed by the patricians, but after a ten year struggle the plan was finally adopted, although the law as passed provided that the commission to codify the law should consist of ten men (decemviri), part of whom should be patricians and part plebeians. The law also provided that the decemviri should hold office for one year with absolute power, all other magisterial offices being suspended.

However, in the election that followed, the patricians did not observe the spirit of the law but succeeded in electing ten patricians upon the commission. These decemvirs acted, however, wisely and with moderation. They codified the greater part of the laws, and published them in ten tables, which were approved and adopted by the senate and by the comitia centuriata, and declared to be the law of the whole people. (451 B. C.)

In the following year, according to the generally accepted story, although much of it is only traditional, Appius Claudius was the only one of the decemvirs who was re-elected. Three of the nine new members were plebeians. Two additional tables were added to the previous ten, and thus, it is generally told, the immortal Twelve Tables of Roman Law were given to the world.

When the decemvirs had completed their work, Appius Claudius established, it is said, a despotism which was more tyrannical than the worst days of the kings, although this tradition is rejected by many critical writers upon Roman history.[17] The story of Virginia, slain by her father, is connected with this period, and the passage of the Valerian-Horatian Laws at about this time gives color to the tradition of the oppression of the people by the decemvirs. These laws revived the old Valerian Law which gave to every Roman citizen the right of appeal to the comitia centuriata from the judgment of a consul, and also provided that all plebiscita, after approval by the Senate, should bind the whole Roman people.

Up to this period in Roman history marriages between patricians and plebeians were not recognized as legal. The Tribune Canuleius, however, in 445 B. C., secured the passage of a law (the Canuleian Law) legalizing such marriages.

The Twelve Tables mark the real beginning of Roman Law. By the Roman jurists they were considered as the foundation of all law, and Cicero always mentioned them with the greatest reverence.[18] The object of inscribing laws upon official tablets, not by any means original with the Romans, since similar tablets are found among peoples who long antedated the Romans, was to preserve them, and especially to protect the people from the oppression of those in power who claimed alone to know the laws and perverted them to their own ambitious and tyrannical purposes. The Leges Regiae, or the laws ascribed to the period of the Kings, were even then traditional and unimportant, but the Twelve Tables declared the existing laws of the Roman people. Three centuries had passed since the founding of Rome and during that long period there had grown up much customary law. The story reported by Livy[19] that the patricians in the year 454 B. C. themselves agreed to send three

17. W. Ihne, Hist. of Rome, Bk. 2, Ch. 9 & 10.
18. Liddell, Hist. of Rome, Bk. 2, Ch. 11.
19. Livy 3, 31. Dionysius, also, Antiq. Rom. b. 10.

commissioners to Athens to investigate the laws of Solon, and that in consequence of such a visit the commissioners collected much information concerning the methods of codifying laws, and, in fact, incorporated many Greek laws and customs in the ten original tables, is of very doubtful historical value. The probability is that the story is largely mythical.[20] Pomponius, however, who wrote about the middle of the second century of our present era, repeats the story,[21] and says that the custody of the Twelve Tables was given to the College of Pontiffs, a patrician order, at the head of which was the Pontifex Maximus.

The style of the Twelve Tables is brief, terse, imperative. They are a collection of legal principles, covering the general outlines of the law. They were engraved on metal tablets (hence "tables") and set up permanently in the Forum. Cicero describes them as a "summary of all that is excellent." Small copies were made for private use and they were widely distributed. "In my eyes," said Cicero,[22] "the little book of the laws of the Twelve Tables, with regard to the source and principles of law, is preferable to the libraries of all the philosophers that ever lived."

Various attempts have been made by scholars to restore the Twelve Tables only fragments of which remain, but it is not certain that such attempts are accurate. Their original form has undoubtedly been greatly changed by repeated transcriptions. However, there are numerous references to them and quotations from them in the Latin authors, especially in the writings of Cicero, Dionysius, and Gaius, and

20. Lewis, Credibility of Early Roman History, 2, 222; Gibbon, Hist. VIII, 8.
21. Dig. 1, 2, 2, 4.
22. De Or. 1, 44.

from such sources the work of research has been conducted.[23]

II. From the Twelve Tables to the Praetorship

The second period of the political and legal history of Rome extends from the Twelve Tables to the institution of the praetorship in 366 B. C., a period of eighty-six years. During this period the long strife between the two classes of the Roman people, the patricians and the plebeians, continued with unabated force, the plebeians constantly struggling to gain political equality. The plebeians demanded that they should be eligible to the consulship, the highest political office. This demand was bitterly resisted by the patricians, and the contest was carried on for many years. Meanwhile the plebeians were harassed with debt, and although various attempts were made to bring about a better adjustment of the agrarian laws yet very little was accomplished up to the time of the invasion of the Gauls and the burning of Rome in 390 B. C.

In the period of reconstruction that followed, the demands of the plebeians for reforms in the debt and land laws and for representation in the consulship became even more insistent. They again withdrew from the city, in 386 B. C., this event being the third time that they had done so.[24] Finally, ten years later, or in 376 B. C., the tribunes Caius Licinius Stolo and Lucius Sextius Lateranus proposed a group of laws to

---

23. The fragments of the Twelve Tables as reconstructed by the research critics will be found in Ortolan's Hist. of Rom. Law, Eng. Trans., London, 1896, p. 81 et seq. The entire Latin text would have covered but a few pages of a modern book. In short, concise sentences, the Tables declared fundamental principles governing actions at law; various offenses; debtors and creditors; family law; inheritance; property law; trespasses; rural law; rights of citizens; funerals; public worship; and husband and wife.

24. The first secession was in 494 B. C. The second is said to have been during the despotism of the decemvirs.

relieve the burdens of the poor. This proposed legislation is known in Roman history as the Licinian Rogations. The provisions of these bills were as follows:

I. All debts on which interest had been paid, the sum of the interest paid should be deducted from the principal, and the remainder paid off in three successive years.

II. No citizen shall hold more than 500 jugera (about 320 acres) of the Public Land, nor shall feed on the public pastures more than 100 head of larger cattle and 500 of smaller.

III. That henceforth one of the two consuls shall be a plebeian.

The struggle over these proposed laws went on for ten years. Finally, in 367 B. C., they were carried. The chief victory of the plebeians was that hereafter one of the two consuls must be a plebeian. As far as the new laws governing the public land were concerned, they proved a failure. It was intended, of course, that the great landowners should be deprived of their holdings in excess of 500 jugera, but the law was seldom enforced. Licinius was himself convicted of violating the very law that bore his name. Moreover, the Licinian laws "did not fulfil the evident expectations of their author in uniting the plebeians into one political body. This was impossible. What they did was to break up and practically abolish the patriciate. Henceforth were the Roman people divided into the rich and poor only." [25] In accordance with the new law, L. Sextius Lateranus, the former tribune, was, in 366 B. C., elected the first plebeian consul. The patricians, however, in the final days of the bitter struggle over the Licinian Rogations, when the demands for a plebeian consul seemed likely to be

25. Stephenson, Public Lands and Agrarian Laws of the Roman Republic. (Johns Hopkins Univ. Studies, 9th ser., nos. 7-8.)

successful, had refused to yield unless, as a compromise, the executive and magisterial functions, up to that time residing in a consul, should be separated. The patricians insisted that judicial power should be taken away from a consul and reposed in a new official to be known as the praetor, and that this officer should be a patrician. In achieving this result, which was considered by its advocates merely a political victory, a consolation for the loss of a consul, a step was taken which was destined to have the most important consequences in the development of Roman Law. The praetor was elected annually by the comitia centuriata, the same as the consuls. The judicial power, the imperium of the kings and of the consuls, now resided in him. For over a hundred years only one praetor was elected each year. The increasing population then required the services of two praetors. Later, the number was increased to six, and in the times of Sulla, eight. Still later, in the days of Julius Caesar, there were ten, twelve, fourteen, and sixteen. Pomponius says that there were eighteen praetors in his time.[26]

The praetor was a very important official. He was commander in chief of the army in the absence of the consul. In fact, it was customary to elect an ex-consul to the office.

The outstanding prerogative of the praetor was to prescribe the rules of procedure before his court. This was known as the jus edicendi.[27] These rules were made public by his edict, which might be oral or written. It became customary, however to write edicts, and they were written on a white tablet which became known as the praetor's album.[28] The praetor was at-

26. Dig. 1, 2, 2, 32.
27. Gaius, 1, 2.
28. From Latin albus (white).

tended by lictors and fasces.[29] When a second praetor was added in 247 B. C., the first had jurisdiction over matters concerning Roman citizens, while the second presided over trials between aliens. It was this praetor, the praetor peregrinus, who moulded in the years to come the jus gentium, as distinguished from the jus civile, into world-wide law. The climatic period of such "praetorian law" was reached in the last century of the Republic.

The admission of the plebeians to the consulship was believed at the time to mark the close of the long struggle between the classes, and Camillus, the great champion of the aristocrats, founded the temple of Concord as a sign and pledge that the quarrels and divisions between the patricians and plebeians were at an end.[30]

III. From the Praetorship to World Conquest

The third period of Rome's political and legal history covers a long period, namely, from the institution of the praetorship in 366 B. C., to the establishment of the Empire in 31 B. C.

For over twenty years after the adoption of the Licinian laws, there was a period of growth. Successful campaigns were conducted against the Cisalpine Gauls, the Etruscans, and the Volscians. Rome had now gained the mastery over Latium and much of the surrounding territory.

Then, in 343 B. C., began the Samnite Wars, which lasted for over seventy years. They were the wars which marked Rome's struggle for Italy. Her power was ever growing. Latium and the nearby tribes having been subdued, Rome's next plan was the

29. Bundle of rods strapped together with protruding head of an axe. Carried over a lictor's shoulder. The same emblem has been adopted by "Fascist" Italy, to-day.
30. How and Leigh, Hist. of Rome, 92.

subjugation of the entire peninsula. The Samnite Wars, which were the wars with the mountain dwellers of Central and Southern Italy, are usually divided into four periods. The first war lasted for two years. During this time Capua was annexed to Rome. In 339 B. C., Publilius, the plebeian consul, succeeded in putting into effect further statutes which tended to abridge still more the advantages of the patricians. These laws, known as the Publilian Laws, were three in number. The first provided that one of the censors should be a plebeian. The office of the censors had been created about 442 B. C., more than a hundred years before. As in all other offices, originally, only patricians were eligible. The primary duty of the censors was to superintend the taking of the census, which was taken every five years, in early days, the duration of the office being of a similar period. Later, it was reduced to a tenure of eighteen months, there being a vacancy in the last three and a half years of each census period. It was an office of great power. They registered all citizens according to their wealth, and thus determined the divisions of the comitia centuriata. They filled vacancies in the senate, and also had a general supervision over the public revenues, public buildings, and roads. It was a great political gain when the plebeians succeeded in making one of these two officials a member of their own party. The second provision of the Publilian laws made more stringent the already existing law that the resolutions of the comitia tributa, controlled by the plebeians, should have the force of law. The third provision was to the effect that all laws passed by the comitia centuriata or the comitia tributa should receive beforehand the sanction of the senate, thus annulling the power of veto of that body.

In 337 B. C., another step was taken. The office of praetor was made eligible to plebeians. From 326 B.

C. to 304 B. C., occurred the second war with the Samnites. This is known as the Great Samnite War. It lasted for twenty-two years. In 321 B. C. the disastrous defeat of the Romans at Caudine Forks took place. Yet the end of the war saw the Samnites suing for peace, and acknowledging the mastery of Rome.

In 312 B. C., during the second Samnite War, Appius Claudius was elected censor. He was a man of great ability, versatility, and political intrigue. It was he who built the famous Appian Way and the equally famous Appian Aqueduct. In order to insure a partisan control of the Senate, which was the last stronghold of patrician power, Appius filled the senatorial vacancies with some of the lowliest born men in Rome, including even certain sons of freedmen. He also admitted all the freedmen to the Roman tribes. In addition to his radical political views, Appius was distinguished as an author, a poet, a philosopher, and a jurist. He compiled a manual of the law days of the calendar, and it also contained instructions concerning court procedure.[31]

From the year 298 B. C. to 290, the Third Samnite War was fought, the peace after the Second War having lasted only six years. The great Roman victory, in 295 B. C., in the battle of Sentinum, decided the struggle, for although the Samnites held out for five years longer, yet they surrendered in 290 B. C., and Pontius, their great leader, was put to death in the

---

31. See Eliot, The Liberty of Rome, bk. 2, ch. 8 (v. 2). Early Roman Law was greatly influenced by the Pontiffs who were the priests of the state religion. It was customary to consult the Pontiffs in all matters of importance, since business, including judicial business, could be lawfully conducted only on "lawful" or propitious days, dies fasti, other days being known as dies nefasti. Having charge, thus, of the calendar, the Pontiffs, who were patricians, could declare any transaction illegal since it did not take place upon a permitted day. The Pontiffs also were originally the sole source of authority as to the proper method, or form, of procedure before the courts.

dungeons under the Capitoline hill.[32] In 286 B. C., occurred the last secession of the plebs. Hortensius was named dictator, and he succeeded in persuading them to return by providing that all resolutions of the tribes, the comitia tributa, should be binding upon the whole people of Rome. This provision seems to add nothing new to the Valerian and Publilian laws already cited, and there is much dispute as to the exact provisions and construction of the Hortensian law. Nevertheless, "with the passing of this law, the long struggle between the orders came to an end. The ancient patrician gentes remained, but the exclusive privileges of the patriciate as a ruling order were gone."[33]

The last or Fourth Samnite War was carried on from 270 till 266 B. C. At its conclusion the last opposition in the peninsula had been swept away. Italy from Sicily to the Rubicon was under Roman domination, and "for the first time was united into one state."[34] The people in the Latin towns near Rome were given practically self-government locally, but the other communities of Italy, although possessing the rights of citizenship, did not have the right of voting (civitas sine suffragio). They were subject, however, to the burdens of citizenship, the duty to bear arms, and taxation. Roman Law was extended over them, and was administered, says Mommsen, by Roman judges.

We now come to the beginning of the Punic wars, or the wars with Carthage. We have noted the progress of Rome's development of dominion, first, in the mastery of Latium, second, in the subjugation of Italy; and, now, third, we come to the period of her conquest of the world. The Punic wars mark the beginning of Rome's ambition for world-wide sovereignty. These

---

32. Michelet, Hist. of the Rom. Republ. bk. 2, ch. 1.
33. Pelham, Outlines of Rom. Hist. bk. 2, ch. 1.
34. Mommsen, Hist. of Rome, bk. 2, ch. 7 (v. 1).

wars lasted over a century, resulting in the total destruction of the mighty power of Carthage, and left Rome without a commercial or naval rival. The first war continued for twenty-three years (264–241 B. C.). It saw Rome develop into a great naval power. At the conclusion of this first war, Sicily, formerly under the domain of Carthage, became a part of the Roman territory.

In 254 B. C., while the first Punic war was in progress, an important incident happened in Rome. Tiberius Coruncanius, who had become the supreme pontiff (pontifex maximus), and who was also the first plebeian to hold that office, publicly announced that he would instruct all who desired information upon legal questions. Here then, five hundred years after the founding of Rome, we have the beginning of legal instruction. The Digest says:[35] "Of all those who acquired systematic knowledge of our rules of law, no one, according to tradition, made a public profession of it before Tiberius Coruncanius. All who preceded him, desired either to conceal the law, or else to advise only those who consulted them, rather than to devote themselves to systematic instruction." In 247 B. C., the number of praetors was increased to two, one being designated as the praetor urbanus, or the one having jurisdiction in matters preferred by citizens; the other known as the praetor peregrinus, or the praetor to whose court aliens resorted.

From 219 to 201 B. C. the terrible campaigns of the second Punic war were waged. This is the period made glorious by the names of Hannibal and Scipio. Our present object in tracing the historical development of Roman Law does not permit us, however, to tarry, even momentarily, over the history of Rome's wars, save as the story of her military campaigns may serve to explain matters of legal history. After the

35. Digest, 1, 2, 2, 35.

battle of Zama, in 202 B. C., in which Hannibal was defeated by Scipio and twenty thousand Carthaginians were slain, the peace terms, as dictated by Rome, were: (1) Surrender of all Spanish possessions; (2) Surrender of all the Mediterranean islands; (3) Payment annually for fifty years, two hundred talents ($250,000); (4) Destruction of all ships of war save ten; (5) Carthage to undertake no war without consent of Rome.

In the year 198 B. C., Sextus Aelius Catus was consul. Several years previous, 204 B. C., he published a law book called Tripertita. The Digest says [36] of it, quoting from Pomponius who wrote in the second century of the present era: "There exists a book of Sextus Aelius bearing the title Tripertita, a sort of cradle of the law, because in it we have, first, the Laws of the Twelve Tables; then a commentary; and third, the forms of legal actions." This work is sometimes referred to by the name of the Aelian Code. Prof. Sohm calls it the first real Roman Law Book. In 180 B. C., the lex annalis (proposed by the tribune Villius) fixed the minimum age of various Roman officials; e. g., aediles at 37; praetors at 40; consuls at 43.

In 152 B. C., Marcus Porcius Cato, the son of the great Cato, died. He was a distinguished jurist and wrote several legal works. "His father," says the Digest,[37] "wrote some books but the son a great many, and it is on his books as a basis that subsequent books are founded."

The final war with Carthage, the Third Punic War, broke out in 149. It was Cato, the Elder, the father of the jurist just mentioned, who had repeated again and again the famous phrase "Delenda est Carthago" (Carthage must be destroyed). The war continued for three years resulting in the total destruction of Carth-

---

36. Dig. 1, 2, 2, 38.
37. Dig. 1, 2, 2, 38.

OUTLINES OF ROMAN LAW HISTORY

age in 146 B. C. This memorable year also witnessed the Roman campaign against the Achaean League, in Greece, and the destruction of the city of Corinth.

The great and surpassing military conquests of Rome, were, however, beginning to react upon the national character. With the spoils of conquest came corruption. Rome from henceforth began to live upon her subjugated peoples. The conquered territory was turned into vast domains of public lands, and taxes were wrested from the inhabitants. The public domain was farmed out to cattle raisers, and to those who cultivated on vast scales the olive and the vine. Labor was performed by great numbers of slaves whose condition was, in many places, most pitiful. Mommsen says [38] that at the great slave market in Delos, one of the islands of Greece, where the slave dealers of Asia Minor disposed of their wares to Italian speculators, as many as ten thousand slaves were sold on one day. Trades were largely carried on by slaves, mines were worked by them. The plantation system had been carried by the Carthaginians to Sicily, and it was rapidly expanded by Rome after the second Punic war. Capitalists bought slaves instead of employing free labor, and the position of the poor in Rome became more and more critical.

The cruelties practiced upon the slaves resulted in their insurrection in Sicily in 135 B. C. This was known as the First Servile War. Seventy thousand slaves joined in this insurrection and for a time they were the masters of Sicily. In 132 B. C. the rebellion was finally crushed, and thousand of slaves were crucified.

Six hundred years of Roman history had now passed, and it might seem that the government of Rome had been finally established upon democratic ideals, and that after centuries of struggles equal rights had been

38. Hist. of Rome, bk. 4, ch. 2 (v. 3).

won for all freemen. The people elected the magistrates in the popular assembly, and laws were passed only by the voice of the popular will. Plebeians were eligible to all offices. In theory there was equality under the law. But, says a critical writer,[39] "between theory and practice there was a wide difference. Throughout this period the actual sovereign authority in Rome was that of the senate, and behind the senate stood an order of nobles who claimed and enjoyed privileges as wide as those which immemorial custom had formerly conceded to the patricians." In other words, the master politicians of the age, and the wealth of the age, met in the Roman senate. It was there that the administrative policies of Rome, both as to the city itself and also as to its world-wide interests, were planned and approved. The nobles, or the nobility, were largely composed of former plebeians. The term "nobles" was not synonymous with patricians. One who had been elected to high administrative office, to a "curule office" as it was called, became forthwith the founder of a noble family. Official position and wealth built up in time a more arrogant class than the old aristocracy of the patricians. Strictly speaking, the senate had no legal authority. Originally it had been a group of men who were advisors to the king. As a matter of fact, the senate had in time become the organization that controlled the destinies of the Roman world.

At this period of Roman history economic problems of the most serious character reached a perilous crisis. Agriculture was practically ruined. The public land was in the hands of the rich, and the masses of the people impoverished by long wars were in a desperate condition. The small farmer was crushed, and slave labor made free employment almost impossible. Brigands and beggars were numerous in all parts of

---

39. Pelham, Outlines of Rom. Hist. 3, ch. 3.

the country, and Italy was importing most of its food supplies from foreign colonies. The rich were growing richer but the masses were in abject poverty. The two Gracchi, Tiberius and Caius, brilliant and devoted to the cause of the people, and members of a distinguished family, undertook in a spirit of the highest humanity and patriotism to bring about the reforms the times demanded. Tiberius was elected tribune in 133 B. C., and he proposed an agrarian law that would reclaim and redistribute the public lands held by the rich land holders contrary to the Licinian Laws. The land was to be given back to the possession of the poorer citizens who were to pay only a small rent. As was to be expected, this proposed legislation was most violently opposed by the aristocratic class. However, after a bitter struggle the law was passed, but the enemies of Tiberius accused him of aiming at kingly power, and in a riot that followed, inspired by his political foes, he was killed with some three hundred of his followers. In 124 B. C., six years after the murder of his brother, Caius Gracchus was elected tribune. He was abler than Tiberius and at once espoused the cause unfinished by him. He revived the land question, proposed large plans for the colonization of the poor, and provided for the free distribution of food to the needy. Among other things he obtained the passage of a law whereby the judices (jurors) in the trial of law suits should be taken from the middle class known as knights (equites) to the exclusion of the senatorial class which up to this time enjoyed this exclusive right. The fury of the senatorial party knew no bounds. Caius pressing on in his social and revolutionary reforms secured changes in the taxation laws, entered upon various plans of public improvements, and for a while was almost supreme in his political power. The ancient law of appeal, whereby the citizen could demand a hearing before the comitia centuriata was revived and strengthened, new criminal courts were created, and measures to extend the franchise and other civil rights were presented. The old cry that he was subverting the state, and was seeking to make himself king was raised against him, and in the riots that ensued Caius was slain, together with three thousand of his devoted adherents. This was in 121 B. C.

The Gracchi were the victims of their idealism. They aimed not at royal power, but they were politically impractical in the corrupt and sordid Roman state. The old Roman spirit was dead, the masses were disorganized, and the oligarchy that ruled Rome, although utterly selfish and unscrupulous, was, nevertheless, the people's master. The times were "out of joint," and the Gracchi fought for hopeless and impossible things.

"After the death of Caius Gracchus the nobles did what they pleased in Rome. They paid no more attention to the Agrarian Law, and the state of Italy grew worse and worse. The nobles cared nothing for Rome's honor, but only for their own pockets. They governed badly, and took bribes from foreign kings, who were allowed to do what they liked if they could pay enough." [40]

The most important political events in the ensuing twenty years were the war with Jugurtha, the King of Numidia in Africa, who was finally defeated by Marius; the overthrow of the northern tribes, the Cimbri and Teutones likewise by Marius; and the second Servile War in Italy. Marius was elected consul six times, but his brilliant victories were his undoing. His great triumphs and popularity made him feared by the nobles and the accusations of ambition brought against him forced him into a voluntary exile in 98 B. C.

---

40. Creighton, Hist. of Rome (Primer), Ch. 7.

[Roman Law]

It was about this time that Quintus Mucius Scaevola, one of Rome's greatest jurists, wrote his famous treatise on the Jus Civile. It consisted of eighteen "books" or parts. The Digest [41] says that he had a great number of pupils among whom were Gallus, Sextus Papirius, and Juventius. Servius Sulpicius, one of the greatest lawyers of this period, received his first inspiration from Scaevola who had rebuked him for not knowing the law. Sulpicius, thereupon, became a diligent student and the author of one hundred and eighty "books." Among the pupils of Sulpicius was the distinguished jurist, Aulus Ofilius.

In the years 90 to 88 B. C., occurred the Social or Marsic [42] War, brought on by the demands of the Socii, or the Italian allies of Rome, for Roman citizenship. In this war the Samnites, Hirpenians, and Lucanians joined with the Marsians. To gain assistance, a law was passed by the Romans, giving citizenship to the Latini and all other Italian tribes that remained loyal. After several defeats, the Roman army under Sulla put down the revolt.

In the years 88 to 82 B. C., the Civil War between Marius, who returned from exile during the Social War, and Sulla plunged Rome into a series of massacres. It was a war between the adherents of the two greatest soldiers of the time, each ambitious for supreme power. Marius was a plebeian, rude and coarse in his tastes, while Sulla was an aristocrat and a scholar. Marius was the leader of the popular party, Sulla of the nobles, the optimates. Sulla captured Rome and Marius fled to Africa. Then Sulla departed for the East to lead the war against King Mithridates. Marius thereupon returned from exile and, capturing Rome, subjected his enemies to a horrible massacre.

41. Dig. 1, 2, 2, 41–44.
42. From Marsians, one of the leading tribes of Italy.

The following year Marius was elected consul for the seventh time but died a few weeks later. In 83 B. C., three years after the death of Marius, Sulla returned from the Mithridatic War, and was joined at Brundisium by Cnaeus Pompey, then a young man twenty-three years old. Sulla marched upon Rome, captured the city in 82 B. C., and, in turn, took a terrible revenge by slaughtering all who had opposed him. He thereupon made himself Dictator for life. The administration of Sulla was attended with great and radical changes in the laws. He set free ten thousand slaves and made them citizens; declared that only members of the senate should be eligible for the office of tribune; added three hundred new members to the senate; and also restored senatorial eligibility to the office of judex in the trial of law suits which privilege had been taken away by Caius Gracchus.

Sulla abdicated the dictatorship in 79 B. C., dying the following year. Two years before (81 B. C.), Quintus Mucius Scaevola, already mentioned as one of the great Roman jurists,[43] was murdered by one Sembria. The death of Scaevola had been ordered by Marius, but he escaped, at that time, from those sent to slay him.

In 63 B. C., Cicero, the famous orator and lawyer, became consul. Pomponius, one of the distinguished later jurists, said, according to the Digest,[44] that Cicero was the greatest pleader of causes of all his contemporaries

Rome, however, was now in the last throes of the dying Republic, and the plots of revolutionists and anarchists were threatening the end of the state. The rich and the powerful were aiming at absolute power. Cicero, the eloquent patriot and idealist, was the hope of the better elements of Rome who strove for a re-

---

43. Cicero said that Scaevola was the greatest lawyer of his time.
44. Dig. 1, 2, 2, 43.

turn of the old republican ideals. He had been elected praetor in 66 B. C., and was elected to the consulship by an overwhelming majority. His administration was memorable by his suppression of the conspiracy of Catiline, and in the public rejoicing that followed he was hailed by Cato as "the Father of his Country." However, his popularity was temporary, and upon the expiration of his consulship his political enemies charged him with the crime of having put the conspiring nobles of Catiline's associates to death without a trial before the comitia centuriata, and a decree of banishment was pronounced against him. He was, however, recalled from exile in 57 B. C.

In 61 B. C., Pompey returned from his victories in the East, and the following year saw the formation of the First Triumvirate, the powerful, political coalition of Julius Caesar, Pompey, and Crassus. By means of this alliance Caesar was elected consul, and at once undertook strenuous measures to improve the condition of the state. A new agrarian law was passed, and his proposals for punishing the extortions of provincial administrators were also enacted into law. In 58 B. C. he obtained for himself the administration of the province of Gaul, and set out for his new post, leaving Pompey in charge of affairs at Rome. The famous campaigns of Caesar in Gaul made him the idol of the Roman people, but Pompey turned against him, and, in 49 B. C., Caesar with his army crossed the Rubicon, the little stream separating his province from Italy, and took up the gage of battle with Pompey. In the civil war that ensued Pompey was defeated, and his army utterly routed. Pompey fled to Egypt where he was murdered.

The further military successes of Caesar made him the sole master of the Roman state. He was practically an absolute monarch but he undertook great reforms and planned vast enterprises. His assassination in the year 44 B. C. ended the career of the greatest genius that Rome had ever produced.

It was during this period that Aulus Ofilius, the distinguished jurist, lived. He was a friend of Cicero and was intimate with Caesar. Ofilius was the author of several law books, and compiled into a single volume the edicts of the praetors. The great law teachers, Capito and Labeo, were among his pupils.

The year following the death of Caesar the Second Triumvirate was formed by Marc Antony, Lepidus, and Octavius. All of these had been associated with Caesar, Antony being his chief lieutenant, Lepidus, his Master of Horse, and Octavius, then only eighteen years of age, his grand-nephew, adopted son, and the heir of the greater part of his estate. The closing days of the Republic were now at hand. Cicero was murdered by order of Antony in 43 B. C. The battle of Philippi, in Thrace, was fought in 42 B. C., resulting in the defeat of Brutus and Cassius, followed by their suicide. The government of the world was divided among the members of the Triumvirate in 40 B. C., but Lepidus was overthrown by Octavius (now known as Octavianus) in 36 B. C., and finally the end of the struggle between Octavianus and Antony took place in the great naval battle at Actium, in 31 B. C. Here the fleet of Antony was destroyed. He fled with Cleopatra to Egypt where both of them committed suicide. Octavianus was now the sole sovereign of the world, for the date of his victory at Actium "has been formally recorded by historians as signalizing the termination of the Republic and the commencement of the Roman monarchy." [45]

45. Merivale, Hist. of the Romans, Ch. 28.

CHAPTER V

OUTLINES OF ROMAN LAW HISTORY

B. THE EMPIRE TO THE DEATH OF JUSTINIAN

Two years after the battle of Actium, or in the year 29 B. C., the Temple of Janus was closed, signifying that war throughout the Roman world had ceased. It is a frightful record that only twice before in the history of Rome had the doors of this Temple been closed, once in Numa's reign and the second time after the First Punic War.

Octavianus did not assume the name of king although he was the supreme ruler of his people. He was, however, surnamed Augustus (Sublime) by the senate, and had previously taken the name of Caesar from his great uncle. He was also styled Imperator, meaning that he was the head of the army. It was, however, the policy of Augustus to keep alive the old offices of the Republic. "Consuls, Praetors, Quaestors, Tribunes, and Ediles rose from the same classes as before, and moved for the most part in the same round of work, though they had lost forever their power of initiative and real control." [1]

During the Republic the comitia centuriata was the source of legislation, but in the new regime the senate, as the mouthpiece of the emperor, took the place of this popular assembly. In the later days of the Empire the emperor became the sole and absolute law maker.

The rule of Augustus was a brilliant period of empire building. The provinces were divided into sena-

---

1. Capes, Rom. Hist. The Early Empire, Ch. 1.

torial and imperial classes, and the borders of the Empire were extended. Magnificent public buildings were erected at Rome, and public roads were built from Italy to the remotest parts of the Roman world. Order was restored not only in the city but in all parts of the imperial domain. The people were more prosperous and more contented than they had been for years.

It was also the golden age of Roman literature, Vergil, Horace, Ovid, and Livy being contemporaries of this period.

It was likewise in the days of Augustus that learned counsellors at law were first licensed by the state. In former times the right to give professional opinions upon the law (publice respondendi jus) was not a matter of grant or favor on the part of the state, but any one who had confidence in his own learning might advise such as consulted him. The Emperor Augustus, however, provided by edict that, in order to insure greater authority to the law, only such jurisconsults as were expressly licensed by the Emperor should be permitted to render legal opinions.[2] Such jurists were known as jurisprudentes, or simply, prudentes, and their opinions as responsa prudentium.

During the early days of the Empire there developed two distinct schools of juristic thought and law interpretation, known respectively as the Sabinians and the Proculians. The originators of these opposing views were Ateius Capito and Antistius Labeo. Both of these jurists were in their youth pupils of the great Ofilius, mentioned in the preceding chapter as the friend of both Cicero and Caesar. Capito favored the imperial form of government, but Labeo was an ardent republican. Capito was consul at one time, and this office was offered to Labeo by Augustus. Labeo, however, refused the office on the ground that

---

2. Dig. 1, 2, 2, 49.

it would interfere with his legal studies. We read in the Digest[3] that Labeo spent six months of each year with his law pupils at Rome, and the other six months he lived away from the city where in retirement he could write his books. There are many "paragraphs" in the Digest taken from the works of Labeo.

Upon many questions of law Capito and Labeo differed in opinion. The Digest, quoting Pomponius, says[4] that Capito "adhered to the doctrines that had reached him by tradition," while "Labeo, a very versatile man and of wide learning, was disposed to introduce many innovations." It would seem, therefore, that the school, or doctrines, of Capito and his followers may be designated as conservative, while Labeo and his followers were more liberal and progressive.

Neither Capito nor Labeo gave their names to the views of their followers who in the succeeding years became more numerous. Sabinus[5] was an admirer and follower of the views of Capito and Proculus of Labeo. Under the leadership of these respective disciples the rival schools of interpretation became more active, and the term Sabinians was applied to those who accepted the views of Capito, and Proculians to those who favored the opinions of Labeo.[6]

The reign of Augustus was far from being one that was long free from military operations. On the contrary he carried on by the aid of his generals many foreign wars in connection with the extension and subjugation of the imperial domain. His armies made many great conquests, but in 9 A.D., the Romans,

3. Dig. 1, 2, 2, 47–52.

4. Ib. (Pomponius was a Sabinian.)

5. Sabinus enjoyed the friendship of Tiberius, the successor of Augustus. He was also the author of a number of books.

6. The writings of Labeo have caused him to be more widely known than is Capito. Quotations from Labeo will be found in Snedeker v. Waring, 12 N. Y. 170, and in Rolli v. Troop, 157 U. S. 386.

under Varus, were terribly defeated by the Germans led by Arminius (the German Hermann).

Augustus died in 14 A.D., and was succeeded by Tiberius, his step-son. The government of the Empire soon took on a most despotic and cruel character. Tiberius was crafty, suspicious, jealous, and tyrannical. The law of Majestas (Lex de majestate) was revived [7] and extended by Tiberius. This law, which originally applied only to acts against the state, was construed to include every act alleged to be hostile to the Emperor. Informers (delators) sprang up on every hand, and hundreds of accused persons were put to death. Tiberius made Sejanus, a coarse and brutal monster, his chief minister (praetorian prefect), and in the later years of his reign retired to the island of Capreae leaving Rome in the hands of Sejanus. The praetorian troops were quartered near Rome, and thus the military despotism of the empire originated. It was during the reign of Tiberius that Jesus Christ was crucified in Judea.

Upon the death of Tiberius, in 37 A. D., the imperial government for a period of sixty years continued under the iron heel of despotic power. The throne was upheld by the force of the military arm, and corruption and vice, mingled with oppression and cruelty, destroyed almost the last vestige of Roman liberty. Well has Gibbon said: [8] "It is almost superfluous to enumerate the unworthy successors of Augustus. Their unparalleled vices, and the splendid theatre on which they were acted, have saved them from oblivion. The dark, unrelenting Tiberius, the furious Caligula, the feeble Claudius, the

---

7. In the later days of the Republic, various laws were passed punishing crimen majestatis, or treason against the majesty of the state. One of these laws was the Lex Julia Majestatis, passed either in the time of Julius Caesar or of Augustus. This law will be found in Dig. 48, 4.

8. The Decline and Fall of the Roman Empire, Ch. 3.

profligate and cruel Nero, the beastly Vitellius, and the timid, inhuman Domitian, are condemned to everlasting infamy. During four score years (excepting only the short and doubtful respite of Vespasian's reign) Rome groaned beneath an unremitting tyranny, which exterminated the ancient families of the Republic, and was fatal to almost every virtue and every talent that arose in that unhappy period."

Vespasian was emperor from 69 to 79. Government affairs were for a time in better shape. The army, the senate, and the public revenues were reorganized, and many public buildings were erected. Proculus, who gave his name to the Proculians, or to those jurists who followed the views of Labeo, enjoyed great repute under the favor of Vespasian. In the year 70, Titus, the son of Vespasian, captured and utterly destroyed Jerusalem.

In 79, Titus succeeded his father as emperor, and in the following year the Roman Colosseum was dedicated with magnificent celebrations. In 81, Domitian, the brother of Titus, and the last of the "Twelve Caesars,"[9] came to the throne. He remained in power for fifteen years, or until his assassination in 96. His reign witnessed the brilliant successes of the Roman general Agricola in Britain, and saw the extension of the imperial power to the Scottish border. However, the period was one of disorder and despotism, marked with the persecution of all anti-Roman religious sects, including both Jews and Christians.

In 96, Nerva, known as the first of the successive "Five Good Emperors," became the head of the government. He was elected emperor by the senate of which body he was a member at the time. He forth-

---

9. The "Twelve Caesars" were Julius Caesar, Augustus, Tiberius, Caligula, Claudius, Nero, Galba, Otho, Vitellius, Vespasian, Titus, and Domitian. Galba and Otho, Roman generals, were proclaimed emperors by the troops. Each held the office only a few months, in the years 68 and 69.

with set about the correction of abuses and introduced many reforms. His character was in marked contrast to his predecessors. He possessed many virtues and was devoted to the welfare of the state. Trials for treason, so frequent in the past, were abolished. Taxes were diminished and large tracts of public land were divided among the poorer classes. His virtuous reign was all too short in that he died in sixteen months after coming into power.

However, in his adopted son, Trajan, he had a worthy successor. Trajan was the first emperor who was not a native of Italy, having been born in Spain. At the time of his succession he was in command of the Roman legions on the German frontier. For nineteen years (98 to 117) Rome enjoyed a period of great prosperity coupled with a wise and humane administration of public affairs. He was one of the ablest rulers Rome ever had, just and merciful, yet firm and impartial. He was also a patron of literature, the writings of Juvenal, Plutarch, and the younger Pliny belonging to his reign. Trajan carried on two great campaigns against the Dacians across the Danube, his brilliant victories being commemorated by a splendid column in Rome, erected in the year 113, and still standing in excellent condition. He also adorned the city with magnificent buildings, including a new forum, temples, a library, a new theatre, and gymnasium. It was during the reign of Trajan that the Roman Empire reached the limits of its greatest extent.

Trajan died in the year 116 on his homeward journey to Rome after his successful campaign against the Parthians in the far East. He was succeeded by Hadrian who was elected by the senate. He reigned for over twenty years (117–138). He is known as the traveling emperor since he spent nearly fifteen years in traveling through almost every part of his vast domain, visiting, in turn, Gaul, Germany, and Britain. He then proceeded to the East, journeying to Egypt and Syria, returning homeward through Asia Minor and Greece. It was also a period of the building of many public works on a scale of great magnificence. He erected a vast mausoleum on the banks of the Tiber. This structure yet remains, known today as the Castle of Saint Angelo. He also rebult the tomb of Pompey in Egypt, completed the temple of Jupiter in Athens, constructed in Rome the temple of Venus and Rome, built a famous villa at Tivoli, a great wall or rampart, known as Hadrian's Wall, in northern Britain as a barrier against the Scottish tribes, and rebuilt the city of Jerusalem, to which he gave the name Aelia Capitolina.

The reign of Hadrian is of especial interest, however, to students of Roman Law since it marks the renaissance of legal study, and ushers in the dawn of the golden age of Roman jurisprudence. The century that passed from the death of Augustus to the accession of Hadrian was not an age that was conducive to the development of the law. During the greater part of these years oppression and tyranny were supreme. Private law, the law that governed men in their domestic relations, in their business transactions, and in the settlement of their estates upon their death, continued in force as in the years before. The courts, presided over by regular magistrates, heard and decided cases and Roman lawyers cared for the interests of their clients. In these respects there was little change in all this period, but there was little to encourage the spirit of justice in anything. The nominal law making power, the senate, was but the mouthpiece, the puppet, of its imperial master. The emperor, backed by a great army, was supreme. For years, property, liberty, and life itself were at the mercy of a despot. Yet through it all, the Roman sense of order and of legal procedure was so ingrained that everything was said to be done in the name of law. The Republic was not formally abolished. The government did not call itself a monarchy, and the emperor (imperator) did not assume the title of king. The old offices of state nominally remained, but they were filled either by the dictation of the emperor or conferred upon himself. In the time of Tiberius the election of magistrates was taken from the people and transferred to the senate.

There were few laws of any importance so far as private law was concerned that were passed during this tragic period. For the most part the senate was busy in enacting laws designed to enhance the power and prerogatives of the emperor, and to punish all with the severest penalties who were hostile or even unfriendly to him. Hundreds of persons were put to death for the only reason that they had incurred the dislike of a malignant tyrant.

This period was not destitute, however, of notable jurists and writers upon the law. It was, in fact, the age of Capito and Labeo who have already been mentioned. Capito wrote upon the Jus Pontificium, and Labeo wrote upon the Twelve Tables. Sabinus and Proculus also flourished during this first century. There were also other jurists, among them Pegasus and Longinus, who wrote various treatises and commentaries.

In the time of Hadrian, however, there was a revival in scientific jurisprudence. The time of territorial expansion had passed. The Emperor even relinquished some of the provinces upon the far eastern frontier, for there was need of a better organization of the Empire, and of reform and regulation in the law itself. In order to effect this, the jurisdiction of the various courts was settled, and the procedure upon appeal was made more definite.

Another matter of importance was the authority given by Hadrian to the published opinions of those jurists who had been licensed to give opinions upon legal questions.[10] Hadrian decreed that such responsa prudentium if unanimous in their views should have the force of law. However, if they disagreed the judge in a case could follow any of such opinions he preferred.[11]

An even more important event in the reign of Hadrian was the publication, in the year 132, of the Perpetual Edict (Edictum Perpetuum), or a revision and codification of the edicts of praetors and other magistrates in order that they might be cast into permanent form. For centuries, a praetor (both city and peregrine) had upon taking up the duties of his office issued an edict setting forth the rules that were to govern his court during his term. Such edicts were known as edicta repentina (special edicts) and edicta perpetua (general, or standing edicts). The former applied to special cases, the latter consisted of the general rules for the entire term (one year). Each and every praetor was independent and not bound by the edicts of any of his predecessors, and until the year 67 B.C.[12] a praetor was not bound by his own edict but could change it at will. Successive praetors in the preparation of their edicts adopted such rules of procedure in their predecessors' edicts as were satisfactory to them, and also added such other rules as seemed desirable. As the years went on the rules became more and more established, and many praetors merely adopted, without any change, the edict of the preceding praetor. After the establishment of

---

10. It has already been stated that such imperial licenses were first granted in the time of Augustus.

11. Gaius, 1, 7.

12. The Lex Cornelia of that year provided that a praetor should not change his edict.

the Empire the praetor's power to publish edicts was inconsistent with the emperor's supreme power in matters judicial, and new praetorian edicts were seldom issued. Hadrian brought the matter to a climax by directing Salvius Julianus, a prominent jurist, to revise and arrange the magisterial edicts, and the compilation thus made was ratified by the senate. The edictal law thus enacted is known as Hadrian's Edict, also as Julian's Edict, but is generally cited as the Perpetual Edict, signifying that it was permanent and binding from year to year. From this time, changes and modifications in procedural law were not made by means of a praetor's edict but only by an imperial edict or constitutio. The Edictum Perpetuum contained, in addition to matter taken from praetors' edicts, certain edicts of the aediles relating to market regulations. Three of these aedilitian edicts are cited in the Digest,[13] one prohibiting savage animals near public streets; another requiring a vendor to disclose hidden defects; the third providing that one unlawfully injuring the slave of another should be obliged to reimburse the slave's owner.

Only fragments of the Edictum Perpetuum remain, although scholars have made efforts to find others.[14] Quotations from this compilation are found, however, in various places in the Digest.

It is in the time of Hadrian that the century that had the greatest names in Roman jurisprudence began, names that will be forever illustrious in legal history since they are the names of the famous writers from whose works the Digest of Justinian was largely compiled. Celsus, the son of Celsus the Elder, lived in the reign of Hadrian, both of them being very distinguished jurists. Celsus the Younger was consul in 129, and he was also the author of a

---

13. Dig. 21, 1, 48, 1 and 4; 21, 1, 1, 6; 9, 2, 27, 28.
14. See Hoffmann, Hist. Jur. 2, 305; Muirhead, Rom. Law, 291.

work entitled "Digesta," quotations from which are found in the Digest of Justinian. Neratius Priscus, another well known law writer, and the eminent Africanus (Sextus Caecilius) also were contemporaries of Hadrian, and in his reign the great commentator Gaius was born.

Hadrian was succeeded by Antoninus in the year 138. His long reign was a period of peacefulness, prosperity, and content. He was a benevolent ruler, and devoted to the welfare of the state. His sense of justice and his wisdom preserved the government from conspiracies and insurrections which were so characteristic of the first century. In his reign the laws were improved, literature and architecture encouraged, taxes lightened, and peace promoted. The senate conferred upon him the title "Pius" by reason of his devotion to the memory of Hadrian whose name he defended against certain dishonorable charges.

He was succeeded in 161 by his adopted son, Marcus Aurelius Antonius, distinguished as an author, scholar, statesman, and soldier. The reign of the "Two Antonines," Pius and Marcus Aurelius, was conspicuous as being among the wisest and best in Roman history.

During the reign of the Antonines the writings of Gaius, one of the most distinguished of all the great jurists, were produced. It is to Gaius that we owe the chief source of our knowledge of Roman law prior to the times of Justinian. Of Gaius, the man, practically nothing, however, is known beyond his mere name, and the fact that he is mentioned only by a single name, instead of two or three names common to well known Romans, has been made the foundation for the suggestion that he was either a foreigner or even a freedman. This, however, is mere conjecture.

Gaius was a prolific and able writer. Until superseded by the works of Justinian the Institutes of Gaius and other treatises written by him were the authoritative text books in the Roman schools of law. Over five hundred quotations from Gaius are found in the Digest, and the Institutes of Justinian were copied largely from the Institutes of Gaius. For many centuries the Institutes of Gaius were lost, but in the year 1816 a copy of this work was accidentally discovered by Niebuhr, the celebrated German historian, on a palimpsest manuscript in the Cathedral library at Verona. The re-written parchment originally consisted of one hundred and twenty-nine sheets, three being lost. Underneath the second writing on these sheets,[15] consisting of a copy of Saint Jerome's epistles, were faint outlines of some Roman law text which was identified by Niebuhr and Savigny to be the long lost text of Gaius' Institutes. This text was carefully uncovered by experts, and thus the famous Institutes, with some omissions, were restored to the world.[16]

It is believed that Gaius was a law teacher in Rome. Among his other numerous writings were Commentaries on the Twelve Tables, and on the Urban, Aedicilian, and Provincial Edicts; treatises on Verbal Obligations, Mortgages (Hypotheca), and "Trusts" (Fideicommissa); a work on Rules of Law (Regulae); and a work in seven books entitled "Res Cotidianae," or Daily Matters, being a popular, practical work of legal principles intended for every day use. This work was also known by its popular name, "Aurea."

The days of Marcus Aurelius were not as peaceful as those of his predecessor. Rome was engaged in wars against the Parthians in the extreme East, and

---

15. Sixty-three sheets had been written on three times, the text of Gaius being partially effaced to give place to some theological treatise which in time had been erased to give way to the copy of St. Jerome's epistles.

16. The best edition of these Institutes, with English translation, is Poste's, Oxford, 1904.

the whole Empire was devastated by the Asiatic plague which the returning soldiers brought back with them. There were also campaigns of long duration on the northern border of the Empire against the encroaching barbarians.

Aurelius died in the year 180.[17] He was the last of the "Five Good Emperors," and for a hundred years after his death the affairs of the Empire were in a most deplorable condition. The decline of Roman greatness and power set in upon the accession of Commodus, the son of Aurelius, whose reign began what is known in Roman history as the Later Empire, the period from Augustus to Commodus being known as the Early Empire. From Commodus to Diocletian, who became emperor in 284, there were twenty-three emperors, thirteen of whom were murdered by their own soldiers or servants. It was a century of despotism, cruelty and licentiousness. The luxury of the imperial court stood out in sharp contrast to the poverty of the masses.

Commodus, who proved to be a weak and cruel tyrant, was murdered in 192. Pertinax, the city prefect, was proclaimed emperor in 193 by conspirators but he was killed three months later by the leaders of the Praetorian Guard who then sold, at public auction, the Empire to the highest bidder. Didius Julianus, a senator who was immensely rich, was the purchaser. The commanders, however, of the Roman armies in the field, refused to recognize him as their emperor, and two months later Julianus was assassinated. Immediately the legions in various parts of the Empire proclaimed their respective commanders emperor, the soldiers in Britain naming Clodius Albinus; those in Asia, Pescennius Niger; and the legions of Pannonia naming Septimius Severus. Among

17. During the latter part of his reign the massive equestrian statue of Aurelius, still standing, was erected in Rome.

these three rivals for the throne a struggle ensued, but Septimius Severus defeated the other two and remained in sole possession of the imperial power. His reign lasted for eighteen years, or from 193 to 211. To students of Roman Law it is conspicuous in that it was the period in which flourished the most celebrated of all the great Roman jurists, Aemilius Paullus Papinianus, better known as Papinian. He held several public offices under Severus, including that of praetorian prefect.[18] Papinian was a man of the highest character, of great legal learning, of marked ability as a lawyer, and a profound author.[19] Cujacius, the great French jurist, has said, "There never was, nor ever will be, a lawyer that excelled or can equal Papinian." Among his writings are Quaestiones, thirty-seven books; Responsa, in nineteen books; Definitiones, in two books; and several treatises. From his works there are five hundred and ninety-five extracts in the Digest, but only fragments of his writings now remain. His books were studied by law students for several centuries, even long after Justinian's time. Third year students in the law schools of the Empire, in which year of their course they took up the works of Papinian, were, on account of this fact, known as "Papinianistae." Among the personal pupils of Papinian were such later famous jurists as Ulpian, Paulus, Pomponius, Africanus, Florentinus, and Modestinus. Papinian accompanied the emperor Septimius Severus to Britain in his campaign against the Caledonians. The Emperor made his headquarters at Eboracum (York) where he died in 211.

Severus during his reign disbanded the Praetorian Guards who had for many years arrogantly and in-

---

18. This was, at the time, the highest judicial office.
19. A quotation from Papinian will be found in Snedeker v. Waring, 12 N. Y. 170.

solently dominated the imperial power. He, however, established, in their place, a great body of his own troops who served as his body-guard. The commander of these legions was made the emperor's chief executive officer in the administration of the government, all legislative power being taken away from the Roman senate.

Severus left the Empire to his two sons, Caracalla and Geta. Caracalla soon murdered his younger brother, and ruled alone. Caracalla was of beastly ferocity. He put to death all who dared to censure his murder of his brother, including the great Papinian. Caracalla demanded from Papinian a statement that would legalize his crime against Geta but the high minded and courageous jurist replied that he knew of no law that would justify murder. His own death followed in consequence.

In 212, Caracalla conferred Roman citizenship upon all free-born inhabitants in the Empire. His motive seems to have been to increase the imperial revenue, since he also amended the laws [20] whereby the taxes on the granting of citizenship, on inheritances, and on gifts causa mortis were increased from five to ten per cent.

Caracalla was murdered by Macrinus, the commander of the emperor's body-guard. Macrinus then attempted to seize the imperial power, but was in turn put to death by the army who proclaimed Elagabalus, a supposed son of Caracalla. This youth, a sensuous and vicious weakling, was emperor nominally for five years (218-223), and then was killed by his own soldiers who despised him. He was succeeded by Alexander Severus, an able and valorous ruler, who was victorious in war, and also possessed a keen desire for learning. In his reign of twelve years (223-235) some of the most famous men in the annals of Roman Law

20. Leges Julia et Papia.

enjoyed his patronage and friendship. The great Ulpian (Domitius Ulpianus) who had been a pupil of Papinian, was the chief adviser of Severus, who appointed him praetorian prefect. Ulpian wrote many books, including Notes upon the works of Papinian; a work entitled Ad Edictum in eighty-three books; another entitled Ad Sabinum in fifty-one books; a third known as Ad Leges Julias et Papias in twenty books; and a work entitled Liber Singularis Regularum, otherwise known as Fragmenta.[21] The Digest contains 2462 excerpts from the writings of Ulpian, about one third of the subject matter of that entire compilation. This is a larger number of quotations than from any other author. In the year 228, Ulpian was killed during a mutiny of the soldiers.

Another great jurist, Julius Paulus, was a contemporary of Ulpian, and also a pupil of Papinian. He was a native of Padua where a statue has been erected to him. He held, at various times, the offices of praetor, consul, and praetorian prefect. He was the most voluminous of all the Roman Law writers, seventy of his various writings being mentioned in the Digest which contains 2080 extracts from his works. In fact, about a half of all the contents of the Digest is made up from the writings of the two jurists, Ulpian and Paulus. Among the writings of Paulus were Annotations upon the writings of Papinian; his great work in eight books upon the Edict (Ad Edictum); his work entitled Sententiae Receptae; his Quaestiones, in twenty-six books; and his Responsa, in twenty-three books. He died about 235.

Among other jurists of this same period should be mentioned the distinguished Pomponius and Modestinus. Pomponius was one of Papinian's pupils and

---

21. An outline of the Fragmenta of Ulpian is preserved in an ancient MS. in the Vatican Library. It was first published in Paris in 1549.

also an extensive author. There are many excerpts in the Digest from his writings. Modestinus, a reputed pupil of both Papinian and Ulpian, enjoyed the friendship of Alexander Severus, being one of his counsellors. He was also consul in the year 228. He wrote a number of legal works which ranked among the foremost authorities.

Four of the writers of this period attained to the highest distinction in the history of the Roman Law. Two centuries after their death, at a time when the study of law had greatly declined, and when there was much dispute and doubt as to what writers of the past should be accepted as authority, Theodosius II, who was then emperor of the Eastern Empire, issued a proclamation which was adopted by the government of Valentinian III in the Western Empire, declaring that all the writings of Papinian, Paulus, Gaius, Ulpian and Modestinus, excepting one work of Paulus and another of Ulpian, were approved and given legislative authority, and were to be cited in the courts as law.[22] This was the most remarkable honor ever paid to the legal writings of private authors.

Among the works of Ulpian and Paulus mention was made above of their Annotations, or Notes, upon the writings of Papinian. These particular writings were forbidden by Constantine, in 321, to be cited in court against the opinions of Papinian. Likewise, in the Law of Citations of Theodosius and Valentinian III, in 425 and 426, Ulpian's and Paulus' Notes on Papinian were expressly excluded. All writings of Ulpian and of Paulus were to be cited as law except these. Whether this was done because the reverence paid to Papinian was so great that his admirers could brook no adverse criticism of his writings, for the "Notes" of Ulpian and of Paulus show that they did not always agree with

[22]. This "Law of Citations" is often cited as that of Valentinian III. See post.

the master, or whether it was done to put an end to contention and dispute as to the law, has caused some speculation. The latter view would seem, however, to be the more probable.

In striking contrast to the brilliant array of great jurists who adorned the age of Alexander Severus, soon after his death all learning decayed in the years of carnage and corruption that followed. From the time of Alexander Severus to Justinian there were not a dozen prominent names in legal literature. Three jurists, and three only, during this period are quoted in the Digest, Hermogenianus, Aurelius Arcadius, and Julius Aquila.

The emperor Alexander Severus was victorius over the Germans who were threatening the northern boundary of the Empire, and was also successful in his campaign against the Persians in the East. His subsequent attempts to curb the growing arrogance of the army in its disposition to dictate the government cost him his life. He was slain in the year 235 by a mutiny of the troops. The leader of this revolt was a Thracian peasant, Maximin by name, a giant in size, and a ferocious, cruel monster. Upon the death of Severus, Maximin declared himself emperor and marched upon Rome. Before he reached the city, another mutiny arose and Maximin was killed (238).

The period that next followed was one of the most dreadful in all Roman history. It is an awful story of murder after murder of those who wore the purple, the insignia of imperial power. Upon the death of Maximin the army and the senate were unable to agree upon a successor, but finally a compromise was effected whereby Gordian, a boy only thirteen years old, was named emperor. In 244 he was killed by Philip, the captain of the guard, and Philip, an Arabian by birth, seized the throne, and held it for five years. In his reign he celebrated with splendid and magnificent ceremonies and festivals the thousandth year of the founding of Rome, but in the year 249 he was slain in battle by Decius, the commander of the legions on the Danube, who was his rival for the throne. Two years later Decius was killed in battle against the Goths who were again invading Roman territory.

In the succeeding seventeen years (251-268) a period of chaos ensued. This period in Roman history is often called "The Age of the Thirty Tyrants," although during those years not that many assumed imperial rule. The commanders of the several armies in various parts of the empire respectively were proclaimed emperors by their soldiers. The army on the Danube proclaimed Gallus; the army in Moesia, Aemilianus. Yet these same armies soon rebelled, and Gallus was murdered by his own troops in 253, and Aemilianus suffered a like fate three months later. Then the army in Gaul set up their leader, Valerian, as Emperor. He was a brave soldier but mutiny and insurrection were rampant everywhere. He was engaged in constant wars with the Goths, the Scythians, and the Persians. In this last campaign he crossed the Euphrates, only to be surrounded by the Persians, led by Sapor, and was taken prisoner (259). He was kept in captivity till his death, nine years later, being treated with the greatest insolence, barbarity and cruelty. It is said that Sapor used him for a horseblock, contemptuously putting his foot upon his wretched captive, a Roman Emperor, whenever the Persian ruler mounted his horse.

When Valerian was taken prisoner, his son Gallienus was declared Emperor. He made no effort to obtain the liberty of his father, and his sloth and incapacity caused many rivals in the various provinces to seek the throne.[23] The most conspicuous of these

---

23. Among these were Odenatus in Palmyra, Celsus in Africa, and Piso in Thessaly.

was Odenatus in Palmyra but he was soon murdered. His wife was the famous Zenobia who called herself Queen of the East. She was beloved by her subjects and was an able and accomplished ruler. Her capital city, Palmyra, was prosperous and beautiful. Her ambition caused her to declare herself her husband's successor to the Roman seat of power.

Gallienus died in 268, being murdered while on a campaign against Aureolus, one of his rivals, in northern Italy. He had previously declared that Claudius should be his successor, a general of great ability. Meanwhile most of the other aspirants for the throne had fallen in battle. Claudius defeated Aureolus, and then turned his attention towards the East to march against Zenobia, but he died of a pestilence that swept the land in 270. He was succeeded by his brother who was murdered only seventeen days later. Then the army proclaimed Aurelian, one of their generals, Emperor. He was an able man and a great leader. The action of the army was gladly confirmed by the senate at Rome who saw in Aurelian great promise for better days.

The new Emperor immediately took active steps to establish order in the Empire. He drove the Alemanni, composed of a number of German tribes, out of northern Italy, and then began the construction of a new wall around Rome to guard against future invasions.[24] He then defeated the Vandals who had crossed the Danube, and thereupon led his victorious army against Zenobia. His campaign resulted in the capture of this queen [25] and the destruction of the city of Palmyra. Soon after he subdued a revolt in Egypt, and then quelled various insurrections in Gaul, Spain,

24. The ruins of this wall, thirteen miles in circuit, still stand.
25. Zenobia was taken a prisoner to Rome where later she appeared as one of the captives in Aurelian's great triumph. She afterwards was given a villa at Tibur where she resided the remainder of her life.

and Britain, restoring these provinces to the Empire. Returning to Rome he was honored with the greatest triumph in Roman History. The senate conferred upon him the title "Restorer of the Roman Empire." His last campaign was against the Persians. His strict discipline caused, however, a mutiny among his soldiers and during this campaign he was murdered by them (275).

The senate elected Tacitus as the successor of Aurelian, but he died a natural death seven months later. Florian, the brother of Tacitus, was next elected by the senate, but the army in Spain proclaimed Probus. Florian was slain by his own troops, and Probus was thus left without a rival. He was, however, in constant warfare, defeating the Gauls, the Goths, and the Isurians in Asia Minor. Yet, in 282, he suffered the fate of many of his predecessors, being murdered in a mutiny of his soldiers, who proclaimed as Emperor Carus, the commander of the praetorian troops. Carus was successful in a campaign against the Persians, but mysteriously died in a year after assuming the imperial authority. He was succeeded by his sons, Numerianus and Carinus who were soon murdered, Carinus by an angry husband, Numerianus by his own father-in-law, Arrius Aper, the commander of his guard who coveted the throne. Aper in turn was put to death by the army in punishment for his crime.

Such is a brief synopsis of the horrible story of the rulers of Rome from the death of Alexander Severus, in 235, to the beginning of the reign of Diocletian, in 284. Such a terrible record of repeated assassinations of the titular heads of a great state is without parallel in history. The explanation of this direful record is, however, not difficult to understand. It was due to the vast armies of Rome which were constantly engaged in war against hordes of peoples who either comprised, or surrounded the borders of, the great and unwieldy Empire. The masses of the people were helpless against absolute despotism within and constantly advancing enemies without. Anarchy and confusion prevailed everywhere. The greed, avarice, and ambition of military leaders caused them to incite their armies to revolt, and the soldiers, most of them rude and illiterate barbarians, were easily influenced by the promises of plunder to declare their leaders the supreme rulers of the state.

It has seemed amazing to some that Rome with its appalling history of warfare and bloodshed gave, nevertheless, to the world the greatest system of jurisprudence known to men. The state, indeed, suffered terribly in many periods of its history from usurpations of despotic rule, but even in its darkest days the spirit of Roman Law was kept alive by its great jurists. Moreover, it was not in the days of the Roman Empire that Roman Law was born and developed, but in the days of the Republic. Roman praetors, not Roman emperors, were the fathers of that form of Roman Law, the jus gentium, which during the days of the Empire became the law of the world. The great Roman jurists who expounded this law during the last hundred years of the Republic and during the first two hundred and fifty years of the Empire, or until the end of the reign of Alexander Severus, were the preservers of this law for posterity. From the time of this Emperor till the reign of Justinian, a period of about three hundred years, Roman Law was in its "dark ages." There were few legal writings of any great importance, and even the study of the law almost ceased. The senate, as long as it continued to function, now and then enacted laws of more or less value in private jurisprudence, and emperors, even the worst of them, under the advice of wise counsellors learned in the law, likewise, now and then, promulgated new statutes. The great body, however, of

Roman Law, the praetorian law, reached its culmination in the Perpetual Edict published in the reign of Hadrian.

"The Roman senate," says Gibbon,[26] "under the reign of the Caesars, was composed of magistrates and lawyers, and in questions of private jurisprudence, the integrity of their judgment was seldom perverted by fear or interest."

However, during the four hundred years from Hadrian to Justinian both private and public law were in many ways amended and changed by imperial legislation. There were three methods by which this was done, namely, by edicts, decrees, and rescripts. An edict (edictum, constitutio) was a general law, a new statute, which all people were to obey. A rescript (rescripta, epistola) was a written answer from the emperor (usually under the advice of his legal counsellors) in reply to a magistrate seeking instruction upon a question of law. A decree (decretum) was a judgment in a particular case given by the emperor in his capacity as supreme judge. Imperial rescripts and decrees, depending upon the intelligence and prejudice of the particular emperor, were sometimes "good law" and at other times "bad law" but they were authoritative and final, the same as in the case of a modern court of last resort.

Upon the death of Numerianus, in 284, Diocletian, a general in the army that Numerianus was leading against the Persians, was proclaimed emperor by his troops. He was a native of Dalmatia, his original name, Diocles, being changed into the Roman Diocletianus. He was of humble birth but he ascended from the lowest grade of military service to the highest rank. In the early part of his reign he was beset on every side by hostile incursions of barbarians. In order to meet these attacks he appointed (286) as his

---

[26]. Decline and Fall of the Roman Empire, Ch. 44.

colleague, or as joint-emperor, Maximianus, a fellow soldier, and gave to him the title of Augustus, assigning him to the western part of the Empire, the eastern part being reserved by Diocletian for himself. The attacks continuing from every quarter, Diocletian appointed (292) two others, Constantius and Galerius, to assist him in maintaining order. These two were named "Caesars" by the emperor, who then divided the Empire into four areas. Diocletian took the East with headquarters at Nicomedia. To Maximianus was assigned Italy and Africa. Constantius was placed in command of Britain, Gaul, and Spain, and Galerius was given Illyricum and the regions of the Danube. Each was supreme in his own territory, but Diocletian was the emperor of all.

This division of authority and power proved successful, and the enemies of Rome were subdued in all quarters. In 304 Diocletian celebrated a magnificent triumph in Rome, and then returned to Nicomedia. The following year he voluntarily abdicated the throne, desiring to spend his last years freed from the cares of government. He died in the year 313.

"The accession of Diocletian," says Merivale,[27] "marks a new epoch in the history of the Roman Empire. From this time the old names of the Republic, the consuls, the tribunes, and the senate itself, cease, even if still existing, to have any political significance. The government becomes avowedly a monarchial autocracy, and the officers by whom it is administered are simply the nominees of the despot on the throne. The Empire of Rome is henceforth an Oriental sovereignty."

Diocletian upon his abdication in 305, compelled his associate, Maximian, to abdicate also. This resulted, as previously ordered by Diocletian, in the succession of Constantius and Galerius as joint emperors, or

[27]. General Hist. of Rome, Ch. 70.

Augusti (305). Galerius was the son-in-law of Diocletian and he permitted Galerius to nominate the two "Caesars," who would, according to the plan previously formed, be the heirs to the throne. Instead of appointing Constantine, the son of Constantius, or Maxentius, the son of Maximian, Galerius appointed his nephew, Maximin, and Severus, a personal friend. This political blunder aroused all the old strife for supreme power. Constantius died about a year later, and Constantine, his son, was proclaimed Emperor (306) by the army in the West. Soon after a revolt in Rome against Severus caused the senate to declare Maxentius Emperor. In the civil war that followed, Severus was put to death, and Galerius thereupon named Licinius as the successor of Severus. Meanwhile Maximian, the father of Maxentius, had come forward to assert his own claim to the throne, and the Empire had no less than six rivals for the supreme power. In the ensuing military struggles of these contenders, Maximian was put to death; Galerius died of disease; Maxentius was defeated and slain in the battle of Saxa Rubra (312), nine miles from Rome, by Constantine; and Maximin died soon after his defeat by Licinius (313). Finally Constantine, in 323, defeated Licinius, and from that year till his death in 337 he was the sole ruler of the Empire. In the year 330 Constantine selected Byzantium as the imperial capital, giving to the city the new name of Constantinople. Five years before (325) the emperor had formally accepted the Christian faith and made it the state religion.

It was in the reign of Constantine that the Gregorian and Hermogenian Codes were probably published, although some authorities would place the Hermogenian Code at a later date.[28] These codes

---

28. Some place the Code of Gregorianus in the reign of Diocletian,

were not compiled by any imperial order but were merely private works and contained the more important imperial rescripts of the second century. Seventy fragments of the Gregorian Code are still extant, being certain constitutions from the reign of Septimius Severus to that of Diocletian. The extant fragments of the Hermogenian Code are thirty-two in number, consisting of some constitutions of Diocletian and Maximian. Certain constitutions of Valentinian ascribed to this collection by some authorities [29] are believed by other scholars to be a later addition by some unknown compiler.

Upon the death of Constantine (337) the imperial government was divided among his three sons, Constantine, Constantius, and Constans. Peace between these brothers lasted only about three years, and then followed quarrels and wars. Constantine was killed in battle in 340, and Constans was murdered in 350 during a mutiny of his soldiers. Three years later (353) Constantius after the defeat of several new rivals for the throne, was left the sole ruler. He died in 361, and Julian, his nephew, who had previously risen in rebellion against his uncle, became emperor. He is known in history as Julian the Apostate from the fact that he renounced Christianity.

He was killed two years later (363) in his campaign against the Persians. He was succeeded by Jovianus, proclaimed by the army in its retreat from Persia, who lived only seven months, dying before he reached Constantinople. The leaders of the army then offered the throne to Valentinian (364), one of their number. He appointed his brother Valens as ruler at Constantinople, choosing the western part of the Empire for himself, and selecting Milan for his capital.

and the Code of Hermogenianus in the reign of Valentinian, or about 365 A. D.

29. See Huschke, Juris Antejust., pp. 743-745.

In the West, Valentinian was succeeded by his son Gratian (375). Eight years later (383) while residing in Gaul he was killed by the soldiers of Maximus who had crossed the channel from Britain. Maximus, who had been declared Emperor by his army, succeeded Gratian, and was the nominal emperor till 388 when he was delivered by his mutinous troops to Theodosius, the Emperor of the East, and put to death by Theodosius as a usurper. Valentinian II was then placed upon the Western throne by Theodosius, but he was murdered in 392, by Arbogastes, leader of the Frankish troops who made his satellite Eugenius the Emperor. Theodosius again came from the East, defeated Eugenius in battle, and put him, when taken captive, to death. For a year Theodosius was the sole Emperor of both the East and the West, but he died at Milan in 395.

Upon the death of Theodosius, his two sons, Arcadius and Honorius, succeeded him, the father having assigned the East to Arcadius, and the West to Honorius, the latter being a boy eleven years old. This event marked the final division of the Empire. Stilicho, the commander of the imperial forces, an able man and brave soldier, had been named by Theodosius as the guardian of his younger son. Honorius, who was a weakling, remained the nominal head of the West till the year 423. In his reign, the Goths under Alaric, their King, revolted (398), but were finally defeated by Stilicho in 403. However, five years later (408) the Goths again made war. Rome was beseiged for a year, and the Goths withdrew only upon the payment of an immense ransom. The purchase of peace was very unpopular, however, with the Romans, and resulted in the execution of Stilicho by the ungrateful Honorius. Two years later, 410, Alaric invaded Italy once more, and this time Rome was captured and plundered. Honorius died in 423. During the succeeding two years the throne was usurped by an adventurer named John, otherwise called Johannes the Notary, who assumed to act as emperor till he was killed in 425 by the army sent from the East. Valentinian III, the infant nephew of Honorius, was made Emperor by command of Theodosius II, the eastern Emperor, and his reign lasted till the year 455. In his reign (426) the famous "Law of Citations," which had been promulgated by Theodosius II,[30] became the law of the Western Empire, and twelve years later, 438, the Theodosian Code [31] was also adopted for the West.

But the Western Empire was now rapidly approaching its last days. In 451, the Huns, under Attila, who called himself "the Scourge of God," invaded northern Italy and utterly devastated this entire region. Four years later (455), Valentinian III was murdered by Maximus who usurped the throne, who in turn was killed the same year in the sack of Rome by the Vandals under Genseric.

Affairs were now in the utmost confusion. For a few years, the commander of the foreign troops in the Roman army, known as Count Ricimer, was the self constituted dictator of the government, and although he would not take the imperial title yet he made and unmade the nominal emperors at his pleasure. Avitus, proclaimed Emperor in Gaul, was murdered, probably at the instigation of Ricimer. Majorian was then placed upon the throne, only to be soon killed. Severus then was Emperor for five years (461–467), but was, by Ricimer's command, succeeded by Anthemius, a Greek, who held the office till he was killed in 472. A Roman senator, Olybrius by name, was then made Emperor, but both he and Ricimer died that same year. Glycerius, an officer of the imperial guard, wore the crown for a year, but was deposed and succeeded

30. See post.
31. See post.

by Julius Nepos in 473, who soon after was assassinated by Glycerius. Finally the youthful Romulus Augustus, who was ridiculed by the popular name "Augustulus," the Little Augustus, was made Emperor by his father Orestes, the commander of the barbarian troops. Orestes was, however, killed by his rival Odoacer, another barbarian general, who deposed "Augustulus" and usurped the rule as so many of his predecessors had done. This was in the year 476, the year of the, so called, "fall of Rome." The glory of Rome's greatness, however, had departed long before Odoacer's day. Constantinople for over a century had been the real head of the imperial power. This city remained the capital of the Eastern Empire till its capture by the Turks in 1453. The "fall of Rome" really means that in the year 476 the line of Roman emperors ended in the West. "When at Odoacer's bidding," says Bryce,[32] "Romulus Augustulus, the boy whom a whim of fate had chosen to be the last native Caesar of Rome, had formally announced his resignation to the senate, a deputation from that body proceeded to the Eastern court to lay the insignia of royalty at the feet of the Eastern Emperor Zeno. The West, they declared, no longer required an emperor of its own; one monarch sufficed for the world; Odoacer was qualified by his wisdom and courage to be the protector of their state, and upon him Zeno was entreated to confer the title of patrician and the administration of the Italian provinces."

Turning once more to the East, and resuming the outline of its political history from the time when Valentinian, in 364, placed his brother Valens upon the Eastern throne, we find that the Goths and Persians were held in check during the lifetime of Valentinian by their very fear of his well known military prowess. However, upon his death in 375, they resumed their in-

---

[32]. The Holy Roman Empire, Ch. 3.

vasions, and three years later (378) they defeated the army of Valens in the terribly destructive battle of Adrianople, Valens being among the slain. More than 60,000 of the imperial troops fell in this conflict.

The situation demanded a great military leader for the East, and Gratian, who was Emperor of the West at this time, selected Theodosius, an able soldier, who was then living in retirement in Spain, to take the place of his uncle Valens. Theodosius, known in history as Theodosius I, carried on a successful campaign against the Goths and persuaded them to become his allies. In 388, he defeated Maximus, the usurper in the West, and became, as already stated, the sole Emperor of both East and West upon the death of Valentinian II in 394.

Theodosius I died in 395, leaving his two sons, Arcadius and Honorius to succeed him, as previously stated. Arcadius, the older son, was eighteen years old, and to him was given the East. In accordance, however, with the direction of Theodosius, Rufinus was made the guardian of Arcadius, and regent of the Eastern Empire; but Rufinus was soon murdered, and for a few years Arcadius, weak and vacillating, was the puppet of the more powerful minds that surrounded him. He died in 408, leaving the Empire to his son, Theodosius II, then a child seven years old.

Theodosius II reigned for forty-two years. His older sister, Pulcheria, was the dominant power during his youth. His reign is memorable for two very important events in connection with the history of Roman Law. One of these was the famous "Law of Citations," the other being the publication of the Code, known as the Theodosian Code. Due to the long lapse of time since the writings of the great jurists of the second century had been published, there had arisen many differences of opinion among later jurists and judges concerning the most authoritative books of the law. The writings of some of the former jurists were cited as law by some, while others insisted that they were not of equal value to some of the other jurists. There was need, consequently, of some imperial edict as to what writers should be regarded as authoritative. Under the advice of his wise and learned legal counsellors, Theodosius published a constitution ordering that the writings of Papinian, Paulus, Gaius, Ulpian, and Modestinus, together with the writings of all other jurists quoted by them as of authority, should have the effect of law, and should be followed by the courts. In case the five mentioned writers should not agree upon any question, the majority of their opinions should govern; in case they should happen to be equally divided, the opinion of Papinian, if expressed, should control; in case Papinian were silent, and the others were equally divided, then the judge hearing the case should exercise his own discretion. This famous constitution of Theodosius was published in 425, and in the following year it was adopted in the Western Empire then ruled by Valentinian III. This law is often cited as "the Law of Citations of Valentinian III," but it originated in the Eastern Empire, and was later accepted in the West through the influence of Theodosius II.

The second event, The Theodosian Code, took place in the year 438. There had been no compilation of the imperial laws since the Codes of Gregorianus and Hermogenianus in the reign of Constantine, and additional imperial legislation had so accumulated that this branch of the law was in great confusion. Theodosius II, therefore, appointed a commission, consisting of sixteen jurists with Antiochus, the leading jurist of his day, at their head, to collect and arrange the imperial law. The plan was to supplement the former codes with the subsequent material. The work was completed in 438, and was given legislative force by the Emperor. It was also given imperial sanction by Valentinian III in the Western Empire, and thus became the law for both the East and the West.

The Theodosian Code was the law of the Empire till it was supplanted by the Corpus Juris Civilis of Justinian. It was also from the Theodosian Code that much of the law of the Franks, the Burgundians, and the Visigoths was derived when the German Kings, for the use of their Roman subjects, promulgated from time to time certain codes of Roman Law. Thus, the Code known as Lex Romana Visigothorum, or Breviarium Alarici, promulgated by order of the Gothic King, Alaric II, A.D. 506, as the law for the Visigoths in Gaul,[33] was largely an abridgment of the Theodisian Code. Lex Romana Burgundionum, promulgated by Sigismund, in 517; and Edictum Theodorici, promulgated by Theodoric the Great for the Ostrogoths, about 500 A.D., likewise drew from the same source.

The Theodosian Code is largely extant. It contains the imperial laws, or constitutions, from the time of Constantine to Theodosius II (306–438). It is divided into sixteen books, the first five treating of private law, the other eleven being devoted for the most part to public law. The last book deals with religious and church law. The Code has been preserved complete from the latter part of the sixth book to its end, but many parts of the work are missing in the first five and a half books.

It was also during the reign of Theodosius II that a school of law was established at Constantinople. However, even as in the matter of the Code, it is undoubtedly true that the suggestions and efforts of Antiochus, the chief law adviser of the emperor, were the chief factors in bringing this school into existence. A school of law had been established in Rome sometime

33. See Chap. I.

during the preceding century. This second school, the school in Constantinople, was founded in 425. In the time of Justinian, a third school was in existence at Berytus. These schools were public institutions and were controlled by the emperors. In the reign of Justinian, the length of the course of study was fixed at five years. The course of study was prescribed by imperial authority, and legal instruction could be given only by duly authorized persons. Severe penalties were imposed upon any who taught without due license.

Theodosius II died in 450, and the government was administered by his sister Pulcheria for a short time after his death. Later, she married Marcianus (Marcian), an officer of high rank in the army, and made him Emperor. He had a peaceful reign till his death, without issue, in 457. Marcian was succeeded by Leo, known as Leo I, being proclaimed Emperor by the army. He reigned till 474, being engaged in several wars. He gained a victory over the Huns but was unsuccessful against Genseric in Africa.

Leo left an infant grandson, but the throne was usurped by his father, Zeno, the son-in-law of Leo. His reign lasted from 474 to 491, but it was constantly disturbed with domestic revolts and foreign wars. Zeno proved to be utterly incompetent, and in his personal character is described as being cruel and depraved. Upon his death, his widow, Ariadne, married Anastasius and raised him to the throne. The reign of this Emperor continued till his death in 518.

Justinus (Justin), the commander of the bodyguard of Anastasius, succeeded to the throne in 518. He was of barbarian origin as were also many of the emperors who both preceded and followed him. He was a Dacian peasant, born about 450. In early youth he went to Constantinople where he enlisted in the imperial guards of Leo I. He rose step by step until he became commander of the guards, and upon the death of Anastasius was proclaimed Emperor by the soldiers. He was, however, utterly without learning or experience in public affairs, and, therefore, he gave over the civil administration to his quaestor Proclus who proved to be a wise and able administrator. In the year 524, Justin associated with himself in the government of the Empire his sister's son, Justinian, and three years later the old emperor resigned the entire throne to him. During that same year Justin died.

Thus came to the head of the Roman Empire Justinian, a peasant born lad of Dacia, or modern Roumania. He was born on May 11, 483, and was forty-one years old when made Associate Emperor by his uncle Justin. Of his previous life practically nothing is known, but during his thirty-eight years of imperial power he became one of the most celebrated rulers in all Roman history.

In 525, the year following his appointment as sharer of the throne, he married Theodora, a notorious actress of Constantinople, and when he became sole ruler, in 527, he proclaimed Theodora Empress.[34]

Justinian has been represented to have been learned in theology, philosophy, law, poetry, and architecture. He was probably unlearned in all these. His family came from an obscure barbarian stock and he probably grew up with but little education. He was thirty-five years old before his uncle became emperor, and he had attained adult years before Justin had even gained much prominence in the army.

Justinian's name in his native language was, according to the traditions, "Uprauda," meaning, it is said, "just or upright," which translated into Latin became "Justinianus." This, however, is very fanciful since the name was not an uncommon one. Moreover,

---

34. Concerning Theodora, see Gibbon, Decline and Fall of the Rom. Emp. Ch. 40.

Justinian's name was, undoubtedly, derived from the Latin name of Justin, his uncle.

Justinian's great ability lay in his genius for administration. He was an executive of rare qualities. He saw clearly and deeply the needs of his Empire, and had great courage and energy in carrying out his plans. He was a good judge of men and gathered about him for his advisers and co-workers great jurists and great military leaders.

He was also a most zealous advocate and defender of the Christian religion, so much so that he became bigoted and intolerant. Shortly after the beginning of his reign he instituted a most vigorous persecution against the Jews, the Pagans, and heretical Christians. In a revolt that occurred about 532, the great church of Saint Sophia was burned and many thousands of the rioters were killed by the imperial troops. Justinian is reported, however, to have been very lenient towards all those insurgents who were made prisoners. He ordered the church to be rebuilt and it was restored upon a scale of great grandeur and magnificence. It still stands, today, as one of the wonderful edifices of the world.[35]

The building program of Justinian was not limited, however, to the church of Saint Sophia. Extensive operations in the erection of temples, aqueducts, roads, bridges, and fortifications were carried on in many parts of the Empire. His military campaigns were also famous under the leadership of his great generals, Belisarius and Norses, who won notable victories over the Vandals in Africa, the eastern Goths, and the Persians. Their conquests again carried the boundaries

---

35. It was originally built by Constantine, but its reconstruction by Justinian far surpassed the work of the earlier emperor. The name, Saint Sophia, is a translation of the Greek words, meaning "Holy Wisdom."

of the Empire almost to its greatest extent in former times.

The most famous thing, however, in the brilliant reign of this great emperor was the codification of the Roman Law, and his publication of it in that celebrated work later known as the Corpus Juris Civilis. The editorial part of this great task was accomplished under the direction of the eminent jurist Tribonian. It is not Justinian's work in the sense that he was its author or its compiler. Paintings and legends of Justinian's active participation in the work, sitting with and advising the learned jurists in their deliberations,[36] are mere fables. Justinian's part was that of originator. He had the breadth of view, the wisdom, and the statesmanship to call to his aid for the actual performance of the work the master legal minds of his Empire. It was the inspiration and the encouragement that Justinian gave to the great achievement that have justly immortalized his name.

36. As, for example, Constant's beautiful painting, "Justinian and Compilers of the Roman Corpus Juris", in the New York Metropolitan Museum of Art.

CHAPTER VI

THE CORPUS JURIS CIVILIS

The compilation of what was adjudged to be all the then existing law was not only the greatest achievement of Justinian's reign, but it was also the most important event in the history of the law of the Roman people. This great work consisted originally of three parts, the Digest (or Pandects), the Institutes, and the Code. The Digest was a comprehensive collection of extracts from the writings of the accepted legal authorities from the time of the Emperor Trajan to that of Constantine. The Institutes was a small, elementary book for those beginning the study of the law. The Code was a transcript of imperial laws still recognized as in force, and was based upon the former Codes of Gregorianus and Hermogenianus and the Code of Theodosius II.

The title, Corpus Juris Civilis, by which Justinian's great store-house of law is known to us is not found in the work itself, but was given to it by medieval civilians who thereby expressed their view that these writings contained "the whole body" or "the entire substance," of the civil law.

Long before the time of Justinian Roman Law had reached its highest point of development, and at the beginning of that emperor's reign (527 A.D.) it was widely scattered in many manuscripts, or "books." Owing to the divergent views of many writers who lived in periods far apart, it was also in many particulars both conflicting and confusing. The ambition of Justinian was to compile this great mass of law into a symmetrical and consistent whole, and then by his imperial power of legislation to make this compilation the sole law of the Empire.

In addition to the writings of the great jurists, especially those of the classical period of the second and third centuries, there were certain collections of imperial "constitutions," or laws promulgated by various former emperors. These collections were known as "the Gregorian Code," "the Hermogenian Code," and "the Theodosian Code." All of these Codes were still cited as law when Justinian ascended the throne.

The Gregorian Code (about 295 A.D.) and the Hermogenian Code (about 310 A.D.)[1] have previously been mentioned. They were private and unofficial transcripts of various imperial "constitutions" or "rescripts" emanating from emperors from the time of Hadrian to Constantine, a period of about two hundred years. The Hermogenian Code was a sort of supplement to the Gregorian Code. These two Codes are often cited as one; namely, the Codex Gregorianus et Hermogenianus.[2]

In the year 435, Theodosius II, ruler of the Eastern Empire, appointed a commission to collect the edictal laws from the time of Constantine to his own reign. This work was completed three years later (438) and was published under the name of the Theodosian Code. It was, in effect, a continuation of the Gregorian and Hermogenian Codes, and these two former codes, which up to this time had no legislative sanction, were given statutory authority by Theodosius along with his own code. The Theodosian Code was published at Constantinople, and became the law of the Eastern Empire. It was also adopted by the Roman Emperor Valentinian III, the son-in-law of Theodosius, for the Western Empire.[3]

1. Some scholars place the date of this Code as late as 325 A. D.
2. Only scattered fragments from these codes are now extant.
3. The Theodosian Code consists of sixteen books, divided into titles;

Imperial laws that were promulgated from time to time subsequent to the publication of the Theodosian Code were known as "Novels," that is, "new" (novellae) laws (constitutiones). "Novels" between the time of the Theodosian Code and the reign of Justinian are known as the Post-Theodosian Novels.

Another method of establishing the law amid its growing confusion of the later centuries was to give authority by imperial order to the writings of certain jurists. An emperor would merely by his fiat declare that the views of certain eminent writers of the past might be cited as law. Such imperial edicts were known as "laws of citations," of which the most famous was the Valentinian Law of Citations,[4] promulgated in 426 A. D. by the Western emperor Valentinian III.[5] This edict declared that the writings of Papinian, Paulus, Gaius, Ulpian, and Modestinus should be given the force of law. Also certain other famous legal authors of former times, such, for instance, as Scaevola, Sabinus, Julian, and Marcellus and all others whom the first five named jurists were accustomed to quote and approve as authorities were likewise given imperial sanction, and the views and opinions of all these writers were declared to be binding upon the courts, in the same way as the opinions of a supreme court in one of our American states are binding upon the courts of inferior jurisdiction.[6]

We are now able to see just what were the materials

and is extant with the exception of some sections. The greater part of Lex Romana Visigothorum (also known as Breviarium Alarici (506 A. D.) was taken from the Theodosian Code.

4. Theod. Code, 1, 4, 3.

5. This law was really the enactment of Theodosius II, the uncle of Valentinian III who was at this time only about eight years old. Valentinian III was made "emperor" by his uncle in 425 A. D.

6. That the Roman courts and judges should be guided by a majority opinion of these ancient writers in case of any divergent views, and that the opinion of Papinian should control in case the differing views were equal in number, has been previously mentioned.

out of which the great compilations of the law, later known as the Corpus Juris Civilis, were made in the time of Justinian. They may be summarized as follows:

(a) The Writings of the ancient jurists as sanctioned by the Valentinian Law of Citations.

(b) The Gregorian and the Hermogenian Codes.

(c) The Theodosian Code together with the Post-Theodosian Novels.

Nearly a century had passed since the publication of the Theodosian Code when Justinian took his seat upon the throne. It seems to have been his original plan to compile merely the statutory law, that is, the law found in the Gregorian, Hermogenian, and Theodosian Codes, and in the laws enacted by subsequent emperors. Obsolete laws were to be omitted and the compilation was to be made the sole repository of existing statutory law. To carry out this plan he appointed on February 28, 528, a commission of ten distinguished officials and jurists,[7] and they completed the task a little over a year later, namely, on April 7, 529. The new compilation was given statutory authority by Justinian and received the name of Justinianeus Codex. Owing to the fact that this Code was repealed five years later, in 534, being incorporated in the new Code of that year, this compilation of 529 became known as the Codex Vetus or "the Old Code."[8]

Hardly had the Code of 529 been completed when the emperor changed his plan entirely. He was not satisfied merely to compile a substitute for the imperial codes of the past. He desired to achieve a magnum opus. He would revise and consolidate all the existing law, and reduce the accumulated law of

---

7. Tribonian, professor of law at Constantinople, was a member of this commission.

8. This first code of Justinian consisted of twelve books. It is no longer extant.

centuries to a concise and compact form. He would incorporate the writings of the great jurists and the constitutions of the emperors into a single volume, "in unum codicem." Whether this great idea actually originated with Justinian or with his great counsellor Tribonian, or even with one of Tribonian's associates, we cannot tell. At any rate, whether by a just or an ironical destiny, the result immortalized the name of Justinian.

On Dec. 15, 530, the emperor commissioned Tribonian and his associates to execute the great task. In the imperial instructions regulating the scope and plan of the work, Justinian said:

"It was our first desire to amend the constitutions of former emperors, to arrange them in proper order, and to collect them into one book. This work having been done, we now hasten to make a full and complete amendment of the law, to amend and rearrange the entire jurisprudence of Rome, and to present in one volume the scattered books of many authors, a thing which no one has ever dared to hope, the task appearing not only of great difficulty but impossible. However, we have prayed for divine aid, and have undertaken this enterprise, trusting in God who in the greatness of His goodness is able to grant success in matters seemingly hopeless." [9]

The head of the new commission was Tribonian, who was born in Pamphylia about 475 A. D. He served Justinian for many years being appointed quaestor, master of the imperial household, praetorian prefect, and consul. In his edict confirming the Digest, Justinian says: [10] "The entire work has been executed by the illustrious and most learned magistrate Tribonian, ex-quaestor and ex-consul; distinguished both for eloquence and legal knowledge, and also eminent in prac-

---

9. Constitutio Deo Auctore, in preface to Digest.
10. Constitutio Tanta, 9.

tical affairs." Associated with Tribonian were Constantinus, Theophilus, Dorotheus, Anatolius, Cratinus, Stephanus, Mena, Prosdocius, Eutolmius, Timotheus, Leonides, Leontius, Plato, Jacobus, Constantinus (the second of that name), and Johannes. These sixteen fellow commissioners of Tribonian are all mentioned in the edict above, which also pays tribute to their high reputation and renowned juristic ability. The members of this distinguished and eminent commission assembled from various parts of the empire. Theophilus was a law professor in Constantinople; Dorotheus was a law professor at Berytus, as was also Anatolius; Cratinus had likewise been a law teacher in Constantinople. Most of the other members were magistrates or learned counsellors.

Under the direction of Tribonian the commissioners worked efficiently and rapidly. The imperial instructions directed the committee to read and make extracts from the approved law books of the learned men of old, and to distribute and condense the whole law into "fifty books." The committee was also instructed to revise as well as to compile. In other words, any passages in the books examined found incorrectly expressed were to be corrected. The law was collected, says [11] Justinian, from numerous volumes, the very names of some of the authors being unknown. Tribonian uncovered in his researches a great many books, some of which were unknown even by the most learned men. In all, over two thousand "books," or "rolls," were examined, and when the selected matter was arranged under particular titles the result was an encyclopedia of the law as gathered from the writings of the ancient masters.

It will thus be seen that the Digest consists of quotations, or extracts, or "fragments" as they are often called, from the writings of the great jurists. The

---

11. Constitutio Tanta, 17.

great bulk of the material came from the jurists of the second and third centuries, especially from Paulus and Ulpian whose quoted writings alone make up about one half of the entire Digest, there being 2462 quoted extracts from Ulpian's works, and 2080 from those of Paulus. The Digest also contains over 600 extracts from Papinian, over 500 from Gaius, and over 300 from Modestinus. There are also many quotations from other jurists. Justinian ordered a list of the ancient books, together with the names of their authors, from which the Digest was compiled, to be published at the beginning of the work. This list includes thirty-nine names, among which, in addition to those already mentioned, are the famous names of Neratius, Iavolenus, Labeo, Pomponius, Celsus, Julianus, Marcianus, Scaevola, Africanus, Sabinus, Proculus, Marcellus, and others. In addition to these thirty-nine writers, the Digest also incidentally mentions many other jurists whose opinions are quoted from time to time in various passages selected from the works of these thirty-nine.

Despite the injunction of Justinian that all the contradictions of the original writings should be harmonized, contradictions still remain in the Digest. It is but another illustration of the inevitable imperfection of all human work. It is not that the task was done hurriedly, although it was completed in three years, despite the fact, says the preface to the Digest,[12] that at the outset it was supposed it would take over ten years to finish, but because no length of time would probably have been sufficient to remove every cause of criticism. A more serious matter was the liberties that were taken with the original texts. They were mutilated in places. Some writers, moreover, are quoted as saying things never mentioned by them. This was probably due to the policy of "harmonizing"

12. Constitutio Tanta, 12.

as far as possible the independent writings. In fact, Justinian in his instructions to the commission said:[13] "If you find any matters in the ancient authors or laws incorrectly stated, you are to correct the same and state it properly, so that whatever is decided and written down by you shall appear to be true and best and as if the original writing. No one shall be permitted to argue from a comparison of the ancient books that what you have written is erroneous."

The great work was completed by Tribonian and his associates in three years. It was published on Dec. 16, in the year 533,[14] and went into effect as the law of the Empire on Dec. 30 of that year.

"We have given these books," said Justinian in his proclamation to the Senate and All Peoples,[15] "the name of Digest or Pandects because they contain all matters of question and their legal decision." The Emperor further states[16] that the Digest is composed of seven parts, as follows: I. Introduction, comprising Books 1 to 4; II. On Trials at Law, Books 5 to 11; III. On Things, Books 12 to 19; IV. Matters Relating to Hypotheca (Mortgages), the Edilian Edict, Interest on Money, Documents of Title, Witnesses and Presumptions, Betrothals, Marriages, and Guardianship, Books 20 to 27. This fourth part or division, says Justinian, "is placed in the middle of the Digest, and it contains all the most practical and best rules collected from all sources." The fifth division (V) treats of Wills, Legacies, Fideicommissa, and kindred matters, Books 28 to 36; VI. Bonorum Possessio and Intestate Succession in general, Operis Novi Nuntiatio (Notification of New Structure), Damnum Infectum (Apprehended Damage), Gifts, Manumissions, Prop-

---

13. Constitutio Deo Auctore, 7.
14. Constitutio Tanta.
15. Ib.
16. Ib.

erty and Possession, Judgments, Insolvency, Interdicts, and Exceptions, Books 37 to 44. VII. Verbal Obligations, Novation, Discharge of Debt, Private and Public Wrongs, Appeals, and Laws relating to Public Offices, Books 45 to 50.

This sevenfold division of the Digest is, to a modern lawyer, a most curious and strange combination of legal topics. It is very illogical and unscientific. The plausible presumption is that a sevenfold division was deemed appropriate owing to the mystical significance of the number "seven," and that the allotment of topics to these seven parts was largely mechanical.

The law as thus enacted was made the supreme authority. The great jurists from whose writings the Digest had been largely compiled were no longer to be cited. "In every trial or other legal contest," said Justinian,[17] "where rules of law have to be enforced, let no one quote or strive to maintain any rule of law save such as are composed and promulgated by us."

The fifty "books" of the Digest are divided into "titles," or chapters, each title consisting of "fragments" or extracts quoted from the writings of the great jurists who long had been accepted as authorities of the first rank. The titles largely follow the order of the topics set forth in the Edictum Perpetuum as compiled by Salvius Julianus. It was the opinion of Bluhme, the noted German jurist,[18] that the commissioners who worked upon the compilation of the Digest divided their material into three parts, namely, Sabinian material, Edictal material, and Papinian material. The first included formal treatises upon the law (jus civile); the second covered edicts promulgated by praetors; the third was made up from the writings of Papinian and reported cases. This material, according to Bluhme, was arranged under the various titles

17. Constitutio Tanta.
18. Professor of Law at Bonn. He died in 1874.

of the books of the Digest in the order in which the three parts of the material predominated.

Not alone is the general arrangement of the Digest as a whole, particularly as far as the sevenfold division described by Justinian is concerned, artificial and often illogical, but the individual books also present confusing mixtures of legal principles. Each book is supposed to deal with a particular subject. For example, Book 1 treats of the fundamental principles of justice, and the elementary divisions of persons and things; book 2 deals with magistrates and their powers; book 6 treats of real actions; books 7 and 8 of servitudes; book 23 of marriage; books 26 and 27 of guardianship; book 47 of private offenses; book 48 of public offenses; and book 50 of various municipal matters. However, there are many digressions, and topics not at all correlated are often discussed in the same book.

The Digest is cited in various ways. By the older European writers the introductory Latin words of a particular book are first cited, similar to the method employed by English writers in citing old English statutes, such as the Statute de Bonis conditionalibus, or the Statute quia emptores. The method usually employed by most modern writers is to cite, first, the Book, then the Title, and, third, the fragment (or the particular extract) as, for example, Dig. 2, 14, 8. Most of the fragments, however, are subdivided into an introductory part (a few words, or several lines) known as the principium, followed by other parts numbered successively and called "paragraphs." In such cases a citation consists of four parts, as, for example, Dig. 2, 14, 10, pr., or Dig. 2, 14, 10, 2. The former of these illustrations means that the matter referred to is found in the second book, fourteenth title, tenth fragment, and in the principium (or introduction) of the tenth fragment; the second means the second book, the fourteenth title, the tenth fragment, and the second paragraph of such fragment.

The oldest known manuscript of the Digest is the Florentine or the Pisan text. It dates back to the early part of the seventh century, or to a period within a hundred years of the original. It is a copy made by Greek scribes. It was long preserved in the city of Pisa, but when that city was captured by the Florentines in 1406 it was removed to Florence. It is the Florentine manuscript upon which the 1899 Berlin edition of the Digest is based.

A fanciful story that was current in Blackstone's day is repeated by him.[19] It is that a copy of Justinian's Digest was accidentally discovered at Amalfi, in 1137. The book was carried to Pisa, and it was this book, written on thin parchment and bound in two quarto volumes, that was taken to Florence in 1406. According to Blackstone, the Civil, or Roman Law had all but been forgotten when the accidental discovery of this manuscript in 1137 revived its dying embers. Had it not been for this chance event, the Civil Law, it is said, would have disappeared from earth. Lord Holt in the case of Blackborough v. Davis, 1 Peere Williams 52,[20] also says that for five hundred years the laws of Justinian had not been heard of until they were discovered by Lothar at the taking of Amalfi, and were published at the University of Bologna.

However, this story alleging that the revival of the study of Roman Law was due to the finding of the long lost copy of the book of the law at Amalfi, is regarded as apocryphal by modern scholars. The study of the Civil Law at the university of Bologna began long before the times mentioned. Savigny, in his Histoire

---

19. Com. I, 18.

20. 24 Eng. Reprint, 289, citing Selden's Notes on Fortescue, Chap. 18, 19.

Droit Romaine,[21] also Hallam, in his Middle Ages,[22] completely refute the legend.

The Digest was not intended for popular reading or even as a text-book for those beginning the study of the law. It is too voluminous, too abstruse, too complicated for such purposes. It is a vast storehouse of legal erudition, a general repository of the Civil Law. Scholars have spent lifetimes in the study of its pages and have not exhausted its contents.

Justinian clearly realized even before the completion of the Digest that such a "mass of knowledge" (tantae sapientiae molem)[23] was too great a burden for young law students to carry, and, accordingly, he appointed Tribonian who was the director of the whole work, and Theophilus and Dorotheus, who were law professors, the former at Constantinople, the latter at Berytus, as special commissioners to prepare a text-book, consisting of four parts, upon the first principles (institutiones) of the law, and thus enable young men to prepare for heavier and more serious study.[24] This book of "Institutes," the Emperor further directed, should be compiled from those works of ancient authors in which the first principles of the law were to be found, meaning the elementary text-books of recognized authority, particularly the books of Gaius, Paulus, Ulpian, and Marcianus. Accordingly, it was from these books, particularly from the Institutes of Gaius, that the Institutes of Justinian were compiled. The work upon this elementary text-book was completed on Nov. 22, 533, and by order of the Emperor its contents were enacted into law on Dec. 31, the same day the Digest went into effect.

The Institutes consist of four books, each book con-

21. Vol. II, 2, 15.
22. Vol. II, 520.
23. Constitutio Tanta, 11.
24. Ib.

taining several "titles" [25] (or chapters), and each title having an introductory clause known as the "principium," followed by various paragraphs. The Institutes are regularly cited by book, title, and either principium or paragraph.[26]

The order of the discussion of topics follows substantially the threefold order of the Institutes of Gaius, namely, persons, things, and actions.

The first two titles of the first book discuss certain general principles of justice and law, and then the third title takes up the consideration of the law of persons which topic is continued throughout the remainder of the book. Under the law of persons such topics as the status of persons, parent and child, marriage, adoption, and guardian and ward are treated. The second book of the Institutes deals with "things" or property law. This branch of Roman Law with its many subdivisions, including servitudes, gifts, wills, intestacy, obligations, and delicts, consumes all the space of the second book and likewise of the third, and is continued through the first five titles of the fourth book. Actions are then discussed in the following eleven titles of the fourth book, the seventeenth title setting forth the duties of a judge in connection with various actions brought before his court, and the last title, the eighteenth, dealing briefly with public offenses.

The Institutes of Justinian were, however, not merely an introductory text-book for the use of law students but they were the law itself, being given statutory force by the Emperor. This fact made the Institutes the most famous "text-book" upon the law ever published. They presented the actual state of the Roman private law, as far as they declared it, as it

25. The first book contains twenty-six titles; the second twenty-five; the third twenty-nine; and the fourth eighteen.
26. For example, Inst. 2, 9, pr.; and 2, 9, 1.

existed at the time Justinian authorized its publication. The Emperor said:[27] "The work was presented to us and read from beginning to end; whereupon we accepted it willingly and judged it to be worthy of our approval; and we ordered that the books should have the same authority as our own enactments."

The Institutes of Justinian were used as a text-book in the law schools of the Roman Empire, and were also used as a basis of the study of Roman Law in the universities of medieval Europe. Also at the present time they are recognized in all lands by legal scholars as of first importance in connection with the scientific study of legal principles.

In his proclamation announcing the completion of the work of codifying the law [28] Justinian says: "The entire Roman Law has now been compiled in three volumes, one of the Institutes, one of the Digest or Pandects, and lastly one of Constitutions." This third volume, the book of constitutions or imperial enactments, was the Code of the year 529 already mentioned in this chapter. As previously stated, this Code supplemented with subsequent "constitutions" the former codes of Gregorianus, Hermogenianus, and Theodosius II. It was published four years prior to the publication of the Institutes and the Digest, but after the promulgation of these two great works the Code of 529 was not deemed a satisfactory piece of compilation equal in rank and value to the other two. It had many imperfections and, moreover, was not up to date since Justinian during the four years subsequent to its publication had announced a number of new and important laws (constitutions). In order, therefore, to complete the work in a satisfactory way a new "Code" was considered to be necessary.

Accordingly, in the year 534, which was the year

27. Constitutio Tanta, Sec. 11.
28. Constitutio Tanta, Sec. 12, issued Dec. 16, 533.

following the publication of the Institutes and the Digest, a new commission was appointed to revise the former Code of 529. The members of this commission were Tribonian and four associates, Dorotheus, Menas, Constantine, and John.[29] Dorotheus was a professor of law in the school at Berytus. Menas, Constantine, and John were distinguished jurists residing at Constantinople. The work was finished that same year. The necessary corrections were made, the new constitutions of Justinian added, and the new Code (or the "second edition" of the old Code) was confirmed by Justinian on November 16, 534,[30] who further declared that it should become effective on Dec. 29 of the same year.[31]

The new Code consists of twelve books, the same number as the old Code. Each book is divided into titles, and the titles are divided into leges (laws). Frequently a lex is further divided into a principium and paragraphs.

The general arrangement of the Code is the same as the Digest. The laws (leges, constitutiones) of each title are placed in chronological order (that is, from the time of Hadrian to Justinian), each law being regularly preceded by the name of the emperor who declared it.

The old Code was repealed by Justinian, and lawyers when in court were forbidden longer to refer to it as law.[32] In consequence, it became obsolete and in time wholly disappeared. It has been lost for many centuries. Various references are made to "the Code" in the Institutes. These references are, of course, to the old Code, and for that reason were not authoritative after the new Code was enacted.

29. De Emandatione Codicis.
30. Constitutio de Emandationis Codicis.
31. Ib.
32. Const. de Emand. Codicis.

The Code is by English scholars usually cited by book, title, lex, and paragraph, as, for example, Cod. 6, 61, 8, 3. Since it is a revision of the old Code it is sometimes cited as the Codex Repititae Praelectionis,[33] or the Second Edition of the Code.

With the completion of the Institutes, the Digest, and the Code the great work was finished. These three volumes constituted the entire body of the civil law, "the Corpus Juris Civilis," a term not used, however, by Justinian, but given to the collected volumes centuries later by European writers.

The Corpus Juris Civilis, as known to modern scholars, consists of four divisions instead of three, a fourth division known as "the Novels" having been added many years after the publication of the Code. The word "Novels" is from the Latin "Novellae," the phrase Novellae Constitutiones, or new laws, meaning laws enacted by imperial authority subsequent to some preceding codification. Prior to Justinian's time, Theodosius II and his successors had promulgated laws under this title. During his entire reign Justinian was a prolific law maker, many new laws (novels) being enacted by him subsequent to the publication of the Institutes, Digest and Code. These laws modified or amended more or less some of the laws contained in these three volumes. The law of intestate succession, for example, was particularly affected by such later laws. Justinian in his confirmation of the Code announced that he would provide for amendments, if found advisable, by enacting "novellae constitutiones" from time to time. Such new laws were enacted by him, the greater number of them being published during the lifetime of Tribonian who doubtless suggested to the Emperor their advisability. That Tribonian was the leading spirit in all these new laws is evidenced by the fact that of the one hundred and sixty-

---

33. Literally, the Code of the repeated, or second, reading.

eight "novels" that are usually assigned to Justinian's authorship, all but about twenty were published between 534, the date of the new Code, and 543, the year of Tribonian's death. Some of the editions of the Novels that have come down to us contain, moreover, a few laws that were promulgated by emperors who succeeded Justinian, who died in 565.

No official collection of the Novels was ever published in Justinian's lifetime. However, a few years after his death a collection of one hundred and sixty-eight of such laws was made and published. In the middle ages a collection of ninety-seven was published, the civilians of that time being of the opinion that only that many were of general application.[34] Modern collections, however, contain one hundred and sixty-eight.

The Institutes, Digest, and Code were published in the Latin language, the official language of the Empire. Most of the Novels, however, were originally published in the Greek language since Greek was the language of the great majority of the people of the Eastern Empire.[35] Latin translations of the Novels were, however, made from time to time.

Each Novel is cited by its number, as, for example, the 118th Novel or the 127th. A Novel is addressed to some magistrate or other public official, and at times to a private citizen, with a direction to have it publicly proclaimed. Most of the Novels consist of a preface, several chapters, and an epilogue. Chapters are divided into paragraphs. The preface sets forth the purpose of the law, similar to the preamble, or "whereas" clause, of an ancient English statute. The chapter contains the law, often in the form of decisions upon questions that have been raised, and the epilogue consists of an admonition to obey the law. It is a very

34. Savigny, Gesch. Rom. Recht. im Mittel alter, Vol. 3, Ch. 22.
35. Nov. 66, 1, 2.

difficult matter to analyze in connected order the subject matter of a Novel since in the same Novel many matters are often mixed together. The Novels are cited by number, chapter, and paragraph.

It was in the middle ages, long after the time of Justinian, that Roman Law scholars added the Novels as a fourth division to the three divisions mentioned by Justinian, the Institutes, the Digest, and the Code, and gave to the entire fourfold compilation the immortal name, Corpus Juris Civilis.

In the Eastern empire the Civil Law remained in force for more than five hundred years after Justinian's death. The period from the death of Justinian till the capture of Constantinople by the Turks, or from 565 to 1453, is known as the Graeco-Roman or Byzantine period of the Civil Law. This period had many Greek commentators upon the law, and, about 910, the Basilica, a Greek version of the Corpus Juris, a voluminous work of six volumes divided into sixty books, was published. During the latter part of the Byzantine period, the Civil Law became blended with, and gradually was supplanted by, the Canon Law. When the Turks captured Constantinople they established the law of the Koran, but at the present time the basis of private law in Turkey is the Civil Law and it is also the law of modern Greece.

The Canon Law is a system of law that was developed in the course of time for the government and regulation of the Christian, or Roman, Church. The word "canon" means a rule, a standard, and authority. Applied to law it means the law laid down by ecclesiastical councils and by epistles and decretals of the Head of the Church. After Christianity became the state religion of the Roman empire, the bishops of the churches were authorized by the Christian emperors to assume jurisdiction in church matters, and, in consequence, a great mass of church or ecclesiastical law accumulated during the centuries. It was, however, in much confusion. The first collection of this law is said to have been undertaken by Ivo, bishop of Chartres, in 1114, and completed by Gratian, a monk of Bologna, in 1150. This work, known as the Decretum of Gratian, was arranged in three parts or books, and was patterned after the order of Justinian's Digest. It contained the ecclesiastical laws promulgated from the time of Constantine to the time of the compilation of the work. About a hundred years later, or about 1230, another work known as "The Decretals" was published. This work consists of epistles of various popes. It is divided into five parts or books, and contains much matter relating to matrimony, divorce, inquisition of crimes, and other important subjects. About seventy years later (1298) a sixth book, known as "the Sext" (from sextus), was added to the Decretals. Ten years later, or in 1308, "the Clementines," or the constitutions of Pope Clement V, were published. In addition to the foregoing, Pope John XXII, who succeeded Clement V, published further constitutions, to which the name "Extravagants" is given, since they "go beyond" the limits of preceding laws and regulations. Later papal constitutions than those of John XXII are also included in the name Extravagants.

We find, therefore, three divisions of Canon or Ecclesiastical Law, namely, the Decretum of Gratian, the Decretals, and the Extravagants. These three compilations make up what is known as the Corpus Juris Canonici in distinction from the Corpus Juris Civilis. However, in 1917, a new Codex Juris Canonici, containing the later papal constitutions to that date, was adopted in Rome, and was promulgated by the Roman Church and declared to be effective in 1918.

It is easy to understand how in those countries or governments which acknowledged the authority of the

Church as superior to the authority of the King or Emperor, the Canon Law gradually supplanted the Civil Law. While the Canon Law is based largely on the Civil Law, yet it departs from it in many particulars, especially in laws governing offenses and matters of procedure. The Corpus Juris Canonici became the basis of English ecclesiastical law,[36] but the Canon Law never made much headway against the English Common Law as the law of the land.

In the Western empire, the Civil Law, after the death of Justinian, passed through different phases of history in different countries, owing to the vicissitudes and disintegrations of governments. In Italy, however, it continued to exist during all the various conquests and changes there. Upon the revival of learning, the famous law school of Bologna was established by Irnerius. This was in the latter part of the eleventh century. The fame of this school went abroad throughout the countries of Europe and numerous students were attracted to it. Other schools were later organized in other parts of Italy and France. From that time even up to the present day, the Corpus Juris Civilis has been the foundation of legal studies in the universities of Europe.

Irnerius, the reputed founder of the law school of Bologna, is also said to have been the first of the "Glossators." The Glossators (from glossa, a note or comment) were thus named because in connection with their study and teaching of the law they wrote notes, or brief comments, upon the text of the Corpus Juris Civilis. These notes were appended to the text of the Institutes, the Digest, the Code, and the Novels. They were sometimes written between the lines of the text (glossae interlineares), and at other times upon the margin of the manuscript (glossae marginales). As

---

36. See Blackstone, Com. 1, 19, 79, 82.

time went on, the glosses of the jurists of recognized ability were used to explain, analyze, compare, and to sum up matters of the text, and thus the use of glosses became a method of teaching the law. The medieval jurists who followed this plan were called glossators in distinction from the "scribentes" who insisted upon teaching from the text alone. The method of the glossators required an exhaustive study, however, of the text, and in this the glossators differed from the earlier Italian teachers who taught for the most part from hand-books giving only a general outline of the principles of the Roman Law.

Among the best known of the glossators after Irnerius were Bulgarus,[37] Hugo, Vacarius, Azo, and Accursius. Vacarius was called from the law school at Bologna to England by Theobald, archbishop of Canterbury, in 1144, and founded a school of law at Oxford university. Azo (who died about 1220) was also a law professor at Bologna. He wrote a summary of the Institutes of Justinian (Summa Institutionum) and also of the Code (Summa Codicis). Bracton, the English law writer, was largely indebted to Azo for much of his material. Accursius (1182–1260) was a pupil of Azo, and likewise a law professor at Bologna. He made a collection of the notes of the glossators which he published under the name of Glossa Ordinaria. This work is often referred to as "The Great Gloss."[38]

After the times of the Glossators there arose in Italy in the fourteenth century another distinguished school, or group, of jurists who were known as the Post-Glossators, or the Commentators. This latter term was applied to them by reason of the great num-

37. Died about 1165.
38. There is a tradition that the son of Accursius also lectured at Oxford in the time of Edward I. See Swetland v. Curtiss Airports Corporation, 41 Fed. Rep. (2d Series) 929, 934.

ber of writings, or commentaries, they produced upon the Roman Law texts. They exerted a great influence upon the law of Italy by bringing more and more into unity that law with the Roman Law. Italian law of the middle ages was largely local law, the law of the various Italian cities. The commentators by their historical methods enabled their readers to realize the common origin of many of their laws, and in this way a much greater uniformity in law was developed. It has also been said [39] that "the commentators raised Roman Law for the second time in history to the rank of universal law."

The most famous of the commentators were Cinus, Bartolus, and Baldus.[40]

Cinus (1270–1336) was a professor of law at various schools including those of Perugia and Florence. He wrote a Commentary on the Codex which brought him great fame. He was the contemporary of Dante and Petrarch, the great Italian poets, and of Boccaccio, the famous novelist, all of whom were his intimate friends.[41] Petrarch and Boccaccio are said to have attended the lectures of Cinus.

Bartolus (1313–1356) was also a law professor at Perugia. He began the study of law under Cinus. He was the most distinguished of the Commentators. "The central figure," says Sohm,[42] "in the general legal history of the Middle Ages is neither Irnerius nor any one of the Glossators, but Bartolus. His commentaries dominated the practice of the courts. . . . The creation of the common law of Italy was due first and foremost to the labors of Bartolus."

Baldus was a native of Perusa, and was born about

---

39. Sohm, Inst. Rom. Law, Ledlie's Trans. 2d Ed. p. 27.
40. These names are Latinized from the Italian Cini, Bartoli, and Baldi.
41. Dante and Petrarch both speak affectionately of Cinus in their poems.
42. Inst. Rom. Law, Ledlie's Trans. 2d Ed., p. 28.

1327. He was a pupil of Bartolus, and later was a teacher of law in various universities, Bologna, Perugia, Pisa, Florence, Padua, and Pavia. He was also a voluminous writer. He died about 1400.

Among many other great names of European civilians should especially be mentioned Cujas (1523–1590), Doneau (1527–1591), Domat (1625–1695), Pothier (1699–1772), and Ortolan (1802–1873) of the French school; Grotius (1583–1645) of the Dutch; and Zaze (1461–1535), Heinecke (1681–1741), Hugo (1768–1844), Savigny (1779–1861), and Mackeldey (1784–1834) of the German school.

Cujas, whom Hallam pronounces "the greatest of all civil lawyers," was professor of law at Bourges, the chief law school of its day in France. Students from all nations of Europe attended his lectures. Among his writings are commentaries upon the Institutes and the Digest.

Doneau also taught law at Bourges. He was forced, however, to flee from France to escape the massacre of Saint Bartholomew, and later taught law at Heidelberg, Leyden, and Altorf. His writings upon the Civil Law are very highly esteemed.

Domat was for many years king's advocate in the court at Clermont, his birthplace. He was distinguished as a lawyer and as an author, his great work, entitled "The Civil Laws in Their Natural Order" (1689), placing him among the great civilians.

Pothier was professor of law at Orleans. He was the author of various books, his greatest being "The Pandects of Justinian digested in New Order." This work, in three volumes, was published in 1748–1752. He also produced a valuable treatise "On Obligations." The compilers of the Napoleanic Code made extensive use of the writings of Pothier.

Ortolan, of Toulon, published, in 1827, his "Historical Explication of the Institutes of Justinian," in three volumes. He was also the author of other writings, all of authoritative value.

Grotius, born at Delft, was one of the world's great scholars. He was eminent both in law and in theology, and his writings have been accorded the highest praise. From the standpoint of jurisprudence his most celebrated work is his great treatise on International Law ("De Jure Belli et Pacis"), which has been translated into many languages.

Among German writers upon the Roman Law Zaze (or Zazius) enjoys a very high reputation. He was born at Constance and became professor of law at Freiburg. His "Method of Law" (Methodus Juris) is perhaps the best known of his works.

Heinecke, professor of law at Halle, was distinguished both as a theologian and a jurist. He was the author of numerous works, the scholarly character of which caused them to be ranked as classics. He wrote, among other books, "The Elements of the Civil Law according to the Institutes," "The Elements of the Civil Law according to the Pandects," "Elements of the Law of Nature and Nations," and a "History of Roman and German Law."

Hugo (Gustav), another German jurist, was born in Baden. He became professor of law at Göttingen. His great work in seven volumes, "Manual of a Course in Civil Law," places him among the valuable contributors to the cause of legal knowledge.

Savigny was born in 1779, at Frankfort-on-the-Main. He was a descendant of a French family that had migrated to Germany to escape religious persecution. He became a professor of law at Marburg, also, later, at Landshut, and, in 1810, was called to the University of Berlin where he taught law for thirty-two years. Savigny's name is one of the great names among modern civilians, since he gave a great impetus to historical methods of teaching jurisprudence. His chief writings are "Right of Possession" ("Recht des Besitzes"); "A History of Roman Law during the Middle Ages," in six volumes; and "System of Modern Roman Law," in eight volumes. He died in 1861.

Mackeldey (Ferdinand) was born in 1784, at Brunswick. He was professor of law, successively, at the universities of Helmstedt, Marburg, and Bonn, being the first law professor in the latter university. He was the author of numerous writings but his "Handbook of Modern Roman Law" gave him a very high reputation. This book went through a number of editions and has been translated into all of the most important European languages.

CHAPTER VII

THE LAW OF PERSONS

A. Introduction

Roman writers on elementary law thought it important that a law student should have at the outset a clear notion of what the word "law" (jus) means, and the Digest opens with a quotation from the Institutes of Ulpian which reads as follows: "When one is about to give himself to the study of the law (jus) he ought first to know the origin of the term. It is derived from justitia, and according to the excellent definition of Celsus, it is the art of what is good and fair (ars boni et aequi)."[1] The Institutes of Justinian also say in their introductory words: "Justice (justitia) is a resolute and constant purpose to render to every man his due."[2] They further say:[3] "To live honestly, to wrong no one, to render to every man his due are the commandments of the law (jus)."

The word "jus" is in Roman jurisprudence the general term for "law." The word "lex," commonly translated "law," means, literally, that which is laid down, fixed, established, which is also the literal meaning of our English word "law;" technically, however, the word "lex" meant among the Romans a statute passed by the whole Roman people, in the comitia centuriata, upon the proposal of a consul or other magistrate.[4] The word "jus," on the other hand, has the same root

1. Dig. 1, 1, 1, pr.
2. Inst. 1, 1, pr.
3. Inst. 1, 1, 3.
4. Inst. 1, 2, 4.

as our English word "just," meaning literally, that which is fair, impartial, right. It was used by the Romans in several senses, meaning, first that which was fair and right in the abstract, as in "natural law;" secondly, that which was serviceable to all the people in a particular state, as in "civil law;" thirdly, says Paulus,[5] the word "jus" is applied to the place where the law is administered, the name being transferred from the thing done to the place where it is done. Whatever place the praetor fixes for dispensing justice (jus dicere), that place is rightly called "jus."

It has been said that the conception of law as expressed by Roman jurists, who based law upon fundamental ideas of right, was due to the influence of an idealistic, Greek philosophy. Whether this be true or not, and it certainly is subject to doubt, the Roman jurists did, in fact, constantly insist that law and justice should be in accord.[6] The Roman jurists accepted the theory of the divine origin of law, and to them jurisprudence was the knowledge of things divine as well as human.[7] Law embraced the religion of the Roman people.[8]

There are two branches of the law, says Ulpian,[9] public law and private law. Public law deals with matters affecting the administration of government. It is connected with political power, sovereign dominion,[10] and regards the welfare of the State, which included, in Roman days, matters of religion and was concerned

5. Dig. 1, 1, 11.
6. For a view that such an accord may not always be desirable, see Duncan v. Magette, 25 Tex. 245, pp. 252-254.
7. Inst. 1, 1; Dig. 1, 1, 10, 2.
8. People v. Ruggles, 8 Johns. (N. Y.) 289.
9. Dig. 1, 1, 1, 2; Inst. 1, 1, 4.
10. See Brown v. Gerald, 100 Me. 351; Bardes v. Herman, 62 Misc. (N. Y.) 428; Corvallis, etc. R. Co. v. Benson, 61 Oreg. 359; Oakland v. Oakland Water Front Co., 118 Cal. 160.

with public officers, sacred rites, and priests.[11] Private law deals with matters relating to the interests of individuals.[12] It is concerned with private ownership, or the right, title, and dominion of a private owner as distinguished from public ownership or public rights.[13]

Private law is derived from three sources, natural law, the jus gentium, and the jus civile. Natural law, or the law of nature, is that law which nature teaches all animals, not man alone, but all animals of land, and sea, and air.[14] The jus gentium, or the law of nations, is the law of mankind, law that is common to all men alike. It is the law which reason has established for men in general. It is called jus gentium because it is the law which all peoples recognize,[15] such as duty to God, to parents, and country.[16] By jus gentium wars arose, nations and governments were established, rights of property determined, boundaries fixed, and mutual obligations in connection with trade, buying and selling, letting and hiring came into being.[17] Jus civile, or civil law, is that law which any nation establishes for itself, the law which belongs to a particular state, as the civil law of Athens, or the civil law of Rome. It is taken in part from natural law, from the law of nations, and added to by the laws which a people creates for itself. Thus the laws of every nation are partly common to all mankind and partly peculiar to itself.[18]

The Roman civil law, says the Digest, is partly

11. Dig. 1, 1, 1, 2.
12. Dig. 1, 1, 1, 2.
13. See cases in note ten, supra.
14. Dig. 1, 1, 1, 3.
15. Dig. 1, 1, 9.
16. Dig. 1, 1, 2.
17. Dig. 1, 1, 5.
18. Dig. 1, 1, 6, pr.; Inst. 1, 2, 1.

written, partly unwritten.[19] The written law is found in statutes (leges), plebiscites, decrees of the senate (senatus consulta), constitutions of the emperors, edicts of magistrates, and the opinions of those learned in the law.[20] The edicts of praetors make up what is known as the praetorian law. This law is also called the honorary law, by reason of the honor connected with the praetor's office. The edicts of the aediles also constitute a part of the honorary law.[21]

The unwritten law is the law of approved usage, or custom. Where there are no written laws, the law is that which use and custom has established, for an immemorial custom is as binding as a statute. The statutes themselves are binding merely because they have been approved by the people, and what is the difference, asks the Digest, whether the people declare their will by their votes or by their practices and conduct?[22]

B. Status of Persons

All our law, says the Digest, quoting Gaius, relates either to persons, or to things, or to actions, and the Institutes of Justinian deal with the elementary principles of law that are founded upon this threefold division.[23]

Various are the titles or subjects that are considered under the law of persons, covering, as it does, such topics as freemen and slaves; citizens and aliens; and persons who are sui juris and alieni juris. The law of persons also involves family law, including the law of marriage, husband and wife, parent and child, adoption, and the law pertaining to guardian and ward.

A "person," in contemplation of Roman Law, is

19. Dig. 1, 1, 6, 1.
20. Dig. 1, 1, 7, pr.; Inst. 1, 2, 3; Gaius, 1, 2.
21. Dig. 1, 2, 2, 10; Inst. 1, 2, 7.
22. Dig. 1, 3, 32, pr. 1.
23. Dig. 1, 5, 1; Gaius 1, 8, 12; Inst. 1, 2, 12.

something entirely different from a mere human being. Slaves were human beings, but they were not persons, they were chattels or things;[24] something not capable of exercising ownership and of exercising legal rights, but property over which ownership could be exercised. A person was a being that was capable of ownership, a being that possessed legal capacities and legal rights. To be a "person," therefore, was to have a legal standing, a status, a legal capacity, a caput.

Persons are divided into two classes, natural persons and juristic persons. Natural persons are individuals having legal capacity, capacity to own private property. The term includes conceived but unborn persons, those who are in esse, as we say in our law, but called nascituri by the Romans. Juristic persons are artificial persons created by law. They are what we would call corporations in our law, particularly public or municipal corporations, since juristic persons, in Roman Law, were persons having capacity to hold public property, or property to be used for the public welfare. Thus the state, a town, a city, having capacity to own public property, was a person.

All human beings were, under Roman Law, either free or slaves.[25] There was a middle class known as freedmen, being those who had once been slaves but had been set free. Those who were free born were called ingenui. They always enjoyed a higher social position than freedmen, and were alone entitled to wear the gold ring, a common fashion during the Empire followed by all free born persons. One was born free when born of free parents, lawfully married, regardless of the free birth of the parents. That is, a free born person's parents may be either free born or freed persons. One is also free born even though his father may be a slave providing the moth-

24. Inst. 1, 16, 4; Dig. 4, 5, 3, 1.
25. Dig. 1, 5, 1.

er is free, since a child in such a case followed the condition of the mother. Likewise, if the mother is free, the child is also free born even if the father is unknown.[26] A man could also be declared "free born" by the emperor even though he were born a slave. This was sometimes done by an imperial order bestowing upon a freedman the right to wear the gold ring (jus aureorum anulorum). Justinian conferred this right upon all freedmen,[27] consequently in his day all distinctions between free born persons and freed persons were extinguished. The fact that a person was free born did not make him a Roman citizen, since a free born man might be a Latin, that is, a Roman colonist, or an alien (peregrinus).

Freed persons were manumitted persons, that is those who had been set free from a previous lawful slavery. They were called libertini, that is, those who had been given liberty. In early Roman Law, libertini, or freedmen, were of three grades or classes, depending upon the terms of their respective manumissions. These were "citizens," "Latins," and "enemies surrendered at discretion" (dediticii). In Justinian's time, however, all such distinctions were abolished and freedmen were all made citizens.[28]

Until the law was changed by imperial statute, freedmen were excluded from all magisterial offices. Moreover, at different periods of the Roman Law, the slave who had been set free owed many legal duties to his former master, and was under various legal disqualifications. He could not institute a lawsuit against his former master, henceforth known as his patron, and he could not marry his patron's daughter or his patron's widow. The laws also discriminated between free born and freed men in connection with their in-

26. Inst. 1, 4.
27. Nov. 78, 1, 2, 5.
28. Inst. 1, 5, 3.

testate estates. Under the praetorian law, the former master, the patron, was entitled to one-half of the estate of a deceased freedman. Freedmen were also frequently under a legal duty to render particular services (known as opera) to their former masters. It was customary for a master before setting free a slave to bind him by an oath to perform certain things for the master's benefit. These obligations included service and gifts of property. It was also a freedman's duty to render support and maintenance to his patron in case of the latter's lack of means.

Slaves:

Slavery existed in the Roman state from its earliest days. It did not, however, originate with the Romans but was a custom practiced by many ancient peoples. It had its origin in war. It is unknown to the law of nature (jus naturale) for by that law all men are born free, says Ulpian, and liberty, says Florentinus, is a natural right to do what one desires to do except as he is prevented by force or by law.[29] Slavery is a creation of the law of nations [30] whereby, contrary to the law of nature, a man is subjected to the ownership of another.[31] "From the earliest times," says Marshall,[32] "war has existed, and war has conferred rights in which all have acquiesced. Among the most enlightened nations of antiquity, one of these was that the victor might enslave the vanquished, and although throughout Christendom this harsh rule has been ex-

---

[29]. Dig. 1, 1, 4; 1, 5, 4; Inst. 1, 3, 1. Compare the opening words of the Declaration of Independence: "All men are created equal; endowed by their Creator with certain inalienable rights; among these are life, liberty, and the pursuit of happiness."

[30]. That is, the jus gentium, the custom of mankind in general. The Roman jus gentium is quite different from what we call "International Law."

[31]. Dig. 1, 5, 4; Hodges v. U. S., 203 U. S. 1, 17.

[32]. The Antelope, 10 Wheat. (U. S.) 66, 120.

ploded, yet what was the usage of all could not be pronounced repugnant to the law of nations."

Among the Romans, slavery usually originated in three ways, captive enemies taken in war, birth, and condemnation for crime. The war captives belonged to the state and were either sold for the benefit of the public treasury, or were compelled to work upon public improvements. Such persons were called "slaves" (servi) from the fact that military commanders spared, or "saved," their captives and sold them instead of putting them to death.[33]

In addition to the three sources of slavery already mentioned, a free man over twenty years of age might, by the jus civile, become a slave by permitting himself to be sold by one fraudulently pretending to be his master, in order that he might share the purchase money with his accomplice.[34] Under the jus civile such a person could at any time claim his free born status, but as a punishment for such a fraud a statute provided that one who had thus voluntarily permitted himself to be sold, should be estopped from claiming his freedom and should be held as a slave.[35] It was also a statutory law of Rome that a free woman who had sexual relations with a slave might herself be reduced to slavery. This statute was repealed, however, by Justinian.[36]

It was also possible that a freedman might lose his freedom and be relegated to his former condition of slavery by any act of great violence or wrong upon the person or to the reputation of his former master.[37]

The Twelve Tables provided that a debtor might be sold by his creditors, and also that a thief taken in

33. Dig. 1, 5, 4, 2; Inst. 1, 3, 3.
34. Dig. 1, 5, 5, 1; Inst. 1, 3, 4; Westbrook v. Mitchell, 24 Tex. 560.
35. Senatus Consultum Claudianum, Dig. 40, 3, 5.
36. Gaius 1, 91, 160; Codex 7, 24.
37. Dig. 25, 3, 6;. Code 4, 10, 1.

open theft should be delivered in bondage to the owner of the stolen property.[38] These ancient laws were obsolete, however, long before the reign of Justinian.

The child born of a slave mother, regardless of the status of the father, was a slave,[39] and persons condemned for the commission of heinous crimes were often, as a punishment, reduced to the condition of slavery, the loss of the status of freedom being a result of the character of the penalty. Thus, a free man condemned to death, or to labor in the mines, or to fight with gladiators or wild beasts became a slave. Such persons were said to be slaves of the state, or slaves without a master.[40] Slavery for crime was, however, abolished by Justinian.[41]

In the early days of Rome, slaves were very few, being mostly household servants, and were regarded as members of the family. However, as Rome's conquests extended, the number of slaves vastly increased, and in the days of the later Republic and the Empire their great numbers imperiled the state both socially and politically. Every person of means had slaves, and some wealthy Romans are said to have owned as many as ten thousand.[42] In the days of Augustus, fully a half of the entire population of the Empire, estimated to be about one hundred and twenty millions, were slaves.[43] The fact that all manual work, both agricultural and domestic, was performed by slaves made free labor degrading. This was one of the chief causes of the deterioration of Roman character and of the subsequent degeneration and destruction of Rome.

38. 12 Tab. 3, 6; 8, 14.
39. Inst. 1, 3, 4; 1, 4, pr.; Gaius 1, 82, 89; Dig. 1, 5, 5, 2; Guess v. Lubbock, 5 Tex. 536; Cartwright v. Cartwright, 18 Tex. 636.
40. Inst. 1, 12, 3; 1, 16, 1; Dig. 48, 19, 8, 11 and 12; 48, 19, 17, pr.
41. Inst. 3, 12, 1; Nov. 22, 8.
42. Hume, Essay on the Populousness of Ancient Nations.
43. Gibbon, Decline and Fall of the Roman Empire.

THE LAW OF PERSONS 189

The condition of all slaves was one and the same.[44] While many of them were barbarians, yet, on the other hand, there were numerous Roman slaves who were superior to their masters in intelligence, culture, and attainments. A man or woman of refinement and education might by the accident of war become the slave of some coarse, ignorant Roman master.

By the jus gentium and the jus civile a slave had no rights at all. He was a thing to be possessed, a chattel.[45] He could be sold, pledged, or given away. Everything acquired by the slave belonged to the master,[46] and the master had a power over the slave (potestas dominica) corresponding to the power of the paterfamilias over his son (potestas patria). By virtue of this legal power a master could put a slave to death with or without any just cause.[47] In imperial times, however, the arbitrary power of masters over their slaves was curbed, and more humane laws were passed respecting the treatment of slaves. Masters were not permitted to kill their slaves merely because they fell sick and were consequently useless,[48] or to condemn their slaves to be torn by wild beasts in the arena except as a punishment for wrong and except also that such punishment was approved by a magistrate.[49] The Emperor Antoninus declared that a man who wilfully killed his own slave should be punished just as if he had killed the slave of another,[50] that is, should be punished for murder.[51] Constantine enacted that a master should not be held liable for killing a

44. Inst. 1, 3, 5.
45. Dig. 4, 5, 3, 1. The term Mancipium was often applied to a slave, meaning a thing taken, or possessed. Dig. 1, 5, 4, 3.
46. Inst. 1, 8, 1; Dig. 41, 1, 32.
47. Gaius 1, 52; Inst. 1, 8, 1; Dig. 1, 6, 1, 1.
48. Suetonius, Claudius 25.
49. Dig. 48, 8, 11, 2.
50. Gaius 1, 53; Inst. 1, 8, 2.
51. Dig. 48, 8, 2; 48, 8, 3, 5.

slave in the course of proper punishment, as by flogging, but if the slave's death was due to wilful abuse of such authority, it would be murder on the part of the master.[52] It further became the law that in cases of cruelty, or of insufficient sustenance, or of indecent assaults, slaves might prefer their complaints before a magistrate,[53] and that in the case of the sale of a group of slaves, as in the settlement of an estate, slaves who were near relatives should not be separated, if avoidable, but that, if possible, they should be sold together.[54] There were, however, rigid laws punishing slaves who tried to escape from their bondage, and the law severely punished any one who harbored a runaway slave.[55] Persons, however, who became slaves by being taken captive in war could regain their freedom by making a successful escape and recrossing the boundary line of their own country (postliminium).

A large part of the business transactions of Rome was carried on by slaves, many of whom were men of ability, and some of great ability. Slaves were employed in every sort of occupation, including mechanics, clerks, stewards, artisans, business managers, actors, physicians, surgeons, teachers, shopkeepers, farmers, and many other forms of labor and business. The master of a ship engaged in the carriage of goods or the transportation of passengers might be a slave, and often large and important business interests were managed by men who were only the slaves of others.

In connection with their employment slaves were often entrusted by their masters with money or other property. Sometimes one or many slaves would be put under the control and direction of another slave[56] for

52. Codex 9, 14, 1.
53. The City Prefect, in Ulpian's day, Dig. 1, 12, 1, 8.
54. Dig. 21, 1, 35; Codex 3, 38, 11.
55. Dig. 11, 4, 1, 1; Codex 6, 1, 4, 7.
56. Gaius 4, 7, 3; Inst. 4, 7, 4. . A slave under the control of another slave was called a vicarius.

the purpose of managing the master's business. Over the property thus placed in their hands slaves were very commonly given the absolute control, and in such cases the property was called peculium, that is, the individual or peculiar property of the slave. It did not, however, belong to the slave. It remained the master's property,[57] and he could demand it at any time at his will and pleasure,[58] although the slave was permitted to keep and manage it as his own. Likewise, many slaves through their industry and thrift earned much money, and, at times, talented slaves, such as artists, actors, physicians, and surgeons, were the recipients of valuable gifts. All these gains belonged, however, to the owner of the slave, but in many instances the master gave permission (concessio) to a slave to treat such property as his peculium.[59]

In dealing with others in connection with his master's business, or with relation to his own peculium, a slave had no contractual capacity. However, by order, or permission of his master a slave could make a contract which would bind the master, although no action could be brought against the slave, the gains and losses of such transactions being the master's. The fact of a peculium also made it possible for a master and slave to enter into agreements with each other, and this was often done, the master permitting the slave to retain whatever profit he thereby made, although such agreements were not, of course, enforceable by action.[60] When a slave was permitted by his master to make contracts with third persons in relation to the slave's peculium, the master thereby became bound, in case of loss, to the extent of the pe-

57. Dig. 41, 1, 37, 1.
58. Dig. 15, 1, 8.
59. Dig. 15, 1, 4, pr. and 2.
60. Gaius 1, 78; Dig. 15, 1, 49, 2.

culium. The master was liable for delicts (torts) committed by his slave, but the slave was alone liable for his crimes.

Slaves could not legally marry. What was called the marriage of slaves, contubernium, was merely a permissible cohabitation.[61] However, the offspring of such a relation were recognized as having a natural or blood relationship (cognatio) which relationship prevented them from marrying each other if they ever became free.[62]

There were various ways by which slaves could obtain their liberty, and in the course of Roman history many thousands of slaves were set free. Postliminium has already been mentioned. By this law one made a slave by being taken prisoner in war became free when he returned to his own country.[63] The most common method, however, of liberating slaves, was manumission by the voluntary act of the master.[64] Under the old law manumission was effected in three ways, per vindictam, censu, and testamento. The first was effected by means of a judicial order, although it did not have to be pronounced in open court. A master wishing to set free a slave informed the magistrate of this desire. Whereupon the magistrate declared the slave to be free. The name per vindictam given to this method of manumission is said to be derived from the fact that one of the lictors, always in attendance upon a praetor when engaged in official business, placed his rod or staff (vindicta) upon the slave, when the praetor pronounced him free, in token of

---

61. The marriage of slaves was permitted under the Spanish civil law, also the intermarriage of a free person with a slave. By the marriage of a free man to a slave woman the slave became free. Pearson v. Pearson, 51 Cal. 120; Wells v. Lane, 9 Johns. (N. Y.) 144.

62. Dig. 23, 2, 14, 2.

63. Gaius 1, 129.

64. Inst. 1, 5, pr.

his freedom.[65] In imperial days, magisterial manumission was very common. Masters were accustomed to present such requests to magistrates even when they met them on the streets, as when a praetor, or proconsul, or a governor of a province was going to the baths or to a theatre.[66]

A slave could also be liberated censu, that is, by having his name enrolled, by order of his master, among the list of freemen as shown by the census[67] which list was made up at Rome by the censors every five years. Likewise a master could by his will (testamento) give freedom to his slave.[1]

Under the old law, a slave manumitted by any of the preceding methods became both a freeman and a Roman citizen.[2]

In the imperial days there were other ways in which slaves could be set free, very little formality being required. The Institutes state that manumission may occur in various ways, as by an announcement in holy church, or by default in a fictitious suit of ownership, or by a declaration in the presence of friends, or by letter, or by testament or any other expression of a master's last will. In fact, continues Justinian, there are many other ways either provided by the constitutions of earlier emperors or by our own.[3]

The setting free of a slave in church, in ecclesia, dated from the time of Constantine. The master announced in the presence of the bishop and the congregation that the slave was free, and a record of the declaration was made.[4]

It was the general rule that a slave upon his manu-

65. Livy 34, 16; Dig. 40, 2, 8; 40, 2, 23.
66. Gaius 1, 20; Inst. 1, 5, 2.
67. Cicero de Orat. 1, 40; Ulp. Frag. 1, 7.
1. Ulp. Frag. 1, 22; Dig. 41, 4, 43; Gaius 2, 267; Inst. 2, 24, 2.
2. Gaius 1, 17.
3. Inst. 1, 5, 1; Code 1, 13, 7, 6.
4. Code 1, 13, 1; 1, 13, 2.

mission became a citizen, but under some of the imperial modes of granting freedom to slaves citizenship was not necessarily a sequence.[5] However, in Justinian's time all forms of manumission were followed by citizenship.

In addition to freedom being obtained by the voluntary act of the master, various laws at different times bestowed liberty upon slaves, either in recognition of some meritorious service on the slave's part or as a penalty upon an unjust master. Thus slaves were set free as a reward for detecting and exposing various sorts of criminals,[68] and masters forfeited their slaves for abandoning them in sickness[69] or in infancy[70] or in selling them, if females, for the purpose of prostitution.[71]

It may seem strange that laws should have been passed to curb or limit the power or authority of masters to set free their slaves, but such was the fact.[72] The chief reason for restraints upon manumission was probably the same as in the case of restraints upon immigration, to-day, in some modern countries. The freeing of slaves, many of them of an undesirable class, caused additions to Roman citizenship that were not for the best interests of the state. It is also believed that some masters used the bribe of freedom in order to persuade their slaves to enter into conspiracies against the government. At any rate, the lex

5. The famous Dred Scott Case, 19 How. (U. S.) 393, held that in this country a descendant of an African slave could not, though he had been emancipated, become a citizen of a State in the constitutional sense of citizen.

68. Dig. 4, 8, 5; Code 7, 13, 1; 7, 13, 2; 7, 13, 3.
69. Dig. 40, 8, 2.
70. Code 1, 4, 23; Nov. 153.
71. Code 1, 4, 12; 1, 4, 14.
72. In the United States, in slavery days, some states forbade the manumission of slaves. Hall v. Hall, 38 Ala. 131; Cowan v. Stamps, 46 Miss. 435; Charlotte v. Chouteau, 11 Mo. 193; Guess v. Lubbock, 5 Tex. 536.

[Roman Law]

Aelia Sentia (4 A. D.) provided that a slave who had committed a crime should not, upon being set free, become a Roman citizen; that no slave under thirty years of age should be manumitted except for special reasons approved by a magistrate; and that manumissions by an insolvent in fraud upon his creditors should be void.[73] Likewise the lex Fufia Caninia (A. D. 8) placed a restriction upon the number of slaves a man could set free by his will, permitting him to liberate one-half if he owned up to ten slaves; one-third if he owned between ten and up to thirty; one-fourth if from thirty to one hundred; and one-fifth from one hundred to five hundred.[74] Since this statute applied only to manumissions by will, a master could set free all his slaves by some other way, such as vindicta, or censu, or inter amicos.[75] On account of this inconsistency Justinian abolished the law.[76]

In the course of time, the Roman Law system of slavery became merged in the serfs of the European middle ages and in the villeins of the early English law. When African slavery was introduced into our own country and became an established institution, our American courts looked to the Roman Law for rules applicable to it,[77] since it resembled the Roman system,[78] and because slavery was entirely unknown to the English Common Law.[79]

Slavery was introduced into America by African slave traders, but was chiefly perpetuated by birth.[80] Under the early laws of some of our American colonies

---

73. Gaius 1, 36 and 37; Inst. 1, 6, pr.; Gaius 1, 38–41; Inst. 1, 6, 4.
74. Gaius 1, 42, 43.
75. Gaius 1, 44.
76. Inst. 1, 7, pr.
77. Neal v. Farmer, 9 Ga. 555.
78. Neal v. Farmer, 9 Ga. 555; Douglass v. Ritchie, 24 Mo. 177.
79. Neal v. Farmer, 9 Ga. 555.
80. Jones v. Wootten, 1 Harr. (Del.) 77; Lee v. Sprague, 14 Mo. 476.

and states, Indians when taken prisoners in battle became slaves, and their descendants followed their status.[81] Questions relating to slavery are not even yet in this country wholly things of the past. Matters connected with the property rights of persons who are the descendants of slaves are still from time to time presented to our courts.[82]

Persons Sui Juris and Alieni Juris:

In connection with the law of persons, individuals were also classed as either sui juris or alieni juris. This classification was based upon the family law of Rome by virtue of which members of the household or familia were under the legal power or authority of the family head, the paterfamilias. Individuals who were thus dependent upon or subject to another's power or control were said to be alieni juris, while persons who were their own masters, that is, were independent of, and subject to no other's authority, were said to be sui juris.[83]

Individuals were alieni juris who were either in the "power" (potestas) or "hand" (manus), or bondage (mancipium) of some other person.[84] Accordingly, slaves in the power of their masters, children in the power of their paterfamilias, wives in the "hand" (manus), of their husbands, and bondmen in the control of their creditors were not sui juris but alieni juris. Only those persons who were independent of all such authority or control were sui juris.

It is clear, therefore, that age had nothing to do with this classification. A man forty years old might be in the power (patria potestas) of his grandfather or

---

81. Marguerite v. Chouteau, 3 Mo. 540; State v. Van Waggoner, 6 N. J. L. 374; Jenkins v. Tom, 1 Wash. (Va.) 123.

82. For a case as late as 1925 see Bryant v. Bryant, 190 N. C. 372, 130 S. E. 21.

83. Gaius 1, 48; Inst. 1, 8, pr.; Dig. 1, 6, 1.

84. Gaius 1, 49.

father and, therefore, be alieni juris, while a child a few days old might, owing to the decease of his paterfamilias, be sui juris. Again, persons might be sui juris and yet devoid of legal capacity, as persons under guardianship.

According to Gaius, individuals were said to be in mancipio because they could be set free (emancipated) by the legal transaction known as mancipatio.[85] This was the ancient formal sale per aes et libram. By the extension of the ancient doctrine of the transfer of chattels by this ceremony, human beings could also be bought and sold by mancipatio. Consequently slaves were said to be in mancipio, likewise wives who were in manu, also children in potestate, and freemen who were in bondage.[86]

However, the term mancipium, although often applied to a slave,[87] was generally limited in its use to a free person in bondage. Such a person was still a freeman and a Roman citizen. He was not reduced to the status of a slave, although his actual condition was in loco servi.[88] He was one who had either voluntarily bound himself to another, as a pledge for debt, or one who by the old fiction of sale by mancipatio was transferred to another, as in the case of the emancipation of a son.[89]

The law of bondage in the earlier days of the Roman Republic was evidently cruelly abused. The creditor often not only compelled his bondman to work incessantly, but kept him in chains and flogged him just as if he were actually a slave instead of being a Ro-

---

85. Gaius 1, 116 et seq.
86. Gaius 1, 116–123.
87. "Slaves (servi) are so called because generals are accustomed to save (servare) their captives for public sale; they are also called mancipia because they are taken by hand (manu capiantur) from the enemy." Dig. 1, 5, 4, 3.
88. Gaius 1, 138.
89. Gaius 1, 140, 141.

man citizen. Bondsmen became thousands in numbers in the times of great poverty and distress, and it was said that every patrician's dwelling was a private prison-house.[90]

The old law of bondage was practically obsolete, however, in the time of Justinian. In the Institutes and Digest the only illustrations of individuals who are alieni juris are children in the power of their paterfamilias, and slaves in the power of their masters.[91] The old law of manus, or the subjection of wives to their husbands, had also passed away.

It is pertinent to observe in connection with the Roman law of bondage that it has its analogies in our own law. The system of villeinage in early English law is an example. A villein was not a slave. He had some legal rights, yet he was bound to render service to another.[92] Bond servants were also common in England for centuries, and in our early colonial days some of them came to this country with their masters, and others, in consideration of their passage being paid, bound themselves to service for a period after their arrival here. The children of paupers are yet bound out by overseers of the poor, and probably in all our states minors with parental consent may voluntarily bind themselves to masters as their apprentices.

Cives and Peregrini (Citizens and Aliens):

For a long time in the history of Roman Law, one of the most important matters in the law of persons was the division of freemen into two classes, citizens (cives) and aliens (peregrini). Roman law was founded upon this distinction. The very term jus civile meant citizen law, the old jus civile applying exclusively to Roman citizens. Foreigners, or aliens, had no part in it. As previously stated, the Pa-

90. Livy 6, 36; Muirhead Rom. Law, 3d ed., 85; Roby, 2, 296.
91. Inst. 1, 8, pr.; Dig. 1, 6.
92. See Co. Litt. 1236; Coke II Inst. 4, 45.

THE LAW OF PERSONS 199

tricians in early times alone possessed the full rights of citizens and for many years there was a continuous struggle on the part of the Plebeians to obtain equal rights under the law.

The legal rights possessed by a man under the Roman Law constituted his status, but all men did not have the same status. To be a "person" in the legal sense, was to have legal capacity, and in order to have full legal capacity three things were necessary, freedom (libertas), citizenship (civitas), and membership in a family (familia).

Citizenship originated either by birth or by grant. Citizenship by birth depended upon the status of the father and mother. If there had been a valid marriage, the child followed the status of the father at the time of conception. In case there was no marriage, the Roman Law gave to a child the status of the mother at the time of birth. A child born of a slave mother was held to be free providing the mother had been free at any time during the pregnancy, but the same rule did not apply to citizenship. Even though the mother had been a citizen at any time during the pregnancy, yet if she were not a citizen at the time of birth, the child would not be a citizen by birth.[93]

Under the Roman Law, a citizen had the public rights of voting (jus suffragii) and of eligibility to public office (jus honorum); his private rights were marriage (jus connubii) and the right to acquire and transfer property by Roman Law (jus commercii). A citizen's marital right was the right to marry a Roman woman according to the jus civile, and thus to have a family entitled to the rights of Roman Law.[94]

---

93. Gaius 1, 76-92.

94. See paterfamilias and potestas, post. In order to have a marriage valid under the jus civile both parties had to be Roman citizens. For this reason the marriage of Antony and Cleopatra caused great resentment among the Romans.

Under the jus commercii a citizen's title to property was protected by the same law; a citizen could dispose of his property by will, and could also be a beneficiary under a will; he also had the right to bring actions in the courts.

One might, however, be a Roman citizen in a limited sense, that is, without enjoying the full benefits of citizenship. Accordingly we hear of citizens optimo jure and citizens non optimo jure, the former meaning citizens possessing both public and private rights. Citizenship was also described at times as sine suffragio, or without the right to vote, as where citizenship was conferred upon the inhabitants of a friendly town or community in recognition of its allegiance. Women could be Roman citizens [95] as well as men, yet female citizens did not have the public rights of citizenship. They had no voice in the national assembly, the comitia centuriata, and they were not eligible to public office.[96]

Aliens, or peregrini, could not invoke the privileges of the Roman Law since it did not apply to them. In latter days, when foreigners became numerous in Rome, it was necessary, as we have seen, that a special magistrate should be elected in order to adjust many matters that necessarily arose in their family and commercial relations. Accordingly, this magistrate, the praetor peregrinus, decided their disputes not by the jus civile, the citizens' law, but by the principles of conduct that theoretically ought to govern mankind in general, the jus gentium as it was called, or as we might say by equitable principles.

The legal rights and privileges of citizens in contrast with the rights and privileges accorded to aliens is not peculiar to Roman Law. Every state has recognized a similar doctrine. Civil rights are merely

95. Gaius 1, 90-92.
96. Dig. 50, 17, 2, pr.; Code 2, 13, 4 and 18.

the rights that appertain to one by virtue of his citizenship, and such rights include the rights of property, marriage, and freedom of contract.[97]

Our English word "citizen" is derived from the Roman word civis, its primitive meaning being a person who is vested with the freedom and privileges of a city.[98] When the word came to be applied to the inhabitants of a state, it carried with it the same significance, with reference to the privileges of the state, which had been implied by it with reference to the members of a city. It is in this sense that the term citizen is used in this country, and this is the sense in which the word is used in our federal Constitution in speaking of "the privileges and immunities of citizens in the several states."[99] As said in Gardina v. Jefferson Co., 160 Ala. 155, "The word 'citizen' has come to us from the Roman Law. In Roman Law it designated a person who had the freedom of the city of Rome and could exercise the political and civil privileges of the Roman government.[100] It was both an honor and a sacred privilege to be a Roman citizen." Again in White v. Clements, 39 Ga. 232, 259, it is said: "Citizens were the highest class of subjects at Rome, to whom jus civitatis belonged, and those who had it possessed all rights and privileges, civil, political, and religious."

There is also a peculiar sense of pride and dignity in the word "citizen." Every nation must necessarily have a people, a population, and various names have been applied to the units of a country's members, such as "inhabitant," "subject," "citizen."[101] The term citizen, however, is never employed, said the supreme

97. Friendly v. Olcott, 61 Oreg. 580, 588.
98. White v. Clements, 39 Ga. 232, 259. See also Thomasson v. State, 15 Ind. 449; Amy v. Smith; 1 Litt. (Ky.) 332.
99. Amy v. Smith, 1 Litt. (Ky.) 332.
100. Quoted from Kent's Com. II, 76 n.
101. Minor v. Hoppersett, 21 Wall. (U. S.) 162.

court of Georgia in an early case, to designate the people of a monarchy, since it involves an idea not enjoyed by "subjects," namely, equality, together with the inherent right to share in the government.[102]

Despite the theoretical correctness, at one time, of this judicial utterance, nevertheless the term "citizen" was employed in the Roman state during all the days of the Empire, even in the periods of its most absolute despotism. And it could hardly be said, to-day, that British "subjects" do not have an inherent right to share in the government.

In the Roman Law citizenship embraced both civil and political rights. In the course of time, however, there was developed a sort of partial citizenship which possessed some civil rights but no political rights.

Citizenship by Grant; Naturalization:

Although in the early days of Roman Law, all freemen were either citizens or peregrini, whether they were Latins or Italians, yet as the power of the Roman state expanded over Latium and the other districts of Italy, certain privileges were granted to these peoples which resulted in a class of rights midway between the rights of full Roman citizenship and the position occupied by peregrini. Freedmen (libertini), says Gaius,[103] are divided into three classes, citizens, Latins, and persons who are regarded as being in the position of enemies who surrender at discretion (dediticii). This last class was created by the Lex Aelia Sentia,[104] which provided that slaves who had been punished by their masters with chains, or who had been branded, or subjected to torture in connection with an examination upon a criminal charge, or who had been condemned to fight with men or beasts, should, in case of their subsequent manumission by

102. White v. Clements, 39 Ga. 232, 260.
103. Gaius 1, 12.
104. 4 A. D.

THE LAW OF PERSONS 203

their masters, be in the condition of enemies surrendered at discretion.[105] Such persons possessed practically no legal rights at all. They were incapable of taking under a will, the same as peregrini, nor could they make a will.[106] They could not, moreover, at any time in the future become citizens,[107] and were forbidden to reside within a hundred miles of Rome.[108]

However, the inhabitants of many of the Latin towns were given certain privileges enjoyed by Roman citizens. They possessed, in general, the private right of commercium but not the right of connubium. The rights of the Latins varied according to the particular privileges granted to different towns. Some towns were given citizenship (civitas) without the privilege of the public right of voting (sine suffragio). As Rome's territory increased, the same policy of limited citizenship, known as Latinitas or as jus Latii, was extended to the provinces.

As the years went on, the number of Roman citizens became greater and greater. In 90 B. C., the lex Junia, passed at the close of the Social War, gave full citizenship to the people of the Latin towns. The following year, the lex Plautia Papiria conferred Roman citizenship upon all aliens (peregrini) who were citizens of the Italian federated states. Subsequent laws extended citizenship to many inhabitants of the provinces.

In 19 A. D., it was provided by the lex Junia Norbana that certain manumitted slaves should be placed in the same status as the former Latin colonists.[109]

Our word "naturalization" is derived from the Roman naturalis, a native born person. As a legal term

105. Gaius 1, 13.
106. Gaius 1, 25.
107. Gaius 1, 26.
108. Gaius 1, 27.
109. Gaius 1, 22–24.

it means an act or proceeding whereby an alien has conferred upon him the rights and privileges of a native born citizen.[110]

The conferral of citizenship upon an alien is an act of sovereign power, and every independent state has an inherent right to determine under what conditions both native born persons and aliens shall exercise the rights of citizenship. In early times, in Rome, citizenship was granted by the people in their public assembly, the comitia centuriata. In later times, citizenship (jus civitatis) was granted by magistrates. Still later, generals and emperors conferred citizenship upon entire populations or classes. Various laws were enacted from time to time upon the question. Mention has already been made of the lex Junia by which citizenship was granted to all the Latins of Italy. An earlier law, the Acilian law, about 121 B. C., conferred citizenship upon an alien who successfully prosecuted a provincial magistrate for abuse of power. There was also a law that gave citizenship to one who established a home in Rome. This law was later amended since it caused too many to leave the smaller towns of Italy. The emperor Caracalla extended citizenship to all free born persons (ingenui). Justinian extended it to those who had been set free from slavery (libertini).[111] Thus, in time, the very name peregrini became obsolete. The word Barbari was used to designate all who were not Romani.

Citizenship could, however, be lost by capitis deminutio or change of status.[112] Such a change might happen in three ways, known respectively as the greatest change (maxima capitis deminutio), the middle or intermediate change (media capitis deminutio), and

---

110. Bouvier Law Dict.
111. Inst. 3, 7, 4.
112. Gaius 1, 160–162; Inst. 1, 16.

the least change (minima capitis deminutio).[113] The first was loss of liberty, which necessarily involved the loss of citizenship; the second was loss of citizenship without loss of liberty; and the third was a change in a Roman's agnatic family. This last form of change of status occurred upon the marriage of a daughter, the emancipation or bondage of a son, or the adoption of one into another family. Such a change in family status did not, however, affect citizenship.[114]

Maxima capitis deminutio, or the loss of both liberty and citizenship, took place when a Roman citizen was taken captive in war, or when upon conviction of crime he was condemned to the mines or to the wild beasts, and thus made "a slave of punishment," or when a freedman was reduced to slavery for ingratitude towards his patron, or when one permitted himself to be sold in order to share the price thus received.[115]

However, where one suffered change in status by being taken captive in war, if he escaped from his captors or was set at liberty by them, then, in case he returned to his Roman home he was restored to his former rights, including the right of citizenship. This was the doctrine known as jus postliminii. For, even as the threshold (limen) is the boundary of a house, so the boundary of the Roman state was termed a threshold. A Roman prisoner of war who was also retaken on the defeat of the enemy was said to come back to his former status by postliminium.[116]

The Roman Law doctrine of jus postliminii has been applied analogously in our own law in connection with property taken in time of war by the enemy but later coming under the power of the country to which it

---
113. Ib.
114. Gaius 1, 162; Inst. 1, 16, 3.
115. Gaius 1, 160; Inst. 1, 16, 1.
116. Gaius 1, 129; Inst. 1, 12, 5.

originally belonged.[117] An American private ship, however, captured by the enemy and sold as a prize to an enemy merchant, and then in turn recaptured from the enemy, has been adjudged public property and not the property of the former owner.[118]

Media capitis deminutio, or loss of citizenship without loss of liberty, occurred when a Roman citizen was exiled or banished by being forbidden to use fire or water (interdictio aquae et ignis) within four hundred miles of Rome.[119] Augustus introduced a form of exile known as deportatio, or banishment to a particular place, usually to some island.[120] This also caused a loss of citizenship. There was a third form of exile, known as relegatio, whereby one was prohibited, either for a limited period or for life, from entering some particular district. This did not occasion loss of citizenship or of property.

Media capitis deminutio also took place when a Roman citizen emigrated from Rome to a colony, or when he became a citizen of some foreign city. In the time of Justinian, however, when citizenship was extended throughout the empire one did not lose his citizenship by emigration, but only in case of his interdiction of fire and water or his deportation.

In our own law, citizenship may be lost by expatriation. The English Common Law never recognized, however, the right of a subject to sever his allegiance except with the sovereign's consent, but the courts of this country have from early times declared that such a right was inherent. Citizenship may also be lost by conviction of felony. At Common Law, an attainder of treason or other felony resulted in the civil death

---

117. See The Venus, 8 Cranch (U. S.) 253, 309; Leitensdorfer v. Webb, 1 N. M. 34, 44.
118. The Star, 3 Wheat. (U. S.) 78. And see U. S. v. Rice, 4 Wheat. (U. S.) 246.
119. Gaius 1, 161; Inst. 1, 16, 2.
120. Inst. 1, 16, 2.

(civiliter mortuus) of the person so attainted, and in many of our states there are statutes which provide that a person convicted of felony shall be deemed to be civilly dead.

Associated with the Roman Law doctrine of loss of citizenship was the doctrine of the loss or impairment of civic honor (minutio existimationis). The status of citizenship gave to one a civic reputation (existimatio), a position of esteem recognized by the law. However, some of the rights of citizenship, as the right to vote (suffragium) and the right to hold public office (honores), might be forfeited by such disgraceful conduct as amounted to infamia.

Existimatio was a Roman citizen's condition of unsullied honor, according to the standards set by the laws and customs of Rome.[121] It did not depend upon the social standing of a citizen as affected by his birth, rank, or wealth, but signified a reputation that qualified him to perform the duties of citizenship and to be entitled to all its privileges and honors.

An untarnished reputation was the Roman theory, at least, of complete civic qualifications. "The honor of a Roman citizen" was at one time an inspiring and ennobling phrase. When ideals were high, and Roman character strong and sturdy, civic reputation, or existimatio, was an essential element of Roman citizenship. Of course, different times had different standards, or morals, and were governed by different ideals. In our own time the word "honor" conveys a different meaning to different classes or groups of men. For example, the "honor" of the army, or of the navy, has particular significance to army and navy officers. In the learned professions, "professional honor" also has its special meaning.

As early as the Twelve Tables, we find a provision that where a necessary witness to a legal transfer of

---

[121]. Dig. 50, 13, 5, 1.

property later refused to testify to such fact of transfer, he became thereafter "infamous," incapable of being a witness and unworthy to have testimony given by another in his own behalf. In later days, the censors had great power in placing a stigma upon a Roman citizen's reputation. No doubt this power was usually exercised with justice, yet it was open, of course, to great abuse and political influence. The censors divided the citizens into classes in connection with the organization of the comitia centuriata, also of the comitia tributa. They likewise filled vacancies in the lists of senators and knights. In connection with such duties "a note of censure" (nota censoria) was at times made against a name in the list of citizens, signifying that the individual was morally unfit or unworthy, by reason of his disgraceful conduct or occupation, to render service to the state, and was, therefore, excluded from public office, or from the army, or from membership in the senate, or even in the comitia.

This decision of a censor was arbitrary and being controlled by no fixed standards depended upon the views of the individual holder of the censorian office. Moreover, all such decisions could be set aside by a succeeding censor,[122] and in the course of time many decisions were devoid of general respect. In fact, the practice seems to have become obsolete towards the close of the Republic, and instead of censorian decrees declaring what persons are unfit to exercise public duties, we find the praetors by their edicts declaring what persons shall be deemed infamous, and thereby to be without right to bring any action in a praetorian court. While the censors barred infamous persons from public rights, the praetors barred them from the exercise of certain private rights.

122. The two censors were elected by the comitia centuriata every five years.

Julianus in writing upon the Edict [123] says [124] that a man was deemed to be stigmatized with infamy who is dishonorably discharged from the army; or who appears on the stage as an actor; or who is engaged in the business of a procurer; or who is a false accuser in a criminal action; or who has been convicted of theft, robbery, injuria, or fraud; or who has had judgment given against him in an action founded on his duty in a personal matter of guardianship, mandatum, or depositum; or who gives in marriage a widow under his paternal authority before she has completed her period of mourning; or who knowingly marries a widow before she has legally completed such mourning; or who permits one under his paternal power to marry a widow under such circumstances; or who for himself or for one under his paternal power arranges for two betrothals or for two marriages at the same time.

Infamy was said to be of two sorts, immediata and mediata. The former attached, ipso facto, upon the very happening of the cause, as where a soldier was dishonorably discharged, or a citizen engaged in a disreputable business. Infamia mediata attached only in consequence of some judicial decision, as for example, where one was convicted of crime. It did not attach at the time the crime was actually committed but only upon the conviction of it. Another illustration of mediate infamy was the disgrace or infamy that attached to one when, upon a judicial decision, it appeared that he had been guilty of a dishonorable breach of duty in connection with fiduciary matters, as in the case of a guardian or a partner.

In the time of Justinian, the effects of infamia so far as they were concerned with public rights or privileges had passed away. In fact suffragium and the right of holding public office (honores) were of little,

---

123. The Perpetual Praetorian Edict.
124. Dig. 3, 2, 1. See also, Gaius 1, 182.

if any, value. Infamia had become to mean only such unworthiness as a judge before whom a case was brought might deem one unfit to testify, or to be appointed to some fiduciary office, as that of guardian, or to take under a will.[125] The old exceptions, or defenses, against plaintiffs on account of their infamy were expressly abolished.[126]

Under our own law, the term infamous may signify the mode of criminal punishment inflicted, or may refer to the fact that one is disqualified from testifying in a court of justice.[127] It is in this latter sense that our law is similar to the Roman Law concerning infamia. In our law, it is only crime that works infamy and renders, in consequence, the criminal incompetent as a witness. The crimes that so result are treason, felony, and every species of crimen falsi, such as forgery, perjury, subornation of perjury, false pretenses, public cheating, and any other similar offense which involves falsehood and affects the public administration of justice.[128]

Our legal term "moral turpitude" is a broader term than "infamous" since it is associated with all infamous crimes and also with many other forms of misconduct. However, what constitutes moral turpitude is not entirely clear.[129]

It has been broadly defined as an act of baseness, vileness, or depravity in the private and social duties which a man owes to his fellow man or to society in general.[130] It is also said to be anything done con-

125. Inst. 2, 18, 1.
126. Inst. 4, 13, 11.
127. Ex parte Wilson, 114 U. S. 417, 422; State v. Clark, 60 Kan. 450; Com. v. Shaver, 3 Watts & S. (Pa.) 338.
128. Davis v. Carey, 141 Pa. 314.
129. Pullman's Palace Car Co. v. Central Transp. Co., 65 Fed. 158.
130. State v. Mason, 29 Oreg. 18; Baxter v. Mohr, 37 Misc. Rep. (N. Y.) 883.

[Roman Law]

trary to justice, honesty, principle, or good morals.[131] It is a term used at times in our law to mark the limit of permissible civic or professional conduct. This suggests a similarity to the loss of existimatio in ancient Rome. Thus under our Federal laws, an alien may be barred from entering this country when guilty of misconduct involving "moral turpitude." Likewise, for a similar reason, an attorney may be barred from the practice of his profession.[132]

131. In re Coffey, 123 Cal. 522.
132. In re Kirby, 10 S. D. 322; In re Smith, 73 Kan. 743.

CHAPTER VIII

THE LAW OF PERSONS, *continued*

MARRIAGE; HUSBAND AND WIFE; DIVORCE

A very important part of the law of persons is the law of the family. This is particularly true in Roman Law owing to the paternal power that the head of the family exercises over all its members. In fact, Sir Henry Maine has said that the entire law of persons has developed from the idea of the family as held together by the patria potestas.[1]

With us the word "family" although derived from the Roman word "familia" is, nevertheless, capable of many different meanings according to the connection in which it is used.[2] Its ordinary meaning is a household living under one roof, consisting of parents, children, and other relatives who may be permanent members of the same house.[3] In the Roman Law, the word familia has a much wider significance than that. It means all the descendants of a living ancestor, including adopted persons, also the servants and slaves, that were under the legal power (potestas) of the ancestor who was called the paterfamilias.[4] It might include what we, in our ordinary use of the word, would call

---

1. Maine's Anc. Law, 147.
2. In re Bennett, 134 Cal. 320; Wentz v. Chicago, etc. R. Co., 259 Mo. 450.
3. Cheshire v. Burlington, 31 Conn. 326; Danielson v. Wilson, 73 Ill. A. 287.
4. Pringle v. McPherson, 2 S. C. Eq. 524; Export v. Meason, 5 Berlin, (Pa.) 167; Race v. Oldridge, 90 Ill. 250. Note. There is another meaning at times given to the word "familia", namely, all the goods belonging to the paterfamilias.

a dozen or more, "families." For example, a great grandfather might have a number of children, all of them married and having their separate houses, and they likewise having children and grandchildren many of them likewise residing in independent homes, yet all of these descendants with their wives and children, and children's children, constituted but one "familia" whose legal or civic head was the oldest living male ancestor, the paterfamilias. It will thus be seen that the Roman family was not a household group, as we understand the term, but a purely artificial creation of law. It had its origin in the old days of the patrician aristocracy.

In the development of Roman family law, we find certain technical terms which require consideration, namely, gens, agnatus, cognatus, affinitas, and patria potestas. The gens has previously been mentioned in connection with the early history of Rome, and it has been pointed out that the gens included all those patricians who were able to trace their ancestry to a common source. It was a line of freemen in whose blood there never had been a taint of slavery.[5] To each gens were attached the respective clients and freed slaves, and also the descendants of members of the gens. In time, consequently, a gens often became a numerous and powerful aggregation, like unto a medieval Scottish clan. Each gens had its own traditions, its own religious rites, its own customary laws.

A gens might contain a number of "families." A family, as previously stated, consisted of those persons who were under the authority of the same paterfamilias. Such persons were called agnates (agnati). They were usually related through male ancestors,[6] but not necessarily so. A son by blood was agnate to a brother by adoption, and a son's wife was agnate to

---
5. Cicero, Top. Para. 6.
6. Inst. 1, 15, 1.

her husband, since they were all under the same paternal authority. This bond of common allegiance to the head of the household, the paterfamilias, was called agnatio. It had no necessary connection with natural, or blood, relationship which was called cognatio, such relatives being called cognates (cognati). While two or more persons could be both agnates and cognates, as the children of two brothers under the same paternal authority, yet persons related only by female ancestors, as, for instance, the son of a brother and the son of a sister, were cognates but not agnates. Children were members of their father's family and not of their mother's previous to her marriage.[7]

Under the jus civile, cognatio had no legal significance, the only legally recognized relationship being agnatio. Since this was a status created by law it could be taken away by law, and capitis deminutio of any degree (maxima, media, or minima) usually resulted in the loss of all agnatic rights.[8]

Affinitas, or affinity, was the relationship created by marriage between either one of the married pair and the cognates of the other spouse. It had no legal significance under the older Roman Law, the jus civile, but within certain degrees was a bar to marriage in the later law.

Patria potestas, paternal power, was the legal authority which the oldest living head of a Roman family, the paterfamilias, exercised over all the members of his agnatic family.

The mutual rights, duties, and liabilities of husband and wife in general depend upon the character of the legal relation that exists between them. In primitive times, among peoples yet rude and barbarous, marriage, in a legal sense, did not exist. Promiscuous living was the custom, and when in the course of time

7. Inst. 1, 15, 1.
8. Inst. 1, 15, 3.

the relation of husband and wife became more or less recognized, the woman was practically a slave, the captive or purchase of her master. As the social life advanced there was more or less ceremony in connection with the selection of a wife, and the man's control of her person and his dominion over whatever property she possessed came to be regarded as law.[9]

The development of the law of husband and wife in both the Roman and English Law was largely due to the custom of monogamy that prevailed among the early Roman and Teutonic peoples.

Among the Romans, marriage (nuptiae, matrimonium) was the union of a man and woman in a life long consortium.[10] It was the foundation of family law. Roman citizens were married when they were united according to law, the male having attained the age of puberty and the female being of marriageable age.[11] Puberty, originally, was a matter of fact, governed by the individual case. Justinian fixed the time, however, by declaring it to be fourteen years in males, and twelve in females.[12]

In France, the civil code fixes the age of puberty in males at 18 years, and in females at 15 years.[13]

Under the Roman Law, unless the parties were sui juris, the consent of the fathers of the bride and groom was a necessary prerequisite.[14]

If children contracted a marriage without the father's consent, in a case in which the father could be consulted (not in captivity, absent, or imbecile), the marriage was void.[15]

9. Burdick, Husband and Wife, Cyc. of Law and Procedure, Vol. 21, p. 1143.
10. Inst. 1, 9, 1; Dig. 23, 2, 1.
11. Inst. 1, 10, pr.
12. Inst. 1, 22, pr.; Dig. 33, 1, 2, 4.
13. Civil Code, Sec 93.
14. Inst. 1, 10, pr.; Dig. 23, 2, 2.
15. Dig. 23, 2, 2, 18-35; Inst. 1, 10, 12.

A woman (virgin or widow) under 25, although emancipated, had to obey her father as to her marriage, unless he commanded an improper marriage.[16]

In case a man was sui juris, that is, no longer under paternal authority (patria potestas), he could marry without consent. A woman, however, was always, in theory, under the power or protection of her father, or in case of the father's death, under the authority of her guardian.

The question has arisen, say the Institutes,[17] whether the daughter or the son of an insane man can legally contract marriage, owing to the lack of parental consent. To settle any doubt, Justinian decreed that, in such a case, either the son or the daughter might marry without such consent.[18]

Under the modern civil law of France, minors must obtain the consent of their father and mother, or at least of one parent.[19] The codes of other Civil Law countries contain similar provisions but with varying particulars. In Germany, the father's consent is necessary up to twenty-one years;[20] in Japan, the consent of both parents is required up to thirty years in males, and twenty-five years in females;[21] in Spain, and several other countries, the consent of both father and mother is required if the male is under twenty-one and the female under eighteen.[22] However, in case the law does not declare a marriage invalid if parental consent is not first obtained, the general rule is that such a marriage is not void, although it may be voidable.[23]

16. Dig. 23, 1, 12.
17. Inst. 1, 10, pr.
18. Ib.
19. Civil Code, art. 148.
20. Civil Code, art. 1305.
21. Civil Code, art. 772.
22. Spanish Civil Code, art. 45, 46.
23. See Ferris v. Public Administrator, 4 Brad. Surr. (N. Y.) 28,

The consent of the parties themselves to the marriage was for a long time in Roman Law ignored. Marriage was a matter to be arranged by the heads of the respective families. The fathers of the bride and groom married them regardless of their consent. In later times, however, the consent of the married pair becomes a necessary element of a valid marriage. While such consent had to be voluntary, yet reverential fear of a parent was not compulsion.[24] But force, fear, insanity, or drunkenness, whereby the person may be deprived of his senses, made the marriage void.[25]

The existence of a prior and undissolved marriage was a bar to a subsequent marriage. Roman Law was strictly monogamous, in theory, a person not being permitted to have two wives or two husbands at the same time.[26]

Moreover, there were certain restrictions upon the right of marriage (jus connubii). At different periods in Roman Law, marriages between patricians and plebeians, citizens and aliens, freeborn and freedmen, and, in later times, between Christians and Jews were forbidden. Marriage with a prostitute was also an illegal marriage.

In time, these impediments were, however, removed. The Lex Cannuleia, as early as 445 B. C., gave the plebeians the right of the Roman connubium,[27] and, in 9 A. D., the Lex Papia Poppaea, made lawful marriages between the freeborn and freedmen.[28] In Justinian's day, all the old restrictions as to social conditions were practically abolished.[29] Religious discrim-

---

100, 101; Aguilar v. Lazaro, 4 Phil. 735, 737; Lerma v. Mamaril, 9 Phil. 118.
24. Cod. 5, 4, 14.
25. Cod. 5, 4, 14; Dig. 23, 2, 18.
26. Inst. 1, 10, 6; Dig. 3, 2, 1.
27. A law exacted by the Tribune Canuleius, Livy, Hist. 4, 6.
28. Livy, Hist. 29, 19.
29. Cod. 5, 4, 23; Nov. 89, 15; Nov. 117, 6.

inations, however, continued. The age of Justinian should not be pointed out as peculiar in its spirit of intolerance. It has taken many centuries for the world to learn the lessons of liberty, both civil and religious. Pagan Rome persecuted the Christians. In turn, "Christian" Rome persecuted heretics, apostates, and Jews. To this latter class was denied many legal privileges. The Jews were excluded from Roman marriage, from magisterial offices, and from testifying in court against Christians.[30] Such injustice and intolerance were blots not alone upon the later Roman Law, but also upon English and American law till comparatively recent times. Religious intolerance and persecution drove Englishmen to seek new homes in America, and in America human slavery existed until within the memory of living men. Equality before the law has long been the ideal of jurists but it is not yet recognized over all the earth.

Others declared by Roman Law to be incapable of entering into marriage were eunuchs.[31] In Justinian's time, monks and nuns,[32] also clericals of high position were forbidden to marry.[33] Married men were not excluded from the clergy by Justinian, but unmarried priests after attaining positions of influence in the Church could not marry.

Concerning marriages forbidden on account of relationship, only close relatives were forbidden by custom in early times, but the law gradually developed until in Justinian's day the restrictions were many.

Marriage was forbidden between all ascendants and descendants, such unions being incestuous and crim-

30. Cod. 1, 1–11.
31. Dig. 23, 3, 39, 1.
32. Nov. 5, 8; Nov. 6, 1; Nov. 123, 14, 29.
33. Nov. 6, 5; Nov. 22, 42; Nov. 123, 12.

incl.[34] This law applied to adopted persons even after the dissolution of the adoption.[35]

As to collaterals, marriage was forbidden between brother and sister except between a brother and sister by adoption providing the adoption had been previously dissolved;[36] between an uncle and niece;[37] and between an aunt and nephew.[38] Marriage was permitted, however, between first cousins,[39] contrary to the law, however, in the time of Ulpian.[40]

Affinity, or relationship by marriage, was, also, in certain cases, a bar to marriage. A man could not marry his son's wife, or his own wife's daughter by a former marriage.[41]

A widow, in case she entered into a second marriage, was required by social custom to wait a year ("year of mourning") after the decease of her former husband. If she married before the expiration of a year she incurred infamia.

In Roman Law, the betrothal, or the engagement to marry, was a formal matter. It was not legally necessary but was a well established custom. It involved a moral obligation, an obligation of honor, although its breach did not give rise to an action for damages. One incurred infamia, however, by being engaged at the same time to marry two persons.

The betrothal was called sponsalia, from sponsio, a solemn engagement or promise to perform some act.[42] The betrothed man was known as the "sponsus," the betrothed woman as the "sponsa." It was not a formal

---

34. Inst. 1, 10, 1.
35. Inst. 1, 10, 1.
36. Inst. 1, 10, 2.
37. Inst. 1, 10, 3. It was not so in earlier times. The Emperor Claudius married the daughter of his brother.
38. Inst. 1, 10, 5.
39. Inst. 1, 10, 4.
40. Ulpian 5, 6.
41. Inst. 1, 10, 6.
42. Dig. 23, 1, 1–2; Codex 5, 1.

contract between the parties, since the woman did not personally make any promise. It was a promise on the part of her paterfamilias, or her tutor, to give her in marriage to the man. This promise was accepted by the man, if he were sui juris, otherwise by his paterfamilias. It was customary to give the woman a betrothal ring which she wore on the same finger as is used in our own times.[43]

Since there was no formal contract of betrothal, the paterfamilias of the woman could legally renounce his promise.[44] However, in the district of Latium, there was, according to Gellius,[45] a formal contract (stipulatio) the breach of which was actionable.

Under the codes of most modern Civil Law countries it is the general rule that no action lies for a breach of promise to marry,[46] although in Louisiana [46a] and in the Philippines [47] it is held actionable.

The earliest form of marriage among all primitive peoples was probably capture, the woman being seized by the man and taken forcibly to his place of habitation. As civilization advanced, the man purchased the woman from her father or from those who had her in their control. There was no form or ceremony, the husband's rights being based upon the consent of the woman's father who delivered her to the man who bought her. In the course of time certain customs became established and still later these customs ripened into law.

Among the ancient Romans, a valid marriage (justae nuptiae, justum matrimonium) was one that con-

43. Gellius 10, 10.
44. Dig. 23, 1, 10.
45. Gellius 4, 4.
46. Germany, Civil Code, art. 1297; Italy, Civil Code, art. 53; Spain, Civil Code, art. 43; Switzerland, Civil Code, art. 91.
46a. Smith v. Braun, 37 La. Ann. 225; Morgan v. Yarborough, 5 La. Ann. 316.
47. Garcia v. Del Rosario, 33 Phil. 189.

formed to the jus civile.[48] Such a marriage might be either with manus (cum manu) or without manus (sine manu).[49]

The term "manus," literally "hand," was in very early Roman times applied generally to the power or authority of a man over the things that he owned, things that were within the control and grasp of his hand. Later, it became a term designating the authority of the head of a house over all its members and possessions. All were "in his hand," in manu. Still later, it became a legally technical word meaning, specifically, the legal rights of the husband with respect to the property and person of his wife, the term patria potestas being used for the broader term of general power over the entire family.

A woman, by the Roman Law, was always under the legal and protective care of some male relative, either her father, her husband, or her guardian (tutor). A marriage cum manu automatically extinguished her father's legal authority (patria potestas), and substituted for it the authority of her husband (manus). In other words, the wife cum manu passed into the familia of her husband if he were sui juris; otherwise, into the familia of his living ancestor.[50] All her property likewise passed to the husband or his paterfamilias,[51] and her status was technically that of a daughter to her husband.

On the other hand, a marriage sine manu left the woman in the family of her own paterfamilias. If she were sui juris and married sine manu she retained her property with the same rights as if she were single. The husband had no legal right to it. The doctrine of community property of husband and wife, found in

48. Ulp. 5, 1, 2.
49. Ulp. 26, 7.
50. Gaius 2, 159.
51. Gaius 2, 96, 98.

some modern Civil Law countries, particularly France and Spain, and existing in some of our own states, through derivation from such sources, was unknown to the Roman Law.

At a very early period three modes or forms of marriage cum manu were recognized by the Roman Law, confarreatio, coemptio, and usucapio.[52]

Confarreatio was the patrician formal marriage. It was characterized by a solemn ceremony of a religious nature, attended by the pontifex maximus and a priest (flamen) of Jupiter. There were also ten witnesses, representing, it is said, the ten curiae of old Roman days. The auspices were observed in connection with preceding sacrifices, in order to determine whether the day was propitious for the marriage celebration. The word confarreatio is derived from the word far or farreum meaning a cake or loaf of bread, referring to the offering of bread which was a part of the religious ceremony.

The bread was offered, in sacrifice to Jupiter,[53] and then was broken by the priest and given to the bride and groom to eat. After the ceremony, which was of considerable length, a wedding procession (deductio) conducted the bride, at dusk, to the home of her husband. Torches carried by friends lighted the way,[54] and flute players usually preceded the throng. Arriving at the house the bride was carefully lifted by her companions over the threshold[55] in order that the evil omen of touching with her foot that which was sacred to the virgin goddess, Vesta, might be avoided.

Confarreatio was exclusively a patrician ceremony. Among plebeians, the usual form of marriage was known as coemptio, or the formal purchase of the bride

52. Gaius 1, 110.
53. Gaius, 1, 112.
54. Catullus, 62, 1.
55. Catullus, 61, 166.

from her father. Coemptio was an ancient method of transferring rights in property and called, technically, mancipatio. In the presence of five witnesses, an official weigher of money (aes, copper), called the libripens, weighed the purchase price which was handed to the vendor. Thereupon, the vendee, with words of ownership, placed his hand upon the thing sold (manu capere), thus transferring the title. It was by this form of sale that marriage by coemptio was celebrated, and the bride came into the power, or manus, of her husband.[56]

There was a third way in which marriage with manus could be contracted, and that was usus, or usucapio. Under the jus civile, one of the methods of acquiring ownership in movable property was usucapio, or long continued possession. Under the old law the necessary time of such use and possession was one year. It was an original title like our modern adverse possession and prescription. Under the doctrine of usucapio, if a man and woman lived together, for a year, as man and wife, despite the fact that there had been no formal marriage, no confarreatio or coemptio, the result was a legal marriage with manus. The intention of the parties was manifested by the fact of cohabitation, and the length of the cohabitation, one year, was sufficient to constitute a valid union. Marriage by usus, says Professor Sohm,[57] was probably the outcome of the most ancient form of marriage, that is, marriage by capture, whereby after a certain period following the woman's abduction the relationship was regarded as a marriage. Under the Roman Law, the husband's rights of property in the wife, or, in other words, his manus, followed marriage by usus in the same way that the same method of acquisition applied to movable property in general.

56. Gaius, 1, 110–113.
57. Inst. of Roman Law, Eng. Trans., 3d. Ed. p. 454, note.

That marriage by usus was a very ancient form of marriage among the Romans is shown by the Twelve Tables (450 B. C.) which provided that a wife not married by confarreatio or coemptio, who desired to prevent the legal consequences of manus, could do so by absenting herself from her husband's house for three consecutive nights each year (trinoctium), and thus interrupt the usus of each year.[58]

It is obvious, therefore, that, at a very early time in Roman Law, there were cases where for various reasons it was desirable that a married woman should remain under the legal authority of her father or guardian rather than pass to the authority of her husband. Such a marriage, where the usus was broken by the wife's absence, was equally legal, although sine manu, with a marriage cum manu. It merely differed as to the husband's legal rights.

However, long before the time of Justinian, all these modes of marriage, confarreatio, coemptio, and usucapio, together with their doctrines of manus, had become obsolete. Gaius, writing in the second century of the present era, says that in his day all that part of the old law relative to marriage by usus was a thing of the past, being changed partly by new laws and partly by disuse.[59] The change in the old jus civile was caused by the gradual adoption of the marriage law of the jus gentium. When it is said that aliens and some other classes were excluded from the Roman right of marriage, the jus connubii, it does not mean, of course, that such persons could not marry among themselves, but that their marriages did not have the same legal results in Roman Law, as did Roman marriages. In other words, marriages under the jus gentium did not involve the doctrine of "manus," the wife remaining "free" from the power of her husband even

[58]. XII Tab. VI, 4; Gaius 1, 111.
[59]. Gaius 1, 111.

as before marriage. It can easily be understood, therefore, how the notion of marriage according to the jus gentium, otherwise called "free" and "informal" marriage, supplanted marriage under the jus civile with its consequent manus. Accordingly in time, the "free marriage" of the jus gentium entirely superseded during the Empire the old idea of marriage of the jus civile. Under the old law, the wife was known as materfamilias, under the jus gentium as uxor. Under the old law of manus, the husband had the power to chastise, sell or even kill the wife,[60] having the same authority over her as over his child. In fact, the doctrine of manus made, legally, the wife a member of her husband's agnatic family and a sister to her own children.[61] Under manus, the husband acquired the wife's property, his power was absolute and her identity was completely merged in his.[62] Of course this theoretical power was seldom invoked, and the theory itself was confined to very primitive times,[63] and some writers question whether the power arising from manus ever extended to a power to kill.[64] The doctrine of the marital power of the old type must, however, have become objectionable at a very early state of the development of Roman Law, as evidenced by the early statute of the Twelve Tables which provided for marriage without manus. The only rights of the wife under manus were her support, and a share of her husband's property at his death, as one of his heirs.[65]

Under the marriage law of the jus gentium, the mutual consent of the parties took the place of the old time ceremonies. Consensus facit nuptias,[66] said the

60. Sohm's Inst. p. 93.
61. Gaius 1, 115, 136.
62. Gaius 2, 98; 3, 83, 84.
63. See Bryce Studies Hist. and Jur. 787.
64. See Hunt. Rom. L. (3d Ed.) 224.
65. Bryce Studies Hist. and Jur. 787; Sohm's Inst. pp. 94, 109.
66. Dig. 50, 17, 30. (Ulpian).

jurists, although it was contended by some authorities that traditio, or delivery of the possession of the wife to the husband was a necessary element of marriage. The delivery was understood to be made by the conduction of the wife to the home of the husband. It was accordingly held that a man by mere message delivered by another could enter into marriage provided the woman was taken to his home. His presence was not necessary. A woman could not, however, by her letter or message be married unless she was afterwards taken as wife to the abode of her husband.[67] The leading of the woman to the house of the man was regarded as evidence of the present intent of the parties, an essential to the bond of the marriage, since a consent to be husband and wife at the time the consent is given is quite a different thing from a consent to marry in the future.

In marriage under the jus gentium, the wife remained a member of her own family, not passing, as under manus, into the family of the husband. Moreover, according to the early view, the children of free, or jus gentium, marriages followed the family of the mother. However, this theory became changed in time, and it was held that while the wife did not pass into the family of her husband, nevertheless the children of the marriage were in the family of the father and under his patria potestas.

Under consensual, or free marriage, the husband and wife were regarded as partners.[68] The wife retained all her antenuptial property and liabilities. The marital rights of the husband were the right to choose the domicile, the right of his wife's companionship (consortium), the right to regulate household expenses, and the right of custody and education of the children. It was the husband's duty to support the

---

67. Dig. 23, 2, 5; Dig. 24, 1, 66, 1; Cod. 5, 3, 6; Cod. 5, 4, 21.
68. Wylly v. Collins, 9 Ga. 223; Sohm's Inst. p. 93.

[Roman Law]

wife, but he had no legal control over her actions as in the case of manus.[69]

The Roman Law of marriage has influenced the marriage law not only of modern Civil Law countries but also of those where the English Law obtains. It is the general rule that marriage, the entering into the marital relation, is, legally, a civil contract. The mutual present assent to immediate marriage (in distinction from an agreement to marry in future) by persons capable of assuming that relation constituted a marriage at the Roman Law and likewise constitutes a marriage at our Common Law. Statutes may require certain formalities but no formality either civil or religious is necessary at Common Law.

The Canon Law governed the law of marriage during the Middle Ages, and the Council of Trent in the sixteenth century [70] provided that marriage should be performed by a priest in the presence of witnesses. Such is the law in some Catholic countries today, although most Civil Law countries require a civil ceremony, that is, a marriage performed by a state official.[71]

As to the minimum marital age our Common Law is the same as Justinian's law, fourteen years in males and twelve years in females. However, under our Common Law, parental consent is not necessary, although statutes usually require such consent if the male is under twenty-one and the female under eighteen.

In our American states where mere consent of the parties constitutes a marriage, generally called a Common Law marriage, it would seem, following the rule

69. Bryce, Studies Hist. and Jur. 790; Sohm's Inst. pp. 93, 94; Hunter, Rom. L. 679.

70. This Great Council of the Church was held at Trent, Austria, during the years 1545–1563.

71. For example, France C. C. art. 165; Germany C. C., art. 1317; Italy C. C., art. 93.

of the Roman Law, that the presence of the man is not requisite. It has in fact, been held that a marriage like any other contract may be effected by correspondence.[72] In 1924, the United States District Court for Massachusetts also held that a Portuguese woman who in her own country had married by proxy a man domiciled in Pennsylvania was his lawful wife under the laws of the United States, since such a marriage was valid by the law of Portugal.[73] There are other Civil Law countries which also recognize the validity of marriage by proxy.[74]

A survival in a limited sense of the Roman Law doctrine of the wife's subordination to the authority of her husband is found in a number of modern Civil Law codes. In the light of the insistence of many women in this country that the word "obey" shall be omitted in the marriage ceremony, it is interesting, at least, to note that the Civil Code of France and of some other countries expressly declare that the wife owes obedience to her husband.[75] The French law also makes it the mutual duty of husband and wife to support each other,[76] which is likewise the law in some other Civil Law jurisdictions.[77]

One of the greatest changes in our own law of husband and wife is that which relates to the property of a married woman. By our Common Law, the woman's personal property in possession passed immediately upon marriage to her husband, while her choses in action became his upon exercising dominion over

72. Great Northern Railway v. Johnson, 254 Fed. 683, 166 C. C. A. 181.

73. Ex parte Suzanna, 295 Fed. 713.

74. Spain, Civil Code, art. 87; Cuba, Civil Code, art. 87.

75. France, C. C. art. 213; Italy, C. C. art. 132; Mexico, C. C., art. 192; Spain, C. C., art. 57.

76. French Civil Code, art. 212.

77. Italy, C. C., art. 132; Japan, C. C., 790; Louisiana, C. C., 119; Portugal, C. C., art. 1184.

them. In her freehold estates in real property the husband had a usufruct during the marriage. The slow development of the doctrine of a married woman's equitable separate estate was followed only in comparatively modern times by statutes creating her statutory separate estate. Our most liberal statutes, however, upon this subject give married women no greater control and enjoyment of their separate property than was given to them by the Roman Law many centuries ago in connection with free marriage, or marriage without manus. Despite the doctrine that a woman, single or married, was, theoretically, always under guardianship, yet in the administration of her separate property her guardian was required to authorize all her transactions. It was this fact that prompted Cicero, the best known lawyer of his day, to say: "Our ancient laws intended to put the woman under the authority of a guardian; the jurisconsults have put the guardian under the authority of the woman." [78]

In marriage without manus the husband had no rights at all in the property of his wife. She could acquire property the same as if unmarried. Her earnings belonged to her alone. She could also dispose of her property without any right of interference on her husband's part. His only compensation was that he was not liable for her antenuptial debts.

There was, however, another kind of property brought, usually, by the wife to the marriage which did belong to the husband for all practical purposes. This was the wife's dos, or dowry, which was her contribution for the household expenses. Over this property the husband exercised control for the purpose intended, although he could not sell or mortgage it, in Justinian's time, without the consent of the wife.[79] A

78. Cicero, Pro Mur. 12.
79. Inst. 2, 8, pr.

counterpart to the wife's dowry was the husband's marital gift to his wife, the donatio ante nuptias. This belonged to the wife but the husband had the control of it.

In distinction from her dowry, or dotal property, the wife's separate property over which her husband had no control was called her paraphernal property, a term derived from Grecian law.[80] This term is still used in modern Civil Law codes, the French code, for example, declaring that "all the property of the wife which has not been included in the settlement of dowry is paraphernal."[81] However, in most Civil Law countries, the power of married women to make contracts and to convey property is limited. Even her separate property is managed by her husband in some countries,[82] although in France and some other jurisdictions the wife has the management and enjoyment of it.[83] However, of the community property, the husband is the sole manager,[84] and it is the general rule, with some exceptions, that a married woman cannot without the consent of her husband convey, mortgage, or acquire property, or bind herself by contract.[85]

CONCUBINAGE:

Under the Roman Law, an unmarried man and an unmarried woman might lawfully live together as hus-

---

80. Code 5, 14, 8.
81. French Civil Code, art. 1574. See, also, German Civil Code, art. 1363; Louisiana Civil Code, art. 2383; Spanish Civil Code, art. 1381.
82. Germany, C. C., art. 1363; Japan, C. C., art. 801 et seq.; Switzerland, C. C., 201.
83. France, C. C., art. 1536, 1576; Louisiana, C. C., art. 2384; Spain, C. C., art. 1384; Hellwig v. West, 2 La. Ann. 1; Casalla v. Enage, 6 Phil. 415. In Porto Rico, a married woman has all the rights of a feme sole as to her separate property. Altuna v. Ortiz, 12 P. R. 318, 326; Arias v. Registrar, 19 P. R. 1115, 1117.
84. France, C. C., art. 1421; Germany, C. C., art. 1443; Italy, C. C., 1433; Louisiana, C. C., 2404; Spain, C. C., art. 59, 1412.
85. France, C. C., art. 217, 1576; Germany, C. C., art. 1395; Italy, C. C., art. 134; Louisiana, C. C., 122; Spain, C. C. art. 61.

band and wife. This relationship was known as concubinatus, and was legalized during the reign of Augustus.[86] Although it resembled marriage in many respects, yet it was not regarded as honorable as marriage, and a concubine was not socially respected. It was a purely monogamous relation, since a man could not have a wife and a concubine, or two concubines, at the same time.[87]

While children born of a Roman marriage were under the patria potestas of their father, the offspring of concubinage were not within such power although by a law first enacted by Constantine they could be brought within it by the subsequent marriage of their parents.[88] The children of concubinage were not "legitimate children," that is, children recognized by the law, since only marriage could produce such children, yet, on the other hand, they were not bastards (spurii), that is, children of illicit intercourse. A different term was applied to them. They were known as "natural children" (naturales liberi) or illegitimate children. Such children inherited from their mothers but had no rights of succession in connection with their fathers' estates. However, under later laws they could be legitimatized by their fathers and accordingly made heirs.[89] Whether or not a man and woman living together were cohabiting as husband and wife or merely in concubinage depended upon the intent.[90] In the former case there must be affectio maritalis, that is, an intent to live together in lawful wedlock. Consequently, in marriage by mutual consent, the parties usually declared their consent before witnesses. In fact, articles of marriage now so familiar in Civil Law coun-

86. Dig. 25, 7, 3, 1.
87. Dig. 50, 16, 144; Cod. 5, 26, 1.
88. Nov. 89, 11.
89. Inst. 1, 10, 13; Cod. 5, 27, 3 and 9.
90. Dig. 25, 7, 4.

tries, whereby the parties affix their names to the agreement, were commonly used in imperial Roman days.[91]

The concubinal relation was theoretically a permanent one, like unto marriage, but could, like marriage, be dissolved by the parties.

Parties who could not lawfully marry were enabled, in some cases, to live in concubinage. For example, a freeborn man might legally have a freed woman for his concubine although he could not legally marry her.[92] Likewise, a provincial official could not take a foreign woman for his wife but he could have her for his concubine.[93]

Concubinage as a matter of legalized cohabitation was abolished by Emperor Leo in 887, A. D. Henceforth there was no legal distinction between "natural children" and "bastards" (spurii).

Contubernium:

Slaves could not marry. They were permitted, however, to cohabit, the relation being known as contubernium.

Although no legal rights followed from such a union of slaves, yet the children born of contubernium were regarded as being related by blood (cognati). It followed, therefore, that if such children became free they might be prohibited from intermarriage, the same as other free persons, by reason of consanguinity.[94]

Dissolution of Marriage: Divorce:

In the Roman Law, marriage was dissolved by death, captivity, slavery, or divorce.[95]

In case of the unexplained absence of the husband, it being uncertain whether he was dead or in

---

91. These written agreements were known as the marriage tablets.
92. Dig. 25, 7, 3, pr.
93. Dig. 25, 7, 5.
94. Dig. 23, 2, 14, 2; Inst. 1, 10, 10; Cod. 5, 4, 4.
95. Dig. 24, 2, 1.

captivity, a wife might marry again after an interval of five years.[96]

The right of a man to put away his wife by divorcement probably existed from the earliest times of Roman history. Plutarch says that divorce was recognized in the days of Romulus.[97] Granting that Plutarch's narrative of Romulus was only legendary, yet Cicero's reference to the divorce procedure as laid down in the Twelve Tables,[98] would seem to establish the antiquity of the doctrine. There are those who, in their admiration of the traditional sturdy character of the ancient Romans, say that for the first five hundred years of Rome there was not a single instance of divorce.[99] This legend is based upon the story attributed to Aulus Gellius [100] that the first Roman to divorce his wife was Carvilius Ruga, in the 523d year of Rome,[101] who divorced his wife, it is said, because of her barrenness. It has been suggested that Gellius merely meant to say that this was the first divorce granted in Rome for such a cause.[102] The statement that "the early Romans out of regard for ancient form and stability of family life held marriage inviolable," [103] is erroneous. There is not a word in Roman Law that upholds the doctrine of indissoluble marriage. The clergy in the time of Justinian persuaded him to curtail in many ways the unlimited right of divorce, but the restrictions that Justinian imposed were swept away again by his successor [104] within a few months after Justinian's death. It is the doctrine of the

96. Dig. 24, 2, 6.
97. Life of Romulus.
98. Cicero, Phil. 2, 28, 69.
99. See Gibbon's Rome, Ch. 44; Schouler Husb. and W. p. 5.
100. Gell. 4, 3, 2.
101. About 230 B. C. See Mackenzie's Rom. Law, 7th Ed. p. 119; Savingy, Verm. Schriften, 5, 1-4.
102. Colq. Rom. Law, p. 655.
103. "Corpus Juris," New York, 1920, Vol. 19, p. 16, art. Divorce
104. Justin II, Nov. 140, 1.

Canon Law that marriage cannot be terminated by divorce,[105] and that doctrine became dominant in medieval Europe, but such was never the doctrine of the Roman Law. In fact, under the Roman Law a covenant between parties to a marriage that the marriage should never be dissolved by divorce was held invalid as depriving the parties of their vested rights.[106] Moreover, what is sometimes called a limited divorce, a divorce mensa et thoro (from board and bed), which is nothing but a legal separation and called a limited divorce in distinction from absolute divorce, a vinculo matrimonii (from the bond of marriage), was not known to the Roman Law. Divorces in Roman Law were all absolute. The marital separation known as divorce a mensa et thoro, which is recognized in some states, but which is not a divorce at all since the parties still remain married, was the creation of the Canon or Ecclesiastical Law.[107] The state of South Carolina grants no divorces, but it does grant separations a mensa et thoro.[108]

Under the early law, the wife being in the power (manus) of her husband, there was, doubtless, but little thought given to the doctrine of divorce. The wife had no legal right to divorce the husband since, in theory, his power over her was absolute, involving the power of life and death. It is probably quite true that for a long time in the early history of Rome, there were very few cases of divorce. The Roman theory of family law rather than superior virtue was doubtless the explanation. However, in the later days of the republic and during the empire divorces were scandal-

105. Harmon v. Harmon, 1 Cal. 215.
106. Cod. 8, 38, 2.
107. See, in general, Pick v. Pick, 99 Neb. 433, 156 N. W. 769; P. v. Cullen, 153 N. Y. 629, 47 N. E. 894; Head v. Head, 2 Ga. 191; Sharpe v. Sharpe, 134 Mo. A. 278, 114 S. W. 584; Hodges v. Hodges, 22 N. M. 192, 159 Pac. 1007.
108. McCreery v. Davis, 44 S. C. 195, 22 S. E. 178.

ously prevalent. Many in the highest places set the example. Caesar, Pompey, Cicero, Mark Antony, the Emperor Augustus, the Emperor Tiberius, and countless others, repudiated their wives, and wives quite equally repudiated their husbands.

It was the theory of the later republican days that when the marital state had been created by consent, it could, likewise, be dissolved by consent, either by mutual consent or at the pleasure of either party. Divorce by mutual consent was called divortium bona gratia, while divorce at the pleasure of only one of the parties was known as divortium mala gratia. No judicial proceedings were necessary, no application to any official required. The parties either divorced themselves mutually or one of them simply declared that the marriage was dissolved.

If the parties had been married by confarreatio or by coemptio, the mere expressed intent of the parties was not sufficient in law to dissolve the marriage. Under the jus civile, one of the usual methods of discharging an obligation was by what was known as a contrarius actus. If an obligation had been entered into by the expression of solemn words, it could be extinguished only in the same way, namely by the "unsaying" of the words in the same way and manner in which they had been originally spoken. In other words, if A and B had, in accordance with Roman Law, bound themselves to some agreement by the utterance of certain words, a common way, in fact, of entering into a contractual obligation, they could not mutually release each other, as far as the law was concerned, by mere mutual intent. They were required to undo or to unbind the thing that had been done or bound by employing the same formula by which it had been created, but expressed negatively where it had been originally expressed positively.

There arose from this fact a curious custom. A

marriage solemnized by confarreatio could be dissolved only by a counter ceremony known as diffareatio. The presence of the pontiff or priest was essential as at the marriage, for the parties could be unmarried only in the same manner in which they were married. If the pontiff, disapproving the dissolution of the marriage, should refuse to act, then the parties remained married, the legal dissolution being impossible.

The same principle of undoing a legal act applied to marriage by coemptio, or the marriage by purchase from the bride's father. It was necessary by the legal procedure known as remancipatio to sell the wife back to her father or to the proper representative of her family. Marriage by usus was also legally dissolved in the same way, that is, by remancipatio.

It was "free marriage," marriage without manus, marriage by the consent of the parties, the form of marriage which was practically observed by all Romans after the later days of the republic, that could be dissolved by mere intention of the parties, and it is this form of dissolution of marriage to which the word divorce or divortium is applied. It was strictly a private act.

In case of divorce by mutual consent no further step was necessary. In the same way in which the parties had been married they were unmarried, and that was all the law required. In case, however, of divorce by the intention of only one of the parties, it was necessary to communicate the intention to the other party and the practice was to do this orally, or by letter sent by a messenger. This notice of the exercise of one's right to dissolve the marital relation was called repudium. The Digest, quoting from Gaius, says [109] that such words as "Tuas res tibi habito" (look after your own affairs) have been approved as a fit-

---

109. Dig. 24, 2, 2, 1.

ting formula for this notice. Under the more ancient procedure, it seems that when a husband took away from his wife her possession of the household keys, or drove her forth from his doors, it was proof of his divorcement of her.[110] In the time of Augustus, it was provided by the Lex Julia de adulteriis that the declaration of divorce should be made in the presence of seven witnesses who were citizens and had attained the age of puberty. In addition, a freedman of the declarant was required to be present.[111]

Repudium meant originally, says the Digest,[112] the breaking of an engagement to marry, while divortium was more appropriately applied to the dissolution of a marriage since the word signifies that the parties go their different ways.

Some commentators upon Roman Law speak of divortium as meaning divorce by mutual consent and of repudium as divorce by the wish of only one of the parties, an ex parte act. Whether, however, the marriage was dissolved by mutual agreement or by the pleasure of only one of the spouses, the word divortium is correctly used. The word repudium came, in time, to be synonymous with a divorce effected by the will of one party since such a divorce was accompanied by a repudium, that is, an expression of the intention of divorce. No cause or grounds were required for a Roman divorce. That one or both wished it was sufficient. One could divorce an insane spouse since the will of one party was all that was required.[113] A divorce declared in a momentary fit of anger was not, however, a divorce since it did not express the real intention of the declarant. Nevertheless, the other par-

110. See Cicero, Phil. 2, 28, 69.
111. Dig. 24, 2, 9.
112. Dig. 50, 16, 101, 1; Dig. 50, 16, 191.
113. Dig. 24, 2, 4.

ty might accept it as a divorce, and in such a case the one so accepting becomes the divorcer.[114]

As previously stated, Justinian rigidly restricted the freedom of divorce. He denied all divorces except in case of the impotency of the husband; the wish of either party to enter a religious association, a monastery or a convent; or in case either became a prisoner of war.[115] These restrictions were removed, however, by Justin II, the successor of Justinian.[116]

There was another form of divorce that was possible under the old law, and at times it was arbitrarily and ruthlessly employed. This was the right of a father whose daughter upon marriage remained in his power (patria potestas), in case she married without passing into the manus of the husband (marriage sine manu), to divorce her regardless of the wishes of the married pair. The father could simply take his daughter away from her husband and the marriage was thus dissolved. It was not until the time of the emperor Marcus Aurelius that this paternal right to divorce a daughter was curtailed. That emperor forbade the exercise of such a power except in very grave and justifiable cases.[117]

Ordinarily the consent of the wife's parents had nothing to do with the question of her divorce by her husband. In case, however, the marriage dowry had been furnished by either of the parents of the bride, and her divorce, with consequent loss of dowry, would affect injuriously the property rights of such parent, she could not be divorced without such parent's consent.[118]

In case there were children, they were disposed of,

---

114. Dig. 24, 2, 3.
115. Nov. 117, 10–12; Nov. 134, 11.
116. Nov. 140, 1.
117. Cod. 5, 17, 5.
118. Nov. 22, 19.

usually, by the agreement of the parties. By a constitution of Diocletian and Maximian it seems that the parties if they could not agree might apply to a court which could allot the children according to its discretion. The father was required to support the children even as during the marriage. However, if the father was unable to provide for the children's support but the mother had ample means, the obligation of their support rested upon her.[119]

The scandal of frequent divorces which were often followed immediately by new marriages became so great that Julius Caesar had a law enacted requiring divorced persons to await six months before marrying again, and Augustus increased the interval to eighteen months. In Justinian's time, if a woman divorced her husband for any other than a serious cause, she was forbidden to marry for five years thereafter.

The adjustment of property rights upon divorce varied with the different periods of Roman legislation. As a rule, if a husband divorced his wife without justifiable cause she recovered her dowry and also retained the husband's marital portion, the donatio ante nuptias. In case a wife unjustly divorced the husband she lost her dowry. By the Lex Julia et Papia-Poppoea, in the time of Augustus, a husband who divorced his wife for adultery was permitted to retain one-sixth of her dowry. Justinian provided that a wife who divorced her husband for certain specified statutory causes could recover her dowry and also keep the donatio ante nuptias.

In modern Civil Law countries the doctrines of the Church or Canon Law that marriage is sacred and the tie indissoluble, remained the law for a long time. In fact, it was also the law of England till the Divorce Act of 1858. Scotland has recognized divorce on the ground of adultery since the Reformation, and by a

---

[119]. Cod. 5, 24, 1; Nov. 117, 7.

later statute [120] made malicious desertion also a ground. The Code Napoleon, 1804, allowed divorce for adultery, violence, cruelty, gross insults, condemnation to an infamous punishment, and, under certain circumstances, even if the parties mutually wished it. This last provision was subsequently repealed, but the other causes still remain.[121] Many other Civil Law countries also permit divorce for adultery,[122] and some of them for other causes in addition. In a few countries, however, no absolute divorce is recognized, although the parties may sue for a judicial separation.[123]

Divorce should be distinguished from an annulment of marriage. The former is based upon a valid marriage entered into legally, the parties having lawful capacity to marry. Annulment is based upon the ground that the marriage was voidable owing to the incapacity of the parties. Even under the Canon Law the annulment of such a marriage is permissible.

120. 1573, c. 55.
121. French Civil Code, art. 229–232.
122. Germany, art. 1565; Louisiana, art. 138; Japan (adultery of wife), art. 813; Switzerland, art. 137.
123. Italy, for instance, Civil Code, art. 148.

CHAPTER IX

THE LAW OF PERSONS, *continued*

A. Parent and Child

The absolute power which the law of Rome gave to a father over his children is one of the most striking differences between the Roman and the English Law. The head of the Roman agnatic family, the paterfamilias, was king and priest of his household. His will was the supreme law, and there was no appeal from his authority whether it was exercised with love and kindness or with despotic cruelty. This legal power which was possessed by every Roman citizen who was the head of a family was called patria potestas. It was a lifelong power, residing in the oldest, living male ancestor. In our law every person who reaches legal majority is free from paternal control. In Roman Law, however, the patria potestas was perpetual. The rights of the paterfamilias and the duties of the members of the family continued without interruption as long as the head of the household lived. "The difference between a society like ours," says Judge Hamersley of the Supreme Court of Connecticut,[1] "based on the principle that each member on reaching his majority is his own master, a responsible unit, with control of each of his own children until and only until the child becomes of age, and a society based on the principle of the patria potestas is organic. With us the legal rights and duties existing between parent and child exist only during the minority of the child.

---

1. Appeal of Woodward, 81 Conn. 152.

After that, the duties arising from the natural relation are not legal but moral, unless by force of statute some specific legal duty is created."

In our own law, moreover, a father's authority extends only to his own children. In Roman Law it extended to his grandchildren, and to all his other descendants.

The term child included offspring begotten in lawful wedlock[2] and children by adoption. It was not until the days of the later Empire that illegitimate children of Roman citizens might also be brought under patria potestas by legitimation. The first law upon the subject of legitimation was enacted by Constantine who decreed that children born in concubinage ("natural" children) should, upon the subsequent marriage of their parents be deemed legitimate.[3] In the reigns of Theodosius and Valentinian (442) legitimation was extended by a provision that natural children, if males, could also be made legitimate by becoming members of a municipal curia, or, in case of a natural daughter, by marriage to a member of such a curia.[4] Justinian added a third mode, that of an imperial rescript, which was the emperor's written sanction and grant of a father's petition that his natural child might be placed under his potestas, and, consequently, made legitimate.[5]

Under the first form of legitimation (per subsequens matrimonium), only "natural" children, that is, children born in concubinage could be made legitimate. This law never applied to "spurious" or bastard children.[6] Moreover, in the time of Justinian,

2. Gaius 1, 55; Inst. 1, 9 pr.; Dig. 1, 6, 6, pr.
3. Code, 5, 27, 3-9; Nov. 89, 11.
4. Codex 5, 27, 3.
5. Inst. 1, 10, 13; Nov. 89, 10. See note to Stevenson v. Sullivant, 5 Wheat. (U. S.) 207, 265.
6. See Pettus v. Dawson, 82 Tex. 18.

it was further necessary that during the concubinage no legal impediment existed to the marriage of the child's parents, that the subsequent marriage was duly proved, and that the child, if old enough, did not object to his legitimation.[7] In case of legitimation by imperial rescript, it was necessary that the father should show that marriage to the child's mother was impossible either by reason of her death or other marriage of the parties, or on account of the mother's disappearance or unworthiness.[8] The child himself could also apply for a rescript if the father in his will had stated that such was his desire.[9]

It is sometimes said that by Roman Law a natural child might be made legitimate by the mere declaration of the father in his will, and the 117th Novel of Justinian[10] has been cited by some in support of such a statement. However, there was no such thing in Roman Law as legitimatio per testamentum, or the making legitimate of a known illegitimate by testamentary declaration. A father could in his will declare that it was his wish that his natural child should be made legitimate, but such a declaration had to be approved and confirmed by the emperor before it became effective.[11] The 117th Novel merely states a rule of evidence: "If any one shall say in his will that a son or a daughter (born to him of a woman to whom it was possible for him to have been married) is in fact legitimate and not illegitimate, such a child shall be regarded legitimate and shall have all the rights of legitimates.[12]

Legitimation by curial membership (per oblationem curiae) was effected by the father's purchase of a

7. Code 5, 27, 10.
8. Nov. 74, 2, 1.
9. Nov. 89, 10.
10. Nov. 117, 2.
11. Nov. 89, 10.
12. See Gaines v. Hennen, 24 How. (U. S.) 601.

membership for his natural son in the local governing body (the curia) of a provincial town.[13] Such an office (decurio) was one of dignity, and, in order to meet the cost of the social and public entertainment connected with it, the incumbent was obliged to incur considerable expense. It was, simply, a way in which a rich father could buy legitimacy for his natural son. The law was, doubtless, inspired by the desire of the emperor Theodosius to have men of means in such positions, and to keep up the membership of such bodies.

Following the imperial Roman Law, it is the general rule in modern Civil Law countries that an illegitimate child may be made legitimate by the subsequent marriage of its parents.[14] Some of the codes distinguish, however, between "natural" and "spurious" children, the former term being applied to children between whose parents there existed no impediment to marriage at the time of conception. Usually, in addition to the marriage, it is necessary that the parents should acknowledge the child by some official instrument.

Likewise, in accord with the Roman Law, some of the codes define a legitimate child as one conceived, not merely born, in lawful wedlock.[15] The French and a number of other codes declare, however, that the presumption of legitimacy applies to a child if born not earlier than one hundred and eighty days after the marriage.[16] Likewise, a child is presumed by most Civil Law countries to be legitimate if born within

13. Code 5, 27, 3, 4; 5, 27, 9; Nov. 89, 2, 1-6.
14. French C. C. art. 331; Germany, art. 1719; Italy, art. 194; Japan, art. 836; Louisiana, art. 198; Spain, art. 120. See Hart v. Hoss, 26 La. Ann. 90.
15. French C. C. art. 312; Italy, art. 159; Louisiana, art. 184. Contra, Germany, art. 1591.
16. French C. C. art. 312; Germany, art. 1591; Italy, art. 160; Spain, art. 108.

three hundred days after the dissolution of the marriage.[17] This period of three hundred days is derived, probably, from a Roman law which made a posthumous child an heir (suus heres) if born within ten months after the death of him who would have been, had he lived, the child's paterfamilias.[18]

Contrary to the Roman and the modern Civil Law, our English Common Law takes no account of the interval between the marriage and the birth. If the child is born in wedlock, irrespective of the time of conception, it is legitimate. Our law, moreover, fixes no exact number of days after the termination of marriage within which legitimacy will be presumed. Medical testimony is admissible in a disputed case to show that the circumstances may lead to the inference that a longer or a shorter period of gestation than the usual time took place.

To our Common Law the legitimation of an illegitimate child is unknown. Under English Law a bastard can be made legitimate only by an Act of Parliament.[19] In this country the rights of legitimacy have also been conferred by special legislative acts in the absence of any general statutory provisions.[20] In a number of states, moreover, there are statutes which provide that illegitimates may be made legitimate by the subsequent marriage of their parents, providing they are acknowledged by the father,[21] while in some other

17. French C. C. art. 315; Italy, art. 160; Louisiana, art. 186–187; Spain, art. 108; Switzerland, art. 252. The German Civil Code specifies three hundred two days. Art. 1591–1592.

18. Dig. 5, 4, 3, pr.

19. Kent's Com. 2, 209; Beall v. Beall, 8 Ga. 210; Robinson v. Ruprecht, 191 Ill. 424.

20. Beall v. Beall, 8 Ga. 210; Houghton v. Dickinson, 196 Mass. 389; Miller v. Miller, 91 N. Y. 315.

21. Stevenson v. Sullivant, 5 Wheat. (U. S.) 207; Miller v. Pennington, 218 Ill. 220; Breidenstein v. Bertram, 198 Mo. 328; Rockingham v. Mount Holly, 26 Vt. 653.

states there are statutes authorizing legitimation upon the father's public acknowledgment alone.[22]

England, on the other hand, has always refused to accept the Roman Law doctrine of legitimation by subsequent marriage of the child's parents. At the parliament of Merton, the ecclesiastics endeavored to enact such a law, but "all the earls and barons, with one voice, answered that they would not change the laws of England which had hitherto been used and approved."[23] The only change in the English law upon the subject has been to recognize and accept legitimation by subsequent marriage providing the father of the child was domiciled both at the time of the birth and at the time of the subsequent marriage in a country which has such a law, although the two domiciles need not be in the same country. It thus results that a father domiciled in England at the time of his illegitimate child's birth can not by subsequent marriage to the mother in any country legitimatize the child in England.[24]

Adoption:

Adoption into the Roman agnatic family could be effected in two ways, by arrogatio and by adoption proper (adoptio). The former is the older method and applied only when the adopted person was sui juris, that is, not within the patria potestas of some ascendant. It was called arrogatio, or adrogatio, because the Roman people, in its legislative assembly, was "asked" to authorize the proceeding.[25]

22. In re Jones, 166 Cal. 108; Murphy v. Murphy, 146 Iowa, 255; McLean v. McLean, 92 Kan. 326.

23. 1 Blk. Com. 19, 456; 2 Kent's Com. 209; Statute of Merton (1236), 20 Hen. III, c. 9.

24. Birthwhistle v. Vardill, 7 Cl. & Fin. 895; Re Grove, 40 Ch. D. 216; Munro v. Munro, 7 Cl. & Fin. 842.

25. Gaius (1, 99) says that arrogatio is so called because the one adopting is "asked" whether he wishes to make his son the one he desires to adopt, also because the one about to be adopted is "asked"

The purpose of arrogatio was to provide a son, or heir, for one who was childless and had no reasonable expectation of having a child of his own. Consequently, the law provided that the arrogator, that is, the man who wished to adopt another by arrogation, should be married, also more than sixty years old, and without children.[26]

Only one person could be arrogated, but if he were himself the head of a family all those who were under his patria potestas passed as a result of the arrogation into the power of the arrogator, the children of the arrogatus becoming the grandchildren of the one who had adopted their father.[27] Whatever property the arrogated person possessed also passed to the new paterfamilias.[28]

A younger man could not adopt an older. Justinian declared that it was a violation of nature that a son should be older than his father, and, therefore, one taking to himself a son, whether by arrogation or adoption, should be at least eighteen years (the full age of puberty) older than the person adopted.[29]

The procedure in arrogation, during the times of the Republic, was conducted, first, before the comitia curiata, and, later, before the comitia centuriata, hence arrogation is sometimes called adoptio per populum. Upon the question being presented to the assembly,

if he consents, and finally because the people are "asked" if they will approve.

26. Cicero, pro Domo, 13, 14; 13, 15; Dig. 1, 7, 15, 2; 1, 7, 15, 3; 1, 7, 17, 3. Cicero (pro Domo, 13, 14) mentions the irregular adoption of Publius Claudius, a Roman Senator, who induced Fonteius, a plebeian only twenty years old, to adopt him, so that Claudius might be eligible to the plebeian tribuneship.

27. Gaius 1, 107; Inst. 1, 11, 11. Justinian says (1, 11, 11) that Augustus adopted Tiberius only after Augustus had made Tiberius adopt Germanicus, so that the latter should be the grandson of Augustus.

28. Gaius 2, 98 et seq.; Dig. 1, 7, 15, pr.

29. Inst. 1, 11, 4.

the arrogation, if approved, was effected by a formal act of legislation.[30] To the Roman mind arrogation involved something more than the mere wishes of the parties. It was a question of public policy. By it an entire Roman family with its traditions and sacred rites might cease to exist. Consequently it was regarded as a matter that should be sanctioned only by a legislative act on the part of the people. Moreover, since the parties interested had to appear before the assembly, arrogation could take place only at Rome,[31] and because women could not appear in the assembly they could not be arrogated.[32] Likewise, since the consent of the arrogatus was required, an impubes, or one under the age of legal consent, could not be the subject of arrogation.[33] When, however, in the days of the Empire, the procedure was changed, and arrogation was effected by the permission, or rescript, of the emperor,[34] boys under the age of puberty and also women could be arrogated.[35]

Adoption proper, or adoptio, in distinction from arrogatio which was the adoption of a person sui juris, was the adoption of a person alieni juris, that is, one under the patria potestas of another. This was not a matter of public concern, but merely a private affair. It was, in effect, a transfer of the patria potestas from one paterfamilias to a new paterfamilias. The person so transferred was, by the jus civile, in the power of the adopter the same as his actual children.[36] This transfer of paternal power was accomplished under the old law by selling the son three times in succession. By virtue of his patria potestas the head of a

30. Cicero, pro Domo, 29.
31. Gaius 1, 100.
32. Gaius 1, 101; Dig. 1, 7, 21.
33. Ulpian, Frag. 8, 5.
34. Inst. 1, 11, 1; Cod. 8, 48, 11.
35. Ulpian, Frag. 8, 5; Dig. 1, 7, 21; Inst. 1, 11, 3.
36. This was changed by Justinian. See infra.

family could "sell" a child to a creditor provided he was a Roman citizen. This in effect, was a sale of the child's services who thus became a bondman of the creditor. However, by the Twelve Tables, a paterfamilias could do this in case of a son only three times, since "If a father sell a son three times, the son shall be free from the father."[37] This procedure of three sales, or three mancipations (per aes et libram), was employed, in the case of a son,[38] both for adoption and for emancipation. When adoption, instead of actual emancipation, was intended, the adoptive father, upon the third sale, appeared in court and claimed the son as his own. The actual father did not interpose any objection, and the magistrate, thereupon, adjudged the subject of the adoption to be the son of the adopter.[39] This form of adoption, in distinction from the procedure in arrogation known as adoptio per populum, was called adoptio per praetorem, or judicial adoption. In the time of Justinian the old cumbersome procedure of fictitious sale and vindicatio (the claim in court) was abolished, and upon the written agreement of the parties, both of whom appeared before the court, the adoption was declared to be accomplished.[40]

Although arrogation could take place only in Rome (prior to the method of imperial rescript), yet judicial adoption was allowed in the provinces before the magistrates.[41] Persons who were not married could adopt others,[42] and Justinian permitted women who had lost children to adopt other children as a means of consola-

37. Table IV; Gaius 1, 132.
38. In case of other issue, a daughter or grandchildren, a single sale was sufficient, Gaius 1, 134.
39. Gaius 1, 134.
40. Inst. 1, 11, 1; 1, 12, 8.
41. Gaius 1, 100, 101.
42. Dig. 1, 7, 30.

tion.[43] Persons of either sex and of any age could be adopted,[44] and adoption, in distinction from arrogatio, did not affect the previously born children of the adoptee since they remained in the power of the actual ancestor. Children of the adoptee born subsequent to his adoption came, however, within the control of the adopting father.[45] While one who had been adopted could be given in adoption to another,[46] yet in such a case he could not be again adopted by the first adopter, and, likewise, if an adopter emancipated his adopted child his re-adoption was not permitted.[47]

One could adopt another person as his son, or even as his grandson, or granddaughter, although he had no son. However, if having a son, one adopted someone as a grandson the consent of the son was necessary in such a case, since the son could not be compelled to have as his heir a person thus forced upon him. A grandfather could give, however, his grandson in adoption without the consent of his son.[48]

An important change in the law governing the legal effect of adoption (adoptio) was made by Justinian. He distinguished between an adoption made by an ancestor, either paternal or maternal, and an adoption made by a stranger to the blood. In the former case, the adopted person passed, as under the old law, into the power of the adopting parent. As, for example, where a grandfather adopted a son's child born after the emancipation of his father, or where a father gave his son in adoption to his maternal grandfather. In case, however, a filius familiae was

---

43. Inst. 1, 11, 10.
44. Gaius 1, 101, 102.
45. Unless the pregnancy of the adoptee's wife took place before the adoption. In such case the offspring was within the power of the actual ancestor. Just. 1, 12, 9.
46. Gaius 1, 105; Inst. 1, 11, 8.
47. Dig. 1, 7, 37, 1.
48. Inst. 1, 11, 5–8.

given in adoption to a stranger, the paternal power of the natural father was not dissolved. The adoptee had a right of succession to his adopting father if he died intestate, but the adopted son was not in his power since he remained in the family of his natural paterfamilias.[49] This latter form of adoption is called by the commentators adoptio minus plena, the term adoptio plena being applied to adoption by an ancestor.

Adoption is recognized in the laws of many modern Civil Law countries.[50] Various restrictions and conditions are placed, however, upon the right. In France, the person adopting must be over fifty years of age, without children or legitimate descendants, and at least fifteen years older than the person adopted.[51] In Louisiana, the adopting person must be of the same sex as the one adopted unless the adoption is made by husband and wife.[52]

In our English Common Law, adoption is unknown.[53] The first statute upon the subject in this country, outside of Louisiana,[54] was in 1846. Prior to that time, the meaning of adoption as expressing a legal status was that derived from the Roman Law.[55] "The statutes of our states, however, that have been enacted upon the subject of adoption differ widely in their terms, and so far as they confer upon any adopted

---

49. Inst. 1, 11, 2; Code 8, 48, 10.

50. As to Spanish and Mexican Law, see Eckford v. Knox, 67 Tex. 200, 204.

51. French C. C. art. 343 et seq.; see also Germany, art. 1744; Italy, art. 202.

52. Louisiana C. C. art. 214. See Dupre's Succession, 116 La. 1090, 1094.

53. Matter of Thorne, 165 N. Y. 140; Matter of Ziegler, 82 N. Y. Misc. 346, 350; Ross v. Ross, 129 Mass. 243; Morrison v. Estate of Sessions, 70 Mich. 297.

54. Adoption was authorized in this state in the Code of 1808; abolished by the Code of 1825; and re-established in 1865. Dupre's Succession, 116 La. 1090, 1094.

55. Hammersley, J., in Appeal of Woodward, 81 Conn. 152.

person a capacity, more or less limited, of succeeding to the property of one not his actual parent, must be understood and applied in accordance with the terms of each statute, in view of our own conditions, and their meanings and effect are not necessarily controlled by the analogies of a Roman adoption."[56] However, such states as Louisiana and Texas have drawn their law concerning adoption largely from the Civil Law, and other states have to a great extent followed them.[57] England, following the Common Law upon this matter, has held that adoption is not recognized by the law of that country,[58] but most, if not all, of our American states have statutes upon the subject[59] and these statutes are based upon the law of Rome.[60] "It is therefore reasonable and proper," says Judge Watson of the supreme court of Vermont, "to look to the Civil Law for the proper definition of the term (adoption), and in aid of the interpretation of the provisions (of our statutes)."[61] Likewise the supreme court of Indiana has recognized the Civil Law as the source from which the statutes upon adoption in this country have been borrowed, and has applied that law in the solution of problems connected with the subject.[62] However, it has also been said that since adoption is unknown to our Common Law, the entire matter being

56. Ib.
57. Vidol v. Commagere, 13 La. Ann. 516; Eckford v. Knox, 67 Texas 200; Bray v. Miles, 23 Ind. App. 432; Hockaday v. Lynn, 200 Mo. 456.
58. Halsbury Laws Eng., Vol. 17, 111; Humphrys v. Polak (1901) 2 K. B. 385. C. A.
59. Keegan v. Geraghty, 101 Ill. 26; Gray v. Holmes, 57 Kan. 217; Clarkson v. Hatton, 143 Mo. 47, 55.
60. In re Walworth's Estate, 85 Vt. 322. And see Power v. Hafley, 85 Ky. 671; Reinders v. Koppelmann, 68 Mo. 482.
61. In re Walworth's Estate, 85 Vt. 322, holding that the children of an adopted child are the grandchildren, and therefore heirs, of the adopting parent.
62. Markover v. Krauss, 132 Ind. 294. See also, Power v. Hafley, 85 Ky. 671; Clark v. Clark, 76 N. H. 551.

statutory with us, "analogies drawn from Roman Law are to be applied with caution when they concern our family law." [63]

Over the Roman agnatic family, consisting of all his legal and legitimatized descendants, all adopted persons with their descendants, and the wives of all such descendants and adopted persons, excepting from these all males given in adoption and females given in adoption or marriage to other agnatic families, the patria potestas of the oldest living male ancestor extended.[64] It was a power exercisable only by a Roman citizen. It could not be exercised by a woman or by an artificial person (corporation).[65]

The head of the agnatic family and the possessor of the family power was known as the paterfamilias. Each male under the paternal authority was designated filiusfamilias, each female, filiafamilias. The mother of children, when married with manus, as previously stated was designated by courtesy and respect as materfamilias. Under the law, however, the mother was merely a daughter of the family, a filiafamilias, occupying no higher plane of civic rights than her children. In the eyes of the law, the mother was merely a sister to her children. However, when a daughter married, the patria potestas of her father was terminated since she was no longer a member of his agnatic family. She became a member of her husband's agnatic family, and thus merely substituted the power of one paterfamilias for another.

The actual number of persons subject to the authority of an individual paterfamilias varied, of course, very much. A young married man twenty-five years old might have no living ancestors and no children. In such a case his wife alone would constitute his

63. Fowler, S., in Matter of Ziegler, 82 N. Y. Misc. 346.
64. Inst. 1, 9, 3.
65. Gaius 1, 104; Inst. 1, 11, 10.

"family" of which family the young man would be the paterfamilias. In another case, an aged man of eighty years might have a dozen living children, all of them married, and they, in turn, might have been the fathers, and even grandfathers, of numerous offspring. It was possible that an agnatic family might include hundreds of individuals, all of them being under the potestas of one paterfamilias.

Gaius says,[66] and the Institutes of Justinian repeat his words,[67] that the Roman doctrine of paternal power is peculiar to the law of Rome. "Our children," he says, "who are born of legal marriage are in our power. This law is peculiar to Roman citizens, for no other people have such power over their children as we have."

The patriarchal power of the head of a family did not, however, originate with the Romans. Such a power is found among many primitive peoples. The Hebrew patriarchal system was similar to it, and like comparisons have been observed in other tribal populations living in a crude age. In semibarbarous times it was doubtless the only system that could maintain order and obedience. Even as an ancient great ruler, chief or king ruled as the father or lord of all his tribe or people, so the head of a family held sway over his household. Such a power was, in reality, a miniature kingdom.

The Roman patria potestas dates back to the earliest days of Roman history. The Twelve Tables but confirmed laws that were then very old when they set forth the right of a father to put deformed offspring to death, and declared that a father should as long as he lived have power over his children. "The father," it is stated,[68] "has power to imprison or to scourge his

66. Gaius 1, 55.
67. Inst. 1, 9, 2 pr.
68. Table IV.

son, to keep him at work in fetters, and even to put him to death. This is his power although the son should hold the highest office in the state."

The literal power of life and death which under the old law, the jus civile, the Roman paterfamilias possessed, was on several occasions actually exercised. Voigt cites [69] six instances of such magisterial authority: Lucius Junius Brutus, in 508 B. C., put his two sons to death;[70] Marcus Fabius, in 222 B. C., executed his son for theft;[71] Fulvius Nobilior, in 64 B. C., inflicted the death penalty on his son for taking part in the Catilinian conspiracy;[72] Pontius Aufidianus killed his daughter because of her immorality,[73] and Alilius Philiscus punished his daughter in the same way for a like offense;[74] the sixth case was that of Tricho who put his son to death.[75]

It seems to us in modern times a thing incredible that any such absolute power on the part of a paterfamilias could be authorized by law. When, however, one reflects that in comparatively modern times great nations have been ruled by despotic power, the sovereign will arbitrarily decreeing life or death, it is not impossible to understand how a rude and harsh age could justify an unlimited parental authority. It was believed to be the best and wisest policy. Human nature was the same then as now. Paternal care, pride, and love were experienced by Roman fathers, but rigid discipline in the household was characteristic of old Roman days, and that discipline was made effective in the only way it seemed to Roman Law was possible. That a few instances of the extreme exer-

69. The Twelve Tables (Zwölf Tafela), 2, 94.
70. Plut. Popl. 6, 7.
71. Oros. 4, 13.
72. Vol. Max. 5, 8, 5; Sal. Cat. 39.
73. Vol. Max. 6, 1, 3.
74. Vol. Max. 6, 1, 6.
75. Sen. de Clem. 1, 15, 1.

cise of parental authority have been recorded should not cause us to believe that the patria potestas resulted in any widespread practice of domestic cruelty.

Moreover, as would be expected, as time went on the harsh feature of this absolute power was more and more modified. Even in the days of the Republic the censors probably had a positive influence in curbing abuses of parental authority. The censors often intervened in various matters to prevent injustice and to punish disregard of public duty. It has been stated in a previous chapter that the censors marked with "infamy" the names of citizens who had been guilty of dishonor or perfidy. Our modern term "censure" is derived from such official practices of the Roman censors. While we have no express record of any interference on the part of a censor with the internal affairs of a Roman household so far as it relates to the power of a father over his child, yet it is recorded that the censors removed from the Roman senate a member who had not followed the required procedure in divorcing his wife.[76] The fact that the censors had authority to punish conduct that disregarded public opinion, served doubtless as a check at times upon parental tyranny. Down, however, to the time of the Empire, the ancient doctrine of patria potestas had been little changed by positive law.

The rule that a filiusfamilias was absolutely devoid of property rights was mitigated in the time of the emperor Augustus. In the case of slaves, whatever had been acquired by them through special effort or by way of gift for various services was permitted by their masters, by long established custom, to remain with them as their own property. Such property was called peculium. Legally, it belonged to the master but most masters observed the accustomed practice

---

76. Namely, in not first laying the matter before the family council. Lucius Annius, in 307 B. C. Val. Max. 3, 9, 2.

and allowed their slaves to retain it. In the same way, there grew up in very early times a custom of permitting a son or a daughter to exercise dominion or ownership over his or her individual possessions. Doubtless then as now, some children were indulged, some were strictly curbed. Some were permitted to possess great wealth as their own, others were limited to scant resources. The law, however, was the same for all. The title of the property possessed by a filiusfamilias, no matter how old or how individually competent he may have been, was in the name of the paterfamilias, although the peculium, or the private possessions of a filius was everywhere recognized by common practice as belonging to himself.

It was Augustus who gave the first legal status to what had previously been parental permission. That emperor declared that whatever had been acquired by a filiusfamilias in connection with military service should be subject to his right to dispose of it by will. At first, this concession was granted to veterans. The result of this imperial legislation was that soldiers, active or discharged, might give their property (called peculium castrense) by will to the person named by them as heir. In case of intestacy, the peculium castrense went to the paterfamilias, but during the lifetime of the soldier his personally acquired possessions remained his own, and his father could not take them.[77]

The concession granted at first to military men was later extended to certain classes of privileged civilians, state officials and church dignitaries. The doctrine of patria potestas included all ranks and social grades. A man might be consul of the Roman state and yet be within the power of his living ancestor. However, the law governing paternal authority was a part of the private law (jus privatum) and had nothing to do with the public law (jus publicum), conse-

---
77. Inst. 2, 12, pr.

quently, the paternal power had no jurisdiction over a man's right to vote or to hold office, or over his official acts, yet so far as a Roman official's private rights, his property rights, were concerned, they were governed by the paternal law. By analogy to the peculium castrense of soldiers, the individual acquisitions of officials of the Imperial Palace, consuls, provincial officials, and others, were given the same privilege.[78] Such exempt property was called peculium quasi-castrense. A similar right was later extended to all public officials, lawyers, and the clergy.

In the time of Constantine the goods inherited from a mother (bona materna) were also excepted from the ownership of the paterfamilias. Later emperors extended the exemption to property coming from any source through the maternal line.[79] In all such property, known as peculium adventitium, the paterfamilias had, however, a usufruct during his lifetime.[80]

Under the law of the Twelve Tables, a paterfamilias could sell a member of his household into slavery, and it was not until the time of Diocletian that this particular law was abolished. Constantine, however, restored the law in part by permitting such sales when the father was in extreme poverty.[81]

The father's power of life and death which is recognized in the law of the Twelve Tables continued to exist in theory for a number of centuries. The emperor Alexander Severus limited, however, the father's right of punishment to chastisement,[82] while Constantine declared that a father who wilfully killed his son should receive the punishment of a parricide,

78. Inst. 2, 11, 6; Code 12, 31.
79. Code 6, 60, 1, 2.
80. Ib.
81. Code 4, 43, 1, 2. Possibly to prevent the exposure and abandonment of helpless children. There were instances of the children of the very poor being killed by their parents.
82. Code 8, 47, 3.

[Roman Law]

THE LAW OF PERSONS   259

namely, that he should be placed in a sack with a viper, a cock, and an ape, and thrown into the water and drowned.[83] The absolute authority of the paterfamilias extended also to the disposal of his children in marriage. He could also give them away in adoption. A son or daughter under his potestas could not marry without his consent,[84] unless the paterfamilias were insane,[85] or a captive, or had disappeared for three years.[86] However, under the later law, if the paterfamilias refused his consent unreasonably, one in his power could marry with the consent of the magistrate.[87] The paterfamilias could also, under the old law, dissolve by divorce the marriage of his daughter if she had been married without manus, but under imperial law he was not permitted to exercise this power except for an important and lawful reason.[88]

Patria potestas was extinguished by the death of the paterfamilias, but only the immediate children of the pater became sui juris, since grandchildren, if any, merely passed into the potestas of their own fathers if living. It was also extinguished in case of the emancipation of the child under power; or in case of the loss of status (capitis deminutio maxima, media, or minima) of the pater. Likewise, the sire's power ended upon the marriage with manus of a filiafamilias, or upon the adoption of a child into another family.

Moreover, under the old law, the power of the paterfamilias terminated in case the son became a priest of Jupiter (a dialis) or the daughter a vestal virgin.[89] In the time of Justinian, the power ceased if the son

83. 318 A. D.; Code 9, 17.
84. Inst. 1, 10, pr.
85. Inst. 1, 10, pr.
86. Dig. 23, 2, 10; 23, 2, 9, 1.
87. Dig. 23, 2, 19.
88. Code 5, 17, 5.
89. Gaius 1, 130; 3, 114.

became emperor or a bishop of the church.[90] It was also the later law that the father's power should be taken away as a punishment in case he abandoned a child or made a daughter a prostitute.[91]

A paterfamilias could free a son from his power by emancipating him, and this was frequently done in order to make a son sui juris. Under the patria potestas a paterfamilias could sell or pledge a child to a creditor, provided such creditor was a Roman citizen. The child did not become a slave by such a transfer, but was merely bound to the creditor. The Twelve Tables provided that in case a father should thus sell a son three times, the son would thereupon become free from the father's power.[92] This provision suggested to the old lawyers a convenient method of emancipating a son. A fictitious sale was made to a friendly person who immediately liberated or returned the child to the father. A second sale and a second manumission followed, succeeded by a third sale which resulted in the extinguishment of the potestas. This old method of emancipation was later replaced by an imperial rescript. Still later, the parties were authorized by law to go before a competent court and, in the presence of a judge, a paterfamilias could free his sons or daughters, grandsons or granddaughters, from his power. Thereupon, the paterfamilias had the same rights over the property of the emancipated child as a patron had over the property of a slave he had freed.[93] A paterfamilias having a son and also a grandson through that same son could emancipate either and retain the other in his power.[94] A son by birth or by adoption could not compel his father to

90. Code 12, 3, 6, Nov. 81, 2.
91. Code 1, 4, 12; 11, 40, 6.
92. Table IV.
93. Inst. 1, 12, 6.
94. Dig. 1, 7, 28.

emancipate him,[95] but where a boy under age had been adopted, he had the right upon attaining full age to apply to the magistrate for emancipation, the decision resting in the discretion of the judge.[96]

In case a man had been emancipated, he could again come under patria potestas by adoption.[97] However, a man having a son and a grandson through that son, if he emancipated the son and afterwards adopted him, the grandson upon his grandfather's death did not come under the potestas of his father.[98]

Traces of the Roman parental authority can be discerned in the modern Civil Law. Many of the Civil Law codes provide, for example, that "a child at all ages owes honor and respect to his father and mother;"[99] that "a minor child cannot without permission, leave his father's house;"[100] that "a father may, as a means of correction, have his minor child incarcerated without judicial proceedings;"[101] that "a parent shall have the use of the property of his minor children."[102]

It has been said that, in Civil Law countries, adult children, as a rule, submit to and acquiesce in, the authority of parents more readily than is the case in English Law countries. However, with this view the writer cannot agree. The Civil Code of Louisiana[103] contains substantially the same provisions concerning paternal authority as the Civil Law codes of other peoples. It is presumed, however, that filial devotion, obedience, and respect are no more marked in Louisiana than in other American states. In European Civil

95. Dig. 1, 7, 31.
96. Dig. 1, 7, 32; 1, 7, 33.
97. Dig. 1, 7, 12.
98. Dig. 1, 7, 41.
99. French Code, art. 371; Spain, art. 154; Quebec, art. 242.
100. French Code, art. 374; Quebec, art. 244.
101. French Code, art. 376-380.
102. French Code, art. 384-387; Spain, art. 156.
103. See Rev. C. C. art. 215-226.

Law countries the exercise of paternal authority is no more noticeable than is, in England, the exercise of the authority given to parents under our Common Law. After all, filial honor and respect originate in the divine law, or, at least, in the law of the jus gentium. The ancient Hebrew Law, as formulated in the Mosaic Code, "Honor thy father and thy mother," and as incorporated in the moral law of Christian nations, has probably had more influence in promoting filial duty than had the paternal power doctrine of the Roman Law. Excepting the usufruct of minor children's property given by modern Civil Law codes to the parent, and the greater authority given to the father in the matter of his consent to the marriage of children under certain ages, there is very little practical difference in the law of parent and child, as it obtains to-day, in both English and Civil Law countries.

B. Guardian and Ward

The extinguishment of the patria potestas did not, in Roman Law, necessarily leave one free from protective control. Persons who were sui juris, that is, not subject to ancestral power were, nevertheless, classed either as persons subject to guardianship or persons not subject to guardianship.[104]

In our law the terms "infant" and "minor" are synonymous. The Roman Law, however, divided minors into three classes, (1) infants, (2) impuberes, and (3) puberes less than twenty-five years old. An infant was a person under the age of seven.[105] An impubes was one between seven and puberty, the later law fixing the age of puberty at fourteen in males and twelve in females.[106] Persons between the age of puberty and twenty-five were known as puberes less

104. Gaius 1, 142; Inst. 1, 13, pr.
105. Dig. 23, 1, 14; 26, 7, 1, 2.
106. Inst. 1, 22, pr.

than twenty-five years old. A person who had attained the age of twenty-five years, the full age of majority without distinction of sex,[107] was called a major.

The guardianship of children under the age of puberty and of women during their entire lives was a very ancient doctrine of the Roman Law. It was intended not alone for the care and protection of persons of tender years but also for the protection of family rights in property. The Twelve Tables recognize both these forms of guardianship, a paterfamilias having the right to appoint a guardian by his will, or, in case he died intestate, the male agnates became guardians by operation of law.[108]

The guardianship of women and of children under the age of puberty was known as tutela, the former being tutela mulierum, the latter tutela impuberum. There was another form of guardianship known as cura. This was a guardianship of the property of puberes under the age of twenty-five.

Tutela, says Justinian,[109] is, as Servius defined it, a right and power over a free person, authorized by the jus civile for the protection of one who by reason of his age is unable to protect himself.

Under the old law, tutela was a sort of potestas, although much less authoritative than the paternal power. The one who exercised this power was called a tutor, and the one subject to it was termed a pupillus or pupilla. The word tutor was derived from the Latin word meaning "to protect," because a tutor protected and defended those under his care.[110]

The tutorship of children under the age of puberty was a guardianship of both the person and the property of the child. The paterfamilias of a child was,

---

107. Cod. 6, 45, 5.
108. Twelve Tables, V.
109. Inst. 1, 13, 1.
110. Inst. 1, 13, 1.

if living, his "tutor," but upon the death of the paterfamilias the child, although sui juris by the decease of his paterfamilias, was placed under the tutorship of some other person. The duties of a tutor were, in general, to exercise a supervision over the pupillus, to look after his education with proper care,[111] to give legal sanction, or authority (auctoritas) to the business transactions of the child, and to manage the property possessed by him. A tutor did not necessarily have the actual custody of the child, nor did a tutor act as a teacher of his ward. Our modern terms, tutor and pupil, although derived from these Roman Law terms, are applied to the relationship of a teacher and his student, but nothing of the sort was necessarily involved in tutela. The mother of the child, if she survived the father, had the personal care of the ward,[112] unless the father had provided otherwise in his will. If the mother were dead, the custody of the child's person was usually given to some other near relative.

In connection with the ward's property the tutor's duty was to protect it and to manage it with care. This management was known as gestio. However, the possession of property by a ward was not a requisite for tutorship, since a ward might not, in fact, have any property. Consequently, in tutela, gestio might or might not exist, depending upon the fact of the ward's possession of property.

In every tutorship, however, the tutor's right and duty were to guard and protect the ward in all his business and contractual acts. A ward under seven years of age could not perform any legal act that was binding upon him. Above that age he could, moreover, do no act that might prove disadvantageous to him without the sanction (auctoritas) of his tutor. Trans-

---

111. Dig. 26, 7, 12, 3; 27, 2; Code 5, 49.
112. Horace, Ep. 1, 1, 22; Livy, 39, 9, 1.

actions, however, to his advantage were valid, as far as he was concerned, without the sanction of his tutor.[113] But even these could not be enforced against him. When, for example, the ward stipulated that something should be given to him the sanction of a tutor was not necessary.[114] But in obligations that were mutual, as in transactions of buying, selling, letting, hiring, mandates, or deposits, if the tutor did not give his authorization the person dealing with the ward was bound but the ward was not bound.[115] Consequently, in order to enable a ward to enter into such contracts with persons who otherwise would be unwilling to bind themselves when he would not be bound, the consent of his tutor was always necessary. This consent or authorization was known as auctoritatis interpositio, and such consent made the ward's act legal. The consent had to be given, however, at the time of the transaction. A subsequent confirmation, or a consent given by letter was without legal effect.[116] The tutor was not given arbitrary power to refuse his consent since it was his duty to assent to any transaction that appeared to be advantageous to his ward.[117]

Tutors were appointed either by will, by a magistrate, or were designated by the law. A father, that is a paterfamilias, having children in his power who had not attained the age of puberty could by his will appoint a tutor for them.[118] A tutor appointed by will was known as a testamentary tutor. A tutor designated by the law was called a tutor legitimus,[119] or a legal or statutory tutor. The Twelve Tables made

113. Gaius 3, 107.
114. Inst. 1, 21, pr.
115. Inst. 1, 21, pr.
116. Inst. 1, 21, 2.
117. Dig. 26, 7, 10.
118. Inst. 1, 13, 4. Compare the Statute of 12 Car. II, in English Law.
119. Inst. 1, 15; Dig. 26, 4.

the nearest agnate the tutor, but Justinian gave the tutorship to the next of kin, whether agnate or cognate.[120] Where there was no testamentary tutor or no person qualified to act as a "legal tutor," a tutor was appointed by a magistrate, tutor dativus.[121]

Only citizens who had attained majority, that is, twenty-five years of age, were qualified to act as tutors.[122] A man under paternal power was competent, however, since the office of a tutor was regarded as a public office, the law of patria potestas not affecting public law.[123] Women, however, were not qualified to serve as tutors, although Justinian provided that a mother or a grandmother might serve as the tutor of her child or grandchild.[124] A qualified person having been regularly appointed a tutor could not refuse to accept the position since the service was regarded as a public duty.[125] Exemptions from service were, however, allowed in the case of persons over seventy years of age,[126] state officials,[127] teachers,[128] physicians,[129] and parents of three or more living children.[130]

A tutor's office was one of honor and duty. He was not permitted to charge for his services,[131] nor was he allowed to reap any advantage from his office. He could not authorize any act on the part of his ward that would result in enrichment for himself.[132]

Upon assuming his office, it was his first duty, if

120. Inst. 1, 17, pr.; Nov. 118.
121. Inst. 1, 20; Code 1, 3, 52.
122. Inst. 1, 25, 13.
123. Inst. 1, 14, pr.; Dig. 27, 10, 1, 7; Dig. 1, 6, 9.
124. Nov. 118, 5.
125. Dig. 26, 7, 5, 7.
126. Inst. 1, 25, 13; Dig. 27, 1, 2, pr.
127. Inst. 1, 25, 1.
128. Inst. 1, 25, 15.
129. Inst. 1, 25, 15.
130. Inst. 1, 25, pr.
131. Dig. 26, 7, 33, 3.
132. Dig. 26, 8, 1, pr.

there was property, to see that an inventory of it was made.[133] Any money on hand was to be safely invested within a reasonable time,[134] or to be expended in the purchase of land.[135] Lands belonging to the ward could not, however, be sold unless so directed by the will of the ward's father or by order of the Praetor.[136] The prohibition against an unauthorized sale of land was extended, in Constantine's day, to all sorts of property unless it chanced to be trivial in value.[137]

Tutorship of children extended to the age of puberty. An infant (in-fans, voiceless) meant one who possessed no legal capacity at all. An impubes had some legal capacity. He could act with legal efficacy in matters that were wholly beneficial to him, and in such instances, as previously stated, no sanction of a tutor was required to make the transaction binding. An impubes could not, however, repudiate a contract and retain its benefit. For example, he could not keep a purchased article and refuse to pay for it, unless the article was no longer in existence.[138]

During the existence of the tutorship, the tutor was at all times bound to care for the interests of his pupil with all the care of a prudent man.[139] If a tutor acted corruptly, as, for example, by deliberately returning a false inventory, or by fraudulently disposing of his ward's property, he was liable to a criminal punishment.[140] It was the tutor's duty to manage the property of the ward with as much care as he managed his own property. He was liable not only for fraud but

133. Codex 5, 51, 13.
134. See Dunscomb v. Dunscomb, 1 Johns. Ch. (N. Y.) 508, 511.
135. Codex 5, 37, 24.
136. Dig. 27, 9, 1, 2.
137. Codex 5, 72, 4.
138. Dig. 44, 1, 4.
139. Dig. 26, 7, 33, pr.
140. Dig. 1, 12, 1, 7.

also for negligence,[141] and a tutor who showed incompetence could be removed from his office.[142] Prior to the time of Justinian a tutor could resign when he was no longer willing to serve, but that emperor permitted no such resignation except for a cause approved by the magistrate.

When the male ward arrived at the age of puberty, fourteen years old, it was the duty of the tutor to make an accounting.[143] If this was not done voluntarily the ward could bring an action to compel it. It was also the tutor's duty to inform and advise the ward of his need now of another kind of guardian, a curator, to care for his property until the youth should become a major, that is, a man of full age, namely, twenty-five years old.[144]

The second kind of tutela was the guardianship of women (tutela mulierum). This guardianship did not cease when a female ward arrived at the age of puberty (twelve years old) since a woman who was not either under patria potestas or under the manus of a husband was always in perpetual tutela.[145] The ancient Roman Law regarded women as being in a sort of perpetual nonage.[146] However, when a girl arrived at the age of twelve the tutor did not continue to manage her property, but his sanction (auctoritas) was still necessary to give validity to her alienation of mancible things.[147] If she married and came into the manus of a husband the guardianship of the tutor came to an end. However, by the Lex Claudia in the early Empire, the guardianship of women was practically abolished, and in the reigns of Theodosius and Hon-

141. Dig. 27, 3, 1, pr.
142. Gaius 1, 199.
143. Dig. 27, 3, 1, 3.
144. Dig. 26, 7, 5, 5.
145. Gaius 1, 144.
146. Beauregard v. Piernas, 1 Mart. (O. S.) (La.) 280.
147. Gaius 1, 190; 2, 80.

orius it entirely disappeared.[148] It was unknown in the time of Justinian.

The tutorship of a boy under the age of puberty came to an end, as previously stated, when the ward reached the age of fourteen years. A boy of that age who was sui juris could legally transact all business matters for himself, and was entitled to the management of his property. Under the ancient law he had no further guardian.

At no time in Roman Law did a youth between the age of puberty and twenty-five years require the sanction of a guardian's auctoritas in order to give validity to his business transactions. He had full legal capacity, provided he was freed from potestas, or, in other words, was sui juris. It was always possible, however, for such a minor to complain of unfair dealing whenever he was dissatisfied with the outcome of any transaction with an adult, and, on the other hand, it often happened that older persons did actually take advantage of the inexperience of such youths. Even prior to the year 183 B. C., the Lex Plaetoria,[149] which seems to have been the first law that was passed upon the subject of minors, provided that anyone who defrauded a minor should be publicly punished, and the law further permitted a minor in certain cases to apply to the magistrate for the appointment of a curator to manage his property.

Moreover, the praetor in connection with his granting of actions introduced the action and the exception of fraud in transactions alleged to be fraudulent, and also further provided that a minor who had received any injury from any transaction could generally petition for restitution. Such a restitution restored everything to its former condition (restitutio in in-

---

148. Code 8, 58, 1.
149. This law is mentioned by Plautus, Psued. 1, 3, 69, who died in the year 183 B. C.

tegrum).¹⁵⁰ The minor recovered what he had transferred and returned whatever he had left of that which he had received in consideration.¹⁵¹ The minor's right to a restitution continued for four years after he attained his full majority (twenty-five years), or until he was twenty-nine years old.¹⁵² It was not necessary for a minor to charge fraud in order to recover his property, a statement to the effect that his youth had caused him to agree to a bad bargain was all that was needed.¹⁵³

Of course the inevitable result was that adults would not transact matters of any importance with minors unless they were under curatorship, and the curator's approval given to the transaction. In such a case a minor could not rescind a contract and demand restitution unless there had been actual fraud.¹⁵⁴

However, a boy having attained the age of fourteen years was not, except in certain cases, obliged to have a curator against his will.¹⁵⁵ The exceptions were in case of a lawsuit;¹⁵⁶ in case of receiving the payment of a debt;¹⁵⁷ in case of settling a tutor's accounts;¹⁵⁸ and in case of the minor's arrogation.¹⁵⁹ In such cases the party dealing with a minor could insist upon the appointment of a curator for the particular occasion in order to protect himself against any subsequent charge of dealing unfairly with one of immature years.

According to Gaius,¹⁶⁰ it was not until the time of Marcus Aurelius that a minor could apply to have a

150. Gaius, 4, 57; Dig. 4, 4, 3, 4; 4, 4, 2, 1; 4, 4, 47, pr.
151. Dig. 4, 4, 27, 1; 4, 4, 47, 1.
152. Code 2, 53, 7.
153. Dig. 4, 4, 44; Code 2, 22, 5, pr.
154. Dig. 45, 1, 101.
155. Inst. 1, 22, pr.
156. Inst. 1, 23, 2; Dig. 42, 1, 45, 2.
157. Dig. 4, 4, 7, 2.
158. Code 5, 31, 7.
159. Code 1, 7, 8.
160. Epit. 1, 8.

curator appointed to look after his property generally. A minor was never obliged to ask for the appointment of a general curator, but a minor having valuable property seldom failed to do so. Curators were appointed by the same magistrates that appointed tutors,[161] and were appointed only by magistrates. A father might in his will nominate a curator for his minor child but such a testamentary provision was discretionary with the court which could confirm or refuse to confirm the nomination.[162]

The chief distinction between a tutor and curator was that a curator was not appointed for the care and maintenance of a ward, but was appointed to manage and protect his ward's property. A curator possessed no general power (auctoritas) to give validity to the transactions of his ward, since a minor having a curator could bind himself and his property without the curator's consent,[163] except in those matters where the law required a special curator to be appointed upon the request of the party dealing with the minor. The curator's sanction was requisite in such cases to give validity to the transactions involved. Also a constitution of Diocletian required the curator's consent, providing the minor had a curator, in case of the minor's sale or mortgage of his property.[164]

In the management of a ward's property curators were governed by practically the same rules as in the case of tutors. Security was usually required to the end that they would diligently care for the property of their wards, and curators could be removed by the magistrate for incompetency or fraud.[165] In case of the sale of property belonging to a minor under cura-

161. Inst. 1, 23, 1.
162. Inst. 1, 23, 1.
163. Dig. 45, 1, 101; 34, 3, 20, 1; 4, 4, 16, pr.; 14, 6, 3, 2.
164. Code, 2, 22, 3.
165. Dig. 45, 1, 101.

torship the transaction usually required the approval of the magistrate to make it conclusive.[166] The office of a general curator ceased upon his death or that of the minor,[167] when either the curator or the minor suffered maxima or media capitis deminutio, or when the minor attained his full majority which was the age of twenty-five years.[168] A curator appointed for a specially required purpose served only till the contemplated transaction had been performed.[169]

In addition to the curatorship of minors, curators were also appointed for persons who were either mentally or physically incapacitated to protect their affairs. Insane persons and spendthrifts, although more than twenty-five years old, were, as early as the law of the Twelve Tables, placed in the care of curators.[170] In the time of Justinian, the guardian care of the helpless was extended to persons of unsound mind, the deaf, the dumb, and the incurably sick, since such were unable to manage their own affairs.[171]

The modern law of guardianship, both in Civil and Common Law countries, has been largely derived from the Roman Law, and the terms tutor and curator have been preserved in many modern Civil Law codes.[172]

In Louisiana, the Roman Law term "tutor" corresponds in general to our word guardian,[173] and curators may also be appointed to care for the interests of absentees,[174] and also for the management of the property of insane persons, and of other persons who by

166. Code 5, 71, 16; 5, 37, 22. See Means v. Robinson, 7 Tex. 502, 512, for a similar provision in Spanish and Mexican law.
167. Inst. 1, 22, 3.
168. Inst. 1, 23, pr.
169. Inst. 1, 21, 3; Dig. 27, 1, 10, 8.
170. Inst. 1, 23, 3.
171. Inst. 1, 23, 4.
172. For example, Germany, arts. 1909-1921; Japan, art. 908; Mexico, Lib. 1, tit. 11.
173. Louisiana Rev. C. C., tit. VIII.
174. Rev. C. C. art. 47 et seq.

reason of infirmities are unable to care for their own affairs.[175] Provision is also made for the appointment of a tutor or a curator "ad hoc" [176] in cases of emergency,[177] a temporary guardian corresponding to the special curator of the Roman Law.[178] In some countries, a sort of assistant guardian, known as an undertutor, is also appointed in every tutorship. His duties are to act for the minor when his interests conflict with those of the tutor.[179]

In the state of Missouri the term "curator" has been adopted from the Civil Law, but is applied to the guardianship of the estate of the ward as distinguished from the guardianship of his person.[180]

175. Rev. C. C. art. 31–33.
176. Rev. C. C. art. 313, 369.
177. In re Fortier, 31 La. Ann. 50, 51.
178. See Derepas v. Shallus, 15 La. 371, 373; Brian v. Bonvillain, 52 La. Ann. 1794, 1808.
179. French C. C., art. 420–426; Italy, C. C., art. 264–267; Japan, C. C., art. 910; Louisiana, Rev. C. C., art. 273–280; Spain, C. C., art. 233–236. See Monget v. Tessier, 5 La. Ann. 165, 166.
180. Duncan v. Crook, 49 Mo. 116; Larned v. Renshaw, 37 Mo. 458; State v. Greer, 101 Mo. App. 669.

CHAPTER X

ARTIFICIAL PERSONS OR CORPORATIONS

In our own law corporations are often classed with "persons," being described as "artificial" or "legal" persons, that is, persons created by law. Moreover, modern writers upon Roman Law frequently call corporations in that legal system "persons," and many of the present day Civil Law codes expressly define corporations as juristic or juridical persons.[1]

But whether Roman lawyers, even up to the time of Justinian, ever conceived of a "corporation" as a person, a "persona" within the meaning of the Roman Law, is questionable. Gaius, in his Institutes, divides Roman Law into three heads, persons, things, and actions, yet omits in that elementary work all discussions of corporations.[2] He treats of corporations in other writings, however, yet in the various passages from his works inserted in the Digest he does not speak of a corporation as a person.

Moreover, neither the Institutes of Justinian nor the Digest define a corporation (universitas). Chancellor Walworth of New York, in one of the early leading cases in this country upon corporations,[3] says that "the terms used by one of the Roman jurisconsults to describe the nature of a corporation, or associated body of individuals, under the laws of the Republic, are perhaps as appropriate as any general language which can be used to describe a corporation aggregate

---

[1]. As, for example, the Spanish Civil Code, art. 35.
[2]. He speaks, however, of corporate property (res universatatis) 2, 11.
[3]. Warner v. Beers, 23 Wend. (N. Y.) 103, 123.

at the present day, without referring to the specific object for which any particular corporation is organized." The learned chancellor then translates a Digest passage of Gaius [4] as follows: "Those who are permitted to form themselves into a body under the name of a corporation, society, or other community, have within their peculiar jurisdiction property in common, and a common chest or treasury, and an agent or head of the corporation or society by whom whatever is necessary to be done for the benefit of the community may be transacted."

However, these words of Gaius state rather some of the privileges and functions of a corporation than its nature.

What the Roman jurists themselves conceived the nature of a corporation to be we can only conjecture by the light of the comparatively few passages upon the subject found here and there in the Corpus Juris of Justinian. The passage already quoted is one of such passages. The Roman jurists, however, were given very little to philosophical theory or speculation. They were intensely practical. There came a time in the evolution of Roman Law when there arose a need of a theoretical ownership of property and of property rights in connection with community interests; or ownership that should be entirely apart from, and independent of, the individuals who comprised the community. The Roman jurists supplied this need without any discussion of its philosophic nature. The great thing that the Roman lawyers developed was the idea that legal rights and liabilities could be predicated of a body or a group, a universitas, considered as an entity entirely apart from its individual members. In this sense, the whole, the corpus, may be regarded as having a personality, or may be considered as having rights and privileges and obligations like

[4]. Dig. 3, 4, 1, 1.

unto a person. There are modern commentators upon the Roman Law who dispute whether the idea of a corporation constitutes a fictitious or an actual "person," that is, whether it is "fictitious" in the sense that it is *created* by law, or whether it is actual or "real" in the sense that its legal personality actually exists, and is not created but is accepted by law.[5] The Roman lawyers, however, evidently did not think it important to consider the question and the Digest is silent upon it.

A "person" in Roman Law is, as previously stated, an individual, a human being, capable of possessing and exercising legal rights. It is one who has legal capacity to acquire and possess property; who may sue and be sued, and in other ways may exercise legal privileges. When a universitas, a corporation, was recognized as having rights as a collected whole, a unit, apart and separate from the individual members that composed it, it surely, for legal purposes, had a sort of personality, or, at least, must have been treated as a sort of person. The Digest in various places speaks of a corporation as having certain characteristics or qualities that are usually attributed to a person, persona, and that, after all, is practically all that is meant when lawyers speak of a corporation as a person. That a corporation is an artificial person, a juristic person, a legal person, a legal fiction, or that it is intangible, or invisible, are the products of philosophic reflection. Such views were not expressed by the Roman lawyers. Regardless of academic speculation and dispute upon the extent of the development among the Romans of the idea of legal personality in a corporation, the important thing is the fact that they developed the corporate idea. A corporation is one thing and the nature of a corporation is another thing. That what we call corporations were recog-

5. See Sohm's Inst. Rom. Law, 3rd Ed. p. 193, note.

nized as a part of Roman Law there is no question, and from the Roman Law of corporations our English fundamental law upon the subject is derived. Blackstone, who ordinarily could find little to admire in Roman Law, even went so far as to give the Roman lawyers the credit of inventing the corporate idea. The honor, says he, of inventing the plan belongs wholly to the Romans.[6] A German writer, however, has said that "from the earliest times and among all nations organized bodies have been recognized, over and above separate individuals, as subjects of legal rights and duties, and the only changes that have occurred, have been changes in the form in which the personality of these bodies had found expression." [7]

It is, of course, true that the Romans did not originate or invent the plan or custom of two or more persons combining their resources for the purpose of accomplishing desired results. Such combinations are purely natural. They belong to all ages and peoples, and involve no technical legal ideas or theories. The thing achieved by the Romans, in connection with such combinations or organizations, was the conception of a legal entity, a sort of legal personality, apart from and independent of the individual members that composed the associated group. The corporation law of every modern nation, whether its system of general law be the Civil Law or the so-called English Law, is based upon this conception of the Roman Law.

"Every system of law in western Europe," say Pollack and Maitland,[8] "adopted and turned to its own use an idea of non-human persons, ideal subjects of rights and duties, which were gradually discovered in the Roman law books. From the nature of the case it is not often that jurisprudence can make a discov-

6. Com. I, 468.
7. Gierke, Deutsche Privatrech, I, 468.
8. Hist. Eng. Law, I, 469.

ery comparable to the discoveries made by other sciences or arts, for it has to await rather than to forestall the slow changes of common opinion. But here there is something that we may fairly call a discovery, though it was made by no one man and by no one age—in order that the relationships between men may be adequately and succinctly stated, we must in thought institute a new order of persons who are not men."

Of one thing we may be quite sure, and that is that the story of the way corporations originated among the Romans, as narrated by Blackstone and attributed by him to Plutarch, is purely mythical.

According to Blackstone, corporations had their beginning in the days of King Numa. That ruler, finding the city of Rome torn to pieces by the two rival factions who comprised the population, the Sabines and the Romans, thought it would be a prudent and politic measure to divide these two groups into many smaller ones, by instituting separate societies of every manual trade and profession. These trade groups or guilds were, as Blackstone intimates, the first corporations.

However, turning to Plutarch himself, we see that the passage in question does not support the statement that Numa organized "corporations." It merely refers to his device of dividing the people into associations or guilds of tradesmen. Plutarch says: "The most commended of all the acts of Numa was his division of the people by their trades into groups or guilds. Since the city was divided into two different tribes, the diversity between them could not be quelled. This fact prevented unity and gave rise to perpetual tumult and ill feeling. Reflecting upon the fact that hard substances do not readily mix when in lumps, but may, if beaten into powder, be mingled, Numa decided to divide all the people into a number of small groups, hoping in this way to obliterate the original and great difference which would be effaced among smaller parts. Consequently, classifying the population by their various arts and trades, he created guilds of musicians, goldsmiths, carpenters, dyers, shoemakers, tanners, braziers, and potters. Moreover, he grouped and made into single guilds all other craftsmen, appointing for each guild its separate court, council, and religious rites. In this way, all factions began, for the first time, to cease, no one being longer spoken or thought of as a Sabine, a Roman or as a follower of Romulus or of Tatius. The new division was a cause of general harmony and good will." [9] While this legend, from Plutarch's "Life of Numa," does not belong to critical history, but presents a traditional origin of the Roman trade guilds, yet it affords no authority for the statement that Numa created "corporations." The early Roman guilds, or collegia, were not corporations, no more so than unincorporated groups of artisans or tradesmen of to-day. Centuries after the legendary Numa, various Roman guilds became "corporations" or "universitates" as the Romans called them, but the Roman conception of a "universitas" was a thing undreamed of in the days of the Kings. It belongs to a much later period of the development of the Roman Law.

Chancellor Kent shows a clearer understanding of Roman corporations when he says: "The powers, capacities, and incapacities of corporations, under the English Law, very much resemble those under the Civil Law, and it is evident that the principles of law applicable to English corporations were borrowed chiefly from the policy of the municipal corporations established (by the Romans) in Britain and other Roman colonies." [10]

9. Life of Numa.
10. Com. II, 269, 13th Ed.

It was, indeed, due to the development of Rome's system of government, a government of states (civitates), municipalities (municipia), colonies (coloniae), and villages or districts (vici), that, as far as Rome is concerned, the idea of a corporation was born. This idea, however, was of slow growth, and seems to have been developed as a public necessity. It originally had nothing to do with private interests. Much misapprehension and confusion have been caused by assuming that the trade guilds or "collegia" of ancient Rome were corporations.

Associations of individuals of the same trade or crafts, as also those of the same convivial or social habits, are, doubtless, as old as civilization. They have been common to all peoples. Such associations existed in ancient Rome. They were known as societates and sodalitates, the former being applied to trade groups, the latter to social companies or clubs. They were also called collegia, or colleges, meaning a group of persons gathered or collected together. Gaius says that the right of the members (sodales) of a "college" to make their own by-laws, provided they are not inconsistent with public law, is as old as the Twelve Tables, the doctrine being taken from Solon.[11] Some have supposed from this passage that "corporations" among the Romans were as old as the Twelve Tables. Such was evidently the opinion of Chancellor Walworth when he said: "Such associated bodies as were, in the language of the constitution (of New York), at the time of its adoption by the people in January, 1822, called bodies politic and corporate, had been known to exist as far back at least as the time of Cicero; and Gaius traces them even to the laws of Solon of Athens, who lived some five hundred years before. These associated bodies or communities of individuals, with certain rights and privileges belonging to them by law

11. Dig. 47, 22, 4.

in their aggregative capacity, were styled by the Romans Collegium, and sometimes universitas; as Collegium Tibicinum, Collegium Aurificum, Collegium Architectorum; the society, corporation or community of Flute Players, Goldsmiths, Architects, etc." [12]

However, in the passage above cited, Gaius was not speaking of a "corporation." He merely stated what the members of a collegium could do. These early Roman societies (or collegia) had no proprietary capacity "in their aggregative capacity," no rights or ownership as a group, as a collective whole. Whatever property such a society possessed was purely private property, the property of the individual members, either separately or jointly. The society, or college, owned nothing as belonging to itself, and could not acquire anything for itself. It was not thought of as having any rights or any liabilities in its own name.

The same thing was likewise true of a partnership, which was also called societas in Roman Law. A partnership, as with us, was a contractual relation between two or more persons for some common purpose. The partners (socii) owned the property, and the partnership had no separate existence, no entity, no legal independence.

Even older than the collegia of tradesmen and artisans were, doubtless, the collegia of various groups of persons connected with religious rites and observances, such as priests of various temples, the vestal virgins, and others.

The Roman doctrine of a corporation originated with the need of a workable or practical theory concerning the ownership of *public* property; not of *private* property as in the case of ordinary collegia or of partnerships, but of *public* property, the property of a municipality, a municipium. It was not until the closing days of the Republic, after the system of the

12. Warner v. Beers, 23 Wend. (N. Y.) 103, 122.

government of towns and cities, municipia, had become established, that the doctrine of municipal or corporate ownership was recognized. Concerning property, or "things," say the Institutes of Justinian, some kinds of property may be owned by individuals; other kinds cannot be so owned. Some things are by the law of nature common to all; some are public; some belong to a corporation (universitas); and some belong to no one. Examples of things belonging to a corporation (universitas), and not to individuals, are theatres, race courses and such other similar things as belong in common to cities.[13] The original of this passage is found in the Institutes of Marcianus, quoted in almost identical words in the Digest.[14]

Although when the Institutes and Digest were published private as well as public corporations had long been recognized, yet it seems to be evident that the fundamental meaning of corporate property, res universitatis, was, even then, the property that belonged to cities or states (civitates) in their governmental or municipal capacities. It was for the purpose of designating the ownership of public property that the term universitas which we translate "corporation" came into use. The phrase res universitatis, or university property, called by us corporate property, meant, originally, property that was owned by the municipality, the use being in the public. Consequently the original notion of a corporation in Roman Law was what we would call a municipal, or a public, corporation, and not a private corporation.

The term "universitas" means, literally, the whole, the whole number of beings considered as a unit, the one single whole. However, as a technical legal term it meant something different from all the members who comprised it. It did not mean that the property of a

13. Inst. 2, 1, pr. and 6.
14. Dig. 1, 8, 2, pr. and 6.

university, or corporate property, was owned by all the members jointly, for it was only private property that could be so owned, but it means that apart and distinct from the individual members there was an abstract something that had rights and liabilities. Our term "university" took its name from the fact that in the Middle Ages (12th and 13th centuries) teachers, or students, formed corporations (universitates) for the promotion of higher education. Schools were originally connected with cathedrals and monasteries, but later became independently incorporated. The university of Paris was incorporated by its teachers, likewise those of England and Germany. The university of Bologna was incorporated by its students, as were also the other universities of Italy and those of provincial France.

The Roman jurists treated law under two divisions, public law and private law. Public law deals with the affairs of government, private law with the interests of individuals.[15] Under the old Roman Law, the jus civile, property known as public property was not subject to any sort of ownership. It was said to be extra commercium. An entirely new theory was injected into the law when public property was made subject to the ownership of a corporation, a universitas. In other words, the doctrine of private ownership, a part of the jus privatum, was extended to include public property, a part of the jus publicum. Moreover, ownership, or the dominion over property, could be exercised only by an individual, a "person." It was, consequently, another notable advance in the progress of Roman Law when the universitas, something different from all the individuals or "persons" who composed it, was recognized as a legal owner. In that sense it had some of the qualities of a "person." In the same way that municipal property had by the doctrine of

---

15. Dig. 1, 1, 1, 2.

corporate capacity been brought within the law of private ownership, and that ownership vested in the entire corporate body, similar rights were, in imperial days, granted by law to various collegia, societies, and other groups. Still later, the Public Treasury (fiscus) was made a corporation, and, in Christian days, after it had become a state institution, the Church. In all these incorporations, however, the public welfare was supposed to be served. Corporations were not originally created, theoretically at least, for the sake of the private gain of any group, but only that the welfare of the state might be promoted. Roman writers upon the law did not, however, classify corporations as public and private, because, originally, the idea of a corporation (universitas) was confined to public property. However, such corporate bodies suggested the practicability of such organizations for private as well as public benefit, and in time, we know not just when, private corporations came into existence patterned upon municipal corporations.

The Digest, quoting from Gaius, says: "Those who are permitted to form a corporation (corpus habere) for the purpose of a collegium or a societas or any other similar body, have the right, after the manner of a municipality (ad exemplum rei publicae), to have common property, a common chest, and an actor or syndicus by whom, just as in a municipal body (tamquam in re publica), anything that has to be transacted or done for the common welfare may be so transacted and done." [16]

As already said, the word "universitas" was the general name for a corporation. Other terms, such as "collegium" and "corpus," were, however, used to express the same thought. The phrase "habere corpus" is regularly used in the Digest in the sense "to form

---

16. Dig. 3, 4, 1, 1.

a corporation."[17] Universitas was the usual term for a public or municipal corporation, while the term collegium in imperial days when private corporations were created was the usual term for a private corporation.[18] In fact, collegium is the oldest term for an association, being originally employed to designate both religious and trade associations. The later use of the word collegium is largely responsible, doubtless, for the opinion that a collegium in the early days of Rome was a corporation. Our word "corporation" is derived from the word "corpus." As late as 1691, Lord Holt, Chief Justice of England, used all these Roman terms in defining a corporation, saying, "a corporation is an ens civile, a corpus politicum, a collegium, an universitas, a jus habendi et agendi."[19]

The most important private corporations of the imperial days appear to have been combinations of persons for farming the public revenues, shipbuilding, and working mines of gold, silver, and salt.[20] There were other incorporated private enterprises but these are especially mentioned by the Roman writers. One of the greatest sources of private gain was collecting the public revenue, and this privilege was leased or "farmed out" to the highest bidders. Large amounts of money were invested by the rich in tax farming. Foreign trade was also monopolized by powerful companies, even as in England centuries later. As a writer upon modern corporation law has said: "The genius of the Roman people for conquest and government led naturally, as with the English speaking races, to industrial organization and new modes of business of a large scale."[21]

17. Dig. 3, 4, 1, 1. See Dig. 27, 1, 17, 3; 27, 1, 41, 3; 34, 5, 20; 47, 22.
18. See Dig. 47, 22, De Collegiis, etc.
19. Laws of Eng. VII, 301.
20. Dig. 3, 4, 1, pr.
21. Cook, on Corporations, a 1, 1923 Ed.

Corporations could be created only by the sovereign power, the state. They could not be brought into being by the mere agreement of the persons who desired to form them. An express permission of law was a necessity.[22]

The Digest, quoting from Gaius, says:[23] "A societas or a collegium or a similar corporation (corpus) is not a common right. This is a matter that is controlled by statutes (leges), decrees of the senate, and imperial constitutions. It is only in a few cases that such corporations have been allowed, such as to partners in the collection of the public revenues, and in the operation of gold and silver and salt mines. There are also at Rome certain collegia whose corporate existence has been created by decrees of the senate and imperial constitutions, such as collegia of bakers and certain others, also of shipowners, colleges of whom are also found in the provinces."

Back of the restraint upon the liberty of voluntary association was a governmental policy of self protection. In imperial days all clubs and other associated groups were closely watched by state officials since they afforded peculiar opportunities for breeding political dissension.

Municipal corporations were a very important part in Rome's system of government, and Rome's policy in the administration of conquered cities and towns demonstrates her genius in organization and control. To Rome government was a science. The history of the rise and growth of municipal management is long and varied. First, there were the towns near Rome, then the towns of all Italy, and then, in time, the towns and cities of the rest of the world. In the development of Rome's policy, there was a desire to leave, as far as safely possible, the control of local

22. Dig. 47, 22.
23. Dig. 3, 4, 1, pr.

affairs in the hands of the local people. By the time of Julius Caesar, practically all the towns of Italy were municipia, having their local differences, but under a common type of government, patterned largely upon the model of Rome's own government. Self-government under Rome's political supremacy was the ideal. In imperial days, after the conquest of Britain, the same system of municipal government was planted there, and upon the models of these governmental corporations, England, centuries later, built her own public corporations, municipal, ecclesiastical and educational, and, in time, her commercial and industrial corporations. We, in turn, received these models from English Law.

It is not to be supposed, however, that the Roman idea of a municipal corporation was an instantaneous creation. It was an evolution. In very early days, as already stated, the doctrine of corporate property was unknown. Step by step the idea grew, and finally became a recognized legal principle. The corporation, or the universitas, became a distinct entity having not merely collective rights and liabilities but its own rights and liabilities. Whatever, says the Digest,[24] was owed to the corporation was not owed to the members as individuals, but to the corporation. Likewise, whatever the corporation owed, the members as individuals did not owe.

Here we have the idea that was finally evolved, a corporate right to own and possess for itself, and a corresponding duty to perform its own obligations.

A municipal corporation had even greater juristic capacity to acquire property than an individual. The latter could acquire only private property, while the municipal body could acquire both public and private property. When, however, private property was acquired by a municipality it became res universitatis,

24. Dig. 3, 4, 7, 1.

and, thus, public property, the property of a public corporation. Accordingly, a municipal corporation could own a slave, who, upon his purchase, became the slave of the corporation and not the slave of its members.[25] From this fact it resulted that although a slave owned by a citizen could not be compelled to testify against his master, yet the slave of a municipality could be even tortured to force him to give information, if legally necessary, against any one or more of its citizens.[26] Likewise, a freedman could not cite, that is, summon, his former master, for the purpose of a legal action; but a slave set free by a city could bring action against any individual member of the city, since the former slave was not the freedman of any individual citizen.[27]

A municipal corporation could also get title to property by usucapio,[28] that is, long time possession, like unto our adverse possession. It could also be the owner of the use, or usufruct, of property.[29] A usufruct is the right to enjoy the use, income, or produce of the property of another without impairment of the substance.[30] It could be created by means of a legacy.[31] It is in connection with a municipal corporation's capacity to be the legatee of a usufruct that the doctrine of such a corporation's possible immortality is raised. The Digest, quoting from Gaius, says that there was a question formerly whether a municipal corporation should be permitted to be the beneficiary of a use since there was a danger that such use might become perpetual, because it would not be lost by death or by capitis deminutio. To put such a question at rest,

25. Dig. 48, 18, 1, 7.
26. Dig. 48, 18, 1, 7.
27. Dig. 2, 4, 10, 4.
28. Dig. 41, 2, 2.
29. Dig. 7, 1, 56.
30. Dig. 7, 1, 1.
31. Dig. 7, 1, 3, pr.

Gaius says, further, that the municipality's enjoyment of the use has been limited to a hundred years since such a period of time would be the utmost extent of a human life.[32] Modestinus, however, says, in the Digest,[33] that if a usufruct is bequeathed to a city and later the ground of the city is ploughed up, as in the case of Carthage after its destruction, it ceases to be a city, and consequently loses the usufruct by death. A municipal corporation could also be an "heir" in trust of legacies known as fideicommissa.[34]

The governing body of a municipal corporation was called the curia, an assembly of notables corresponding to the Roman senate. The members of the curia were called decuriones or curiales. The presence of two-thirds of the members of the curia constituted a quorum.[35] The curia was authorized to appoint a general agent or manager, called a syndic (syndicus), also to appoint a special agent known as an actor, particularly in case of bringing lawsuits.[36] In connection with suits against municipalities, the Digest, quoting from Javolenus, says that if a municipality when sued fails to defend the action by the syndic who manages the property, and there is no tangible property that can be levied upon by the judgment creditors, the latter should be permitted to satisfy their judgments out of debts owing to the municipality.[37] The individual members of the municipality are not liable, however, for the corporation's debts, and if an agent (actor) is appointed to institute legal proceedings he is not to be regarded as the agent of any group of individuals but as the agent of the

---

32. Dig. 7, 1, 56.
33. Dig. 7, 4, 21.
34. Dig. 36, 1, 27.
35. Dig. 3, 4, and 4; 50, 1, 19; 50, 9, 2, 3; Code 10, 31, 45.
36. Dig. 3, 4, 1, 1; 3, 4, 2.
37. Dig. 3, 4, 8.

corporation, since he does not appear for the members individually.[38]

In connection with its various transactions, a municipal corporation was regarded the same as a single individual in case of any duress on its part. In other words, an action would lie against it for the restitution of property exacted by intimidation or fear (metus) practiced upon one.[39] As to fraud (dolus), Ulpian was of the opinion that a municipality as a corporation could not be guilty of a fraud. However, he held that if a municipality had received any benefit through the fraud of its agents, an action ought to be allowed against it.[40]

As to private corporations the same general rules of law were recognized as in case of municipal corporations. As already pointed out, they could be created only by the express permission of law, which in imperial days meant the consent of the emperor. Like municipal bodies, they were authorized to hold corporate property, to have corporate funds, and to appoint a syndic or an actor by whose agency the corporate business could be transacted.[41] As in the case of municipal corporations, the agent, if appointed, was the agent of the corporation and not of its members individually or collectively.[42] The business affairs of the corporation were in the hands of its members who were usually called associates, or socii. The property of the corporation belonged, however, to the corporation and not to its individual members.

It required at least three persons to constitute a private corporation,[43] and in the reign of Caracalla it

38. Dig. 3, 4, 2.
39. Dig. 4, 2, 9, 1.
40. Dig. 4, 3, 15, 1.
41. Dig. 3, 4, 1, pr.; 3, 4, 1, 1.
42. Dig. 3, 4, 2.
43. Dig. 50, 16, 85.

became the law that a man could be a member at the same time of but one corporation.[44] The probable explanation of such a law is that it was not deemed politic to give a man too many opportunities for amassing wealth.

A corporation could sue and be sued,[45] buy and sell, and enter into contracts connected with its business. It could also be a legatee in trust under a will.[46] Individual members were not liable for the debts of the corporation.

Since in imperial days labor was mostly performed by slaves, the law permitted private corporations to own slaves.[47] They could also set their slaves free.[48] A corporation slave upon obtaining his freedom was qualified to bring an action, if needs be, against any member of the corporation since he was not the freedman of any individual man in it.[49]

As in the case of a municipality, so a private corporation could be made to restore what it had exacted through duress or fear.[50]

The continuity of a business regardless of the death of some of those interested in it must, even at an early day, have impressed itself as a great economic need upon the thoughts of men engaged in important affairs. The idea of a corporation supplied this need, continuity regardless of changes in the personnel. Ulpian says, in the Digest,[51] that in the case of corporations it matters not whether all the members remain unchanged, or a part are changed, or all are changed.

44. Dig. 47, 22, 1, 2.
45. Dig. 3, 4, 7.
46. Dig. 34, 5, 20; Gaius, 2, 195.
47. Dig. 40, 3, 1.
48. Ib.
49. Dig. 2, 4, 10, 4.
50. Dig. 4, 2, 9, 1.
51. Dig. 3, 4, 7, 2.

Even if a corporation is reduced to one member, it is still a corporation, and the one remaining member can sue and be sued in the name of the corporation. Upon the death, however, of all its members, it would seem, according to Roman Law, that a corporation would be dissolved.[52] A corporation moreover could be dissolved by the state, if its object was found to be illegal or its further existence detrimental to the public interests.[53] Upon the dissolution of a corporation its property was divided among its members.[54]

Lord MacKenzie, in his Studies in Roman Law, says:[55] "Besides the corporations where several individuals are united into one body, and which in England are called corporations aggregate, the Romans recognized another class of artificial persons as capable of rights and obligations, bearing some resemblance to the corporation sole of the English Law. Of this description were the state itself; the prince, in so far as he was regarded as the depository of sovereign power; every public office, considered with reference to the rights and duties attached to it; the public treasury or fisc; and, finally, the inheritance of a deceased person (hereditas jacens), so long as it was not taken up by anyone as heir."

The learned judge of the Scottish Court of Session meant that such groupings of rights and obligations around an abstract idea were merely like unto corporations, since they were not, in fact, corporations under the Roman Law. That system did not recognize the existence of a corporation sole.[56] It is true, however, that the State, that is, Rome, or the Roman peo-

52. Dig. 7, 4, 21.
53. Dig. 47, 22, 3, pr. and 1.
54. Dig. 47, 22, 3 pr.
55. Studies in Rom. Law, 7th Ed. p. 162.
56. See Blk. Com. I, 469.

ple, might be an owner and could exercise the rights of an owner. Public things (res publicae), such as rivers, harbors, public roads, were state property. The title, or ownership, was in the State, the use in the public. There were other things, however, owned by the State, such as the public lands, various state mines, and slaves, over which the State had the rights of a private owner. The State did not own and exercise the rights of ownership, however, as a corporation, that is, as a body created by the State, by itself, but as a sovereign. In the same way, the fiscus, or the public treasury, was treated as an ideal whole, a something having prerogatives and privileges, yet, strictly, it was not a corporation, a universitas. For all practical purposes the fiscus was the State itself. Where the Romans said that certain property belonged to the fiscus, we would say that it belonged to the State. Thus, a lapsed devise or bequest went to the fiscus,[57] also fideicommissa (testamentary trusts) for the benefit of aliens, they being incapacitated to take.[58] Likewise, inheritances forfeited by the misconduct of heirs became fiscal property.[59] The fiscus, however, upon receiving the benefits of a forfeited inheritance, became liable for its obligations.[60]

As to an inheritance (hereditas jacens), or the estate of a deceased person before it has been accepted by one called a voluntary heir, that is, one who may either accept or refuse it, it is true that some writers call it a person, or a juristic person, following the language of the Digest that an inheritance like unto a municipium or a decurio or a societas is regarded in the light of a person (hereditas personae vice fungi-

57. Lex Julia et Papia Poppaea.
58. Gaius, 2, 286.
59. Dig. 34, 9, 5, 6; 34, 9, 5, 19.
60. Dig. 34, 9, 5, 4; 30, 50, 2.

tur, sicuti municipium et decurio et societas.).[61] Such an inheritance might receive new rights and liabilities between the time of the death of the deceased and its vesting in his successor. Roman lawyers thus considered it as being the subject of rights and liabilities, but in no sense of the word was it a "corporation." It would, moreover, seem to be the better opinion that such an inheritance represented for the time being the person of the undetermined heir, and had no personality of its own.[62] It was in the same way that in the later imperial days the Christian Church was spoken of as a person, as a subject of juristic rights. Under the early law there were various collegia of priests connected with Roman temples, and, as previously stated, they were probably the oldest of all such bodies in Rome. These collegia owned property and, after their analogy, the Christian Church was, in turn, looked upon as a subject having capacity of ownership. It was not, however, a corporation. It was particularly in connection with bequests for religious or charitable purposes that the quasi corporate character of the Church, similar to the fiscus, was recognized. Under the old law, such temples as were expressly designated by some statute could be made an heir. In Justinian's time, the Church was a general trustee of charitable gifts. When a testator made a bequest to some particular saint, or archangel, or martyr, as was frequently the case, the church dedicated to such saint or martyr in the place where the testator was domiciled was made the beneficiary; if there was no such church in the place, then the bequest went to the same saint's church in the capital city. If even there no such particular church existed, then it went to the

---

61. Dig. 46, 1, 22; 41, 3, 15, pr.
62. See Dig. 46, 2, 24.

church, irrespective of its patron saint, of the testator's residence.[63] In many a will, property was given to "Jesus Christ." Justinian declared that in such cases the bequest should go to the church where the testator lived.[64]

It was sufficient for a donor to make a mere declaration of a charitable gift, either by way of transfer inter vivos or by a will. In such cases, the church managed the property through the agency of its bishop or other official. Such benefactions for the cause of religion, the relief of the poor, the encouragement of education, and the promotion of charitable objects in general, were known as piae causae.[65] Such charitable gifts are sometimes spoken of as "subjects of rights," and as "persons," and even as "corporations." They were, however, foundations, created by their donors and administered by the Church. They were like unto our own modern "charities" or public trusts. In fact, our law pertaining to charities is derived from the Roman Law,[66] and the supreme court of the United States has said the whole English system of charitable donations was borrowed from the Roman Law, and copied almost verbatim into the Common Law writers.[67]

As already stated, the idea of a corporation in modern Civil Law countries is based upon the fundamental doctrines of the Roman Law.[68] The Quebec Civil

63. Codex 1, 2, 25 (26), 1.

64. Codex 1, 2, 25 (26), pr.

65. See, in general, Codex 1, 3; Novel 120.

66. Church of Jesus Christ v. U. S., 136 U. S. 1; Fordyce v. Woman's Christian Nat. Library Ass'n. 79 Ark. 550, 96 S. W. 155; Klumpert v. Vrieland, 142 Iowa, 434, 121 N. W. 34; Jackson v. Phillips, 14 Allen (Mass.) 539; Buchanan v. Kennard, 234 Mo. 117, 135 S. W. 415; White v. White, 1 Bro. Ch. 12, 28 Reprint, 955.

67. Inglis v. Trustees, etc. 3 Pet. (U. S.) 140.

68. See Spain, C. C. art. 35-39; Cuba, C. C. art. 35-39; Mexico, C. C. art. 38-42; Germany, C. C. art. 21 et seq.; Louisiana, Rev. C. C. art. 427-447; Quebec, C. C. art. 352-373; Switzerland, C. C. art. 52-89.

Code, for example, defines a corporation as "an artificial or ideal person whose existence and succession are perpetual, or sometimes for a fixed period only, and which is capable of enjoying certain rights and liable to certain obligations." [69] Louisiana defines a corporation as "an intellectual [70] body, created by law, composed of individuals united under a common name, the members of which succeed each other, so that the body continues always the same, notwithstanding the change of the individuals which compose it, and which, for certain purposes, is considered as a natural person." [71] Further the same code says that "corporations legally established are substituted for persons, and their union which renders common to all those who compose them, their interests, their rights and privileges, is the reason why they are considered *as one single whole.*" [72]

The civil codes, as a rule, lay down only fundamental conceptions regarding corporations. In many Civil Law countries the general law governing corporations will be found in the commercial codes. In Louisiana it is found in special statutory provisions. The constitution of that state, as in many other American states, provides that the legislature shall enact a general law for the creation of corporations. There are statutes regulating the formation, rights, duties, and liabilities of corporations organized for literary, scientific, religious, and charitable purposes; for the transaction of any kind of legitimate business in general; and for such special kinds of business as banking, insurance, and building and loan associations. In Civil Law countries, as well as in England and this

69. Quebec C. C. art. 352.
70. Meaning, perceptible to the intellect alone, that is, artificial, ideal.
71. Louisiana Rev. C. C. art. 427.
72. Louisiana Rev. C. C. 433. This is an excellent definition of the Roman "universitas."

country in general, corporation law has grown with the advancing needs of modern times until it has everywhere become a special branch of the law. The fundamental principles, however, are common to all these countries and they still preserve the conceptions of the Roman Law.

CHAPTER XI

THE LAW OF PROPERTY

INTRODUCTION, DIVISIONS OF PROPERTY

The law of "things" (res), or, as we say, the law of property, is, in Roman Law, a very broad subject, comprising, according to Gaius,[1] the law of all matters not included in persons or actions. It deals with the divisions or classifications of property; with titles, including the acquisition of one's own property, and also of rights in the property of others; with the law of wills, legacies, fiduciary bequests, intestacy, and descent. In addition, it includes personal rights in property or rights arising from obligations, namely, contracts, quasi contracts, delicts, and quasi delicts.

It will thus be seen that the law of "things" in Roman Law covers a much wider range than the law of property in our own system of law. The Institutes of Gaius make a three-fold division of the law, persons, things, and actions.[2] The first of his four books is devoted to persons, the second and third to "things," and the fourth to actions. The Institutes of Justinian follow this same division,[3] the first book treating of persons, the second, third, and a part of the fourth dealing with "things," the remaining part of the fourth book being given to the consideration of actions.

The treatment of the law of property, or "things," in these elementary works of Gaius and Justinian seems unscientific, cumbersome, and even confusing.

1. Gaius, 1, 8.
2. Gaius, 1, 8.
3. Inst. 1, 3, pr.

However, property law among the Romans was very slowly developed, the simple notions of the early days becoming more and more complicated in the progress of the centuries. Long before the time of Gaius the legal conceptions and theories of "things," or property, had been greatly influenced by the forms of actions, and "things" that were the subjects of property, or of ownership, were associated with rights in property, whether rights in one's own property (jura in re sua) or in property belonging to another (jura in re aliena).

The name given in general to all sorts of property and to property rights was "res." The term as thus used has no precise equivalent in our law. It is a broader term than our word "property" despite the fact that we employ the word "property" to designate both the subject matter, whether corporeal or incorporeal, of ownership, such as lands, tenements, hereditaments, goods, chattels, patent-rights, and rights of user, and also to designate any other valuable right or interest that one may possess or to which he has a legal claim. However, "res" in the Roman Law is applied, at times, to things not capable of being owned. It is also broader than our word "thing" as commonly used, since to us the word "thing" usually conveys the meaning of something corporeal or material. However, in a wider sense, the word "thing" may represent, in our language, an incorporeal right, an object of thought, an abstract idea, a status, and it was with a similarly broad significance that the word "res" was often used in Roman Law.

In English Law from very early times the word "goods" has been both colloquially and legally employed to designate practically all kinds of personal property. While there have been some critical distinctions made between "goods," "wares," and "merchandise," and while "goods" is not entirely identical with personal property, money, for instance, not being embraced within the term, yet it substantially includes all chattels personal. In the same way, among the Romans, "bona," i. e., good or beneficial things, was popularly applied to all kinds of property. It was not limited, like our word "goods," to personal property but included land as well as chattels. In an early Massachusetts case,[4] it is said, " 'Bona,' as used in the Civil Law, is almost as extensive as personal property itself." As a matter of fact, it is more extensive than personal property, since it covers all sorts of property, both movable and immovable. It is from this term, "bona," that a number of modern Civil Law countries have derived their legal term for property in general.[5]

The popular use of the word "bona" among the Romans developed into a legal term under the praetorian law, or the law of the jus gentium. In cases before his court the praetor used the word to designate both movable and immovable things.

In our own modern law, property is classified either as real property or personal property. These terms are unknown to the Roman Law, and have been in use in English Law for only about three hundred years. They were hardly known when the Jamestown and Plymouth colonies were planted in this country. The older writers upon English law spoke of "lands, tenements, and hereditaments" instead of real property, and of "goods and chattels" instead of personal property.

4. Tisdale v. Harris, 20 Pick. 9, 13.
5. France, C. C. art. 516, "All property (Tous les biens) is either movable or immovable." In the Italian Code the word is "beni;" in the Spanish, "bienes." "The term 'bienes' appears to be of comprehensive import, and includes all things, not being persons, which may serve for the uses of man." Larkin v. U. S., 14 Fed. Cas. No. 8,091. The Louisiana Code retains the word "things." The Quebec Code employs the word "property."

It is somewhat curious that, although the terms "real" property and "personal" property are not Roman Law terms, they, nevertheless, have come to us indirectly through the Roman Law. They arose out of the use of the so-called "real actions" and "personal actions" in the English Common Law courts. The descriptive names of these actions were transferred to the property with which they were usually associated. Real actions came to mean, in time, actions affording remedies for the recovery of land, while personal actions were actions for damages. The former actions were called "real" because they were said to be enforceable against the res, the land; the latter being called personal since they were brought against the person. Even though certain personal actions, such as detinue and replevin, were employed to recover, specifically, goods and chattels, and so, logically, might have been regarded as "real" actions since their object was the recovery of a thing, the res, yet since in such actions a defendant, if judgment were against him, might compensate the plaintiff in a money payment instead of returning the chattel in question, the name "personal" was applied to them.

The terms real actions and personal actions were coined by the English jurists from the Roman Law terms "actiones in rem" and "actiones in personam." Bracton seems to be the first English writer to employ these terms.[6] In the Roman Law an actio in rem was brought when the plaintiff desired to assert his ownership of, or title to, a "res." Such an action might be founded upon a claim of ownership of some corporeal thing, or upon an alleged particular right in a thing, such as a right of use or usufruct of the property of another,[7] or upon a right growing out of a legal status, such as paternal power, or a claim of being a

6. Lib. 3, cap. 3, par. 1, fol. 101 b.
7. Gaius, 4, 3.

free man instead of a slave. An action in rem could be brought to establish ownership to a chattel as well as to a piece of land. This, of course, was quite different from the English notion of a real action.

As previously stated, the word res was applied to anything that could be the object of rights, proprietary rights whether corporeal or incorporeal. Whether a plaintiff in a Roman action was claiming a corporeal thing (res), movable or immovable, or whether he was claiming an incorporeal right (also res), his action was an action in rem. In such an action there was no particular defendant. In fact, no defendant was named. It was a remedy to establish a right against everybody, and enforceable against everybody.

On the other hand, in an action in personam, the action was brought against a person, and the person, or defendant, was expressly named. It was an action to force such person to make amends for some breach of duty he owed to the plaintiff. It was an action arising out of an obligatory right possessed by the plaintiff, in which action he sought to compel the defendant, owing to the latter's tort or breach of contract, to make some sort of satisfaction for his wrong.[8]

The English writers who transferred these terms, actiones in rem and actiones in personam, from the Roman Law to the English Law did not, however, employ them in the same sense as did the Roman lawyers. "Actiones in rem" was translated "real actions," and "actiones in personam" "personal actions." In time, "real actions" came to mean nothing more than actions for the specific recovery of land, while personal actions were actions for damages. Actions were said to sound in the realty or in the personalty. The result was that it became the common practice among English lawyers to speak of "lands, tenements, and heredit-

8. Gaius, 4, 2.

aments" as "real property" and of "goods and chattels" as "personal property." Leasehold interests, or terms for years, were not, originally, specifically recoverable, and they were, consequently, classed as "chattels" or "personal property." [9]

English lawyers applied the names "real" and "personal" to property, but medieval commentators upon Roman Law called rights protected by such actions "real rights" and "personal rights." A "real right" was said to be a right maintainable against all persons unlawfully dealing with or disturbing the "res" of another whether the subject of a right or the right itself. A "real right" thus came to mean a right which a Roman lawyer used to say could be "vindicated" against any one, vindicatio rei being the remedy whereby the owner of property (res) enforced his right against anyone violating it.

Between the doctrines of the Roman Law and of our Common Law relating to property there is a greater difference than between any other doctrines of these systems. One of the most striking features in our law of property is the distinction made between the law of real property and the law of personal property. In no other legal system is there such a wide divergence of principles in property law. In Mohammedan Law, no distinction is made between the law of movable and immovable property. Both kinds of property are governed by the same rules. "In the eye of that law the sale, hire, pledge, and devolution of a piece of land are subject to exactly the same incidents as the sale, hire, pledge, and devolution of a piece of cloth." [10] The same thing is substantially true in the Civil Law. As said in an early case by the supreme court of Texas, referring to the Civil Law formerly

9. See Gaius, 4, 3; Inst. 2, 2; 4, 6, 1; P. & M. Hist. II, 46 et seq.; Reeves' Hist. Com. Law (Finalson ed.), p. 336, notes; 4 L. Q. R. 394.
10. 26 L. Q. R. 24 (1909).

in force there: "The difference in the rule of the Common Law between land and personal property never had existence in this country. . . . These distinctions are unknown to the Civil Law as it prevailed under Spanish modification in Texas; land here was thought to be of comparatively little value, and many a fine league has been transmitted with as little form and ceremony by our early colonists, as would attend the sale of an Indian pony."[11]

There is no distinction in Roman Law between the inheritance of lands and of things that we call personal; there is no preference of males to females as in the English canons of descent; and land may be transferred orally in the same way as may a movable. Roman Law knows nothing of our technical tenures, seizin, and estates. Fee simple, fee tail, curtesy, dower, contingent remainders, executory devises, and conditional limitations are terms of which a Roman lawyer never heard.[11½] Yet, despite all this, there are similarities in a number of matters in the Roman and the English Law of property, and some principles of the Roman Law of things have been engrafted upon our real property law.

Many of the differences in our law of real and personal property are explained in part by the fact that much of our land law was derived from the feudal system, and from the even older Anglo-Saxon law, while our law of personal property has been largely derived from the law merchant. This, however, does not tell the whole story because not a few doctrines of our real property law which differ from those of personal property owe their origin to the influence of the ancient forms of Common Law actions.[12]

In this connection it is interesting to find another

---

11. Thompson v. Duncan, 1 Tex. 485, 488.
11½. Cf. Wemple v. Nabors Oil & Gas Co. 154 La. 483, 97 So. 666.
12. Burdick, Real Prop. p. 9.

link between the Roman and the English Law. The law merchant (lex mercatoria) which influenced in many ways the development of our personal property law was itself largely derived from the Civil Law.[13] Even the feudal law of England, brought there from France by William of Normandy, was not entirely free from Roman Law influence. The very term "feud" seems to be equivalent to the Roman "beneficium," otherwise known as a precarious benefice. A precarium in the Roman law was something granted merely during the will of the grantor. From the precarium was developed in the continental feudal law the beneficium, or an estate upon a conditional tenure. In fact, during the decadent years of the Roman Empire, social conditions were practically feudal.[14] "The system of feudation may, after all," says an English writer,[15] "be derived from the Roman custom of patron and client. At any rate the similarity is striking."

By the Roman and later civilian jurists res or things were divided or classified in various ways, depending either upon their own nature or upon their legal character. Accordingly, we find such natural divisions as things movable and things immovable; things divisible and things indivisible; things consumable and things inconsumable; things considered as a class and things considered specifically; things principal and things accessory. With reference to their legal character, some things are the subjects of property or of property rights, or, in other words, can be reduced to ownership (dominium). Other things cannot be so reduced. Accordingly, the Roman Law further classified things as things which are subject

---

13. "The law of merchants is jus gentium and the judges are bound to take notice of it."—Mogadara v. Holt, Shower (K. B.) 318 (1691).

14. De Coulanges, Les Origines du Système Féodale, p. 206 et seq.

15. Colquhoun, Civil Law, Sec. 124.

to ownership, and things which are not capable of personal ownership, or things which enter into commerce and things which are not in commerce. Things were also divided into things corporeal and things incorporeal.[16]

Gaius says that all things are divided into two main classes, things which are "in our patrimony" and things which are not.[17] Justinian, likewise, in his Institutes,[18] uses the same words. By patrimony is meant private ownership, dominion. It is, therefore, the same as saying that some things are subject to individual ownership and some are not, or, as the Romans otherwise expressed it, in commercio and extra commercium, signifying, respectively, within the law of buying and selling, and not within or subject to such law.

Things are also divided, says Gaius,[19] into things that are subject to divine law and things that are subject to human law. The former consist of "sacred" (sacrae) and religious (religiosae) things.[20] Holy (sanctae) things, such as the walls and gates of a city, also partake of the nature of divine things.[21] Things within the divine law cannot be made the subject of human ownership.[22] Things subject to human law are either public or private.[23] Public things cannot be individually owned since they necessarily belong to all the members of a group who constitute one body, that is, a corporation (universitas), but private things may be made the property of individuals.[24] Gaius further

16. Gaius, 2, 12; Inst. 2, 2, pr.; Dig. 1, 8, 1, 1.
17. Gaius, 2, 1.
18. Inst. 2, 1, pr.
19. Gaius, 2, 2; Dig. 1, 8, 1.
20. Gaius, 2, 3.
21. Gaius, 2, 8.
22. Gaius, 2, 9.
23. Gaius, 2, 10.
24. Gaius, 2, 11.

[Roman Law]

says that things are also either corporeal or incorporeal,[25] and again may be classed either as mancible or not mancible.[26]

The Institutes of Justinian follow substantially the classifications mentioned by Gaius. Most things, he says, are subject to individual ownership,[27] but some things cannot be so owned. "These latter things consist of things that belong to all men in common (res communes); of things that belong to the state (res publicae); of things that belong to a corporation (res universitatis); and of things that belong to no one (res nullius)".[28]

Justinian also classifies things as corporeal or incorporeal.[29] The distinction mentioned by Gaius between mancible things (res mancipi) and things not mancible (res nec mancipi) is not mentioned by Justinian since it was obsolete in his day.

Things that are common to all men are illustrated by the air, running water, the sea, and the shore of the sea.[30]

Public property is represented by rivers, harbors, and public roads.[31] They differ from res communes in that they belong to the Roman people. Common things have no owner, but public things belong to a people, a state, the use being in the public at large. The State could also be the owner of property that was not classed as public property, but as private property, or property in commercio. Over such property, as, for example, the public lands, public mines, public slaves, the State had all the rights of a private owner.

25. Gaius, 2, 12.
26. Gaius, 2, 14 a.
27. Inst. 2, 1, pr.; see also Dig. 1, 8, 2.
28. Inst. 2, 1, pr.
29. Inst. 2, 2, pr.
30. Inst. 2, 1, 1; Dig. 1, 8, 2.
31. Inst. 2, 1, 2–5; Dig. 1, 8, 4, 1.

Res universitatis, or property of a corporation, has been previously considered.[32] In case of a municipal corporation, its property such as theatres and stadia is public property, after the analogy of the public property of a state. However, a corporation may also own private property, such as lands and slaves,[33] as previously stated.

The term res universitatis is used in the sense of municipal property the use of which is in the public. In contrast, the things belonging to individuals are known as res singulorum.[34]

Things that are beyond the domain of human law, since they are subject to the divine law only, are the things that are classified as sacred, religious, and holy.[35]

Although things that are within the domain of human law are usually the property of some particular owner (res alicujus), yet such a thing may be no man's property (res nullius).[36] Thus, wild animals (ferae naturae), wild birds, fishes, bees, pebbles, gems and other things lying unclaimed upon the seashore, as long as they are not appropriated and reduced to one's possession are res nullius. However, such things when captured, tamed, or reclaimed became res alicujus.[37]

A thing that comes under the divine law can, of course, be owned by no one.[38] Hence sacred, religious, and holy things are said to be res nullius.[39]

32. See preceding chapter.
33. See preceding chapter, Corporations.
34. Inst. 2, 1, 6.
35. Inst. 2, 1, 7.
36. Dig. 1, 8, 1, pr.
37. Dig. 1, 8, 3; Inst. 2, 1, 12.
38. Dig. 1, 8, 6, 2.
39. Inst. 2, 1, 7; Dig. 1, 8, 6–11.

Sacred things[39½] are things which have been consecrated by public authority, such as temples and offerings dedicated to the service of God. They cannot be created by individual act, for one cannot legally make a thing or a place "sacred" by private authority. Sacred places may exist either in a city or in the country. Such places are always open to the public. Statues may thus be set up in public places and be officially declared sacred. If a temple is once consecrated, the place on which it stood remains sacred even though the temple may have been destroyed.

Religious things[40] are things that are devoted to the dead, such as tombs and other places consecrated for burial purposes. A place or thing may be made religious by a merely private act, as, for example, the burial of a human body in one's own ground, or in the ground of another providing it be done with the owner's consent; or with the subsequent satisfaction of the owner. Even an empty tomb is a religious thing.

Holy things[41] (Sanctae Res) are things that should be defended against human wrong or injury, such as the walls and gates of a city. One who trespasses against a city's walls is punishable with death, as, for example, where one without public authority, climbs over the walls by a ladder or other means. The walls of a city cannot be repaired without the consent of the emperor, or the praeses in case of a province, the praeses being a proconsul, an imperial legate, or a provincial governor. Roman citizens may lawfully leave the city only by passing through the gates. Any other way is the act of an enemy. Romulus slew even his brother Remus because he sought to climb over the wall.[42]

39½. Dig. 1, 8, 6; 1, 8, 9; Inst. 2, 1, 7-8.
40. Inst. 2, 1, 9; Dig. 1, 8, 6, 4.
41. Dig. 1, 8, 8; Inst. 2, 1, 10.
42. Dig. 1, 8, 11; 1, 18, 1.

The foregoing classification of property as set forth by Justinian may be tabulated as follows:

A. Res in Patrimonio (or in Commercio)
B. Res Extra Patrimonium (or Extra Commercium)
   a. Res Communes
   b. Res Publicae
   c. Res Divini Juris
      1. Res Sacrae
      2. Res Religiosae
      3. Res Sanctae

The Institutes of Justinian, after dealing with the division of things into things capable of private ownership and things not capable of such ownership, thereupon make another division of things into things corporeal and things incorporeal.[43] The same division is made likewise by Gaius.[44]

Corporeal things are tangible things, things discernible by the physical senses, such as land, a slave, a garment, gold, silver, and innumerable other things.[45] Incorporeal things are intangible. They exist merely in contemplation of law. They are legal rights, such as an inheritance, a usufruct, a use, or any sort of an obligation.[46] For although inheritance, usufruct, and obligations have to do with things corporeal, yet the rights they represent are incorporeal. The same is true of rights connected with houses and land, rights known as servitudes.[47]

Such an interpretation of incorporeal things shows why the law of "things," or property, is so much broader in Roman Law than in our own law. It includes not only property in its ordinary sense, but also

43. Inst. 2, 2, pr.
44. Gaius, 2, 12.
45. Inst. 2, 2, 1–2; Gaius, 2, 14.
46. Ib.
47. Ib.

all rights in property, including obligations, that is contracts and delicts (torts). Such a classification of property is a joinder of the objects of rights with rights themselves. Under the Roman classification not only are such "things" property, or "res," as are usually designated property by us, but also servitudes, both praedial and personal; likewise rights of emphyteusis, superficies, and pignus; and, in addition, rights arising either from contract or delict. In one sense, such rights are indeed "property," but they are rather a classification of various rights, rather than a classification of "things." However, after all, it would seem that from the point of view of the Roman jurists themselves the whole law of "res" was, instead of the law of "things" as ordinarily understood by us, the law of "rights." In other words, under "corporeal things" they considered the right of ownership, or the right of dominium in one's own property, and under "incorporeal things" they discussed rights in the property of another, jura in re aliena.

In this connection it is interesting to note that Bracton, the first known writer upon the laws of England, follows the division of things as laid down by Gaius and the Institutes. As has been truly said:[48] "Bracton follows his Roman models in his commentary on the general doctrines relating to things and rights concerning them. He does so especially in regard to the division of things, and the terminology of the Corpus Juris, which he has adopted in his Chapter (Lib. I, Chap. 12) De Rerum Divisione has since remained fixed in the English Law."

In the chapter above referred to, Bracton makes three divisions of things. The first division is into "things that are within our patrimony and things that are beyond it." The second division is into things corporeal and incorporeal. The third division is based

---

48. Güterbock, 85.

upon the nature of the ownership, some things being common, others public, others belonging to corporations, others belonging to no one, and others belonging to individuals. These divisions, it will be observed, are taken from the Roman jurists.

The terms "incorporeal property," "incorporeal rights," and "incorporeal hereditaments" are familiar in our own law. The older writers often speak of "incorporeal hereditaments," meaning inheritable rights not of a corporeal nature but connected with and arising out of corporeal inheritances.[49] Blackstone mentions ten kinds of incorporeal hereditaments, advowsons, titles, commons, ways, offices, dignities, franchises, corodies or pensions, annuities, and rents.[50] In this country, at the present time, incorporeal rights are usually classified as consisting of easements, profits a prendre, rents, and franchises.

Incorporeal property in our law has been defined as "a right issuing out of or annexed to a thing corporeal, and consists of the right to have some part only of the produce or benefit of the corporeal property, or to exercise a right or have an easement or privilege or advantage over or out of it."[51]

Mancible and Non-Mancible Things:

A third division of things set forth by Gaius,[52] but ignored by Justinian since such a classification was obsolete in his day, was things mancible (res mancipi), and things not mancible (res nec mancipi). It was a division of property under the old law, the jus civile, depending upon the mode of the transfer of its title, a subdivision of things that were capable of private ownership. The terms were derived from the word mancipatio, the ancient legal formality required for

49. Burdick, Real Property, 21.
50. II Com. 20.
51. Nellis v. Munson, 108 N. Y. 453, 458, 14 N. E. 939.
52. Gaius, 2, 14 a.

transferring title or ownership in the ordinary farm property of a primitive Roman.

Mancipatio (from manus and capio) means, literally, to take in the hand, to take into one's possession, or power. In ancient Roman days the only method by which important kinds of property could be legally transferred from seller to buyer was by a ceremony in which the buyer literally took hold of the property, laid his hand upon it, and declared it to be his own. In some ways it was analogous to the ceremony of livery of seizin in old English law.

In mancipatio, the two parties to the transaction were present, also at least five witnesses above the age of puberty, likewise an official money weigher known as the libripens. In early days, before the coinage of money, a purchase price was a weight of metal, usually native copper. The libripens having weighed the agreed price, the buyer thereupon placed his hand upon the subject matter of the sale, upon the earth if he were buying land, or holding a bit of the soil in his hand, declaring in formal words that he was its owner, and that he had bought it "per aes et libram," with money and scales. He then struck the scales with a piece of the money (the copper) and handed it to the vendor.[53] This completed the transaction. There was no writing. The five witnesses were there to establish the fact of the transfer should their testimony ever be needed.

In time, things or property, that required this ceremony of mancipatio to effect their transfer were known as res mancipi, while other things not requiring any such formality for their transfer were called res nec mancipi. These latter things were bought and sold by mere delivery. Originally the actual price was carefully weighed. In later days when coined money came into use, the same ceremony was followed although

---

53. Gaius, 1, 119.

the real payment was a separate matter. The piece of money that was then weighed was merely a symbol of the price.

This somewhat cumbersome ceremony was the only way in which important property, such as Italian lands, buildings, slaves, oxen, horses, and mules, and land servitudes could be bought.[54] It was strictly limited to Roman citizens, and, therefore, res mancipi could not be purchased, under the old law, by aliens. This classification of property was unknown, however, in Justinian's time, since it had long been obsolete, having been developed when the Romans were a purely agricultural people.

Immovable and Movable Things:

Another natural division of corporeal things, although such a classification seems to have developed very slowly in Roman Law,[55] was things immovable and things movable, res immobiles and res mobiles. Under the jus gentium the terms bona immobilia and bona mobilia were employed.[56] The word "bona" (goods), as already stated, was a general term for property, not being limited to movable property.

Immovable things included land,[57] its natural productions, and permanent structures erected upon land, such, for example, as buildings,[58] trees,[59] and fruit hanging upon their trees.[60] Corporeal things which from their nature are not stationary and, therefore, can be carried away, including animals which move themselves,[61] are movable.

The generic word for land in Roman Law is solum.

54. Ulpian, tit. 19, § 1
55. Maine, Anc. Law, p. 265.
56. Penniman v. French, 17 Pick. (Mass.) 404, 405.
57. Dig. 43, 16, 1, 3 & 4 & 6; Dig. 43, 16, 3, 15; Dig. 7, 9, 1, 1.
58. Dig. 9, 2, 50; Dig. 41, 1, 7, 10; Dig. 44, 7, 44, 1.
59. Dig. 19, 1, 40.
60. Dig. 6, 1, 44.
61. Dig. 50, 16, 93.

It included, as with us, all things naturally a part of it or made a part of it. A piece of land, such as a farm in the country, or a lot in the city, was called praedium (plural praedia).[62] In connection with servitudes, or easements, the terms praedia rustica and praedia urbana, meaning rural lands and town lands, were commonly used.[63] The word fundus was also employed to designate land, especially land without buildings upon it,[64] although it was also used at times synonymously with praedium.[65] A particular place (locus) with no building upon it was called "area" (lot) if in a city, "ager" if in the country. A city building was called "aedes," a country building "villa." [66]

Things Divisible and Indivisible:

Roman lawyers also spoke of things as being either divisible or indivisible. From their very nature some things are divisible without destroying or diminishing their value, while other things cannot be so divided. Land, for example, may be divided into smaller parts; also wine and grain. A thing, however, which depends upon its unity, or individuality, such as a horse, a slave, a house, or a book is called an indivisible thing. However, whether a thing be naturally divisible or not, yet it may be considered by the law to be divisible so far as it is owned by two or more persons. Such phrases in our own law as "an undivided interest," "an undivided half," "ownership in common," when speaking of land, are found in the Roman Law phrases pro indiviso habere, communem habere. In case two or more owned an immovable in definite parts, they were said possidere rem pro diviso.[67]

62. Dig. 50, 16, 115.
63. Dig. 50, 16, 198. Cf. Dig. 20, 2, 4, 1.
64. Gaius, 2, 42; Ulpian, 19, 1; Inst. 2, 4, 2.
65. Dig. 50, 16, 60 and 115 and 211.
66. Dig. 50, 16, 211.
67. Dig. 6, 1, 8; 10, 3; 27, 9, 5, 16; 41, 1, 29.

Things were further designated as consumable or inconsumable, consumable things being such that their very value depends upon their consumption, such as oil, food, and wine. Other things which may be put to a natural and proper use, and yet kept in their entirety, such as a horse, books, household furniture, and the like, are called inconsumable. The distinction is convenient at times in connection with the doctrine of usufruct, since there can be no "use" of a consumable thing. A usufructuary or the beneficiary of a "use," is required to use the property in question so that the substance of it shall not be impaired.[68] From their very nature, consumable things are limited to movables. This ancient classification of things into consumable and non-consumable is preserved in some modern civil codes.[69]

Things Fungible and Non-Fungible:

Things are also frequently mentioned as being of a class, a genus, in distinction from other things which are mentioned specifically, or, as otherwise said, in specie. One may have a legal duty (an obligation) to perform which may be fulfilled by the delivery of a thing that answers to the class or genus to which the thing in question belongs, or the obligation may be to deliver a particular, a specific thing. Thus, it may be my duty to deliver to you, on a certain date, ten thousand bushels of wheat of a certain grade. This obligation I may perform by delivering to you any such ten thousand bushels, without regard to the particular ten thousand bushels. Had I a million bushels of such wheat, any ten thousand bushels of that entire quantity would satisfy the legal requirement. On the other hand, I might be required to deliver to you a certain horse which we have agreed upon and designated

---

68. See Dig. 7, 5.
69. See, for example, Spanish Civil Code, art. 337; German Civil Code (Wang), art. 92; Austrian Civil Code, art. 291.

as the subject matter of our transaction. It is my duty to deliver to you that particular horse; no other horse can take its place. Things are of the former class, that is, are intended to be understood generically, when they are estimated or valued merely by number, weight, or measure, that is, when obligations connected with such things can be discharged or performed by furnishing the required number, or weight, or measure of units of the same general class.[70]

The medieval writers upon the Civil Law gave the name res fungibiles to things designated by class or genus, and the name res non-fungibiles to things designated by species.[71] Since then the terms are frequently met with in the works of modern writers. These coined phrases are not very happy ones, but they seem to be firmly embedded in modern books upon the Roman Law.

The terms are particularly employed in connection with what are called "loans for consumption," or "loans" where the ownership of the thing loaned passes, a transaction known in Roman law as "mutuum" because as a result, says Gaius, "meum becomes tuum."[72] When such a loan is made, it is repaid not by the return of the identical thing loaned, but by the delivery of its equivalent, another thing of the same nature which is of the same weight, number, or measure, as, for example, where money, wine, oil, grain, copper, silver, or gold is loaned for consumption.[73] Such things are called res fungibiles,[74] or payable, or dischargeable things, that is, things that legally may be substituted to pay or to discharge an obligation.

70. Inst. 3, 14, pr.; Gaius, 3, 90.
71. The term is said to have been first used by the German jurist Zase, in the sixteenth century. Mackenzie, Rom. Law, 7th ed., p. 276, note.
72. Gaius, 3, 90.
73. Ib.
74. From fungi to discharge, to take the place of.

Things that cannot be so used are called res nec fungibiles, or things not fungible. A thing is fungible when an obligation in connection with it can be discharged or performed by the substitution of an equal number, or weight, or measure, of units of the same class.[75] If an obligation can be met only by giving a thing in specie, or an identical thing, then the property in question is non-fungible. In connection with the sale of fungible things the risk remains with the seller until they are weighed, numbered, or measured, or definitely appropriated to the contract.[76] Fungible things, however, can be sold in bulk (per aversionem), in which case, of course, the risk passes without any weighing or measuring.[77]

In modern civil codes, loans for consumption are sometimes called simple loans in distinction from a loan in specie which is called commodatum. The codes generally provide that a person who receives money or any other thing which is consumed by the use is under obligation to return to the creditor an equal amount of the same kind and quality.[78]

It should be noted that under our law, a delivery of goods for consumption, called by the Romans a loan, a mutuum, is at times called by our courts a sale instead of a bailment, since the specific property delivered is not to be returned, but only property of like kind. In such a case, the title of the original property passes to the one receiving it.[79] Technically, of course, since there is no money price in such a transaction, its nature is, in English Law, a barter rather

75. See Arnott v. Kansas Pac. Ry. Co., 19 Kan. 95.

76. Dig. 18, 1, 35, 5; 18, 1, 35, 7.

77. Dig. 18, 1, 62, 2; 18, 6, 1; 18, 6, 4, 2.

78. French Civil Code, art. 1892-1904; Spanish Civil Code, art. 1740-1757; Louisiana Civil Code, art. 2910-2922.

79. Rahilly v. Wilson, 20 Fed. Cas. No. 11,532; Caldwell v. Hall, 60 Miss. 330, 44 Am. Rep. 410.

than a sale, simply an exchange of goods for other goods of a like kind.

Fungible things are often confused with consumable things, the two terms being used by some identically.[80] They are also said by some to be limited to movable things, as is the fact in the case of consumable things. The German Civil Code, for example, defines fungible things as "movable things which are determined by number, weight, or measure." [81]

Fungible things, however, are things whose generic rather than specific character is designated. Their consumable character is only an incident. The distinction between fungible and non-fungible things is not limited to movable things, since immovable things may be treated as fungible, as where, for example, A devises to B one of several houses of a similar kind.[82] Judge Saunders in his "Lectures on the Civil Code of Louisiana" moreover says: "It is not necessary that a thing should be consumed in order that it should be fungible. A spade or a hoe, or any other implement of which thousands are made of the same size and quality is regarded as fungible, and the borrower of a hoe or spade may return not the one he borrowed but any other one of the same size and kind."[83] The soundness of this illustration may, however, be questioned. While usually in such cases the lender would suffer no financial loss since he is put in statu quo, yet a lender may attach a personal or sentimental value to an article and the return to him of another similar article "of the same size and quality" might be far from satisfactory to him. In such a case the lender by proper action could compel the restoration of the original article if retained by the borrower.

80. It is so under some of the modern civil codes. For example, Spain, art. 337; Cal. art. 663; Chile, art. 575.
81. Art. 91, Wang's Eng. Trans.
82. Mackeldey, Rom. Law, Dropsie's Trans., Phil. 1863, p. 142.
83. Lectures on the Civil Code, 1925, p. 153.

THINGS PRESENT AND THINGS FUTURE:

Things may also be designated as things present or existing (res existentes) and things future (res futurae). This latter classification refers to things which have not yet come into existence, but are expected or even hoped for, such as growing crops, the birth of a slave, increase of flocks and herds. Future things may, according to Roman Law, be proper subjects of mortgage or sale.[84] A contract to buy a free man, in case he should ever be a slave, was not valid, however, since it was not lawful to anticipate a thing like that.[85]

Things Principal and Things Accessory:

Principal and accessory things constitute an important division of things, since accessory things followed the ownership of principal things. A principal thing is the main thing, the self-existing thing, the independent thing. An accessory thing is a thing that is connected with a principal thing, a dependent, a subordinate thing. One buys a farm, for example; the farm is the principal thing, but there may be many things accessory to it that would pass to the buyer in connection with the farm. In our law we would call some of such things appurtenances, others we would call fixtures, but in the Civil Law the doctrine of accessory things, including title or ownership by accession, covers a wider field than do our doctrines of appurtenances and fixtures.

Single and Collective Things:

Things may also be distinguished as single or collective, the latter meaning things considered regardless of their number, as, for example, a flock of sheep, a herd of cattle, an inheritance. Things designated as single things were called res singulares or res singu-

[84]. Dig. 20, 1, 15, pr.; 20, 4, 11, 3; 18, 1, 34, 2; 19, 1, 11, 18.
[85]. Dig. 18, 1, 34, 2.

THE LAW OF PROPERTY 321

lae; things considered collectively or as a whole, rerum universitas.[86]

The divisions of property recognized by the Roman Law have been strikingly preserved in many of the modern Civil Law codes. There are variations in details in their classifications of property, but the influence of the ancient law is upon them all. According to the Civil Code of Louisiana, for instance, "Things (extra commercium) are either common or public." [87] "Private estates" (and "the word estate is relative to the word things")[88] are those things which belong to individuals.[89] This division of things into public and private, the same as the Roman Law, is found generally in the other codes.[90]

The provisions of the Roman Law concerning the classification of some things as holy, sacred, and religious, and the nature and inalienability of these kinds of things are yet found in some codes,[91] although they are omitted from others, and in Louisiana expressly abolished.[92] The division of things into corporeal and incorporeal is found in a number of the modern codes.[93]

All the modern codes retain the classification of property as movable and immovable.[94] In no Civil Law country is property designated real and personal. Although for the most part the terms

86. See Dig. 41, 3, 30, pr.; 41, 3, 23, pr.; 43, 24, 8.
87. Rev. C. C. art. 449.
88. Rev. C. C. art. 448.
89. Rev. C. C. art. 459.
90. For example, Italy, art. 406, 425; Quebec, art. 399 et seq.; Spain, art. 338 et seq.; Switzerland, art. 664; Chile, art. 580; Mexico, art. 795.
91. Quebec, art. 2217; see McEmery v. Pargoud, 10 La. Ann. 497, 499; Barlin v. Ramirez, 7 Phil. 41, 52.
92. Rev. C. C. art. 456.
93. Austria, art. 374; Cuba, art. 1464; Louisiana, art. 460; Quebec, art. 374; Spain, art. 1464.
94. For example, French C. C. art. 516; German C. C. art. 92, 029; Japanese C. C. art. 86; Louisiana Rev. C. C. art. 461; Quebec C. C. art. 374; Swiss C. C. art. 655, 713; Spanish C. C. art. 333 et seq.

movable and immovable correspond to our terms personal and real, yet they do not exactly correspond to them. Moreover, the word "movable" in our law is not strictly synonymous with the same word in the Civil Law. In our law, things personal include something more than things movable.[95] Thus "movable goods" have been held in English Law, not to include debts due to an estate,[96] and, in Louisiana, a growing crop, although usually considered immovable property even as it is considered real property by us, is yet classed as movable in connection with the administration of an estate.[97]

In the modern Civil Law, movables are classed as movables by nature and movables by law, the former being things movable of themselves, self-moving, as animals, or things that are moved by extraneous agency or power; the latter, things that are specifically declared to be movables by law. Thus, under the French Code,[98] bonds and shares or interests in financial, commercial, or manufacturing companies are movables by operation of law.

The modern Civil Law codes also recognize what are called "immovables by destination," that is, a movable which by its intended use in connection with land and buildings becomes an immovable, something after our law regarding fixtures. For example, a mule placed on a farm or plantation for use in cultivating the land becomes, "by destination" a part of the land, and, hence, an immovable.[99] Conversely, when a movable by destination ceases to be of service to a

---

95. Blk. 2 Com. 383.
96. Sparke v. Denne, W. Jones 225; Penniman v. French, 17 Pick. (Mass.) 404; Strong v. White, 19 Conn. 238.
97. National Bank of Com. v. Sullivan, 117 La. 163, 41 So. 480.
98. Civil Code, art. 529.
99. See La. Code, art. 468; French Code, art. 524; Moussier v. Zunts, 14 La. Ann. 15; Girard v. New Orleans, 2 La. Ann. 897, 901; Morton Trust Co. v. American Salt Co., 149 Fed. 540.

[Roman Law]

tract of land, or is detached from a building of which it formed a part as an accessory, it returns to its original character of a movable.[100] In general, things immovable by destination include cattle intended for cultivation; implements of husbandry; seeds, plants, fodder; beehives; and machinery for farming work. Moreover, all such things as the owner has attached permanently to the building are likewise immovable by destination.[101]

100. False v. Triche, 113 La. 915, 37 So. 875.
101. La. Code, art. 468.

CHAPTER XII

THE LAW OF PROPERTY, *continued*

THE ACQUISITION OF PROPERTY

The acquisition of property in our law is treated under the topic of "Titles," a term meaning, according to Coke,[1] "the lawful cause of possessing that which is our own." The phrase "lawful cause," or "justa causa," is taken from the Roman Law, and is synonymous with "justus titulus," meaning the legal cause or ground by means of which ownership is acquired, as by reason of a sale, a legacy, dowry, payment of a debt, or a gift.[2]

Among the Romans in primitive times all property rights resided in the gens. In fact, until a late period in Roman Law the gens was, in theory, the ultimate heir of an intestate. By the law of the Twelve Tables the "own heirs," the "sui heredes," of an intestate were first entitled to the inheritance. If there were no persons who came within this class, the agnates took, and in the lack of agnates the estate of the deceased went to the gens.[3] This order of sucecssion continued to be the law for a very long time.

With the growth and development of family law, the property possessed by a family was managed and controlled by the paterfamilias, and by the time of the Twelve Tables the paterfamilias was regarded as the actual owner of the family possessions. Whatever

---

1. Coke, 1, 345 b, "Titulus est justa causa possidendi id quid nostrum est."
2. Codex 3, 32, 34.
3. Gaius, 3, 17.

was acquired by any member of the "family" was vested in the family head.

Our word "property" is derived from the Roman words "proprius" and "proprietas." Proprius means one's own, one's exclusive right of ownership of a thing. In this sense, "property" and "ownership" are synonymous. Proprietas, in Roman Law, means, in fact, ownership, although the more usual word is dominium, which means the mastery or the absolute control over a thing except as one may be restrained by law. The owner, or dominus of the thing owned, is entitled to its use, to its products, or to its entire consumption. He has also the right to dispose of it absolutely (jus disponendi). These elements of ownership constitute what the Romans called jura in re.[4] Dominium is thus what the later commentators called a "real right," that is, a right maintainable against all other persons. These commentators also distinguished between absolute ownership and qualified or limited ownership, calling the former dominium plenum and the latter dominium limitatum.

Property rights in Roman Law are divided into two classes, the absolute rights of property or ownership (dominium) in one's own things (jura in sua re), and rights in the things owned by another (jura in re aliena). This latter class of rights are four in number, (1) servitudes (servitutes); (2) (mortgage or pledge (pignus); (3) superficies; and (4) emphyteusis. These four are limited or partial ownerships, or, rather, certain parts of the total rights of ownership. They are called rights in another's property, since the "property," or ownership (dominium) is in another person.

In Roman Law, however, there is no technical distinction between legal and equitable titles as in our

4. Judge Spencer, In re Morgan R. R. & S. S. Co., 32 La. Ann. 371, 375.

own law. Dominium, or ownership, was an aggregation of an unlimited number or bundle of rights, and the transfer to another of one or any number of such rights, less than all, gave to the transferee a jus in re aliena, or a right in the property or res of another. For example, usufruct (usufructus), one of the forms of servitudes, is the right of using the fruits of the property of another without impairment of the substance (salva rei substantia).[5] It is a real right, but limited in its contents, and, consequently, not ownership (dominium). It is a right detached from the aggregate of rights contained in ownership.[6] In such a case the bare ownership (nuda proprietas) existed in the dominus and the use in another. Such a situation is similar, of course, to our division of a title into the legal and equitable title, but the Roman lawyers conceived no such division of the dominium, the use being but a right in another's property, and when it determined it reverted to and was reunited with the ownership.[7]

However, one person might have "quiritary" ownership of a thing and another person have "bonitary" ownership (in bonis habere) of the same thing.[8] The term "quiritary" refers to the clan law of the early regal period of Roman history, when a Roman's legal rights were based upon his membership in a curia ("quiris"), in contrast to his rights as a citizen (civis) under the jus civile. Quiritary ownership, therefore, was ownership by virtue of the old jus civile, and bonitary ownership was ownership by virtue of the later praetorian law. Under the jus civile ownership could be acquired only in certain prescribed ways, but under the praetorian law other ways (such as tradi-

5. Inst. 2, 4, 1.
6. Inst. 2, 4, 1.
7. Inst. 2, 4, 4.
8. Gaius, 2, 40.

tio) were recognized. One did not acquire the "legal" ownership, that is, the ownership known to the jus civile, by getting possession of the thing under the praetorian law, but the praetor protected this possession by various remedies, and the possessor was said to hold the thing in question as his own property (in bonis habere). The later commentators coined the phrase "bonitary ownership" from this fact. It was not the same thing as alien ownership since the thing thus possessed had to be a thing (res) that might have been acquired according to the old, or quiritary, law, yet was not so acquired. For example, if the owner of a mancible thing, that is, a thing transferable by mancipatio under the jus civile, did not so transfer it, but simply delivered it to another with the intent to transfer it (traditio) no transfer under the jus civile took place. The quiritary ownership still remained with the former, but the bonitary, or praetorian, ownership passed to the latter. However, if the transferee retained it sufficiently long he became the quiritary owner by usucapio, one of the quiritary means of ownership.[9] This distinction between quiritary and bonitary ownership was, however, gradually effaced, and when Caracalla, in 212 A. D., made all free inhabitants of the Empire citizens, all practical difference between these two forms of ownership ceased. Justinian expressly abolished quiritary ownership,[10] although nothing but a possessory, that is, a bonitary, ownership had been in existence for a long time preceding him.

In connection with the acquisition of property it is necessary, at times, to consider possession which is quite different from ownership yet may, in time, under certain circumstances, ripen into ownership. Possession is said to be either "natural" or "civil," the for-

9. Gaius, 2, 41.
10. Codex 7, 25; 7, 31.

mer meaning a mere physical fact, the fact of holding or detaining a thing, the latter meaning a possession that is recognized and protected by law, a legal possession. Natural possession is actually having a thing in one's power.[11] Civil possession is actual or physical possession coupled with an intention of keeping it for one's own (animus retinendi). In other words, natural possession consists of but one element, namely, custody; civil possession consists of two elements, custody and an intention to retain as owner (animus domini).

Either form of possession may be justa or injusta, that is, legal or illegal, in its origin.[12] One's tenant or bailee, for example, has natural possession legally (ex justa causa). A thief may have civil possession illegally (ex injusta causa).

Possession is also said to be bonae fidei and malae fidei, the former meaning a possession without legal right but believed to be legal, the latter a possession on the part of one who knows he has no legal right to it. A possessor in good faith is entitled, for example, to the gathered fruits of land that he has cultivated, but if they have not been consumed they may be reclaimed by the true owner.[13]

Mere intention is not sufficient to constitute possession, but when possession has once been attained, intention is sufficient to retain it in case the possessor leaves the thing possessed with the intention of returning to it.[14]

While possession is not, in itself, ownership, yet it is a badge of ownership, and in case of movable property the ownership is presumed to be in the possessor till there is evidence to the contrary.

11. Dig. 43, 17, 1, 2.
12. Inst. 4, 15, 5.
13. Inst. 2, 1, 35; Dig. 41, 1, 48; 22, 1, 25.
14. Inst. 4, 15, 5.

Possession carries with it certain legal rights. It may be protected with force, if needs be, against illegal disturbance,[15] and if one is expelled by force from the possession of land or building he may recover his possession by means of a judicial remedy.[16] In a dispute over property where the rights of parties seem equal the one in possession has the advantage, the maxim of the law being "In pari causa conditio possidentis melior est."[17] One claiming a right of possession against another who is in possession must establish his right, for as in our English action in ejectment the burden of proof is upon the claimant.[18]

Not all individuals could acquire ownership. In Roman Law a "person," as previously stated, was one who was endowed with legal capacity, one who had the legal power to acquire property. Not all individuals had such power. Thus, as a rule, property could not be acquired by slaves, children under patria potestas, and wives subject to manus. The exceptions to such general restraints on ownership have also been pointed out, as the peculium in the case of slaves, the peculium castrense in case of children under parental power, and the dos, parapherna, and donatio propter nuptias in case of the wife under manus.

Again, under the old law, the jus civile, ownership was restricted to Roman citizens, and the only ownership that aliens could enjoy was bonitary ownership, the praetorian ownership by virtue of the jus gentium, based upon possession.

In considering the modes of acquiring ownership, it is important, at times, to distinguish between the modes of acquiring particular things, res singulares, and the modes of acquiring an entirety of things and

15. Dig. 41, 2, 43; 43, 16, 3, 9; 9, 2, 29, 1.
16. Inst. 4, 15, 6.
17. Dig. 41, 2, 3, 1; 50, 17, 128.
18. Codex 2, 1, 4; 3, 32, 28.

rights, as an inheritance. The latter comprises many different and separate things considered as a whole and known as a universitas rerum, and such ownership is acquired only when one person takes the place of another person who formerly was the dominus or owner of all these things. Arrogatio, already considered, is an illustration of such substitution, likewise the succession of a person to the estate of a deceased person.

With reference to the modes of acquiring ownership of particular things, res singulares, the Roman Law classifies such methods of acquisition as either "civil" or "natural," the former meaning the methods recognized by the old law, the jus civile, the latter the methods introduced by the jus gentium. Under the jus civile, Roman citizens could acquire ownership by mancipatio, addictio, legatum, and usucapio. In the later law, as developed under the jus gentium, traditio, accessio, and prescriptio were recognized as "natural" modes of ownership. In addition to the foregoing an original and primitive form of ownership was that of occupatio.

In the rude age of primitive Roman days, ownership was associated with the thought of power, physical power. Mancipium is the original term for ownership, signifying what one seizes by the hand (manus) and retains as his own. Later, the term acquired a legal significance, meaning the formal legal procedure by which ownership was transferred. In the earliest times, however, it was, doubtless, true that violence and force were the common modes of getting and retaining what one desired.[19]

Mancipium, or mancipatio, was a formal method for the transfer of certain property practiced even before the days of the Twelve Tables. This ancient procedure has already been explained in connection with

---

19. Ortolan, Hist. of Rom. Law, p. 532, London, 1896.

mancible and non-mancible things. It required the presence of at least eight persons, the vendor, the vendee, the official money-weigher, and five witnesses, and the only way in which mancible things could be transferred from citizen to citizen was by this procedure. It was manifestly a cumbersome means of acquiring title, yet in a rude age it served to give formality and publicity to important transactions, and that, of course, was its chief purpose. Mancipatio was not restricted to the mere transfer of rights in corporeal property but afforded the means of transferring other rights, such as marriage by coemptio (purchase), adoption, and emancipation. It was also employed in early times for the transfer of one's entire property in the name of a will, the testamentum per aes et libram.[20] Before the time of Justinian, however, mancipatio had wholly disappeared.

Addictio, meaning a magisterial decree, was also an ancient form of transferring title. The most familiar form of such judicial title was known as in jure cessio, or a surrender in court. Like unto all methods of transfer known to the old law, the jus civile, it was confined to Roman citizens. While not so ancient as mancipatio yet it was recognized even before the time of the Twelve Tables. It was a collusive or fictitious suit whereby the person to whom the property right was to be conveyed claimed in open court to be the owner. Thereupon, the magistrate asked the other party, the present owner, whether he also claimed it. Upon the denial or silence of such other party, the magistrate gave judgment (addicit) in favor of the claimant.[21] As in the case of mancipatio, in jure cessio was available for a number of legal transactions, such as the transfer of res, the purpose of adoption, emancipation, and the creation of servitudes. However, like

20. Gaius, 2, 102–104.
21. Gaius, 2, 24.

unto mancipatio, it became obsolete. Even in the time of Gaius, mancipatio, he says, was generally employed instead of in jure cessio, because it was less difficult to transfer property in the presence of one's friends than to go into court before the praetor.[22]

The method of transferring title by in jure cessio, or surrender in court, was undoubtedly the inspiration of the collusive or fictitious suits in early English law known as fine and common recovery.

Besides in jure cessio there were other forms of addictio, or title by a magistrate's decree, such as venditio sub hasta, assignatio and adjudicatio. Venditio sub hasta, or a sale at public auction, was an ancient form of judicial sale. It was originally employed in the sale of booty acquired in war. A spear (hasta) was erected at such sales for the double purpose of showing that a sale was being held and that it was being conducted under public authority.[23] In later times the word hasta was commonly employed for any sort of auction. Gaius says [24] that the sale of public land under the spear (sub hasta) gave full rights of ownership.

Assignatio was a judicial assignment or grant of public land, the amount of such assignments to Roman citizens and colonists varying under the different agrarian laws. Such land was called agri dati assignati. The oldest assignments seem to have been two jugura to each citizen.[25] Later we hear of seven jugura as being the size of an assignment.[26]

Adjudicatio was another form of judicial title, it being the award made by a magistrate in a suit for the partition of an inheritance among co-heirs, or for

22. Gaius, 2, 25.
23. Cic. de Off. II, 8, 29.
24. Gaius, 4, 16.
25. Varr, 1, c.; Niebuhr, Hist. of Rome, II, 156 ff. The jugerum was 240 ft. long by 120 ft. wide. It contained about ⅝ of an acre.
26. Pliny, Hist. Nat., 18, 18.

the division of the common property among partners, or for the settlement of disputed boundary lines between adjacent owners of land.[27] If the parties could not agree a judicial decree became necessary, in such cases, to determine the ownership. The adjudication itself, as under our own modern statutes, transferred the property in question to the individual. It was the title, or the means by which the dominium, or ownership, was acquired. The term adjudicatio, judgment, was also used in connection with a lawsuit in which rival claimants alleged ownership of the same thing. Such a judgment, however, should not be confused with the term employed in connection with derivative titles.

Legatum, legacy or bequest, was the means by which ownership of particular things (res singulares) was acquired under a will. In such a case possession of the property by the legatee was not necessary, since he became the owner by the mere force of the provisions of the will, that is, by the act of the testator, provided the legacy was made by direct and positive words.[28]

Justinian, in his Institutes,[29] says that things became the property of individuals in many ways. Some are acquired by natural law, that is, by the jus gentium, others are acquired by the jus civile. Occupatio (occupation, occupancy) he says, is a natural mode of original ownership. The modes of acquiring ownership in the time of Justinian may be tabulated as follows:

I. Original Ownership
  1. Occupatio
  2. Accessio
    a. Fructus

27. Gaius 4, 42.
28. See Chapter XIX, post.
29. Inst. 2, 1, 11.

b. Alluvio
c. Adjunctio
   (1) Inaedificatio; (2) Plantatio; (3) Scriptura; (4) Pictura; (5) Satio
d. Confusio
e. Specificatio
3. Prescriptio (developed from Usucapio)
II. Derivative Ownership
1. Traditio
   (Including contract, gift, exchange)
2. Legatum
3. Adjudicatio

Occupatio is a taking possession of corporeal things which have no owner at the time (res nullius) with the intention of making them one's own property.[30] It must have been a very primitive form of ownership, and was doubtless recognized in the earliest times.

Wild beasts, birds, and fish become by the jus gentium, says Justinian, the property of the one who captures them, because that which belongs to nobody is acquired by natural law by the person who first possesses it. Moreover, it matters not whether one captures these wild beasts and birds on his own ground or on the ground of another. However, he who enters the grounds of another for the purpose of hunting can be stopped by the owner if he perceives such a purpose.[31] Wild bees may also be hived and thus reduced to one's ownership.[32]

In the case of wild animals that have been captured and tamed, as, for example, in the case of tame deer that are in the habit of going into the woods and returning again, they are the property of their owner

---

30. Gaius, 2, 66–69; Dig. 41, 1, 3; Pothier, de Proprieté, N. 20; La. Civ. Code, art. 3375; Co. Litt. 416.

31. Inst. 2, 1, 12; Dig. 41, 1, 3; Geer v. Connecticut, 161 U. S. 519, 523.

32. Inst. 2, 1, 14.

as long as they have the intention of returning (animus revertendi). Such animals are supposed, however, to have lost such an intention when they have lost the habit of returning.[33]

Likewise precious stones, gems, and other things found upon the seashore belong to the finder.[34]

In addition to things which never had a previous owner, things may also become ownerless (res nullius) when they are abandoned (derelictio) by their owners. Such things immediately upon their being taken possession of by others with intent to retain them likewise become, by occupatio, the property of such others.[35] Dereliction, or abandonment, requires, however, an intention to abandon. Consequently, things thrown overboard to lighten a vessel in a storm are not derelict.[36]

Treasure trove (thesaurus), or treasure found, which is said by Paulus to be an ancient deposit of something valuable which owing to lack of human memory no longer may be said to have an owner,[37] belonged to the person who found it in his own field,[38] but found in the field of another belonged half to the finder and half to the owner of the land.[39] According to the early English Law, all treasure trove belonged to the finder, unless, of course, the true owner appeared.[40] However, by statute of IV Edw. I, the title was vested in the crown subject to the claim of the

---

33. Inst. 2, 1, 15.
34. Inst. 2, 1, 18.
35. Inst. 2, 1, 47; Dig. 41, 7, 1.
36. Inst. 2, 1, 48; Dig. 14, 2, 8; Livermore v. White, 74 Me. 455; Ralli v. Troop, 157 U. S. 386; Barnard v. Adams, 10 How. (U. S.) 270; The Hyderabad, 11 Fed. 754; Spigener v. Cooner, 64 Am. D. 755.
37. Dig. 41, 1, 31, 1.
38. Inst. 2, 39; Cod. 10, 15.
39. Ib.
40. 1 Blk. Com. 296; 2 Kent Com. 358, 13th Ed.

true owner.[41] Such is the present English law.[42] In this country, the law of treasure trove has been generally merged, it is said, into the law of the finder of lost property, and, as a rule, is held to belong to the finder as against all save the true owner.[43]

Acessio, acession or increase, is another mode of original title. The term includes both accession and accretion as used in our law.

Accession means the acquisition of property in a thing (res) which is produced by, or which is united to, a thing (res) already owned by a person. The thing already owned is known as the principal thing, the added thing being called the accessory thing. The law makes the accessory thing a part of the principal (res accessoria cedit principali).

There are various ways in which accession may take place. It includes the offspring of animals subject to one's ownership;[44] alluvion and other things added to one's land;[45] islands formed in a river adjacent to riparian owners;[46] and things made with materials belonging to another.[47]

The increase of animals and the produce of land were called by Roman lawyers "fruits" (fructus), and, as such they belonged to the owner of the thing which produced them. In the "fruits" of animals are included their young, also milk, hair, and wool.[48] "Fruits" are classed by the later commentators as natural, industrial, and civil. Natural fruits (fructus

---

41. 1 Blk. Com. 296; McLaughlin v. Waite, 5 Wend. (N. Y.) 404.
42. Atty. Gen. v. Moore, 1 Ch. (1893) 676.
43. See Danielson v. Roberts, 44 Oreg. 108, 74 Pac. 913; Weeks v. Hackett, 104 Me. 264, 71 Atl. 858; Livermore v. White, 74 Me. 452. Compare Ferguson v. Ray, 44 Oreg. 557, 77 Pac. 600. Huthmacher v. Harris, 38 Pa. St. 491.
44. Inst. 2, 1, 19.
45. Inst. 2, 1, 20.
46. Inst. 2, 1, 22.
47. Inst. 2, 1, 25.
48. Inst. 2, 1, 19; 2, 1, 37; Dig. 41, 1, 6.

naturales) are the spontaneous products of the soil, the offspring and all other produce of animals. Industrial fruits (fructus industriales) are those produced by hand through cultivation and labor.[49] Civil fruits (fructus civiles) are rents of lands, buildings, and interest on money.[50] These terms are found in some of the modern codes,[51] but not in the classical Roman Law.

At times the fructus or fruits of a thing became the property of a person who was not the owner of the principal thing. This might arise by contract between the parties, as in case of a lessee of a farm, or might follow the ownership of a servitude known as a usufruct,[52] or might be the result of the bona fide possession of the principal thing although owned by another. Where one had obtained the principal thing in good faith, relying upon a legal form of title, ex justa causa, he was not bound to restore the "fruits" obtained by his industry and already consumed by him up to the time of the owner's action, but bound only to restore the principal thing. If, however, the fruits had not been consumed they belonged to the true owner of the principal property. After the possessor had notice of an adverse claim followed by a suit to recover the possession he held as a mala fide possessor and was, as such, liable to restore all the profits accruing from the time of the notice.[53]

The mala fide possessor was required to restore, or to make compensation, for all fruits, whether consumed or not, accruing from the beginning of his possession.

"These doctrines of the Civil Law," the Supreme

49. Dig. 7, 1, 9; 22, 1, 45; 41, 1, 48, pr.; 50, 16, 77.
50. Dig. 22, 1, 36; Paulus, Sent. 3, 6.
51. French C. C. art. 547; Quebec C. C. art. 409, 449; Spanish C. C. art. 354-357.
52. See Servitudes, post.
53. Inst. 2, 1, 35 and 36. See Hernandez v. Hermanos, 7 Porto Rico Fed. 445.

Court of the United States has said,[54] "are not recognized by the Common Law of England. We are not aware of any Common Law case which recognizes the distinction between bonae fidae possessor, and one who holds mala fide. Whoever takes and holds the possession of land to which another has a better title, whether by disseisin, or under a grant from the disseisor, is liable to the true owner for the profits which he has received, of whatever nature they may be, and whether consumed by him or not."

The Roman Law also distinguished between a bona fide possessor and a usufructuary with reference to the ownership of fruits. The former was entitled to all the fruits that were severed, in any way or by any person, from the land. The usufructuary, however, owned only the fruits gathered by himself (perceptio fructuum).[55]

According to the modern Civil Law, the ownership of a thing whether it be movable or immovable, carries with it the right to all that the thing produces, and to all that becomes united to it, either naturally or artificially.[56] These general principles of the Civil Law as to title by accession have also been adopted by our Common Law.[57] For example, where under a chattel mortgage the title is transferred from the mortgagor to the mortgagee, a mortgage of live stock carries a title to their increase.[58] In a Maryland case, the court quotes the Civil Law as laid down by Domat[59] as follows:

54. Green v. Biddle, 8 Wheat. 1, 80.
55. Inst. 2, 1, 36; Dig. 7, 4, 13.
56. French C. C., art. 546; La. C. C., art. 498; Spanish C. C., art. 353.
57. Pulcifer v. Page, 32 Me. 404; Peirce v. Goddard, 22 Pick. (Mass.) 559.
58. Domat, Civil Law, by Strahan, Sec. 1663.
59. Cahoon v. Miers, 67 Md. 573, 11 Atl. 278, citing the Roman Law rule. Compare, however, Winter v. Landphere, 42 Iowa 471; Darling v. Wilson, 60 N. H. 59.

[Roman Law]

"When a stud of horses, a herd of cattle, or a flock of sheep is put in pawn, into the creditor's hands, the foals, the lambs, and other beasts which they bring forth, and which augment their number, are likewise engaged for the creditor's security, and if the herd or flock be entirely changed, the heads which have renewed it are engaged in the same manner as the old stock."

Another form of accession is alluvion (alluvio), the deposit and addition of soil on the bank of a river or the shore of the sea, the deposit being so gradual that no one can conceive how much is added at any moment of time.[60] The proprietor of the land increased by alluvion is entitled to such addition. In the Roman Law, title by alluvion applies only to those lands whose boundaries are natural, such as a river, wood, or mountain, since in case of land held in a specified quantity (agri assignati or limitati), such accessions belong to the state rather than to the owner of the adjacent land.[61]

In distinction from alluvio or the imperceptible increase of one's land by the action of water, an accretion by which one's land was enlarged in a perceptible manner, as where by a flood a considerable part of one's land was deposited by the violence of the water upon another's land, was termed avulsio. Ordinarily in such a case the land remained the property of him from whose land it had been thus torn away. If, however, the owner delayed to claim his land till a time when trees or shrubs on it had be-

60. Gaius, 2, 70; Inst. 2, 1, 20. Jeffries v. East Land Co., 134 U. S. 178, 192; Morgan v. Livingston, 6 La. 19; Municipality v. Cotton Press, 18 La. Ann. 122; County of St. Clair v. Livingston, 23 Wall. (U. S.) 46; Krant v. Crawford, 18 Iowa, 549; Mubry v. Norton, 100 N. Y. 426; Merrit v. Johnson, 7 Johns. (N. Y.) 473; Nebraska v. Iowa, 143 U. S. 359; Smith v. St. Louis Public Schools, 30 Mo. 291; St. L. Ry. Co. v. Mo. Ry. Co., 114 Mo. 13; Warren v. Chambers, 25 Ark. 120.

61. Dig. 41, 1, 16; 43, 12, 1, 6.

come firmly rooted in the other land, it became the property by accession of the owner of the soil upon which it had been deposited.[62]

Another part of the law of title by accession is the law of adjunction (adjunctio), the attachment or union permanently of one thing to another. Thus where one built a house upon another man's land, or used another man's material in building upon his own land (inaedificatio), the building thus erected belonged to the owner of the soil. Solo cedit quod solo inaedificatur.[63]

Among other illustrations of title by adjunction cited by Justinian are planting trees or shrubs (plantatio),[64] or sowing grain (satio),[65] upon the land of another, writing on another's paper (scriptura),[66] embroidery upon another's garment,[67] and painting upon another's tablet (pictura).[68] Owing to a dispute that had long continued whether a painting by one person upon another's tablet should be considered as principal or accessory, Justinian enacted that the painting was the principal, the tablet becoming accessory to the painting. The painter was, however, required to compensate the owner of the tablet.[69]

The term confusio (for liquids) or commixtio (for solids) means mixing together things of the same kind so that they become inseparable, as pouring together

---

62. Inst. 2, 1, 21; 2, 1, 36; Gaius, 2, 71; Dig. 41, 1, 7, 2.

63. Inst. 2, 1, 29, 30; Dig. 41, 1, 7, 10; Aldrich v. Hunter, 131 Mass. 480; Arnott v. Ry. Co., 19 Kan. 95; Pulcifer v. Page, 32 Me. 404; Merritt v. Johnson, 7 Johns. (N. Y.) 473. The owner was required, however, to compensate a bona fide possessor for such permanent improvements. Inst. 2, 1, 32; Dig. 50, 17, 206. See Bright v. Boyd, Fed. Cas. No. 1875, 1 Story 478; U. S. v. Midway Northern Oil Co., 232 Fed. 619.

64. Inst. 2, 1, 31; Gaius, 2, 74; Dig. 41, 1, 7, 13.
65. Inst. 2, 1, 32; Gaius, 2, 75; Dig. 41, 1, 9 pr.
66. Inst. 2, 1, 33; Gaius, 2, 77; Dig. 41, 1, 9, 1.
67. Inst. 2, 1, 21; Gaius, 2, 71; Dig. 41, 1, 7, 2.
68. Inst. 2, 1, 34; Gaius, 2, 78.
69. Inst. 2, 1, 29-38.

wines belonging to different owners, mixing grain, or fusing together metals. Where such mixing was mutually consented to, or was accidental, the owners became joint owners of the mixture.[70]

However, if a mixture of things of the same kind is made without the owner's consent, they have an action in rem for such part of the whole as appears to belong to them respectively.[71] In case the mixture were of different kinds, the law of specification would apply.

Specificatio is the making of a new "species" or substance out of another man's materials, as where, for example, one made wine out of another man's grapes, or oil from another's olives, or a ship or article of furniture from another's lumber. There was a dispute between the Proculians and Sabinians concerning the ownership of the thing thus made, the former contending that the one who had made the article was the owner, the latter insisting that such a fact made no difference in the title to the materials, since the materials were the principal thing and the labor the accessory.[72] As in many other matters, Justinian settled the law by his imperial authority, declaring that if the article thus made was in fact a new kind of property, nova species, and the material could not be restored into its former state, the one who made it, providing he acted in good faith, should be regarded as the owner, although he was bound to pay for the value of the materials used.[73] If the labor and materials of the finished product could be separated, as where one made an article out of another's metal and the metal could be restored to its former condition by melting the article, then the owner of the material became the

70. Inst. 2, 1, 27; Dig. 6, 1, 3, 2; Dig. 6, 1, 5, pr.
71. Dig. 6, 1, 5, pr.
72. Gaius, 2, 79.
73. Inst. 2, 1, 25. See also Dig. 10, 4, 12, 3; 41, 1, 7, 7; 41, 1, 27, 1.

owner of the manufactured article.[74] In case one acted in bad faith and stole the material he worked into a new form he became liable as a thief.[75] If a man steals purple (i. e. costly material), says Justinian,[76] and weaves it into a garment of his own, then, despite the fact that the purple is more valuable than the garment, it goes as an accessory to the garment. The former owner has, however, an action for theft against the one who stole it.

It is regarded illogical by some to place title by specification under either occupatio or accessio. Some authorities, therefore, treat it as a separate form of title. The prevailing view, however, regards it as a form of accession, the materials being treated as accessory to the principal thing, the workmanship or labor, which gives the new product its economic value. In our own law, the doctrine of specification is usually placed under title by accession. Thus where lumber worth twenty-five dollars was converted into barrel hoops worth seven hundred dollars, it was held that there was such a change of identity (nova species) as to give the "operator" title to the hoops.[77] However, in another case where corn was taken by wilful trespass and converted into whiskey, a New York court held that the whiskey belonged to the owner of the original material.[78]

Usucapio, or usucaption, is a form of title, or ownership, resulting from continuous possession for a period of time prescribed by law.[79] While there have been learned disputes concerning the original reasons for such a form of title, the view of most scholars is

74. Gaius, 2, 79; Inst. 2, 1, 25.
75. Gaius, 2, 78; Inst. 2, 1, 34.
76. Inst. 2, 1, 26.
77. Wetherbee v. Green, 22 Mich. 311.
78. Silsbury v. McCoon, 3 N. Y. 379, reversing 6 Hill, 425. See argument of counsel in footnote.
79. Dig. 41, 3, 3.

the same as that of Gaius, namely, that it is a legal fiction adopted in order that the ownership of property might not remain uncertain for too long a time.[80]

Usucapio is frequently confused with praescriptio, otherwise known as longi temporis possessio. The term usucapio, however, is a term of the old jus civile, the citizen or quiritary law, while praescriptio, or longi temporis possessio was a term of the jus gentium introduced by the Roman praetor. Usucapio under the old law (it is called merely usus in the Twelve Tables) seems to have been the length of time that a thing transferred by mancipatio, yet not legally transferred owing to some defect in the proceedings, would have to be possessed by the transferee in order to effect ownership. In other words, it seems to have been a means of curing a defective title. Such a title, however, was available only to Roman citizens, and under the Twelve Tables could be obtained in a year in the case of movables, and in two years in the case of "fundus" or land.[81] It did not apply to lands outside of Italy, nor, with certain exceptions, to servitudes.

In later times when the praetor felt it necessary as a matter of justice to protect the rights of those who were not Roman citizens and who, consequently, could not acquire title by the jus civile, he laid down, as a rule of procedure, that one could not maintain an action for the recovery of property against one who had possession of it in good faith, unless such action was brought within a certain time. It was in the nature of a statute of limitations, an equitable defense allowed by the authority of the praetorian magistrate. This defense of long time possession (longi temporis possessio) was called praescription (praescriptio) for the reason that, under the forms of pleading adopted by the praetor, defenses were written in the "formula"

---

80. Gaius, 2, 44; Dig. 41, 3, 1; 41, 10, 5, pr.; Cicero, Pro Caec. 26.
81. Gaius, 2, 42, 44, 54, 204; Inst. 2, 6, pr.

at the beginning, or before the main part of the substance of the action, the declaratio.[82]

Usucapio was, therefore, a positive means of acquiring title under the old law when the property in question was in one's possession. It was a right in rem. Praescriptio under the praetorian law (the jus gentium) was a defense, sometimes called a negative defense, which barred one from the enforcement of his claim of ownership irrespective of the question of the true title.[83]

The time of the possession as fixed by the various praetors varied. One year was a familiar rule in many praetorian defenses.

In the time of Justinian all technical differences between the old usucapio and the praetorian praescriptio had entirely disappeared, and long possession of property, under the general term praescriptio, became a means of acquiring positive title.[84] He finally fixed the period in connection with movable property at three years, and in case of immovables at ten years if the parties had lived for that period in the same province (inter praesentes), or at twenty years if they had resided in different provinces (inter absentes).[85] If they had lived in the same province a part of the time, and in different provinces a part, two years of absence counted as one year of presence.[86]

These periods were based upon a possession acquired in good faith. Justinian further provided that a period of thirty years should bar all claims of ownership regardless of the manner in which the property

---

82. Gaius, 4, 132.

83. See Townsend v. Jemison, 9 How. (U. S.) 407, 417. The court in this case, however, seems to be of the opinion that praescriptio was limited as a defense in merely obligatory rights. It also applied, however, to the enforcement of real rights.

84. Codex 7, 39, 8, pr.

85. Codex 7, 31; 7, 33, 12.

86. Nov. 119, 8.

might have been acquired, whether in bad faith, or even by theft. In case, however, of church property or mortgaged property the period was made forty years.[87]

The foregoing prescriptive periods applied to the ownership of property, the period in which a right in rem might be maintained. In the case of rights in personam, merely obligatory rights, the right, for example, to sue for a debt, Justinian fixed a general period of thirty years, although in case of an action upon a mortgage debt the time was limited to forty years.[88]

It was not, however, until the year 531 A. D.[89] that Justinian abolished the old usucapio rule of one year in the case of movable property, and the two year rule for land. Consequently in the law of the Digest the ancient periods are to be understood. It was necessary that the possession should be continuous and uninterrupted.[90] If there were an interruption (usurpatio) all the previous time of possession was lost. The tacking of the time of one person's possession to that of another was not recognized till a late date, although an exception was allowed in case of an heir provided his possession followed immediately.[91] However about 200 A. D. the doctrine of tacking (accessio temporis) was allowed in case of any transfer inter vivos,[92] and the Digest also mentions accessio temporis in connection with the transfer of possession by way of gift, dowry, and pledge.[93] To the fact of possession it was necessary to add the possessor's claim of ownership,[94]

87. Codex 7, 39; Nov. 117.
88. Codex 7, 39, 1.
89. The year of Codex 7, 31.
90. Dig. 41, 3, 16; 41, 2, 1, 15.
91. Dig. 41, 3, 20; 41, 4, 6, 2.
92. Inst. 2, 6, 13; Dig. 41, 4, 2, 20; Codex 7, 31, 3.
93. Dig. 44, 3, 5, pr.; 41, 2, 13, 6.
94. Dig. 41, 3, 25; Inst. 2, 6, pr.; Dig. 41, 3, 31, 6.

and the possessor must have originally acquired the possession in good faith,[95] although if he subsequently learned of his error it did not affect the situation. The doctrine of usucapio did not apply to things not in commercio, consequently, as in our English law, no title by such means could be acquired against public property.[96] Moreover, the thing possessed must be corporeal, and servitudes and other intangible rights in another's things (jura in re aliena) were not subject to usucapio, although at a later period they might be acquired by praescriptio or longi temporis possessio.[97] Stolen property was expressly exempted from the law of usucapio by the Twelve Tables.[98]

A further remedy for the protection of a bona fide possessory title was given by the praetor Publicius,[99] known as the actio Publiciana. It availed one who had acquired possession by some defect in the transaction known as mancipatio, or in case of any other bona fide possessor whose possession had not yet ripened into ownership by the statute of limitations, who was dispossessed before the necessary time for usucaption had run. It was a fictitious action in which the one who had lost the possession was permitted to say that the property in question was his by usucaption.[100] By means of this action the plaintiff was enabled to regain the possession unless the defendant could prove that he was the real owner, or could show that he was also a bona fide possessor prior in time to the possession of the plaintiff. In this latter case the legal principle "in pari causa conditio possidentis melior est"[101] applied.

95. Inst. 2, 6, pr.; Gaius, 2, 43; Dig. 41, 1, 48, 1; 41, 4, 2, pr. and 13.
96. Gaius, 2, 46.
97. Dig. 41, 2, 3, pr.; 41, 3, 4, 27; 8, 5, 10, pr.
98. Gaius, 2, 45; Inst. 2, 6, 2; Dig. 41, 3, 4, 6.
99. Inst. 4, 6, 4. When this Publicius was praetor is uncertain.
100. Gaius, 4, 36; Dig. 6, 2.
101. Dig. 41, 2, 3, 1; 50, 17, 128.

THE LAW OF PROPERTY

Derivative Titles:

Thus far we have considered the acquisition of property by original titles. We have yet to consider derivative ownership, or where ownership is acquired from a former owner. In the time of Justinian such means of ownership were three in number, traditio, legatum, and adjudicatio. The last two of these, legatum and adjudicatio, have already been explained. It remains, therefore, to speak of traditio.

The right to dispose of property, jus disponendi, is one of the rights of absolute ownership. As Justinian says: "Nothing is more conformable to natural fairness than that the wish of an owner who wishes to transfer his property to another should be held valid." [102]

Under the old law of Rome, ownership could not be acquired by mere delivery or tradition (traditio). Things not mancible were, undoubtedly, from a very early time put into the possession of another by simple delivery, but it was only by usucaption that the possessor's title in such cases became legal. However, in the course of time, the necessity of transferring ownership by more simple and practical means became more and more apparent. Ulpian says [103] that ownership by tradition, or delivery, applied originally only to non-mancible things (res nec mancipi) and Gaius also says [104] that full ownership may be transferred in nonmancible things, if they are corporeal, by mere delivery.

Under the influence of the jus gentium, however, the transfer of ownership by tradition was applied to all corporeal property, and even before the time of Justinian it was the only way in which such property could be transferred, as far as direct transactions be-

102. Inst. 2, 1, 40.
103. Ulpian, 19, 7.
104. Gaius, 2, 19.

tween the parties were concerned, from one person to another. Justinian calls it a "natural" mode of acquiring things, and his statement that all kinds of corporeal things could be legally acquired thereby, including Italian and provincial land, when based upon some legal ground (causa), such as gift, dowry, or any other legal cause,[105] merely declared existing law. Long before Justinian's day the old methods of acquiring ownership by mancipatio and in jure cessio had become obsolete.

Delivery, or traditio, has both a popular and a legal meaning. The Romans called the former nuda traditio. If I loan my book to you it is a "delivery" of the book but I do not transfer the property in it thereby. Never in Roman Law did a mere delivery, a nuda traditio, transfer ownership since there had to be some legal ground, some justa causa, such as a sale or a gift, which preceded the delivery as evidence of the intent to transfer the title.[106]

Under the praetorian law, traditio required none of the ceremonial or public proceedings necessary to the old transfer of ownership, since it was very informal. A mere agreement, however, to transfer without delivery of possession, even though the agreement was in writing, did not pass the ownership.[107] Under the modern Civil Law, tradition is defined, even as in the Roman Law, as "the transferring of the thing sold into the power and possession of the buyer."[108]

While it is necessary that the person who transfers the property, called auctor in the Roman Law, should be the owner, since delivery (traditio) cannot transfer more to one who receives the property than the one

105. Inst. 2, 1, 40.
106. Dig. 41, 1, 31, pr.
107. Codex 3, 32, 27.
108. Louisiana Civil Code, art. 2477; Mazone v. Caze, 18 La. Ann. 31, 34; French C. C. art. 1604; Spanish C. C. art. 1462.

who delivers it possesses,[109] yet it is not necessary that the owner should make the delivery in person since another may do so with the owner's consent.[110]

Traditio, however, on its legal side, was a mental act. In many instances the "delivery" of small movables was, naturally, an actual handing of the res to the buyer, but such an act even in connection with such subjects of sale was not necessary. Traditio was the voluntary placing by the owner of the thing sold in the possession of the other party, and when the buyer likewise assented to the acceptance of the possession the tradition was complete. Delivery could be either actual or constructive, the latter meaning some symbol of the legal right of possession, as, for example, the handing over of the key of a house.[111]

Immovables as well as movables were transferred by traditio, and lands were thus sold the same as clothing and food.[112] Although the transfer of valuable things was commonly attested by writing,[113] yet Roman Law never required a writing in order to pass any sort of property. Where, however, the parties to a contract had agreed that it should be reduced to writing, Justinian provided that it was not binding until it had been so executed.[114]

There could be a transfer of property by traditio without a consideration, a quid pro quo, since it might be a free gift (donatio). Roman jurists spoke of a justa causa or a justus titulus, and by justa causa they meant a legal ground for the transaction, such as a legacy, a gift, a dowry, or a sale. It was the basis upon which the intention to transfer was evidenced and sustained. Where, however, traditio followed a

109. Dig. 41, 1, 20, pr.
110. Inst. 2, 1, 42.
111. See Inst. 2, 1, 45; Dig. 41, 1, 9, 6.
112. Inst. 2, 1, 40.
113. Codex, 4, 38, 12; 7, 32, 2.
114. Inst. 3, 23, pr.

sale, a price was essential to such a contract, and in such a case a delivery of the thing sold did not pass ownership unless the price were paid or credit given.[115]

There was no implied warranty of title in a sale, whether of lands or movables,[116] although the contrary was true in case of an exchange.[117] Consequently, in a sale one who was not the owner (dominus) could make a valid traditio provided the vendor was in possession,[118] and, on the other hand, one out of possession could not sell although he was the owner.[119] However, the vendor did warrant by the very sale itself the quiet possession of the vendee, and if the latter were evicted the vendor was obligated to compensate him.[120]

When a house was sold, all that which was beneficial to its use and which was commonly regarded as a part of it, in other words what we call appurtenances in our law, was included in the sale.[121] In the case of the sale of a farm growing crops were considered a part of the land.[122] Property could be sold unconditionally or with reservations, conditions, and exceptions as the parties agreed. For example the vendor could reserve a usufruct or a habitatio,[123] or he might except from the sale of land certain quarries upon it.[124] A vendor could also expressly warrant against incumbrances.[125]

According to Justinian, donatio, or gift, is another mode of acquiring ownership, and gifts are said to be

---

115. Inst. 2, 7, pr.
116. Dig. 18, 1, 25, 1; 19, 4, 1, pr.
117. Dig. 19, 4, 1, 3.
118. Dig. 18, 1, 28.
119. Dig. 19, 1, 2, 1.
120. Dig. 19, 1, 3, pr.; 21, 2, 76; 41, 3, 23, 1.
121. Dig. 19, 1, 13, 31; 19, 1, 17, 7; 19, 1, 38, 2.
122. Dig. 19, 1, 17, 1; 6, 1, 44.
123. Dig. 19, 1, 53, 2; 19, 1, 7.
124. Dig. 18, 1, 77.
125. Dig. 50, 16, 90; 50, 16, 169.

of two kinds, mortis causa and inter vivos.[126] Gaius, in his Institutes, does not place donatio among the various modes of acquiring property but treats it as a pact or contract. This is the view, also, of many civilian commentators who regard donatio as a justa causa, or a legal ground or motive, for the transfer of property rather than a mode of transfer. For example, the justa causa in case of traditio may be a sale, that is, a price, or it may be a gift (donatio), but in either case the mode of transfer is by traditio. Moreover, donatio does not necessarily transfer ownership, or dominium, since it may consist merely in the release of a debt. Gifts mortis causa were considered to be forms of legacies rather than an independent mode of transfer,[127] and this is expressly recognized by Justinian,[128] although he declared that donatio was an independent mode of transfer coördinate with traditio. It is very probable that Justinian's law in this particular was influenced by his legislation upon gifts in general, prompted by his desire to make binding the promises of gifts for pious uses. Prior to his time, a mere promise to bestow a gift was not enforceable, being a mere pactum. Justinian, however, made such a promise actionable.[129]

Modern Civil Law: The law concerning the acquisition of property in modern Civil Law countries follows to a great extent the Roman Law. The doctrines of original ownership by means of occupatio,[130] usucapio, prescriptio, and accessio are common to the codes, and the generally recognized modes of derivative ownership are traditio and donatio. In the latter

126. Inst. 2, 7, pr.
127. Dig. 39, 6, 35, pr.; 39, 6, 9; 39, 6, 15; 39, 6, 37, pr.
128. Inst. 2, 7, 1.
129. See Pacts, post.
130. French C. C. art. 713–717; German C. C. art. 937 et seq.; Louisiana C. C. art. 3421; Italian C. C. art. 711–719; Mexican C. C. art. 709 et seq.; Spanish C. C. art. 609.

form of property acquisition the modern codes follow Justinian. The Quebec Code,[131] for example, defines a gift as "an act by which the donor divests himself by gratuitous title of the ownership of a thing" in favor of the donee who accepts it.

Traditio, called "tradition" in the code of Louisiana,[132] is generally defined in the modern codes, the same as in the Roman Law, as the transfer of the possession of a thing with the intent to transfer ownership therein.[133] Although the modern codes require writings, usually called public instruments, in connection with the transfer of real rights in land, yet it was not always so. In the Missouri case of Mitchell v. Tuckers[134] the question to be decided was an oral transfer of land. The court held that in 1815, prior to the time of the introduction of the Common Law in that state, the Spanish law was in force there. Under that law, at that time, a deed was not necessary to convey land, since it could be conveyed by parol. The Spanish law, today, however, provides that a sale of land must be executed by a public, that is, a notarial, instrument.[135]

In Louisiana, all sales of immovable property must be made either by "authentic act" or "under private signature."[136] An "authentic act," as relates to contracts, is executed before a notary public in the presence of two competent witnesses.[137] Yet a verbal sale of immovable property is good against the vendor, as well as against a vendee who confesses it when inter-

131. Quebec C. C. art. 755. See French C. C. art. 894; Louisiana Rev. C. C. art. 1468.
132. C. C. art. 2477.
133. France, C. C. art. 1136, 1264, 1604; Germany C. C., art, 448; Italy, C. C. art. 710, 1125, 1463; Louisiana C. C. art. 2477, 870, 1910.
134. Mitchell v. Tuckers, 10 Mo. 260.
135. Spanish C. C., art. 1280.
136. Civil Code, art. 2440, 2275.
137. Civil Code, art. 2234.

rogated under oath, provided actual delivery has been made of the property thus sold.[138] It has been said that with regard to immovable property in Louisiana registry is essential to the sale, that the owner is not divested until the sale is registered in the conveyance office.[139] The supreme court of that state has held, however, that an unrecorded deed transfers property to a purchaser just as effectually as a recorded deed, as against all the world, except creditors of the vendor, and bona fide purchasers from him, without notice.[140] This certainly is the law of all other states of this country unless some statute requires recording as a prerequisite to validity.

138. Civil Code, art. 2275.
139. Saunder's Lectures, New Orleans, 1925, p. 456.
140. Logan v. Herbert, 30 La. Ann. 732; White v. Sheriff, 32 La. Ann. 130; McCall v. Irion, 41 La. Ann. 1126.

CHAPTER XIII

THE LAW OF PROPERTY, *continued*

JURA IN RE ALIENA

Real rights were of two sorts, rights over one's own property (jus in re propria), and rights over the property of some one else (jus in re aliena).[1] These latter rights are lesser rights than the right of ownership (dominium) yet they make inroads upon and curtail the rights of the owner. The very fact that one person has a right in the property of another person necessarily restricts and abridges the rights of ownership of such other. In other words, the owner of the property has for the time being parted with some of his rights. The rights of ownership, when intact, are said to be unlimited. The rights that one has in the property owned by another are, on the other hand, limited, that is, determined by the terms and conditions of their creation.

The Roman Law recognized four classes of jura in re aliena, namely, servitudes, emphyteusis, superficies, and mortgage (pignus and hypotheca).

Servitudes (servitutes), as the term implies, primarily signify that property owned by one person is not in a free condition of ownership but is subject to a burden or service (servitus) for the benefit of another person.[2] The term is, however, customarily employed in Roman Law to signify the benefit or the right which such other person enjoys. It is a jus in re

---

1. Moyle, Inst. 214.
2. Dig. 39, 1, 5, 9. See Harrison v. Boring, 44 Tex. 255; Henslee v. Boyd, 48 Tex. Civ. App. 494; Laumier v. Francis, 23 Mo. 181.

aliena since no one can have a servitude in his own property, "nulli res sua servit." [3]

Servitudes of the Roman Law are often said to be synonymous with easements in English Law. As pointed out, however, by Lord Chancellor Selborne,[4] servitude is a broader term than easement. With us, an easement is a right which the owner of one parcel of land has, by reason of such ownership, to use the land of another for a certain defined purpose not inconsistent with the general property in the latter. An easement involves no right to take.[5] The right to take a part of the soil or the produce of the land of another is called, in English Law, a profit à prendre. Servitudes, in Roman Law, include both our easements and profits à prendre.[6]

Servitudes in Roman Law are of two kinds, personal and praedial,[7] since they are attached either to persons or to things.[8] Personal servitudes are rights which persons have over the property of others, as usus and usufructus. Praedial servitudes are rights which certain lands or buildings (praedia) have over other near-by lands or buildings, such as a roadway (via), a watercourse (ductus aquae), or a right to light and air. Praedial servitudes are burdens imposed upon immovable property (lands or buildings) for the benefit of other immovables (lands or buildings) regardless of the persons who happen to own the two estates, the dominant and the servient as they are called. A personal servitude, on the other hand, is a mere right, irrespective of any other property he may own, which a person may exercise over the property

3. Dig. 8, 2, 26.
4. Dalton v. Angus, 6 App. Cas. 740 (1881).
5. Race v. Ward, 4 El. & Bl. 702; Wickham v. Hawker, 7 Mees. & W. 63.
6. Dalton v. Angus, 6 App. Cas. 740 (1881).
7. Dig. 8, 4, 1.
8. Dig. 8, 1, 1.

of some other person, whether such property be immovable or movable. It is only personal servitudes that include a right to take, praedial servitudes being, therefore, synonymous with easements in the English Law.

Praedial servitudes are further divided into rural servitudes and urban servitudes.[9] Due to the fact that the former, in early times, were more frequently exercised in the "country" and the latter in the "city," the terms rural and urban became established. They have, however, no such local meaning. There may be a rural servitude in the city, or an urban servitude in the country, since rural servitudes are attached to land, regardless of its location, and urban servitudes are attached to buildings wherever they may be. Paulus, in the Digest, more accurately says that some praedial servitudes are connected with the soil (solo), others with structures above the soil (superficie).[10] Personal servitudes are divided into four classes, usufructus, usus, habitatio, and operae servorum, or usufruct, use, habitation, and the services of slaves.

Usufructus: Usufructus is defined as the right to use and to take the fruits of the property of another,[11] the subject matter or source of the fruits being left intact: "jus alienis rebus utendi fruendi salva rerum substantia."[12] In other words, the use must not diminish the substance. The right lasts for the lifetime of the user unless a different term is fixed at the time of its creation.[13] The person who has the usufruct is called usufructuarius or fructuarius. The owner of the property subject to the usufruct is known as pro-

9. Inst. 2, 2, 3; Dig. 8, 1, 1.
10. Dig. 8, 1, 3.
11. Cartwright v. Cartwright, 18 Tex. 626, 628.
12. Dig. 7, 1, 1; Inst. 2, 4, pr.
13. Dig. 45, 1, 38, 12; Inst. 2, 4, 3. In case the usufruct was enjoyed by a corporation the term was limited to a hundred years unless otherwise provided. Dig. 7, 1, 56.

prietarius or dominus proprietatis, the ownership or the interest of the owner as long as the usufruct endured being a mere nuda proprietas. A usufruct may be created in both movable and immovable property, in lands, houses, slaves, beasts, in fact in everything except what is consumed by the very fact of its use, such as money, food, and clothes.[14] However, even in these things a law of the senate allowed a usufruct in case sufficient security were given to the heir.[15]

The usufructuary was entitled to the possession of the property,[16] and could make any lawful use of it.[17] His use, however, was required to be exercised in such a way that the reversionary interest of the dominus should not be impaired, or as we say in our law he could not commit waste.[18] His duty was to deal with the property as a "bonus paterfamilias."[19] Accordingly, while he could take branches and stakes for his vines,[20] he could not, however, cut down fruit trees.[21] It was incumbent upon him to cultivate land in a husband-like manner, to keep roofs tight, and to make other ordinary repairs.[22] He could not, however, alter the character of the property even though he might thereby increase its value. For example, a pleasure garden could not be converted into an orchard or vineyard;[23] a slave who had been employed in an artistic or literary occupation could not be used for manual

14. Inst. 2, 4, 2.
15. Dig. 7, 5; Inst. 2, 4, 2. Ulpian refers to an usufruct in clothes. Dig. 7, 1, 15, 4; 7, 9, 9, 3.
16. Dig. 41, 2, 12, pr.; 43, 17, 4.
17. See, in general, Dig. 7, 1.
18. Dig. 7, 1, 9, pr.; 7, 9, 1, pr.
19. Inst. 2, 1, 38.
20. Dig. 7, 1, 10.
21. Dig. 7, 1, 13, 4.
22. Dig. 7, 1, 9; 7, 1, 65; Cod., 3, 33, 7.
23. Dig. 7, 1, 13, 4.

labor;[24] a private house could not be used for a shop;[25] buildings could not be erected or torn down,[26] and even a new wing could not be added to a building.[27] He could, however, work stone quarries and clay and sand-pits,[28] and use open mines of gold, silver, copper, iron, and other minerals.[29] He could also, contrary to our English law rule relating to life tenants, open new mines if the land in his possession was of such extent as to justify it.[30]

The usufructuary could release or surrender his right to the owner,[31] but he could not alienate it absolutely to a third person.[32] He could, however, assign by way of pledge or mortgage his interest to another, the actual legal right remaining meanwhile in himself.[33] In case a usufruct was created by a legacy, it was the duty of the usufructuary, in absence of a contrary direction in the testament, to pay the taxes.[34]

Usus: In the same ways by which a usufructus can be created the bare use (nudus usus) of property may likewise be constituted.[35] It is a lesser right than that of usufruct since it is merely a right of user without a right of fructus.[36] The right to take the produce of a thing includes usus, but usus does not include the right to the produce, says Ulpian,[37] who further says that the usus of property may belong to one person, the fructus to another, and the bare ownership to a

24. Dig. 7, 1, 15, 1.
25. Dig. 7, 1, 13, 8.
26. Dig. 7, 1, 13, 6.
27. Dig. 7, 1, 13, 7.
28. Dig. 7, 1, 9, 2.
29. Dig. 7, 1, 9, 3; 7, 1, 13, 5.
30. Dig. 7, 1, 9, 3; 7, 1, 13, 5.
31. Inst. 2, 4, 3; Gaius 2, 30.
32. Inst. 2, 4, 3; Gaius 2, 30; Dig. 23, 3, 66; 10, 2, 15.
33. Dig. 7, 1, 12, 2; 7, 1, 38-40.
34. Dig. 7, 1, 52.
35. Dig. 7, 8, 1, 1; Inst. 2, 5, pr.
36. Dig. 7, 8, 1; Inst. 2, 5, 1.
37. Dig. 7, 8, 14, 1.

third. In such a case, however, the usus would be shared in common by the first two.[38] In other words, usus differs from usufructus in that usus, strictly speaking, is a mere right to use the property of another while usufructus is a right both to "use" and to take the fruits of another's property, or, as said by Ulpian, "Cui usus relictus est, uti potest, frui non potest."[39] To this general rule there are, however, certain exceptions. For example, if the usus is over land with a house, the usuary may occupy the house and take such fruits of the land as may be needed for himself and family;[40] also where the only practical benefit of the property would be its fruits, as the use of a woodland.[41]

Usus is, in general, confined to the personal needs of the usuary, but where one had the usus of a dwelling house he could occupy it together with his family, slaves, servants, freedmen, and guests, although it was questioned in earlier times whether the right included freedmen and guests.[42] The usuary could not, however, alienate the use.[43] Ordinarily the usuary was not bound to make repairs,[44] but if the property yielded no fruits for the owner the usuary was under obligation to repair.[45] The duties generally of the usuary were practically the same as those of a usufructuary, in that he must commit no waste, and must not overstep his rights.[46] He should cause no annoyance to the owner or impede, in any way, persons who are carrying on agricultural work.[47] If the usus is of land and a house,

38. Dig. 7, 8, 14, 2 and 3.
39. Dig. 7, 8, 2; Inst. 2, 5, 1.
40. Inst. 2, 5, 1; Dig. 7, 8, 12; 7, 8, 15, pr.
41. Dig. 7, 8, 22, pr.
42. Inst. 2, 5, 2; Dig. 7, 8, 2, 1; 7, 8, 4.
43. Inst. 2, 5, 1; Dig. 7, 8, 8, pr.; 7, 8, 11.
44. Dig. 7, 8, 18.
45. Inst. 2, 5, 1; Dig. 7, 8, 18.
46. Dig. 7, 8, 22, 2.
47. Dig. 7, 8, 11; 7, 8, 15, 1; Inst. 2, 5, 1.

the usuary has a free use of the place and may forbid the owner to enter, unless the owner and his workmen are there to cultivate the land.[48] In the same way in which the usuary cannot prevent the owner from enjoying the produce of the land, the owner cannot alter the position of the usuary for the worse or prevent him from doing anything a prudent man should do.[49]

Habitatio: Habitatio, or the right to occupy a house owned by another person, is a form of usus, and at one time it was doubted by the ancient Roman jurists whether it really was a right distinct from usus.[50] Papinian admitted that usus and habitatio were in their practical effect substantially the same.[51] One who had the right of habitation could not transfer it to another,[52] although in Justinian's time such a transfer was permitted,[53] and he could allow to occupy the premises only such persons as a usuary could.[54]

It is, however, distinguished from both usus and usufructus in that the right was not lost by non-user or by suffering capitis deminutio.[55] Originally, a habitatio continued for only a year, but later it could be created for life.[56]

Usus and habitatio are real rights, servitudes, and should not be confused with precarium. A precarium was the possession of a house or lands, or of a servitude, and later of movables, at the mere pleasure of the owner.[57] It was called a precarium because the possessor received the property by request (prece).[58]

48. Dig. 7, 8, 10, 4; 7, 8, 12.
49. Dig. 7, 8, 23; 7, 8, 15, 1.
50. Dig. 7, 8, 10; Cod. 3, 33, 3.
51. Dig. 7, 8, 10, pr.
52. Dig. 7, 8, 10, pr.
53. Inst. 2, 5, 5.
54. Dig. 7, 8, 10, pr.
55. Dig. 7, 8, 10, pr.
56. Dig. 7, 8, 10, 3.
57. Dig. 43, 26, 15, 2; 4, pr.; 12, pr.
58. Paulus Sent. Rec. 5, 6, 11.

It was like, in the case of land, unto our tenancy at will.

Operae Servorum: The services of slaves, also a similar right, operae animalium, the services of animals, were rights to the services of slaves or animals belonging to another.[59] Such rights were not considered as separate and independent forms of servitudes by either Gaius or Justinian, and were regarded by some of the ancient jurists as forms either of usufruct [60] or of usus.[61] Ulpian, however, says that such services were not wholly patterned upon usufruct.[62] He who has the use of a slave is not permitted to transfer his right to another person, since it is purely personal.[63] Moreover, in case of a legacy of operae servorum the right did not terminate with the death of the legatee but passed to his heirs being terminated by the death of the slave or slaves.[64] In this respect operae servorum or animalium differed from usufruct and usus which were extinguished by the death of the usufructuary. Another distinction was that the servitude operae servorum vel animalium was not lost by non-usage; likewise they were not terminated by capitis deminutio.

Praedial Servitudes: As already stated, praedial servitudes pertain to land, and require two parcels of land, since it is only where one is owner or tenant of a parcel of land or of a house (praedium), known as the praedium dominans, that he can have a praedial servitude in another's parcel of land or house, known as the praedium serviens. It is this class of servitudes that corresponds to easements in our English law.

59. Dig. 7, 7, 9, 5, 3.
60. Dig. 7, 1, 3, 1; 7, 7, 3. (Gaius).
61. Dig. 7, 7, 5. (Julianus).
62. Dig. 7, 9, 5, 3.
63. Inst. 2, 5, 3.
64. Dig. 33, 2, 2.

Praedial servitudes are divided into rural and urban servitudes.

Rural Servitudes: The most important rural, or rustic, servitudes are various rights of way, such as iter, actus, and via; certain water rights such as aquaeductus, aquaehaustus, and pecoris ad aquam appulsus. Among other rural servitudes are jus pascendi, calcis coquendae, arenae fodiendae, lapidis eximendi, and silvae caeduae.[65] Such illustrations are not exhaustive, however, since there may be many other rural servitudes, or servitudes that one piece of land renders to another.

Iter or Jus Eundi: Iter ordinarily means a footpath, a right to pass, to walk, but not to drive a beast or a carriage.[66] One may, however, be carried in a litter, or a horse may be ridden if the place permits,[67] but the terms of the servitude may expressly limit the right to a footpath.[68] The width of an iter was whatever was determined by the grant,[69] and the right could be granted to as many persons as the owner of the servient land wished.[70]

Actus: Actus is the right of driving a beast of burden, or cattle, or a chariot or cart, but not a laden chariot or cart, over the land of another.[71] It includes the right of iter,[72] and its width as in iter depended upon agreement.[73]

65. Inst. 2, 3, 2; Dig. 8, 3, 3, 1; 8, 3, 3, 2; 8, 3, 3, 6; 8, 1, 15, pr.; 43, 20, 1, 28.
66. Dig. 8, 1, 13; 8, 3, 1, pr.; 8, 3, 1, 12; Inst. 2, 3, pr. See Cater v. N. W. Teleph. Co., 60 Minn. 539; McCann v. Telephone Co., 69 Kan. 210, 214.
67. Dig. 8, 3, 7, pr.; 8, 3, 1, 12.
68. Dig. 8, 1, 4, 1. (semble).
69. Dig. 8, 3, 13, 2.
70. Dig. 8, 4, 15.
71. Inst. 2, 3, pr.; Dig. 8, 3, 1, pr.; 8, 3, 1, 12; 8, 3, 7, pr.
72. Dig. 8, 3, 1, pr.; Inst. 2, 3, pr.
73. Dig. 8, 3, 13, 2. See, however, Varro de L. L. 4, 46, where it is said that the width of actus is four feet.

Via: Via is a more comprehensive term than actus since it includes it, and in addition gives the right to drive a loaded cart or wagon, or even to haul timber and stone.[74] By the law of the Twelve Tables the width of a via was fixed at eight feet where the road was straight but in case of a turn in the road sixteen feet were allowed.[75] However, a via could be created for more or less than eight feet, provided the width was sufficient for the purpose.[76]

Aquaeductus: Aquaeductus is the right to conduct water across or from another's land to one's own land by means of pipes, trenches, or canals.[77] The terms of the grant usually determined the location of such a course, but Paulus says that a grant of a watercourse (iter aquae) across one's land without a designation of the location subjects the whole servient estate to the service.[78]

Aquaehaustus: Aquaehaustus is the right of taking water by means of buckets or other vessels from the spring, fountain, or pond of another.[79] Paulus mentions an imperial rescript, or decision, holding that although there was a non-user of a certain spring, through no default on the part of the dominant owner but owing to the fact that the spring had dried up, nevertheless the right should be restored when the spring began to flow again.[80] When one has a right to draw water he is held to have a right of iter also in order to have access to the water.[81]

Other Illustrations of Rural Servitudes: The servitude pecoris ad aquam appulsus is the right to

74. Dig. 8, 3, 7, pr.; 8, 3, 1, pr.; Inst. 2, 3, pr.
75. Dig. 8, 3, 8.
76. Dig. 8, 3, 23, pr.
77. Inst. 2, 3, pr.; Dig. 8, 3, 1, pr.; 43, 20, 1, 2 and 3.
78. Dig. 8, 3, 21.
79. Inst. 2, 3, 2; Dig. 8, 3, 1; 8, 3, 2, 1; 43, 22, 1, 6.
80. Dig. 8, 3, 35.
81. Dig. 8, 3, 3, 3.

drive cattle to water on the land of another;[82] jus pascendi is the right to pasture cattle on another's land,[83] or the right of agistment in our law; calcis coquendi is the right to burn lime on the servient estate;[84] arenae fodiendi is the right to dig for sand;[85] lapidis eximendi is the right to take stone from another's quarry;[86] and silvae caeduae is the right to cut wood on the land of another. In all of these cases, as in all other true servitudes, there must be two estates the dominant and the servient.[87]

In connection with the law of praedial servitudes some writers discuss certain limitations or restrictions placed upon the exercise of the ownership of land, and refer to such restrictions as "servitudes created or imposed by law." Thus, under the doctrine of the modern Civil Law, a doctrine derived in principle from the Roman Law,[88] lower land is said to be subject to the servitude of receiving the natural flow of surface water from higher and adjoining land. The owner of the lower land cannot, therefore, obstruct the drainage of surface water naturally flowing thereon from higher ground. Outside of Louisiana, this rule seems to have been first adopted in Pennsylvania, and is now followed in many states.[89] Judge Saunders, in his Lectures on the "Civil Code of Louisiana," speaks of this

82. Dig. 8, 3, 1, 1.
83. Dig. 8, 3, 1, 1; 8, 3, 4.
84. Dig. 8, 3, 1, 1.
85. Dig. 8, 3, 1, 1.
86. Dig. 8, 3, 6, 1.
87. Dig. 8, 3, 5.
88. McCormick v. Kansas City, etc. R. Co., 70 Mo. 359, 35 Am. Rep. 431.
89. Southern R. Co. v. Lewis, 154 Ala. 551, 51 So. 746; Sanguinetti v. Pock, 136 Cal. 466, 69 Pac. 98; Barrow v. Landry, 15 La. Ann. 581; Martin v. Jett, 12 La. 501, 32 Am. Dec. 120; Mirkil v. Morgan, 134 Pa. St. 144, 19 Atl. 628; Kauffman v. Griesemer, 26 Pa. St. 407, 67 Am. Dec. 437. See, also Cyc. 40-640, citing decisions from Georgia, Illinois, Iowa, Kentucky, Maryland, Michigan, North Carolina, Ohio, and Texas.

burden which obliges one piece of land to receive the water, or natural drain, from another piece of land that is above it, as a servitude imposed by law.[90] Elsewhere it is said that the upper estate, the dominant estate, has a natural easement to have the water that falls upon it flow off the same upon the field below, which is burdened with a corresponding servitude, the two pieces of land being in the nature of dominant and servient tenements.[91] Under this doctrine the servient owner cannot by embankments stop the natural flow of surface water from the dominant land and thus throw it back upon the latter.[92]

This Civil Law doctrine is contrary to the Common Law doctrine which regards surface water as a common enemy which every proprietor may ward off as he deems best, even though it does throw the water back upon the land of the adjoining proprietor.[93] Some jurisdictions distinguish, however, between urban and rural property, holding that in case of urban property, even in some states following the Civil Law rule in rural lands, that the urban proprietor may fill in a lot so as to bring it up to grade, regardless of the effect it may have in turning surface water upon adjoining lots.[94] The duty of a lower piece of land to receive the surface water flowing naturally from a higher piece of land although owned by another person, is not, however, a "servitude." It is a natural right, not an easement, that the higher land possesses, and a natural duty imposed by law for the public welfare, not a servitude, that the lower land is bound to observe. There is a number of such duties imposed by the Roman

90. Saunders' "Lectures on the Civil Law," p. 176.
91. Peck v. Herrington, 109 Ill. 611; Totel v. Bonnefoy, 123 Ill. 653, 14 N. E. 687; Farkas v. Towns, 103 Ga. 150, 29 S. E. 700; Gray v. McWilliams, 98 Cal. 157, 32 Pac. 976.
92. Gillham v. Madison Co. R. Co., 49 Ill. 484, 95 Am. Dec. 627.
93. See Cyc., Vol. 40, p. 642, citing many cases.
94. See Cyc. 40-643, citing Ala., Iowa, Pa., and other states.

Law, as, for example, the duty to permit one to come upon your land in search of his property, and to remove the same if found there;[95] the duty imposed by the Twelve Tables upon every houseowner in Rome to leave a vacant space two and a half feet wide around any building erected by him as a safeguard against fire; the duty to cut off branches from trees, providing such branches were less than fifteen feet from the ground, which extend over land belonging to an adjacent owner.[96] It was a general duty imposed by Roman Law upon the owner of property that he should not use his property in such a way that it would cause an injury to another. Accordingly one may not erect works upon his own ground hurtful to others. If he does so they have a right to a legal remedy. From this doctrine came, probably, our own Common Law doctrine of abating a nuisance as well as the recovery of damages for the wrong.[97] Such restrictions fall under the head of "wrongs" or delicts, and are no part of the law of servitudes. The duty of lower land to receive the surface water from higher land was discussed by the ancient Roman jurists under the term aqua pluvia, or rain water. The Roman Law permitted an action to be brought (aquae pluviae arcendae actio) either against one who diverted the natural course of rain water and in so doing injured the land of an adjoining owner, or against a lower owner who prevented the water from flowing naturally from the higher to the lower ground.[98] The modern rule, in some jurisdictions, that this natural right applies only to rural and not to urban lands,[99] is derived from the Roman Law which allowed this action only in case of

95. Dig. 10, 4, 15; 39, 2, 9, 1; 19, 1, 25; 43, 28.
96. Dig. 47, 27, 1, pr.; 47, 27, 1, 7-9.
97. See Thurston v. Hancock, 12 Mass. 220; note, 227.
98. Dig. 39, 2; Cicero, Mur. 10, Top. 9.
99. Nininger v. Norwood, 72 Ala. 277; Boyd v. Conklin, 54 Mich. 583.

injury to land and not to injuries caused to a building. The land of an adjoining owner may be subject to a servitude in connection with rain water, by agreement of the parties, but the natural right and duty does not constitute a servitude.

Urban Servitudes: Servitudes connected with buildings, regardless whether the buildings are in the city or in the country, are called urban servitudes, or servitudes which deal with immovables erected upon the land (superficies), in contrast with rural servitudes which affect only the land.[100] The most common servitudes pertaining to buildings are the right of support (oneris ferendi); the right to insert beams in a neighboring wall (tigni immittendi); the right to have part of one's house project over the land of another (projiciendi); the right of rain-drip (stillicidii); the right either to build or to prevent the building of a house high enough to shut off one from the light (altius tolendi or non tolendi).[101]

The owner of a house may have the right to make use of the wall or building of an adjoining owner as a support for his own (oneris ferendi). This "servitude of support" may be a duty upon the servient property to support a part or even the whole of a neighboring building. In either case the servient owner is bound to keep his building or wall in repair so as to furnish the support it owes.[102]

The existence of such a servitude in the city of Rome may seem inconsistent with the statement previously made that a regulation of the Twelve Tables required house owners to leave an open space (ambitus) of two and a half feet in width around their dwellings. This law had, however, long fallen into disuse, and as the city grew it was the custom to erect houses of different

100. Dig. 8, 3, 12.
101. Gaius 2, 14; Inst. 2, 3, 1; Dig. 8, 2.
102. Inst. 2, 3, 1; Dig. 8, 2, 1, 1; 8, 2, 33; 8, 5, 6, 2.

owners with a common wall. It was not until after the great fire in the reign of Nero that the requirement of an open space around each building was re-enacted. The great apartment houses in Rome were called insulae (islands) because they covered an entire "square," and were surrounded by streets as islands are surrounded by water. In these great buildings, often several stories in height, the poorer tenants of Rome dwelt, occupying either "a flat" or a separate room. In the time of the emperors Antoninus and Severus the ancient law was applied to the space to be left around the insulae.[103]

The right to insert a beam, tile, stone, or piece of iron (all classed under the term tigna) in or upon a neighbor's wall was known as servitus tigni immittendi. This right, however, did not impose any legal duty upon the servient owner to keep the wall in repair.[104]

The right of having a part of one's building project over the land of another, as, for example, in case of a projecting balcony, was called servitus projiciendi et protegendi, or a servitude of projecting or overhanging. It involved no right of support or right to insert a beam in another's building, but merely created a right that a certain part of one's building, as, for example, the eaves, a projecting window or a balcony, might overhang the land belonging to another.[105] Like unto our English Law, the owner of land owned all above him, ad coelum, and no adjoining owner could lawfully project his building into the air area above the land of another unless such a servitude existed.

Servitus stillicidii was primarily the right to have the rain water from the roof of one's house to flow in its natural course upon a neighbor's land. Other forms

---

103. Dig. 8, 2, 14.
104. Dig. 8, 5, 8, 2; 8, 2, 2, and 6; 8, 6, 18, 2.
105. Dig. 8, 2, 2; 43, 17, 3, 5 & 6.

THE LAW OF PROPERTY   369

of this servitude consisted in a right to conduct by means of a pipe the rain water from one's roof to adjoining land, or the right to receive such water from a neighbor's house in one's garden or cistern (recipiendi vel avertendi).[106]

It was often a great benefit to have the use of additional water from a neighboring roof. Many Roman houses of the more expensive class were built around a courtyard, the roofs slanting to the interior so that the rain water might run into a cistern (impluvium) in the center of the court. However, the plan of building was not uniform. Some houses had flat roofs with tiled gutters, and some roofs slanted towards the outside.

Servitus stillicidii is connected in our English law with the right of eaves-drip, that is, the easement which the owner of a house may obtain by grant or prescription to have the rain water from his roof and eaves fall upon the land of an adjoining owner.[107]

Another well known urban servitude is the servitude altius non tollendi, or the right which the owner of land has to prevent an adjoining owner from erecting buildings upon his land beyond a certain height.[108] In this way the owner of the dominant property could insure his prospect and light from being impaired. "Light" means a view of the sky, says the Digest,[109] while "prospect" means an unobstructed view over the lower levels.

The owner of a building not subject to a servitude may raise its height as he pleases although it does cut off the flow of light to his neighbor.[110] Lights (lumina)

106. Dig. 8, 2, 17, 3; 8, 2, 20, 3-6.
107. Neale v. Sealey, 47 Barb. (N. Y.) 314. Cf. Bellows v. Sackett, 15 Barb. (N. Y.) 96; Harvey v. Walters, L. R. 8 C. P. 162.
108. Dig. 8, 2, 2.
109. Dig. 8, 2, 16.
110. Dig. 8, 2, 9; 8, 6, 5; 39, 2, 26; Code 3, 34, 8.

[Roman Law]—24

and prospects (prospectus) are not natural rights, but may be created and protected as servitudes.[111]

A servitude preventing the building of a house beyond a certain height, a servitude created by private law, should not be confused with municipal restrictions imposed for the general welfare. To guard against fire and also against the fall of cheaply built insulae, Augustus limited the height of new buildings to seventy feet,[112] and in the reign of Trajan the maximum height was fixed at sixty feet.[113]

In addition to the urban servitudes above enumerated, there are several others mentioned in the Digest. Thus, an owner of a building may have a right to maintain a drain or sewer through neighboring premises (servitus cloacae immittendae);[114] the smoke from the household fire in one home may by a servitude be carried off through the chimney of an upper or a side dweller (servitus fumi immittendae);[115] and one may have a right to have the light of day uninterrupted by any buildings, trees, or other obstructions upon neighboring premises.[116] Moreover, as also in the case of rural servitudes, the enumeration of well-recognized urban servitudes does not close the list. New conditions may require new servitudes, and such may of course be created in accordance with the principles governing servitudes in general.

Real and Personal Servitudes:

It will be observed from the foregoing illustrations of servitudes that the difference between personal and real servitudes lies not in the nature of the service but

111. Dig. 8, 2, 15; 8, 2, 4.
112. Strabo 5, 235.
113. Aur. Victor, Epit. 13.
114. Dig. 8, 1, 7; 43, 23, 1, 4.
115. Dig. 8, 5.
116. Dig. 8, 2, 3, 12, 15–17; 8, 2, 4, 40; Cod. 3, 34, 8.

[Roman Law]

THE LAW OF PROPERTY 371

in the nature of the right to the service. Both personal and real (praedial) servitudes are "real rights," or jura in re and not mere rights to a thing, jura ad rem. The right of a personal servitude attaches, however, to a person, while the right of a praedial servitude attaches to a thing, a res.[117] A personal servitude requires only one res, while a praedial requires two, a dominant and a servient res. The distinction is not that a personal servitude endures for the life of its owner while a praedial servitude runs with the land, since praedial servitudes may be granted for the benefit of a person or may be made perpetual. By express limitation, a personal servitude, such as operae servorum, may also go to a man's heirs.[118] If A grants to B the right to draw water from A's well, the servitude is purely personal, but if A is the dominus of a piece of land and grants such a right to B, the owner of another piece of land, and to all subsequent owners of the same land, the right runs with the land, and thus becomes "real" instead of "personal."

Servitudes are also sometimes classed as negative and positive. A negative servitude is a right to prevent one from doing something which without such restriction he could lawfully do, as where one by right of such a servitude may prevent an adjoining owner from building above a certain height. A positive servitude, on the other hand, is a right to do what one without such right could not lawfully do, as a right to go over the land of another. Servitudes are also said to be passive, that is, merely permissive, since the servient owner merely permits something to be done on his land, or refrains from doing some particular thing.[119] However, in the case of the servitude of support (on-

117. Dig. 50, 16, 86.
118. Dig. 33, 2, 2.
119. Dig. 8, 1, 15, 1.

eris ferendi) the servient owner is bound to keep his wall or building in repair.[120]

Servitudes How Created and Lost:

Servitudes were created under the old law, the jus civile, by legacy, in jure cessio, and adjudicatio. Being incorporeal they are obviously unable to be transferred by delivery (traditio),[121] just as we say in our own law that incorporeal hereditaments lie in grant and not in livery of seisin. However, in Italy, rural servitudes were classed among res mancipi, and, consequently, could be created by mancipatio as well as by in jure cessio.[122] In the provinces, on the other hand, servitudes could be created only by pacts and stipulations since land itself outside of Italy could not be conveyed either by mancipatio or in jure cessio.[123]

The grantor of a valid servitude must be the absolute owner of the praedium serviens, the dominus directus, or, as we say, the owner in fee, since if he is a conditional owner a grant by him of a servitude will be extinguished if his own interest be terminated.[124]

Under the praetorian and the later laws of Justinian, servitudes could be acquired by pacts and stipulations (that is, by agreement of the parties, or grant); [125] by legacy; [126] by prescription; by adjudicatio; and by a reservation on the part of the dominant owner in his transfer of land to another.[127]

According to the jus civile, servitudes being incorporeal were not subject to usucapio, since no "possession" could be obtained of them. Under the prae-

120. Dig. 8, 2, 33; 8, 5, 6, 2.
121. Gaius 2, 28.
122. Gaius 2, 31.
123. Gaius 2, 31.
124. Dig. 8, 6, 11, 1; Cod. 4, 51.
125. Inst. 2, 3, 4; 2, 4, 1; Dig. 7, 1, 3, pr.; 7, 1, 6, pr.
126. Inst. 2, 3, 4; Dig. 8, 2, 31.
127. See Frost-Johnson Lumber Co. v. Salling's Heirs, 150 La. 756.

torian law, however, a quasi possession, or, as we would say, an equitable possession, was recognized, and this kind of possession was protected by praetorian, or equitable, remedies.[128] Such a possession or user had to be, however, under a claim of right,[129] and the claimant was required to show that his use had not been forcible (vi), secret (clam), or permissive (precario). We see in these terms the origin of similar rules in our own law concerning prescriptive rights. In Justinian's time, however, the law of prescription was made a legal mode of acquiring servitudes.[130]

A servitude could also be created by judicial decree (adjudicatio) in the division of an inheritance among the heirs. The judge could impose on one piece of land a service for the benefit of another piece.[131]

In our own Common Law, it is said that easements can be created by grant or by prescription. Owing to this rule the English cases have held that an easement cannot be created by a reservation in favor of a grantor. Our American cases have taken an opposite view, which view is entirely supported by the Roman Law, for by that law if a man sells a piece of land he can subject it to a servitude for his own benefit.[132] In the case of a praedial servitude such a reservation requires two pieces of land, and the service may be imposed either upon the piece sold or the piece retained.[133] A grantor cannot, however, reserve a servitude in favor of anyone but himself.[134] This is also the rule in our own law.

128. Dig. 8, 1, 20; 8, 5, 10; 8, 4, 2.
129. Dig. 8, 6, 25.
130. Codex 7, 33, 12.
131. Dig. 10, 2, 22, 3.
132. Dig. 8, 1, 19. Frost-Johnson Lumber Co. v. Salling's Heirs, 150 La. 756.
133. Dig. 8, 4, 3; 8, 4, 6; 8, 2, 34; 8, 2, 35; 8, 4, 7.
134. Dig. 8, 4, 5.

Under the old law, the jus civile, servitudes were not subject to any limitation of time or conditions,[135] but in the days of Papinian it was well settled that servitudes could be created with limitations both as to the time of user and with conditions imposed concerning the way and manner in which the benefit could be enjoyed.[136]

Servitudes may be lost or extinguished in various ways, depending upon the character of the servitude whether praedial or personal. Moreover, in the case of praedial servitudes a distinction is made between rural and urban servitudes.

Praedial servitudes are lost by merger in case the same person becomes the owner of the two estates.[137] They are also lost by non-user. There is a difference, however, between rural and urban servitudes in regard to non-user. Rural servitudes are lost merely by the fact of non-user for a specific length of time, two years at first, later ten years; urban servitudes are lost by non-user only when the dominant estate ceases to use the benefit and the servient estate at the same time prevents the use of it. For example, if A has the urban servitude of a right to insert a house beam into the wall of B's adjoining house and merely takes out the beam, he does not lose his right; however, if during the same time, B blocks up the cavity from which the beam was taken, then A does lose his right.[138] It is the servient estate's possession of freedom (usucapio libertatis) as much as the dominant estate's non-user that in such cases resulted in the extinguishment of the servitude.

A servitude is also lost by the destruction of the

---

135. Dig. 8, 1, 4, pr.; 8, 1, 8.
136. Dig. 8, 1, 4, 1 and 2; 8, 1, 5, 1.
137. Dig. 8, 6, 1; 8, 1, 18; 8, 2, 30; 8, 3, 27.
138. Dig. 8, 2, 6. (Gaius.)

THE LAW OF PROPERTY   375

property over which the right was exercised;[139] by the expiration of the time limited (one hundred years in the case of a municipal corporation);[140] by breach of a condition imposed;[141] by release or surrender;[142] by death or capitis deminutio of the person entitled in case of personal,[143] but not of praedial, servitudes.[144] Personal servitudes are also lost by non-user;[145] by merger (consolidatio); and where a usufructuary acquires the ownership of the property.[146]

Emphyteusis:

Another real right in the property of another is emphyteusis, a Greek word compounded from "en," upon, and "phuteuo," grafted, that is, "grafted upon," and signifying a right grafted upon the dominium or ownership. It was a long lease, usually a perpetual lease, of large tracts of land, whereby the tenant, known as the emphyteuta, had practically all the rights of an owner, the technical owner (dominus) having only a naked title (nudum dominium). Many have seen in this relationship of emphyteuta, and dominus the prototype of the double ownership of feudal lands.[147]

In early days, land belonging to municipalities was leased for such length of time as a certain rent (vectigal) was paid, that is, leased in a possible perpetu-

139. Dig. 7, 1, 2; 7, 4, 30; Inst. 2, 4, 3.
140. Dig. 7, 1, 56; Inst. 2, 4, 3.
141. Dig. 7, 4, 15; 8, 1, 4.
142. Dig. 8, 1, 6; 8, 6, 8; Inst. 2, 4, 3.
143. Dig. 2, 4, 3; 7, 4, 14; Codex 3, 33, 14; **Inst. 2, 4, 3**. Not in the case of habitatio, however. Dig. 8, 10, pr.
144. Dig. 8, 6, 3.
145. Dig. 7, 4, 25; Inst. 2, 4, 3.
146. Inst. 2, 4, 3.
147. Moyle, Inst. 4th ed., 323–325; Maine, Ancient Law, 299, 302, 303; MacKenzie Rom. Law, 7th ed., 191–193; Muirhead, Rom. Law, 2d Ed., 392–394.

ity.[148] The same thing was done with the public lands of Rome (agri vectigales), and also with lands owned by various corporate bodies. In time private land (vectigale praedium) became the subject of similar contracts, and sometime during the second century of the Christian era the Greek term emphyteusis was applied to the transaction. Ulpian is said to have been the first writer to use the expression.[149]

Some doubt arose among the Roman lawyers as to the nature of this contract. Some, including Gaius, said it was a contract of letting and hiring (locatio-conductio).[150] Others held that the contract was in the nature of a sale of the land, since the emphyteuta had practically all the rights of an owner. The emperor Zeno (475–491) declared by a constitutio that it was neither a contract of hiring or of sale, but a contract sui generis resting on the peculiar nature of the agreement. This view was confirmed by Justinian.[151]

The emphyteuta, or tenant, could keep the land as long as he paid the annual rent (pensio, canon). He could be ejected, however, in case the rent was in arrears for three years.[152] He had all the rights of a usufructuary, and in addition could create servitudes, sub-let, mortgage, or sell the land.[153] He could not, however, impair the property,[154] and in case of sale he was bound to give the owner the right of preëmption.

Upon the death of an emphyteuta, the property went to his heirs. In our own law, perpetual leases, or covenants for continued renewals of leases for years

---

148. Gaius 3, 145 (where such a lease is called a perpetuity, "in perpetuum").
149. MacKenzie, Rom. Law, 7th Ed., p. 191; Dig. 27, 9, 3, 4.
150. Gaius 3, 145.
151. Inst. 3, 24, 3.
152. Codex 4, 66, 1; See Blk. Com. III, 232.
153. Dig. 13, 7, 16, 2; Nov. 7, 3, 2.
154. Nov. 7, 3, 2.

have not been favored since they tend to create perpetuities.[155] Some have been held valid, however, when there is an express covenant to that effect.[156] Thus, it has been held in Pennsylvania that a lease for a term of years, wherein it was provided that the lessee, his heirs and assigns, might hold the premises so long as he and they should think proper, after the expiration of the term, at the same rent, is a perpetual lease at the will of the lessee, "and may be equivalent to a fee simple." [157] The former-time manorial leases in New York have sometimes been called perpetual leases. They were, however, grants in fee subject to a perpetual rent charge.[158] Similar to these are the ground rent conveyances in Pennsylvania.[159] Maryland has, however, a form of lease known as a forever renewable lease.[160] A grant in fee with a perpetual rent charge or a ground rent transfers the ownership of the land, the new owner paying the rental to the former owner. In emphyteusis of the Roman Law, the ownership (dominium) of the land was not conveyed. The dominium technically remained where it was, although the emphyteuta had, as stated, all the practical rights of an owner.

Superficies:

Superficies is a right similar to emphyteusis, in that it is a long or perpetual enjoyment or use of anything built upon land, upon the payment of an annual rent (solarium, pensio).[161] Ordinarily, in case one

155. Nakdimen v. Atkinson Improv. Co., 149 Ark. 448, 233 S. W. 694; Brush v. Beecher, 110 Mich. 597, 68 N. W. 420.
156. See Landlord and Tenant, Corpus Juris. Vol. 35, p. 1017.
157. Effinger v. Lewis, 32 Penn. St. Rep. 367.
158. Van Rensselaer v. Hays, 19 N. Y. 68; Tyler v. Heidorn, 46 Barb. (N. Y.) 439; Millard v. McMullin, 68 N. Y. 345.
159. Bosler v. Kuhn, 8 Watts & S. (Pa.) 183; Ingersoll v. Sergeant, 1 Whart. (Pa.) 337.
160. Banks v. Haskee, 45 Md. 207; Kraft v. Egan, 76 Md. 243. See, also, 16 Ohio St. 478.
161. Dig. 6, 1, 74; 43, 18, 2.

builds upon the land of another, the building, by the law of accession, becomes the property of the owner of the land, superficies solo cedit. In time, however, there grew up a custom whereby the owner of land agreed that another might build upon the land and perpetually enjoy the use of the building by paying an annual sum. The builder, known as the superficiary, was said to have a superficies in the land,[162] and the praetor recognized this as a jus in re which he protected by allowing proper actions for such purpose (interdict de superficie and an actio in rem utilis).[163]

The duration of the right might be forever or for a definite period in accordance with the agreement of the parties concerned. The superficiary had the right to make repairs upon or to improve his building, but he could not commit waste by causing any deterioration of the land itself.[164]

A superficies could be created in a single story of a building.[165]

A superficiary could mortgage or sell his interest, but the owner had no pre-emption right as in case of emphyteusis.[166] Upon the death of a superficiary the superficies passed to his heirs if not previously alienated.

In many respects, says Lord MacKenzie,[167] the jus superficiarium bore a strong resemblance to the long building leases granted by landholders in England, in consideration of a rent, and under the reservation of the ownership of the soil.

The fourth right in the property of another is pignus, the property right known to us as both pledge and

162. Dig. 6, 1, 74.
163. Dig. 43, 17, 3, 7.
164. Dig. 43, 18, 1, pr.; 43, 18, 3.
165. Dig. 43, 17, 3, 7.
166. Dig. 43, 18, 1, pr.; 13, 7, 16, 2.
167. Rom. Law, 7th ed., p. 193.

mortgage. It is a subject of especial value to American law students since our doctrines in regard to mortgage have been derived from the Roman Law. As said by the Supreme Court of the United States,[168] "The Civil Law is the springhead of the English jurisprudence upon this subject."

The study of the forms of mortgage in the Roman Law is valuable for a twofold reason. It shows the evolution of the theory of mortgage in that system of jurisprudence, and also the origin of the equitable theory of mortgage that now prevails in most of our American states. In the Illinois case of Longwith v. Butler, the court said: "It will be conceded by all who have any knowledge of the Roman Law, that all the equitable doctrines now universally prevailing in regard to mortgages, have been derived from that source. The Civil Law, in this as in many other instances, has been the great armory from which the courts of equity, in England, have supplied themselves with the most efficient weapons to ward off the severities of the stern and unrelenting Common Law."

The first form of pledge or mortgage among the Romans was an absolute conveyance, a literal transfer of ownership by mancipatio or in jure cessio, accompanied with an agreement on the creditor's part to reconvey the property to the debtor upon payment of the debt. It was not an absolute conveyance with a defeasance clause as in the English Common Law, a conveyance upon condition subsequent, but a conveyance, a sale of the property, with an ancillary agreement that the creditor would sell back the property when the debt was paid. This transaction was known as fiducia,[169] the borrower being dependent upon the hon-

---

168. Gilman v. Ill. & Miss. Teleg. Co., 91 U. S. 603. See. also, Longwith v. Butler, 8 Ill. 32, 36; Wheeler v. Insurance Co., 101 U. S. 439, 443.

169. Mancipatio fiduciae causa.

or and faith (fides) of the creditor. In this form of mortgage there was no way of compelling the restoration of the property, the res, upon the payment of the debt. The debtor was left to his personal action, the actio fiduciae, an action equitable in its nature, or what the Roman lawyers called an actio bonae fidei, depending upon the magistrate's decision as to what under all the circumstances an honorable man should, in good faith, do.[170] The legal title of the property was in the creditor and he could sell it, if he wished, to some third person. The debtor had no "real" right, that is, no remedy against the property itself.

Under a fiduciary sale, the borrower, therefore, obtained his loan at great risk as far as the recovery of the specific property was concerned. This led, in time of the praetors, to a change in the law. The praetor by his edict provided that instead of making a formal conveyance of the ownership of the property to the creditor, the creditor should be placed in the *possession* of the property, but its ownership should remain with the debtor. This transaction was known as pignus or pledge. The possession of the property pledged as security was in the creditor, but the debtor had all the rights and remedies of ownership.[171] If the debtor paid his debt, and meanwhile the creditor had sold the property, the debtor had an owner's right, a "real" right, to recover it from any one who had obtained possession of it.[172] When property had been pledged by being put into the possession of the creditor, the security extended to all the increase that arose from the pledge, as, for example, in the pledge of cattle.[173]

Upon default of the debtor to meet his obligation when due there was usually an agreement that the

170. See Sohn's Inst., 3d Ed., p. 62.
171. Dig. 13, 7, 35; Casey v. Cavaroc, 96 U. S. 467, 480.
172. Dig. 13, 7, 8, 3; 13, 7, 34.
173. Cahoon v. Miers, 67 Md. 573, 11 Atl. 278.

property might be sold by the creditor who after paying himself out of the proceeds of the sale returned the surplus, if any, to the debtor. In some cases it was provided that the property should become absolute in the creditor upon default of the debtor (lex commissoria). This resembles the English Common Law mortgage upon failure of the mortgagor to pay the debt upon "the law day." However, this harsh provision was declared invalid by a constitution in the time of Constantine.[174]

In the mortgage of property by "fiducia" the ownership of the property passes, as we have seen, to the creditor, while in pignus only the possession is given to him. The last step in the development of the Roman Law of pledge was brought about by a further praetorian edict some time later. Although pignus was in many ways preferable to fiducia, yet it frequently happened that the debtor desired to retain the possession of the property pledged, and the creditor, also, may not have cared to have its possession. By a new action allowed by the praetor, the actio hypothecaria, the debtor was permitted to retain the possession of the property pledged, when an agreement of pledge had been made, and the creditor, upon default of the debtor, was then permitted to have possession. This transaction became the hypotheca of the Roman Law, and this method of pledge and its name were both adopted by the Romans from the Greeks, the word "hypotheca" meaning to place under a charge or obligation.

Upon obtaining, by means of the action allowed by the praetor, the possession of the property upon the debtor's default, the creditor could sell it in satisfaction of his claim. Due notice (denunciatio) had to be given to the debtor of the intention to sell, and it seems

---

174. Codex 8, 35, 3.

that even after the notice the debtor had two years in which to redeem the property before it could be finally sold.[175] The sale had to be made upon a fixed day. If there were a prior creditor he was entitled to have his claim satisfied first. It was also the duty of the creditor who made the sale to see that it was conducted with legal formality, and that the rights of the debtor were protected in good faith.[176]

In Roman Law, both pignus and hypotheca applied to movables and immovables alike. The notion entertained by some that pignus applied only to movables while hypotheca applied exclusively to immovables, is erroneous. Each applied to both classes of property. In the modern Civil Law, however, such a distinction is made, and a pledge of movables is called a pawn (pignus), while "hypothec," or mortgage, is a right to subject immovable property to a charge for the satisfaction of an obligation.[177] Movable property cannot be subjected to hypothec in the modern Civil Law, and a chattel mortgage, as understood in our law is unknown.[178] As previously stated, however, in connection with movable and immovable property, immovables, in the Civil Law, include things intended "by destination" for the use of land. In this sense, therefore, a hypothec of a plantation may include animals on the land.

"By the civil law of Spain and Mexico," says the supreme court of Texas,[179] "mortgage is a contract by which one binds his property to secure the payment of some obligation." This is the theory of the modern

---

175. Codex 8, 28, 5; 8, 14, 10; Inst. 4, 7, 1; Dig. 13, 7, 4; 47, 2, 73.

176. Dig. 6, 1, 65; Codex 8, 30, 2; Dig. 21, 2, 50; Codex 8, 28, 4.

177. See French Civ. Code, art. 2071–2119; Spanish Civil Code, art. 1857–1875.

178. See Moussier v. Zunts, 14 La. Ann. 15; French C. C. art. 2119; Louisiana, Rev. C. C. art. 3278–3289.

179. Coles v. Perry, 7 Tex. 109, 146.

Civil Law in general,[180] and it is also the equitable or the lien theory of mortgage in our own law.

Antichresis:

Another technical term used by the Romans in connection with pledge was antichresis, another Greek word, meaning literally, reciprocal use or wage.. In antichresis,[181] the possession was delivered to the creditor with the express agreement that all the produce or income of the property (fructus) should belong to the creditor in lieu of interest.[182] In the modern Civil Law, a pledge of immovables, whereby possession is given to the creditor with right to collect the revenues, applying them to the interest on the debt, and also, if sufficient, to the reduction of the principal, is likewise an antichresis.[183] Such a pledge corresponds to the old vivum vadium, or live pledge (or mortgage) of the early English law whereby the rents and profits of the land were taken by the pledgee in possession and applied to the reduction of the debt. The pledge was thus said to be alive. In the modern Civil Law antichresis is not, therefore, the same thing as hypotheca. In antichresis the creditor is placed in possession. In hypotheca the debtor retains the possession. Antichresis operates upon the fruits, hypotheca affects the land. There may be at the same time upon the same piece of land a mortgage (hypotheca) in favor of one creditor, and an agreement of antichresis in favor of another creditor.[184]

The Roman Law theories of real rights in the property of others, that is, rights not merely personal, but

180. Duclaud v. Rousseau, 2 La. Ann. 168; McNair v. Lott, 25 Mo. 182; Eglauch v. Labadie, 21 Quebec Super. Ct. 481.
181. Dig. 13, 7, 33.
182. Dig. 20, 1, 11, 1.
183. See French Civil Code, art. 2085-2091. See, also, Livingston v. Story, 11 Pet. (U. S.) 351, 388; Marquise E. Portes v. Hurlbut, 44 N. J. Eq. 517.
184. Pickersgill v. Brown, 7 La. Ann. 297, 314.

rights enforceable against everybody, and the doctrines in connection with such rights that were developed by the Roman jurists, have influenced to an incalculable extent all subsequent law.

The Roman Law of servitudes has been retained in practical entirety in the codes of modern Civil Law countries. Usufruct, use, and habitation are terms still commonly employed,[185] and real servitudes, or burdens imposed on one piece of land for the benefit of another belonging to a different proprietor, under substantially the same rules as are found in the Roman Law, are generally recognized.[186] The old distinction between use and usufruct, in that the former is entitled only to what is necessary for his personal wants and those of his family,[187] while the right of a usufructuary extends to all the fruits produced by the thing of which he has the usufruct,[188] is still made by most of the codes. Emphyteusis also still exists in some Civil Law countries,[189] its duration being usually in perpetuity. In Quebec, however, it cannot exceed ninety-nine years and must be for more than nine,[190] while, in Japan, the period is limited from twenty to fifty years.[191]

185. Brazil C. C. art. 713; French C. C. art. 578; German C. C. art. 1030; Italian C. C. art. 477; Louisiana Rev. C. C. art. 533. See Strausse v. Sheriff, 43 La. Ann. 501, 503; Samuels v. Brownlee, 36 La. Ann. 228, 233; Fisk v. Fisk, 3 La. Ann. 494, 496; Cartwright v. Cartwright, 18 Tex. 626. In Louisiana, usus and habitation are said to be alike and subject to the same rules. Rev. C. C. 635.

186. See, for example, French C. C. art. 687; Mexican C. C. art. 944; Quebec C. C. art. 546.

187. France, C. C. art. 630; Italy, C. C. art. 477; Louisiana, Rev. C. C. art. 533; Quebec, C. C. art. 487; Spain, C. C. art. 524; Switzerland, C. C. art. 776.

188. France, C. C. art. 578; Italy, C. C. art. 521; Louisiana Rev. C. C. art. 626; Quebec, C. C. art. 443; Spain, C. C. art. 467; Switzerland, C. C. art. 745.

189. Germany, C. C. art. 1017; Japan, C. C. art. 270 et seq.; Louisiana, Rev. C. C. 2779; Quebec, C. C. art. 567; Spain, C. C. arts. 1605, 1628.

190. Quebec, C. C. 568.

191. Japanese C. C. art. 278.

In our own law, many of the doctrines of usus, usufructus, and habitatio are found in our law of landlord and tenant. The usufructuarius of the Roman Law corresponds in many ways to the English tenant and the dominus, or owner of the land, to the landlord. There are, of course, many differences in the law of the two systems, yet the basic principles are alike. Our law of easements has been taken almost entirely from the Roman Law of praedial servitudes. There must be two pieces of land, the dominant and the servient estate, just as in the Roman Law. They are themselves incorporeal, yet are imposed upon corporeal property, and not upon the owner thereof. They confer no rights to a participation in the profits, but are imposed for the benefit of other corporeal property. In all these essentials our law follows the Roman. Likewise our modern law of mortgages of land, whereby, according to the equitable theory prevailing in most states, a mortgage deed no longer, as at Common Law, conveys the legal title of the land to the mortgagee, but merely gives him a lien upon it, has been derived, as already stated, from the law of Rome. It should, therefore, be more and more apparent that to that great system of jurisprudence we are indebted for a large part of the law that we call our own.

CHAPTER XIV

THE LAW OF OBLIGATIONS

General Principles

The Roman law of obligations is a voluminous subject, including both our law of contracts and of torts (delicts). By the ancient elementary writers who divided the law into three great branches, Persons, Property (Res), and Actions, obligations were treated, broadly, under the law of Property (Res). This was due to the fact that obligations were not only largely concerned with property but also because the "rights" which were possessed by those who were legally entitled to enforce obligations were regarded as property.

The word obligation as commonly employed in our English speech usually means a duty that one is bound to perform. As used, however, in Roman Law, it is a legal relation, a tie or bond, which holds two (or more) persons together, creating both a duty and a right, the duty of a debtor to pay,[1] and the right of a creditor to be paid.[2]

The legal rights thus far considered, namely, rights connected with ownership (dominium) and rights that one may have in the property of others (jura in re aliena), are designated by writers upon the Roman Law as "real rights" (jura in rem) in distinction from rights arising from obligations. To the latter the name "personal rights" (jura in personam) has been given. They are also known as obligatory rights.

1. Dig. 12, 1, 6.
2. Inst. 3, 28; Dig. 45, 1, 126, 2.

A "real" right, a jus in rem, is a right, say the philosophical writers, exercisable over the "res," the property itself, and is enforceable against everybody. A "personal" right, a jus in personam, is, on the other hand, a right enforceable against some particular person, an individual. In other words, a personal, or an obligatory right, is a right arising from some obligation, a right to enforce by law a duty which, by virtue of an obligation, is owed by one person to another. One who has a right in rem, a "real" right, can maintain, or "vindicate" his right against all persons. It is not, however, a right against any particular person. A right in rem is, therefore, not an "obligation" since an obligation is enforceable against a person. "Real" rights deal with property or with a legal status. Personal rights are connected with duties owed by individuals, and, therefore, are appropriately called "obligatory" rights.

These distinctions concerning "real" and "personal" rights are, however, purely philosophical, and belong to the domain of scientific jurisprudence. They do not, as Ortolan says,[3] belong to the Roman Law. The terms jus in rem and jus in personam, used respectively to designate a "real right" and a "personal right" were coined by medieval Roman Law writers after the analogy of actio in rem and actio in personam. "Every right" says Ortolan,[4] "from the moment it exists, exists with respect to all, and must be protected, if needs be, against all. Only in the case of real rights no person whatever is individually the passive subject of them, whilst in the case of personal rights, a person is individually the passive subject of them. The common expressions, 'real rights' and 'personal rights,' have been accepted by common consent and use, and we adopt them as conventional phrases, though they

3. Hist. of Rom. Law, Eng. Trans. 2d Ed. London, 1896, p. 522.
4. Ib.

do not completely express the idea, and are not altogether correct, because every right, without exception, is personal as to the subject to which it appertains and real as to the object."

It should further be noted that the employment of the term obligatory rights synonymously with personal rights is inaccurate, since personal rights are more extensive than obligatory rights. There were many kinds of personal rights that were not connected with "obligations," as, for example, various family rights including guardianship, and rights connected with judicial proceedings. As said by Ledlie, the translator of Sohm's Institutes of Roman Law,[5] "Obligatory rights are but a particular kind of rights in personam. For example, rights in personam which are based upon family relations (such as the right of a husband to require his wife to give up the custody of a child) are not 'obligatory rights.' In the absence," however, says the same writer, "of any recognized English equivalent the term 'obligatory' right, though open to obvious objections, must serve."

An obligation (obligatio), according to the definition found in the Institutes,[6] is a bond created by law (vinculum juris) whereby one is necessarily compelled to perform something in compliance with the laws of the realm.

Sir Henry Maine in commenting upon Justinian's phrase, vinculum juris (a legal bond), used by the latter in defining an obligation,[7] says: "The image of a vinculum juris colors and pervades every part of the Roman Law of contract and delict. The law bound the parties together, and the chain could only be undone by the process called solutio, an expression still figurative, to which our word payment is only occasionally

---

5. See footnote, Sohm, 2nd ed. 326.
6. Inst. 3, 13, pr.
7. Inst. 3, 13, pr.

and incidentally equivalent. The consistency with which the figurative image was allowed to present itself explains an otherwise puzzling peculiarity of Roman legal phraseology; the fact that 'obligation' signifies rights as well as duties, the right, for example, to have a debt paid as well as the duty of paying it. The Romans kept, in fact, the entire picture of the legal chain before their eyes, and regarded one end of it no more and no less than the other." [8]

As to the object or purpose of an obligation, Paulus says [9] that an obligation does not make some corporeal thing or a servitude our own, but it constrains another to give to us the ownership of property (dare), or to render some service (facere) or to supply something (praestare). "The three words, dare, facere, and praestare, were symbolic words," says Ortolan,[10] "used in the formulas of Roman Law to signify generally the possible object of all obligations." "Dare," to give, meant the transfer of ownership;[11] facere, to do, meant either a positive or a negative act, the actual performance of something or an abstaining from doing a thing;[12] praestare, to supply, meant to perform any other duty the agreement specified.

Obligations arise, says Gaius, from contracts or wrongs (ex contractu and ex delicto),[13] also from various causes (variae causarum figurae).[14] Justinian in the Institutes mentions four sources, namely, contracts, quasi contracts, delicts, and quasi delicts (ex contractu, quasi ex contractu, ex delicto, quasi ex delicto). Modestinus says [15] that they arise from "res,

8. Ancient Law, chap. IX.
9. Dig. 44, 7, 3, pr.
10. Hist. Rom. Law, p. 524. See Gaius 2, 2.
11. Dig. 45, 1, 75, 10; 50, 17, 167.
12. Dig. 50, 16, 175; 50, 16, 218; 45, 1, 75, 7.
13. Gaius 3, 88.
14. Dig. 44, 7, 5 (quoting Gaius).
15. Dig. 44, 7, 52.

verba, consensus, lex, jus honorarium, necessitas, peccatum;" that is, either from the fact that certain property (res) was delivered to another in connection with some mutual understanding; or that certain words (verba) were said by the parties to an agreement; or that there was, in connection with some few particular transactions, a mere mutual consent (consensus); or that the obligation was created by force of some statute (lex) or by some praetorian law (jus honorarium); or that some compulsion (necessitas)[16] or wilful wrong (peccatum) gave rise to it.

These various sources of obligations set forth in the classic writings have been criticised by some modern writers as being both incomplete and inaccurate from the viewpoint of scientific jurisprudence. It should be remembered, however, that the Corpus Juris does not purport to be a scientific treatise of Roman Law. It is merely a vast storehouse of legal principles, and is perplexing and confusing at times in its arrangement.

In the course of time Roman lawyers came to speak of obligations as being either "naturales" or "civiles." In the early days, however, all obligations were "civiles," that is, were only such obligations as were recognized by the jus civile, and, consequently, enforceable by action. In later days, under the influence of the jus gentium and the praetorian law, it became customary to speak of some obligations as merely "naturales," meaning that while certain transactions or agreements might create "moral or natural obligations," yet they were not such obligations as could be enforced by an action at law. For example, an agreement entered into might be invalid (nudum pactum) since it was not made with the formality required by law. It might, nevertheless, be a moral, or a "natural" obligation, and although unenforceable by action, yet if such a moral

---

16. As where a "necessary heir" was under obligation to accept "an inheritance."

debtor performed his obligations, as, for instance, by paying money, he could not maintain an action for its recovery on the ground that he was not, when he paid it, legally liable.[17]

Obligations were also said to be either civil or praetorian,[18] or obligations recognized and enforced by the jus civile or some statute, and obligations created and enforced by the praetor. The latter were also known as honorary obligations.

In connection with actions for their enforcement, obligations were further classified as either stricti juris or bonae fidei. The former were transactions in which the parties had expressly declared their rights and liabilities and called for a strict and literal performance, nothing more. Transactions bonae fidei, on the other hand, involved more than strict performance, more than a compliance with the letter of the agreement, since they involved the good faith of the parties, and called for whatever performance the circumstances of the case in all fairness demanded. It might be more than actually promised or it might be less. Transactions stricti juris were construed by the strict letter of the law, the old jus civile, and involved no questions of equity, but transactions bonae fidei were construed entirely upon equitable principles. It was the Roman praetor who thus distinguished obligations, and all remedies created by him were bonae fidei in their nature. Such equitable defences as dolus, metus, pactum, and conventum could be raised in transactions bonae fidei, which was not true in matters purely stricti juris unless they were specially pleaded. For example, transactions of sale, hire, mandate, and partnership, also those of commodatum, depositum, and pledge, or all consensual contracts and all real contracts except

17. Dig. 46, 1, 16, 4.
18. Inst. 3, 13, 1.

mutuum,[19] were construed as transactions bonæ fidei.[20]

Contracts are further classified by modern writers upon Roman Law as unilateral and bilateral. The former is a contract where only one of the parties has a duty to perform, the other party alone having a right, as, for example, where A owes B a sum of money. A bilateral contract is one where both parties owe reciprocal duties to each other, as, for example, in case of a contract to sell, it is the duty of one party to convey the thing sold and the duty of the buyer to pay the price. Unilateral contracts were stricti juris. Bilateral contracts were bonæ fidei.

Contracts comprise the large part of obligations, and in connection with contracts important general principles relating to their formation, their subject matter, and to the terms or mode of their performance, require consideration. These general principles deal with parties; their agreement or consent; with questions affecting the nature of the alleged consent, whether it was voluntary or induced by duress (vis), fear (metus), fraud (dolus), mistake (error), or illegal consideration (injusta causa, sine causa); with the nature of the subject matter of the contract; and with questions relating to the time, place, conditions, or other terms of its performance.

Parties:

As in our own law, not all individuals were competent to make a contract. A slave could make no contract, not even with his master,[21] although from an early date it was customary for the owners of slaves to permit them to enter into transactions connected with their peculium. The peculium was legally, how-

---

19. As to "consensual" and "real" contracts, see Ch. XVI.
20. Inst. 4, 6, 28.
21. Inst. 3, 19, 6.

ever, the property of the master, and the latter could refuse to abide by any agreement made by his slave wherein the master received no benefit.[22] Under the praetorian law, however, one dealing with a slave acting under the authority of his master could hold the master liable.[23]

Infants under seven years of age had no contractual capacity whatever.[24] Children between the age of seven and puberty (fourteen years in males and twelve years in females) were called pupils, and, as already stated in a previous chapter, no pupil was capable of entering into any transaction without the approval or authority (auctoritas) of his tutor.[25] The term "minor" was technically applied to persons between the age of puberty and twenty-five. Such persons who had no curator or guardian could make binding contracts,[26] although the praetor permitted a minor to rescind his contract if seriously prejudicial to him and provided also he made restitution in integrum.[27]

Insane persons had no legal capacity at all.[28] However, where persons twenty-five years old afflicted with insanity had intermittent periods of lucid minds they might, in such periods of normal intelligence, bind themselves by their contracts.[29] Deaf and dumb persons were also incapable of making contracts, and this incapacity applied to those who were deaf only provided they could not hear at all, since they could not hear the words of the promisor.[30] By our early Common Law, persons born deaf, dumb, and blind were

22. Inst. 4, 7, 3, and 4.
23. Inst. 4, 7, 1.
24. Inst. 3, 19, 10.
25. Inst. 1, 21, pr.; 3, 19, 9.
26. Dig. 4, 4, 7, 3.
27. Dig. 4, 4, 6; 4, 4, 7, 1; 4, 4, 44.
28. Inst. 3, 19, 8.
29. Code, 4, 38, 2.
30. Inst. 3, 19, 7.

classed with idiots being supposed incapable of any understanding, since wanting in all those senses which furnish the human mind with ideas.[31]

Persons under potestas, despite their matured age, were for a long time incapable by the Roman Law of acquiring any rights for themselves. The paterfamilias could transfer to another child or even to a stranger anything acquired by one in his paternal power.[32] Although a filiusfamilias could make a valid contract, yet the benefit of it, if any, accrued to the paterfamilias, while the liability of it, in case the filiusfamilias became a debtor to a third person, was that of himself alone.[33] However, under the imperial law, even as early as the times of Augustus, a filiusfamilias could, in connection with his peculium, acquire property independently of his paterfamilias.[34]

Married women who were in manu were subject to the patria potestas of their husbands, and were legally the same as daughters. As such they had no contractual capacity.[35] If the marriage were sine manu the woman remained in the power of her own paterfamilias, or under that of her tutor. However, even in the time of Gaius, the tutorship of women of full age was a mere form,[36] and in Justinian's time it had entirely disappeared.

Aliens (peregrini) could not make contracts by the old Roman Law, the jus civile, but the praetor recognized and enforced their agreements by principles of the jus gentium.

Consent:

Contracts are founded upon the consent or agree-

31. Blackstone Com., 1, 304; Co. Litt. 42; Fleta, 1, 6, c, 40.
32. Inst. 2, 9, pr.; and 1.
33. Inst. 3, 19, 6; Gaius 3, 104; Dig. 44, 7, 39.
34. Inst. 2, 9, 1; 2, 12, pr.; 2, 11, 6.
35. Gaius 2, 159.
36. Inst. 1, 190.

ment of the parties. Not that in every case consent alone gives rise to an obligation, for often in Roman Law there is some other necessary element, but in every case there must be an accord or meeting of the minds of the parties before a contract is created. There must be both an offer and an acceptance. A mere offer (pollicitatio) is the proposal of one party, and in itself it does not amount to an agreement.[37] The offer must be accepted in order to constitute a consent (consensus). In other words, there must be a determination and a declaration of the will or intent of the parties. Moreover, the expression of the will must be voluntary and actual, free from force, fear, fraud, error, or ignorance.

Force and Fear (Vis and Metus):

By the praetorian law an agreement is voidable if caused by duress (vis) or threats (metus). The older phrase of the law was "force or fear," force (vis) meaning physical force, and fear (metus) covering every kind of mental compulsion on account of immediate or apprehended danger. Later, says Ulpian, the term "vis" was omitted and the word "metus" alone used since that which is done by "force" may be said to be done by "fear" also.[38] The praetorian term "fear" (metus), says Gaius, is understood to mean not the fear felt by a weakminded person but such as might reasonably influence one of firm character.[39]

Under the formal contracts of the old jus civile one who made a promise even when compelled by fear was nevertheless bound.[40] The praetor, however, said, "I will not enforce an act done through fear,"[41] and accordingly he allowed a defense (exceptio metus causa)

---

37. Dig. 50, 12, 3, pr.
38. Dig. 4, 2, 1.
39. Dig. 4, 2, 6.
40. Inst. 4, 13, 1.
41. Dig. 4, 2, 1.

in actions brought upon all contracts bonae fidei in their nature. According to Ulpian [42] fear means present or immediate alarm, and it makes no difference whether the fear is caused by the other party to the contract or by some other person, whether by an individual, a mob, a municipality, a guild, or a corporation, the nature of the defense being in rem and not in personam. Mere threatening language is not "fear,"[43] but a promise obtained by unlawful threat of death,[44] or by unlawful physical restraint of one's person, will not be enforced.[45] Force, even death itself, may, in certain cases, be lawfully applied by a magistrate. It is, however, unlawful force that is here intended, as if, for example, a magistrate or a provincial governor, says Pomponius,[46] should extort money from one by threatening him with death or with flogging.

Accordingly where a man was kept a prisoner in his house until he had agreed to do a certain thing,[47] the promise was not enforceable. Likewise, where one having in his possession the documentary proofs of another's freedom, and threatened to destroy them unless paid for not doing so, the money paid under such compulsion could be recovered.[48]

The action for the recovery of property obtained from one by duress or intimidation was known as the actio quod metus causa. This was a delictual action, and by it one was entitled to recover fourfold damages. Like an action of trover it lay against the actual offender and also against any other person who, even innocently, had profited by the transaction. However, an innocent person was liable only for the actual

42. Dig. 4, 2, 9.
43. Codex 2, 20, 9.
44. Codex 2, 20, 7.
45. Dig. 4, 2, 22; 4, 2, 23, 2.
46. Dig. 4, 2, 3, 1.
47. Dig. 4, 2, 22.
48. Dig. 4, 2, 4; 4, 2, 8, 1.

profit received by him. In addition to this penal action, the wronged person had his remedy of suing for the restoration of the property. If the contract had not been executed, a defendant from whom the promise had been extorted could interpose, if sued, the defense known as the exceptio metus.[49]

Dolus (Fraud):

Dolus, or fraud, may also affect the validity of a contract. However, as in the case of duress (vis, metus), formal contracts under the jus civile were binding regardless of the presence of fraud. It was due to the praetorian law that a defense might be opposed (exceptio doli) to the enforcement of a contract tainted with fraud or deceit, and that an original action (actio doli) might be brought against one who had defrauded another in respect to his property rights.

The Roman Law term "dolus" was a word of very broad import, and not readily susceptible of a definite and certain meaning. It included almost any act that transgressed honest and fair dealing. It might be a statement that was positively false, or one which the one making it did not believe (suggestio falsi), or it might be the suppression or the concealment of a matter that one should in fairness disclose (suppressio veri). For example, one who wilfully made a false representation in the sale of a slave or a piece of land made himself, thereby, liable to an action. The consequences of such misrepresentation often depended upon the nature of the transaction, also of the fraud. Under varying circumstances, the contract might be rescinded, the property restored, the party guilty of the fraud subjected to damages, or even to a penalty. Thus, one who wilfully deceived another in the sale of land was liable to a penalty of double the value of the

---

49. Inst. 4, 13, 1.

land,[50] and if a vendor knowingly misrepresented the skill of a slave and effected a sale thereby, the sale could be rescinded, or the vendor could be sued for damages.[51]

A vendor, likewise, who suppressed the truth, who sold lands without informing the purchaser of burdens or servitudes thereon,[52] or who concealed defects in things sold, such as defects in timber making it unsuitable for building,[53] disease in cattle,[54] or vices in slaves,[55] was bound to make good all damages sustained by his fraud.

Due to the nature of dolus, comprehending as it did many forms of fraud, deceit, and violations of good conscience and fair play, attempts to define it were often unsatisfactory. Ulpian speaks [56] of this difficulty and refers to various definitions that had been given. He then quotes approvingly the definition given by Labeo, namely, "Any craft, deceit, or subterfuge used with the intent to defraud, deceive, or circumvent another."

It is clear that a definition as broad as this includes practically all means that may be employed to take an unfair advantage of another in any legal transaction. However, since dolus required an evil intent to defraud, it became customary to speak of dolus malus in contrast with dolus bonus, the former meaning malicious fraud or deceit, the latter justifiable or excusable deceit, as in the case of concealing money or other property from a robber, or of using deceit against a public enemy.

Of course the reason why dolus made a contract

50. Paulus, Sent. 2, 17, 4.
51. Paulus, Sent. 2, 17, 6.
52. Dig. 18, 1, 66, pr. and 1; 19, 1, 1, 1; 19, 1, 21, 1; 19, 1, 41.
53. Dig. 19, 1, 13, pr.
54. Dig. 19, 1, 13, pr.
55. Dig. 19, 1, 4, pr.
56. Dig. 4, 3, 1.

voidable was because it affected the free consent that was essential to contractual obligations, the defrauded party being induced to assent by reason of the fraud practiced upon him. This made the contract voidable by the deceived party. Where, however, the fraud was practiced by some third person, a stranger to the transaction, the agreement was not affected. In such a case the obligation between the actual parties to the agreement was binding, but an action for the fraud (actio doli) could be brought by the aggrieved party against the third person responsible for the wrong.[57] No one could, however, profit from the fraud of a person acting for him.[58]

In cases of gross fraud the praetor permitted a recovery of the property, restitutio in integrum, requiring the wrongdoer to place the person whom he had defrauded in statu quo ante. Gross fraud was variously called dolus ex proposito (aforethought), claudestinus and manifestus, that is, secret, underhanded, or manifest fraud.

Whether or not in any particular transaction there had been dolus depended upon the facts of the particular case together with the intention, or the fact of the deception and the intent thereby to defraud.[59] Dolus was not presumed, and the burden (onus) of proving it was on the person who alleged it.[60] In no case, however, could a person validly insert a provision in a contract that he would be immune or exempt from the consequences of any dolus that might enter into the transaction.[61]

Error (Mistake):

There can likewise be no agreement, no meeting of

57. Dig. 44, 4, 2, 1.
58. Dig. 50, 17, 49.
59. Dig. 50, 17, 79.
60. Code 2, 21, 6.
61. Dig. 50, 17, 23.

the minds of the parties, where the intent is lacking as in the case of material error or mistake.[62] There can be consent only when the parties agree upon the same thing in the same intent.[63]

Error is said to be either essential (material), or non-essential (immaterial). Essential error, or error that prevented consensus, was known as error in corpore, or, as we would say, in identity; non-essential error, or error that did not in itself prevent a formation of the contract, although it gave in some cases a right to avoid it, was called error in substantia or error in materia.[64]

Essential error, or error in corpore, may arise in three ways, namely, error as to the subject matter of the contract; as to a party to the contract; and as to the character or nature of the contract. For example, if a promisee (stipulator) and a promisor, says Justinian, mean different things no obligation arises. It is just the same as if the offer had not been accepted. Thus, if one offers to sell to you a slave named Stichus, and you accept, thinking he means Pamphilus whose name you suppose is Stichus, there is no contract.[65] However, a mistake in a mere name is nothing provided there is an agreement upon the subject matter.[66] Thus if A agrees to sell to B "blackacre," the correct name of a farm, but B supposes he is buying "whiteacre," a different farm, being mistaken in the name, there is no sale since there is an error in corpore;[67] but if B had the same farm in mind, although he knew it by a different name, the error in the name would be immaterial.

Error as to the party to a contract may also be ma-

62. Dig. 39, 3, 20.
63. Dig. 44, 7, 57, 50, 17, 116, 2.
64. Dig. 18, 1, 9.
65. Inst. 3, 19, 23; Dig. 18, 1, 9, pr.
66. Dig. 18, 1, 9, 1.
67. Dig. 18, 1, 9, pr.

terial (in corpore). If A agreed to make a loan to B, a person of good repute but not known to A, and C brings to A another "B," an irresponsible person, and represents him to be the original B, and A lets the spurious B have the money, there is no contract of loan, and both C and the fraudulent B are guilty of theft.[68]

Again, an error as to the nature of the transaction may prevent a binding obligation. If A and B apparently assent to an agreement concerning a piece of land, but A meant a sale while B meant a hiring of the land, then there is no meeting of the minds, no mutual consent.[69] Likewise if A, intending a mere custody, left a sum of money with B, but B thought it was a loan and spent it, the transaction was neither a depositum nor a loan (mutuum). However, the money being spent by B, he would be liable upon an implied promise to repay it.[70]

As to non-essential error (error in materia or error in substantia), while the Roman jurists were agreed that such error did not render a contract void, yet they did not always agree as to what facts constituted only non-essential error. Ulpian says[71] that the question is asked whether there would be any sale if there were no error in corpore but there was an error in substantia, as, for example, if one sells vinegar for wine, bronze for gold, or lead for silver. Ulpian further says that Marcellus was of the opinion that there would be a sale, since the parties agreed in corpore, although there was an error in materia. Ulpian, however, says that while he agrees with Marcellus as to the wine and vinegar, since they are both the same corpus provided the wine soured, yet if the wine did

68. Dig. 47, 2, 52, 21.
69. Dig. 44, 7, 57.
70. Dig. 12, 1, 18.
71. Dig. 18, 1, 9, 2.
[Roman Law]—26

not become sour but was vinegar, ab initio, then there would be no sale. As to the bronze for gold, or lead for silver, he says there would be no sale although the error was "in materia." Paulus says [72] that if one buys a thing of gold, and it actually is gold although of a poorer quality than the purchaser supposed, the sale is good.

In our own law there are principles similar to the doctrine of error in the Roman Law although we usually employ the term mistake. There can be no contract when there is a mutual mistake as to the person dealt with, or as to the identity or species of the article sold. However, with regard to a mistake in the quality of an article the doctrine of caveat emptor applies. Thus, in an English case,[73] there was a contract for the sale of a cargo of cotton to arrive by the ship "Peerless" from Bombay. The evidence showed that there were two ships named "Peerless," both sailing from Bombay, and that the buyer had one ship in mind and the seller another. It was held that there was no contract since there was no consensus ad idem. In a Massachusetts case,[74] a mistake as to the solvency of a maker of a note sold in market was held to be a mistake as to quality, and, therefore, the contract was valid.

Possibility of Performance:

A contract to be valid must be capable of being performed.[75] If one contracts, for example, with reference to a subject matter that does not and cannot exist, as where one agrees to buy a certain slave who is dead at the time,[76] the contract is invalid. The same is true where the subject matter is regarded as a whole

---

72. Dig. 18, 1, 10.
73. Raffles v. Wichelhaus, 2 H. & C. 906.
74. Hecht v. Batcheller, 147 Mass. 335.
75. Dig. 50, 17, 185.
76. Inst. 3, 19, 1.

[Roman Law]

and a part of it is no longer in existence, as where one agrees to buy two slaves for one price and one of the slaves is dead. The contract is void as to both.[77]

Impossibility is not to be confused, however, with inability. Thus where A agreed to deliver to B a hundred tons of copper, the inability of A to get the copper for delivery does not invalidate the contract. Impossibility exists only when no one can perform the contract.[78]

While there may be a valid contract concerning any property, movable or immovable, that is subject to private ownership,[79] yet if A agrees to sell to B something not subject to ownership (res extra commercium) the agreement is invalid since it is legally impossible.[80] Even if the thing contracted for may be a proper subject of contract at the time, yet if before the performance of the contract it be set apart for public purposes, the contract is rendered invalid.[81]

Illegal Promises:

A contract must have for its object or purpose something that is lawful, consequently a promise or agreement to do an illegal thing, something that is criminal or contrary to public policy or good morals, is absolutely void.[82] Thus a promise to kill someone,[83] to steal,[84] not to sue if any theft or injuria be committed,[85] to marry a person within the prohibited degrees of kinship,[86] to marry for a monetary considera-

77. Dig. 18, 1, 34, 3.
78. Dig. 45, 1, 137, 5.
79. Inst. 3, 19, pr.
80. Dig. 50, 17, 185, 11, 17, 8, 1.
81. Inst. 3, 19, 2.
82. Gaius 3, 157; Inst. 3, 26, 7; Cod. 2, 3, 6.
83. Inst. 3, 26, 7.
84. Gaius 3, 157; Inst. 3, 26, 7.
85. Dig. 2, 14, 27, 4.
86. Dig. 45, 1, 35, 1.

tion,[87] or to agree to conduct a lawsuit for another in return for a share of the proceeds recovered,[88] is invalid. However, a loan of money with interest in order that one might maintain a suit was legal.[89]

Collateral Provisions (Modalities):

There may be various collateral, or incidental, provisions attached to contracts, but they exist only when they are specifically expressed in the agreement. They are not to be presumed but must be proved by the party relying upon them, except in such cases as the very validity of the contract would depend upon them. In the latter cases, the other party must show that such provisions were not to apply or that they had been performed.[90] Among the usual and most important collateral provisions are the time of performance, the place of performance, and conditions connected with the performance. The restrictions thus modifying contracts are known as modalities.

Time of Performance (Dies):

If the contract specifies no particular time for its performance, then it is to be presumed that immediate performance was intended, and this means within a reasonable time.[91] Thus, if one makes a contract for a piece of land or for a slave, he cannot demand performance until a sufficient time has elapsed for the delivery to be made.[92] What constitutes a reasonable time depends upon the circumstances of the particular case. It is a question of fact for the judex to determine how long a reasonably diligent man would need for the performance.[93]

87. Dig. 45, 1, 97, 2.
88. Dig. 2, 14, 53; 17, 1, 7; Cod. 4, 35, 20.
89. Dig. 2, 14, 53.
90. Dig. 45, 1, 10.
91. Dig. 45, 1, 41; 45, 1, 60; 50, 17, 14.
92. Inst. 3, 19, 27.
93. Dig. 45, 1, 137, 2.

Where, however, a particular time, called by Roman lawyers "the day" (dies),[94] is specified for performance, then the promisor has the right to wait till such time before performance can be demanded of him.[95] Yet he has the whole of such day in which to perform, as, for example, in case of the payment of a sum of money, since he would not be in default until the entire day had passed.[96] The same principle applies to agreements to be performed within a month or within a year. The promisor is not in default until the whole of the month or of the year is gone.[97]

The time agreed upon for the performance of a contract was designated either as "ex die," on a certain day, or as "in diem," up to a certain time.[98] Thus a promise to perform a certain obligation, such as the payment of a sum of money, on the Kalends of March, would be an example of a promise "ex die," and an agreement to do something up to the Kalends of March would be a promise "in diem." "Dies" is also either a quo or ad quem, the former meaning the time or day upon which an obligation begins, the latter meaning the time it ends.[99] When an obligation began to exist, Roman lawyers described the time as "dies cedit;" when the time arrived for the performance of it, upon default of which suit might be brought, it was said "dies venit."[100]

Although a certain time be fixed for the performance of an obligation, as the payment of a sum of money on the Kalends of March, yet the debtor could pay before that day, although the creditor could not sue before that time, since the intervening time was

94. Dig. 44, 7, 44, 1.
95. Inst. 3, 15, 2.
96. Inst. 3, 15, 2.
97. Inst. 3, 19, 26.
98. Dig. 44, 7, 44, 1; 45, 1, 124.
99. Dig. 44, 7, 44; 45, 1, 56, 4.
100. Dig. 50, 16, 213, pr.; Dig. 36, 2; Cod. 6, 53.

for the benefit of the debtor.[101] This rule of the Roman Law was applied, it would seem, only to cases where a specific sum, without interest, was payable at a stated time. None of the passages in support of this Roman Law rule contain any allusion to the case of a loan upon interest.[102]

The Roman jurists further speak of time as either continuous (tempus continuum) or as judicial (tempus utile). The former means ordinary reckoning of time measured by uninterrupted days, the latter meaning only those days upon which judicial business may be transacted.[103] In short periods of time it was obviously an advantage to one desiring delay to have his time for performance measured by judicial rather than by continuous days.

Another distinction in the computing of time was known as the enumeration of days (ad dies numerare) in contrast with the enumeration of moments (a momento in momentum computare). Ordinarily time was reckoned by days, and reckoning by moments was exceptional. In computing days, the first calendar day is counted. In computing years, the day preceding the anniversary is regarded as the last. Consequently, one born on January 1, 1910, would complete his twenty-first year immediately after midnight of Dec. 30, 1930.[104] In the protection of rights, there may be cases, however, when time should be reckoned from "moment to moment." For example, Ulpian suggests the case of a minor, one who in Roman Law did not reach full majority till the age of twenty-five. "Should we, in such a case," asks Ulpian, "say that a person is under twenty-five even on his birthday before the very hour at which he was born? Until he is twenty-five he

101. Dig. 45, 1, 38, 16; 45, 1, 137, 2; 46, 3, 70.
102. Chancellor Kent in Ellis v. Craig, 7 John. Ch. (N. Y.) 7.
103. Dig. 38, 15, 2; 44, 3, 1.
104. Dig. 28, 1, 5; 40, 1, 1; 41, 3, 6, 7; 44. 3, 15, pr.; 50, 16, 134.

may get restitution if one imposes upon him." For this reason Ulpian was of the opinion that in such a case the time should be reckoned from moment to moment.[105]

Place:

It is also customary to insert in a contract a particular place for performance, as, for example, at Carthage or at Rome.[106] If the place of performance be stipulated but not the time, then such time as would reasonably enable one to reach the place of performance will be implied.[107] The location of the subject matter of the contract will often determine the place of performance, as a contract to repair a building. The place of delivery of an immovable is obviously where the immovable is located, but in case of movables, in absence of an express agreement to the contrary, the promisor must deliver in the jurisdiction in which he is suable.[108] Where, however, the place of performance is expressly stipulated, the party entitled to the benefit of the performance cannot lawfully demand that the performance should be at some other place.

Conditions (Conditio):

Contracts may be further modified by conditions, that is, made dependent upon future, contingent events which by agreement of the parties are to govern the existence of the transaction in question. A "condition" says Papinian,[109] refers to a future time, and a stipulation, says Justinian,[110] is conditional when performance depends on some uncertain event in the future, so that it becomes actionable only in case something is done or not done.

105. Dig. 4, 4, 3, 3.
106. Inst. 3, 15, 5.
107. Inst. 3, 15, 5.
108. Dig. 45, 1, 137, 4.
109. Dig. 12, 1, 39.
110. Inst. 3, 15, 4.

Sometimes a condition may refer to the present, to the time when a contract is made, as for example, a promise to give one a sum of money if the King of the Parthians is living.[111] However, this is not really a conditional contract. The agreement when made is either binding or not binding according to the actual fact, even though, says Papinian,[112] the parties did not know it was binding. The rule is the same, he adds, when the condition refers to past time.

Conditions of any sort may at the pleasure of the parties be attached to a contract, providing the condition imposed is not something illegal or impossible.[113]

Conditions are said to be either "suspensive" (conditio suspensiva) or "resolutive" (conditio resolutiva), that is, they either suspend or delay the actual beginning, or formation, of a contract, or dissolve or put an end to, a contract already formed. In other words a contract subject to a suspensive condition is binding only in case the condition is first fulfilled; while a contract having a "resolutive" condition attached to it is binding immediately but will cease to have any binding force upon the breach of the condition. It will be observed that these forms of "conditions" are similar, respectively, to our "precedent" and "subsequent" conditions.

An impossible condition, if suspensive, makes a stipulation invalid. An impossible condition, says Justinian,[114] is one which according to the course of nature cannot be fulfilled, as where, for example, one says, "Do you promise to give if I touch the sky with my finger?" However, if the proposal had been, continues Justinian, "Do you promise to give if I do not touch the sky with my finger?" it is regarded as no

111. Dig. 12, 1, 37.
112. Ibid.
113. Gaius 3, 98; Inst. 3, 19, 11.
114. Inst. 3, 19, 11.

condition at all, and consequently the agreement can be sued upon at once. In other words, an affirmative physical impossibility prevents the formation of a contract, but if expressed in negative form the contract is considered unconditional.

In case of a suspensive condition, the title does not pass to a purchaser until the condition is fulfilled, and one in possession under such a conditional sale cannot acquire title by usucapio, and he is not entitled to the profits or produce.[115] Where, however, one buys property under a resolutive condition, the contract is complete and title, or ownership, is in the purchaser as long as the contingency does not occur. Such a purchaser may obtain title by usucapio and is entitled to the fruits and accessions. The risk is also his in case of loss.[116]

If a price which was owing conditionally was paid by some mistake before the condition was fulfilled, then as long as the condition remained suspensive, the payer could bring an action (condictio indebiti) for its recovery. Upon the fulfillment of the condition no such action could, however, be brought.[117]

115. Dig. 18, 2, 4, pr.
116. Dig. 18, 2, 2.
117. Dig. 12, 6, 16.

CHAPTER XV

THE LAW OF OBLIGATIONS, *continued*

CAUSA; CULPA; JOINT OBLIGATIONS

Consideration and Causa:

It is a familiar doctrine of our English Law that a contract not under seal requires a sufficient consideration to support it. An apparent exception is made in the case of negotiable instruments in the hands of innocent purchasers for value, but with the development of the action of assumpsit the equitable doctrine of a quid pro quo became established, and a consideration was deemed necessary to make a mere promise actionable. Without such a consideration a verbal or an unsealed written agreement is declared by English and American courts to be a "nudum pactum,"[1] and it is said that "from a nudum pactum no action arises."[2]

It is also said that in the modern Civil Law an agreement without consideration is void,[3] and that the term "causa" in that law is synonymous with "consideration." In fact, some writers upon the Civil Law, including both the ancient jus civile of Rome and the modern Civil Law, use the term "causa" in the same sense as the word consideration is used in the jurisprudence of England and the United States.[4]

---

1. Rann v. Hughes, 7 T. R. 350, note; Brawn v. Lyford, 103 Me. 362, 69 Atl. 544; Mills v. Wyman, 3 Pick. (Mass.) 207; Hardison v. Reel, 154 N. C. 273, 70 S. E. 463.

2. Ib.

3. Taylor v. Wooten, 19 La. 518; Huie v. Bailey, 16 La. 213; Campbell v. Lambert & Co., 36 La. Ann. 35; Kirby-Carpenter Co. v. Burnett, 144 Fed. 635.

4. Monton v. Noble, 1 La. Ann. 192.

However, in the Roman Law, a "formal" contract did not require a "consideration." Informal agreements (pacta) did require something more than the mere fact of agreement, and this additional element was called "causa." This term conveyed, however, a different meaning from our English term "consideration." It was simply the ground or reason, in any particular case, which distinguished a particular class of agreements from ordinary agreements (pacta), and made this particular class actionable.[5] If a formal contract intended a consideration, and such consideration failed, it was said to be sine causa, and to ask for its performance under such circumstances was said to be unfair or unjust (dolus).[6] For example, A promises to loan B a sum of money, and B before receiving the money makes a formal contract (stipulatio) to pay A the amount at some future day. The day arrives but A has never made the loan. If A now sues B on the contract, B may defeat the action by the defense known as exceptio doli.[7]

The element, the vinculum juris, that turned an agreement into a contract seemed very plain to an ancient Roman jurist. It involved no profound discussion of legal principles. Certain agreements were binding just because long observed custom and practical need had made them so. For this reason they became subject to legal enforcement. The ancient writers indulged in no speculations, so dear to many modern writers, concerning the nature of a contract or of any other sort of obligation.

Modern civilians, however, have introduced an entirely new element into contractual obligations, the element known as causa civilis, and in most of the modern Civil Law codes an essential element of a contract is a

---

5. Pollock, Contracts, 134.
6. Hunter, Rom. Law, 598.
7. Dig. 44, 4, 2, 3.

causa civilis.[8] However, as pointed out by a learned friend of the writer, Professor Peterson,[9] medieval and modern writers have used the term causa civilis in a way never conceived by the ancient Roman lawyers. As Professor Peterson says: "Modern treatises on Roman Law apply the term causa civilis to the res, verba, litterae, and consensus upon which the classes of contract are based, but such a technical term was quite unknown to Roman jurists."[10] The only place in the Digest where "causa civilis" is employed[11] shows that the term was used merely to mean the cause, ground, or reason whereby one was placed under obligation by the law. To the practical and non-philosophical Roman lawyer causa meant nothing more than the reason held sufficient by law for enforcing an obligation. The modern doctrine of causa with its many refinements was unknown to them. The modern doctrine of causa is really a psychologic inquiry into the motif of the obligor, an effort to determine why he entered into the obligation. The question is not simply why one owes, but why did he promise.[12] Modern civil codes patterned upon the French Code, generally make "causa" in this refined and scientific sense, an essential element of all contracts. Some of these codes even define "causa."[13] The Code of Portugal, however, makes no mention of "causa," and "in the German Code,[14] 'causa' is certainly not viewed as a universal essential for the formation or existence

---

8. Thus in the French Civil Code, "une cause licite," art. 1108. See also, art. 1131, 1132, 1133. Likewise in the Civil Code of Louisiana.

9. "The Evolution of Causa in the Contractual Obligations of the Civil Law," bulletin of the University of Texas, No. 46, 1905.

10. Ib. citing Accarias, Preecis droit romain, 4th Ed., II, 16, note.

11. Dig. 15, 1, 49, 2, (quoting Pomponius).

12. Prof. Peterson, ibid.

13. Spain, art. 1261, 1274; Chile, art. 1467.

14. Burgerliches Gesetzbuch.

of a contractual obligation."[15] In the Spanish Code,[16] as also in the Cuban, Porto Rican, and Philippine Codes copied from the Spanish, "causa" is made a contractual requirement, and as far as the American courts established in Porto Rico and the Philippines are concerned they have given to the notion of "causa" the broad meaning of "consideration" as understood in our American law.[17]

However, the maxim taken from the Roman Law, ex nudo pacto non oritur actio, has been often misunderstood and misapplied by some writers upon our own law. In Roman Law, an action did not arise upon a mere pact (nudum pactum), but only upon the formal agreement (stipulatio) which reduced a pact to an obligation. No consideration, however, as that word is generally used, was necessary to support a stipulation.[18] Moreover, in later times in Roman Law, actions would lie on certain pacts known as pacta vestita in distinction from pacta nuda.[19]

Turpis Causa:

No agreement made for an illegal or immoral purpose or inducement (injusta or turpis causa) could be enforced.[20] If action were brought it could be defended by an exceptio doli.[21] For example, Ulpian says[22] that if a man detected in the act of adultery pays to be permitted to go, there is no right of action to recover the money. Celsus says,[23] however, that where

15. Prof. Peterson, supra.
16. Art. 1261, 1274.
17. Villegracia v. Vlibare, 24 Phil. 371; Standard Oil Co. v. Codina Arenas, 19 Phil. 363; Bigelow v. Porto Rico Planters Co., 7 Porto Rico 463; Guerra v. Porto Rico Treasurer, 8 Porto Rico 280.
18. Mouton v. Noble, 1 La. Ann. 192.
19. See Chapter XVII.
20. Codex 4, 7, 1; 4, 7, 5.
21. Dig. 12, 5, 8.
22. Dig. 12, 5, 4, pr.
23. Dig. 12, 5, 4, 2.

the immoral conduct occurs on the part of the receiver alone, there may be an action for the recovery of the money, as where A gives B money to keep B from doing wrong to A.

Culpa (Negligence):

In connection with obligations the doctrine of culpa, or negligence, is at times an important matter, since certain contracts from their very nature impose as a matter of law, without any express agreement of the parties, certain duties of diligentia or care in performance of the obligation. A failure to exercise the care or diligence thus required renders one liable in damages for any injury that may result from his negligence (culpa). Persons who are under contractual obligations are required to protect each other not only from wilful harm (dolus malus) but also from damage by culpa.

Culpa, variously translated as negligence, wrong, fault, carelessness, blame, is a term of broad significance. At times it is used synonymously with dolus (fraud) and at other times is distinguished from it, dolus, or dolus malus being used to mean intentional, or wilful wrong, and culpa to mean unintentional wrong resulting from negligence.

Culpa in a general sense covers any wrongful act or omission,[24] and in this general sense it would include dolus malus.[25] Culpa also in a legal sense may result from a positive act of commission or from a negative act or omission, since it is the failure to exercise the care or diligentia which a transaction according to the circumstances of its particular case legally requires. It is for this reason that "culpa" in its technical sense is not susceptible of a brief, concise defini-

24. Dig. 49, 16, 14, 1; Cod. 9, 4, 2.
25. Dig. 9, 2, 5, 1.

tion, since what would be culpa, or failure to take due care, in one case would not be culpa in a different case.

However, various terms were used by the Roman jurists to describe various degrees of culpa, such as lata,[26] latior,[27] latissima, magna,[28] gravior,[29] levis, and levissima, although these terms were more academic than practical. In the same way writers upon our own law have described our corresponding term "negligence" as being "slight," "great," "ordinary" (?), and "gross." In both systems of jurisprudence such terms are often misleading, since there is no fixed standard of "culpa" or of "negligence" and because the same conduct might under one set of circumstances be considered only "slight" negligence (or culpa) and "great" in another set of circumstances. It is the failure to exercise the care (diligentia) that the particular circumstances call for, or the "due care," that care which it is one's legal duty to exercise in any particular case, that gives rise to negligence or culpa.

Culpa and diligentia are, therefore, inseparably associated, since culpa is the lack of due diligentia, and the degree of diligentia or care required in any given case regulates inversely the degree of culpa or negligence that will subject one to liability in case of loss. Culpa and diligentia are terms used in obligations arising ex delicto and also in obligations arising ex contractu, and each class of obligations has its own rules as to the amount of diligence required.

The Roman jurists speak of two degrees of diligentia in connection with contract, (1) the diligentia that "a good paterfamilias" should exercise, otherwise called exacta diligentia, and (2) the diligentia that is ordinarily shown by a person in the management of

26. Dig. 50, 16, 213, 2.
27. Dig. 16, 3, 32.
28. Dig. 41, 2, 1, 5.
29. Dig. 41, 1, 54, 2.

his own affairs (quanta in suis rebus diligentia). In the first, or higher degree of diligentia, one was held responsible for "slight" (levis) culpa, but in the second only for "great" (lata) culpa or negligence. In all contracts or quasi-contracts involving good faith (bona fides), such, for example, as sale, hire, partnership, commodatum, mandatum, negotiorum gestio, fiduciary relations between guardian and ward, and any other business relations of trust and confidence, the doctrine of diligentia or due care applied. If a party to such obligations did not exercise the care required of him he was answerable for the consequences.

However, the requirements of diligentia were not always the same for both parties. In the contract of commodatum, for example, the duty of the borrower (commodatarius) to exercise care was greater than that of the lender (commodans). The borrower was required to use "exacta diligentia" [30] and was, therefore, liable for "levis culpa," but the lender who received no benefit from the transaction was liable only in case of dolus malus or "lata culpa." The borrower is bound to employ a greater care than he is accustomed to take of his own property, for if it is lost and it appears that a more careful person might have guarded it, he will be liable.[31] On the other hand, a person with whom a thing has been left for safe-keeping (a depositary) receives no benefit (the contract of depositum being gratuitous) and he is responsible only for wilful wrong (dolus malus).[32] The depositor, however, the one for whose benefit the contract is made, must exercise exacta diligentia and therefore is liable for "levis culpa" on his part. The depositary, in contrast with the depositor, is required to use only such diligence as he in person is accustomed to use in

---

30. Inst. 3, 14, 2.
31. Inst. 3, 14, 2.
32. Inst. 4, 1, 17.

his own affairs.[33] This is, of course, a very variable standard, yet it is the rule of diligence applied in the case of vendor and vendee,[34] in contracts of letting and hiring,[35] pledge,[36] partnership, and agency (negotiorum gestio).

Plurality of Parties:

In the great majority of obligations there are only two parties, a single debtor and a single creditor, yet there may be an obligation where a single debtor has two or more creditors, or where two or more debtors have a single creditor, or where two or more debtors have two or more creditors.[37]

In our own system of law we have the familiar terms "joint obligations" and "joint and several obligations," that is, obligations where the parties may be held, in the one case, collectively, and, in the other, collectively and individually.

In the Roman Law, an obligation having a plurality of parties may be an obligation where each of a number of creditors may be entitled to only a part (pro rata) of the indebtedness, or each of a number of debtors may be bound to pay only a part.[38] Again, such an obligation may be what Roman lawyers called an obligation in solidum, or in solido,[39] that is, an obligation where in case of several creditors each may lawfully demand the whole debt, or where in case of several debtors each is bound to pay it in full. Modern writers have applied the term solidarity to this Roman form of joint obligation.

However, instead of joint debtors being obligated

---

33. Johnson v. Reynolds, 3 Kan. 251.
34. Dig. 18, 6, 3.
35. Dig. 19, 2, 25, 7.
36. Dig. 13, 7, pr.
37. Inst. 3, 16, pr.
38. Dig. 45, 2, 11, 1 & 2.
39. Solidum in this use means whole or entire. See Carroll v. Waters, 9 Mart. (O. S.) 500 (La.)

to pay either pro rata or in solidum, the nature of the obligation when there was a plurality of parties on one side or on both sides might be what modern Roman Law writers term "correal."

In the Roman Law various names were given to the parties to a contract. In the verbal contract, stipulatio, the person to whom the promise was made was called the stipulator and the person who made the promise was called the promisor. The term "reus" was a general term used in all kinds of obligations, and its original meaning was the party who was subject to a demand, and in this sense was regularly applied to a defendant in an action. However, it was commonly applied to any party to a contract, stipulators being called "rei stipulandi," and promisors "rei promittendi."[40] The term adstipulator was also used to describe a party who joined with a stipulator,[41] and the term adpromisor to an additional promisor.

Modern writers upon Roman Law coined a Latin term "correus," from "con" and "reus," meaning a co-party or a joint party, equally applicable to joint debtors and to joint creditors. From this term "correus" are derived the further words "correal" and "correality," certain kinds of obligations being called "correal obligations," and certain debtors and creditors being called "correal debtors" and "correal creditors." The term "correality" is used to mean the doctrine of "correal obligations," that is, obligations where there is either a plurality of debtors or of creditors, or of both, and where each or all of several creditors may enforce an obligation against a single debtor, or against each or all of several debtors for the entire amount (in solidum).[42] Such a form of obligation was obviously created for the benefit of

---

40. Inst. 3, 16, pf; Dig. 45, 2, 1.
41. Gaius 3, 110.
42. Savigny, Obl. R., sec. 16.

[Roman Law]

creditors since it was an advantage to have several
persons who could enforce an obligation, and it was
also a greater security if there were several persons
who could be held responsible for the whole debt. As
applied to several co-debtors such an obligation was
said to be passive, but called active when applied to
several co-creditors.

It would seem from the preceding statements that
there was no difference between correal obligations
and obligations in solidum, or between solidarity and
correality. They did, indeed, agree in the right of
each creditor to exact the whole amount due and in
the duty of each debtor to pay the entire amount, but
in their nature obligations in solidum and correal
obligations were entirely different, and, in consequence, were governed by different principles of law.
A correal obligation, like an obligation in solidum, has
a plurality of parties, and, also, a single objective
based upon the same act of performance or forbearance, but there is only one obligation, only one bond
(vinculum juris) between all the parties. An obligation in solidum, on the other hand, is an obligation
where there is a separate and individual contract (vinculum juris) between each debtor and creditor. In
correal obligations there is a plurality of parties and
only one obligation, but in obligations in solidum
there is both a plurality of parties and a plurality of
obligations.

It follows, therefore, that in a correal obligation
any act or event that discharges or extinguishes the
bond or tie between any one or more creditors and
any one or more debtors, extinguishes the obligation
as to all, since there is but one bond (vinculum) that
holds them together. Accordingly, in a correal obligation not only a payment by one debtor releases all
the other debtors,[43] but the release of a single debtor

43. Inst. 3, 16, 1.

by one creditor (acceptilatio) breaks the bond of all, likewise a novation made by one creditor and one debtor. Again if one creditor brings suit against a single debtor the very joinder in issue, the litis contestatio, extinguishes the obligation of all.

An obligation in solidum, on the other hand, could be extinguished only by actual compensation (solutio), that is, by satisfying the common object of the obligation. A mere release of one debtor, or a joinder in issue in an action against him has no effect upon the other parties, either creditors or debtors.

Moreover, in correality there is no right of contribution (regressus). If one debtor pays the whole amount he cannot compel his co-debtors to reimburse him pro rata.[44] Solidarity, however, carries with it the right of contribution.

Whether or not co-debtors are liable only pro rata, or in solidum, or as "correi," depends either upon the intention of the parties to a contract,[45] or upon a rule of law, irrespective of intent, in certain kinds of obligations. The ordinary rule governing joint liability in Roman Law is that debtors are liable pro rata. They may agree, however, to be bound in solidum, or in correality.

The usual origin of correal agreement was a joint stipulation,[46] but it might also arise by testamentary provision. For example, several bankers may give credit to one debtor for the same debt and stipulate that the debt may be enforced by them all in solidum. There is but one contract and one debt, but each creditor can enforce the entire obligation.[47] This, therefore, is a correal obligation. Likewise, a testator may

---

44. At least, such is the weight of opinion among modern civilians. Savigny, however, is of the opinion that there is a right of contribution in correality.
45. Dig. 45, 2, 9, pr.
46. Inst. 3, 16, pr.
47. Dig. 2, 14, 9, pr.

charge several heirs with the duty of paying a certain legacy. Here, again, there is but one obligation having the same objective, but it would be enforceable as to the whole legacy against any one of the heirs in severalty.[48] Again, the co-owners of a slave are individually rendered liable by a rule of law for any damage caused by the slave.

On the other hand, the liability of several persons for a joint delict committed by them is an illustration of solidarity. In such a case there are as many obligations as there are wrongdoers, but all the obligations have the same objective, compensation for the damage. They are severally liable in solidum, and payment by one of them will discharge the others from that particular liability.[49] However, if the law also imposed a penalty for the delict, in addition to compensation for damages, such obligations would be individual and each and all could be compelled to pay the same.

The law also imposed an obligation in solidum upon joint tutors for dolus or culpa in the management of the estate of their ward,[50] and persons by their contractual agreement might likewise become liable in solidarity.[51]

In the time of Justinian there was very little practical difference between correality and solidarity. In either case, it seems that if an action against one debtor did not result in a payment of the entire debt, another co-debtor could be sued,[52] and contribution (beneficium divisionis) was allowed in the case of correal debtors if it appeared that the one who had been com-

48. Dig. 30, 8, 1.
49. Dig. 2, 10, 1, 4; 4, 2, 14, 15.
50. Dig. 16, 3, 1, 43.
51. Dig. 17, 1, 60, 2; 16, 3, 1, 43; 13, 6, 5, 13.
52. Code, 8, 41, 28.

pelled to pay the entire debt had actually originally received only a part of the benefit.[53]

Suretyship (Fidejussio):

Connected with the Roman Law of joint obligations is the law of suretyship, for suretyship (fidejussio) is a form of a correal obligation. It is also a form of what is known in Roman Law as intercessio, that is, the assumption of a debt owed by another. When one assumed the already existing debt of another, and thereby relieved the debtor from all liability, such an intercessio was called privative intercession. This was, in fact, a sort of novation, the creditor accepting by a new obligation the intercessor in place of the former debtor, the first obligation being thereby extinguished. When, however, one agreed to be responsible for an obligation in futuro of another, this was a form of intercessio known as cumulative intercession, and was specifically called suretyship.

In different periods of Roman Law, suretyship existed under the forms of sponsio, fidepromissio, and fidejussio. All of these terms derived their respective names from the technical words used in the creation of the obligation. Sponsio (from spondeo, I solemnly promise) was the jus civile form of suretyship and was limited to Roman citizens.[54] Fidepromissio (from fidepromitto, I pledge my faith, or credit) was a later formula and could be used by aliens. The rules which governed these forms of suretyship were, however, similar.[55] They could be used only in connection with verbal contracts,[56] and the heir of such sureties was not bound by their guaranty.[57] Both sponsio and fidepromissio were obsolete in the time of Justinian, the

53. Nov. 99.
54. Gaius 3, 93.
55. Gaius 3, 118.
56. Gaius 3, 119.
57. Gaius 3, 120.

only form of suretyship then existing being fidejussio.[58]

Fidejussio (from fidejubeo, I bid you trust my faith, or credit) dates from the last century of the Republic and superseded the older forms of suretyship by reason of the greater security afforded by it. It could be applied to any form of contract and even to delict.[59] In case of more than one fidejussor each was liable for the whole debt,[60] and the heir of a fidejussor was also bound.[61] This contract of suretyship could be created either before or after the principal obligation to which it was accessory,[62] and could be created by writing, by formal words, or by mere consent of the creditor and the surety.[63] The consent or even the knowledge of the debtor was unnecessary.[64] The surety could bind himself for a less amount than the principal debtor but not for a larger sum.[65] He was primarily liable with the principal and the creditor could elect to sue either, but in Justinian's time a fidejussor could require that the principal if solvent should be first sued before recourse to the surety.[66] The emperor Hadrian also provided that a creditor should seek his remedy, in case there was more than one surety, from all the solvent sureties proportionally.[67] A fidejussor had no right of contribution from another fidejussor, but he could recover from the principal debtor,[68] and

58. Inst. 3, 20.
59. Inst. 3, 20, 1; Gaius 3, 119 a; Dig. 46, 1, 26.
60. Inst. 3, 20, 4.
61. Inst. 3, 20, 2.
62. Inst. 3, 20, 3.
63. Inst. 3, 20, 1.
64. Dig. 13, 5, 27; 46, 1, 30.
65. Inst. 3, 20, 5; Gaius 3, 126.
66. Nov. 4.
67. Inst. 3, 20, 4; Gaius 3, 121.
68. Gaius 3, 127.

was entitled to be subrogated to any pledges or other securities held by the creditor.[69]

In addition to the ordinary form of suretyship known as fidejussio, there were also in Justinian's time two other ways of obligating one's self to pay the debt of another. One of these was known as constitutum, the other as mandatum qualificatum. The former was an informal agreement, that is, a pact, to pay the debt of another on a fixed date (pactum de constituta pecunia).[70] The latter was a direction to another to lend money to a third person.[71] In such a case, if the borrower failed to pay the loan the law imposed a duty upon the mandator to do so.[72]

It is of interest to note that according to the Roman Law, an extension to the principal debtor of the time for payment did not discharge the surety.[73] However, under some of the codes of the modern Civil Law, such an extension without the consent of the surety does operate as a discharge of the latter,[74] thus making the modern Civil Law rule conformable to the general rule in our own law.

Agency: Representation:

In our English Law, contracts, both express and implied, are often made by a person acting through an agent. In the Roman Law, however, the doctrine of agency, or of "representation" as often called by Civil Law writers, was only partially developed. It was utterly unknown in the early law of contracts, and never in the entire history of Roman Law did it reach the importance it has attained in English Law. In our law the doctrine of principal and agent is based upon

69. Dig. 46, 1, 17; 46, 1, 59.
70. Dig. 13, 5, 5, 3.
71. Dig. 17, 1, 12, 13.
72. Gaius 3, 127.
73. Pothier on Obligations, 381.
74. Mouton v. Noble, 1 La. Ann. 192.

three elemental propositions: first, the creation by contract, express or implied, of the relation; second, the non-liability of the agent for contracts made in the name of his principal; and third, the liability of the principal for contracts made by his duly authorized agent. The Roman Law of contract never developed, however, agency to such an extent as this.

A fundamental idea in the Roman Law was that rights and liabilities were acquired or incurred only by the persons making the contract; third persons were not considered.[75] To the old formal contracts, such as mancipatio, cessio in jure, and stipulatio, the doctrine of agency never applied. The formal, ceremonious words employed to create such obligations bound only the persons who actually uttered them. It was the act of the individual, his solemn declaration, which bound him, and according to the theory of the old Roman Law he could not speak for another but only for himself.

While, in the old jus civile, a paterfamilias could acquire rights through agreements made for his benefit by a son or by a slave, yet this fact was not an illustration of agency but merely an incident of the patria potestas. The son or slave had no independent personality, he was not sui juris, and his act if accepted by the father or master, accrued to the latter's benefit by reason of his legal power. What the slave or the son acquired belonged to the master or the father not by the fact of agency, but by a positive rule of law, regardless of the knowledge or even contrary to the command of the master or father.[76]

The prevailing custom of employing slaves in connection with business transactions afforded, in many instances, a satisfactory substitute for an ordinary

---

75. Orleans Navigation Co. v. Mayor of New Orleans, 2 Mart. (O. S.) 10.

76. Inst. 3, 17, 1; Dig. 45, 1, 62.

agent, and this was the reason, no doubt, why the law of agency was so little developed by the Romans.

It was the rule of the old Roman Law that while the master or the father might acquire benefits by agreements made by his slave or his son, yet he was not bound by them.[77] However, under the praetorian law, a father who commanded a son, or a master who commanded a slave, to contract with a third person, was liable for the whole amount of the debt contracted, since the creditor in such a case relied upon the credit of the father or the master.[78]

In the course of time the praetor extended the operation of such actions. The growth of commerce required that many persons should be represented by others in business transactions, and many competent and able slaves, oftentimes more able than their masters, were made managers of various business enterprises. Thus a master would appoint a slave a commander (magister) of a ship, and in the course of the ship's business it would be necessary for the commander to enter into many various transactions. The person to whom the daily profits of the ship belonged was called an exercitor,[79] regardless of whether he was the actual owner or charterer of the ship. For all contracts made by the ship's commander in connection with the ship's business or repairs the exercitor could be sued in an action granted by the praetor and known as an actio exercitoria.[80] The creditor was allowed to choose between the exercitor or the commander, and could bring his action against either.[81] The exercitor did not, however, have an action against persons who contracted with the commander, but was confined to

77. Inst. 2, 9, pr. and 1; Dig. 44, 7, 39; Cod. 4, 26.
78. Gaius 4, 70; Inst. 4, 7, 1.
79. Inst. 4, 7, 2; Dig. 14, 1, 1, 15.
80. Inst. 4, 7, 2; Dig. 14.
81. Dig. 14. 1, 17.

his action against the latter,[82] who as time went on was frequently a freeman and sui juris.

Similar to the actio exercitoria was the actio institoria. An "institutor" was the manager of another's business, a shop, an inn, a bank, for example.[83] As in the former action, the person who contracted with the institutor could sue either the institutor or his employer, but the employer could not sue the one who dealt with the institutor.[84]

The contract of mandate (mandatum) in the Roman law was also a common, every day means whereby one person authorized another person to do something for him,[85] but mandate was not identical with agency. The person who procured another to act for him was called a mandator (mandans), the one who agreed to act was called a mandatary (mandatarius). The service was always gratuitous, however. Any promise whereby, without compensation, one agreed to do some lawful act for another, was a mandate, and it would seem that such a contract would cover practically the whole field of what we call agency. As far as practical service was concerned it substantially did so. As far, however, as the legal effect of agency is concerned, it did not do so. In a mandate, if A (the mandator) authorized B (the mandatarius) to transact some business for him, and if in connection with that business B made a contract with C, then in case of any subsequent breach of that contract, A (the mandator) had no action against C, nor C against A. The contract was made by B and C, and as far as C was concerned, B (the mandatarius) was the responsible party, not A (the mandator). This legal result is not, of course, the same as in our English law of agency.

82. Dig. 14, 1, 1, 18.
83. Dig. 14, 3, 4; 14, 3, 3; 14, 3, 5, 5; 14, 3, 5, 1; 14, 3, 5, 2.
84. Inst. 4, 7, 2.
85. See mandatum, next chapter.

In the modern Civil Law, however, the doctrine of mandate has been extended so that it has become synonymous with agency. In the Roman Law, mandate was confined to gratuitous services. In the modern Civil Law, any contract whereby one undertakes to act for another, either gratuitously or for compensation, is known variously as mandate, agency, or procuration. In some Civil Law jurisdictions, the term "procuration" is confined to an authority or appointment expressed in writing. In the state of Louisiana, "a mandate, procuration, or letter of attorney is an act by which one person gives power to another to transact for him and in his name, one or several affairs. The procuration is gratuitous unless there has been a contrary agreement."[86] In that state, it is held that the contract of mandate may be tacit as well as express; and the acts of the principal must be fairly and liberally construed towards those who contract with the agent, as well as toward the agent.[87]

Donations (Gifts):

A gift is distinguished from a contract in that it does not give rise to reciprocal duties and rights, but is merely an intended benefit conferred upon another by motives of friendship, generosity, or liberality.[88] It is a consensus in that there is a purely voluntary offer of a benefit by one party and an acceptance by the other, although no formal acceptance is necessary since the law presumes acceptance on the part of the donee.

In addition to gifts known as propter nuptias, the husband's gift to his bride already referred to in connection with the law of marriage, gifts are classed as gifts between living persons (donations in vivos) and

---

86. La. Rev. Civ. Code, arts. 2985, 2991.
87. Ball v. Bender, 22 La. Ann. 493.
88. Inst. 2, 7.

gifts made in contemplation of death (donations causa mortis).

For a long time in Roman Law, a mere promise to make a gift was not enforceable by any action, being a mere pactum. The donee acquired no right of property until the gift had been actually delivered to him. However, in the time of Antoninus Pius, promises of gifts between ascendants and descendants were made enforceable,[89] and in Justinian's time such promises were binding in general, and could be enforced by action.[90]

A striking difference between our law and the Roman Law was that gifts could be revoked on the ground of base ingratitude on the part of the donee. Prior to Justinian's time this was true only in case of gifts made by parents to their children or by patrons to their freedmen.[91] Justinian, however, extended the right of revocation in connection with all gifts where the conduct of the donee justified it.[92]

There were various restrictions in the long history of the Roman Law that were imposed upon the freedom of donation. As early as 204 B. C., the lex Cincia declared that gifts, except in the case of near relatives and patrons, should be invalid beyond a certain amount. Various imperial laws limited the amount in value of gifts unless they were duly evidenced by a court record (insinuatio), and Justinian fixed the amount at five hundred solidi.[93] Any excess of that sum was invalid unless duly recorded.[94]

From the earliest times it was the Roman Law that gifts between husband and wife were void. However,

89. Theod. Code, 7, 12, 4.
90. Inst. 2, 7, 2. Code, 8, 54, 35, 5.
91. Dig. 29, 5, 31, 1. Code 8, 56, 7; 8, 56, 8.
92. Code 7, 56, 10.
93. The solidus was the gold unit of value. Five hundred solidi in Justinian's time has been estimated to be worth about $1200.
94. Inst. 2, 7, 2.

in the time of the Emperor Septimius Severus, donations between husband and wife were upheld provided the donor died without having revoked the gift.[95] Reasonable presents, however, on the Roman New Year's Day (the Kalends of March), and on birthdays and other festal occasions were not included in the prohibition.[96]

Justinian speaks of another kind of donation inter vivos which was wholly unknown, he says, to the ancient jurists.[97] This was the donatio ante nuptias and its associated donatio propter nuptias. This marital gift was not, however, a mere gift between husband and wife, but was a provision made by the husband, as a counterpart to the wife dowry (dos), for her maintenance and support.

Donations Causa Mortis:

A gift between living persons became effective immediately upon the promise to bestow the benefit, but a gift causa mortis, made in contemplation of death, was conditioned upon the death either of the donor or of some third person.[98] Consequently, such a gift could be revoked any time prior to the death contemplated. The gift was also revoked in case the donee predeceased the donor.[99] The form of the gift might be attended with immediate delivery, upon condition that the property should be transferred to the donor in case the expected death should not occur, or the delivery might be postponed until the event of the death in question, in which case the property remained that of the donor until the death contemplated.

95. Dig. 24, 1; Code 5, 16.
96. Dig. 24, 1, 31, 8.
97. Inst. 2, 7, 3.
98. Dig. 39, 6, 11.
99. Dig. 39, 6, 23. See further as to "Donations" Chap. XVII in connection with "Pacts."

CHAPTER XVI

THE LAW OF OBLIGATIONS, *continued*

CONTRACTS

Obligations ex Contractu:

An obligation arises from contract when two or more persons enter into an agreement that is enforceable at law. The word contract (contractus) means, literally, a drawing together, and its juridical significance is a mutual agreement of the parties concerned.[1]

The terms consensus, pactum, pactio, and conventio were also used by the Romans in the general sense of agreement. They all signify the consent of two or more persons to the same thing.[2] The word conventio (a coming together, a convention) is a general term applying to all matters about which men, in their mutual dealings, agree either for the purpose of entering into a business agreement or of settling some dispute.[3]

However, even though there is an agreement there is not, necessarily, a contract. The fact that the parties agreed to do or not to do a certain thing did not always give rise to an obligation, even though they intended to create an obligation. There must be some legal cause or reason whereby the agreement becomes a contract, something that makes the agreement a legal bond or tie (vinculum juris). To the consent of the

---

1. Dig. 50, 16, 19.
2. Pactio est duorum pluriumve in idem placitum consensus, Dig. 2, 14, 1, 1; 50, 12, 3, pr.
3. Dig. 2, 14, 1, 3.

parties another element was necessary in Roman Law. The agreement had to be entered into in some way or form recognized by law, or else it had to be an agreement connected with some special subject matters.

At the time of the Twelve Tables, all legal contractual dealings between Roman citizens were limited to two primitive and formal transactions known as nexum and mancipatio. The ceremonial mancipatio with its five witnesses in addition to the two parties and the official money-weigher, the libripens, has already been described in connection with the division of property, under the old law (the jus civile), into things mancible (that is, things capable of being transferred by mancipatio) and things non-mancible. Nexum is believed to have preceded mancipatio, and is therefore, generally considered to be the oldest form of contract in Roman Law. Its exact nature and scope is a matter of dispute among the Roman writers themselves, but it is generally agreed that it was originally a solemn transaction for effecting a loan of money, there being five witnesses and a libripens just as in the case of mancipatio (per aes et libram). By force of the ceremony and the accompanying words the debtor stood bound (nexum) to repay the loan. It seems to have been similar to a confession of judgment, in that the creditor in case the debtor failed to pay, was not required to bring an action to obtain judgment. Under the old Roman Law the unpaid creditor could proceed forthwith against the person of the debtor, casting him into prison, and even selling him into slavery.[4] Although nexum was originally a contract of a loan of money, yet it was probably extended to cover any transaction involving a money indebtedness.

The terms obligatio and contractus belong to a later period than the time of the Twelve Tables. It is believed, however, that the terms verbis and literis,

---

4. See Livy 2, 24; Dionys, 6, 29, 37.

familiar in the later law of contract, are traceable to the form of words used in the ancient ceremony of nexum in connection with "the bronze and scales" (per aes et libram).

Both of these ancient forms of contract, mancipatio and nexum, had long been obsolete even before the time of Justinian, having been replaced by informal and more practical methods.

Other ancient forms of contract, but all later than the Twelve Tables, were mutuum, stipulatio, expensilatio, syngraphae, and chirographa.

Mutuum was another contract of loan but it differed from nexum in many ways. The time of its first appearance in Roman Law is unknown but it was one of the earliest transactions of the jus gentium. It was informal, being the oldest of the contracts originating "in re," that is, a contract connected with the delivery of a thing (res). A mutuum, or mutui datio, dealt, however, only with fungible things, things which are reckoned by number, weight, or measure, such as money, bronze, silver, gold, corn, wine, oil. The res thus loaned became the property of the borrower, his only duty being to return an equal number, amount, and quality of things of the same kind.[5] The most common loan connected with mutuum was a loan of money. The borrower did not stand in the shoes of a debtor who had confessed judgment, as in the case of nexum, but an action was necessary to enforce the contract upon the failure of the borrower to perform. The action was, however, stricti juris in character, rather than bonae fidei, meaning that the borrower could be held only to the letter of his agreement, namely, to return an equivalent of what he had received without being liable for any interest on a money loan or for any charge for the use of any other thing. Since the borrower in mutuum became the

5. Inst. 3, 14, pr.

owner of the res in distinction from the later contract known as commodatum,[6] the duty to return an equivalent in kind was not extinguished by the loss or destruction of the thing borrowed.[7]

The Civil Law contract of mutuum has been referred to in a number of American cases, and in some instances its principles have been adopted and followed.[8]

Another very ancient form of contract was known as stipulatio, a verbal contract, or a contract arising verbis. One party to the contract, the stipulator, put a formal question to the other party (the promisor) who returned to the stipulator a formal affirmative answer. The ancient Romans held that one who had thus been asked by certain binding words, and had also promised in a similar solemn, legal form, was obligated to perform. In early times the only words that were effective for this purpose, and they were valid only between Roman citizens,[9] were "Spondes?" (Do you solemnly promise?) and "Spondeo" (I do solemnly promise).[10] The same intention if conveyed and returned by the employment of other words of similar meaning would not suffice. This seems to be very strange to modern readers but it was for a long time the Roman Law. The origin of this form of contract is not known, but the particular words were probably connected with some ancient religious custom of the Romans whereby one invoked the gods in testimony of a solemn promise. The old religious

6. See infra.

7. See Inst. 3, 14, 2; Coggs v. Bernard, 2 Lord Raymond's Reports, 909, quoting Bracton.

8. See, in general, Thompson v. Riggs, 5 Wall. (U. S.) 663, 671; Rahilly v. Wilson, 20 Fed. Cas. No. 11,532; Caldwell v. Hall, 60 Miss. 330; Payne v. Gardner, 29 N. Y. 146, 167; Fosdick v. Green, 27 Ohio St. 484.

9. Gaius 3, 93.

10. Gaius, 3, 93, 179; Plautus, Capt. 4, 2, 117; Cicero, Pro Caec. 3, 7.

[Roman Law]

ceremony became obsolete but the ancient words remained probably with the significance of a solemn oath. Stipulations were doubtless made before witnesses in order to prove the fact of their being made but the law seems to have required no witnesses.

As time went on, the rigid rule concerning the exclusive use of spondes and spondeo relaxed, and other words, like promittis and promitto, dabis and dabo, facies and faciam, became binding by force of custom.[11] In the time of Justinian any words might be employed provided by their use the parties intended to create an obligation.[12]

On account of its simplicity stipulatio became in time the prevailing form of contract for a multitude of transactions. By stipulation (stipulatio) an informal promise (pactum) could be converted into an actionable one. It could not only originate obligations but transfer them either by changing the parties to an obligation, or by changing one obligation for another.

A stipulatory promise could also be made to a second person in addition to the creditor himself. Such a person was called an adstipulator. He was a sort of trustee for the stipulator, and by virtue of the promise being made to him he could bring action to enforce it.[13] Likewise, a second person known as an adpromisor could make the same promise as a surety for the promisor.

The three other early forms of contract, expensilatio, syngraphae, and chirographa, were, in addition to mancipatio and nexum, obsolete in Justinian's time. These three were all "literal" contracts (literis) in that they were originated by some form of writing.

Expensilatio was an entry made by a creditor in his account book of an expensum incurred for the

---

11. Gaius 3, 93; Inst. 3, 15, 1.
12. Inst. 3, 15, 1; 3, 19, 17; Codex 8, 38, 10.
13. Gaius 3, 111, 114.

benefit of a debtor.[14] The entry, to be binding upon the debtor, had to be made with the debtor's assent.[15] Syngraphae and chirographa, according to Gaius,[16] were literal contracts (literis) used by persons not Roman citizens (peregrini) and consisted, in the case of syngraphae, of a written acknowledgment of debt signed by both debtor and creditor, and in the case of chirographa such an acknowledgment signed by the debtor alone.

Chirographa and syngraphae are Greek words and were doubtless adopted as legal terms by the Romans in connection with their dealing with colonists and aliens. Chirographum literally is one's own handwriting,[17] an autograph. In the language of business it meant a written memorandum, a note, a bond, an obligation. A chirographum was a note or memorandum in writing signed by a debtor and delivered to the creditor, while syngraphae were two such notes or memoranda, one being executed by the debtor and one by the creditor, which were exchanged by the parties. They were in daily use in the Roman busi-

14. Gaius 3, 137.
15. Cicero, Pro Rosc. Com. 1, 5.
16. Gaius 3, 133, 134.
17. "And may be applied to any writing." Gibbs v. Usher, 10 Fed. Cas. 303. In Coke's Commentaries on Littleton (Litt. 2, ch. 12, sec. 217; Coke, 143 b) there is an interesting reference to the word chirographa. Coke says that in ancient times a deed indented (a deed with a toothed or notched edge) was called charta chirographa, because each party had a part (alluding to the fact that deeds of indenture were executed in duplicate). In a footnote to Coke's statement (Ed. of 1817) it is said that Mr. Maddox takes exception to it because many "chirographa" were not indented. It is further said, in the same note, that anciently (in England) deeds of two parts were written on the same paper with the word "Chirographum" in capital letters between the two parts, and were afterwards divided by a cut through the middle of the letters. The footnote further observes that some apply Coke's statement to "syngrapha," and make "chirographa" deeds of one part. The editor of the edition (1817) says, however, that doubtless by English lawyers in Coke's time the words "chirographa" and "syngrapha" were used synonymously.

ness world for many years, but as formal contracts (literis) they had long been obsolete in the time of Justinian. In that emperor's day all the old written contracts had become merged in stipulatio, the contract verbis. "In times past," say the Institutes,[18] "an obligation was created by writing, said to be created by names (nominibus). These names (nomina) are not, however, in use at the present time." The term "name" (nomen) here employed by the writer of the Institutes had long been used as a legal term to signify a bond, a note, or a debt, owing to the fact that the names of debtors were entered by creditors in their account books (expensilatio), or were signed to the written notes or memoranda (chirographa, syngraphae) given by debtors to their creditors.[19]

When it is said that written contracts (literis) were no longer in use in Justinian's time, it means that the creation of a contract by the fact of some writing was no longer the law. Written memoranda, however, of contracts created by words (verbis, stipulatio) were universally employed, and this practice has caused some misunderstanding, since some have supposed that a new form of written contract had merely taken the place of the old written contracts, the contracts literis. The memorandum of a verbal contract (contracts verbis) was called cautio [20] and had been in use long before Justinian's day and was still in use when the Institutes were written. It is highly probable that the use of a cautio, or written memorandum of a debt, was the outgrowth of the old contracts literis. It was merely evidence, however, of the contract verbal, the stipulatio. In the older law, the writing (expensilatio,

---

18. Inst. 3, 21.
19. Cic. Verr. 2, 1, 10, sec. 28; Fam. 7, 23, 1.
20. Literally caution or safety; hence in a secondary and legal sense the means by which one puts himself or another in safety, as by a bond, a security, a warranty, a bail. A cautio might be oral or written. See Cic. Fam. 7, 18, 1; Dig. 12, 1, 40.

chirographum, or syngraphae) created the obligation. In the later law, the writing (cautio) was not the foundation of the obligation but merely the evidential written memorandum of an obligation created by the words employed in the stipulatio. If at any time a dispute arose between the parties to a stipulatio upon the question whether or not the proper words to create a stipulatio had been actually uttered, the written memorandum (the cautio) was prima facie evidence that they had been spoken. Such evidence could be rebutted, however, by proof that the party who was thus said to have uttered the binding words was not present at the time and place when and where the contract was alleged to have been made. Moreover, despite the written cautio held by the creditor, the burden of proof, in case of a loan, was upon the creditor if the alleged borrower denied that he had ever received such a loan.[21] However, if the cautio were not thus denied by the debtor within five years he was, under former imperial constitutions, barred from making any defense to it. Justinian limited the period to two years.[22]

In the time of Justinian the only ways outside of so-called "innominate contracts" [23] and certain "pacts," in which contractual obligations could be created were three, namely, re, verbis, and consensu.[24] Contracts "re" were four in number, namely, mutuum and commodatum which dealt with loans; depositum; and pignus (pledge). They were all called "real" contracts since they were confined to the delivery of the ownership or possession of property (res).

Mutuum has already been described. Commodatum was the gratuitous loan of a res for the use of the bor-

21. Cod. 4, 30, 3; 4, 30, 1.
22. Inst. 3, 21; Cod. 4, 30, 14, pr.
23. See next chapter.
24. Inst. 3, 13, 2; 3, 14; 3, 15.

rower. In such a case, since the borrower is the one benefited by the use he is required by the law to exercise omnis diligentia in keeping and preserving the property in order that it may be duly restored to the owner.[25] In mutuum, the loan, money or other thing, was to be returned in kind, but in commodatum the specific property loaned had to be returned, as in case of a slave, a horse, or a garment. The borrower was not liable for any deterioration caused by the natural and reasonable use of the article, but for any damage caused by the borrower's negligence in excess of such ordinary wear he was liable.[26] Losses, however, arising from accident or violence, or other causes beyond the borrower's control were not chargeable to him.[27]

The borrower could not lawfully use the loan for any other purpose than the one for which it was lent, or permit another to make use of it since the loan of commodatum is a strictly personal favor. Losses occurring in such cases of misuse fall upon the borrower.[28]

Depositum is where one gratuitously receives the possession of property for the purpose of keeping it safely for the benefit of the owner. Here, in contrast with commodatum, the position of the parties is reversed. If A loans B a book for B's use (commodatum), the benefit is solely for the possessor (B); but if A leaves, for his own convenience, a book with B (depositum), the benefit is for the owner and not for the person who has the custody of the book. In depositum, the person with whom the thing is left is responsible only for wilful wrong (dolus malus) since

---

25. Dig. 13, 6, 5, 3 and 5.
26. Dig. 13, 6, 3, and 18, and 23.
27. Inst. 3, 15, 2; Dig. 13, 6, 5, 4; 13, 6, 20.
28. Dig. 13, 6, 5, 7 and 8; 47, 2, 40; Coggs v. Bernard, 2 Ld. Raym. 915; Bringloe v. Morrice, 1 Mod. 210. And see **Davis v. Shaw**, — La. —, 142 So. 301.

there is no advantage accruing to the person with whom the deposit is made (depositary).[29] If the depositary gives to the thing deposited the same care that he gives to his own things, he fulfills his entire duty. If the property is stolen from him he is not liable, even if a more careful man would have prevented the theft, for one who leaves his property in the keeping of a careless friend has only himself to blame.[30]

The receiver was not entitled to make any use of the property,[31] and it was his duty to return it on demand.[32]

In depositum, the depositary receives no reward or compensation for his service. If a remuneration in money is paid for the keeping of a thing the contract is no longer one of deposit, for it then becomes a contract of locatio-conductio (letting-hiring). However, even in depositum the parties might agree that a greater degree of care should be exercised by the depositarius than that imposed upon him by law.[33]

A depositum made in a time of emergency when the depositor had no opportunity to select a depositarius, as in case of fire or shipwreck, was called a depositum necessarium or a depositum miserabile, and in such a case the depositarius was liable in double damages for any loss occasioned by his wilful wrong.[34]

Pignus, or pledge, is the delivery of property to another for the purpose of securing some debt or other obligation. The pledgeor remains the owner of the property, the creditor merely requiring a possessory right in the property pledged.[35] The creditor did not

29. Dig. 13, 6, 5, 2; Inst. 3, 14, 3; Dig. 16, 3, 1, 7; 16, 3, 32.
30. Inst. 3, 14, 3; Johnson v. Reynolds, 3 Kan. 257.
31. Code 4, 34, 3.
32. Dig. 16, 3, 1, 45; 16, 3, 1, 24.
33. Dig. 16, 3, 1, 6 and 35.
34. Dig. 16, 3, 1, 1.
35. Dig. 13, 7, 35, 1.

have the use of the pledge, and in case of profits arising from it they were applied to the debt.[36] By express agreement, however, of the parties, the creditor could take the profits in place of interest (antichresis).[37] A pledge was beneficial to both parties, to debtor and to creditor, and for that reason the creditor being in possession of the property was required to practice exact diligence, that is, the care or diligence of a prudent man. If he did this and yet by some accident the property was lost or destroyed, he was not liable for the loss and could still recover from his debtor.[38]

Pignus has previously been considered in connection with the development of the Roman Law of mortgage.[39]

The second class of contracts in the time of Justinian was known as verbal contracts or contracts verbis, that is, contracts arising from the use of certain words in the form of question and answer. This form of contract has already been considered in connection with the contract known as stipulatio. The verbal contract of Justinian's time was a very informal one in comparison with the use of the "solemn words," spondes and spondeo, of the earlier law. If the parties understood each other and agreed to the same thing the particular words of the agreement were immaterial. In the time of Justinian the term stipulatio was synonymous with verbal contract, and stipulatio was used universally in all sorts of contracts. It always retained, however, its form of question and answer, although as already stated, any words might be used.[40]

The third class of contracts in Justinian's time was

36. Code 4, 24, 1.
37. Dig. 20, 1, 11, 1.
38. Inst. 3, 14, 4.
39. Chapter XIII, ante.
40. Inst. 3, 15, et seq.

known as consensual contracts. In such contracts there was no delivery of property as in the case of contracts re; no question and answer were required as in the case of verbal contracts (stipulatio), but the mere consent (consensus) of the parties was sufficient to create the obligation.[41] It was, however, only in the case of a few very common contracts that an obligation could arise by mere consent, and these few were exceptions to the general rule that a mere consensus was not actionable. Consensual contracts owed their existence to the jus gentium, and were made exceptions to the general rule on account of the daily conveniences and needs of business. As population increased, and commercial transactions multiplied, the need of contractual obligations other than re and verbis was obvious. Accordingly, under praetorian law, certain entirely informal agreements were recognized as binding. In other words, the praetor granted an action to enforce such agreements. However, as already said, they were few in number and had their origin in economic necessity.

The contracts that were in time thus recognized as being created by mere consent consisted of four classes, as follows: (1) Contracts of buying and selling, or sale (emptio-venditio); (2) contracts of letting and hiring, or hire (locatio-conductio); (3) contracts of partnership (societas); and (4) contracts of mandate (mandatum).[42] Beyond these four classes, the doctrine of consensual contracts was not extended.

The contract of sale in Roman Law (emptio-venditio) is not, as in our law, a contract transferring the general title in a thing for a price consisting of money or money's worth, but it is an executory contract, like unto our contract to sell. It is a contract to deliver

41. Inst. 3, 22; Gaius 3, 136.
42. Inst. 3, 22, pr.

to another for a price [43] the undisturbed possession of a thing (res). The contract was binding as soon as the parties had agreed upon the thing and the price.[44] No writing was required unless the contract itself provided that the terms or provisions of the transaction should be expressed in writing.[45] In case of a written contract the sale was not complete until the writing was completed and signed by the parties. Till this was done, either party could retract without liability, providing no earnest had been given. In case earnest (arra) had been given, then regardless whether the contract was to be written or unwritten, the buyer, if he refused to pay, forfeited whatever had been given as earnest, and the seller, if he refused to deliver, was liable for double its value.

Although the contract was duly formed yet the seller was not bound to deliver the thing sold till the buyer paid the price, unless credit had been given.[46] Moreover, title did not pass until the property was delivered to the buyer, although the risk (periculum rei) was the buyer's upon the completion of the contract. Consequently, if the subject matter of the sale was lost, stolen, or destroyed after the completion of the contract and before the time of delivery, without fault on the seller's part, the buyer was nevertheless liable for the price.[47] However, as an offset to this liability on the buyer's part, if there were, on the other hand, any increase, fruits, or accessions to the property after the completion of the contract, the seller was bound to deliver them all to the buyer.[48]

The price had to be in money.[49] It was disputed by

43. Inst. 3, 24; Dig. 18, 1, 2.
44. Gaius 3, 139; Inst. 3, 23, pr.; Dig. 18, 6, 8.
45. Inst. 3, 23, pr.; Dig. 44, 7, 2.
46. Inst. 2, 1, 41.
47. Inst. 3, 23, 3.
48. Inst. 3, 23, 3.
49. Inst. 3, 23, 2.

the ancient jurists whether the price could be something besides money, as a slave, a piece of land, or a toga.[50] However, the view that such latter transactions were barter (permutatio) and not sales prevailed.[51] Moreover, the price must be fixed by the parties and if it were left for a third person to determine, Labeo said the contract was invalid, although Proculus thought it good.[52] Justinian enacted that the contract in such a case should be binding if the third person did actually fix the price, but if he failed to act the contract should be void.[53]

The contract of sale, like all the other consensual contracts, was governed by good faith (bona fides). It was the duty of the seller to exercise exacta diligentia (the care of a prudent man, a "bonus pater familias") in the care and preservation of the thing sold till it was delivered to the buyer.[54] The seller was not an insurer, however, and for acts of mere force, violence, or casualty, not connected with fault or negligence on the seller's part, he was not liable.[55] Accordingly, the subject of the sale being a slave, a house, or a field, if, before delivery, the slave dies or is injured, or if the house is burned, or if the field is damaged by flood or tempest, the loss is upon the buyer although he has not received the property.[56]

Upon payment by the purchaser, it was the duty of the seller to deliver (tradere rem), that is, to deliver to the buyer the free and undisturbed possession. The contract did not require the seller to make the buyer the owner (dominus) of the thing sold, but only its

50. Gaius 3, 141; Inst. 3, 23, 2.
51. Inst. 3, 23, 2; Dig. 19, 4, 1, 2; Code 4, 64, 3.
52. Gaius 3, 140.
53. Inst. 3, 23, 1.
54. Dig. 18, 1, 35, 4; 19, 1, 36.
55. Inst. 3, 23, 3; Dig. 18, 6, 7.
56. Ib.: see Osborn v. Nicholson, 13 Wall. (U. S.) 654, 660; Viterbo v. Friedlander, 120 U. S. 707, 712.

undisturbed possessor. Even if it proved to be true that the seller did not own the goods, and, therefore, could convey no title, yet that fact alone was not a breach of the contract, and gave the buyer no right to rescind.[57] As long as the buyer was left undisturbed in his free use and possession of the goods he could not complain. If, however, he were ousted by a judicial proceeding from his possession by some third person having a superior title, then there was a breach of the contract and the seller was bound to indemnify him.[58]

In addition to this warranty against eviction, the seller was also liable on an implied warranty of quality, and was answerable for defects unknown to the buyer in quality or quantity.[59] Such was not the early law of Rome, since the jus civile made the seller liable, in such cases, only for fraud on his part, or unless he had expressly made such a warranty. The curule aediles, among whose duties was the general charge of the markets and trade, especially in grain, cattle, and slaves, imposed at an early day, however, an implied warranty of quality upon things sold in the open market, and in time the principle became a recognized rule of law in all sales.[60] It was, however, competent for the parties to stipulate that the seller should not be held responsible for any implied warranty of quality, and, on the other hand, the buyer could bind the seller to an express warranty instead of relying upon the implied warranty.

As said in the New York case of Wright v. Hart, 18 Wend. 449: "The rule of the Civil Law is caveat venditor, and, therefore, if the seller wishes to secure himself from future responsibility, in the case the article sold should afterwards be found to be different

---

57. Dig. 21, 2, 41, 1.
58. Dig. 41, 3, 23, 1; 21, 2, 6; Code 4, 52, 5.
59. Dig. 19, 1, 13, 1.
60. Dig. 21, 1, 31, 20; Code 4, 49, 14.

in kind or quality from what the parties supposed it to be, he must take care or provide against such a responsibility, by a particular agreement with the purchaser. The rule of the Common Law, on the contrary, is caveat emptor, which implies that the purchaser must take care to examine and ascertain the kind or quality of the article he is purchasing, or provide against any loss he may sustain from his ignorance of the kind or quality of the article sold, or from his inability to examine it fully, by an express agreement of warranty." [61]

In case the seller made an express warranty of quality, or had been guilty of fraud (dolus) in concealing defects, he was liable in case of breach upon the actio empti,[62] and there was, originally, no limitation placed upon this action, although in the time of Theodosius II (424 A. D.) it was limited to thirty years.[63] An implied warranty, in case of breach, was enforced by two actions, the actio redhibitoria, and the actio aestimatoria or quanti minoris. The former action, limited to six months, was a suit for the recovery of the purchase price, with interest, accompanied with a return (redhibitio) of the goods.[64] The latter action, limited to one year, was not based upon a rescission of the contract but enabled the buyer to sue for a recovery of a part of the price in proportion to the defects in quality or quantity.

The seller, on the other hand, had the actio venditi, which like the actio empti was a "direct" or jus civile action.[65] The seller was entitled to interest if the price was not paid at the time agreed,[66] and if it appeared

61. See also Waring v. Mason, 18 Wend. (N. Y.) 425; Eagan v. Call, 34 Pa. St. 236; Bulkley v. Honold, 19 How. (U. S.) 390; Co. Lit. 102 a.
62. Dig. 19, 1, 13.
63. Code 7, 39, 3.
64. See Macurty v. Bagnieres, 1 Mart. (O. S.) (La.) 149.
65. Dig. 18, 1, 75; 19, 1, 11, 1. See Actions, post.
66. Dig. 19, 1, 13, 20.

that a thing had been sold for less than half of its real value, (laesio enormis), the emperor Diocletian enacted that the seller could rescind the sale unless the buyer agreed to pay a fair price.[67]

A sale could be absolute or conditional,[68] but a sale of a thing known to the buyer to be not subject to sale (extra commercium), such as a temple, a forum, or a public building, was void.[69] However, if the buyer were deceived by the seller as to the salable character of the property, the seller was bound. The buyer could not get the property, but he could compel the seller by the actio empti to pay to him whatever would have been the reasonable value of it.[70]

Locatio—Conductio (Hire):

The second form of consensual contracts, or locatio-conductio [71] was of two sorts, namely, (1) locatio-conductio rei, the rental of the use of property; and (2) locatio-conductio operarum, the rental of hired services, or of work and labor. Some writers upon Roman Law recognize a third kind, locatio-conductio operis, or the delivery of a thing or materials to another to work upon, but by other writers this is included in the second class. In our English Law contracts for work and labor correspond to conductio-locatio operarum, and certain forms of our bailments would be included in locatio-conductio operis.

Letting and hiring (locatio and conductio) was governed by rules similar to those of sale. The sum paid (merces) had to be fixed before the contract was complete,[72] and the compensation had to be in money. Ac-

---

67. Code 4, 44, 4 and 8; Copley v. Flint, 1 Rob. (La.) 125; see, also, Nott v. Hill, 2 Ch. Cas. 120.
68. Inst. 3, 23, 4.
69. Inst. 3, 23, 5.
70. Inst. 3, 23, 5.
71. Locatio, a placing, a letting, a lease; conductio, a hiring, a renting.
72. Gaius 3, 142; Inst. 3, 24, pr.

cordingly, if the payment were left to a third party to fix, or if property were let in return for the use of other property, the contract was not one of locatio-conductio,[73] and, therefore, could not be enforced by an actio locati on behalf of the letter (locator, or lessor), or by an actio conductio in favor of the hirer (conductor, or lessee). The contract in such cases was what is called by modern writers an innominate contract,[74] and was enforceable only by an action praescriptis verbis.[75]

The contract of sale and the contract of hire are so similar, says Gaius,[76] that in some cases it is a question whether a contract is one or the other. For example, land leased in perpetuity, as is the custom, says Gaius, in connection with municipal lands which are leased as long as the rent is paid, is by the better authority a contract of locatio and conductio. Where, however, a band of gladiatorial slaves is delivered upon an agreement that for the performance of each who leaves the arena uninjured twenty denarii shall be paid, and that for each one slain or disabled a thousand denarii shall be given, the prevailing view was that the slaves who escaped injury were let and hired, while those who were killed or injured were bought and sold, the contracts whether of hire or of sale being conditional, or dependent upon the outcome.[77]

Locatio-conductio rei was the letting and hiring of the use of a thing (res) for money. The res could be anything that might be the subject matter of a sale, that is, a movable or an immovable thing, or an incorporeal thing, as a usufruct.[78] The letting of houses and of lands was a common illustration of this form of

73. Gaius 3, 143–146; Inst. 3, 24, 1 and 2.
74. See post.
75. Inst. 3, 24, 1 and 2.
76. Gaius 3, 145.
77. Gaius 3, 146.
78. Dig. 7, 1, 12, 2.

contract, the lessee of a house being called an inquilinus (a renter, a lodger), and the lessee of a farm a colonus (a husbandman, a farmer).

The lessee had the right to the possession, and fruits if any, of the property during the time specified. The lessor (locâtor) remained, however, the owner (dominus) of the property and could sell it to some third person, who, contrary to our law, could evict the lessee, in absence of a stipulation to the contrary. The locator was liable, however, to the conductor in damages for the eviction.[79] Also, contrary to our English Law, the locator was bound to keep the property in reasonable repair and convenience for the use of the lessee. For example, where A let a house to B, and C, an adjoining owner, erected a building which shut out the light from B, the latter could rescind the contract, as, also, he could do if the doors and windows of the rented house became out of repair and were not restored by the locator.[80]

In our law, there is, by the great weight of authority, no implied warranty of fitness for the use intended in the lease of property, but the Roman contract of hire required good faith between the parties. Consequently, the lease of pasture land that was unfit for pasture by reason of injurious herbs,[81] or the lease of wine vats that would not hold wine because the vats were rotten,[82] made the lessor responsible in damages.

A lessee was bound to pay the agreed rent,[83] to care for the property with exacta diligentia,[84] and to return it, at the end of the contract, in as good condition, less

---

79. Dig. 19, 2, 25, 1. See Dig. 19, 2, 30, pr. and 1.
80. Dig. 19, 2, 25, 2.
81. Dig. 19, 2, 19, 1; 19, 2, 60, pr.
82. Dig. 19, 2, 19, 1.
83. Dig. 22, 1, 17, 4; see Christy v. Casanane, 2 Mart. (N. S.) 451 (La.).
84. Inst. 3, 24, 5; Code 4, 65, 28.

[Roman Law]—29

ordinary wear and tear, as he received it. Even as in our own law, a lessee could not deny his lessor's title. Although the lessee claimed to be the owner of the property, he was obliged to deliver it before beginning an action for its recovery.[85]

If the lessee died during the term, his heir succeeded to his rights.[86] If the lessee of a farm (colonus) held over his term he was liable for the rent of another year, unless the lease were in writing. In the latter case he became a tenant at will unless a new written lease was executed.[87]

Locatio-Conductio Operarum:

The contract locatio-conductio operarum, or the contract of paid labor or employment, was a contract where the locator agreed to give his services to the conductor for a fixed sum (merces). If the locator contracted that the conductor should do or make some specific thing, with materials furnished by the locator, as to build or repair a house or a ship, or to carry goods, the contract was called locatio-conductio operis (faciendi).[88] Where the agreement was to pay a lump sum for the entire employment, instead of a per diem or other payment period, it was said to be made per aversionem, or by the job.[89] In any case, the compensation had to be fixed. Work done on a quantum meruit agreement was not a contract of locatio-conductio but an innominate contract.[90]

It should be noted that there is an inversion of the terms locator and conductor in the contract for services (locatio-conductio operarum) and the contract for making some specific thing (locatio-conductio op-

---

85. Code 4, 65, 28.
86. Inst. 3, 24, 6.
87. Dig. 19, 2, 13, 11.
88. Dig. 19, 2, 19, 9.
89. Dig. 19, 2, 35, pr.; 19, 2, 36.
90. See post.

eris). In the former, he who "lets" his services, that is, the one who is to do the work, is called the locator, the same as in the letting of a thing for hire (locatio-conductio rei), and the one who pays for the services is called the conductor. However, in the contract locatio-conductio operis, the one who does the work is called the conductor and the one who pays for it is called the locator. This produces some confusion in terms, but the Roman jurists looked upon the one who took the property of another in order to do work upon it as the hirer (conductor or redemptor operis) and the owner of the property as the locator, or the one who let out the work to be done.[91]

In connection with the contract of hire of services (locatio-conductio operarum) only such work as was usually considered to be compensable with money could be the subject of this contract. The services of professional men, such as advocates, physicians, teachers, and other skilled persons were not regarded as being measured by a mere monetary valuation, and contracts for such services were void. It was customary, therefore, to give an honorarium for services of this character.[92]

In connection with contracts made with a common carrier (a form of locatio-conductio operis) the Rhodian law of jettison (Lex Rhodia de Jactu) was adopted by the Roman Law, or rather was introduced into Roman Law by the praetorian magistrates. By the Rhodian Maritime Law, when a cargo was thrown overboard from a ship in order to lighten the load when the vessel was in distress on a stormy sea, so that the ship itself and, possibly, a part of the cargo might be saved, the owners of the sacrificed cargo were entitled to apportion their loss among the owners of

[91]. Dig. 19, 2, 13, 5; 19, 2, 59; 19, 2, 62.
[92]. Dig. 50, 13, 1, pr.; 50, 13, 1, 12.

the ship and also the owners of the part of the cargo that may have been saved.[93]

This doctrine of jettison was an equitable doctrine, based upon the principle that a loss incurred for the benefit of all should be made good by the contribution of all.[94] A ransom paid to pirates to redeem a ship was governed by the same rule.[95] The obligation to contribute in such cases was not founded upon contract but was created by law and was therefore a quasi-contractual obligation,[96] but, in practice, there was no action against the owners of the cargo or of the ship that may have been saved by the jettison, the remedy being brought against the master of the ship by virtue of his contract of hire, the purpose of the action being to compel the master to hold the goods till the respective owners who had been benefited should contribute their shares of the loss.[97]

In our own law, the maritime doctrine as to general average is derived from this Rhodian Law, as adopted in Roman jurisprudence.[98]

Societas (Partnership):

The agreement of two or more persons to form a partnership (societas) was also a consensual contract, that is, a contract requiring nothing more than mutual consent.[99] A partnership is a contract whereby two or more persons unite themselves for the purpose of accomplishing a lawful common object with the intent to participate in the resulting profit or loss.[100] The rule, in absence of agreement to the contrary, is that

93. Dig. 14, 2, 1; 14, 2, 9.
94. Dig. 14, 2, 1.
95. Dig. 14, 2, 2, 3.
96. See post.
97. Dig. 14, 2, 2, pr.; 14, 2, 2, 2.
98. Columbian Ins. Co. v. Ashby, 13 Pet. (U. S.) 331; Bradhurst v. Columbian Ins. Co., 9 Johns. (N. Y.) 9.
99. Gaius 3, 135; Dig. 17, 2, 4, pr.
100. Dig. 17, 2, 57.

the individual partners shall share both profits and losses equally,[101] but it is competent for the partners to agree in what proportion the profit and loss shall be divided among them.[102] An agreement, however, to the effect that one partner shall take all the profits and the other partner shall bear all the losses, called facetiously by Roman jurists a lion's share partnership (societas leonina), was void.[103]

Partnership among the Romans was of various forms, namely, universal partnership (societas universorum bonorum, or societas omnium); special or particular partnership (societas negotiationis alicujus); and partnership for general trading (societas omnium quae ex quaestu veniunt).

A universal partnership extended to all the property of the partners.[104] It seems to have been a sort of communistic arrangement whereby all the property, both movable and immovable, of each partner was placed in a common fund and became the joint property of all.[105] All the expenses and contractual debts of each partner were paid from the common purse,[106] but the partnership fund was not liable for damages arising from a delict unless the fund had profited by such means.[107]

Property subsequently acquired by each partner, such as legacies, inheritances, and gains in trade, was contributed to the joint possessions, since this form of partnership did not contemplate the holding of private property by an individual.[108] It is obvious that such a partnership was not an ordinary trading or

101. Inst. 3, 25, 1.
102. Gaius 3, 149–150; Inst. 3, 25, 1–3; Dig. 17, 2, 76–80.
103. Dig. 17, 2, 29, 2.
104. Inst. 3, 25, pr.
105. Dig. 17, 2, 1, 1; 17, 2, 2; 17, 2, 74.
106. Dig. 10, 2, 39, 3; 17, 2, 3; 17, 2, 27.
107. Dig. 17, 2, 73; 17, 2, 55.
108. Dig. 17, 2, 3, 1; 17, 2, 65, 16; 17, 2, 73–74.

commercial partnership, but an arrangement whereby two or more persons were to own and share all things in common.

A particular or special partnership (societas negotiationis alicujus) was a partnership for the accomplishment of some particular object or purpose. It might be for the carrying on of some particular business, or it might be limited to a single transaction. Partnerships for the buying of slaves for the market,[109] or for farming the public revenues (societas vectigalis) were illustrations of this form. In partnerships of this sort only the property contributed for the common purpose and the profits derived therefrom belonged to the partnership.[110]

The ordinary commercial partnership in general was the societas omnium quae ex quaestu veniunt, or a partnership in all property which comes from gain in business transactions.[111] The gains might arise from the capital, skill, or labor of the partners. Only the property invested in the business belonged to the firm, and, therefore, each partner might be the owner of private property, and whatever came to a partner by way of gift or inheritance belonged to himself.[112]

The contract of partnership was bilateral and required good faith (bona fides) on the part of each member.[113] Unless there was an agreement to the contrary, each partner shared equally in the gains and the losses.[114] It was the legal duty of partners to care for the common property with the same diligence as he cared for his own personal affairs,[115] and the mutual duties and responsibilities of partners could be en-

109. Gaius 3, 148.
110. Dig. 17, 2, 5, pr.; 17, 2, 58, pr.
111. Dig. 17, 2, 7 and 13.
112. Dig. 17, 2, 9; 17, 2, 71, 1.
113. Gaius 3, 137.
114. Gaius 3, 150.
115. Inst. 3, 25, 9.

forced by the action pro socio.[116] The rule, however, of our law that a partner within the scope of the partnership business is the implied agent of the firm, and binds the firm by his transactions relating to the business of the firm, was unknown to the Roman Law. If all the partners jointly contracted with a third person, they could sue and be sued in connection with such a contract, but a contract made with a third person by one partner, even with reference to partnership business, gave the firm no right to sue, and, likewise, ordinarily gave the third person no right of action against the firm, or any one of its members except the one who was a party to the contract. There were some exceptions to this rule, especially in the case of bank partners (argentarii) and partners engaged in the slave trade, and shipmasters.[117] Partners who transacted business through the captain of a ship or the manager of a shop were individually liable for contracts made by such a representative. As a general rule, however, a partner was not personally liable for the act of another partner unless the former had subsequently made an express agreement to be bound. The very slight development of the law of agency in Roman jurisprudence is illustrated in this rule of nonliability. In Roman Law the rights and liabilities of partners were limited to themselves. They did not extend to third persons. In case a partner was obliged to pay a debt contracted for the benefit of the firm he had his remedy (actio pro socio) for contribution against his fellow partners,[118] but this action was confined to the partners themselves.[119]

The duration of a partnership depended upon the continuance of mutual consent. No one was required

116. Inst. 3, 25, 9.
117. Dig. 21, 1, 44, 1; 14, 1, 25, 1-4.
118. Dig. 17, 2, 27; 17, 2, 38.
119. Dig. 17, 2, 43.

to remain in a partnership against his will, and the withdrawal of any one member dissolved the partnership.[120] However, if, in a case of universal partnership (omnium bonorum), a partner withdrew because he secretly planned to acquire for himself alone an inheritance to which he was soon to succeed, he could be made to share the inheritance with his fellow partners since he did not act in good faith. It would have been otherwise if he had withdrawn without any selfish motive, and afterwards had succeeded to an inheritance.[121]

A partnership is also dissolved by the death of a partner,[122] by the loss of status (capitis deminutio) of a member,[123] not including, however, the loss of agnatic family (capitis deminutio minima),[124] by forfeiture of a partner's property for crime,[125] or by insolvency.[126] A partnership also came to an end when the object for which it was formed was accomplished,[127] or when it was terminated by the expiration of the time it was to continue.[128] Likewise, a partnership was dissolved when a partner filed an action in court for the division of the partnership property.[129]

The rule that a partnership was dissolved by the death of a partner had one exception. In a partnership for farming the public revenue (societas vectigalis), the heir of a deceased partner could by express agreement take the place of the deceased.[130]

In addition to the forms of partnership already mentioned there was a form of joint ownership which

120. Gaius 3, 151; Inst. 3, 25, 4.
121. Gaius 3, 151.
122. Gaius 3, 152; Dig. 17, 2, 1.
123. Gaius 3, 153.
124. Dig. 17, 2, 58, 2; 17, 2, 65, 11.
125. Inst. 3, 25, 7; Gaius 3, 154.
126. Inst. 3, 25, 8; Gaius 3, 154.
127. Inst. 3, 25, 6.
128. Dig. 17, 2, 65, 6.
129. Dig. 17, 2, 65.
130. Dig. 17, 2, 35 and 59.

might or might not be a partnership according to the circumstances of its creation. The Romans called this form of joint ownership a societas rei unius, a partnership in a single thing, or a societas certarum rerum, a partnership in certain things. Two or more persons could, of course, agree to be the partnership owners of a single thing, and in such a case, the mutual consensus of the parties created a legal partnership. However, a legacy might be given to two or more persons jointly, and, in this case, they would be joint owners not by their own agreement but by the act of a third party. This did not create a strict partnership although they were joint owners as in the first case. The remedies of the two cases were, however, different. In the first case the partners had against each other the actio pro socio, the regular partnership remedy. In the second case, the remedies were the actio communi dividundo (partition), or the actio familiae eriscundae, the former action being the general action for partition in case of joint ownership arising by any means; the latter was a special action for the division of an inheritance.[131]

Mandatum:

The fourth and last form of consensual contracts was mandatum, the only gratuitous contract created by mere mutual consent. In the preceding consensual contracts already considered, there was always an element of compensation, but mandatum had no monetary consideration. A contract for services to be paid for at an agreed upon price was a contract for hire (locatio-conductio),[132] and services to be paid for at an unfixed price was an "innomitate"[133] contract.

Mandatum, or mandate, is a contract whereby one person, the mandator, or mandant, requests, without

---

131. Inst. 4, 6, 20; Gaius 4, 42.
132. Gaius 3, 162; Inst. 3, 26, 13.
133. See post.

compensation, another person, the mandatarius, or mandatary, to do or to give something either for the benefit of the mandator or for some third person, and the mandatarius promises to do so.[134]

In our own law "mandate" is often defined as a form of bailment, namely, the delivery of a chattel to another who is to carry it, or to do some work upon it gratuitously.[135] However, this is only one of many forms of mandate in the Roman Law. Mandate does not require the delivery of any property (res) in order to create the contract. It may be a request and a promise to do any sort of lawful business for another.

Mandate, as a contract, has nothing in common with the term "mandate" used in the sense of a judicial command. The contract is a purely voluntary matter, and the person who is requested to act for another, the mandatary, may accept or refuse the request at his pleasure.[136] Moreover, even after the request has been made and accepted, either party can withdraw from the agreement up to the time the service is actually begun, providing reasonable time is given to the mandator to obtain someone else.[137]

The contract of mandatum, says Justinian,[138] may be of five forms: (1) for the mandator's benefit only; (2) for the mutual benefit of the mandator and the mandatarius; (3) for the benefit of some third person only; (4) for the benefit of the mandator and some third person; (5) and for the benefit of the mandatarius and some third person. There can be no mandate for the sole benefit of the mandatarius, since

---

134. See Richardson v. Futrell, 42 Miss. 525, 543.
135. Coggs v. Bernard, 2 Ld. Raym. 909; Hanes v. Shapiro, 168 N. C. 24; Montgomery v. Evans, 8 Ga. 178, 180; Eddy v. Livingston, 35 Mo. 478, 492; Maddock v. Riggs, 106 Kan. 808.
136. Gaius 3, 159; Inst. 3, 26, 9, and 11.
137. Inst. 3, 26, 11.
138. Inst. 3, 26, pr.; Gaius 3, 155.

this would be a mere matter of advice, and involves no obligation.[139]

The possible illustrations of mandate are infinite. The most common form is the first above cited, where the mandator requests the mandatary to perform some service for the sole benefit of the mandator. The service may consist of a single transaction or a multitude of transactions. For example, A requests B to buy a slave for him (A), or to take charge of his entire business.[140] An illustration of mutual benefit would be where A requests B to lend money with interest to C who is to use the money for the benefit of A's property.[141] A mandate for the benefit of a third person is illustrated where A requests B to buy a farm for C.[142] Under the fourth form would be a mandate whereby B agrees, at request of A, to transact some business in which A and C are jointly interested.[143] A mandate would be for the benefit of the mandatary and a third person where A requests B to lend money with interest to C.[144]

The third form of mandate, or a mandate for the sole benefit of a third person, is a form of suretyship and has been previously mentioned in connection with that subject. It has been called by modern writers mandatum qualificatum. Thus where A requests B to loan money to C (without interest),[145] it was an implied guaranty on A's part that he would pay B in case of C's failure to do so, and B had the actio mandati contraria against A if C did not pay.[146]

It is obvious that mandate is a sort of agency so far

139. Gaius 3, 156; Inst. 3, 26, 6; Dig. 17, 1, 2, 6.
140. Gaius 3, 155; Inst. 3, 26, 1.
141. Inst. 3, 26, 2.
142. Inst. 3, 26, 3.
143. Inst. 3, 26, 4.
144. Inst. 3, 26, 5.
145. Inst. 3, 26, 5.
146. Gaius 3, 127; Inst. 3, 20, 6; Dig. 17, 1, 12, 13.

as one person acting for another is concerned, and the term "mandatum" is often translated "agency," the mandator being the "principal" and the mandatarius the "agent." [147] However, the idea of agency, or representation, developed very slowly in Roman Law, since the fundamental doctrine was that only the person who entered into a contract with another could sue or be sued upon it. Consequently, a third person with whom the mandatarius dealt had no direct action against the mandator and vice versa. In later times, however, equitable actions (actiones utiles) between a mandator and third persons dealing with a mandatarius were granted by the praetor.

Mandate originated in the need, often arising, of having some person to act for another. However, since such a transaction could be enforced only by the actual parties to it, it was essential that the person who thus acted for another should be one in whom the person requesting him to act had trust and confidence. Mandate in its origin was probably a trust reposed in a friend, a commission given with the hand clasp (manu datum) of friendship and confidence to another, and as a service of friendship and honor it was not placed upon a commercial basis of pay but was always regarded as gratuitous.[148]

Any commission that was lawful and not for the exclusive benefit of the one accepting it could be the subject of mandate.[149] No particular form or way of creating the contract was required; it might be by words, or by writing, as a letter.[150] When the commission was accepted, it was the duty of the mandatary

---

147. See Williams v. Conger, 125 U. S. 397, 422.

148. Dig. 17, 1, 1, 4. Sohm is of the opinion that the oldest form of mandate was the familiae emptio, the first form of a private will. Rom. Law, 3d ed., 543.

149. Gaius 3, 157; Inst. 3, 26, 7; Dig. 17, 1, 22, 6.

150. Dig. 17, 1, 60, 1.

to execute it with diligence,[151] and to account to the mandator for all that was received in connection with the business transacted.[152] It was the mandator's duty to reimburse the mandatary for all expense properly incurred by him.[153] To enforce the mandatary's duty the mandator had the actio mandati directa, and the mandatary could sue the mandator by the actio mandati contraria to recover his expenses. Either party guilty of bad faith suffered the penalty of infamia.[154]

Although the element of compensation was never a part of the contract mandatum, yet an honorarium might be agreed upon by the parties.[155]

151. Gaius 3, 161; Inst. 3, 16, 11; Dig. 17, 1, 5, pr. and 1; 17, 22, 11; Code 4, 35, 13.
152. Dig. 17, 1, 10, 2; 17, 1, 10, 9.
153. Dig. 17, 1, 10, 9 and 10; 17, 1, 12, 9; 17, 1, 27, 4.
154. Gaius 4, 182; Dig. 3, 2, 1; 3, 6, 5.
155. Dig. 17, 1, 6; see Gurley v. New Orleans, 41 La. Ann. 75, 79.

CHAPTER XVII

THE LAW OF OBLIGATIONS, *continued*

INNOMINATE REAL CONTRACTS; PACTS; QUASI-CONTRACTS

The contracts considered in the preceding chapter fell within defined classes according to the manner of their creation, namely verbis; re; and consensu. They also had distinguishing names, such as stipulatio; mutuum, commodatum, depositum, and pignus; sale, hire, partnership, and mandate. Moreover, each of these contracts had its own form of action for its enforcement, and, as previously said, if agreements did not conform to the requirements of some one of these particular contracts then none of the actions provided for them could be maintained.

However, as the Roman Law developed with the growing needs of business transactions, there were other agreements which in time were regarded as contracts and were made enforceable by new actions. These agreements thus made enforceable were of two classes, one called by modern writers "innominate" real contracts, or contracts re having no particular names, the other class being known as pacts.

The first class partook somewhat of the nature of contracts re and also of contracts consensu. They became enforceable during imperial times. They did not fall strictly within any of the forms of the four contracts re or of the four contracts consensu to which particular names had been given. However, they were connected with the delivery of property or with the performance of some other act, relating usually to money or labor, and were consequently regarded as a special kind of "real" contracts (contracts re). In order to distinguish these contracts from true real contracts, mutuum, commodatum, depositum, and pignus, modern writers have applied to them the term "innominate real contracts," and they call the four contracts which have specific names "nominate real contracts."

It is sometimes said that "innominate real contracts" are distinguished from "nominate real contracts" in that the latter are based upon an obligation to return the specific property delivered (or its equivalent in case of mutuum), while in "innominate real contracts" the party to whom the property is delivered is bound to give something else in return. However, the agreements called "innominate" varied indefinitely and were not necessarily connected with the return of property or with the delivery of other property.

These agreements also contained an element of consensus, yet they were not enforceable, as were true consensual contracts, by virtue of the mere fact of consent.[1] Moreover, instead of there being a mere mutual consent to one particular thing, there was a performance by one party in consideration of the other party doing some other thing. Mere promises were not sufficient to create an innominate contract, since a second element was necessary, namely, the performance by one of the parties of his promise. By these two elements, mutual promises and performance of his promise by one party, the obligation was created.[2] It was the equitable doctrine of part performance that caused the praetor to give an equitable action to compel the other party to carry out his part of the agreement, the remedy being known as the actio

1. Dig. 19, 4, 1, 2.
2. Dig. 2, 14, 7, 2.

in factum praescriptis verbis.³ This action was like unto our Common Law action of trespass on the case, the circumstances of the plaintiff's case being set out in the pleadings (praescriptis verbis).

Ulpian says,⁴ "Some agreements founded on the jus gentium give rise to actions and some to exceptions (defenses). Those that give rise to actions are not mere 'agreements' but are classed under special names such as sale, hire, partnership, mutuum, depositum, and similar names. However, if the matter does not come under one of these special contracts, yet if there is a sufficient additional ground (causa), an obligation is created. For example, I give you one thing on the agreement that you give me another; or I give you a thing with the understanding that you should do something. This says Aristo is equivalent to a synallagma."⁵ The sufficient additional ground (causa) mentioned by Ulpian in such contracts, in modern times called "innominate," is the part performance of the party that gives something.

According to Paulus,⁶ there were four classes of such enforceable agreements which he numerates as follows:

1. Do ut des, I give to you that you may give;
2. Do ut facias, I give that you may do;
3. Facio ut des, I do that you may give;
4. Facio ut facias, I do that you may do.⁷

It will be noted that in all these four classes there is a performance, either in the giving or in the doing of something by one party, upon the consideration that the other party gives or does some other thing. The possible number and forms of innominate contracts are many. The most common illustrations come

---

3. Gaius 3, 143, 144; Inst. 3, 24, 1 and 2; Dig. 2, 14, 7, 3.
4. Dig. 2, 14, 7, 1 and 2.
5. Greek for "contract."
6. Dig. 19, 5, 5, pr.
7. See Blackstone's Comments upon these distinctions. Com. II, 444.

under the head of agreements known as permutatio (exchange or barter; aestimatum; and precarium).

Permutatio according to the facts of a particular case might resemble various forms of nominate contracts, such as sale, hire, mutuum, commodatum, and deposit. It was, however, none of these and, consequently, not suable as such. For example, in a sale there must always be a price in money, therefore, if A gives a vase to B in consideration of B's promise to give A a horse, there is no sale, but there is an exchange (permutatio), and it is enforceable as such.[8] It is an illustration of a contract "do ut des," I give that you may give. Moreover, it differs further from a sale in that while a contract of sale is complete as soon as there is a mutual consent (consensus), yet exchange or barter (permutatio) does not become an obligation until one of the parties gives to the other the agreed-upon property.[9] There is a further difference between sale (emptio-venditio) and exchange (permutatio). In sale there is no obligation to make the purchaser the owner of the property, no warranty of title, the duty being merely to deliver and to warrant quiet possession. In permutation there is an obligation to make the other party a true owner of the property, a warranty that the title is good.[10]

Again if A loans to B the use of a slave in return for one of B's slaves who is to work for A, the agreement resembles hire but it is not a contract of hire (locatio-conductio) since there is no price in money fixed for the services of either slave. It is another illustration of an innominate contract, "do ut des."[11] Where, also, A had agreed to erect a building on B's land in consideration of B's erecting a building on

---

8. Inst. 3, 24, 1 and 2; Dig. 19, 4, 1, 2; 19, 4, 1, 4; 19, 5, 5, 1.
9. Dig. 19, 4, 1, pr.
10. Dig. 12, 4, 16.
11. Dig. 19, 5, 25.

A's land, there is here no consensual contract, but if A carries out his part of the agreement B is bound by a contract "facio ut facias," I do that you may do, and A, in case of B's failure to perform has his action in factum praescriptis verbis.[12]

Aestimatum was the name given to an agreement whereby property was delivered to one with an option either to pay for it at a stated price (aestimatum) or to return it. This was not a sale, a contract of hire, or a mandate.[13] A, for example, delivers to B a pearl, to be paid for at its estimated price of ten aurei, or to return it. A may not sue by any of the real or consensual contract actions, but by an action in factum he may compel B either to return the pearl or to pay for it.[14] Again, if A and B are walking by the banks of a river, and A upon B's request hands to B a ring for him to inspect, and B while examining the ring carelessly lets it fall and it rolls into the river and is lost, this transaction is not a commodatum, for the mere inspection of the ring is not a use of the ring. It was, however, an agreement "do ut des," and B is liable in an action in factum (praescriptis verbis) for not performing his obligation to return the ring.[15]

Precarium, or permissive occupancy, was originally a tenancy at will of land or of a servitude.[16] Later it was extended to the possession of movable property.[17] It was analogous to commodatum, yet differed from it in that the tenant or holder had a recognized legal possession against all except the true owner,[18] to whom it was the duty of the tenant to

12. Dig. 19, 5, 5, 4.
13. Dig. 19, 3, 1, pr.; 19, 5, 13, pr.
14. Dig. 19, 3, 1, pr.
15. Dig. 19, 5, 23.
16. Dig. 43, 26, 15, 2.
17. Dig. 43, 26, 4, pr.
18. Dig. 43, 26, 15, 4.

[Roman Law]

surrender the possession upon demand.[19] Moreover, the tenant was not, like a commodatarius, bound to exercise diligentia,[20] although he was liable for wilful wrong. It further differed from commodatum and also from hire (locatio-conductio) in that it could be revoked at the pleasure of the owner without any liability for damages on his part. In commodatum and hire the use of a thing was revocable only after the agreed-upon term had expired. In the precarium if the possessor refused to deliver the property upon demand of the owner, the latter could enforce his right of recovery either by the interdict de precario or by an action in factum praescriptis verbis.[21]

Pacts:

Innominate real contracts closed the list of Roman Law contracts, and all other agreements not falling within the classes already considered were known as mere pacts, nuda pacta, which were not enforceable by action, for, as Paulus says,[22] ex nudo pacto inter cives Romanos actio non nascitur.

However, in the course of time, some pacts were regarded as natural, or moral, obligations, and, as already pointed out, if one in performance of such an obligation had paid money that he had promised to pay, he could not sue for its recovery on the ground that his promise was a mere pact.[23] Likewise, in time, such pacts although not giving a plaintiff a right of action, yet might be set up as a defense (exceptio) by a defendant. Hence arose the maxim, nuda pactio obligationem non parit, sed parit exceptionem.[24]

Further, as a still later development, certain pacts

---

19. Dig. 43, 26, 8, 3.
20. Dig. 43, 26, 8, 3.
21. Dig. 43, 26, 4, 2; 43, 26, 2, 2; 43, 26, 19, 2.
22. Sent. rec. 2, 14, 1.
23. Dig. 46, 1, 16, 4.
24. Dig. 2, 14, 7, 4.

became actionable, either because they were made collaterally at the time binding transactions bonae fidei were made; or because the praetor allowed an action for their enforcement; or because some statute made them actionable. Of these three classes of pacts the first were called pacta adjecta, that is, pacts "added" to binding agreements; the second, praetorian pacts; and the third, pacta legitima. Later writers upon the Justinian law applied the term "Pacta Vestita," that is, "clothed" with legal power of enforcement, to all these three classes of pacts. They were thus distinguished from other pacts by being practically regarded as contracts, all other pacts remaining as before, unenforceable in an original action.

Pacta adjecta were frequently connected with sales, which were negotia bonae fidei, and often expressed in the form of a condition. For example, A agrees to buy a piece of land from B, provided that B will inclose it with a wall. The agreement to buy and to sell emptio-venditio is a consensual contract and valid as such, but the "added" agreement does not fall within the list of transactions (namely, sale, hire, partnership, and mandate) that may be enforceable by the mere fact of the consent of the parties. If, however, this added agreement is a part of the original transaction, it is included in it so as to give ground for an action for its breach.[25] However, if the agreement to inclose the land with a wall was made "after an interval," that is, subsequent to the agreement to sell, it would be a mere pact (nudum pactum) and, consequently, would be of no force so far as the plaintiff was concerned.[26] Moreover, had the agreement to sell the land been made by stipulatio, which was a stricti juris transaction, the added consensual agreement to build the wall, although made at the same time, could not

---

25. Dig. 2, 14, 7, 5.
26. Ib.

be enforced since it was only in connection with transactions bonae fidei that the rule applied.

Praetorian pacts were informal agreements that were upheld by the praetor, provided that they were in good faith and were not prohibited by any law.[27] A pact made with an intent to defraud one would not be upheld by the praetor,[28] and the law of the state could not be varied by any agreement of private persons.[29]

The most important praetorian pacts were receptum argentariorum; constitutum debiti; hypotheca; and receptum arbitrii. The first of these, receptum argentariorum, or banker's agreement, was a promise made by a banker to the creditor of a customer of the bank that the banker would pay to the creditor a certain sum of money out of any deposit the customer might have at the time or afterwards made. The reason for making such an agreement enforceable was business convenience. A stipulatio could be made only when the parties to the contract were present[30] and entered into the verbal agreement by speaking the necessary words.[31] A pact, however, could be made by one absentee to another, by means of a message or a letter,[32] and the action allowed by the praetor to make such a promise valid in case of a banker's agreement was known as an actio receptitia.[33]

The praetorian pact of constitutum debiti, or fixing a day for the payment of an existing debt, was an informal agreement to pay a present debt at some fixed day in the future. It might be a promise to pay one's

27. Dig. 2, 14, 7, 7.
28. Dig. 2, 14, 7, 10.
29. Dig. 2, 14, 38 (Papinian).
30. Inst. 3, 19, 12.
31. For this reason deaf and dumb persons could not make such a contract. Inst. 3, 19, 7.
32. Dig. 13, 5, 5, 3.
33. Inst. 4, 6, 8.

own debt or to pay the debt of another. Such an agreement could be made, of course, by a stipulatio, but such a formal agreement required, as said before, the presence of the parties. The enforcement of such an informal agreement, regardless of the presence of the parties, was merely an extension by the praetor of the actio receptitia, the new action being known as an actio de pecunia constituta.[34]

This action originally lay merely for the recovery of a money debt but it was extended by Justinian to cover all sorts of debts.[35]

A constitutum debiti could be made regardless of the ground (causa) of the debt, that is, irrespective of the kind of contract to pay a specific sum or an un- liquidated amount, and whether based upon a sale, or upon money payable as dowry (dos), or in connection with guardianship matters, or any other sort of contract.[36] Even a debt arising from a moral (natural) duty would support a constitutum debiti,[37] and one liable for a delict, such as injuria, theft, or robbery was bound by such a constitutum.[38] A constitutum did not amount to a novation, however, since it was no bar to the recovery of the debt upon the original obligation. Accordingly where one promised by a constitutum to pay the debt of another the latter was still bound,[39] since one could bind himself to pay the debt of another even without the debtor's consent.[40] However, when payment was made in performance of the constitutum the original debt was discharged.[41]

34. Dig. 13, 5, 1; Inst. 4, 6, 8. Justinian later merged both these actions in the actio constitutoria. Cod. 4, 18, 2, **pr.**
35. Inst. 4, 6, 8, 9; Cod. 4, 18, 2.
36. Dig. 13, 5, 1, 6.
37. Dig. 13, 5, 1, 7.
38. Dig. 13, 5, 29.
39. Dig. 13, 5, 28.
40. Dig. 13, 5, 27.
41. Dig. 13, 5, 18, **3.**

One by a constitutum could agree to pay at an earlier day than the maturity of the original debt,[42] although if he promised to pay a larger sum he was liable only for the original amount.[43]

As already stated, the promise may be made to pay the debt of another, or to pay one's own debt also.[44] When the promise is to pay another's debt the difference between such an enforceable promise and the ordinary contract of suretyship (fidejussio), which was regularly created by a stipulatio, seems to be that a constituens (the promisor in a constitutum) was under a stricter obligation than a surety (fidejussor). A surety was liable only after the principal debtor had been ineffectively sued;[45] the formal release of the principal debtor also released the surety;[46] a surety might bind himself for less than the principal debt, or place some condition upon his liability; and a surety could refuse to pay unless the creditor should assign to him his rights against the principal debtor.[47] The liability on a constitutum, on the other hand, was not secondary but primary, and a constituens was released only by payment, or by the acceptance of other security on the part of the creditor.

Although a constitutum was an entirely informal promise, yet it seems that it did not arise from the mere words of the promisor unless he intended at the time to create a constitutum. Accordingly where one attempted to make a formal contract (a stipulatio) but the same was invalid by reason of some technical defect, it was held that the creditor could not treat the defective stipulatio as a constitutum, and sue upon

42. Dig. 13, 5, 4.
43. Dig. 13, 5, 11, 1; 13, 5, 12. He could promise to pay a less amount. Dig. 13, 5, 13.
44. Inst. 4, 6, 9; Dig. 13, 5, 3.
45. Nov. 4, 1.
46. Dig. 46, 1, 60; 46, 1, 68, 2.
47. Dig. 49, 14, 45, 9; Cod. 8, 41, 21.

it as such, since the intention was to create a stipulatio and not a constitutum.[48]

The praetorian pact known as hypotheca has been discussed in a previous chapter, in connection with the law of pignus, or mortgage. By the old law, it was necessary to deliver the property into the hands of the creditor in order to create a mortgage upon it, but the praetor allowed a pledge, or mortgage, to be created by any simple, informal agreement without the necessity of the delivery of the property in question,[49] and gave the creditor an action to enforce his claim.[50]

Receptum arbitrii (an arbitration agreement) was an informal agreement to settle a dispute by arbitration. Its object was to put an end to litigation, and the praetor allowed an action, when the arbitrator selected by the parties had made an award, to recover the amount determined, providing it was not voluntarily paid.[51]

The third class of enforceable pacts consists of what are known as pacta legitima, that is, pacts made binding by legislative authority,[52] either by direct enactment of the people in the comitia centuriata, by decrees of the senate, or imperial decrees. A right of action might be given or taken away by such a statutory pact.[53] However, there seem to have been only a few pacts in this third class, the most important being pactum donationis, or an informal promise of a gift, and pactum de dote, an informal agreement to provide a dowry.

Under the jus civile a mere promise to give something to another was not binding, the rule being the

48. Dig. 13, 5, 1, 4.
49. Dig. 20, 1, 4; 20, 1, 23, 1.
50. Actio hypothecaria.
51. Dig. 4, 8.
52. Dig. 2, 14, 6.
53. Ib.

same as in our English Law. The emperor Constantine, however, made such promises enforceable provided they were expressed in writing. Justinian made even oral promises of gifts pacta legitima,[54] providing they did not exceed five hundred solidi in value.[55]

The gifts here mentioned are gifts made to living persons (inter vivos) in distinction from gifts causa mortis. The gift became effectual when the donor declared his intention, it then being the duty of the donor to deliver the gift in accordance with his promise.[56] Gifts in excess of the maximum legally permitted were invalid only as to the excess,[57] but gifts of a value above five hundred solidi might be legally made if publicly registered.[58] Gifts for certain purposes, such as gifts on account of marriage (donatio propter nuptias),[59] and gifts to redeem captives, or to restore buildings destroyed by fire,[60] were valid without registration although in excess of that amount.

Ordinarily gifts to a living person were irrevocable, but Justinian provided that in case of base ingratitude on the part of the donee, as where he lays violent hands upon his benefactor or otherwise seriously wrongs him, or does not fulfil the conditions imposed in connection with the gift, the donor might revoke the benefit conferred.[61]

The solidus in imperial times was a gold coin previously called an aureus. It was worth about twenty-five denarii, but varied in value in different periods of Roman history. The denarius was a silver coin

54. Codex 8, 54, 35, 5.
55. Inst. 2, 7, 2.
56. Inst. 2, 7, 2.
57. Cod. 8, 54, 34, 1.
58. Inst. 2, 7, 2.
59. Nov. 119, 1.
60. Cod. 8, 54, 36, 3.
61. Inst. 2, 7, 2; Cod. 8, 54; Cod. 8, 56, 10; Dig. 39, 5.

about mid-way in size between our "dime" and "quarter."

The pactum de dote was an informal promise made by the father or other paternal ascendant of a bride, or at times by some other person, to furnish a dos, or dowry, as the wife's contribution upon marriage, to the marital expenses (onera matrimonii). The formal mode of providing for the dos was by stipulatio, but from the time of the emperor Theodosius II, a mere informal promise to provide a dos was binding.[62]

Obligations Quasi Contractu:

Thus far we have considered obligations arising from contract (ex contractu). There is another class of obligations which do not spring from contract, neither do they take their origin from delict (ex delicto), yet seem to rise, say the Institutes,[63] "as if from contract" (quasi ex contractu). "Quasi contracts" are not, however, contracts at all. They have naught to do with the mutual consent of parties or with any of the other grounds upon which contracts in Roman Law arise. They are analogous to contracts in that the law treats the parties as if they had made a contract, but the obligation arising quasi ex contractu arises from the circumstances of the case, ex variis causarum figuris says Gaius,[64] and is imposed, not as the result of the actual or presumed consent of the parties, but by the law itself as a matter of public policy. For example, such obligations may be imposed as duties, or obligations, arising from a status, a legal relation, such as that of husband and wife or parent and child. Just as one would be obligated by a contract, so likewise one may incur an obligation due to certain facts irrespective of his volition. In contract one is bound

62. Cod. Theod. 3, 13, 4; Cod. 3, 11, 6.
63. Inst. 3, 27, pr.
64. Dig. 44, 7, 1, pr.

because he consented to be bound; in quasi contract one is bound by operation of law, and not because he agreed either expressly or impliedly to be bound.

In our own law "quasi contracts" have often been confused with implied contracts, due to the fact that where the procedure of the Common Law prevails, the fiction of a promise, where none in fact exists, permits the favorite remedy of implied assumpsit.[65] This is illustrated in cases brought to recover money paid by mistake, or obtained by fraud, likewise in cases where necessaries have been furnished an insane person, or a neglected wife or child. "In all these cases no true contract exists. They are by many authors termed quasi contracts, a term borrowed from the Civil Law."[66] A quasi contract is no contract or promise at all. It is an obligation which the law creates in the absence of any agreement. "Duty, and not a promise or agreement or intention of the person sought to be charged, defines it."[67]

Quasi contract is, however, a comparatively modern term so far as its general use is concerned in our law. It is very rarely employed in our reports prior to sixty years ago. "It has been customary to regard all obligations as arising either ex contractu or ex delicto," says Professor Ames,[68] and thus it is readily seen why obligations created by law have been called contracts. They are, however, "more aptly defined as obligations quasi ex contractu than by our ambiguous 'implied contracts.'"[69]

65. Columbus, etc. Ry. v. Gaffney, 65 Ohio St. 104.

66. Ibid; and see Hertzog v. Hertzog, 29 Pa. 465; Miller v. Schloss, 218 N. Y. 400.

67. Miller v. Schloss, 218 N. Y. 400; Parsons v. Moses, 16 Iowa 440; Bright v. Boyd, 1 Story 478; Culbreath v. Culbreath, 7 Ga. 64; McSorley v. Faulkner, 18 N. Y. Supp. 460; Moses v. Macferlan, 2 Burr. (K. B.) 1005.

68. The History of Assumpsit, 2 Harv. L. R. 53.

69. Ibid.

Illustrations of obligations quasi ex contractu in the Roman Law, although these illustrations are not exhaustive, are given in the Institutes of Justinian [70] as follows:

(a) Negotiorum gestio, or voluntary agency.

(b) Certain obligations arising from the relation of guardian and ward.

(c) Communio, or obligations imposed upon those who have received a joint gift, inheritance, or legacy.

(d) Solutio indebiti, or payment by mistake of money that is not owed.

(e) The obligation imposed upon an heir to pay a legacy.

Negotiorum Gestio:

The literal meaning of negotiorum gestio is the management of affairs, and in a legal sense the term was ordinarily applied to the voluntary assumption on the part of one person to undertake the management of the affairs of another who was absent. It is distinguished from mandate in that mandate was a contract, an express authorization to act for another, while negotiorum gestio was never authorized and was undertaken even without the knowledge of the absent principal. One might be compelled to leave in haste, without having entrusted the management of his affairs to anyone, and, in order to prevent loss and injury thereby, one who voluntarily undertook to look out for such an absent person's interests, was permitted to recover by action, if needs be, any expenses he may have incurred in so doing.[71] The right to bring such an action arose by virtue of a praetorian edict, and it was at times a matter of great importance to absent persons to have some one, although unauthorized, to see to it that their property should

---

70. Inst. 3, 27. See also, Dig. 44, 7, 5.

71. Inst. 3, 27, 1; Dig. 3, 5, 2. And see Police Jury v. Hampton, 5 Mart. (N. S.) 389 (Louisiana).

not, as a result, for instance, of defaulted actions brought against them, be sold to pay their debts, or be impaired or lost unfortunately in other ways.[72] Consequently, those whose affairs were thus cared for were bound by an obligation, although they had no knowledge at the time of what was being done in their behalf, to repay the gestor (the voluntary agent) whatever money he might have spent in good faith in the interest of the absent person.[73] The business thus transacted for an absent principal must have been such, however, that was demanded by necessity or by its important character.[74] The management of one's "affairs" (negotia), says Ulpian,[75] means one affair or several. While in most cases it was the business of an absent person that was thus transacted, yet one might as a gestor attend to the affairs in which another was concerned at his death,[76] or to the affairs of a lunatic.[77]

In addition to illustrations previously given, one might have an action on negotia gesta for repairing a house that was in danger of falling, or for furnishing medical assistance to a sick slave,[78] or for furnishing food for household slaves.[79] Papinian says[80] that where a mother appropriated presents made to her daughter by a man betrothed to her, the daughter having no knowledge of the gifts, the daughter could not sue on mandatum or depositum but could sue on negotia gesta. And Scaevola further says[81] that a divorced husband who manages affairs on behalf of

72. Dig. 3, 5, 1.
73. Dig. 3, 5, 2.
74. Dig. 44, 7, 5, pr.
75. Dig. 3, 5, 3, 2.
76. Dig. 3, 5, 3, pr.; 3, 5, 12.
77. Dig. 3, 5, 3, 5.
78. Dig. 3, 5, 10, 1.
79. Dig. 3, 5, 22.
80. Dig. 3, 5, 22, 1.
81. Dig. 3, 5, 35, pr.

his former wife may be sued by her on a similar action. A special form of action in connection with negotia gesta was allowed in case of the burial of the dead when the person whose duty it was to bury the deceased was unable or failed to act.[82] As an exception to the usual rule governing such rights of action, it could be maintained although the one upon whom the legal duty to bury was imposed had forbidden the one who acted to do so.[83]

Again, when some great profit or advantage to an absent person suddenly presented itself, which demanded immediate action if the benefit were to be gained, he who voluntarily acted in the matter had his right of action for the expenses involved in the transaction.[84] In all these foregoing matters, and they are but illustrations of innumerable possible transactions, he who acted in good faith placed him for whose benefit he acted under an obligation arising not by contract but arising by operation of law, quasi ex contractu.

It was essential, however, to his right of action that the gestor should have acted for the benefit of another person and not for his own benefit.[85] Yet even in such a case the gestor is entitled to his expenses for whatever he did in enriching the other.[86] The gestor was bound to exercise the utmost diligentia,[87] and in addition to his liability for negligence he was sometimes liable even for accidents as where one undertakes to do something that the absent principal himself would not have undertaken.[88] Labeo said that if one purely out of good will volunteered to act for

82. Dig. 11, 7, 14, 3.
83. Dig. 11, 7, 14, 13–17.
84. Dig. 15, 3, 11.
85. Dig. 3, 5, 6, 2–4.
86. Dig. 3, 5, 6, 3.
87. Dig. 3, 5, 11; Inst. 3, 27, 1.
88. Dig. 3, 5, 11.

another to prevent the loss of his property, he would be liable only for deliberate fraud (dolus).[89] It was the duty of a gestor when once he had undertaken the management of the affair of another, to carry it through to its completion.[90] He was also required to account to the principal, and to deliver up to him all property coming into his hands by virtue of his undertaking.[91]

It will thus be noted that negotiorum gestio gave mutual rights of action. As the gestor makes the absent principal liable to him by an obligation, so the gestor is bound to render an account of his management.[92]

Obligations between Guardian and Ward:

Tutors and curators in their business relations with pupils and minors are not bound by contract, for there is no contract in such cases, but are bound quasi ex contractu.[93] There are reciprocal actions in such cases, just as in the case of negotiorum gestio.[94] Not only has the pupil an action known as actio tutelae against his guardian, but the guardian has also a contrary action against his ward in case the guardian has incurred expense in connection with the property of the ward, or has become personally liable for the ward, or has pledged his own property to the ward's creditors.[95]

Communio:

Likewise, says Justinian,[96] in cases where property is common to joint owners who have no contractual

89. Dig. 3, 5, 3, 9.
90. Dig. 3, 5, 21, 2; 13, 6, 17, 3.
91. Dig. 3, 5, 2. See Succession of Richmond, 35 La. Ann. 858.
92. Inst. 3, 27, 1.
93. Inst. 3, 27, 2.
94. Ib.
95. Ib.
96. Inst. 3, 27, 3.

relations of partnership (societas), as where they have received a joint legacy or a joint gift, if one of them has alone received the income of the property, or if his co-owner has incurred necessary expense in connection with the property, he is liable to the action communi dividundo. Such a one cannot be said to be bound by a contract, because the parties never made any contract, but he is bound quasi ex contractu.

The action communi dividundo was one of the three judicia divisoria, or partition, actions, the other two being the actio familiae erciscundae and the actio finium regundorum. The first of these three actions was brought for a division of property held in common; the second for the partition of a joint inheritance; and the third for the determination of a common boundary to adjoining lands.[97] In the action communi dividundo, not only a division of the common property might be obtained, but one joint owner might recover from another any excess profit that the latter had received. If the property was not susceptible of division, as a slave or a mule, the same was sold and the purchase price divided.[98]

Solutio Indebiti:

Solutio indebiti, or the payment of something that is not owed, as where one through mistake of fact pays money to another, or does any other service, which was believed to be owed, is another illustration of an obligation arising quasi ex contractu. He who receives such a payment of money, or other performance of a benefit, is bound just as he would be bound in a case of mutuum.[99] However, if one pays what he knows is not owed, he has no right of recovery, since in such a case the payment will be treated as a gift.[100]

97. Inst. 4, 6, 20.
98. Inst. 4, 17, 4 and 5; Dig. 17, 2, 6, 10; Dig. 10, 3.
99. Inst. 3, 27, 6; Dig. 12, 6, 1.
100. Dig. 12, 6, 1.

Solutio ("payment") is a broader term than the payment of money, and the obligation to restore imposed upon one who has been unjustly enriched by another's mistake applies to any property given or delivered to another by mistake, such as crops or accession.[101]

The money paid, or property delivered, must not be for a debt actually owed although paid before it was due, and no recovery can be obtained where the duty to pay or to perform was a moral, or natural obligation.[102] The mistake must generally be one of fact, but there are some instances where a mistake of law will authorize a recovery.[103] For example, those who from their peculiar circumstances were not supposed to know the law, such as minors,[104] women,[105] or peasants,[106] or those who were unable to obtain advice as to the law, such as soldiers in active service,[107] were made exceptions to the rule that ignorance of law constitutes no excuse.

The action for the recovery was known as the action condictio indebiti.[108]

Acquisitio Hereditatis:

Upon the acceptance of an inheritance by the heir named in a will, an obligation was imposed upon him to pay all legacies given by the testator. The heir, says Justinian,[109] is not obligated by a contract, since the legatee cannot be said to have made any contract either with the heir or with the testator, consequently he is said to be obligated quasi ex contractu.

101. Dig. 12, 6, 15, pr.
102. Dig. 12, 6, 10; 12, 6, 13; 12, 6, 26, 9; 12, 6, 38, pr.; 12, 6, 40, pr. Cf. Perrillat v. Puech, 2 La. 428.
103. Dig. 12, 6, 1, 1; Cod. 4, 5, 6.
104. Dig. 22, 6, 10.
105. Dig. 22, 6, 9, pr.
106. Dig. 22, 3, 25, 1.
107. Dig. 22, 6, 9, 1.
108. Dig. 12, 6.
109. Inst. 3, 27, 5.

Receptum Nautarum, Cauponum, Stabulariorum:

There were various other transactions in Roman Law which are classed by some writers as arising out of contract and by others as arising from quasi contract. The Rhodian Law of jettison already mentioned is placed by some under quasi contract. Likewise the transaction known as datio ob causam quae non sequitur (transfer of property for a purpose which becomes impossible) is said by some to be an illustration of another form of quasi contract, in that the law places a duty upon the one who received the property to restore it. Others, however, regard this transaction merely as a form of solutio indebiti.

Another obligation, known as receptum nautarum, cauponum, stabulariorum, or the duty of shipowners, innkeepers, and stablekeepers to keep in safe custody the property of travellers received by them in connection with their business, is mentioned by some modern writers (not, however, by the Roman classic writers) as another illustration of quasi contract, although others regard it as an implied contract. By the Roman Law, the duties of such persons arise either by contract, such as depositum or locatio-conductio, or by quasi delict.

The praetorian remedy known as the actio de recepto could be employed by a traveller when he had left his property in charge of such persons and loss or damage had resulted. The defendant could plead, however, the negligence (culpa) of the traveller, or that the loss had occurred by unavoidable accident (vis major).[110] There were also delictual remedies given to travellers in connection with the damage or theft of property, by the servants of such person.[111]

---

110. Dig. 4, 9, 3, 1. And see Thickstun v. Howard, 8 Blackf. (Ind.) 534, 536; Colt v. McMechen, 6 Johns. (N. Y.) 160.

111. Inst. 4, 5, 3.

THE LAW OF OBLIGATIONS 483

These remedies will be considered, however, in a subsequent chapter.[112]

The Roman Law of obligations has been largely retained in modern Civil Law countries. In fact, almost the entire general outline of Roman obligations is literally preserved in many jurisdictions, the Roman terms being translated into the local language. Thus, obligations are said to arise from (1) contract; (2) quasi contract;[113] (3) delict; and (4) quasi delict. Contracts are classed as verbal, real, and consensual. Under real contracts we find the Roman divisions of mutuum;[114] commodatum; depositum;[115] and pignus.[116] Contracts dealing with pignus are frequently called pignorative contracts and include pignus or pledge, hypotheca, and antichresis, with substantially the same distinctions as in Roman Law, pignus being limited to movable property, hypotheca to immovable. Some countries also include within such contracts a sale and return.[117] Consensual contracts, as in Roman Law, comprise sale; letting and hiring (locatio-conductio); partnership (societas); and mandate (mandatum). Permutatio, or exchange, classed by the lat-

112. See Delicts and Quasi Delicts, post.

113. France, C. C. art. 1370; La., Rev. C. C. art. 2292; Quebec, C. C. art. 983; Spain, C. C. art. 1089.

114. France, C. C. art. 1897; Italy, C. C. art. 1822; Louisiana, Rev. C. C. art. 2913, 2915; Quebec, C. C. art. 1780; Spain, C. C, 1754.

115. France, C. C. art. 1915; Germany, C. C. art. 688; Italy, C. C. art. 1835; Japan, C. C. art. 657; Louisiana, Rev. C. C. 2926, 2963; Spain, C. C. art. 1758.

116. France, C. C. Bk. III, tit. 17 and 18; Italy, C. C. Bk. III, tit. 19, 20, and 23; Japan, C. C. Bk. II, c. 9 and 10; Louisiana, Rev. C. C. Bk. III, tit. 20 and 21; Germany, C. C. Bk. III, Div. 8 and 9; Quebec, C. C. Bk. III, tit. 16 and 17; Spain, C. C. Bk. IV, tit. 15.

117. The vente à rémère of the French law, C. C. art. 1659–1673. See, also, Germany, C. C. art. 497–503; Louisiana Rev. C. C. art. 2567–2588; Spain, C. C. art. 1507–1520.

er civilians as an "innominate" contract, is also generally included within the consensual contracts.[118]

Quasi contracts in the modern Civil Law preserve the distinction made by the Roman Law between them and contracts, in that they are not contracts at all, but are obligations which arise without any contract between the parties, being purely voluntary acts of an individual.[119] The principal kinds of such obligations are the voluntary transaction of another's business, the negotiorum gestio of the Roman Law,[120] and the payment of a thing not due or payment by mistake, the solutio indebiti of the ancient law.[121] The quasi contractual obligation concerning the proper use of property belonging to co-owners, including the duty to contribute for expenses incurred by one owner, and the right of compensation in connection with an unequal division of the property, all of which are considered under the term communio in the Roman Law, is also found in some of the modern codes.[122]

118. France, C. C. art. 1702, 1703; Louisiana, Rev. C. C. art. 2660, 2661; Quebec, C. C. art. 1596; Spain, C. C. art. 1538.
119. France, C. C. art. 1370, 1371; Louisiana, C. C. art. 2292, 2293; Quebec, C. C. art. 983, 1041; Spain, C. C. art. 1089.
120. France, C. C. art. 1160; Louisiana, C. C. art. 2295; Quebec, C. C. art. 1045; Spain, C. C. art. 1889.
121. France, C. C. art. 1377; Louisiana, C. C. art. 2302; Quebec, C. C. art. 1048; Spain, C. C. art. 1895. See Harper v. Terry, 16 La. Ann. 216.
122. Called "comunidad" in Spanish. See Civil Code of Chile, art. 2304; Peru, art. 2138; and see Germany, art. 741 et seq.

CHAPTER XVIII

THE LAW OF OBLIGATIONS, *continued*

Delicts and Quasi Delicts

In addition to obligations created ex contractu and quasi ex contractu, certain wrongs against persons or property likewise give rise to obligations. Such wrongs are called delicts in the Roman Law and are analogous in many respects to our torts. Whenever one commits a delict he is "bound" (obligated) to pay a penalty to the person he has wronged, and also to compensate him for any damage done. According to the Institutes of Justinian,[1] all obligations connected with delicts arise from the fact of some wrongful act (ex ipso maleficio), such as furtum (theft), rapina (robbery), damnum (damage), or injuria (injury).

The Romans distinguished [2] between public wrongs, or crimes (publica crimina) and private or civil wrongs, the latter being called privata delicta, or simply delicta.

Public wrongs, or crimes, were wrongs against the state or community as a whole, and were prosecuted before some public tribunal. Private wrongs were wrongs against private individuals, and gave rise to suits for penalties or damages. The idea of public wrongs or crimes was slow in developing, however, and the long prevailing theory as to the proper method of dealing with wrongs was that the individual who had suffered a wrong should pursue his own remedy by a civil action. The growing needs of so-

1. Inst. 4, 1, pr.; Gaius 3, 182.
2. Dig. 21, 1, 17, 18.

ciety demanded, however, more adequate and satisfactory remedies for the suppression of great wrongs and consequently, from time to time, laws were passed providing courts and procedure for the trial and punishment of many offenses. Ulpian says that in his time one had his election either to sue in a civil action upon a delict, or to prosecute the offender criminally. He also adds that furtum was, as a matter of fact, usually prosecuted as a crime,[3] due, doubtless, to the fact that most thieves were without financial resources, and that a suit for damages would, therefore, be fruitless.

The nature of the wrong in case of a delict was said to be a violation of a "real" right, that is, an individual's right to a "res," a property right. This might be one's right to property in the physical sense, or one's right to any incorporeal property right, such as personal liberty, personal security, or a right to a good reputation. In this respect, a delict is distinguished from a breach of contract. The latter is a violation not of a real right, a right existing over some "res," and, therefore, enforceable against everyone, but a violation of a personal right, a right created by the parties. The right that is violated by a delict is a right arising not from convention but from the law itself.

A delict is not necessarily, however, a wilful or an intentional act, since it may be the result of negligence. The original notion of the obligation arising from delict seems to have been the duty of paying a penalty for the harm caused by the wrong or fault of one person to the person or property rights of another. In addition to the penalty thus recoverable by proper action, the injured party could also recover compensation for the damage suffered by him. Delicts, moreover, did not include all private wrongs indiscrimi-

---

[3]. Dig. 47, 1, 3; 47, 2, 56, 1; 47, 2, 92.

nately, but only such wrongs as the jus civile, in distinction from the praetorian law, specified and, by legislation, made remediable by some particular action. In the ancient law there seems to have been only two delicts, theft (furtum) and injury (injuria), both being intentional wrongs. Later, theft (furtum) was distinguished from robbery (rapina), and an action was also allowed for wrongs to property occasioned by negligence. Consequently, in the Institutes of both Gaius and Justinian, delicts are divided into the four forms known as furtum, rapina, damnum, and injuria. An evil intent (dolus malus) was an essential element in all of these except in the case of damnum.

Furtum:

Furtum, or theft, is defined in the Institutes as the unlawful appropriation of property either in its entirety, or merely for the purpose of making use of it, or of getting possession of it.[4] Paulus, in the Digest,[5] adds the words lucri faciendi gratia (for the sake of gain). This latter phrase is the origin of the lucri causa doctrine held by some in connection with the English Law of larceny. However, such a doctrine is not generally held, and in the Roman Law the words lucri faciendi gratia were not limited in meaning to pecuniary profit, but included any kind of advantage, gain, or satisfaction, even the mere malicious pleasure of the owner's loss. Blackstone's statement[6] that the Civil Law words lucri causa are equivalent to animus furandi, the intent to steal, is not accurate. It is the "unlawful" or fraudulent (fraudulosa) appropriation or handling (contrectatio) of another's property that constitutes furtum. Evil intent (dolus malus) is necessary,[7] but not an intent to deprive the

4. Inst. 4, 1, 1.
5. Dig. 47, 2, 1, 3.
6. Com. IV. 232.
7. Paulus, Sent. 2, 31, 1; Inst. 4, 1, 7.

owner permanently of the property. The animus furandi[8] of the Roman Law is an intent to commit furtum, and not confined to what we call larceny or stealing.

Furtum is a broader term than our modern "larceny" since furtum includes embezzlement. The element of trespass, essential in modern days in larceny, is not a requisite in furtum. Any kind of physical appropriation of goods belonging to another, without the consent of the owner whether at the time of getting possession or subsequently, is covered by furtum,[9] as, for example, to use a thing that is left in one's keeping, as a mere deposit, or to borrow a thing for one purpose and then to use it for another, or to hire a horse for a short ride and then take it far away.[10] However, a borrower who used a thing for a different purpose than that intended by the owner was guilty of furtum only in case he had reason to know that the owner would not permit it, since, as already stated, it was the evil intent that constituted the offense.[11]

According to some of the ancient jurists, furtum was of four sorts, or kinds, namely manifestum, nec manifestum, conceptum, and oblatum.[12] Labeo, however, recognized only two kinds, manifestum and nec manifestum.[13] Such is also the doctrine of Justinian's Institutes, the terms conceptum and oblatum merely stating circumstances which affected the form of the action.[14] Manifest or open theft (furtum) is not necessarily visible theft, but a theft that is obvious or self-evident, as where one is detected in the act, or where the theft is discovered while the thief is still

8. Inst. 4, 1, 7.
9. Gaius 3, 195.
10. Gaius 3, 195; Inst. 4, 1, 6; Dig. 47, 2, 54.
11. Inst. 4, 1, 7.
12. Gaius 3, 183.
13. Ib.
14. Inst, 4. 1, 3.

upon the premises, or before he has carried the stolen property to its intended destination.[15]

Any furtum, or theft, that is not manifest, is called nec manifestum.[16]

Furtum conceptum was the discovery of stolen goods in another's house after a search therein by the owner of the goods. In case stolen property was thus sought and found, the owner of the house, although not the actual thief, was liable as a receiver of stolen goods.[17]

This ancient right of the owner of stolen goods to prosecute a search within the house of a suspected person was, doubtless, connected with the owner's right to question any person suspected of having possession of the property.[18] Probably only in cases where the replies were unsatisfactory was the right to search the house enforced. It was a search by the owner of the goods, a private person, and not a search by a public officer, under the authority of a search warrant. If the occupier of the house prevented the owner of the stolen property from making his search he became liable to an action (actio furti prohibiti) given by the praetor involving a penalty of fourfold the value of the thing stolen.[19] The Twelve Tables provided that the searcher must be naked, except a loin cloth (licium), and must carry a dish (lanx) in his hands.[20] Gaius says that such a law was ridiculous (ridicula),[21] and that it is not clear what the loin cloth and dish meant. The usual explanation given was that a searcher clad only in a loin cloth and carrying a dish in his hands could not, in consequence, take

15. Gaius, 3, 184; Inst. 4, 1, 3.
16. Inst. 4, 1, 3.
17. Inst. 4, 1, 4.
18. Paulus, Sent. 2, 31, 22; Plaut. Poen. i. 1, 51f.
19. Gaius 3, 192.
20. Gaius 3, 192.
21. Gaius 3, 193.

anything into the house and later pretend that it had been found therein. Gaius, however, pertinently says that such an explanation would be absurd if the stolen article was of such a size that it could not be carried by hand into the house. This mode of search was obsolete long before Justinian's time and search was made simply in the presence of witnesses. Anciently, if the stolen property was found within the house, the owner, providing he was also the thief, was liable to the fourfold penalty of furtum manifestum, and even if he was not the thief the penalty for having stolen goods in his possession was three times the value of the property.[22] In the time of Justinian the old actions of furti concepti and furti prohibiti were no longer in use, and those who knowingly had received and concealed stolen property were liable to the twofold penalty of furtum nec manifestum.[23]

The right given by the Roman Law to a private person to search upon his own initiative the house of another for stolen goods is in marked contrast to the English Law in that particular. In our law, the right of a householder to occupy his home free from arbitrary search has for centuries been protected by the courts, from Magna Charta to the present time, and is guaranteed in every bill of rights.[23½] Even a search warrant in the hands of a public officer "is a sharp and heavy police weapon, to be used most carefully. It was unknown to the early Common Law, and came into use almost unnoticed in the troublous times of the English Revolution."[24] Lord Coke denied the lawfulness of granting warrants to search for stolen goods,[25] but finally the courts and parliament, recog-

22. Gaius, 3, 191, 192.
23. Inst. 4, 1, 4.
23½. McClurg v. Brenton, 123 Iowa 368, 98 N. W. 881.
24. State v. Guthrie, 90 Me. 448, 38 Atl. 368.
25. Coke's Inst. 4, 176; Entick v. Carrington, 2 Wils. C. P. 275, 95 Eng. Reprint 807.

nizing its great efficiency, contented themselves with carefully restricting and controlling its use. In the constitutions of the United States and of all the individual states it is provided that the people shall be secure in their persons and property from all unreasonable searches and seizures.

The fourth form of furtum mentioned by the ancient jurists was furtum oblatum. This consisted in giving stolen property to an innocent person, or in placing it in his house, in order that he might be thought to be the thief. The person who was thus imposed upon had an action known as actio furti oblati, carrying a threefold penalty against the wrongdoer whether he was the actual thief or not.[26] However, as in the case of the action furti concepti, the action furti oblati was obsolete when the Institutes of Justinian were published, and the person guilty of furtum oblatum was punishable for furtum nec manifestum.[27]

The subject matter of furtum was movable property only, although in ancient times some Roman jurists thought there could be a theft of land.[28] The thing stolen must belong to someone, and accordingly res nullius, such as animals ferae naturae, could not be the subject of furtum.[29] One's slave could, however, be stolen, and even a free person, if in the power of another, as a child in patria potestate, or a wife in manu.[30] Likewise one may commit furtum of his own property from a pledgee.[31]

By the law of the Twelve Tables, the penalty for furtum manifestum was flogging and bondage to the owner of the property if the thief was a freeman,

26. Gaius, 3, 187.
27. Inst. 4, 1, 4.
28. Dig. 41, 3, 38; 47, 2, 25.
29. Dig. 47, 2, 26.
30. Gaius 3, 199; Inst. 4, 1, 9.
31. Gaius 3, 200; Inst. 4, 1, 10.

or, in case of a slave, a flogging.[32] According to Gellius, a slave guilty of theft was scourged and then killed by being thrown from the Tarpeian rock. It is probable, however, that in most cases the masters of slaves ransomed them by paying for the damage caused by them.

In later times, manifest theft whether committed by a slave or a freeman was punished by a praetorian edict with fourfold damages, while not-manifest theft was subject to the penalty of twofold damages.[33] The fourfold and double damages were purely penal; the owner of the property could further recover either the stolen goods by a real action (vindicatio), or damages for their loss by a personal action (condictio furtiva). The former action lay against the possessor of the goods whether the thief himself or some other person. Condictio lay against either the thief or his heir.[34] An accomplice was equally guilty and liable with the principal,[35] and an action of theft could be brought by anyone who had an interest in the property at the time it was stolen, as in case of theft from a pledgee, or from one, like, for example, a tailor, to whom the property had been entrusted for repairs.[36]

In the protection of one's property, it was lawful, under the Twelve Tables, to kill a nocturnal thief, and even in the daytime if the thief defended himself with a weapon.[37]

The actio furti did not lie in case a husband or wife stole from the other, but the action rerum amotarum could be brought for the restoration of the stolen prop-

32. Gaius 3, 189.
33. Gaius 3, 189–190; Inst. 4, 1, 5.
34. Inst. 4, 1, 19.
35. Gaius 3, 202; Inst. 4, 1, 11; Dig. 47, 2, 36; 47, 2, 54.
36. Inst. 4, 1, 13–16.
37. Gell. 11, 18, 6, 7. But see Dig. 9, 2, 4, 1; 48, 8, 9. And see note 50, infra.

erty if the theft took place in expectation of divorce which actually followed.[38]

Rapina:

Rapina, or vi bona rapta, is robbery, or the malicious taking of the property of another by force. It is a form of furtum for which the praetor gave a special action known as actio vi bonorum raptorum.[39] Cicero says [40] the action was created in the days of the civil wars of Rome when thefts by bands of robbers became common. In later times, however, the action was applied to any person, irrespective of an armed band, who was guilty of theft by any violent means. The action could be brought within a year after the robbery, and a fourfold penalty recovered.[41] No additional action lay, as in case of furtum manifestum, for the value of the thing stolen, since the value was included in the penalty.[42] Moreover, if the action were not brought till a year or more had elapsed, only the simple value of the stolen property could be recovered.[43] There may be a rapina, however, of a thing of the most trifling value.[44]

The taking must be malicious, that is, with evil intent (dolo malo); therefore, in case one takes with force property not his own but which he honestly believes to be his own, he is not liable for rapina.[45] Nevertheless he would be liable for taking the law into his own hands and forcibly seizing property under a claim of ownership since various imperial constitutions provided that no property, movable or immovable, should be forcibly taken or detained under

38. Dig. 25, 2, 3, 2; 25, 2, 6, 3; 25, 2, 17.
39. Gaius 3, 209; Inst. 4, 2, pr.
40. Cicero pro Tull. c. 8.
41. Inst. 4, 2, pr.
42. Inst. 4, 2, pr.
43. Inst. 4, 2, pr.
44. Inst. 4, 2, pr.
45. Inst. 2, 4, 2.

claim of ownership but that the alleged owner should seek his remedy by legal action. In case of violation of this law, the offender was required to return the property, even if his own in fact, and to renounce all ownership of it. In case he were not the owner and acted in good faith under mistake, he was required to return the property and also to pay its value.[46]

The foregoing imperial laws against unlawful or violent self-redress were laws in the furtherance of public peace and good order, and had nothing to do with lawful self-defense or the retaking on the spot of goods seized by a thief. Human nature permits a man to defend himself.[47] Therefore, if one kills another's slave who lying in wait attempts to rob him he is justified.[48] One may lawfully repel force with force,[49] but one is liable who kills a thief when it was in his power to take him into custody; only such force as the circumstances justify is lawful.[50]

The fourfold value recoverable for rapina included, as already said, the value of the property. Consequently, the owner of the forcibly stolen goods could not recover as much as in case of furtum manifestum which involved a fourfold penalty in addition to the value. While the penalty under the actio vi bonorum raptorum was greater than the twofold penalty of secret theft (furtum nec manifestum), yet a robber, says the Digest,[51] is necessarily a manifest thief since his violence implies the resistance of the possessor of the goods. However, the action for rapina was only an elective remedy, and the owner of the goods could bring instead, if he so wished, an actio furti. The circumstances probably guided the form of action. A

46. Inst. 2, 4, 1.
47. Naturalis ratio permittit se defendere, Dig. 9, 2, 4, pr.; 43, 16, 17.
48. Ib.
49. Dig. 43, 16, 3, 9.
50. Dig. 9, 2, 5, pr.
51. Dig. 47, 2, 80, 3.

depositary, having the mere custody of property, although not its possession, could bring the actio vi bonorum raptorum,[52] which was not the law in case of actio furti. Also a robber might be punished in a criminal prosecution, a Lex Julia providing for banishment in case of violence with a weapon, and for confiscation of a third of the criminal's property in case of unarmed violence.[53]

Damnum Injuria Datum:

Damage unlawfully caused was also another important delict in the Roman Law. It consisted in damaging either wilfully (dolo malo) or negligently (culpa) the corporeal property of another,[54] the element "injuria," or the violation of another's right, including either an intentional act or one due to carelessness. Damage caused by mere accident (casu), or in lawful defense of property, was not actionable.[55]

The Twelve Tables gave remedies for particular kinds of damage to another's property, but those actions became obsolete in time owing to the enactment of a law known as the Lex Aquilia. This law was a partial repeal of all previous laws relating to damnum injuria (unlawful damage). It was a plebiscite, the tribune Aquilius being its author,[56] and it was passed, according to Theophilus,[57] at the time of one of the secessions of the plebs, probably the third secession in 467 A. U. C., or 286 B. C.

The first part of the Lex Aquilia provided that the unlawful killing of a slave or of a four-footed animal of the class of pecudes (such as sheep, goats, kine, horses, mules, asses, and swine) belonging to another,

52. Inst. 4, 2, 2.
53. Inst. 4, 18, 8.
54. Gaius 3, 211.
55. Gaius 3, 211; Inst. 4, 3, 2 and 3.
56. Dig. 9, 2, pr. and 1; Inst. 4, 3, 15.
57. Theophilus, Para. Inst. Just. 4, 3, 15.

made the wrongdoer liable to the owner in an amount equal to the highest value of such property at any time in the year past.[58] The statute put, says Gaius, a man's cattle on a level with his slaves.[59] The term "pecudes" did not, however, include dogs, or wild beasts such as bears, lions, and panthers, but elephants and camels, being beasts of burden, were included.[60] The second chapter of the Lex Aquilia, relating to stipulators and adstipulators,[61] a matter having no connection with delicts, was obsolete even in the days of Ulpian.[62] The third chapter provided that wrongful damage to all other things, besides slaves or cattle, by "burning, tearing, or breaking"[63] them, would render the offender liable in damages for whatever was the value of the property within the previous thirty days.[64] A very broad construction was given by the jurists to the word "breaking" (ruptum), and the Institutes say that it included the ruining (corruptum) of any thing, such as cutting, bruising, spoiling, or in any way destroying a thing. For example, one who put anything into the oil or wine of another so that its goodness was destroyed, was held liable under this section of the law.[65] It was necessary, however, that there should be some corporal damage to a thing, something "datum corpori," since merely depriving the owner of a thing did not warrant a remedy under this law. Moreover, the cause of the damage must be direct or immediate, that is, caused by one's own body, corpore suo, since indirect causes of harm were not in-

58. Dig. 9, 2, 2, pr.; Inst. 4, 3.
59. Dig. 9, 2, 2, 2.
60. Dig. 9, 2, 2, 2.
61. Gaius 3, 215.
62. Dig. 9, 2, 27, 4.
63. "Ustum aut ruptum aut fractum," Inst. 4, 3, 12.
64. Dig. 9, 2, 27, 5; Inst. 4, 3, 5.
65. Inst. 4, 3, 13.

cluded.[66] For example, the killing of a slave by a direct blow, by actually striking him, was actionable, but leaving a cup of poison in his way with the intent that he should by his own act drink of it, was not within the statute. Further, the right of action under the Lex Aquilia belonged only to the owner of the property,[67] and not to one having merely a special interest in it, such as a pledgee or a usarius. For example, if A loaned clothing to B, and C, either wilfully or carelessly, tore the clothing while in the possession of B, the action could not be brought by B but only by A.[68]

These early refinements in connection with the Lex Aquilia were rendered meaningless, in time, by various praetors who extended, in the interest of practical relief, the remedies afforded by it. This was done by allowing actions known as in factum and utiles. Often the precise action given by the jus civile did not cover a case clearly within its spirit but not strictly within its letter. The most important legal reforms inaugurated by praetorian law consisted in allowing, at such times, an action known either as an actio in factum (an action upon the case), or as an actio utilis (a serviceable action), or, as we might say, an equitable remedy. Thus, under the letter of the Lex Aquilia, where A even wilfully pushed B, in consequence of which B was thrown against C, a slave, causing C to fall to his death, B was not liable, because he was not guilty of any wrong, and A was not liable because he did not kill the slave with his own person (corpore suo). The praetor, however, allowed an action in factum against A.[69] Likewise, a person having the mere use of a thing had no action for unlawful damage done to it, but the praetor allowed him an actio utilis, the

66. Inst. 4, 3, 16.
67. Dig. 9, 2, 11, 6.
68. Dig. 9, 2, 11, 9.
69. Dig. 9, 2, 7, 3.

damages being assessed in proportion to the value of his usufruct.[70] The Roman jurists, like lawyers of all ages, became very technical, however, in their views concerning the correct application of a regular action under the law (an actio directa) and an actio in factum or utilis. Thus, Julianus held that if A set his dog on B and the dog bit B while A had his hand upon the dog, an actio directa, under the statute, would lie. However, if A was not holding the dog, the action must be in factum. Proculus, however, was of the opinion that even if the owner did not hold the dog a direct action under the statute (Lex Aquilia) would lie.[71] However, in any case, if no harm is done by one's body (corpore suo) to another's body (corpori), or as expressed by the Roman lawyers corpore corpori, yet if harm is done in some other way, as where, for example, A having pity for a fettered slave looses his bonds to help him to excape, then neither an actio directa nor an actio utilis is applicable, since an actio in factum is the only remedy.[72]

Dolus Malus and Culpa:

As already said, the harm or damage done to another's property that will support an actio legis Aquiliae must have been either a deliberate or wilful act (dolus malus) or a negligent one (culpa). Labeo defined "dolus malus" as any pretence, deceit, or means employed for the purpose of circumventing, deceiving, or ensnaring another.[73] It includes an intentional act of wrongdoing, and except in the delict known as damnum injuria datum, dolus was an essential element in every delict.

Culpa, which in addition to dolus malus may give rise to an action based upon damnum injuria datum, is

70. Dig. 9, 2, 12.
71. Dig. 9, 2, 11, 5.
72. Inst. 4, 3, 15.
73. Dig. 4, 3, 1, 2.

an unintentional violation of the rights of another coupled with some omission or neglect of legal duty. It is the fact of negligence not its degree that justifies the action since the slightest amount of negligence (levissima culpa) is sufficient.[74] In connection with certain quasi delicts the defense of contributory negligence is taken into account but was not, originally, in case of damnum injuria datum. The doctrine applied, however, to actions brought under the Aquilian Law, and Paulus says that in a great many cases relief was refused if it was in the power of one who had run into danger caused by another's negligence to avoid the danger.[75]

Criminal Liability for Causing Death:

In addition to the private remedy given to the owner of a slave unlawfully killed, the owner could also bring a capital charge against the guilty person.[76] The unlawful killing of any one, even a slave, was punishable under the Lex Cornelia de Sicariis, passed about 80 B. C., during the dictatorship of Sulla. The penalty under this law was banishment and forfeiture of property. However, under the Empire, this punishment was limited to the upper classes, the common people being subject to the death penalty.[77]

Pauperies:

Where damage was done by a four-footed, domesticated animal, contrary to the ordinary nature of the animal, without any accompanying legal wrong on the part of the owner, such damage was known as pauperies, and the action de pauperie lay for the value of the harm done.[78] Under the Law of the Twelve Tables the animal had to be a quadrupes pecus, that is, a

74. Dig. 9, 2, 44, pr.
75. Dig. 9, 2, 28, 1.
76. Inst. 4, 3, 11.
77. Dig. 48, 8, 3, 5; 48, 8, 16.
78. Dig. 9, 1.

four-footed animal usually classed among cattle, sheep, or goats. Later the law was extended to dogs, and, still later, practically all domestic animals were included. The law distinguished between a domesticated and a wild animal. It was only for damage caused by the former that the action de pauperie was given, although the law gave an action for damage caused by wild animals if they were in the possession of one who was guilty of negligence in properly confining them. However, if a wild animal, such as a bear, escaped from its master and did damage, the master was not liable since upon the escape of the animal it became res nullius,[79] but under a later law certain animals, such as a dog, a boar, a bear, or a lion were forbidden to be kept along a public road, and in case damage was done in disobedience of this law, the owner was liable for the same.[80]

Pauperies was damage occasioned by the animal itself without any accompanying legal wrong on the part of the owner.[81] For example, if an animal carrying a load upset the load on a passer-by because too large a load had been put upon it, or because the driver of the animal was negligent, or because the road was rough, the action de pauperie did not lie, but an action for damnum injuria datum.[82] Likewise, if a dog did damage because someone urged it on, the action de pauperie did not lie.[83] The action did not lie, moreover, unless the animal did damage "contrary to its ordinary nature." For example, if a horse struck by someone kicked because excited by the pain of the blow, any other person injured by the horse had no action against its owner, although he would have had action

79. Inst. 4, 9, pr.
80. Inst. 4, 9, 1.
81. Dig. 9, 1, 1, 3.
82. Dig. 9, 1, 1, 4.
83. Dig. 9, 1, 1, 6.

against the person who struck the horse. However, if a horse upon being merely stroked or patted kicked one, there was ground for the action.[84]

Upon being sued de pauperie, the owner of the animal had the election either to surrender the animal or to pay the damages.[85]

Injuria:

The fourth general delict was known as injuria, meaning, literally, any unlawful act, an act contra jus,[86] something done non jure.[87] In a special or a separate delictual sense, injuria means insult (contumelia), a wrong to one's personal rights as distinguished from a wrong to one's property (damnum). It includes not only bodily wrongs, such as assault, battery, false imprisonment, and kidnapping, but also wrongs against one's reputation, honor, dignity, and peace. Injuria may be caused, said Labeo, either by a physical act or by mere words.[88] It embraces libel, slander, public shame, abuse, or insult, and the unlawful entry of one's house. There may be injuria not only by direct insult to one's self but also by insult offered to members of one's family, or even by defaming one's dead relatives.[89] Injuria may be committed, say the Institutes,[90] by striking or beating another with the fist or with a club, or lash, by loud abusive words (convicium), by maliciously attaching one's goods, by publishing defamatory writings or songs, by persistently following a respectable married woman, or a young boy or girl, by attempting to corrupt one's chastity,[91] and also by many other acts. In-

84. Dig. 9, 1, 1, 7.
85. Dig. 9, 1, 1, pr. and 14.
86. Dig. 9, 2, 5, 1.
87. Dig. 47, 10, 1, pr.
88. Dig. 47, 10, 1, 1.
89. Dig. 47, 10, 1, 4; 47, 10, 27.
90. Inst. 4, 4, 1.
91. Gaius 3, 220; Dig. 47, 10, 15, 22; 47, 10, 10.

juria might also arise when one's right of privacy was unlawfully invaded. As said by the supreme court of Georgia:[92] "The punishment of one who had not committed any assault upon another, or impeded in any way his right of locomotion, but who merely attracted public attention to the other as he was passing along a public highway or standing upon his private ground, evidences the fact that the (Roman) law recognized that a person had a right 'to be let alone,' so long as he was not interfering with the rights of other individuals or of the public." Further evidence of one's right of privacy was the fact that it was a case of injuria to enter one's home against the owner's will, even though the intruder was seeking to serve a summons.[93] The elements of injuria may be, therefore, summarized as follows: (1) Any unjustifiable act; (2) violating the person, reputation, or dignity of another; (3) with malicious intent.[94]

The intent may be inferred from the circumstances and from the very nature of the act, but an infringement of another's right by mere negligence is not sufficient to constitute the delict of injuria. Julianus cites a case[95] where a shoemaker, who was instructing a free-born boy who was doing his work badly, struck the boy on the neck with a last in order to chastise him. As a result, however, the boy's eye was put out. Julianus said there was no injuria here since the man did not strike with the intent of committing an injuria, but only to correct the boy. An action in such a case would lie, however, against the shoemaker on the Lex Aquilia,[96] since the latter action lies in case of damnum caused by negligence, and an unreasonable chastise-

92. Pavesich v. New England Life Ins. Co., 122 Ga. 190, 50 S. E. 68.
93. Dig. 47, 10, 23; 47, 10, 15, 5.
94. Animo injuriandi. Gaius 3, 220; Dig. 47, 10, 3, 3.
95. Dig. 9, 2, 5, 3.
96. Dig. 9, 2, 5, 3.

ment on the part of a teacher is considered as negligence.[97]

Injuria included public vituperation, slander, and libel. The name convicium was applied to public insult which might consist of slanderous words, or of any other abusive public act such as gathering a crowd about one or around his shop or his house for the purpose of disturbing or annoying him.[98] The insult, or injuria, was said to be "direct" when an individual was personally maligned, and "indirect" when some one in his family or under his protection was the object of the vituperation, such as his child, slave, or wife.[99] In such cases of indirect injuria, the action could be brought by the paterfamilias or husband. Not all the acts that would constitute injuria in case of a wife or child would amount to injuria in case of a slave. In the case of a slave, something would have to be done that would humiliate the master. For example, abusive words addressed to a slave, or even a blow with the fist did not constitute injuria, but an aggravated assault, such as a flogging administered to another's slave, did give the master the right to sue for damages.[100]

Injuria was said to be aggravated or atrocious (atrox) when either from its character, or by reason of the place in which it was committed, or on account of the rank or station of the person injured, its wrongful or outrageous nature was conspicuous. For example, the malicious breaking of a bone, an insult in a public place such as the theatre or forum, or an outrage done to a magistrate by some ordinary person, or an injury done to a parent by a child, were instances

97. Dig. 9, 2, 6.
98. Dig. 47, 10, 15; 2–12.
99. Inst. 4, 4, 2.
100. Inst. 4, 4, 3.

of atrocious injury.[101] In such cases the punishment or the damages were greater. By the Law of the Twelve Tables, the penalty for wilful and grievous bodily injury was retaliation, an eye for an eye; other injuries were punishable either with flogging or with fines graduated according to the offense. In later days, an action for damages took the place of these penalties, the wronged person alleging his own estimate of the damage, and the judex, as in case of the modern jury, determining the amount of the judgment.[102] A person who was the victim of injuria had, however, his option to sue for damages or to have the wrongdoer prosecuted criminally.[103] Liability for injuria applied not only to the person who actually committed the delict but also to an accessory before the fact.[104]

Injuria was an illegal or an unjustifiable act, consequently reasonable chastisement on the part of teachers and others in authority was not included in this offense,[105] and self-defense was always recognized as a good plea to the charge.[106] Moreover, in the Roman Law, defamatory words had to be false in order to constitute libel, therefore the truth of an alleged libel could always be shown.[107] Our familiar maxim, "injuria non fit volenti" is also derived from the law of injuria since by that law a person could not designate as an "injury" any act inflicted upon himself to which act he had given his lawful consent.[108]

Quasi Delicts:

In addition to wrongs that were recognized as delicts by the jus civile, there were unlawful acts which in the

101. Inst. 4, 4, 9; Dig. 47, 10, 7, 8.
102. Inst. 4, 4, 7.
103. Inst. 4, 4, 10.
104. Inst. 4, 4, 11.
105. Dig. 9, 2, 6.
106. Dig. 1, 1, 3; 9, 2, 4, pr.; 43, 16, 3, 7.
107. Dig. 47, 10, 18, 4.
108. Dig. 47, 10, 1, 5 (Quia nulla injuria est, quae in volentem fiat).

course of time came to be regarded sufficiently offensive to justify the granting of actions against those who were held responsible for them. They were all of praetorian origin and do not appear as a separate class of obligations prior to the time of Justinian, who designates them as obligations arising neither from delict nor from contract but "as if" (quasi) from delict (ex delicto), in the sense that such wrongs are similar or analogous to delicts.[109]

Quasi is, therefore, a term of classification and when used as such in the Roman Law it implies a close resemblance but negatives the notion of identity.[110] Quasi delicts were actionable wrongs which were not included in the list of delicts covered by the statutory actions of the jus civile. They were, moreover, wrongs not resulting from the malice of the offender, but rather from his fault, ignorance, or negligence. Pothier describes them as the acts of a person who, without malignity, but by an inexcusable imprudence, causes an injury to another.[111] Quasi delicts were wrongs that belonged to a somewhat advanced stage of civilization, not primitive wrongs like unto delicts. In fact, they were never recognized as wrongs judicially till long after the class of wrongs known as delicts had become fixed. It was, therefore, quite logical to describe a wrong, sufficiently reprehensible to warrant a penalty or a suit for damages, but not included in offenses known as delicts, as an obligation like unto a delict (obligatio quasi ex delicto).

The Institutes of Justinian mention four forms of quasi delicts although it is not to be understood that such a list is exhaustive. They were, however, the principal quasi delicts of Justinian's time, and were as follows: (1) An unjust judgment due to the favor

---

109. Inst. 4, 5, pr.
110. Maine's Ancient Law, 332.
111. Pothier, Oblig. 116.

or ignorance of a judex; (2) throwing or pouring anything from an upper window to the injury of passers-by; (3) hanging dangerous articles over public thoroughfares; (4) damage to or thefts of property committed by servants of shipmasters, innkeepers, and stablekeepers.[112]

An injury caused by the clear unfairness or ignorance of a judex, or, as Justinian says "where a judex makes a cause his own," [113] gave to the aggrieved party a quasi delictual action against the judex. The term "judex," sometimes translated "judge," does not refer to a magistrate, but to the referee or juryman (who was not a lawyer but a layman) who was appointed by the real judge (the praetor) to hear and decide a case.[114] While a praetor was usually careful in the appointing of a judex, and although the list from which the names of judices were taken was as a rule carefully prepared, yet it happened at times that prejudice, fear, ignorance, or corruption influenced the conduct and decision of one to whom a case had been assigned.[115] For example, a greater amount than the pleadings authorized might be awarded by a judex,[116] or judgment might be unjustly given to one of the parties despite the clear evidence to the contrary. A judex was not responsible for honest mistakes or for an erroneous opinion providing it was not the result of actionable ignorance. He always had the opportunity and privilege of consulting men learned in the law (prudentes), who also were always ready to sit with him as counsellors (assessors), and it was a good defense if he followed the opinions thus obtained. The amount of damages recoverable against a judex "qui

112. Inst. 4, 5.
113. Inst. 4, 5, pr.
114. See Actions, post.
115. Dig. 5, 1, 15, 1.
116. Gaius 4, 52.

litem suam fecit" rested in the equity of the case as determined by the conscience of the judex before whom the case of the offending judex was brought.[117]

The quasi delict known as dejectum effusumve aliquid, was the liability of the occupier of a house, whether owner or not, for damage caused by anything being thrown or poured from the house.[118] An action lay for double the amount of the damage caused,[119] but if it resulted in the death of a freeman the penalty was fifty aurei.[120] The offense applied to places where people commonly pass, and it was immaterial whether the place in question was public or private provided it was a common gathering or passing place.[121] The action was against the actual occupier of the house, not necessarily the owner of it,[122] but it did not apply to a guest since a guest is not an "occupier." [123] However, if a number of persons occupied the same apartment, each was individually liable for harm caused by something being thrown or poured from it, since it was impossible to know which one was the actual offender.[124] If a filius familias had a hired upper room, not in his father's house, and someone was injured by something poured or thrown therefrom, the father was not liable, the action being against the son.[125]

The action for "things poured down and thrown out" was maintainable by the heir of the person injured, although not against the heir of the wrongdoer.[126]

The third quasi delict mentioned by Justinian was known as suspensum, or the placing or suspending

117. Inst. 4, 5, pr.
118. Inst. 4, 5, 1.
119. Inst. 4, 5, 1; Dig. 9, 3, 1, pr.
120. Inst. 4, 5, 1; Dig. 9, 3, 1, 5.
121. Dig. 9, 3, 1, 2.
122. Dig. 9, 3, 1, 4; 9, 3, 1, 9.
123. Dig. 9, 3, 1, 9.
124. Dig. 9, 3, 1, 10; 9, 3, 2.
125. Dig. 9, 3, 1, 7; Inst. 4, 5, 2.
126. Dig. 9, 3, 5, 5.

things in such a way above a place used for passing that someone was liable to get hurt by the falling object. It was not necessary in this quasi delict that anyone should be injured or harmed, since the wrong was the mere putting the passer-by in danger from the possible fall of such suspended objects.[127] The Edict [128] declared that anyone who placed anything on the eaves or on a projecting roof over a place where persons are accustomed to pass or stand, which article would be likely to hurt someone if it fell, should be liable in an action in factum for ten solidi.[129] The liability extended to anyone who placed in a dangerous position the object, whether the individual lived in the house or not,[130] and the spot where the object was placed might be the roof, or other part, of a private room, or lodging, or warehouse, or any other building, providing it was over a place where people commonly pass.[131] One also was held to have suspended or placed such an object who permitted it to remain in a dangerous position although he may not have placed it there himself. Accordingly, if one's slave placed the object, and the slave's master permitted it to remain, the master was liable, not in a noxal action, but directly.[132]

The words of the Edict are "eaves or a projecting roof," [133] consequently when a shield or a picture was hung upon the wall of a building, and the picture fell and injured a passer-by, Servius said the action in question did not lie, but contended that another action like unto it should be allowed.[134]

The action might be instituted by anyone (popu-

127. Dig. 9, 3, 5, 11.
128. The Julian or Perpetual Edict.
129. Dig. 9, 3, 5, 6.
130. Dig. 9, 3, 5, 8.
131. Dig. 9, 3, 5, 9.
132. Dig. 9, 3, 5, 10.
133. Dig. 9, 3, 5, 8.
134. Dig. 9, 3, 5, 12.

laris), or could be brought by the person aggrieved or by his heir. It did not lie, however, against the heir of the wrongdoer since the action was penal in character.[135]

The fourth quasi delict previously mentioned related to the wilful damage or theft of the property of shippers or travellers committed by the servants or slaves of shipowners, innkeepers, and stablekeepers.[136] "Shipowners" (nautae) meant those who were carriers of goods by water, and the word "ship" included all forms of sea or river craft.[137] Innkeepers (caupones) were keepers of public houses for the reception of travellers.[138] Stablekeepers (stabularii) were those who cared for beasts of burden, particularly for the feeding and shelter of such animals when used by travellers.[139]

For any loss suffered by wilful damage or theft in a ship, inn, or stable, the owner was liable in an action quasi delicto provided the wrong was not done by himself personally but by someone employed by him in the business.[140] If the owner were himself guilty of the offense, an action would lie against him as a direct action ex delicto, either the action of theft (actio furti)[141] or of unlawful or wilful damage (actio damni injuria dati). However, in such actions the plaintiff must prove that the wrong was done by the defendant in person. In the quasi delictual action, which was an action based upon particular facts of the case (actio in factum), the plaintiff sues for the loss on the theory that it was caused by the servants of the defendant.[142]

135. Dig. 9, 3, 5, 13.
136. Inst. 4, 5, 3; Dig. 4, 9, 1, pr.
137. Dig. 4, 9, 1, pr.; 4, 9, 1, 2; 14, 1, 1, 6.
138. Dig. 4, 9, 4, 1.
139. Dig. 4, 9, 1, 5.
140. Inst. 4, 5, 3.
141. Dig. 47, 5, 1.
142. Inst. 4, 5, 3.

This quasi delictual remedy is sometimes confused with the quasi contractual remedy, the actio de recepto, previously mentioned. This latter remedy arises from the law-imposed obligation of public carriers and entertainers to receive travellers and to care safely for their property. In that action it matters not whether the loss was caused by the proprietor or by his servants. The loss itself is the basis of the action, and the shipowner or other owner is liable as if (quasi) by contract. In the quasi delictual action, the shipowner or other owner is liable quasi ex delicto (or maleficio) on the theory that he is, to some extent at least, a careless or negligent man in employing wicked servants.[143]

If the person doing the wrong was a slave of the shipowner or the innkeeper, or stablekeeper, then the action was what was called a "noxal" (from noxia, harm) action.[144] It was a particular kind of a quasi delictual action, and could be brought only during the lifetime of the slave.[145] Moreover, a master sued in a noxal action could avoid all further liability by surrendering the noxa (slave) to the plaintiff.[146]

In the ordinary action for damage done by servants in ships and taverns, the plaintiff was entitled to recover double the amount of his loss.[147] If the business was conducted by two or more owners each was liable only to his proportionate share in the business.[148]

Quasi Torts and Quasi Crimes:

The term "delict" in Roman Law is applied to both private and public wrongs, or what in our

143. Inst. 4, 5, 3.
144. Gaius 4, 75 et seq. The offender was called "noxa;" the wrong itself noxia.
145. Dig. 9, 4, 7, pr.
146. Inst. 4, 8, 3; Dig. 9, 4, 1.
147. Dig. 4, 9, 7, pr. and 1, 44, 7, 5, 6.
148. Dig. 4, 9, 7, 5.

law are called torts and crimes. In a previous chapter, in connection with quasi contract, it was said that the term "quasi contract" had not till comparatively recent years won its proper place in our legal vocabulary. Likewise, it may be that, in time, the term "quasi tort" will also be found useful. If so, it will be another illustration of the fact that writers upon English Law constantly appropriate terms of the Roman Law for the purpose of classification and definition.

In our own law we speak of harms that are not torts, and there is, at times, a very narrow border line between such harms and those harms which are recognized as torts. However, we do not distinguish between torts and quasi torts. A harm is either a tort or it is not, that is, it is actionable or is not actionable. Harms which in one age may be considered as not giving rise to an action may, however, in a later age, be considered serious enough to warrant an action. In other words, new torts may be recognized under different conditions of society. In the same way delicts grew, or became more numerous, in the Roman Law. A "quasi delict" was a "delict" in the sense that it was an actionable wrong, but it was not suable under the ancient, fixed forms of actions. Consequently, the praetor supplied an action for the wrong just "as if" it were one of the ancient delicts. Delicts and quasi delicts were, therefore, originally classified as such on account of the limitations of certain forms of actions. In our own system of pleadings there has been a strikingly analogous parallel, namely, in the origin of our Common Law action known as trespass on the case, which action lies for injuries caused by the wrongful act of another, unaccompanied with force actual or implied.[149] It originated in the necessity of a writ for which no form could be found in the register of writs.

---

149. 1 Chit. Pl. 132, 133; III Blk. Com. 122.

The Statute [150] made it the duty of the officers of Chancery to issue a writ in any case for which no writ could be found, but which was similar to cases for which writs were issued. These writs, finally, always sounded in tort, and actions brought under them were classed as actions ex delicto.[151] Lord Mansfield might almost have been speaking of the differences between actions ex delicto and actions quasi ex delicto in the Roman Law when, in the case of Bird v. Randall,[152] he said: "There is an essential difference between actions of trespass and actions on the case; the former are actions stricti juris, but an action on the case is founded upon the mere justice and conscience of the plaintiff's case, and in the nature of a bill in equity, and in effect so, . . . because the plaintiff must recover upon the justice and conscience of his case and on that only."

In the ancient Roman Law certain wrongs (quasi delicts) could not, likewise, be cast in the mold of the existing forms of action, due to the fact that the ancient delictual remedies were based upon wilful wrongs, and upon wrongs committed by the person against whom the action was brought. The quasi delicts were not wilful wrongs, but wrongs resulting, in general, from one's negligence, imprudence, or want of skill, and the remedy was, usually, in the nature of a vicarious remedy, that is, not against the actual wrongdoer but against some third person.

While the term "quasi tort" has no generally recognized standing as a term of English Law, yet it has been used by some writers. For example, it is said that it may be conveniently used to classify torts in which one who has not actually committed a tort is, nevertheless, liable as if he had, as, for example, where

150. Westminster II, 1285 A. D.
151. 1 Chit. Pl. 125, 133.
152. 3 Burr. 1253.

a master is held liable for wrongful acts done by his servant in the course of his employment.[153] This would be using the term in nearly the same sense as it is used in the Roman Law. The term, however, has been used by other English writers to describe a class of cases that may be grounded upon either contract or tort. For example, in the English case of Taylor v. Manchester, etc., Ry. Co.,[154] Lindley, Lord Justice, said: "Every one who has studied English Law will know perfectly well that there is a debatable ground between torts and contracts. These are what are called quasi contracts and quasi torts; and it is sometimes not easy to say whether a cause is founded on contract or on tort." Likewise, in an English work on torts,[155] it is said that cases sounding in both contract and tort "are classified by some writers as quasi torts." This use of the term is, of course, a departure from its Roman Law significance.

In the modern Civil Law the term "quasi delict" is still retained. "Agreements arising in connection with a fact, personal to the party who is bound, result either from quasi contracts or from delicts (delits) or from quasi delicts," reads the French Civil Code.[156] The Louisiana Civil Code contains the same article,[157] using, however, the words "offenses and quasi offenses" in place of the words "delicts and quasi delicts" of the French code. Quasi delicts, or quasi offenses, are further mentioned as including wrongs done by one's negligence, imprudence, or his want of skill,[158] or, as has been said judicially, "quasi offenses are those which cause injury to another, but proceed only from

---

153. Broom, Com. Law, 690; Underhill on Torts, 29.
154. 1 Q. B. D. 134 (1895).
155. Ringwood, Outlines of the Law of Torts, p. 6 (London 1898).
156. Art. 1370.
157. Revised Civil Code (1920), art. 2292.
158. La. Civ. Code, art. 2316; French Civ. Code, art. 1383.

error, neglect, or imprudence."[159] "The marked differences between a quasi contract and an offense or quasi offense," says the supreme court of Louisiana,[160] "is that the act which gives rise to a quasi contract is a lawful act, and therefore is permitted; while the act which gives rise to an offense or quasi offense is unlawful, and therefore is forbidden."

The term "quasi crime" has likewise been used in comparatively modern times, both in constitutional and statutory provisions. "The constitutional provision to the effect that the criminal court of Cook county shall have jurisdiction in cases of a quasi criminal nature, means," says the supreme court of Illinois,[161] "all offenses not crimes or misdemeanors, but in the nature of crimes, and which are punished not by indictment, but by forfeitures and penalties. It includes all qui tam actions, prosecutions for bastardy, informations in the nature of a quo warranto, and suits for the violation of ordinances."

159. Edwards v. Turner, 6 Rob. (La.) 382; Perrillat v. Puech, 2 La. 428; Lovell v. Cragin, 136 U. S. 130, 150.

160. City of New Orleans v. Bank, 31 La. Ann. 566; Knoop v. Blaffer, 39 La. Ann. 23, 6 So. 9.

161. Wiggins v. City of Chicago, 68 Ill. 372, 375. And see State v. Snure, 29 Minn. 132; Woodward v. Squires, 39 Iowa, 435, 438; Pittsburgh, etc. R. Co. v. Ferrell, 39 Ind. App. 515.

[Roman Law]

CHAPTER XIX

THE LAW OF OBLIGATIONS, *continued*

The Dissolution of Obligations

An obligation, as previously stated, could be created in the Roman Law only when some legal bond or tie (vinculum juris) gave it efficacy. By a similar doctrine it was dissolved only when in some method authorized by law its legal bond or tie was broken.

Roman jurists distinguished, however, between the legal extinction of an obligation and the mere inability to enforce an obligation. In the latter case the obligation was not dissolved and continued to have a technical legal existence despite the fact that it was unenforceable and to all practical effects invalid. Certain events, acts, or transactions operated by force of law (ipso jure) to extinguish obligations, that is, they dissolved the legal bond (vinculum juris) by which an obligation was created. Other events, acts or transactions while not legally extinguishing obligations yet made them unenforceable since the praetor allowed, in such cases, a defense or "exception" which barred (ope exceptionis) any action upon them.

Obligations were extinguished by law (jus civile), by performance (solutio), by formal release (acceptilatio), by novation (novatio), by prescription (praescriptio), by merger (confusio), and by impossibility of performance. In addition to these modes of legal extinction, obligations were rendered unenforceable (ope exceptionis) by praetorian edict when a plaintiff had made an agreement not to sue (pactum de non petendo). Also when once an issue had been formulated by the praetor (litis contestatio) in any action, no suit upon the same obligation, regardless of the outcome of the original action, could again be brought. Likewise, by praetorian extension of the right of set-off, or compensatio, to actions stricti juris,[1] obligations might be totally or partially extinguished so far as any further action upon them was concerned.

Solutio:

The natural and usual method of extinguishing an obligation is by performance, the technical Roman Law term being solutio. It might consist in the payment of money in liquidation of a debt, or it might be many other things. Whoever did what he promised to do dissolved his obligation.[2] Gradually, the term solutio acquired a broader meaning and was used to signify the loosing or extinction of obligations in general, whether by performance or by some other method.[3]

The "performance" of an obligation meant, however, a different thing in the later law of Rome than in the early years. Solutio, in the strict sense of performance or payment, under the later jus gentium, meant the payment of money due or the doing of something else in its place, with the consent of the creditor. Such acts by their own force discharged the obligation.[4] However, under the ancient law it was necessary in order to extinguish a contractual obligation that the legal tie (the vinculum juris) should be unbound in the same formal way it had been bound. In addition to mere payment, or other satisfaction of the creditor, certain formal acts or words of release were necessary. If A had legally bound himself (that is, by nexum) to pay B a sum of money, A could

1. Infra.
2. Dig. 50, 16, 176.
3. Dig. 42, 1, 4, 7; 46, 3, 54; 50, 16, 17.
4. Inst. 3, 29, pr.

not by a mere payment legally dissolve the obligation. A formal procedure was necessary to do that. It was the legal right, the law, that had to be extinguished, not merely B, the creditor, that had to be satisfied. Consequently, in connection with the ancient formal contract of loan, known as nexum, whereby one bound himself per aes et libram, the obligation thus created could not be dissolved by the mere repayment of the loan, since only by again going through the ceremony per aes et libram (bronze and scales) in the presence of five witnesses, and in connection with the utterance of certain formal words, could the legal tie be loosed.[5] The custom and tradition of this ancient theory of performance influenced Roman Law for centuries, being the foundation of the doctrine of release in the later law.[6]

The solutio of the later law was payment or the performance of what one had agreed to do under the terms of his obligation. The debtor must render to the creditor the specific thing, money or other thing, to which the creditor is entitled. However, if one owes money and cannot pay it when due, he may, nevertheless, discharge his obligation by giving something else to the creditor providing the creditor accepts it in lieu of payment. This was called datio in solutio.[7] The Proculians said that the substitution of something else in place of what was actually due did not, as a matter of law (ipso jure) even with the consent of the creditor, extinguish the obligation, but only gave the debtor the right of a defense on the ground of fraud (exceptio doli mali) if after such acceptance by the creditor he should attempt to sue upon the unextinguished contract.[8] The Sabinians,

5. Gaius 3, 173–175.
6. See Acceptilatio, infra.
7. Dig. 12, 1, 2, 1; Gaius 3, 168; Inst. 3, 29, pr.
8. This theory is like unto the English doctrine of equitable estoppel.

however, held that a datio in solutum put a legal end to the obligation.[9]

Payment may be made by the debtor personally or by some other person acting for him.[10] Even an unauthorized person may discharge the obligation by paying the creditor,[11] regardless whether the debtor knew it or not, and even contrary to his will.[12] Where, however, an obligation consists in the rendering of personal service, such a debt can be paid only by the debtor himself.[13] Payment by the debtor discharges not only his obligation but also the obligation of all who may have been his sureties. In the same way, payment by a surety frees both himself and the principal debtor.[14]

Payment must be made to the creditor or to some third person authorized by the creditor to receive it, and payment to an agent previously duly authorized but whose authority had, unknown to the debtor, been revoked, was held a valid payment.[15]

Payment should be made at the time and place agreed,[16] but in absence of express agreement payment may be made at any reasonable place.[17] It was held, however, by the Roman jurists that although a certain day was fixed for payment, yet the debtor, on the theory that the time of payment was set for his benefit, could pay the creditor, even against his consent, before the fixed day, unless it appeared that

9. Dig. 13, 7, 24, pr.
10. Inst. 3, 29, pr.
11. Inst. 3, 29, pr.; Dig. 3, 5, 38.
12. Inst. 3, 29, pr.
13. Dig. 46, 3, 31, pr.
14. Inst. 3, 29, pr.; Dig. 46, 3, 43.
15. Dig. 22, 1, 41, 1; 46, 3, 12, 2 & 4; 46, 3, 34, 3; 46, 3, 38, 1.
16. Inst. 4, 6, 33; Dig. 13, 4; Cod. 3, 18.
17. Dig. 46, 3, 39.

the day was appointed for the benefit of the creditor.[18]

In order to discharge the obligation the debt must be paid in full, and a debtor cannot ordinarily require a creditor to accept a partial payment.[19] Julianus, however, says the better view is that a debtor should be permitted to pay what he can, thus reducing the obligation proportionately.[20]

As to the appropriation of payments where a debtor owed two or more debts to the same creditor and the sum paid was not sufficient to discharge them all, if at the time of payment neither creditor nor debtor made the appropriation, then certain rules of presumption governed the same. At the time of payment, the debtor, the same as in our law, had the right to specify the debt to which the money should be applied. However, if the debtor made no application, then the creditor might do so, provided it was done at once and was equitable.[21] In case neither debtor nor creditor made any application, then the payment was properly applied to the debt which it was most advantageous to the debtor to discharge.[22] For example, an undisputed debt should be paid in preference to a disputed one; a debt which is due in preference to one that is not; a debt drawing interest in preference to one without interest; a debt that is secured by a pledge in preference to one that is not.[23] It was a further rule of law that where the equities were equal, and the debtor had no interest in discharging one in preference to another, then the payment should be applied to the debt oldest in time. Where, however, the debts were all of the same date

---

[18]. Dig. 45, 1, 38, 16; 45, 1, 137, 2; 46, 3, 70; Vinnius in Inst. 3, 16, 2, 4; Ellis v. Craig, 7 John. Ch. (N. Y.) 7 (1823).

[19]. Dig. 22, 1, 41, 1; 12, 1, 21.

[20]. Dig. 12, 1, 21.

[21]. Dig. 46, 3, 1.

[22]. Cod. 8, 43, 1.

[23]. Dig. 46, 3, 3, 1; 46, 3, 103; 46, 3, 5, **pr.**

and the equities were equal, then the payment should be apportioned equally to each.[24]

Tender:

In connection with solutio a formal and proper tender of a sum of money due, was, by Roman Law, equivalent to payment and extinguished the debt. Its effect was not merely to put an end to subsequent interest, but to release all securities, to relieve the debtor from any loss in case he deposited the money, and to dissolve the obligation.[25] This is quite different from our law since with us a tender of money does not ordinarily operate as a payment, but merely discharges a debtor from interest, costs, or damages accruing after the tender. However, even in our own law it has been held that a tender of specific articles at the time and place agreed upon for the delivery of such articles, followed by a refusal or a failure of the tenderee to receive the same, discharges the obligation and vests the property in the creditor.[26] Also in our law a tender of a debt when due usually discharges liens given in security, although it does not discharge the debt itself.

In the Roman Law, a formal tender, consisted of three parts, an offer to pay (oblatio), a sealing of the money in a bag (obsignatio), and depositing (depositio) the same in a temple, or in some other place designated by a court.[27] When this was done, after a creditor had refused to accept without cause, the deposit amounted to a payment and extinguished the debt.[28] Marcellus even held that if a man owed a certain sum of money and duly offered the same, and

24. Dig. 46, 3; Pothier, Oblig. by Evans, n. 528 to 535; 561 to 572; Pattison v. Hull, 9 Cow. (N. Y.) 773.
25. Dig. 22, 1, 1, 3; 45, 1, 105; 46, 3, 72, pr.
26. Mitchell v. Merrill, 2 Blackf. (Ind.) 87, Singerland v. Morse, 8 Johns. (N. Y.) 474.
27. Dig. 4, 4, 7, 2; 26, 7, 28, 1; Cod. 4, 32, 19; 8, 43, 9.
28. Ib.

the creditor without legal ground refused to accept it, the subsequent loss of the money by the debtor without any fault on his part would release him from the debt.[29] Likewise, the mere sealing and depositing of the amount due might be sufficient in some cases to discharge the obligation without any offer of the money, as where a debt was due a minor who had no curator, and the debtor would have no protection in case he paid the minor.[30] On the other hand, it was held that no deposit was necessary in the case of a penalty of higher interest upon the debtor's default in paying the original interest, where the debtor made a tender at the proper time of the original interest due.[31] In case of a deposit, it was necessary to keep the money deposited, or, as we say, necessary to keep the tender good, since if the debtor withdrew the deposit, he thereby revived his obligation as it existed before the deposit was made.[32]

Acceptilatio:

An obligation could also be extinguished by acceptilatio, that is, by a formal release, or acknowledgment of performance. It originally applied to verbal contracts, that is, contractual obligations created by the saying of certain formal words. It was analogous to the ancient dissolution of nexum by the ceremony per aes et libram, and was called by Roman jurists a fictitious performance (imaginaria solutio).[33] Its legal effect was to discharge the obligation whether there had been actual performance or not, if the creditor was willing to release what a debtor owed him under a verbal contract (stipulatio).[34] The technical

29. Dig. 46, 3, 72, pr.
30. Dig. 4, 4, 7, 2; 45, 1, 122, 5; Cod. 4, 32, 6.
31. Dig. 22, 1, 9, 1; Cod. 4, 32, 9.
32. Cod. 4, 32, 19; 8, 28, 8.
33. Gaius 3, 169; Inst. 3, 29, 1.
34. Gaius 3, 169; Dig. 46, 4, 16 and 19.

form of acceptilatio was a contrarius actus to the stipulatio which was to be released. The debtor said to the creditor "What I promised to you have you received (acceptum)?" The creditor thereupon replied "I have." [35] An informal agreement to cancel a debt, that is, an agreement made by words other than the words prescribed, had no legal effect. Even the giving of a written receipt (apocha) did not extinguish the obligation since the creditor could rebut the evidence of the receipt by showing that no payment had in fact been made.[36] The formal acceptilatio was, however, conclusive. It was necessary that the parties to the obligation should be the parties to the acceptilatio, although if dead the release might be made by their heirs. An acceptilatio, moreover, had to be unconditional, and refer to a present and not to a future obligation. It further acted as an immediate release and could not be made to take effect at a subsequent date.

Acceptilatio destroyed the obligation entirely, consequently if this formal release was given to a surety it also released the principal. There could be, however, a release of a part of a debt,[37] since a part of a debt could be paid.

Although acceptilatio released only such obligations as arose from verbal contracts (stipulatio),[38] yet by the device of novation an obligation originally created in any other legal way could be changed by the parties into a stipulatio, and, then, this stipulatio could

---

35. Gaius 3, 169; Inst. 3, 29, 1. See also Dig. 43, 4, 7, where the word facio is used instead of habeo.

36. An informal release might, however, operate as an agreement (pact) not to sue, and such a pact (see infra) might, under praetorian law, be pleaded in defense to an action. Dig. 46, 4, 19, pr.

37. Inst. 3, 29, 1; Dig. 46, 4, 13, 1. This was a doubtful question when Gaius wrote. Gaius 3, 172.

38. Gaius 3, 170; Inst. 3, 29, 1.

be extinguished by acceptilatio.[39] In the same way a future debt could be converted, by stipulatio, into a present debt and then the present debt could be wiped out by a formal release. In the last century of the Republic, Aquilius Gallus, who, as stated by Pomponius,[40] was considered by the people as the greatest lawyer of his day, invented a formula whereby every sort and kind of an obligation that one owed to another, both present and future, could be reduced, by novation, into a single, present, verbal obligation, and, then, this one obligation could be extinguished by acceptilatio. This formula, known as the Aquilian stipulatio, is set forth in the Institutes of Justinian.[41] By this means several or a multitude of obligations could be extinguished at once. The Aquilian stipulation superseded and extinguished all preceding stipulations and, in turn, was extinguished by the acceptilatio.[42] Any rights of action, however, says Papinian,[43] that the parties did not have in mind when the agreement was made, were not extinguished.

A written receipt (apocha) given in acknowledgment of a payment of money was valid only in case the money was actually paid, but a discharge of an obligation by acceptilatio required no other legal ground ("consideration") to make it valid than the formal acknowledgment of performance irrespective whether there was any actual performance or not.[44] It was for this reason that even in cases of actual performance acceptilatio was more satisfactory to a debtor than a mere receipt (apocha). In the course of

39. Gaius 3, 170. The novation destroyed the original obligation, and then the new verbal contract was destroyed by the acceptilatio.

40. Dig. 1, 2, 2, 42.

41. Inst. 3, 29, 2; Dig. 46, 4, 18, pr.

42. Dig. 2, 15, 4.

43. Dig. 2, 15, 5.

44. Dig. 46, 4, 19, 1.

time, however, an informal pact not to sue superseded, in practice, acceptilatio.[45]

It is familiar doctrine in our law that a release is void unless supported by a consideration. Yet a release under seal is good at Common Law regardless of the payment of any money, the seal being often said to "import" a consideration. However, as a matter of fact, it was the *form* of the release, the solemn use of a seal, that originally made the release valid rather than the purported consideration. Our early Common Law was as much influenced by form and ceremony in some matters as was the Roman Law. Moreover, by statute in some of our states receipts and releases if in writing, whether sealed or not, will be valid, if such was the intention of the parties, without any consideration to support them.[46] Even where consideration is required, it need not be adequate, for if no fraud be practiced and the releasor acts understandingly, a trifling sum will be sufficient.[47]

Novatio:

Novation, or the substitution of a new obligation for a former one, was another means by which an obligation could be dissolved.[48] "It was," says the Digest, "the transfer of a prior debt to another obligation, whether the new obligation was valid by the jus civile or merely a natural obligation. The result was that the prior debt was extinguished by the creation of the new one. A prior obligation of any kind could by verbal contract be subjected to novation, provided that the substituted obligation was binding civilly or naturally, as where a ward made an agreement without his tutor's consent."[49]

45. Post.
46. See, for example, Miller v. Fox, 111 Tenn. 336, 76 S. W. 893.
47. Missouri Pac. Ry. Co. v. Goodholm, 61 Kan. 758, 60 Pac. 1066.
48. Gaius 3, 176; Inst. 3, 29, 3.
49. Dig. 46, 2, 1. Some make novatio synonymous with merger

Novation consisted either in a change of parties or in a change of the nature or subject matter of the obligation.[50] Change of party could be either of the debtor or of the creditor. For example, A might stipulate with B that he (B) would pay a debt owed to A by C, a change of debtor; or C might stipulate with B, providing A consented, that the debt he (C) owed to A might be paid to B, a change of creditor. A change in the nature, or the creative form of an obligation occurred when the parties, for example, substituted a verbal obligation (stipulatio) for a real or a consensual obligation,[51] or when the original obligation was modified or changed either by striking out certain matter, or by inserting new provisions, as a condition, or a time of payment, or a surety.[52]

A transaction substituting a new debtor for a prior one was termed either delegatio or expromissio according to the presence or absence of the prior debtor's consent. If the original debtor agreed to the change the transaction was called delegatio, the new debtor being delegated (delegatus) to take his place. There could be, however, a change of parties, by consent of the creditor and the new debtor, without the knowledge and even against the consent of the original debtor. Such a transaction was called expromissio. The consent of the creditor was always required, however, since one could not be compelled to accept a new debtor in place of another.[53] In either case, whether the new debtor was substituted by delegatio or expromissio, the new obligation took the place of the old, and the original debtor was released from all

(Sharp v. Fly, 9 Baxt. (Tenn.) 4). The term confusio, however, is more like our merger.

50. Gaius 3, 176; Inst. 3, 29, 3.
51. As appointed out in connection with Acceptilatio, supra.
52. Gaius 3, 176, 177; Inst. 3, 29, 3.
53. Cod. 8, 42, 1 & 6.

claims of the first obligation.[54] The result was the same as if there had been performance (solutio) by the original debtor. The first obligation was extinguished, and any securities or pledges that had been given in connection with it were likewise released.[55] Even should the new debtor for any reason be not bound or should become insolvent, nevertheless the original debtor could not be held liable.[56] For example, if the new debtor should stipulate that he would pay after his death, or if a woman or ward, as the new debtor, should stipulate, without a tutor's sanction (auctoritas), to pay the debt, the new stipulation would be void but the original debtor would be discharged.[57] A new debtor, however, who had been fraudulently induced by the original debtor to take his place could not plead such fraud against the creditor when sued by him.[58]

Novation could also be effected, although the debtor and creditor remained unchanged, either by substituting a new form of obligation for the one previously in existence, or by changing the original obligation by inserting or striking out a condition, or terms as to time and place of performance. However, in order to substitute a new obligation for a preceding one, the terms being unchanged, the first obligation had to arise in some other way than by stipulation, as by re or consensus, since novation was made only by a verbal contract (stipulation).[59] In case the prior obligation was also a verbal contract, a new stipulation upon the same

54. Gaius, 3, 176.
55. Dig. 46, 2, 9 & 29.
56. Dig. 46, 2, 1, 1; 46, 2, 20, 1
57. Gaius 3, 176; Inst. 3, 29, 3.
58. Dig. 44, 4, 4, 20.
59. Dig. 46, 2, 32; 46, 2, 34, 2. Under the older law novation could be made either by the written contract known as expensilatio or by verbal contract (stipulatio). The former form of contract (expensilatio) became obsolete, and stipulation remained as the only way in which novation could be accomplished. Dig. 17, 2, 71, pr.

subject matter did not operate as a novation unless it appeared that a novation was intended. For example, A stipulates with B for a farm, and afterwards A stipulates with B for the value of the same farm. It was held that as the objects were different in the two stipulations there was no novation unless such was the intention.[60] Where, however, A stipulated with B for a footpath (iter) and later stipulated for a wagon-road (actus) a novation was held to have been made since the intention was clear. But if the prior stipulation had been for a wagon-road (actus) and the second for a footpath (iter), the second stipulation would have been void, since it was included in the first.[61]

When, therefore, there were two stipulations, a first and a second, identical in terms, the second did not effect a novation, and therefore did not extinguish the first. In order to effect a novation, with consequent extinguishment, the parties remaining the same and both obligations created by stipulation, the terms of the first obligation had to be changed, as stated above, by the addition of new matter or by the cancellation of some previous matter.[62] For example, the first obligation may have been a conditional obligation, and the second an absolute obligation, or the first absolute and the second conditional. In this latter case, the insertion of a condition, the ancient jurists were not agreed as to the time the novation took place. Servius Sulpicius contended that the novation and the extinguishment of the prior obligation took place immediately upon the formation of the new obligation, regardless whether the inserted condition was ever fulfilled or not.[63] Gaius, however, insisted that there

60. Dig. 46, 2, 28.
61. Dig. 46, 2, 9, 2.
62. Gaius 3, 177; Inst. 3, 29, 3.
63. Gaius 3, 179.

was no novation at all unless the condition was performed, and if it was not performed the prior obligation remained in force.[64] Justinian adopted [65] the view expressed by Gaius, and to set at rest the many disputes among jurists as to the intention of parties concerning a novation when they entered into a second obligation, he provided that all presumptions one way or the other as to the existence or non-existence of such an intention should be swept aside, and that a novation should take place only when the parties expressly declared that it was their intention in making a new obligation to extinguish a former one. In absence of such an express declaration he further provided that the former obligation should remain in force, and that the new one should also constitute another binding contract.[66]

Praescriptio:

The term "praescriptio" was originally used in Roman Law as a word of art in connection with the pleadings used in the formulary procedure of the praetors. In drawing up a formula a clause modifying or limiting the scope of the action was sometimes "written before" the regular parts of the formula, from which fact the term praescriptio was derived.[67] However, in imperial days praescriptio was used synonymously with exceptio, a term meaning a special plea in bar in behalf of a defendant.[68] Praescriptio, like the word "limitation" in our own law, became in time associated with different meanings, one, a means of acquiring property by long, continued, adverse pos-

---

64. Gaius 3, 179. However, if the creditor sued upon the prior obligation before such performance or fulfillment he could be met by the defense of dolus or the pact not to sue. Dig. 23, 3, 50.

65. Inst. 3, 29, 3.

66. Inst. 3, 29, 3.

67. Gaius 4, 132.

68. Gaius 4, 116.

session; another, the barring of an action by lapse of time.[69] In this latter sense praescriptio corresponds to our phrase statute of limitations.

In the old Roman Law all actions were said to be perpetual, that is, they could be brought at any time. Under the later procedure, however, the praetors fixed various limits to the right of bringing actions, and still later, in imperial days, such limitations were established by various constitutions.[70]

Actions granted by the jurisdiction of a praetor were usually limited to one year. The emperor Theodosius II, in the year 424, enacted a law whereby all actions, whether in rem or in personam, were limited to thirty years.[71] Justinian also fixed the period at thirty years for nearly all actions,[72] but the action to enforce a mortgage, actio hypothecaria, when brought against the debtor or his heirs, was limited to forty years.[73]

Praescriptio began to run from the time the action accrued,[74] but payment of a part of the debt was a renewal of the right to sue and marked a new beginning of the period.[75] The limitation did not run, however, against persons under the age of puberty, whether they had tutors or not.[76] It was necessary that the term of praescriptio should be unbroken for the whole period, and the term did not end till the last hour of the last day had entirely passed.[77]

When the Roman Law provided that an action could be barred by praescriptio, another means was there-

---

69. See Chenot v. Lefevre, 8 Ill. 637, 642.
70. Inst. 4, 12, pr.
71. Cod. 7, 39, 3.
72. No limit was placed upon actions by the state for taxes. Cod. 7, 39, 6.
73. Cod. 7, 39, 7, 1.
74. Dig. 13, 7, 9, 3; Cod. 5, 12, 30; 7, 39, 3; 7, 39, 7, 4; 40, 1, 1.
75. Dig. 13, 5, 18, 1.
76. Cod. 7, 39, 3.
77. Dig. 44, 7, 6.

by created for extinguishing an obligation. When after a certain lapse of time one's previous legal right to enforce a legal duty was denied him, the extinguishing of the right to enforce also, to all practical results, extinguished the right itself.

While it is the general rule, in our own system of jurisprudence, that, so far as debts are concerned, statutes of limitation bar the remedy but do not extinguish the cause of action, yet some decisions hold that the effect of such statutes is to extinguish the right. The creditor's claim is taken away with his remedy. "The law deals," as said in a Wisconsin case,[78] "only with enforceable rights, and if such a right be changed into a mere moral obligation, in a legal sense it no longer exists at all."

Confusio:

The term confusio in Roman Law was used in different senses. Its original meaning was the mixing together things of the same kind so that they became inseparable, as, for example, where materials belonging to different owners, such as wines, or melted gold or silver, were poured together.[79]

The term also meant the union of a right and duty in the same person, as where a creditor became heir to his debtor.[80] In such a case the right and the duty were merged, and both were extinguished. Confusio, or merger, therefore, was another way by which an obligation could be dissolved.[81] It was only, however, a corresponding or reciprocal right and duty that

---

78. Eingartner v. Ill. Steel Co., 103 Wis. 373, 376. And see Woodman v. Fulton, 47 Miss. 682, where the court says: "The bar created by the statute of limitations is as effectual as payment or any other defense, and when once vested cannot be taken away even by the legislature."

79. Inst. 2, 1, 27.

80. Under the Roman Law of inheritance the heir was regarded as the successor of the deceased.

81. Dig. 34, 3, 21, 1.

[Roman Law]

could merge, for if a creditor became heir to his debtor's surety, the surety's obligation was extinguished but not the principal's debt.[82] In all joint obligations confusio in case of one of the parties did not destroy the obligation.[83]

The reason why confusio, or merger, took place when a creditor became heir to his debtor was because by the Roman Law it was the duty of the heir to pay the debts of the deceased although the heir may have received no property from the one who made him heir.[84] Consequently, if the heir were also a creditor of the deceased he was bound by the law to pay the debt to himself, and thus the creditor and the debtor became the same person. This extinguished the obligation.

However, in the time of Justinian, an heir was bound to pay the deceased's debts only to the amount of the property actually received by the heir.[85] And that emperor further enacted that an heir who made an inventory of the property of the deceased should be classed among his creditors, if in fact the heir was a creditor. The deceased and the heir were then different persons as to their respective estates, and he could pay a debt owed to him by the deceased just as he could pay any other creditor.[86] The heir who did not make an inventory was liable for all debts as under the previous law.[87] An obligation therefore might still be extinguished by confusio in the case of an heir who made no inventory, but since the making of an inventory became the general custom, the doctrine of confusio became practically obsolete.

82. Dig. 46, 3, 43.
83. Dig. 34, 3, 3, 3; 46, 1, 71.
84. Dig. 37, 1, 3, pr.
85. Inst. 2, 19, 6.
86. Cod. 6 30, 22, 14.
87. Cod. 6, 30, 22, 1; 6, 30, 22, 12.

Impossibility of Performance:

One who has obligated himself may be unable to perform his promise through no fault of his own, owing to some supervening act which makes performance a physical impossibility.[88] The subject matter of a contract may have been destroyed by pure accident (casus fortuitus), as where, for example, A agrees to deliver a slave to B and, before the time of delivery, the slave dies. In such a case A is released from his obligation.[89] If, however, A had killed the slave, without lawful excuse, he would have been bound to pay to B the value of the slave.[90] It was essential in order to extinguish an obligation by impossibility of performance that the promisor should be without wilful injury (dolus), negligence (culpa'), or default (mora).[91] Moreover, impossibility does not mean the mere inability of the promisor to perform, but the inability of any human being to perform.[92] The fact that A who promised to deliver a hundred tons of copper to B has not got the copper when the time of performance arrives, does not release him from his contract.[93] Where, however, A agrees to obtain for B a small piece of ground owned by C, and then C buries a dead body there, the ground thus becoming a res religiosa and extra commercium, A's obligation is extinguished.[94] But if A had agreed to transfer a piece of his own ground to B and had buried a body there himself, the obligation would still be binding. A could not transfer the land but he would have to pay B what the land was worth.[95] That A lost a sum

88. Dig. 46, 3, 92.
89. Dig. 45, 1, 33; 45, 1, 83, 5.
90. Dig. 45, 1, 23; 45, 1, 96.
91. Dig. 22, 1, 32, pr.
92. Dig. 45, 1, 137, 5.
93. Dig. 45, 1, 137, 5.
94. Dig. 45, 1, 91, 1.
95. Ib.

of money he had promised to pay to B would not relieve him from his promise, since an equal amount of any other money would satisfy his obligation. But if the promise had been to give to B certain coins in a particular box, and through no fault of A the box and its contents had been destroyed, A would be under no obligation to give or pay to B an equal sum.[96]

The death of one of the parties to an obligation might also extinguish a duty to perform. While it was the general rule in Roman Law that the liability of a debtor descended to his heirs, yet delictual actions, such as actions arising from rapine, injury, and unlawful damage died with the wrongdoer.[97] Moreover, a partnership was dissolved by the death of a partner,[98] and a mandate was also extinguished if before its execution the mandator or the mandatary died.[99] Likewise, contracts, for personal service and contracts depending for their performance upon the peculiar qualifications of the promisor were dissolved by the death of the debtor. Debts owed by one who gave himself in adoption were by the jus civile, extinguished by his loss of status (capitis deminutio).[100] By praetorian law, however, in order to prevent such an extinction of obligations by one who permitted himself to be adopted (arrogated), an action was granted which by a fiction ignored the debtor's capitis deminutio.[101] The extinguishment of the obligations of an arrogated person was, moreover, by the jus civile limited to debts arising from contract, and an arrogatus remained still liable for his delicts.[102]

In connection with the extinguishing of obligations

96. Dig. 45, 1, 37.
97. Gaius 4, 112; Inst. 4, 12, 1.
98. Inst. 3, 25, 5.
99. Inst. 3, 26, 10.
100. Gaius 3, 84.
101. Gaius 4, 38.
102. Dig. 4, 5, 2, 3.

by the accidental destruction of the subject matter it was necessary, as already pointed out, that there should be no default or delay in due performance on the part of the obligor. A debtor who did not perform at the time he agreed to perform, and especially after a lawful demand for performance, was said to be in mora.[103] If while he was in mora the destruction of the subject matter (interritus rei) occurred, all loss was thrown upon him.[104] It was for this reason that one who had stolen property was not relieved from his liability to pay for it even though it had been accidentally destroyed, since a thief was said to be in mora from the time he stole a thing since it was his duty to return it at once.[105]

Of course it was always possible for parties to make a contract whereby even in case of loss without fault the promisor agreed to assume the risk.

Agreement Not to Sue (*Pactum de non Petendo*):

In a previous chapter it has been pointed out that there is a difference between a contract and a pact. Contracts arise by the use of a prescribed form, as in stipulatio; by some act dealing with the subject matter, known as real contracts (re), as mutuum, commodatum, depositum, pignus, and innominate contracts; and by consensus, such as sale, hire, partnership, and mandate. An agreement not falling under any of these classes, or not made valid by some special statute or edict was called a pact, and a bare agreement (nudum pactum) that is, an agreement not rendered binding in law owing to the absence of some legal ground (causa) mentioned above, did not produce an obligation.[106] Such an agreement did produce, how-

103. Dig. 22, 1, 32, pr.
104. Dig. 7, 1, 37; 44, 7, 45; 45, 1, 91, pr.; 45, 1, 91, 3.
105. Dig. 5, 3, 40, pr.; 43, 16, 1, 34.
106. Dig. 2, 14, 7, 4.

ever, by praetorian law a defense (exceptio),[107] and the Praetorian Edict declared that pacts not made with malicious intent, and not contrary to any statute, plebiscite, decree of the senate, or imperial edict, and free from fraud, would be upheld.[108]

Pacts made with malicious intent (dolo malo) were pacts made with deceit and cunning, where in order to entrap the other party the promisor pretends one purpose when he has another purpose in view.[109]

Among pacts was the pact known as pactum de non petendo, or an agreement not to sue. It depended upon no form of words or upon any particular act, but upon the intention. It could be an express agreement or it might be made tacitly. Even a dumb man could make a pact.[110] Where a creditor returned to his debtor a written undertaking executed by the debtor, it was held that there was an agreement on the part of the creditor not to sue, and if he did the debtor would have a good defense (exceptio).[111] However, where an article pledged for a debt was returned by a creditor to his debtor, the creditor could still sue upon the debt unless it was expressly proved that the creditor did not intend to sue.[112]

Pacts not to sue might be in rem or in personam. They were in rem when the agreement was not to sue anyone who might be legally liable for a debt, and in personam when the agreement was not to sue a particular person.[113] Whether the pact was in rem or in personam depended upon the intention of the parties. Very often the name of some particular person was mentioned in a pact, says Pedius, not with the

107. Dig. 2, 14, 7, 4.
108. Dig. 2, 14, 7, 7.
109. Dig. 2, 14, 7, 9.
110. Dig. 2, 14, 4, 1.
111. Dig. 2, 14, 2, 1.
112. Dig. 2, 14, 3.
113. Dig. 2, 14, 7, 7.

intent to make the pact in personam, but in order to make it clear who the party was.[114] If a man made a pact that no action should be brought against him, but only against his heir, the pact would be in personam, and the heir could be sued.[115] And where a father made a pact that no action should be brought either against him or against his daughter, and the daughter subsequently became the heiress of her father, it was held that the daughter could be sued as heir since such a pact could not be applied to a subsequent event.[116]

In case there were several joint creditors or joint debtors with reference to the same debt in its entirety, an agreement made by one creditor with one debtor might give rise to some perplexing questions.[117] Paulus said that a pact made in rem with one co-debtor applied to the other co-debtors when it was to the interest of the one who made the pact to free all the co-debtors from liability. Hence, a pact made with a principal debtor that he should not be sued became a defense to his sureties,[118] unless, as Ulpian said, it was the intention to relieve only the principal.[119] A pact made, however, with a surety would not relieve a principal because the surety would have no interest in not having the principal sued.[120] Where, on the other hand, one of two partners makes a pact that a partnership debtor shall not be sued, the jurists held that the other partner could still sue for the whole debt even though the pact had been made in rem.[121]

A pact could be made not to sue for a specified time,

114. Dig. 2, 14, 7, 8.
115. Dig. 2, 14, 17, 3.
116. Dig. 2, 14, 17, 4.
117. Dig. 2, 14, 21, 5.
118. Dig. 2, 14, 21, 5.
119. Dig. 2, 14, 22.
120. Dig. 2, 14, 23, pr.
121. Dig. 2, 14, 27, pr.

and this was binding only for such time.[122] Likewise, a pact not to sue might be nullified by a second pact that suit might be brought.[123] In case suit was brought and the debtor pleaded an exceptio by reason of the first pact, the exceptio could be rebutted by a replicatio based upon the second pact.[124]

The making of a pact not to sue did not usually extinguish the obligation. The debtor still remained bound so far as the law was concerned.[125] It was the equitable defense by way of an exceptio granted by the praetor that prevented, however, the enforcement of the obligation by action.[126] Some rights of action, contrary to the general rule, were, however, actually extinguished by a pact not to sue, namely, the delictual actions for theft and injuria.[127]

The pact not to sue was practically an informal release. Acceptilatio was a formal release, and, as we have seen, could be created only by the formal words of a stipulatio. Such a release destroyed the entire obligation, but a pact not to sue might be conditional, or temporary, or might apply only to some of the parties bound. It was so convenient and useful that in time the informal pact superseded, in practice, the formal release. Under acceptilatio, a crafty creditor might take advantage of a void release, as where a creditor pretended to give a release, but knew at the time the acceptilatio was void, and it was held that legally he could still sue.[128] Under the praetorian law, however, it was declared that a void formal release

122. Dig. 2, 14, 27, 1.
123. Dig. 2, 14, 27, 2.
124. Dig. 2, 14, 27, 2.
125. Inst. 4, 13, 3.
126. Inst. 4, 13, 3.
127. Dig. 2, 14, 17, 1.
128. Dig. 46, 4, 8, pr.

would be held to amount to a tacit agreement not to sue.[129]

Litis Contestatio:

The joinder in issue of the parties to a lawsuit, or, in other words, the commencement of an action (litis contestatio), was for a long time in Roman Law another means of extinguishing an obligation.[130] According to the Roman doctrine, when once the parties submitted their dispute to the magistrate they mutually waived their conflicting claims and substituted for them the decision of the court. It was in effect a sort of novation,[131] both parties agreeing that whatever their respective rights and duties may have been before, all should now depend upon the outcome of the litigation. It was also the law that when once a matter had been submitted to the magistrate it could not be litigated a second time.[132]

Under the ancient oral procedure, known as the statutory, or legis actio, procedure, the issue was joined, or the contest of the suit (litis contestatio) began, when the praetor referred the dispute to a judex. During the formulary procedure the litis contestatio commenced when the praetor finished the drawing up of the pleadings, that is, the formula. In the later empire, under the procedure known as the extraordinary procedure, the litis contestatio started when the magistrate began to hear the case.[133]

Under the legis actio procedure an obligation was extinguished by litis contestatio by direct operation of law.[134] In the formulary period it seems that the obligation continued as a natural one even after issue

129. Dig. 2, 14, 27, 9; 2, 14, 41.
130. Gaius 3, 180.
131. Dig. 45, 2, 2, 16; 46, 2, 11, 1 & 29.
132. Gaius 3, 181; 4, 108.
133. Cod. 3, 1, 14, 1; 2, 59, 2, pr.
134. Gaius 4, 108.

THE LAW OF OBLIGATIONS 539

was joined,[135] but if the plaintiff brought a second action upon the same question he could be met with an exceptio alleging that the case had been decided (res judicata) or that issue had been joined (res in judicium deducta).[136] When the formulary system was superseded by the extraordinary procedure, about 294 A. D., the technicalities of litis contestatio were no longer observed, and a joinder in issue had no effect upon the existence of an obligation. However, a plea of res judicata could always be interposed when a matter once decided was presented to a magistrate a second time. In the time of Justinian the law was the same, and regardless of the form of an action, whether in rem or in personam, an obligation still existed after suit was brought. In strict law, a second action could be brought upon the same question, but a defendant was protected by the exceptio rei judicatae.[137]

Compensatio:

Compensatio, meaning, literally, a weighing together, a balancing, was in a business and legal sense, a balancing of accounts, or the weighing of one obligation against another. Modestinus defines it as the mutual contribution of a debtor and a creditor.[138]

The doctrine of compensatio as a recognized means of legally extinguishing an obligation seems to have been of slow development in Roman Law. Gaius says [139] that bankers in suing their debtors were compelled to set off any credits in their favor and to bring suit only for the balance, the balance being expressly stated in the written pleadings (formula). For example, if a banker (A) owed his customer (B) ten

135. Dig. 12, 6, 60.
136. Gaius 4, 106.
137. Inst. 4, 13, 5.
138. Dig. 16, 2, 1.
139. Gaius 4, 64.

thousand sesterces,[140] and the customer (B) owed the banker (A) twenty thousand,[141] the statement of the issue (intentio) and the clause directing the judgment (condemnatio) ran as follows: "If it is proved that B owes A ten thousand sesterces more than A owes B (intentio), condemn B to pay ten thousand sesterces to A; if it is not proved, acquit B (condemnatio). According to the law of Roman procedure in the trial of actions, if A claimed a larger balance in the intentio than was due him, even one sesterce more, he lost his entire claim.[142] This seems harsh, but a set-off (compensatio) in case of a suit by a banker, or money broker (argentarius), was, says Gaius,[143] limited to claims of the same genus and nature, money against money, wheat against wheat, or wine against wine. It was the duty of an argentarius to keep correct accounts, and therefore the law held him strictly to his claim for any balance due.

Likewise, again says Gaius,[144] if the purchaser of an insolvent debtor's estate (bonorum emptor) brings an action against a debtor of the insolvent, he must insert a deductio in his formula in case the purchaser owes the defendant anything. The reason for this was that, by Roman Law, an emptor bonorum took the place of the insolvent, and any debts owed by the emptor to a debtor of the insolvent could be deducted from the claims of the emptor. This deductio from the claim of the purchaser of an insolvent estate differed, however, from the compensatio, or set-off, in the case of a banker. A deductio was not confined to claims of the same genus and nature, but was a debt

140. Not a personal debt, but credits in favor of the customer as shown by the account books.
141. That is, debits in favor of the banker.
142. Gaius 4, 53.
143. Gaius 4, 66; 4, 68.
144. Gaius 4, 65.

of a different genus.¹⁴⁵ For example, if the purchaser of the insolvent estate sued for a money debt he would have to deduct from the claim whatever he owed the defendant for corn or wine.¹⁴⁶ Moreover, a deductio was not inserted in the intentio, as was a compensatio, but was placed in the condemnatio, and, in such a case, the plaintiff ran no risk in losing what was actually due him although he may have claimed too large an amount.¹⁴⁷

In addition to these special rules applicable to suits brought by bankers and purchasers of insolvent estates, there grew up under the praetorian law, in connection with bonae fidei actions, the practice of setting off against the claim of a plaintiff whatever might be the counterclaim of a defendant in the same transaction. This was obviously a natural and equitable adjudication of mutual claims, and from this practice compensatio, in its legal and technical meaning, was developed. It was merely a recognition by a magistrate of what men of their own accord had practiced in their business transactions from the earliest times. They were accustomed to set off one debt against a counterdebt, and if both debts were equal, both were regarded by them as extinguished. This private act of the parties was what Roman lawyers called compensatio voluntaria in distinction from a set-off in judicial proceedings which was termed compensatio necessaria. In this latter sense compensatio corresponds to our own legal terms set-off and counterclaim.

In Roman Law, personal actions were classed as either stricti juris or bonae fidei. The former were actions based upon the jus civile, and in such cases judgment followed the strict law of the question sub-

---

145. Gaius 4, 66.
146. Gaius 4, 66.
147. Gaius 4, 68.

mitted, no equitable matters being considered. Actions bonae fidei, on the other hand, were praetorian in their origin and equitable in their nature. In such actions the parties were required to do what in good faith they ought to do, considering all the equities of the case. Actions of purchase and sale, letting and hiring, voluntary agency (negotiorum gestio), mandate, deposit, partnership, guardianship, commodatum, pledge, dotal property, partition of inheritance, partition of property held in common, and, in Justinian's time, the demand of an inheritance were the most important actions bonae fidei.[148]

In bonae fidei actions full power was given to the judex, the referee who tried the case,[149] to estimate how much was equitably (ex bono et aequo) due the plaintiff, taking into consideration, also, any counterclaim of the defendant in the same transaction, giving judgment in favor of the plaintiff for whatever balance might be due.[150] The judex was not obliged to consider a counterclaim of the defendant (compensatio) since he was not expressly instructed so to do by the formula, but the authority to consider such a claim was assumed to be given to him by the equitable nature of an action bonae fidei.[151] The law (that is, the jus civile) recognized the justice of compensatio in an action bonae fidei, but it was not a legal *right* and was allowed only in the discretion of the judex.

The doctrine of compensatio was extended, however, by the emperor Marcus Aurelius. He provided that a counterclaim, or set-off, might be pleaded even in an action stricti juris by an allegation of fraud,

148. Gaius 4, 62; Inst. 4, 6, 28.
149. Under the formulary procedure, the magistrate made up the pleadings (formula) and then referred the case for trial to some other person, known as a judex. This latter person was not a "judge" but a referee. See Actions, post.
150. Gaius 4, 61; Inst. 4, 6, 30.
151. Gaius, 4, 63.

exceptio doli mali,[152] probably for the reason that it was a fraud upon the defendant for a plaintiff in any sort of action to demand more than was his due. From the very nature of an action stricti juris, based upon a unilateral contract in distinction from an action bonae fidei which was bilateral in its nature, compensatio from counterclaims could arise only from different transactions (ex dispari causa) instead of from the same transaction (ex eadem causa) as in the case of an action bonae fidei. It is from this period that the *right* to a set-off was acknowledged, since a defendant having a counterclaim could insist that it be inserted in the formula by means of an exceptio (defense). Consequently, it could now be said that an obligation could be extinguished by operation of law (ipso jure), not, however, by the jus civile but by the praetorian law from which the doctrine of an exceptio was derived.

In the time of Justinian, a still wider latitude was given to compensatio. The right of set-off was given in all kinds of cases, both in personam and in rem, and claims ex dispari causa were equally admissible with those arising ex eadem causa. There was only one exception, namely, the action of deposit, in which action the Emperor did not think it just to allow any claim of compensatio, lest one might thereby be defrauded in the recovery of the property deposited.[153]

In order to make compensatio available it was necessary that the debt should be actually due from the plaintiff to the defendant; a debt not yet due could not be set off against a debt that had matured.[154] A natural obligation could, however, be set off against a legal one since compensatio was equitable in its application. A debt to be set off was also required to

152. Inst. 4, 6, 30; Dig. 16, 2, 4, 5 and 10.
153. Inst. 4, 6, 30; Cod. 4, 34, 11.
154. Cod. 4, 31, 9.

be easily proved (liquidum), and had to be certain and not conditional.[155] In case a compensatory debt could not be conveniently proved in connection with the trial, the defendant could forego the defense of a set-off and could bring a cross action (reconventio). A cross action could be brought at any time, even after the litis contestatio, and could, if desirable, be tried at the same time as the original action or subsequently to it.[156]

Compensatio was available not only to a principal and an original debtor, but also to a surety or to an heir.[157] It was not available, however, in cases of purchase money due the state,[158] or in actions brought against one for delinquent taxes,[159] or in an action of eviction from property of which the defendant had taken unlawful possession.[160]

The Roman Law doctrine of compensation was carried over into the civil codes of modern states whose jurisprudence is based upon that of Rome. Reference to these codes shows that practically the same principles that were recognized in the time of Justinian remain as law to-day.[161] Obligations are said to be extinguished by mere operation of law where debts equally liquidated and demandable are reciprocally due.[162] And the United States Supreme Court has said:[163] "By the Civil Law, where there are cross claims between a plaintiff and a defendant which are so connected with each other that the establishment of one can legitimately defeat, reduce, or modify the other, the defendant is always entitled to insist that

---

155. Dig. 16, 2, 7, pr.; 16, 2, 16, 1.
156. Dig. 2, 1, 11, 1; Code 7, 45, 14; 9, 35, 10; Nov. 69, 2.
157. Dig. 16, 2, 4, 5; 16, 2, 18, pr.
158. Dig. 16, 2, 12, pr.; 49, 14, 46, 5; Code 4, 31, 1.
159. Cod. 4, 31, 3.
160. Cod. 4, 31, 7.
161. See, for example, Civil Code of Louisiana, Art. 2207-2216.
162. Stewart v. Harper, 16 La. 181; Dorvin v. Wiltz, 11 La. 520.
163. Cumberland Glass Mfg. Co. v. DeWitt, 237 U. S. 447, quoting from Langdell, Eq. Pld., sec. 118.

his own claim shall be litigated with that of the plaintiff; that both shall be disposed of by one sentence; and that the plaintiff's recovery shall be limited to what he shall be entitled to, if anything, as the result of adjusting both claims and striking a balance, if necessary, between them."

The right of compensation, or set-off, was recognized in courts of Equity,[164] although the right was unknown to our English Common Law. At law, a defendant was left to his cross action. It was not till the Statute of 2 George II (1729) c. 22, p. 13, that mutual debts could be set one against the other, and proved under the general issue, or pleaded in bar, notice of the particular debt being previously given. At the present time in this country, set-off under Common Law procedure and counterclaim under our code procedure are regulated by the statutes of the various states.

164. Adams, Equity, 222; Story, Eq., 3, p. 1436.

CHAPTER XX

THE LAW OF SUCCESSION

Intestate Succession

Intestate Inheritance:

The Roman Law of inheritance is a part of the law of "succession," but it is so large a part that the terms inheritance (hereditas) and succession (successio) are often used synonymously.[1]

Succession, as a legal term, means an entering into the place and property rights of another. It is a mode of acquiring legal rights; a certain kind of derivative acquisition whereby the rights of one person are transferred to another, so that the latter takes the place of the former. However, not every derivative acquisition is a succession. For illustration, if A acquires from B a servitude, as, for example, a right of way over B's land, there is no succession, since the right thus acquired by A is a new right, and this right of A and the rights of B in the land are separate and different. Where, however, A acquires the ownership (the dominium) of a piece of land from B, the new owner, A, succeeds to the title of B, and a succession results.

There may be a succession to a single or a particular right of another, or to any number of such rights, including all the rights another may own, considered apart by themselves, and there may also be a succession to all the proprietary rights and duties of another considered as a whole, that is, an entire estate, including its assets and its liabilities, formerly belong-

---

[1]. As in Dig. 5, 2, 19; Cod. 6, 20, 1.

ing to another person. The former kind of succession is called "singular succession" (successio singularis or successio in singulam rem), the latter is called "universal succession" (succession universalis or successio per universitatem). The term "universitas rerum" in this connection means an aggregate of all of one's proprietary rights.[2]

Succession may take place with reference to living persons (inter vivos), or one may succeed to the property rights of a deceased person (causa mortis).

Property is acquired, says Gaius,[3] in universal succession in five ways: (1) by heirs (heredes); (2) by the praetor's equitable decree (bonorum possessio); (3) by the purchase of the estate of an insolvent (venditio bonorum); (4) by the adoption of one sui juris (arrogatio); and (5) by marriage. Justinian[4] speaks of two other ways of acquiring universal succession, one by a judgment awarding an inheritance in order to provide for the freedom of slaves (addictio bonorum libertatis causa), and the other by means of a statute known as the Senatus Consultum Claudianum.[5] A judgment awarding a universal succession in order to protect the emancipation of slaves was grantable in cases where an heir appointed by some will which set free one or more slaves, refused to serve by reason of the insolvency of the estate. In Roman Law, the "heir" named in a will was the executor, and without an "heir" or executor no will could stand, all legacies, gifts, including gifts of freedom to slaves becoming null and void. To remedy this situation, especially for the purpose of securing the liberty of the slaves set free by such a will, the magistrate could appoint

2. See Gaius 2, 97; Dig. 21, 3, 3; 23, 3, 3, 1; 29, 2, 37; 39, 2, 1; 43, 3, 1, 13.
3. Gaius 2, 98. And see Inst. 2, 9, 6; 3, 12, pr.
4. Inst. 3, 11, pr. and 1.
5. Tacitus Ann. 12, 53; Inst. 3, 12, 1.

some person as "heir" who would thus become a universal successor.[6]

The Senatus Consultum Claudianum provided that a freewoman who persistently cohabited with a slave should become also a slave of her paramour's master. With the loss of her freedom her entire property rights also passed to her owner. This barbarous law was abolished, however, by Justinian.[7]

Universal succession on the part of heirs (heredes) might take place in two ways, by intestacy, and by will.

The estate of a deceased person was regarded as an entity, a res incorporalis, which passed to his heirs. This estate, viewed as a whole (universitas), was known as hereditas.[8] It included all the rights and liabilities of the deceased, both his assets and his debts,[9] except such rights and liabilities as were personal, that is, during his life, which were terminated at his death. The person or persons who had the legal right to succeed to a decedent's estate, known as heres (heir) or heredes (heirs) under the jus civile, entered into, or succeeded to, the place of the deceased, and assumed all his rights and obligations. This entry of the heir or heirs was called an inheritance succession (successio in universum).

The term familia, or familia pecuniaque, was also sometimes employed to mean a succession, but this was in connection with an ancient form of will whereby the testator, a paterfamilias, conveyed by form of a sale (mancipatio) his family and property rights to a successor (familiae emptor).[10] This term does not necessarily refer, however, to inheritance (hereditas).

The inheritance which devolved upon an heir or

6. Inst. 3, 11, pr. and 1.
7. Inst. 3, 12, 1; Cod. 7, 24, 1.
8. Dig. 50, 16, 24.
9. Dig. 37, 1, 3, pr. and 1; 5, 3, 50, pr.
10. Gaius 2, 104; Inst. 2, 10, 1.

heirs under the law of intestacy was called hereditas legitima or ab intestato. One could dispose of all his property, if he desired, by will (testamentum), but he could not thus dispose of a part of it. A Roman could not leave a part of his estate testate and a part intestate,[11] as may be done under our law, but it had to be either testate or intestate in toto. In case he did by will name but one heir, and gave expressly only a part of his estate to such an heir, the entire estate was taken by this heir.[12]

Under the jus civile, heirs were divided into two classes, domestic heirs (heredes domestici) and extraneous heirs (heredes extranei).[13] Domestic heirs were heirs belonging to the "house" or familia of the decedent. They were also called necessary heirs (heredes necessarii) since they were not at liberty to refuse the succession. Extraneous, or outside, heirs, were heirs who were not members of the household or familia. They were also called voluntary heirs (heredes voluntarii) since they could lawfully refuse to accept the succession.

Since the succession, or inheritance, involved the liabilities as well as the assets of the deceased, an inheritance of an insolvent estate was a hardship. For this reason, heirs not of a decedent's familia were not legally required to take his place as his successors or heirs.

Domestic heirs (heredes domestici) consisted of three possible classes: (1) sui heredes or "own heirs"; (2) grandchildren whose fathers survived the decedent; and (3) slaves of a testator who were made free and also named as heirs.[14]

A testator who was insolvent sometimes appointed

11. Except a soldier, Inst. 2, 14, 5.
12. Inst. 2, 14, 5.
13. Gaius 2, 152.
14. Gaius 2, 153.

a slave as his heir. This was done, says Gaius,[15] so that if the hereditas, or estate, was not sufficient to pay the decedent's debts, the property might be sold as the property of the heir instead of as the property of the testator. In this way the testator preserved his reputation from the taint of insolvency, the ignominy attaching to the heir rather than to the testator. The slave thus set free and made an heir was a necessary heir, and therefore was required, whether he was willing or unwilling, to accept the succession.

Sui heredes consisted of children who were in the paternal power (patria potestas) of a decedent at the time of his death, also of grandchildren, or other lineal descendants, whose fathers, either by death or emancipation, in the decedent's lifetime, had ceased to be within his parental control.[16] All such heirs were both sui and necessary heirs. They were called "sui" because they were domestic heirs, and because even in the lifetime of the paterfamilias were considered, in a sort of way, owners of the property.[17]

Grandchildren, or other lineal descendants, whose fathers survived the decedent were domestic heirs but not sui heredes.

The law governing intestate succession was different in the various periods of Roman Law, and in order to obtain a general survey of this law it will be necessary to consider it as it existed under (1) the old law, that is, the jus civile; (2) under the praetorian law, when the ancient law of hereditas was supplanted by the praetorian law of bonorum possessio; and (3) under the imperial law in the time of Justinian.

One died intestate who either made no will at all, or who made an invalid will, or who made a will and revoked it, or who made a will which was set aside

15. Gaius 2, 154.
16. Gaius 2, 156.
17. Gaius 2, 157.

because it was unjust, or because the testator had undergone a change of status by capitis deminutio, or because the heir named in the will would not accept the inheritance.[18]

Under the jus civile, the law of intestate inheritance was based upon membership in the agnatic family. The "family" included adopted as well as blood children, and excluded emancipated sons and daughters married cum manu.[19] A wife married cum manu was in the same status as a daughter, and a son's wife, married cum manu, was in the status of a granddaughter.[20] In case of marriage cum manu, the widow of a paterfamilias who died intestate took the share of a child. If the wife had not been married cum manu she did not become a member of her husband's agnatic family.

By the law of the Twelve Tables, intestate succession devolved in the following order:

1. Sui Heredes.
2. Agnates of same degree.
3. The gens.

The sui heredes were the primary succession.[21] Children or grandchildren who were in the patria potestas of the decedent, and who became sui juris at his death, shared the inheritance, the children of predeceased sons taking the share (per stirpes) that would have gone to their father had he survived.[22] For example, suppose A upon his death, his wife not surviving, had left six children and six grandchildren as follows: two married sons, A and B; two unmarried sons, C and D; one daughter, E, married cum manu; one unmarried daughter F; two grandchildren

18. Inst. 3, 1, pr. And see "Testamentary Succession," post.
19. Gaius 3, 2 and 3.
20. Gaius 2, 159; 3, 3.
21. Gaius 3, 1; Inst. 3, 1, 1.
22. Gaius 3, 8; Inst. 3, 1, 6.

by one of the married sons; three grandchildren by a predeceased son, G; and one grandchild born to the married daughter, E. One of the two married sons was an adopted son, and one of the two unmarried sons, C, had been emancipated by his father. In such a case the inheritance would have passed in the following shares: one share to each of the married sons, an adopted son sharing equally with an own son; one share to D, the unmarried son; the other unmarried son, C, being by reason of his emancipation no longer in his father's agnatic family, would not be an heir; one share to the unmarried daughter, F; the other daughter by reason of her marriage cum manu would be in her husband's family; one share, the fifth share, would be divided among the three grandchildren of G, the son who had died. The two children of the married son would not be heirs, since they are not sui juris, but pass into the patria potestas of their father; the child of the married daughter would not share in any case since he belongs to another agnatic family.

The inheritance would thus be divided into five shares, A, B, D, and F each having a share, or one fifth each of the inheritance, and the three grandchildren, the children of G, would take their father's share, which would give to each of them one third of one fifth, or one fifteenth of the inheritance.

Posthumous children who would have been in the paternal power of the father had they been born during his lifetime were also heirs,[23] and an emancipated son who was manumitted after the death of his father was likewise counted as a suus heres.[24]

In case a decedent left no sui heredes, the Twelve Tables gave the inheritance to the nearest agnates.[25] Agnates (agnati) are those who are related through

23. Gaius 3, 4.
24. Gaius 3, 6.
25. Gaius 3, 9.

male ascendants, such as brothers and sisters by the same father, or such brothers' sons, or an uncle on the father's side. Persons who are related through female ascendants are cognates. For example, an uncle and his sister's son are not agnates but cognates. The children of agnatic brothers are agnates, but the children of a brother and of a sister are cognates. Likewise the son of one's aunt, whether on the father's or on the mother's side is not one's agnate but cognate. Children follow their father's family not their mother's.[26]

The nearest agnates (agnati proximi) were those agnates other than sui heredes who in case one died intestate were nearest in degree to the decedent at the time of his death.[27] In case, however, one died leaving a will, and it became ineffective for lack of an heir, the nearest agnate was not determined till it became certain there would be an intestacy. This sometimes took a long time, and meanwhile he who was the nearest agnate at the death of the testator may have died, and another person may have thereby become the nearest agnate.[28]

Brothers and sisters born of the same father as the deceased were his nearest agnates in degree. They were also called consanguinei. If there were only one brother or one sister such agnate succeeded to the entire inheritance. The nearest agnate was alone considered,[29] all those who were further removed having no claim. For example, if the deceased left a brother and a nephew by another brother predeceased, the nephew did not take his deceased father's share, but the entire inheritance went to the surviving brother.[30] Moreover, the nephew would not take even if the

26. Gaius 1, 156; 3, 10.
27. Inst. 3, 2, 6.
28. Gaius 3, 13; Inst. 3, 2, 6.
29. Gaius 3, 11.
30. Gaius 3, 15.

brother refused the inheritance (as he could since he was not a necessary heir like a suus heres), or even in case the brother died before entering upon the inheritance, because in title by agnation under the law of the Twelve Tables there was no succession, that is, the agnates of the next degree were not admitted to the inheritance.[31] If, however, there were several agnati of the same degree, several brothers and sisters for example, and any one or more of them refused to accept his share, or died before signifying his acceptance, the remaining members of the group divided equally the inheritance among them.

If the deceased left no brother or sister, then the sons of deceased brothers, but not of deceased sisters, were the nearest agnates. They did not take, however, per stirpes but per capita. For example, if there were two sons of one brother, four of another, and one of a third brother, the inheritance was divided into seven parts, each nephew taking one part.[32]

The daughters of brothers were excluded by the provisions of the ancient law which did not include within the rights of inheritance any females beyond sisters born of the same father. A sister, by the jus civile, could be the heir of a sister or of a brother by the same father, but the sister of a father or the daughter of a brother was not an heir.[33] This preference of male heirs to female heirs has its counterpart in the canons of the English law of descent.

It was the further law of the Twelve Tables that if there were no nearest agnati then the inheritance went to the gens. It has been explained in another connection that the gens included all those persons who derived their origin from some common male ancestor. They bore a common name, the middle name

31. Gaius 3, 12.
32. Gaius 3, 16.
33. Gaius 3, 14.

of the three names possessed by Romans of ancient families being known as the name of the gens. For example, Caius Julius Caesar indicated that the great Caesar was a member of the Julian line or gens. However, long before the time of Gaius the law relating to the inheritance of the gens in the absence of nearest agnates had passed away.[34]

Moreover, the law in general of the Twelve Tables governing the succession of inheritances was replaced, likewise long before the time of Gaius, by the rules laid down by the praetors in their edicts. Gaius mentions many objections that were made to the ancient laws.[35] Emancipated children, he says, had no right to their own father's estate. Agnates who had suffered capitis deminutio were not admitted, since capitis deminutio of any degree extinguished membership in the agnatic family. If the nearest agnate did not accept the inheritance, the next degree could not succeed, and female agnates, except consanguinei, that is, sisters by the same father, had no rights. Cognates, or those who are related by female ancestry, were not admitted, so that even a mother had no succession to her children or they to her, unless by her marriage by manus she had become an agnatic "sister" to them.

It was also the old law that children given to another family in adoption, or married cum manu were excluded from inheritance, and since an adopted or arrogated person was in the same status as a son born to a paterfamilias, an adopted son took in preference to an own son who had been emancipated.

However, in the course of time, the technicalities and unfairness of the old law were corrected by the praetors in the exercise of their magisterial powers.[36] Under the changes thus introduced the law known as

34. Gaius 3, 17.
35. Gaius 3, 18-24.
36. Gaius 3, 25.

praetorian succession, or bonorum possessio, became established.

Upon the origin of the law of bonorum possessio, one of the most important reforms in the history of Roman Law, the authorities have much speculated. The extant writings of the ancient jurists afford but little help in the solution of this perplexing question. Various theories have been suggested, but the matter still remains obscure. How did it happen that during the time the jus civile was yet in existence, when it was the law that governed Roman citizens, a Roman magistrate, without the aid of legislation, could award the right to the possession of an inheritance (bonorum possessio) to one who was not by law (jus civile) entitled to it? The theory that it originated in connection with the praetor's jurisdiction over intestate estates of aliens (peregrini), to whom the civil law rules of intestate succession (hereditas) did not apply, and that in awarding the succession in such cases the praetor applied the rules of natural equity, is plausible and would seem very reasonable.[37] Most authorities, however, do not take this view, but believe that the doctrine was slowly developed from its original application by the praetor to certain special cases in connection with Roman citizens and in connection with the jus civile itself. Some writers connect it with the jus civile action of petitio hereditatis, an action brought by an heir against one in possession of the inheritance for the purpose of determining the question of the legal heirship. It is suggested that the praetor gave merely temporary possession of the inheritance (bonorum possessio) to one of the claimants pending the settlement of the dispute. Others think it may have originated in cases where the inheritance had been seized by one who had no legal title, bonorum possessio

---

37. For an exposition of this view, see Hunter, Rom. Law, 4th ed. p. 846.

being temporarily granted for the purpose of preventing meanwhile any conflict over the property. The title would thus be protected against an unlawful possessor who by a year's possession (usucapio pro herede) might get a legal title to the inheritance.

It is not known when bonorum possessio was first introduced, but it was sometime during the latter half of the Republic. It was undoubtedly the recognized practice long before the time of Cicero,[38] and was probably developed by many successive praetors. When Gaius wrote in the second century of the present era, the doctrine had long been established in its perfected form.

The explanation of practically all of the changes and reforms in the old jus civile was the praetor's magisterial power to administer the law (juris dictio), and also to enforce his decrees by judicial commands under penalties imposed by him (imperium). In his administration of the law he announced by his edict the rules that were to govern the procedure of his court during his term of office. Papinian says [39] that praetorian law was introduced by the praetors for the purpose of aiding, or supplementing, or correcting the jus civile (adjuvandi, vel supplandi, vel corrigendi juris civilis gratia). Justinian says [40] that the praetor sometimes granted bonorum possessio neither for the purpose of amending nor impugning the old law, but rather for the purpose of confirming it (neque emandendi neque impugnandi, sed magis confirmandi gratia). Gaius had previously said this same thing.[41] In most instances, however, both Gaius and Justinian say, bonorum possessio was granted for the purpose of amending the ancient law.[42]

38. In Verr. 2, 1, 45, 117.
39. Dig. 1, 1, 7.
40. Inst. 3, 9, 1.
41. Gaius 3, 33b.
42. Gaius 3, 25; Inst. 3, 9, pr.

The explanation of these different purposes of the praetor in his granting bonorum possessio is found in the fact that bonorum possessio was not confined to intestate succession. What was contained in the first praetorian edict upon the subject nobody knows. The law comes down to us from a time when it had become highly developed, and at that time the praetorian edict declared that bonorum possessio would be granted in three classes of cases to those who made application, namely, (1) Contra Tabulas; (2) Secundum Tabulas; and (3) Intestati.[43]

Bonorum possessio contra tabulas or the granting of the possession of an inheritance contrary to the provisions of a will, was allowed when children, including emancipated children, had not been mentioned in the will. They had not been expressly excluded from the inheritance, but had been passed over without being named at all. The heir or heirs named in the will were not excluded by the praetor, but in addition to such heir or heirs the praetor declared that any child omitted from the will should receive jointly with them the possession of the inheritance, provided he would bring into hotchpot (bonorum collatio) with the designated heirs all property possessed by him at his father's death.[44]

Bonorum possessio secundum tabulas, or according to the will, was granted when there were no applications in behalf of such persons as the praetor would admit to the inheritance contra tabulas.[45] The praetor, moreover, gave the right of possession to the heirs named in the will even though the will was informal, or technically defective at law.[46] Possession granted according to a will which was originally not in legal

43. Gaius 2, 119, 148; 3, 25 et seq.; Inst. 3, 9, 3; Dig. 37, 1, 6, 1.
44. Dig. 37, 6; Cod. 6, 20.
45. Dig. 37, 11, 2.
46. Gaius 2, 118–122; 2, 147–151a.

form, or which was made conformably to law and afterwards was revoked or rescinded, was said to be bonorum possessio cum re, or in fact, when the possession could be successfully defended against adverse claimants.[47] If, however, the possessor could be evicted by a superior legal title the possession was said to be sine re, that is, merely nominal, or not in fact.[48] For example, an heir duly appointed by a will according to the jus civile, or one who is heir by the jus civile in case of intestacy, can evict by a superior legal (jure) title one to whom the bonorum possessio has been granted. However, should such an heir, in either case, assert no claim within the time allotted for bringing such actions, then the possession would be effective (cum re). In no case, could the possessor be deprived of the property by one having no legal title.[49]

The most important changes, however, in the ancient law of inheritance were made by the praetor in connection with the estates of persons dying intestate (bonorum possessio intestati). He declared that he would give the possession of the property to certain classes of persons according to an order of preference established by him. Some of these persons were entitled to the inheritance by the rules of the jus civile but others were not so entitled. In the case of those who were the recognized legal heirs, that is, legal according to the jus civile, the praetor's grant to them of the possession was said to be for the purpose of "aiding the civil law" (juris civilis adjuvandi gratia), but in the case of those who were not recognized as legal heirs the grant was undoubtedly for the purpose of amending or correcting the law (juris civilis corrigendi gratia).

47. Gaius 2, 148.
48. Gaius 2, 148.
49. Gaius 2, 149.

The principal classes of persons to whom the praetor in his edict declared he would give an intestate succession (bonorum possessio) were fixed by him in the following order:
1. Children (Liberi).
2. The legal or statutory heirs (Legitimi).
3. Cognates (Cognati).
4. Husband and wife (Vir et uxor).

These four did not comprise all the classes specified by the praetor but they covered the law of intestate succession relating to free persons. Justinian mentions eight classes contained in the praetorian edicts but four of these applied only to freedmen.[50] The above four principal classes are cited by the Roman Law writers as "unde liberi," "unde legitimi," "unde cognati," and "unde vir et uxor," respectively, the same being abbreviations of "ea pars edicti unde liberi (or unde legitimi, or unde cognati, or unde vir et uxor) vocantur," meaning "that part of the edict where the children (etc.) are named."

The four classes thus designated by the praetor were admitted to the succession in the order enumerated. The liberi, or children, had the first right. In case there was no claimant in this class, then the legitimi, or the heirs designated by the old law, the jus civile, were next entitled. Legitimi failing, then cognates were next in order, and if there were no cognates within the degrees recognized, then husband and wife (vir et uxor), that is, those married without manus, were permitted to inherit, the one from the other, reciprocally.

A formal application (agnitio) to the praetor was necessary in order to obtain the award of the possession of the property. Parents and children were given a year in which to make their claims; other persons

---

50. Inst. 3, 9, 3.

were given a hundred days.[51] No claimant appearing in a preceding class within the limitation designated, claimants in the next succeeding order could apply.[52]

To the applicant, or applicants, in the order specified the praetor merely gave the right to the possession of the property. The bonorum possessor did not, by the praetor's decree, get the legal title (that is, title by the jus civile) to the inheritance, but merely an equitable title, otherwise called a "bonitary" title.[53] Persons given this equitable right of possession did not thereby become the "legal heirs" (heredes), for the praetor could not make any one an "heir" (heres), since only a statute, or a decree of the senate, or an imperial constitution could do that,[54] but they did become the possessors of the equitable right to the inheritance which right was protected and enforced by the praetorian interdict known as quorum bonorum.

To modern American lawyers, there is nothing strange or unusual in such a judicial procedure. The same principle was followed centuries later in the English Court of Chancery whereby, under various circumstances, one person was declared to have an equitable right to the possession of certain property although the technical legal title might be held by another. The Roman praetor's decree in connection with the right of possession of an intestate inheritance extended by means of equity (ex bono et aequo), says Justinian,[55] the rules of succession which by the law of the Twelve Tables were limited by very narrow bounds.

The person who applied to the praetor for the right of possession (bonorum possessio) might already be in possession of the property, or the actual possession

51. Inst. 3, 9, 8.
52. Inst. 3, 9, 9.
53. Gaius 3, 80.
54. Gaius 3, 32; Inst. 3, 9, 2.
55. Inst. 3, 9, 2.

[Roman Law]—36

might be in some other person. The interdict quorum bonorum,[56] already mentioned, was issued only when the successful applicant was not in possession, either in whole or in part, and its purpose was to compel some other person, who either as heir or as a mere possessor did have possession of all or of a part of the inheritance, to deliver the same to the bonorum possessor.[57] One was said to possess as heir (pro herede) who considered himself to be the heir, and one was said to possess as a mere possessor (pro possessore) who with no legal inheritable right, and knowing that the property did not belong to him, nevertheless had control of the whole or a part of the inheritance.[58]

The praetor's decree giving an applicant the right of inheritance was not, however, final. It was temporary or provisional, a sort of interlocutory or an interim order. Although the equitable right was protected by the interdict quorum bonorum, yet the final validity of the bonorum possessio depended upon the fact that there was no subsequent showing of a superior right in another person. If the bonorum possessor could successfully maintain his right against one claiming by the jus civile, the grant of the possession was said to be real or final (cum re), but if he were compelled to yield his right to one having a superior claim it was said to be merely nominal (sine re). If the bonorum possessor was not ousted by a superior title within the time specified by law his equitable title became a legal title by usucaption.[59] During the period of his praetorian possession, the possessor had the right to sue for the recovery of claims due the inheritance, and he was also subject to be sued by its creditors. However, since his title was equitable and

56. The form of this interdict is given in Dig. 4, 3, 2, 1, pr.
57. Inst. 4, 15, 3.
58. Inst. 4, 15, 3; Dig. 5, 3, 11–13.
59. Gaius 3, 80.

not legal, he could neither sue nor be sued as the legal heir by means of direct or legal actions. No debtor was bound by the jus civile to pay him, neither could he claim to be the legal owner of the property of the intestate. The praetor, however, permitted equitable actions (actiones utiles) to be employed in such cases by means of a fiction, whereby the judex was instructed to give judgment "just as if the bonorum possessor were the legal heir."[60]

It is very possible, and even probable, that the origin of the law of praetorian intestate succession was connected with disputes in early times between opposing claimants, and that the praetor, following the jus civile, awarded the inheritance to the person or persons who satisfactorily proved to be the legal heir or heirs. In the course of time, for the doctrine of bonorum possessio was doubtless of slow development, the praetor probably extended, in the spirit of fairness and equity (ex bono et aequo), the meaning of heirs (sui heredes), and, perhaps, still later admitted cognates to the succession upon the failure of agnates. When the doctrine became fully developed, there were then two ways or means by which title to an intestate inheritance might be obtained, one by the legal title of the jus civile, the other by means of the equitable title in accord with the praetor's edict, or bonorum possessio.

The praetor sometimes granted bonorum possessio to one who already had the legal title and in such cases the two titles were merged. At other times, the possession was granted to one who did not have the legal title, and in those cases the possessor might or might not be evicted by one who had the legal title. At times, the legal title holder stood upon his legal rights, and made no effort to apply for the praetorian possession of the property. At other times, and prob-

60. Gaius 3, 81; 4, 34; Dig. 43, 2, 2.

ably very frequently, persons who might be entitled to an inheritance by the jus civile did make application for the praetorian possession, finding it to their advantage to do so since they could thereby much more speedily get actual possession of the property, and could protect that possession by means of the interdictum quorum bonorum which applied only to cases of bonorum possessio. It thus very probably resulted that the praetorian rules of succession were generally accepted, in time, as more satisfactory and beneficial to all concerned.

Under the later development of bonorum possessio in imperial times, no formal or express demand for the possession was required. Any act within the permitted time showing that one had the intention to claim the possession was sufficient.[61] The possessor was given by means of the possessory action petitio hereditatis the same remedies as a legal heir,[62] and, finally, Justinian by imperial constitution gave to the possessor the legal title.[63]

Of the praetor's eight classes of intestate succession four, as already stated, applied to free persons and four to freedmen.[64] The four classes of free born persons (ingenui), namely, (1) liberi, (2) legitimi, (3) cognati, and (4) vir et uxor, need only be considered, since in the time of Justinian they were the only classes recognized owing to the fact that the successions of freedmen (libertini) and free born persons had become substantially the same.[65]

Liberi:

The first persons admitted by the praetor to an intestate inheritance were "liberi," that is, "children" or

61. Inst. 3, 9, 10.
62. Dig. 5, 5.
63. Inst. 3, 9, pr.
64. Inst. 3, 9, 3.
65. Inst. 3, 9, 4–6.

"descendants." This class took the place of the sui heredes, the first successors under the jus civile. The term "liberi," however, was more comprehensive than sui heredes. The latter consisted of a deceased person's children together with the children of his predeceased sons. A deceased person's "children" included, as previously stated, his sons and unmarried daughters, his widow (if in manu at her husband's death) and adopted children (in potestate).[66] The praetorian term "liberi" included all these and, in addition, emancipated sons.[67] The representatives of a predeceased son took their father's share, that is, per stirpes. An emancipated son was required to bring into hotchpot (collatio bonorum) whatever property he possessed in order that it might be divided as a part of the inheritance.[68]

Legitimi:

The second group of successors was known as "legitimi," that is, the "legal" or statutory heirs of the jus civile known as agnates.[69] This group succeeded only in case there were no successors who claimed as members of the first class (liberi), and they took, as under the jus civile, according to the degree of their agnatic relationship, that is, the proximi, or nearest, agnates. Sui heredes who had not applied for the bonorum possessio within the year allowed for such an application were permitted by the praetor to apply as members of this second class.

Cognati:

The third class to whom the praetor gave the bonorum possessio was called cognati,[70] that is, persons

---

66. Children who had been given to another for adoption were not included. They were classed among "cognati."
67. Gaius 3, 26.
68. Dig. 37, 6, 1, pr.
69. Inst. 3, 9, 3.
70. Inst. 3, 5, pr.

who were related by consanguinity with the intestate. This class was permitted to petition for the inheritance only in case there were no claimants in either of the two preceding classes. Cognate successors were previously unknown in Roman Law. Agnates, as already stated, were those persons who were members of the same agnatic family, those who were connected by the tie of a common paterfamilias, even though the original head of the family had long since deceased. Cognates were those who were related by the tie of blood. The daughter of a paterfamilias was his agnate, for example, as long as she remained unmarried, but upon her marriage she passed into the arnatic family of her husband. She remained, however, irrespective of her marriage, a cognate of her father. Likewise, the son of a father's sister was not an agnate of the father's son, but he was a cognate.[71]

Cognates included all descendants, irrespective of their being married (if females), or being emancipated, or given in adoption,[72] likewise female agnates beyond the degree of sisters.[73] Persons who were related by the ties of maternal blood only were also cognates, although they were not agnates.[74] Consequently, as a cognate, a child could inherit from its mother or a mother from her child.[75] Under the jus civile, only the proximi agnates were admitted to the succession, but by the praetorian law more remote agnates, who were thus excluded by the jus civile, might be eligible to succeed as cognates.[76]

Agnates might be admitted to an inheritance, both by the law of the Twelve Tables and by the praetor's edict relating to "legitimi," in any degree however

71. Inst. 1, 14, 1; 3, 2, 4.
72. Gaius 3, 27 and 31.
73. Gaius 3, 29.
74. Gaius 3, 30.
75. Inst. 3, 3, pr.
76. Inst. 3, 2, 7.

remote, providing such degree was the nearest (proximus);[77] but cognates, while also admitted according to proximity, were recognized only as far as the sixth degree, except in case of consobrini, that is, children of a second cousin, who were admitted to the seventh degree.[78]

Degrees of cognatic relationship are reckoned, in Roman Law, in the case of lineals by counting the number of generations. Accordingly, a father and son are related in the first degree, a grandfather and grandson in the second degree, a great grandfather and great grandson in the third degree, and so on. Collateral degrees are reckoned by counting upwards, from either of the two collaterals, to the common ancestor, and then downwards to the other collateral, counting a degree for each generation both ascending and descending. In other words, the sum of the two lines is counted. Accordingly, brothers are related in the second degree, an uncle and a nephew in the third degree, first cousins in the fourth degree, second cousins in the sixth degree. To his second cousin's children (consobrini) a man is related in the seventh degree.[79] This rule of the Roman and the modern Civil Law, which is different from the Canon Law rule,[80] has been adopted by most of our American jurisdictions.[81]

Under the praetorian law of Rome, cognates who

77. Inst. 3, 6, 12; 3, 5, 5, (where the text says "even to the tenth degree," but merely as an illustration).
78. Inst. 3, 5, 5.
79. Inst. 3, 6.
80. The method of computing degrees in the Canon Law, adopted into the English Common Law, is to begin with the common ancestor and count downwards, separately, to each of the two collaterals in question, and in whatever degree the two persons or the more remote are distant from the common ancestor, that is the degree in which they are related. 2 Blk. Com. 206–207.
81. In re Nigro, 172 Cal. 474; Campbell's Appeal, 64 Conn. 277; Lyon v. Crego, 187 Mich. 625. In a few states the Canon, or Common Law rule, has been adopted by statute. Ector v. Grant, 112 Ga. 557; Paul v. Carter, 153 N. C. 26.

were nearest in blood to the deceased, providing there were no claimants, as already stated, among the classes called "liberi" and "legitimi," shared per capita. The doctrine of representation (per stirpes) did not apply. The time of determining what cognates were nearest (proximi) was not at the death of the deceased but at the time the bonorum possessio was given to them.

Vir et Uxor:

The fourth and last class of praetorian successors were husband and wife (vir et uxor) providing the marriage had been without manus.[82] A widow who had been married with manus (cum manu) was placed in the praetor's first class of successors, "liberi," and was permitted to apply for the succession as a daughter of her husband, or as a sister to her children. In marriage, however, without manus a widow was admitted to the succession (under the praetorian law) only after there were no claimants in any of the three preceding classes, the liberi, legitimi, and cognati. The rights of succession of husband and wife were reciprocal, the survivor being the successor in absence of claimants in the preceding classes. There being no claiming survivor in this fourth and last class the succession escheated to the public treasury (fiscus).[83]

The praetorian law of succession was amended in some particulars, in imperial times, by special legislation. The Emperor Claudius enacted that a mother could succeed to the legal inheritance of her deceased children, as a consolation for their loss[84] By the praetorian law, a mother could succeed only as a cognate,

---

82. It has been previously pointed out that as early as the Twelve Tables there might be a jus civile marriage without manus (per trinoctium), and that in consensual marriage the doctrine of manus gradually disappeared.

83. Code 6, 18, 1.

84. Inst. 3, 3, 1.

that is, a member of the third class.[85] The Senatus Consultum Tertullianum, passed in the reign of Hadrian, provided, however, that mothers, but not grandmothers, should have the right of succeeding to their children, providing that a mother, born of free parents, had three children, or a freedwoman had four children.[86] In 178 A. D., the Senatus Consultum Orphitianum, in the reign of Marcus Aurelius, gave children the right to succeed to the estates of their intestate mothers thus permitting children to succeed a mother, as "liberi," the same as in the case of succession to a father. Previously children, so far as succession to a mother was concerned, were in the third class, the cognati.[87] Later constitutions of Valentinian, Theodosius, and Arcadius, provided that grandchildren might be called to the legal succession of grandparents on the mother's side, or of a grandmother on the father's side.[88] In 503 A. D., a constitution of Anastasius allowed emancipated brothers and sisters to inherit as agnati, that is, in the second class (legitimi), instead of being placed, as formerly, in the third class (cognati).[89]

In the reign of Justinian other changes were made by that emperor in the law of the praetorian bonorum possessio. He retained the four classes of successors, liberi, legitimi, cognati, and vir et uxor, but the rules governing the order of succession were amended by various enactments. A mother was given the right to inherit from her children regardless of the previous law limiting this right to free born mothers of three children, and freed mothers of four children.[90]

85. Inst. 3, 3, pr.
86. Inst. 3, 3, 2.
87. Inst. 3, 4, pr. Even children of unknown fathers could inherit from their mothers by this law. Inst. 3, 4, 3.
88. Inst. 3, 4, 1; Cod. 6, 55, 9.
89. Inst. 3, 5, 1; Cod. 6, 58, 11.
90. Cod. 8, 58, 2.

Legitimi, or agnates, were extended to include a deceased person's mother, brothers and sisters of the whole or half blood (whether agnates or cognates), and the children of deceased brothers and sisters. The descendants of a daughter or sister were permitted to succeed to her regardless of the exclusion of agnates.[91] Justinian also gave to agnates, previously limited to the proximi, the same right to succeed in successive grades as the praetor gave to cognates.[92]

However, the Roman world had now reached an age when the many details and complications of the praetorian succession had become impractical. The old distinctions between agnates and cognates were rapidly disappearing, and it was by no means a simple matter to determine in just what class of successors the possible various claimants came. Moreover, the ancient law of hereditas, the law of the jus civile, still existed, never having been repealed, and, in theory, and also in practice in some instances, there were yet two methods of intestate inheritance, the strictly legal method of the old law (hereditas) and the equitable method of the praetorian law (bonorum possessio).

The praetorian law of intestate succession had been the law of Rome for centuries. It was a great improvement upon the ancient law, but, in its turn, it had served its purpose and was now unsuited to the changed conditions of society.

Justinian, therefore, resolved to change the whole system, and, in the year 543, his famous enactment (the 118th Novel) was promulgated. He states in the opening lines of this Novel[93] that its purpose is to correct the existing complexity, confusion, and artificiality of the law of succession, and to base it upon the natural law of blood relationship (cognitio) rather

---

91. Cod. 6, 55, 12.
92. Inst. 3, 7, 2; Cod. 6, 4, 4, 20.
93. Nov. 118, pr.

than upon the law of agnation (agnatio). In fact, he repealed all the old law relating to the succession of agnates, except in the case of adopted children whose rights to the succession of an adopted father remained.

Justinian also repealed the law of succession set forth in his Institutes, and made four new classes of heirs. His new laws of succession applied to all property, both movable and immovable, and were as follows:

I. Descendants:

Upon the death of an intestate, whether man or woman, the descendants, whether male or female, and whether affected by loss of agnatic family or not (that is, whether a daughter was married by manus, or a child adopted, into another family) took the inheritance. Adopted children were treated the same as children by birth. It thus resulted that an adopted child could succeed to both parents, to his own father by blood (cognation) and to his adoptive father by agnation. This, however, was the last trace of agnation left in Justinian's law. Descendants in the first degree took per capita, but descendants of remoter degrees took per stirpes.[94] Thus, if A died leaving one living child B, and two children of a deceased child C, and three children of another deceased child D, A would take one-third of the inheritance, each of the children of C would take one-sixth, and each of the children of D would take one-ninth.

II. Ascendants and Brothers and Sisters of Whole Blood:

If there were no descendants, then the intestate inheritance passed to the nearest ascendants and brothers and sisters of the whole blood.[95] In case there were ascendants only, one-half passed to the paternal and one-half to the maternal ascendants. In case of

---

94. Nov. 118, 1.
95. Nov. 118, 2.

ascendants and also brothers and sisters, or in case there were only brothers and sisters, the inheritance passed to them equally per capita.[96] By a later constitution,[97] Justinian provided that the children of a deceased brother or sister should take their parent's share, that is, per stirpes. Thus, suppose A died leaving a father, mother, one brother, and one sister. Each of these would take one-fourth. In case A died leaving a grandfather, and a grandmother on the father's side, a mother, a brother, and two children of a deceased sister, each of the grandparents would take one-eighth, the mother and the brother a fourth each, and the children of the deceased sister one-eighth each.

III. Brothers and Sisters of the Half Blood:

Failing any successors in both the preceding classes, the inheritance went to brothers and sisters of the half-blood, including brothers and sisters by adoption. These took per capita, the children of a deceased member of this group[98] taking a parent's share per stirpes.[99]

IV. All Remaining Collaterals:

There being none to take in any of the three preceding classes, then all remaining collaterals who were nearest in degree, including both whole and half blood, shared equally, provided that they were all of the same degree. Children of a predeceased collateral of the same degree did not, however, share in the inheritance. The rule, under the praetorian law, as to the sixth and seventh degrees of cognatic inheritance, was repealed, the nearest collaterals of any degree being entitled to the succession.[100]

The 118th Novel made no provision for the succession of a husband to his wife or of a wife to her hus-

96. Nov. 118, 3, pr; 118, 4.
97. Nov. 127, 1.
98. Nov. 118, 3, pr.
99. Nov. 118, 3, pr.
100. Nov. 118, 3, 1.

band. Only those persons who were related by blood were included in this law. However, the praetorian law of bonorum possessio remained as to the right of a husband or of a wife to succeed to the other, in case there were no cognatic, or blood-related, successors. If there were any successor in any of the preceding classes, including collaterals however remote, neither had the right to inherit from the other. The explanation of this apparently harsh law lay in the fact that it was the custom of the Romans to provide a dowry for a bride, and, also, at the marriage a settlement was often made by the husband upon his wife. Justinian, however, provided that in case a widow had no dowry, no means of her own, she should be entitled to a fourth part of her husband's property. The same rule applied to a widower who was in need.[101] This law is often cited as "the marital portion," or "the marital fourth." [102] This right of a widow was amended by a later law of Justinian [103] which gave to her, in case there were more than three children, only an equal portion with them. Accordingly, by this law, if there were five children the widow received one-sixth; if there were not more than three children, or no children at all, she received one-fourth as previously. It was a further provision of this later law that the widow's share, in case there were children, was but a usufruct for life, the ownership (dominium), or "fee" as we say, being in the children.

This provision of the Roman Law for the benefit of the widow has been preserved in the modern Civil Law. Upon this "marital fourth" doctrine the supreme court of Louisiana has said: [104] "The spirit which inspired the legislation originally in Rome, in

101. Nov. 53, 6.
102. Smith v. Smith, 43 La. Ann. 1140.
103. Nov. 117, 5.
104. Succession of Justus, 44 La. Ann. 721.

France, and in Spain, and which dictated its insertion in the body of laws which govern Louisiana, was that where the husband or wife dies rich, without issue, leaving the survivor in a state of penury, the latter shall have the right to take from the succession of the deceased one-fourth of its residue, in full property, after payments of the debts, in order that he or she may not, after a life of ease and comfort, be suddenly thrown into abject poverty." [105]

Students of English real property law will not fail to see also in this Roman Law provision for a widow a striking analogy to the law of dower. The analogy is even greater when we consider that, like unto dower, the widow's portion in the Roman Law was a vested right, a right created by law, and could not be taken from her by the will of her husband. There is also an analogy to our Common Law of curtesy in the surviving husband's reciprocal right to a share in his deceased wife's property. However, an English writer [106] is of the opinion that the English law of curtesy is possibly an application of the law of Constantine [107] as to a child's peculium adventitium, the property that came to a child through its mother's will or by her death intestate. This law gave to a father a life interest (usufructus) in all the property of his children thus acquired by them. However, by a constitution of Arcadius and Honorius, this usufruct of a father applied to all property of children coming from any degree of maternal ancestors,[108] and Justinian enacted that whatever a son acquired by any means, except through his father, should be subject to his father's usufruct.[109]

105. See Rev. Civ. Code (La.) art. 2382; Pelloat's Succession, 127 La. 873; Crockett v. Madison, 118 La. 728; Kunemann's Succession, 115 La. 604, 613.
106. Scrutton, Rom. Law and The Law of England.
107. Cod. 6, 60, 1.
108. Cod. 6, 60, 2.
109. Inst. 2, 9, 1.

This life estate of the father was, however, only a limitation placed upon the father's ancient right of absolute property, under the doctrine of patria potestas in property acquired by those in his power, and it is doubtful whether it is a forerunner of our law of curtesy.

By the Justinian law, the reciprocal rights of husband and wife to succeed to an intestate spouse was the last possible succession. This failing, an intestate estate escheated to the public treasury (fiscus).

The Roman Law of intestate succession as enacted by Justinian has had great influence upon our own modern law of descent and distribution. The English canons of descent, based upon the feudal law, applied to real but not to personal property. The Roman Law, however, regulated intestate succession of both kinds of property, movable as well as immovable.[110] The English statute of distribution of personal property was borrowed to a large extent from the 118th Novel of Justinian,[111] and in our own country, our statutes of both descent and distribution are mainly based upon this same Novel rather than upon the English Common Law rules which were not in harmony with our general system of laws, or adapted to our views of equality.[112]

"Justinian's celebrated 118th Novel has become," said the supreme court of Missouri,[113] "as it were, the law of the civilized world, on account, we may suppose, of its expressing the general sentiment of mankind

---

110. Rountree v. Pursell, 11 Ind. App. 522.

111. Carter v. Crawley, T. Raym, 496, 83 Eng. Reprint 259. In re Curry, 39 Cal. 529; In re Lander, 100 Misc. Rep. (N. Y.) 635.

112. Bates v. Brown, 5 Wall. (U. S.) 710; Wall v. Pfanschmidt, 265 Ill. 180, 184; Decoster v. Wing, 76 Me. 450; Sheffield v. Lovering, 12 Mass. 490; Prescott v. Carr, 29 N. H. 453; McKinney v. Abbott, 49 Tex. 371.

113. Cutter v. Waddingham, 22 Mo. 206, 259. And see Kelsey v. Hardy, 20 N. H. 479.

in reference to the distribution of a man's property after his death. The great difference between the Roman and the English laws of descent is, that the former looked alone to the intestate, and called his kindred to his succession according to their proximity of relationship, the nearer excluding the more remote, without any reference to the source from which the property was derived. The Common Law, proceeding upon feudal reasons, after the descendants of the last owner were exhausted, looked to the source from which the property came, and by its sixth canon . . . excluded all the collateral kindred of the last proprietor that were not of the full blood of the intestate. Again, the Roman Law, still proceeding upon the same principle, called the three principle lines of kindred to the inheritance in order of natural affection: first, lineal descendants, then lineal ascendants, and lastly, collaterals; while the Common Law, upon the same feudal reasons, excluded the lineal ascendants. The Civil Law, therefore, paid no regard to the line from which the property came, nor to quantity of blood, except in the case of brothers and sisters of the whole blood, and their descendants, who took before and to the exclusion of the brothers and sisters of the half blood."

In concluding this chapter upon intestate inheritance, it is pertinent to add that even inheritance taxes, or rather taxes on the right of succession are traceable to the Roman Law. Such taxes were imposed by the Romans and from them the policy has been extended to the Civil Law countries of continental Europe, to England, to our federal government and to many of our individual states.[114]

---

114. Gibbon, Decline and Fall of Rom. Emp. I, 163-4; State v. Alston, 94 Tenn. 674; Magoun v. Illinois Trust and Savings Bank, 170 U. S. 283; Knowlton v. Moore, 178 U. S. 43.

CHAPTER XXI

THE LAW OF SUCCESSION, *continued*

Testamentary Succession

A will has often been defined in our own law, as a disposition of one's property to take effect after his death. A more satisfactory definition is given in an English work [1] which says that "a will (or testament) is the declaration in a prescribed manner of the intention of the person making it, with regard to matters which he wishes to take effect upon or after his death." This definition of a will corresponds very closely to the definition of a will (testamentum) in the Roman Law which defines a testamentum as "the declaration in a form prescribed by law (justa sententia) of one's will (voluntas) concerning that which he wishes to be done after his death." [2] It is not necessary even in our law that a will should dispose of any property. It may merely appoint an executor, a guardian for some minor child, or may merely revoke a former will. In the Roman Law, the object of a will was not the disposal of property but the appointment of an heir or successor of the testator.

The term testament, from the Latin testamentum, does not mean, as sometimes erroneously supposed, a declaration established by other persons as witnesses (testes), but is derived, says Justinian,[3] from two words, testatio and mentis, meaning a declaration in evidence of, or in witness of, one's own intention.

---

1. Laws of Eng., Vol. 28, 505.
2. Modestinus, in Dig. 28, 1, 1.
3. Inst. 2, 10, pr.

In other words, it is the declaration in the form and manner prescribed by law, of the declarant's intent that constitutes his "testamentum."

The disposal of a man's property after his death in accordance with his expressed will or intent is not a natural right, but a privilege given to him by law. In our own system of jurisprudence while folkland could be devised by will in Anglo Saxon days in England, yet under the feudal system there was no general power to devise lands. Such a power was opposed to the policy of holding lands inalienable without the consent of the lord.[4] In the time of Henry II, only one-third of one's personal property could be disposed of by will, the other two-thirds going to the widow and children.[5] Even the famous Statute of Wills in the reign of Henry VIII,[6] although giving power to devise lands held in socage, placed restrictions upon the power to devise lands held by knight service.

The supposition, expressed by some, that the right of testamentary disposition is an incident of the right of property, is, therefore, erroneous. In fact, the very notion of individual ownership in things either movable or immovable was an evolution. Primitive men did not hold things in individual and exclusive control but only in common with other members of the tribe, clan, or group to which they belonged. In time, the power of a strong man to hold for himself alone what had previously been regarded as the common possession of several or of all, gave him the recognized mastery, dominion, or "ownership" of the thing. In further time, ownership, originally enjoyed by the powerful few, became gradually the recognized right of many.

---

4. Magoun v. Bank, 170 U. S. 283; United States v. Fox, 94 U. S. 315; In re Fox, 52 N. Y. 530, 533.
5. Glanville, 7, 5.
6. 32 Hen. VIII, A. D. 1540.

[Roman Law]

In the development of Roman Law, the things we call property belonged in early times to the family, the "family" in the Roman sense, the familia, and in more primitive times all things belonged to the gens. It was a community ownership, evolving in time to a possession and control on the part of the head of the family, the paterfamilias, and, finally, the things which were possessed and controlled by him were regarded as being owned by him. The ancient law of intestate succession, first to the sui heredes, then to the nearest agnates, and then to the gens, probably was based upon the theory of the progressive steps of ownership in the history of the Roman people.

Ownership and property have become synonymous terms. The original meaning of "property"[7] is one's exclusive right to, in, and over a thing. It is a bundle or collection of rights. It is in a secondary sense that the word "property" is applied, generally, to the thing itself over which the right is exercised.

Even after property, or individual ownership, had become recognized, first, as a privilege of the few, and then as a custom of the many, human laws regulated the rights of owners in their use of things over which they claimed dominion, and even declared who should have any such rights at all. Ownership was not regarded as a natural right, not an inherent right of a human being, but only of such human beings as those who made the laws were pleased to recognize. Slaves had no legal rights at all, and, therefore, no rights of property. Likewise, among all primitive peoples, after they had established laws, or rules for their mutual protection and comfort, property rights were further restricted by considerations of sex and childhood. Even in the case of those recognized as having full rights of ownership, those rights were limited to a man's lifetime. Neither to the law of nature, nor to

---

7. From Latin "proprius," belonging to one, one's own.

the early law of man, did it seem comprehensible that any legal rights could exist longer than the span of a human life.

Accordingly, when a man died being at his death the possessor of property, the law, and this law was again very slowly developed, declared who should be his successor in its ownership. Such laws of successorship developed long before the evolution of any privilege granted to an individual to predetermine for himself to whom the things he owned during his life should be given upon his death.

However, the privilege of declaring one's will or intent concerning the disposal of his possessions after his death, became recognized in time among many ancient peoples. In the time of the patriarchal Hebrews, Abraham,[8] and Isaac,[9] and Jacob [10] made various declarations concerning the inheritances that were to pass to their sons who were regarded as their fathers' heirs; and Solon, who was born about 640 B. C., is reputed to have introduced wills among the Athenians.[11]

Blackstone says [12] that wills were unknown in Rome till the laws of the Twelve Tables were compiled. This statement, however, is historically incorrect. Wills were in use among the Romans, even before the period of the Twelve Tables. The privilege of a paterfamilias to declare his will concerning his property after his death is recognized by the Twelve Tables,[13] but this provision was only declaratory of existing custom.[14]

8. Gen. 15, 2–4; 25, 5.
9. Gen. 27.
10. Gen. 48.
11. Plato, de Leg. 11, 679; Plutarch, Solon, 90.
12. Blk. Com., II, 491.
13. Table V, 4; Dig. 50, 16, 120.
14. The words of the Twelve Tables are "Uti legassit suae rei, ita jus esto" (As one shall have bequeathed his property, so shall it be the law). It is generally accepted that this provision merely confirmed the previous practice.

In the Roman Law, the fundamental purpose of a will (testamentum) was to appoint, or, as the Roman lawyers said, to "institute" an heir. "The institution of an heir," says Gaius,[15] "is the source and foundation of a will, because a will derives its validity by the fact of the institution of an heir." Probably the original idea of a will among the Romans was to provide a successor (heres) for a Roman citizen who had no heir of his own (suus heres), that is, no son or descendant of a son in his potestas. The immemorial law of intestate succession in such a case gave the inheritance to the nearest agnates, and, failing agnates, the inheritance went to the gens.[16] In many instances such a failure of an immediate heir or successor was undoubtedly both a disappointment and a hardship. Plans were wrecked and possessions scattered. In the Roman Law, the term "heir" (heres) meant something entirely different from the word "heir" in our Common Law. In our law an heir is he upon whom the law casts the descent of the estate in lands, tenements, or hereditaments. In the Roman Law, an heir is one's successor, he takes the place of the deceased, inheriting all the rights and all the liabilities of the deceased, the assets and also the debts, even though the deceased left nothing but debts. In Roman Law, an heir was one who succeeded either by intestacy or by will, and he succeeded to all kinds of property alike, both immovable and movable. The heir was not only the personal representative of the deceased, his administrator or his executor, but he was also, in many respects, legally identical with the deceased. The heir carried on just where the deceased left off, for the theory of a Roman inheritance (hereditas) like that of an established monarchy was a series of continuous successions. It never died. As previously stated in another

15. Gaius 2, 229.
16. See preceding chapter.

connection, the status of a hereditas jacens, as the estate of a deceased person was called in the case of a merely voluntary heir pending its acceptance by such heir has caused some perplexity. Even as in the old English law the question of seisin of an inheritable estate before the entry of the heir presented some difficulty, so some civilians have called a hereditas jacens a person, while others merely regard it as representing for the time being the person of the undetermined heir.[17]

Forms of Wills:

In primitive times there were two kinds of wills among the Romans, one known as the testamentum calatis comitiis, the other as the testamentum in procinctu.[18]

The testamentum in calatis comitiis was probably the oldest form. The assembly (comitia) was the comitia curiata in which the heads of families (patresfamilias) assembled according to their respective curiae. It was specially called together (calata) twice a year for the purpose of giving efficacy to wills.[19] A will, therefore, in these primitive days of Rome was an act of special legislation, a public act whereby the usual and regular law of succession was, in an approved case, set aside and another order of succession permitted. Nothing is known as to the procedure in such cases, and wills of this sort must have been confined to the early days when the population of the city was comparatively small, and when, probably, the applicant and the circumstances of the case were known to the assembled people. In fact, many authorities are of the opinion that the testamentum calatis comitiis was a legislative act sanc-

17. Chapter X, Artificial Persons, or Corporations; Dig. 46, 1, 22; 46, 2, 24.
18. Gaius 2, 101; Inst. 2, 10, 1.
19. Gaius 2, 101.

tioning the adoption of a son by a person who had no son of his own rather than a will in its ordinary meaning.

The second ancient form of a will was known as a testamentum in procinctu, or a will declared by a soldier before going into battle, the word "procinctus," according to Gaius,[20] meaning an army ready for battle (armatus expeditusque). This was a special privilege given to military men who, on the verge of battle, were permitted to name, in the presence of witnesses, the person whom they wished to make their heir. This particular form of a will was obsolete long before Gaius wrote, being replaced by other forms of military wills.

Another form of early Roman will, but not so ancient as the preceding two, was the testamentum per aes et libram (by bronze and scales).[21] One who had not made a will either in the comitia calata or in procinctu could, in apprehension of death, convey his family property (familia) to some friend who was requested to carry out, after the death of the testator, his wishes as to the distribution of his property. This form of a will was a transaction inter vivos, and is known as the mancipative will since it was made by mancipation, that is, a sale per aes et libram.[22] The "purchaser" of the estate, called the familiae emptor, took the place of an heir (locum heredis),[23] and was like unto an executor in our law. This method of making a will superseded the old forms of wills but was itself modified in the course of time. In the days of Gaius, the ancient form of mancipation per aes et libram was still in use merely to give validity to the proceedings, but the person named as heir was a dif-

20. Gaius 2, 101; Inst. 2, 10, 1.
21. Gaius 2, 102; Inst. 2, 10, 1.
22. Gaius 2, 102.
23. Gaius 2, 103.

ferent person from the familiae emptor.[24] The testator having written his will summoned five witnesses (all being Roman citizens fourteen years old at least) and a libripens, as in the case of an ordinary mancipation. The estate was sold pro forma to a friend, still called the familiae emptor, who made declaration that he accepted it in order to make the transaction legal. Then, the testator holding the tablets upon which his will was written said: "This estate as written in these tablets I so give and declare and testify, and do you, citizens (meaning the five witnesses) bear witness for me." These words were called the testator's public declaration (nuncupatio) and by them whatever the testator had specifically written upon the tablets was said to be published and confirmed.[25]

The ancient wills known as comitiis calatis and in procinctu were public wills, that is, wills whose validity depended upon the publicity given to an oral declaration. The mancipative will was the first form of a private will, the forerunner of wills in the modern sense. Under the earlier mancipative will the familiae emptor acted as heir (in loco heredis), but in the later form the heir was named in the written instrument although his name was not necessarily published until the will was opened after the death of the testator. In either case, the sale, the mancipation of the estate, was intended to be fictitious, merely a formal transaction between faithful friends, and the testator retained the property during his life, and, if it proved desirable, the property could be remancipated to him again, and other disposition made of it.

Just when the testamentum per aes et libram became obsolete is not known. The first two forms of wills,

24. Gaius 2, 103.
25. Gaius 2, 104.

says Justinian,[26] disappeared in ancient times, and the third form, the testamentum per aes et libram, was not commonly used. The reason was that a new kind of will had gradually taken the place of the mancipative will, and generally known as the praetorian will, in distinction from the three earlier forms already mentioned which were jus civile wills.[27] Instead of being, however, a different form of will, the so-called praetorian will was rather the praetor's judicial declaration as to what should be construed as a will in his court. As stated in the previous chapter,[28] the praetorian doctrine of bonorum possessio, or the awarding of the right of the possession of an inheritance, was not confined to intestate successions but applied also to cases known as contra tabulas and secundum tabulas. In other words, the praetor in some cases granted the possession of an inheritance contrary to the provisions of a will, and in other cases according to the provisions of a will even though the will was informal or technically defective by the jus civile. The praetor declared that if the tablets of a will were attested by the seals of seven witnesses he would grant the possession of the inheritance to the persons named in the will.[29] Accordingly, the so-called praetorian will, which practically took the place of the mancipation of the family estate per aes et libram, was merely a tablet or tablets sealed, or closed, with seven seals. The seven seals, or witnesses, represented the five witnesses, the libripens, and the familiae emptor of the legal, or mancipative will. The formal procedure of mancipation was not required, and, consequently, no familiae emptor. It was necessary that the testator should have been a Roman citizen and

26. Inst. 2, 10, 1.
27. Inst. 2, 10, 2.
28. "Intestate Succession."
29. Gaius 2, 119; Inst. 2, 10, 2; 3, 9, pr.

sui juris at the time of his death,[30] and that the tablets should be sealed. The necessity of seals was introduced by the praetor, jus civile wills not requiring them.[31]

The praetorian will, or tablets with seven seals, was the regular and usual form of will during the latter part of the Republic. Such wills did not affect the validity of "legal" wills, that is, wills made per aes et libram according to the law, and, as explained in connection with intestate inheritance,[32] the praetor's grant of the bonorum possessio in connection with informal wills conveyed only an equitable title to the possessor who was protected by interdicts. Accordingly, for a long time after the introduction of the praetorian will, the heir thus recognized by the praetorian law was not the "legal" heir, and a testator had two ways of making a will, either a formal and "legal" will by mancipatio (jus civile), or an informal and praetorian will by tablets with seven witnesses and their seals. An imperial rescript, however, of Antoninus Pius, or of Marcus Aurelius, provided that an heir at law of an intestate should not be permitted to thwart the last wishes of a testator on the ground that his will was not executed with the formalities of the jus civile.[33] This rescript, therefore, probably made legally valid the informal will of the praetorian court.

Before the time of Justinian the law governing the form of a will was further modified. The rules of the civil and praetorian law regarding testaments had gradually become blended, and in order to make a valid will it was necessary that one should either orally make known and declare his intentions in the presence

30. Gaius 2, 147.
31. Inst. 2, 10, 2.
32. See preceding chapter.
33. Gaius 2, 120.

of seven witnesses,[34] or, in case of a written will, it was necessary for the testator to acknowledge it in the presence of seven witnesses, to subscribe it, and then the seven witnesses were required to sign their names and to affix their seals.[35] This form of will was derived, says Justinian,[36] from three sources (jus tripertitum); the witnesses from the jus civile; the signing by the testator and the witnesses from the imperial law;[37] and the number of the witnesses (seven) and the affixing of their seals from the praetorian law.[38]

In addition to the foregoing forms of oral (or nuncupative) wills and written wills, a special form of will was allowed in the case of soldiers (testamentum militis). One in actual military service, or in the state's naval service,[39] could make a written will without the necessity of witnesses, or could declare orally to witnesses, expressly summoned for the purpose, what his wishes were.[40] The validity of a soldier's will continued during the term of his service and for an additional year after honorable discharge.[41] Ulpian says that Julius Caesar was the first to give this special privilege to soldiers, the practice being later followed by Titus, Domitian, and Nerva, and finally made permanent law by Trajan.[42]

34. Inst. 2, 10, 14; Prince v. Hazleton, 20 Johns. (N. Y.) 502, 519.

35. Inst. 2, 10, 3; Cod. 6, 23, 26; Adams v. Norris, 23 How. (U. S.) 353.

36. Inst. 2, 10, 3.

37. The constitutions of Diocletian and Maximian, Cod. 6, 23, 12; and the constitutions of Thedosius and Valentinian, 439 A. D., Cod. 6, 23, 21, pr.

38. Inst. 2, 10, 3.

39. Dig. 37, 13, 1, 1.

40. Dig. 29, 1, 1, pr.; 29, 1, 19, pr.; Inst. 2, 11; Hubbard v. Hubbard, 8 N. Y. 196, 200.

41. Dig. 29, 1, 21; Inst. 2, 11, 3.

42. Dig. 29, 1, 1, pr.

Execution of Wills:

The early public wills of the Romans were oral, and the first form of a private will, the testamentum per aes et libram, was likewise oral. The object and the essential part of a Roman will was to institute or to name an heir, and an heir, says Ulpian, can be instituted either orally (nuncupare) or by writing (scribere).[43] Although a mancipative will (per aes et libram) did not have to be written, yet in its later form tablets were used, and upon them the testator wrote and then formally declared to the witnesses that the tablets contained his will. In Justinian's time, an oral or nuncupative will [44] was still valid but most wills were written.

Originally, the tablets used for a written will consisted of thin sheets of wood coated with wax. It was the common use of such tablets (tabulae) in connection with wills that the term "tabulae" became synonymous with "testamentum" (will). In early times the tablets were white and were coated with black wax, and a pointed metal stylus was used to cut through the wax leaving the written words traced in white. In later times, parchment, papyrus, the prepared bark of trees, and even ivory were employed for tablet material;[45] and in the case of parchment or papyrus, in imperial days, an ink made of a solution of lamp-black or soot was used.

Wills were required to be written in the Latin language until a law enacted by Theodosius and Valentinian permitted also the use of Greek.[46] A testator could write his will himself, or he could have some other person,[47] even another's slave,[48] write it for him.

43. Dig. 28, 1, 21; Inst. 2, 10, 14.
44. Dockum v. Robinson, 26 N. H. 372, 383.
45. Inst. 2, 10, 12.
46. Cod. 6, 23, 21, 6; (439 A. D.).
47. Dig. 28, 5, 9, 3; 29, 1, 40, pr.; 20, 6, 1, pr.
48. Dig. 28, 1, 28.

Only one side of a tablet or piece of parchment or papyrus was ordinarily used for the writing, although in some instances both sides were used. In case of a will being written upon three or more tablets the inner tablets were usually written on both sides, the practice being to tie the tablets together with a cord and to leave the outside of the enveloping tablets blank.[49] In this way the contents of the will were secret until opened after the death of the testator.

In the time of Justinian the testator "subscribed" the will, and then the seven witnesses subscribed and affixed their seals. However, if the will itself had been written entirely by the testator and that fact was stated in the will, Justinian's law did not require any further subscription by the testator.[50] If a testator could not write at all or was unable at the time to write by reason of physical infirmity, some other person called the "eighth subscriptor," could subscribe for him.[51] The seven witnesses subscribed and affixed their seals in the testator's presence and in the presence of each other, and the failure of any one of the seven to both subscribe and seal rendered the will invalid.[52] Witnesses sealed by making an impression with a ring or some other article upon soft wax.[53] A witness could use his own seal or the seal of another witness. In fact, the entire seven witnesses could use the same seal,[54] because the name of each witness was placed opposite a seal thereby making it his individual seal. When several tablets were used, it was customary for the witnesses to place their names and seals

49. Dig. 37, 11, 1, 11.
50. Cod. 6, 23, 28, 1.
51. Cod. 6, 23, 21, 1.
52. Cod. 6, 23, 12.
53. It was the usual custom for a Roman citizen to wear a gold ring on the third finger of the left hand. This ring often had upon it a raised figure or emblem which was used for sealing. Dig. 50, 16, 74.
54. Cod. 6, 23, 12; Inst. 2, 10, 5.

upon the outside cover in addition to their subscriptions at the bottom of the will. The tablets were bound together with a cord, and with the seals of the witnesses this cord was fastened to the tablets in such a way that the will could not be opened without breaking all the seals.

When a will was duly signed and sealed it was said to be solemnized.[55] It was then usually placed in the care of some friend or deposited in the archives or the strong-box of some temple, there to remain till upon the testator's death it was opened in the way and manner prescribed by law. Copies of wills were often made in order to guard against their loss or destruction.[56]

Upon the death of a testator it was the duty of the person having the will in charge to present it to the praetor for its opening and inspection. The witnesses were summoned, and after identifying their seals the same were broken and the will opened and read. One who opened a will without due magisterial authority was liable to a heavy fine.[57]

Capacity to Make a Will:

In order to make a will valid three things were necessary. First, the testator had to have legal capacity to make a will; second, the will had to be executed in the form required by law; and, third, a competent heir or heirs must be instituted, or appointed, with proper words. A will might be executed, as far as its outward form was concerned, in strict compliance with the law, yet it might not be valid owing to the fact that the testator was not legally competent to make a will.

Legal capacity in connection with wills was known

55. Cod. 6, 23, 21, pr.
56. Dig. 31, 1, 47.
57. Dig. 29, 3; Paulus, Sent. 4, 6.

as testamenti factio.⁵⁸ This term was applied in three ways; capacity to make a will; capacity to witness a will; and capacity to take under a will.⁵⁹

Under the jus civile a testator must be a Roman citizen, of the age of puberty, sui juris, and of sufficient physical and mental ability.⁶⁰ Individuals in potestate, wives in manu, aliens, and slaves were, consequently, incompetent.⁶¹ Mutes (muti), deaf persons (surdi), insane persons (furiosi), and prodigals (prodigi) under guardianship were, likewise, denied testamentary power. Prodigals, or spendthrifts, under guardianship were considered to be too weak-minded to be capable of making a will.⁶² The deaf (surdi) and dumb (muti) were originally classed with imbeciles, and for that reason did not have "animus testandi." The same rule was applied in English Law in the case of persons born deaf, blind, and dumb.⁶³ The Roman Law was, however, modified by Justinian who provided that deaf and dumb persons might have the power of making a will if under the facts of each case such persons had sufficient intelligence to do so, a distinction being made between persons deaf and dumb from birth and those whose hearing or speech had been lost by accident or disease.⁶⁴ A blind man could make a will, under a constitution of Justin, the father of Justinian, provided the testator had the assistance of a notary (tabularius), or an eighth witness was present at the time of the execution of the will to do the writing.⁶⁵

58. Dig. 28, 5, 49; Inst. 2, 19, 4.
59. Inst. 2, 19, 4.
60. Inst. 2, 12, 1. Our Common Law rule that one of the age of puberty may make a testament of chattels is derived from the Roman Law. Davis v. Baugh, 33 Tenn. 477.
61. Dig. 28, 1, 6, pr.; 28, 1, 8; 28, 1 19.
62. Inst. 2, 12, 2.
63. Blackstone, Com. II, 497.
64. Inst. 2, 12, 3; Cod. 6, 22, 10.
65. Inst. 2, 12, 4; Cod. 6, 22, 8. In the Institutes Justinian calls Justin who adopted him "my father."

In early times, women whether married or not had no testamentary capacity. This was true under the old form of will, the testamentum in calatis comitiis, since women were not permitted to take any part in the business of the comitia [66] where such wills were publicly declared by the testator. In later times, however, women who were not in potestate or manu could make wills with the sanction (auctoritas) of a tutor,[67] and finally in imperial times they had equal testamentary capacity with men.

Sons in the power of an ancestor (patria potestas) could not make a will since they were not sui juris, and because they had no property of their own to dispose of by will.[68] However, family sons who were soldiers were permitted during the Empire to bequeath whatever property they had acquired by means of their military service,[69] such property being known as peculium castrense, and Constantine gave the same right in connection with property known as peculium quasi castrense, property acquired by public officials or ecclesiastics by means of their salaries, or by honoraria given to advocates and other professional men. Gifts bestowed by the Emperor could also be disposed of by will by those who were yet under paternal power.[70]

A Roman citizen lost his right to make a will by being captured as a prisoner of war. In such a case he was regarded as being reduced to the status of a slave,[71] and a will made by him during his captivity was invalid even if he afterwards regained his freedom.[72] However, if a citizen had already made a will

66. Gell. 5, 19.
67. Gaius 1, 115a; 150, 157; 2, 112.
68. Dig. 28, 1, 6, pr.; 28, 1, 19.
69. Gaius 2, 106; Just. 2, 12, pr.; Dig. 14, 6, 2; 49, 17, 11.
70. Cod. 12, 31; 12, 29; 12, 37.
71. Inst. 2, 12, 5; Dig. 28, 1, 8, pr.
72. Inst. 2, 12, 5; Dig. 28, 1, 8, pr.

before he was captured by the enemy, such a will was regarded valid, in case of his return, by the law of postliminy,[73] and if he died while held a captive, the will was declared valid by the Lex Cornelia, since, in such a case, a Roman citizen was presumed to have died at the moment he was captured, and, therefore, died a freeman and not a slave.[74]

A Roman citizen who also lost his citizenship in consequence of his commission of a crime could not make a will,[75] and, in case he had made a will previous to his condemnation the will was invalid, in imperial times, by reason of his subsequent loss of liberty (capitis deminutio maxima).[76] However, in the case of a soldier condemned to death for a military offense, the law permitted him to make a will of property acquired by his military service (bona castrensia) provided that privilege was expressly given in connection with the sentence.[77]

Qualifications of Witnesses:

A valid will required not only a competent testator, but also competent witnesses. Under the old law governing the will per aes et libram, witnesses were required to be Roman citizens of the age of puberty, and members of the family of the purchaser of the estate were disqualified.[78] However, members of the family of the heir or legatee could be witnesses as could also the heir himself, although, as Gaius says,[79] such a practice was not advisable. Ulpian, however, says that an heir cannot be a witness to the will in which he is instituted as an heir, but that the rule is

73. Inst. 2, 12, 5; Dig. 28, 3, 6; Inst. 1, 12, 5.
74. Inst. 2, 12, 5; 4, 18, 7; Dig. 48, 1, 1.
75. Dig. 28, 1, 8, 2; 48, 20, 1, pr.
76. Dig. 28, 1, 8, 4; 48, 20, 1, pr.
77. Dig. 28, 3, 6, 6.
78. Gaius 2, 104–107.
79. Gaius 2, 108.

different in case of a legatee.[80] Such was also the law in the time of Justinian.[81]

In addition to being Roman citizens at least fourteen years old, witnesses were also required to be of good repute. They were required to have the qualifications of witnesses in general and no person who had incurred infamy was competent.[82]

In consequence of the foregoing necessary qualifications, women, males under fourteen years of age, aliens, slaves, insane persons, deaf and dumb persons, prodigals, and infamous persons could not be witnesses to a will.[83] In later imperial times witnesses were also required to be of the Christian religion.[84] In Justinian's time not only was an instituted heir incompetent as a witness, but also anyone in his power. Likewise, a person in whose power the heir was, or his brother in the power of the same father was not competent.[85] Persons, however, taking under a will as legatees or as fideicommissary heirs, and also persons who were members of their families could be testamentary witnesses, since legatees and fideicommissary heirs were not successors to the rights of the deceased.[86]

The qualifications of a witness were determined as of the time he was called upon to act as one. Consequently, if he was a qualified witness at the time the will was executed he was competent. The fact that he afterwards became disqualified did not affect the validity of the will.[87]

80. Dig. 28, 1, 20, 6.
81. Inst. 2, 10, 10; 2, 10, 11.
82. Papinian in Dig. 22, 5, 14; Ulpian in Dig. 47, 10, 5, 9; Inst. 2, 10, 6.
83. Dig. 2, 10, 6, 1; 26, 5, 12; 27, 10, 1; 28, 1, 20; Inst. 2, 10, 6.
84. Cod. 1, 7, 3, 4; 1, 5, 44.
85. Inst. 2, 10, 10.
86. Inst. 2, 10, 11.
87. Dig. 28, 1, 22, 1.

[Roman Law]

Witnesses to wills had to be requested to act as such by the testator (rogatio testium),[88] and it was necessary that they should act freely and voluntarily without any compulsion.[89] Their seals had to be attached in the presence of the testator,[90] but it was not necessary that they should know the contents of a written will. Since it was necessary in case of a sealed will for the witness to identify his seal when the will was opened after the testator's death, a blind man could not be a witness in such a case. Whether or not he could be a competent witness in the case of an oral (nuncupative) will is a disputed question.

Who May Be Made an Heir:

In order to make a valid will an heir must be instituted, and the person or persons who were thus named as heirs had to be persons who were legally competent to act as such.

Not all persons could be testamentary heirs, for the term testamenti factio, or testamentary capacity, was applied to heirs as well as to testators and to witnesses, although applied in different senses. Accordingly, one might be competent to be an heir although incompetent to make a will. Thus, an insane person, a dumb person, a posthumous child, a son in the power of his father, or a slave belonging to another was competent to take under a will, although incompetent to make one.[91]

It was the general rule that no person could be named as heir in a will who was not capable of being an intestate successor. Consequently, aliens [92] and persons convicted of a capital offense [93] were excluded.

88. Dig. 28, 1, 21, 2.
89. Dig. 28, 1, 20, 10.
90. Dig. 29, 3, 4.
91. Inst. 2, 19, 4.
92. Gaius 2, 110; Dig. 28, 5, 6, 2; 28, 5, 49.
93. Dig. 37, 1, 13.

A Roman could appoint his own slave as his heir,[94] or the slave of another Roman citizen,[95] but the slave of an alien could not be appointed.[96] Under the law of Justinian, a slave who was made his master's heir became free upon the death of his master by the very fact of the appointment.[97] In former times, however, it was necessary that the slave should be expressly set free in the will in order to make him a competent heir.[98] If a testator made the slave of another his heir, it depended upon the slave's master whether the slave took the inheritance or not. He was compelled to do so if his master so ordered.[99] In such a case, the slave was merely acting as the slave of his master who was entitled to all benefits arising from the inheritance while avoiding all its liabilities. A testator's own slave, however, was obliged to accept the inheritance since he became by his institution as heir a "necessary" heir. This rule of law enabled a testator who was insolvent to leave a successor who was obliged to carry the burden of his debts.[100]

Another rule governing the capacity of instituted heirs was that an uncertain person could not be appointed heir, neither could he be a legatee.[101] An uncertain person is one, says Gaius, of whom the testator has no definite thought, as, for example, where a testator orders a legacy to be given to the first man who comes to his funeral.[102] Bequests, continues Gaius, to "every one who comes to my funeral," "to any person who gives his daughter in marriage to my

94. Inst. 2, 14, 1.
95. Inst. 2, 14, 1; 2, 19, 4.
96. Dig. 34, 8, 3.
97. Inst. 2, 14, 1; 2, 19, 1.
98. Gaius 2, 153–155.
99. Inst. 2, 14, 1.
100. Inst. 2, 14, 1; 2, 19, 1.
101. Gaius 2, 238, 242; Ulp. Frag. 22, 4.
102. Gaius 2, 238.

sons," or "to those who first after the making of my will are elected consuls," are further illustrations of uncertain persons and all such bequests are void.[103] However, a definite designation of a present unknown person among a definite class of existing persons was held not to be uncertain, as "whoever of my relatives now alive first comes to my funeral." [104]

A posthumous "stranger" was an uncertain person and, therefore, could not be appointed as an heir;[105] children not conceived at the death of the testator were also uncertain persons.[106] A posthumous stranger was one who at the time of his birth would not be included among the testator's sui heredes; for example, the posthumous son of A's emancipated son was a "stranger" (alienus) and not suus heres to A.[107]

Originally, no juristic person, that is, no corporation, including municipalities, could be an heir since such was uncertain and there was no definite natural person to accept or to "enter upon the inheritance." [108] The fiscus, or public treasury, however, was always an exception, and by a decree of the senate municipalities, could be instituted heirs by their freedmen.[109] Likewise, in the absence of a statute, temples dedicated to the gods could not be made heirs,[110] but in Justinian's time there were many such special laws, and churches, piae causae, and saints, or their shrines, were often instituted as heirs, and even Jesus Christ was so named, the appointment being construed as that of the church where the testator lived.[111]

103. Dig. 37, 11, 3; Gaius 2, 238; see also Inst. 2, 20, 25.
104. Gaius, 2, 238; Inst. 2, 20, 25.
105. Gaius 2, 242.
106. Dig. 37, 11, 3.
107. Gaius 2, 241; Inst. 2, 20, 26.
108. Ulp. Frag. 22, 5.
109. Ulp. Frag. 22, 5.
110. Ulp. Frag. 22, 5.
111. Cod. 1, 2, 25 (26).

The laws governing the capacity of persons either to be instituted heirs or to take under a will varied with the different periods of Roman Law. Moreover, certain classes of persons were disqualified at different times by special statutes, and, again, persons who were incapacitated to take under an ordinary will might be qualified to be heirs under a soldier's will. For example, aliens could not be heirs in case of an ordinary form of testament, but they could be under the will of a soldier.[112] By the Voconian law, a woman could not be made an heir by a testator rated in the census as possessing a hundred thousand sesterces, although she could take under a will by means of a fideicommissum.[113] The purpose of such a law was to prevent large estates from coming into the control of women. By a constitution of the Emperor Leo, a second husband or wife could not be given more by a will than an amount equal to the smallest amount given to any child of the first marriage. Any share given in excess of this amount was said to escheat or lapse (caduca) and was equally divided among the children of the first marriage.[114] By a provision of the Lex Julia, which was intended to promote marriage, unmarried persons were disqualified from taking inheritances [115] unless they became married within a hundred days after the decease of the testator.[116] According to Ulpian,[117] this rule, by the Lex Papia, applied to unmarried men up to the age of sixty, and to unmarried women under fifty. Likewise, by the Lex Papia married persons twenty-five years old in the case of men, and twenty years old in the case of women, who had no children, could take only one-half

112. Gaius 2, 110.
113. Gaius 2, 274.
114. Cod. 5, 9, 6, pr.; 5, 9, 9. Nov. 22, 27.
115. Gaius 2, 286.
116. Ulp. Frag. 16, 1, 17, 1; 22, 3.
117. Ulp. Frag. 16, 1.

of any property left to them.[118] In later imperial days, however, these provisions of the Julian and Papian laws were repealed.[119] In Justinian's time those who were incompetent to take under a will included aliens (barbari), persons incapacitated by commissions of crimes, widows who violated their year of mourning by marriage,[120] and persons not of the Christian religion.[121]

Soldiers were given special privileges. They could institute as heirs persons who in the case of ordinary wills would be incompetent, as aliens and celibates.[122]

Institution of the Heir:

A valid will required a competent testator and an execution according to the requirements of law,[123] but even these were not sufficient [124] because in addition to the testamentary capacity of the testator and the proper execution of the will it was necessary that certain provisions of a will should be expressed in a formal and prescribed manner. A will, therefore, which failed to possess all of these essential elements, testamentary capacity, proper execution, and requisite contents properly expressed was said to be a testamentum injustum (illegal) or nullum (no will at all).

A will might be very short or very voluminous. It was possible for a will to contain nothing more than a single clause instituting an heir in proper words. Every will had to contain at least that much. It could contain, however, many clauses, each governed by special rules. A fair illustration of the contents of an ordinary Roman will, and the order of these contents,

118. Ulp. Frag. 16, 1.
119. By Constitutions of Constantine and of Honorius and Theodosius. Cod. 8, 57 (58).
120. Novel 22, 22; Code 5, 9, 1.
121. Cod. 1, 5, 4, 5; 1, 7, 3.
122. Gaius 2, 110–111.
123. Gaius 2, 114.
124. Gaius 2, 115.

prior to the time of Justinian, would be as follows: first, a disinheriting clause; second, the institution of the heir or heirs; third, a clause providing for a substituted heir, in case the instituted heir should fail; fourth, one or more legacy clauses. In many wills there were still further clauses, such as clauses providing for gifts in the nature of trusts (fidei commissa); clauses emancipating slaves; and, possibly, clauses setting out directions concerning the funeral and burial of the testator.

The primary purpose of a Roman will was to institute an heir, and it was of the utmost importance that the heir should be instituted "in a solemn form."[125] Unless this was done, then, regardless of the capacity of the testator and the regular execution of the will, the will was of no effect. The proper, or solemn, form, says Gaius,[126] to institute an heir is, "Be Titius my heir" (Titius heres esto), although "I order that Titius be my heir" may also be used. However, such an institution as "I wish Titius to be my heir" is not permitted, and even such forms as "I institute Titius my heir," or "I make Titius my heir," are held by most authorities, continues Gaius, to be improper. In other words, the heir had to be instituted by positive, imperative words. Mere precatory words were always insufficient, and even a simple declaration not expressed in the form of a positive order was considered by most lawyers as inoperative.

It is not difficult to understand why the Romans placed so much stress upon the importance of instituting an heir with solemn and formal words. A Roman heir (heres) was, as already stated, quite different from an English "heir." With us an heir does not take by will (devise) but by descent only. A Roman "heir" was a successor of the deceased, suc-

125. Gaius 2, 116.
126. Gaius 2, 117.

ceeding to all of the property, movable as well as immovable. He inherited, moreover, not only the assets but also the liabilities,[127] and his rights and also his duties covered a wide range. He was an executor of the will and also its residuary legatee, and he was responsible for the debts of the deceased as well as being the beneficiary of his bounty. In the eyes of the law, he was the reincarnation of the man who had died. It was an important and serious matter to appoint such an heir, and it is not strange that the early Roman Law required that it be done in a formal and solemn manner.

Lawyers of all ages have been conservative and have learned by experience the importance of not departing from approved forms in the drafting of legal documents. There can be cited illustrations in our own Common Law that show in its early practice as great subserviency to the absolutely necessary word as in the case of the institution of an heir in a Roman will.

However, even as our own modern statutes have abolished, in some instances, the need of using certain particular words in certain transactions, so the Roman Law similarly progressed. Two hundred years before Justinian's time, or about 340 A. D., Constantius did away with the necessity of using precise and formal words in order to institute an heir. It was still necessary that an heir should be instituted, but the law of Constantius declared that it was immaterial whether imperative and positive words were used providing the intent of the testator was clearly shown. "It is a matter of indifference," says this constitutio,[128] "whether one says 'I institute,' 'I make,' 'I

---

127. It is interesting to note that in England in the time of Henry II, the heir was bound to make up any deficiency out of his own property if the effects of the deceased were insufficient to pay his debts. Glanvil, 8, 8.

128. Cod. 6, 23, 15.

wish,' or 'I desire' such a one to be my heir. Each is equally as good as 'Be such a one my heir.' "

A Roman testator could, if he so desired, institute one heir or two or more joint-heirs. He could also provide for one or more alternate heirs, to cover the possibility that the instituted heir might be either legally incompetent or unwilling to accept, or enter upon, the inheritance. Heirs were classed as "necessary heirs" (necessarii); "own and necessary heirs" (sui et necessarii); and "extraneous heirs" (extranei).[129] A testator's slave was a "necessary heir."[130] One's sui heredes (own heirs), including one's children in his power together with the children of predeceased sons, were likewise necessary heirs.[131] Heirs not of the household were called "extranei," and were "voluntary heirs."[132]

Due to the fact that an heir succeeded to the debts and other obligations of the testator, the acceptance of a testate succession might involve great burdens. Nevertheless, a necessary heir was obliged to accept, the jus civile casting upon him that obligation,[133] but a voluntary heir had the privilege of either accepting or refusing. This fact coupled with the possibility that the appointed heir might die before the testator, or might even prove incompetent to act, led to the practice of instituting an alternate heir. This was known as "substitution," the alternate heir being substituted for the heir first named.[134] Several heirs might be substituted in place of one, or one in place of several.[135] An ordinary substitution of one heir for

129. Inst. 2, 19, pr.
130. Inst. 2, 10, 1.
131. Inst. 2, 19, 2.
132. Inst. 2, 19, 3.
133. Under the later praetorian law, the heir was permitted, however, to keep his own property separate from the inheritance.
134. Gaius 2, 174; Inst. 2, 14, pr.
135. Gaius 2, 175; Inst. 2, 14, 1.

another, as "Be Lucius Titius my heir; if not, then be Mevius my heir," with further substitutions if desired, was called common or vulgar substitution.[136] Where a testator's child was under the age of puberty, but was nevertheless, instituted as heir, such a child, upon the father's death, might enter upon the inheritance, with his tutor's authority, and yet die before he reached the age of puberty. To guard against such a possibility, another heir could be substituted in the father's will.[137] This was practically making a will for the child, since the substituted heir would be the heir of the child and not the heir of the father. However, this authority was given, in such a case, to a parent by long custom. This form of substitution was called pupillary substitution.

Where two or more joint heirs were instituted in a will they shared equally in the inheritance in absence of provisions to the contrary. In case one died before accepting the succession, or refused to accept, or was incompetent to accept, then, by the doctrine of jus accrescendi, the share that would have gone to such instituted heir was divided equally among the other heirs or in such shares as may have been set forth in the will. There was never an undisposed of part of an inheritance in case of a Roman will, since it disposed of all the estate. An estate could not be, as in our law, part testate and part intestate. In case of lapsed legacies the property in question went to the heir or heirs.

When a will was opened upon the death of a testator, the inheritance was said to be offered (delatio) to the heir. The heir's acceptance or "entrance" upon the inheritance was called aditio. The time given for an heir, other than a necessary heir, to decide

---

136. Inst. 2, 15 (title).
137. Gaius 2, 179; Inst. 2, 16, pr.

whether or not he would accept was called cretio.[138] A testator could fix in his will the time for such a decision, the limit usually being a hundred days, although the jus civile allowed a longer or a shorter period to be fixed. The praetor, however, in his discretion could shorten a longer period.[139] In the time of Justinian, the time for decision could be all the way from one hundred days to nine months, and even a year might be allowed by imperial authority. In case no election were made within the prescribed period, then upon the application of legatees or of creditors the instituted heir was held to have accepted, but if the application was made by a substituted heir or by an intestate heir, then the instituted heir was regarded as having refused the inheritance. In case the instituted heir died before the expiration of the cretio, his own heir succeeded to the right to decide for the remainder of the prescribed period.[140] Justinian also changed the whole law concerning the liability of an heir to pay the debts and legacies of a testator by providing for an inventory of the inheritance. This privilege was known as the beneficium inventarii. It was optional with the heir to have an inventory made or not. If made, the heir was liable for the debts and legacies only up to the amount of the estate after deducting necessary expenses and his own "Falcidian Fourth."[141] If the heir called for no inventory within the time allowed for such right, thirty days after notice that the will had been opened and that he had been instituted heir, then he was liable for all the debts and legacies, and could not claim against creditors and legatees his "Falcidian Fourth."[142]

138. Gaius 2, 164.
139. Gaius 2, 166-173.
140. Inst. 2, 19, 507; Dig. 28, 2, 28; Cod. 6, 30, 19.
141. See post.
142. Cod. 6, 30, 22; 1-3; 6, 30, 22, 12; Nov. 1, 2, 1-2.

The Disinheriting Clause:

Prior to the time of Justinian, the disherison clause preceded the clause instituting the heir. Justinian, however, dispensed with such a requirement, declaring it immaterial whether the clause preceded or followed the clause which named the heir. It was still necessary, however, as in former times, that a will should expressly institute an heir or heirs, or else disinherit all the persons who would be entitled, as successors of the deceased, to a share of the inheritance in case of his intestacy. These were the testator's "sui heredes." It was not necessary to make any of them the "heir" or the "heirs," since a testator could name as his heir any one he wished providing, of course, that the person designated was qualified to be an heir. It was, however, absolutely essential to name in some way each suus heres. If a paterfamilias had a son in his power he could make him his heir, or leave to him a legacy, or expressly disinherit him. If, however, he failed to mention the son at all, such a silent passing over (praeteritio) of the son invalidated the will.[143] Even should a son thus passed over die before his father, nevertheless, the heir named in the will could not take since the will was void from the beginning (ab initio).[144] Likewise, if after a will was made, correct in all essentials at the time, another son should be born prior to the death of the testator, the will was thereby rendered invalid (ruptum) since all sui heredes at the testator's death must be mentioned in the will.[145] The same result happened in case of the subsequent legitimation or adoption of a suus heres,[146] but this could be prevented by a clause in a

---

143. Inst. 2, 13, pr.
144. Inst. 2, 13, pr.; cf. Gaius 2, 123.
145. Gaius 2, 138. However, in Justinian's time a will could provide for the institution or disherison of a possible after born son and if this were done the will was good if such a son were born.
146. Gaius 2, 138.

will providing for such a future contingency.[147] The failure, however, expressly to institute as heirs, or to disinherit, a daughter or the children of deceased sons, although they were sui heredes and properly should be named, did not make a will invalid, but such passed over heirs were granted, nevertheless, an equal share with the instituted heir if he were a suus heres, and if he were not a suus heres then they were entitled collectively to a half of the entire inheritance. For example, if a testator having three sons instituted them as heirs but was silent as to his daughter, she was entitled to a fourth part of the estate; in case he had only a daughter and named a stranger as his heir, the passed over daughter could claim a half.[148]

The rule requiring the express mention of a testator's sui heredes, either in terms of institution as heirs or of disherison was founded, probably, upon the primitive doctrine of the Roman family. From ancient times the family was the basis of the whole system of the jus civile, and in the early period of this law the family property was regarded as the joint property of the paterfamilias and his sui heredes, the latter being looked upon as co-owners even during the lifetime of the paterfamilias.[149] The manager and controller of the property was the paterfamilias, and by his will he could still exercise this right of control by allotting this property to whom he would, providing he expressly excluded from it those persons who would be entitled to it in case he died intestate. The rule of the necessity of express disherison was common to both the jus civile and the praetorian law, the latter law requiring emancipated sons and also grandsons (whose fathers were deceased) to be expressly

147. Dig. 28, 3, 18.
148. Gaius 2, 124; 2, 129; Inst. 2, 13, pr.
149. Gaius 2, 157.

instituted or disinherited the same as sons.[150] Justinian went even beyond this, and required that ascendants as well as descendants must be either formally instituted as heirs or else expressly disinherited.[151]

The rule that an heir must be instituted with proper words applied also to the disherison of a suus heres. The usual and approved form was "Be Titius my son disinherited." However, if the testator had but one son, the words "Be my son disinherited" were sufficiently definite.[152] Daughters and grandchildren could be disinherited by some general inclusive term, such as, "Be all my other heirs disinherited."[153]

The right of a testator expressly to disinherit his children and to institute even a stranger as the heir of the family estate resulted, in time, in a reaction. It was looked upon as unjust and contrary to the policy of the law that a testator should be permitted utterly to ignore those bound to him by the ties of natural affection. Accordingly, during the latter part of the Republic, the family rights to the property of a deceased person were further protected by giving persons who would have been entitled to the inheritance in case the deceased had died intestate a remedy based upon the complaint of an unjust or unduteous will, querela inofficiosi testamenti.[154] The action granted in such a case was in the nature of an action to set aside the will, and it was brought in the court of the centumviri[155] which court had a general jurisdiction in matter relating to inheritances. The action was based on the theory that the testator was not in his right mind when he made his will, not that he was

150. Gaius 2, 129.
151. Nov. 115, 3.
152. Gaius 2, 127; Inst. 2, 13, pr.
153. Gaius 2, 128; Inst. 2, 13, pr.
154. Cicero In Verr. 1, 42; Dig. 5, 2; Inst. 2, 18, pr.
155. Dig. 5, 2, 13.

actually insane, since in such a case the will would be void ab initio, but that he was unduly prejudiced or influenced against those whom he had disinherited.[156] At first, no particular share of the inheritance was regularly set apart by the court to a successful complainant, each case being adjudged according to its merits. Later, after the passage of the Falcidian Law,[157] it became the custom to grant to such a complainant one-fourth of what would have come to him if the deceased had died intestate.[158] This share or portion was known as the pars (or portio) legitima,[159] variously translated as the legal or statutory portion, the birthright portion, and the "legitim." By the 18th Novel,[160] Justinian provided that a testator with four or less children must leave to them at least one-third of his property, the same to be divided among them equally, and in case there were more than four children a half of the estate at least must be divided equally among them.

An action to set aside an unduteous will was given, as the rights of intestate succession were expanded to include new classes of heirs, not only to children but also to parents and brothers and sisters who were unjustly passed over by a testator. In the time of Justinian, children and parents could bring such an action only when nothing at all had been left to them. If they had been given anything, no matter how small the amount, the action did not lie, but the fourth part of the amount to which they would have been entitled, had the deceased been intestate, they could, nevertheless, recover by another remedy (actio ad suplendam

---

156. Dig. 5, 2, 2-5; Inst. 2, 18, pr.
157. The Lex Falcidia, 40 B. C., limiting testators to gifts by way of legacy of not more than three-fourths of their estate, thus leaving at least one-fourth for the heir.
158. Ulpian in Dig. 5, 2, 8, 6.
159. Cod. 3, 26, 28.
160. Nov. 18, 1.

legitimam) brought against the instituted heir.[161] In the case of a brother or sister, the action upon an unduteous will could be maintained only when the instituted heir was unworthy (turpis) to receive the benefits of the will.[162] The action based upon an unduteous will could be brought at any time within five years from the acceptance of the inheritance by the instituted heir.[163] In case the court decided against the will and in favor of the complainant, the will was declared void or rescinded (rescissum), and the complainant was declared to be the heir or the bonorum possessor according to the nature of the claim. The setting aside of the will necessarily made all its provisions as to legacies and other matters invalid.[164]

Justinian provided, however, that descendants and ascendants could be totally disinherited for just cause, the cause being stated in the will, and being such a cause as was recognized by law.[165] The grounds for such permitted disherisons were based chiefly upon ingratitude,[166] such as striking a parent; accusing him of crime; attempting to take his life; neglecting to care for an insane parent or to redeem, if possible, a parent from captivity; refusing to be a surety to obtain a parent's release from prison; and any other serious wrong to a parent. Moreover, a son who followed the disgraceful profession of an actor or of a gladiator, or a daughter who became a prostitute could be legally disinherited, and likewise a child who did not accept the Christian religion.[167] Children could

161. Inst. 2, 18, 3; 2, 18, 6; Cod. 3, 28, 1–8.
162. Inst. 2, 18, 1.
163. Dig. 5, 2, 8, 17; 5, 2, 9; Cod. 3, 28, 36, 2.
164. Dig. 5, 2, 8, 16.
165. These grounds are set out in Nov. 115, 3; see, also, Cod. 3, 28, 11; 18–20; 33, 1.
166. See Riggs v. Palmer, 115 N. Y. 514; Ellerson v. Westcott, 148 N. Y. 149, 155.
167. Nov. 115, 4.

also disinherit parents for attempting to take their lives or for accusing them of crime, and likewise brothers and sisters could disinherit each other for the same causes.[168]

Testamentum Ruptum:

A will, however, may have been legally and properly executed in all respects and yet be rendered void (ruptum) by some subsequent event.[169] Various terms, such as ruptum, irritum, and destitutum were applied to such a broken will.

A will might be revoked or broken by the execution of a second valid will; by its intentional destruction by the testator; by the testator's erasure of the name of the instituted heir; by the death of an instituted heir either in the lifetime of the testator, or even after his death if prior to the time of acceptance of the inheritance; by the heir's refusal to accept; by the heir's refusal to comply with the terms and conditions of the will; and by the heir's incompetency to take under the will (by virtue of the Lex Julia et Papia Poppaea) on account of his being unmarried, or, if married, being childless. When a will failed because an instituted heir, no substitute heir having been provided, was either unwilling or incompetent to take, it was said to be destitutum or desertum (abandoned).[170]

A testator could make as many different wills as he pleased. It was "the last will" that controlled, since any subsequent will that did not confirm any preceding will operated as a revocation of all former wills.[171] A subsequent will could institute, however, a new heir, and confirm the general provisions as to legacies and

168. Nov. 115, 3; 115, 4; 22, 47, pr.
169. Dig. 28, 3, 1.
170. Inst. 3, 1, 7; Dig. 26, 2, 9; 50, 17, 181.
171. Dig. 34, 4, 4.

[Roman Law]

other matters set forth in a former will. In such a case, the subsequent will did not invalidate the terms of the former will so far as they were applicable to the new heir.

A mere intention to revoke a will was not sufficient to produce that result, since some act was necessary in evidence of the intent.[172] Under the law of Theodosius a will was valid for only ten years after its execution,[173] but Justinian provided that mere lapse of time would not invalidate a will, although a will ten or more years old could be revoked by an oral declaration before three witnesses.[174]

A will was also broken if the testator subsequently suffered a loss of status (capitis deminutio).[175] In such a case a will was said to be ineffectual (irritum).[176] In case of a testator's loss of liberty by being made a prisoner of war, the law of postliminy applied upon his return to his country, and by the later provision of the Lex Cornelia the will was good even if he never returned. Moreover, under the praetorian doctrine of bonorum possessio, a will invalidated by loss of the testator's status could be given efficiency by the praetor secundum tabulas, providing the testator was restored to his former status of citizenship and legal capacity (sui juris) before his death.[177]

Codicils: [178]

In our own law a codicil is an addition to, or a qualification of, a will, being a part of the will itself. With us there can be no codicil without a will. In the Roman Law, however, while there might be both

172. Inst. 2, 17, 7.
173. Cod. Theod. 4, 4, 6.
174. Cod. 6, 23, 27.
175. Inst. 2, 17, 4.
176. Inst. 2, 17, 5.
177. Inst. 2, 17, 6.
178. Dig. 29, 7; Inst. 2, 25; Cod. 6, 36.

a will and a codicil, there could also be a codicil or any number of codicils although there was no will (testamentum) at all. The word "codicil" originally meant a small writing tablet, and it does not seem to have been used as a legal term prior to the time of Augustus. Justinian says codicils were first employed by Lucius Lentulus who, when dying in Africa, wrote several letters (codicilli) to Augustus, his heir, requesting him to do something as a trust (fideicommissum). The emperor was in doubt as to the legal efficacy of such letters, but being advised by learned jurists whom he consulted that they should be given the recognition of law, since they were convenient and even necessary methods of disposing of one's property, especially when a Roman citizen was far from home and unable, possibly, to obtain a sufficient number of competent witnesses to a will, the emperor decided to give them legally binding force. In later times, the great Labeo himself made codicils, and after that the validity of a codicil was never questioned.[179]

Thus there were established two ways by which a Roman citizen could provide for the disposal of his property after his death, one by means of a will, the other by means of a codicil. There was, however, a distinct legal difference between a will and a codicil, particularly as to their form and in the scope of their effect. Codicils originally were informal letters requesting friends to see that certain gifts by way of trust (fideicommissa) were duly made out of the writer's estate after his death. Codicils were often made after a will had been made for the purpose of imposing such a trust upon the heir instituted in the will. They were also made by persons who left no will for the purpose of placing such a trust, or trusts, upon the intestate successor or successors. Likewise, after a codicil had been made by one who at the time

[179]. Inst. 2, 25, pr.

had executed no will, a subsequent will might refer to and confirm the previously made codicil. In any case, while a man could leave but one will (testamentum) he could leave, if he wished, any number of codicils.

Paulus says that codicils were of four kinds:[180] (1) codicils confirmed by a subsequent will; (2) codicils confirmed by a previous will; (3) codicils resulting from a clause in a will; and (4) codicils made by an intestate.

The first two kinds of codicils were called by Roman jurists "confirmed codicils." The third class was said to be "unconfirmed." There was a reason for such a distinction since different rules of law applied.

It has already been pointed out that the primal and chief purpose of a will was to appoint an heir. It was, moreover, only by a will that an heir could be appointed. No codicil could legally institute an heir.[181] The chief purpose of a codicil was to impose either upon an heir already instituted, or later to be instituted, in a will some trust (fideicommissum), or, in case there was no will, to impose such a trust upon the heir or heirs who took by intestate succession. A codicil, likewise, could not disinherit an heir,[182] such an instrument being unable either to give or to take away an inheritance (hereditas) directly, but a codicil could require an heir to transfer the inheritance, or a part of it, to some third person (fideicommissum).[183] Moreover, a codicil could not place a condition upon an heir or make a direct substitution of an heir.[184] Likewise, a legacy (legatum) could not be given by a mere codicil, a codicil ab intestato, but a legacy given

180. Dig. 29, 7, 8, pr.
181. Dig. 29, 7, 10. Inst. 2, 25, 2; Cod. 6, 36, 7.
182. Gaius 2, 237; Inst. 2, 25, 2.
183. Gaius 2, 273; Inst. 2, 23, 10; 2, 25, 2.
184. Gaius 2, 273; Dig. 29, 7, 6, pr.; Inst. 2, 25, 2.

in a codicil that was confirmed by a will was held to be a valid gift.[185]

A testamentary clause known as the clausula codicillaris was often inserted in a will stating that it was the wish of the testator that if for any reason the instrument should be held invalid as a will it might, nevertheless, be regarded as a codicil. In such a case, if the will failed to stand there would be no testamentary heir, but any provisions for fideicommissa would be good.[186]

While the legal capacity to make a codicil was the same as was required in the case of a will,[187] yet there seems to have been no requirement as to the formality of their execution, either as to signing or sealing.[188] The Emperor Theodosius, however, enacted that five witnesses should be required and that the witnesses should be present at the same time.[189] He also provided that if the codicil were written the witnesses must sign it.[190] In the time of Justinian, no solemnity of execution was required, and codicils, as in former times, could be either oral or written.[191]

Legatum (Legacy):

After the disinheriting clause and the institution of an heir, whatever legacies a testator wished to give were, next in order, inserted in his will. Under the jus civile, a legacy given before the heir was instituted was void.[192] Justinian, however, abolished this requirement.[193]

The term legacy (legatum) has been previously used

185. Gaius 2, 270a; Inst. 2, 23, 10.
186. Cod. 6, 36, 8, 1; Dig. 28, 1, 29, 1; 29, 1, 3; cf. 29, 7, 1.
187. Dig. 29, 7, 6, 3.
188. Dig. 29, 7, 6, 1-2.
189. Cod. 6, 36, 8 3.
190. Ib.
191. Inst. 2, 23, 12.
192. Gaius 2, 229.
193. Inst. 2, 20, 34.

in connection with the acquisition of property as a means of acquiring ownership under a will.[194] It is, in that sense, a kind of title,[195] or a method of acquiring the ownership of definite things (res singulae), in contrast with the acquisition, as in case of an heir, of a totality (universitas) of rights and obligations. Originally, the word "legare" was employed in a general sense, meaning the disposition of one's property by will, and it is so used in the Twelve Tables.[196] Its special meaning in later times, as defined by Ulpian, was "That which, in an imperative form as required by law, is left by will. For the things which are left with mere precatory words are called fideicommissa."[197] Justinian defines a legacy as a kind of gift left by a deceased person.[198]

A legacy might consist of any sort of property, corporeal or incorporeal,[199] as a farm, a house, a slave, a horse, a field, a sum of money, a release from debt, or a grant of freedom to a slave. A usufruct could be created by a legacy;[200] a debt due the testator from a third person could be given to a legatee; and a legacy might consist of some service, as where the heir was directed to rebuild the house of a certain person.[201] A gift, however, by a testator to his creditor of what the testator owes him was void, being no legacy at all, since the creditor would get nothing beyond what was due him. However, a sum owed conditionally by a testator if given absolutely to the creditor would be a valid legacy.[202] It was also possible

194. Chap. XII.
195. Gaius 2, 191.
196. Uti legassit suae rei, ita jus esto (As one shall have disposed of his property by will, so let it be the law). Gaius 2, 224.
197. Frag. 24 (De Legatis), 1.
198. Inst. 2, 20, 1.
199 Inst. 2, 20, 21.
200. Dig. 7, 1, 3, pr.
201. Inst. 2, 20, 21.
202. Inst. 2, 20, 14.

by means of a legacy to give not only the property of a testator, but also the property of third persons. A legacy of that latter sort merely meant that it was the heir's duty to purchase, if possible, the property in question and to deliver the same to the legatee, or failing its purchase to pay to the legatee its value.[203] If mortgaged property were given as a legacy it was the duty of the heir to pay the mortgage so that the legatee might receive it without incumbrance.[204] If property were given in a will and then subsequently sold by the testator, it was the opinion of most jurists that this avoided the legacy,[205] but in the time of Justinian the opinion prevailed that such a sale did not revoke the legacy unless it was the intention of the testator to do so, and, in absence of such intention, it was the duty of the heir to pay to the legatee the value of the property.[206]

Under the old law, a legacy had to be given in accord with certain set forms. The "imperative" form mentioned by Ulpian meant that the gift must be expressed in a positive way and in the manner required by law. In time, four forms of legacy were recognized, and in the days of the Republic and also in the early years of the Empire, a legacy could be given only in one of these four ways, namely, (1) by vindication (per vindicationem); (2) by condemnation (per damnationem); (3) by permission (sinendi modo); and (4) by preception (per praeceptionem).[207] These names were derived either from the form in which the gift was made, or from its legal effect. Thus, "I give to Lucius Titius my slave Stichus" was a legacy by vindication,[208] since in case of such a form of legacy

203. Gaius 2, 202; Inst. 2, 30, 4.
204. Inst. 2, 20, 5; 2, 20, 12.
205. Gaius 2, 198.
206. Inst. 2, 20, 12.
207. Gaius 2, 192.
208. Gaius 2, 193.

the title to the gift vested in the legatee immediately upon the acceptance of the inheritance by the heir, and, if the heir refused to deliver it, the legatee could sue by a real action, an action of ownership (vindicatio) for its recovery.[209]

A legacy by condemnation was given as follows: "Be my heir condemned to give my slave Stichus to Lucius Titius." [210] Such a form of gift did not, per se, give the ownership of the property to the legatee, but it did give the legatee an action in personam against the heir for its conveyance.[211] Since by such an action the heir could be condemned (adjudged) to convey the property, this form of legacy was called per damnationem. By this form, property belonging to a third person could be given to a legatee, the heir being required to purchase and deliver the same, or else pay the legatee its value. Things not in existence at the time the will was made, as, for example, the crops to be produced on a certain farm, or the future children of a female slave, could also be given by this form of legacy.[212]

A legacy in the form, "Be my heir condemned to permit Lucius Titius to take and to have for himself my slave Stichus," was a legacy by permission.[213] By such a form of bequest a testator could give either his own property or the property of the heir. It did not apply, however, to the property of a third person.[214]

The fourth form of legacy, a legacy by preception (per praeceptionem), was made thus, "Let Lucius Titius first take my slave Stichus." [215] This form of legacy, according to the Sabinians, of which school

209. Gaius 2, 194.
210. Gaius 2, 201.
211. Gaius 2, 204.
212. Gaius 2, 203; Dig. 7, 1, 3, pr.
213. Gaius 2, 209.
214. Gaius 2, 210.
215. Gaius 2, 216.

Gaius was a member, could be employed only in case one of several co-heirs was given the right to take certain property for his own before the inheritance was divided; the Proculians, however, held that it applied equally to a legatee who was not an heir.[216]

Due to the technicalities of form, and other particulars connected with the law of legacy, testators often failed to observe the requirements, resulting in many legacies being held invalid. Not only was it necessary that the legacy should be given in a proper form, but the property itself must be such as could be given by a legacy, and, further, the legatee must be capable of taking as a legatee.[217] An alien (peregrinus) could not be a legatee, and an uncertain person, as already stated, could not be named either as an heir or a legatee.[218] Penal bequests were also invalid, as, for example, "If my heir does not give his daughter in marriage to Titius, I order him to pay ten thousand secterces to Titius." [219] Likewise, prior to Justinian's time, legacies to take effect after the death of the heir were void.[220]

Due, however, to the growth of the use of codicils and of gifts in the nature of trusts (fideicommissa) made by such instruments, as already pointed out, and especially due to the fact that fideicommissa were not restricted by the laws governing legacies (legata), testators more and more resorted to bequests made as fideicommissa. The final result was that Justinian abolished all distinctions as to legacies and fideicommissa, making all legacies legally the same as fideicommissa, and applying the same laws to both.[221]

216. Gaius 2, 217–223.
217. Inst. 2, 20, 24.
218. Ante; Gaius 2, 238; Inst. 2, 20, 25.
219. Gaius 2, 235.
220. Gaius 2, 232.
221. Inst. 2, 20, 3.

Restrictions upon Bequests:

Under the law of the Twelve Tables and during a period of more than two hundred and fifty years thereafter, a testator could dispose of his entire estate by legacies leaving nothing to the instituted heir but an empty name.[222] However, in 183 B. C., by the Lex Furia, a legacy of a thousand asses was the largest amount that could be left by the same person to a single legatee.[223] This law did not prevent, however, a testator from disposing of all his estate by way of bequests to different legatees providing he gave no more than the permitted maximum to each. In 169 B. C., the Lex Voconia provided that no legatee should be given more than the heir. Yet, as before, the heir could be limited to a very small amount if the testator divided his property among a large number of legatees.[224] In consequence of this, the Falcidian law (40 B. C.) was passed, restricting the total of all legacies to three-fourths of the entire estate. The heir could retain one-fourth for himself even if more than the permitted three-fourths had been bequeathed. This was the law at the time that Gaius wrote in the latter part of the second century, A. D.[225] Justinian, however, provided that a testator could in his discretion prohibit an heir from taking his Falcidian Fourth.[226]

Fideicommissa:

In connection with codicils and legacies it has already been stated that fideicommissa, or gifts, precatory in form, and in the nature of trusts, could be informally bequeathed. Such gifts did not require the execution of a formal will, although they could be

---

222. Gaius 2, 224.
223. Gaius 2, 225. A penalty of four times the excess was imposed upon such a legatee. Ulpian, Frag. 1, 2; Gaius 4, 23, 24.
224. Gaius 2, 226.
225. Gaius 2, 227.
226. Nov. 1, 2; Nov. 119, 11.

created by will, and they were not subject to the technicalities regulating legacies. They originated in a request or wish that one's heir should deliver or transfer to a designated third person some specific property or some portion of the estate of the one who made the request.

Fideicommissa are often referred to as "trusts." They were, indeed, gifts in the nature of trusts, and there is some similarity between the fideicommissum of the Roman Law and the "use" of the English Law.[227] Fideicommissa, moreover, were not binding by the jus civile, and originally they were left to the honor and faith [228] of those charged with their execution. However, they were not "trusts" as that word is employed in our law. With us, a "trust" involves a separation of the titles to the trust property, the legal title being vested in, and for the purposes of the trust retained by, a trustee, the equitable title with all the beneficial enjoyment of the property being vested in another. The Roman Law, however, did not recognize such a dual system of ownership. A fideicommissum was a request that the property in question now owned by one person should be transferred to another person, the transferee being substituted for the former owner. The person to whom the request was made was known as the fiduciarius, the beneficiary being called the fideicommissarius.

Any declaration of one's wishes, however informal, was sufficient to create a fideicommissum. Such words as "I commit it to your good faith;" "I request;" "I wish;" "I beg" and similar words were commonly used.[229] Such a bequest could be made in a will, a codicil, or, in Justinian's time, orally, the bequest in

---

227. Succession of Meunier, 52 La. Ann. 79; Mathurin v. Livaudais, 5 Mart. N. S. 303.

228. Hence the word "fideicommissum," committed to one's good faith. Inst. 2, 23, 1.

229. Ulpian, Frag. 25, 2; Gaius 2, 249; Paulus, Sent., 4, 1, 6.

the latter case being established either by five witnesses or by the beneficiary first swearing to his own good faith, and then requiring the heir either to deny under his oath such a trust or else to perform it.[230]

Fideicommissa were, before the time of Augustus, merely moral obligations on the part of the one to whom the request was made,[231] but that emperor made them legally binding,[232] and placed the matter of their enforcement in the jurisdiction of the two consuls. The Emperor Claudius transferred this jurisdiction to two specially appointed praetors, the number being reduced to one (praetor fideicommissarius) by the Emperor Titus.[233] The court was always open for such cases, at Rome, during the entire year, although in matters pertaining to legacies litigants were required to await the regular days for the trial of actions.[234]

The freedom of fideicommissa from legal technicalities caused their extensive use. Persons who were legally incompetent to take a legacy could, nevertheless, be beneficiaries under a fideicommissum. Aliens, for example, could originally so take, and Gaius says that this was the chief reason why such forms of bequest originated.[235] Other classes of persons who were by various statutes ineligible to accept legacies were held eligible as fideicommissarii, such as unmarried persons who were excluded as heirs or legatees by the Lex Julia[236] and childless persons by the Lex Papia.[237] In fact, for a long time any one could be a beneficiary under a fideicommissum. However, in the course of time the same restrictions were placed

---

230. Inst. 2, 23, 12; 6, 42, 32.
231. Cicero in Verr., 2, 1, 47; Inst. 2, 23, 1.
232. Inst. 2, 23, 12.
233. Pomponius, Dig. 1, 2, 2, 32.
234. Gaius 2, 279.
235. Gaius 2, 285.
236. Gaius, 2, 286.
237. Gaius, 2, 286a.

upon those who could take under a fideicommissum as under a legacy, and only such persons as had capacity to accept a legacy could accept fideicommissum,[238] the Lex Pegasianum applying to fideicommissa the same rules that governed legacies.[239]

The duty to pay a legacy was imposed upon the heir instituted in the will, but in case of a fideicommissum the duty to transfer the property could be charged upon any one who had received a benefit from the decedent's estate. Accordingly, the fiduciarius might be an heir or a legatee in case of a will, or an heir by intestacy. If no designation of a fiduciarius were made, then the duty was presumed to rest upon the heir, or in proportion to the benefits respectively received in case there were two or more heirs.[240]

All kinds of property and rights in property could be bequeathed as fideicommissa as in the case of legacies. This included incorporeal as well as corporeal things. Even property belonging to the fiduciarius or to a third person could be given, the fiduciarius being bound, as in case of an heir in connection with a legacy, to transfer his own property,[241] or in case of a third person's property, to purchase the same, if possible, and then transfer it to the fideicommissarius.

A gift by way of fideicommissum did not pass the title to the property to the beneficiary, but gave him only the right of an action in personam against the fiduciarius.[242] However, in the time of Justinian, a fideicommissarius to whom had been given a specific thing owned by the decedent, could assert his right to the property by a real action.[243]

A fideicommissum could be employed to transfer

238. Ulpian, Frag. 25, 6.
239. Gaius 2, 286a.
240. Dig. 31 33, pr.; Cod. 6, 51, 8.
241. Paulus, Sent., 4, 1, 7.
242. Paulus, Sent., 4, 1, 18.
243. Cod. 6, 43, 1.

from one heir to another the whole of a testator's estate.[244] This was known as a universal fideicommissum in distinction from a fideicommissum rei singulae, or the transfer of some particular thing. When the entire estate or inheritance (hereditas) was thus transferred the fideicommissarius was substituted for the originally instituted heir, and all the assets as well as all the liabilities went with the transfer. It was a means by which a testator could appoint two or more heirs in succession, and persons not having capacity to act as an heir instituted by a will could, by means of such a fideicommissum, succeed the heir first legally instituted. Moreover, all such testamentary provisions were governed by the rules pertaining to fideicommissa instead of the more technical rules applicable to legacies. A person not yet born or even in esse at the time of the testator's death could thus be named as a fideicommissarius, and a universal succession could be created for an indefinite period, even as long as there were any members in the family of the testator. Hence, a perpetuity was thus possible, such a fideicommissum being called, in fact, perpetuum. Justinian, however, placed a limit of four generations upon such family trusts,[245] his legislation in this particular matter being a historical forerunner of our own modern rule against perpetuities.

When universal fideicommissa first came into use, the one who received the inheritance from the regularly instituted heir was regarded as a purchaser of the inheritance, since a successor to a living person was entirely incompatible with the principles of the jus civile. Consequently, it was customary for the fideicommissarius to pay a small coin as the price of the fictitious sale.[246] To carry out further the forms

244. Gaius 2, 246–259; Inst. 2, 23.
245. Nov. 159, 2; Portis v. Hill, 30 Tex. 506, 539.
246. Gaius 2, 252.

of law, mutual stipulations were entered into whereby the heir agreed that any property belonging to the estate and coming subsequently into his hands should be transferred to the "purchaser," and that the "purchaser" should, as the procurator or cognitor of the heir, have full power to maintain actions in all matters pertaining to the estate. The "purchaser" also stipulated that he would reimburse the heir for all payments of money he might be required to make on account of claims against the estate.[247] However, about 60 A. D., in the reign of Nero, a statute known as the Senatus-consultum Trebellianum, made all such proceedings obsolete, since that statute provided that the very act of transferring the estate should give the fideicommissarius the right to sue and to be sued to the same extent as the heir himself.[248] A later act, known as the Senatus-consultum Pegasianum, passed in the reign of Vespasian, further provided that an heir transferring an inheritance should have the same right to retain a fourth of the inheritance as an heir, by virtue of the Lex Falcidia, had in connection with the payment of legacies.[249] The Lex Falcidia applied only to legacies, and a testator by bequeathing fideicommissa could exhaust his estate leaving nothing to the heir. The result was that an heir might refuse to accept the inheritance and, in consequence, the fideicommissa would fail since there was no fiduciarius to make the transfer. The Sc. Pegasianum further provided that if an heir refused to accept the trust, the praetor might, upon the petition of the beneficiary, order the heir to make the transfer.[250]

There were various detailed provisions set forth in the Sc. Trebellianum and the Sc. Pegasianum [251] which,

247. Gaius 2, 252.
248. Gaius 2, 253; Dig. 36, 1, 102; Inst. 2, 23.
249. Gaius 2, 254; Inst. 2, 23, 5.
250. Gaius 2, 258.
251. See Inst. 2, 23, 4–6.

Justinian says,[252] Papinian and many other authorities did not approve, and this dissatisfaction having increased throughout the years, Justinian revised these statutes, merging them into one, but retained the name Trebellianum for the combined law. Under this legislation, the heir was permitted to retain or to claim a fourth part of the estate, and in such a case, both heir and fideicommissarius were proportionately liable for all debts and charges connected with the estate. However, if the heir voluntarily allowed the fideicommissarius to take the entire inheritance, all actions connected with it were maintainable only by or against that beneficiary. In case the heir should refuse to accept, the fideicommissarius could compel a transfer by proper action, the heir, as a result, being deprived of his right to one-fourth, yet, at the same time, being discharged of all liability.[253]

The substitution of one heir for another, in connection with family fideicommissa, continued for centuries on the continent of Europe, after the time of Justinian, and "served to accumulate wealth in a few families at the expense of the interest of the community." [254] Substitutions of this character were forbidden in the Code Napoleon, and all fideicommissa are forbidden in the present code of Louisiana.[255]

252. Inst. 2, 23, 7.
253. Inst. 2, 23, 7.
254. Mr. Justice Campbell in McDonough's Executors v. Murdoch, 15 How. (U. S.) 367.
255. Civil Code, art. 1520. The article is as follows: "Substitutions and fideicommissa are and remain prohibited.

"Every disposition by which the donee, the heir, or legatee is charged to preserve for or to return a thing to a third person is null, even with regard to the donee, the instituted heir or the legatee."

"In consequence of this article the Trebellianic portion of the Civil Law, that is to say, the portion of the property of the testator, which the instituted heir had a right to detain, when he was charged with a fideicommissa or fiduciary bequest is no longer a part of our law." Gaines v. Chew, 2 How. (U. S.) 619, 650; Succession of Mc-Can, 48 La. Ann. 145.

[Roman Law]—40

CHAPTER XXII

THE LAW OF ACTIONS

The Roman Law of actions, or the judicial procedure whereby a Roman enforced his legal rights, was very slowly developed. Its history is long. All that can be attempted within the limits of the present chapter is to point out the more conspicuous steps of its progress and to set forth in a general way the systems that were in use at different periods of time.

The institution of courts and magistrates for the hearing and settling of disputes in accordance with established rules of procedure belongs to a somewhat advanced stage of civilization. Primitive men guard and defend their possessions and their other personal rights by their own individual methods of craft or force, self help being the earliest means of maintaining and enforcing rights. In time, as various rights become generally recognized by groups of men they learn that it is safer and more convenient to refer their disputes to some trusted arbiter selected by the joint consent of the disputants. When groups of people become organized into a state or government under some chieftain, lord, or king, the ruler, while the state is small, becomes naturally the one to whom important matters of dispute are brought for settlement. As the state increases in population, special magistrates are appointed to relieve the ruler of this burden.

Through these various steps in the evolution of litigation the Roman people passed. In the development of their judicial procedure there were in succession three principal systems known respectively as Legis

Actiones, or the procedure fixed by statutory law; the Formulary Procedure; and the Procedure Extra Ordinem.

I. LEGIS ACTIONES:

Concerning the details of the civil procedure known as Legis Actiones there is much difference of opinion among Roman Law scholars since there is very little definite information upon the subject. This procedure antedated the Twelve Tables and was obsolete long before any of the extant writings of the Roman jurists. Our knowledge of these actions has to be gleaned from various extracts found in the fragments of the Twelve Tables and from a very incomplete account of them given by Gaius [1] who mentions them only as a matter of antiquarian interest. He says that the actions used by the ancients were called legis actiones either because they were created by statutes or because they followed the words of the statutes.[2] He also says that there were five forms of these actions, namely, Sacramento (by wager); per Judicis Postulationem (by demanding a judex); per Condictionem (by notice to the defendant); per Manus Injectionem (by laying hands on a judgment debtor); and per Pignoris Capionem (by seizing a pledge).[3]

In connection with these ancient actions there was no judicial summons. The plaintiff had to see to it that he got the defendant into court. He personally cited the defendant to accompany him to the magistrate, and in case the defendant refused to go the plaintiff, after calling upon some person to witness the summons and refusal (antestatio), was legally permitted to take him by force if he could. However, if the defendant based his refusal upon the ground of

1. Gaius 4, 11-30.
2. Gaius 4, 11.
3. Gaius 4, 12.

illness or age, the plaintiff was required to furnish a beast for him to ride.[4]

If the defendant upon being cited settled forthwith the demands of the plaintiff the matter was ended.[5] He could also avoid going before the magistrate by getting a defender to take his place (vindex).[6] Any one could be a vindex for a proletarius,[7] but a higher class of property holders required a vindex of responsible means.[8] The parties, if the case was contested, were required to appear before the magistrate in the Forum before the noon hour. In the event that the defendant, or his vindex, did not appear by that time judgment was given for the plaintiff. Likewise, if the defendant alone appeared judgment was given in his favor. When both appeared and presented their respective claims the hearing could be prolonged until sunset.[9] If for any reason the case was not concluded by that time, bail (vades) might be required for an appearance upon continuance.

The forms of the various legis actiones and the particular demands for which they were respectively brought are not very clear, owing to our scant information. Gaius says that the action by wager (sacramento) was the general action since it was available in cases where no special action was provided by law.[10] It seems to have been regularly employed in disputes over the ownership of property. Gaius gives an illustration of the procedure in such cases.[11] The subject matter of the dispute, if a movable, such as a slave or

4. Twelve Tables.
5. Dig. 2, 4, 22.
6. Gaius 4, 46.
7. Twelve Tables. The proletarii were the lowest property class in the comitia centuriata.
8. Twelve Tables.
9. Ib.
10. Gaius 4, 13.
11. Gaius 4, 16.

an animal, was brought into court, that is, before the magistrate holding court in the open Forum.[12] If the property in question was such that it was not practical to bring it into court, as, for example, a ship, a column, a building, a piece of land, or a herd of cattle, some part or symbol of it was brought in, as a piece of the ship or column, a tile from the building, a clod from the land, or one sheep or other animal from a flock or herd.[13] The question before the court was the ownership of the property thus brought in toto or in part into the presence of the judge. The claimant, or plaintiff, holding a rod which represented a spear, the most ancient and most authoritative symbol of ownership, (that of property obtained by conquest in war), placed his hand upon the property before the court and said, "I say that this is mine according to the law of the citizens of Rome (Quirites)." Thereupon he also laid his rod, or staff, upon the property in token of his absolute ownership. The adversary or defendant, thereupon, said the same words and went through the same ceremony with his rod. Each of the parties having thus asserted his adverse ownership, the magistrate ordered them to take off their rods, whereupon the plaintiff demanded of his adversary why he had made his claim. He answered by saying, "I acted lawfully when I laid on my rod." To this the plaintiff made denial, saying, "Since you have made an unlawful claim, I challenge you by a wager (sacramento) of five hundred pounds of copper."[14] To which the other replied, "Likewise do I challenge you." Gaius says[15] that the wager (sacramentum) was for five hundred asses when the property in dispute was worth one thousand asses

12. Gaius 4, 16.

13. Gaius, 4, 17.

14. "Five hundred asses," says Gaius. An "as" was originally a pound of copper.

15. Gaius 4, 16.

or more, but if the value was less than that the wager was fixed at fifty asses. Bail or security was given by each party for the amount of the "wager," the losing party forfeiting the sum wagered by him to the public treasury.[16] The word sacramentum, "devoted," was originally used, it is said, because the forfeited wager was applied to the maintenance of the sacred rites in the temples.[17]

The wager being duly made, the magistrate gave the temporary possession of the disputed property to one of the parties, requiring security for its delivery to the other party should he be successful in the outcome of the suit.[18] Then a judex or arbitrator was appointed by the magistrate to hear the case.

Up to this point, the proceedings were said to be in jure, that is, before the magistrate who made up the issue. During the period of the legis actiones and likewise during the times of the subsequent formulary procedure, there were regularly two phases or parts to a lawsuit. The first was the proceedings in jure, or the proceedings conducted by the magistrate preliminary to the trial. The second was the proceedings in judicio, which was the hearing or the trial itself, conducted not by a magistrate, (a consul or a praetor) but conducted by a layman, a judex or juror, selected from an official list. In the early days, only citizens of senatorial rank were eligible as judices, but in later times other classes of citizens were added to the list.

The judex being appointed, a day was set for the hearing. On that day the parties appeared before the judex and stated their respective claims. How witnesses were summoned and what was the procedure in general at the trial Gaius does not say. It would seem that the sole question before the judex was which one

---

16. Gaius 4, 16.
17. The reader will see here an analogy to the English "deodand."
18. Gaius 4, 16.

of the claimants was right. If the successful party did not have possession of the subject matter of the suit, the magistrate doubtless granted the necessary execution to obtain it, and also returned to him his sacramentum.

Such is the outline of the procedure in the legis actio sacramento as set forth by Gaius in actions of ownership, either of movables or immovables, that is, actions in rem. The action sacramento was also available in personal actions, that is, actions to recover loans or for claims for damage, but as to such actions Gaius gives no information.

Of the second action mentioned by Gaius, the legis actio per judicis postulationem, practically nothing is known, since his account of it is not extant. It would seem that it applied to cases where the parties were not sure of their legal rights and, accordingly, appeared before the magistrate and began the action by stating the nature of the dispute and "requesting the appointment of a judex" to determine their respective claims. It is supposed that such an action was applicable, for example, when boundaries to adjoining lands were in dispute, or when an inheritance was to be divided among various heirs, or when an accounting was to be made between a guardian and his ward. Gaius says that one could sue by sacramentum or by judicis postulatio for something that ought to be given (quod dari oportet) to him,[19] and it has been supposed by some that this means that the action per judicis postulationem could be used to recover a claim for a definite sum of money. Others, however, are of the opinion that the words of Gaius were used in a broad sense, applying to one's rights in general, including both certain and uncertain rights, and that it was for the latter that the action per judicis postulationem lay. What, however, was the actual scope of this remedy, or what

---

19. Gaius 4, 20.

was the particular procedure connected with it, can be only conjectured.

The actio per condictionem, or an action by notice, was an action in personam whereby the plaintiff sought the recovery of a definite sum of money. It was shorter than the actio sacramenti in that the preliminary proceedings were omitted. It received its name from the fact that the plaintiff gave notice (condictio) to the defendant to appear in court in thirty days to have a judex appointed.[20] Gaius says that this action was created by the Lex Silia and the Lex Calpurnia, the former providing for its use in connection with the recovery of a debt certain, the latter extending the action for any other thing certain.[21] The dates of these two statutes are very uncertain, scholars placing the Lex Silia from 440 B. C. to 240 B. C.[22] The Lex Calpurnia is believed to date about 235 B. C. The name "condictio" was preserved for a long time in Roman civil procedure. It was used in many actions in personam in the time of Gaius, both in actions ex contractu (except bonae fidei actions) and in actions ex delicto. Gaius says that the name condictio was, however, improperly given in his day to personal actions for the recovery of what was due, since a formal notice was no longer the practice.[23]

The next action of the ancient procedure mentioned by Gaius was the actio per manus injectionem, or the action "by the laying on of hands." It was rather a proceeding, originally, for the enforcement of a judgment than an "action" in our modern use of the word. This action was brought, says Gaius,[24] in such cases as were provided by statute, as, for instance, upon a judg-

20. Gaius 4, 18.
21. Gaius 4, 19.
22. Voigt between 443 and 425 B. C.; Ihering between 350 and 300 B. C.; others as late as 240 B. C.
23. Gaius 4, 18.
24. Gaius 4, 21.

ment under a law of the Twelve Tables. The judgment creditor addressing his debtor in formal words, stating the fact of the judgment and the amount, arrested him by taking hold of him. The debtor could not legally resist this arrest, but was required either to pay the judgment or to find a vindex to conduct the case for him if he desired to contest the validity of the judgment before the magistrate. The debtor was not permitted to act for himself. Unless he paid the judgment or furnished a vindex, he was taken to the house of the creditor and bound in chains.[25] The Twelve Tables provided [26] that the creditor could hold the debtor in bonds for sixty days. During this time he was brought before the magistrate on three successive market days and the amount of his debt was publicly declared. After the third market day the debtor could be either put to death or sold as a slave. If there were two or more creditors they were even permitted to cut and divide the body into parts, each creditor taking his proper share, and if a creditor cut more or less than his just portion he was not guilty of any wrong.[27]

It seems incredible that even at a period in Roman history as early as the Twelve Tables such a useless, senseless, and repulsive law in connection with judgment debtors could be in existence. If it be suggested that less than three hundred years ago English Law punished traitors with the quartering of their bodies, it is sufficient to say that the punishment of treason was an entirely different matter from the treatment of one who failed to pay his private debts. It is probable that such a practice was never followed. Dion Cassius, who wrote near the beginning of the third century says [28] that he never read of such a thing be-

25. Gaius 4, 21.
26. Table III.
27. Twelve Tables.
28. Fragm. 17, 8.

ing done. The probabilities are that the judgment debtor who failed to pay was sold as a slave and that the proceeds of the sale were divided among his creditors. Even this procedure was abolished at a very early day, probably by the Lex Poetilia as is generally believed.[29]

The action per manus injectionem was not confined to the enforcement of judgment debts. Gaius says [30] that other statutes made it available to a surety (sponsor) who having paid out money was not reimbursed by the principal debtor within six months; also against one who had received by way of legacy or gift causa mortis more than the law permitted.[31] In these cases the debtor was allowed to resist arrest and act for himself without obtaining a vindex.[32]

The last of the five ancient actions mentioned by Gaius, the legis actio per pignoris capionem (the taking of a pledge) seems to have been a sort of distress. It was entirely extrajudicial [33] and for that reason Gaius did not regard it as an "action," although most jurists, he says, classed it among the legis actiones since the taking of a pledge was accompanied with certain formal words in order to make it legal. The pledge was usually taken in the absence of the opposite party and could be taken even on days on which it was not lawful to hold court.[34] The remedy was brought, says Gaius, in some cases by force of custom, while in other cases it was statutory. It was by custom that it was used in military cases as where a soldier whose pay was in arrears took a pledge from the paymaster

---

29. About 325 B. C.
30. Gaius 4, 22.
31. Gaius 4, 23.
32. Gaius 4, 24, 25.
33. Gaius 4, 29.
34. That is, dies nefasti. Days on which a magistrate could sit were known as dies fasti. There were at one period only 45 such days in the Roman calendar. Mommsen, C. I. L., I, 373.

for the amount due him; or for the money with which he had to buy a horse and also grain for its use. By force of statute, says Gaius, a pledge might be taken from one who had not paid for a sacrificial animal, or from one who had not paid for the hire of a beast of burden one had let in order to get money for a sacrificial feast, or a farmer of the public revenue might take pledges from those who had not paid the tax imposed by any statute.[35]

All these legis actiones, says Gaius,[36] gradually became hateful. Their excessive technicalities were such that the slightest error caused a man to lose his suit. They could be used only by Roman citizens. An alien could neither sue nor be sued. The exact words of the statute under which the legis actio was brought had to be literally followed, and a suit when once brought could not be brought again on the same matter. The commencement of the action extinguished the claim.[37] The Lex Aebutia [38] and two Leges Juliae,[39] says Gaius,[40] practically abolished these actions, and a new method of procedure came into use whereby suits were begun by drawn up statements or formulae. However, in two cases, continues Gaius,[41] a legis actio was allowed, one in the case of threatened damage (damnum infectum), the other in a trial before the Centumviri.[42] Even to the time in which Gaius wrote, a trial by the Centumviri was preceded by a legis actio, still called

35. Gaius 4, 27, 28.
36. Gaius 4, 30.
37. Gaius 4, 108.
38. Date uncertain. Voigt places it about 240 B. C.
39. Time of Augustus.
40. Gaius 4, 30.
41. Gaius 4, 31.
42. The Centumviri, the court of The Hundred Men, was established during the Kingdom and continued in existence till the end of the Western Empire. It was presided over by the praetor. Its chief jurisdiction was in matters relating to various rights in land and inheritances, concurrent with the jurisdiction of a single judex.

sacramentum, before the praetor urbanus or peregrinus. The legis actio, however, in cases of threatened damage (damnum infectum) was obsolete, since a plaintiff found it more advantageous to bind his adversary by a stipulation than by the ancient pignoris capio.

II. THE FORMULARY PROCEDURE:

The second period of civil procedure in the Roman Law is known as the formulary period. Its name is derived from formula, the written statement drawn up by the praetor for the purpose of instructing the judex who was to try the case. It was a brief, concise statement setting out the claim of the plaintiff and the duty of the judex to find either for the plaintiff or for the defendant according to the evidence presented. The date of its introduction as a method of procedure is not certain. Gaius says it originated with the Lex Aebutia,[43] but it was first used, doubtless, by the praetor in connection with the suits of aliens (peregrini) since the ancient legis actiones were available only to citizens. By reason of its simple and practical method it was gradually employed more and more by citizens, until in time it became the established procedure for all litigants. It lasted for about five hundred years, and was the procedure in use during the classical period of Roman jurisprudence. In the later Empire it was, in turn, superseded by the procedure known as extra ordinem.

Under the formulary procedure the plaintiff gave a personal summons to the defendant to appear before the magistrate (in jus vocatio). Failure to appear was punished by a fine.[44] Exceptions were made, however, in certain cases. One could not summon his parents,

---

43. Some authorities place this statute as early as 240 B. C. Others think it was as late as 150 B. C.

44. Gaius 4, 183.

patrons, or patronesses without the permission of the praetor.[45] Moreover, public officials, such as a consul, prefect, praetor, proconsul, or other magistrate, were not ordinarily subject to summons, nor one who was being married, nor a judex while hearing a case, nor one presenting a case to the praetor, nor one attending a funeral in his house.[46] Gaius also says that by weight of authority one could not be summoned while within his house at any time since a man's house is his most secure shelter and retreat.[47]

The law court was located in the Comitium, a small space in the upper part of the Forum. Here white tablets were conspicuously posted informing the citizens of Rome on what days they could lawfully bring their suits (dies fasti).[48] The two praetors, the praetor urbanus and the praetor peregrinus, held their courts here for many years, or until the building of the first basilica, or hall of justice, in 184 B. C.[49] Other basilicas were subsequently built, twenty in number, in the history of the city of Rome. The famous Basilica Julia was begun by Julius Caesar and was completed by Augustus. Basilicas were all of the same general plan, rectangular in shape, the width about a half or a third of the length. There was a long central nave, lined by columns on each side. At one end of the nave was a semicircular niche containing the tribunal of the praetor. When engaged in his duties as a magistrate the praetor wore the toga praetexta, a white toga with a purple stripe woven in the garment. His chair of office was the sella curulis, its frame made of ivory, without a back, and having curved legs. The seat was made of plaited leather strips. It could be folded, like

45. Ib.
46. Ulpian, Dig. 2, 4, 2 & 3 and 4, pr.
47. Dig. 2, 4, 18, 21.
48. Liv. 9, 46.
49. The Basilica Porcia. Livy 39, 44, 7.

a modern camp-stool, and was easily carried. In the city of Rome a praetor was usually attended by two lictors,[50] bearing the fasces.[51] Whenever the praetor appeared in public the lictors preceded him, warning all persons, excepting matrons and vestal virgins, to make way for him and to honor him with due obeisance.

Judicial proceedings under the formulary procedure consisted of two parts, just as under the legis actiones. The first part, the proceedings before the praetor, was known as the proceedings in jure, and the trial proper, or the proceedings before the judex, was known as the proceedings in judicio. The object of the proceedings before the praetor was to settle the issue (litis contestatio). This being done, the praetor prepared the formula which named a judex, appointed by the praetor, to try the case, and set forth the necessary instructions for the guidance of the hearing.

Actions could be brought or defended by the parties in person or by "agents" known either as cognitors or procurators. They were not advocates but persons who took the place of the real parties. Such a procedure was not possible under the ancient legis actiones, but was available under the formula by substituting the name of one person for another. A cognitor was an agent appointed by formal words in the presence of the opposite party.[52] A procurator was substituted for the principal in a suit without any set form, even by a mere mandate, and even in his absence, and without the knowledge of the other party.[53] When parties

50. Six lictors in the provinces.
51. A bundle of wooden rods, with a protruding axe-head, tied together with a red strap. The fasces were carried by the lictors over the left shoulder. The modern term "fascism" is derived from this emblem of authority, and the same official emblem has been adopted by the present government of Italy.
52. Gaius 4, 83.
53. Gaius 4, 84.

were thus represented by others the name of the substitute instead of the name of the principal was inserted in the condemnatio clause of the formula.[54]

In certain cases third persons were required to represent others. Persons under seventeen years of age, and deaf persons were not competent to sue,[55] and persons under guardianship were represented by their tutors or curators.[56]

The parties having appeared before the praetor, the plaintiff (actor) stated his case. Then the defendant (reus) told his side of the matter. These proceedings were all oral and were intended to bring out the issue and at the same time to ascertain all the equities of the case. The time required to do this varied in length according to the nature of the case. Sometimes the proceedings in jure were very brief, but at other times they were prolonged. If they were not completed on the same day, the defendant was required to give security (vadimonium) either a promise or bail (vades) for his appearance upon continuance to some subsequent day.[57]

It has at times excited the wonder of some that a Roman praetor whose term of office was but a year, and who seldom was trained in jurisprudence since many Romans prominent in public life, including statesmen, military leaders, and politicians, were at some time in their careers elected to the office, could have succeeded so well as a magistrate, and have possessed the necessary legal ability to guide and direct all classes of litigants in the days of Rome's greatest population. The answer to this apparent puzzle is that a praetor had the assistance of men learned in the law (juris consults) known officially as assessors, lit-

54. Gaius 4, 86.
55. Dig. 3, 1, 1, 4.
56. Gaius 4, 82; Inst. 4, 10, pr.; Dig. 3, 1, 1, 6.
57. Gaius 4, 184, 185.

erally, "those sitting with one." In the early days a praetor chose whom he would to assist him in his magisterial duties. In later times no magistrate was allowed to sit without one or more official assessors, and in the days of the Empire assessors were paid regular salaries.[58] Assessors had no magisterial authority, and a praetor was not bound to follow their opinions. They were, however, amici curiae and indispensable to the ordinary magistrate. There were, of course, from time to time, many very able lawyers, men of great legal attainments, who were elected praetors. Such a one, for example, was Cicero. Nevertheless, the great majority of Roman praetors needed the constant legal advice of wiser men.

The Formula:

After hearing the parties, the praetor summed up the essential points involved, including the claim of the plaintiff and the defense or defenses (exceptiones), if any, of the defendant. These he reduced to a brief, terse statement in writing, for the purpose of giving the judex, who was designated in the instrument, his instructions. This short, concise bill of instructions, laying down the matters the judex was to ascertain and then to pass judgment upon, was the formula.

The regular parts of a formula following the naming of the judex were the demonstratio, the intentio, and either the adjudicatio, or the condemnatio.[59] The demonstratio stated the subject matter of the dispute, such as the cause of action, the nature of the plaintiff's right, or the basis of his claim, as, for example, "Whereas Aulus Agerius sold a slave to Numerius Negidius," or "Whereas Aulus Agerius deposited a slave in the hands of Numerius Negidius."[60] The intentio stated the specific claim of the plaintiff (actor),

58. Dig. 1, 22; Cicero de Orat. 1, 37.
59. Gaius 4, 39.
60. Gaius 4, 40.

as, for example, "If it be proved that Numerius Negidius ought to pay ten thousand sesterces [61] to Aulus Agerius;" or "Whatever it be proved that Numerius Negidius ought to pay to Aulus Agerius;" or "If it be proved that the slave lawfully belongs to Aulus Agerius." [62]

The adjudicatio was that part of a formula which directed the judex to make the proper transfers of ownership in actions for the distribution of an inheritance among co-heirs, or for partitioning common property between partners, or for fixing boundaries between adjoining landowners. For example, "As much of the property as should be adjudged to Titus do thou, judex, adjudge." [63]

The part of the formula known as the condemnatio instructed the judex either to condemn or to absolve the defendant. For example, "Do thou, judex, condemn Numerius Negidius to pay to Aulus Agerius ten thousand sesterces, but if it is not proved, absolve him;" or "Do thou, judex, condemn Numerius Negidius to pay to Aulus Agerius a sum not exceeding ten thousand sesterces, but if it is not proved, absolve him;" or "Do thou, judex, condemn Numerius Negidius to pay Aulus Agerius," etc., without specifying a limit of the sum to be paid.[64]

A complete formula of a very simple type ran, therefore, by way of example, as follows; "To Titus who is appointed judex: Whereas Aulus Agerius [65] sold a

---

61. During the Republic and the first 300 years of the Empire, money was reckoned in sesterces. Ten thousand sesterces were approximately $425, a sestertius being a copper coin worth a little over four cents.

62. Gaius 4, 41.

63. Gaius 4, 42.

64. Gaius 4, 43.

65. The names Aulus Agerius and Numerius Negidius were used illustratively by the Roman jurists as we, in our law, use the names John Doe and Richard Roe. The parties' real names were, of course, inserted in the formula.

slave to Numerius Negidius (demonstratio), if it be proved that Numerius Negidius owes Aulus Agerius ten thousand sesterces (intentio), do thou condemn Numerius Negidius to pay Aulus Agerius ten thousand sesterces; but if it is not proved, absolve him" (condemnatio).

However, not always were these usual parts of the formula employed. A formula might consist of the intentio alone as in a formula directing the judex to decide whether a man is a freedman, or to ascertain the amount of a dowry, and many other inquiries.[66] The demonstratio, the adjudicatio, and the condemnatio, on the other hand, were never used alone, since they were meaningless without some other part. A demonstratio always required an intentio and either an adjudicatio or a condemnatio, while an adjudicatio or a condemnatio would have no force without a demonstratio or an intentio.[67]

A formula was not always as brief and as simple as the illustration above. Besides the usual three parts, the demonstratio, intentio, and condemnatio,[68] there was always a clause appointing a judex and often other matter such as an exceptio or a praescriptio was added. The exceptio which was in the nature of a plea was made a part of the intentio. This might be followed by a replicatio, or a reply on behalf of the plaintiff.[69] In turn, the replicatio might be qualified by the duplicatio, a further addition in aid of the defendant.[70] Likewise, the duplicatio was subject to a possible triplicatio in the interest of the plaintiff [71] in case the du-

66. Gaius 4, 44.
67. Gaius 4, 44.
68. The adjudicatio was used instead of the condemnatio only in the three classes of cases already mentioned.
69. Gaius 4, 126.
70. Gaius 4, 127.
71. Gaius 4, 128.

[Roman Law]

plicatio did not fairly meet all the aspects of the case.[72] In some instances the great variety of possible circumstances might require even further additions.[73]

The Exceptio:

The formula did not provide for a plea of the general issue, or a general denial, since that was included in the very form of the intentio and the condemnatio, as, for example, "If it be proved that Numerius Negidius owes, etc., condemn him to pay, etc., but if it is not proved, absolve him." The exceptio was in the nature of a special plea in bar, which pleaded some defense, against the claim of the plaintiff. Exceptions were expressed in the form of a negative condition. For example, if one compelled by fear, or induced by fraud, or misled by error entered into a stipulation to pay money which he did not owe, he could when sued defend by an exception.[74] In case the defendant alleged fraud (dolus malus), the exception read: "If in that matter there was and is no fraud of Aulus Agerius."[75] Likewise, if instead of alleging fraud the defendant alleged that he had entered into a pact (an informal agreement) with the plaintiff whereby the plaintiff agreed not to claim the money, the informal agreement while not extinguishing the obligation to pay, could, nevertheless, be pleaded by way of exception, as, "If Aulus Agerius and Numerius Negidius did not agree that the money should not be demanded."[76] In addition to such equitable defenses as these mentioned,

---

72. The intentio of the formula corresponded to the declaration of our common law pleading. The exceptio would then correspond to the plea, the replicatio to the replication, the duplicatio to the rejoinder, and the triplicatio to the sur-rejoinder.

73. Gaius 4, 129. In such cases the additional pleadings, quadruplicatio and quintuplicatio, would correspond, next in order, to the common law rebutter and surrebutter.

74. Inst. 4, 13, 1.

75. Gaius 4, 119.

76. Gaius 4, 119.

other defenses, including those created by the praetor and those given by virtue of some statute, could be taken advantage of by means of an exceptio.[77]

Exceptions were either peremptory (absolute) or dilatory.[78] Peremptory exceptions were always available, without limitation as to time, such as fraud, duress, res judicata, some opposing statute, or an informal agreement not to sue for the debt in question.[79] Dilatory exceptions were those which could be pleaded only at certain times or only against some particular person,[80] as, for instance, an informal agreement not to sue for five years in which case the exception would not be valid after five years, or an exception taken against one suing as a cognitor who was not lawfully appointed as another's representative.[81]

As already stated, an exceptio might be answered by a replicatio, which in turn might be countered by a duplicatio, which could be followed by a triplicatio. Where, for example, a creditor makes an informal agreement (pact) with his debtor not to sue upon the debt, and then, subsequently, makes another agreement (pact) that the original right to sue shall stand, if the debtor later pleads the first pact as an exceptio to his creditor's action upon the debt, the plaintiff creditor can reply (replicatio) by setting up the second pact.[82] In such a case, the formula would run about as follows:

"Titus is appointed judex. Whereas Aulus Agerius stipulated for 10,000 sesterces from Numerius Negidius (demonstratio), if it be proved that Numerius Negidius ought to pay Aulus Agerius 10,000 sesterces (intentio), provided that Aulus Agerius and Numerius

---

77. Gaius 4, 118.
78. Gaius 4, 120.
79. Gaius 4, 121.
80. Gaius 4, 122, 123, 124.
81. Gaius 4, 122, 123, 124.
82. Gaius 4, 126.

Negidius did not agree that the money should not be demanded (exceptio), and if there was no subsequent agreement that Aulus Agerius might sue (replicatio), do thou, judex, condemn Numerius Negidius to pay Aulus Agerius 10,000 sesterces, or if it be not proved, do thou absolve him."

Praescriptio:

The pleadings might be further modified by a praescriptio or a clause written before the formula proper. In the early times of the formulary procedure a praescriptio was available to either the plaintiff or the defendant, but later it was restricted to the use of the plaintiff. The cases where it had previously been employed by a defendant, namely, when pleading res judicata and the limitation of an action by lapse of time (praescriptio temporis [83]) were later covered by the use of exceptions.[84]

A praescriptio was regularly introduced by the words ea res agatur (let only this question be considered). Its purpose was to confine the judex to the determination of a particular matter, disregarding all other questions. Ordinarily a formula covered the entire subject and might include a number of matters incidental to the case. When the cause of action was determined and stated by the praetor in the formula, it was the final settlement of the issue or issues to be tried (litis contestatio). It covered the whole transaction set forth in the demonstratio and no subsequent action was granted. Accordingly, in order to preserve one's possible other rights, present or future, connected with the same matter, it became the practice to limit the inquiry by prefixing a clause to the formula showing the sole question at issue at the time being. For example, if one were suing for the conveyance of

83. Whence the term prescription in our law.
84. Gaius 4, 130–133.

land which he claimed to have bought, if he did not limit his action he might subsequently, in case he wished the possession of the land to be delivered to him, be unable to maintain such an action. Consequently, to preserve this right to sue, he had the praetor prefix to the formula the clause, "Let the sole question be the conveyance of the land." [85] Likewise, in further illustration, if one were entitled to money in a series of annual or monthly payments, some of which were due, others being payable in the future, unless a praescriptio expressly provided that the only question to be considered was the money now due, any recovery of money due would bar all future actions for sums falling due in the future.[86] A praescriptio, therefore, narrowed the issue, leaving the plaintiff to sue upon any future claims connected with the transaction.

Formulas in Factum or in Jus:

In the drawing up of formulas the form of the intentio may be said to be either conceived in fact (in factum concepta) or conceived in law (in jus concepta). That is, the claim set forth in the intentio might present either a question of fact or a question of law. In each case, however, the law or the fact was to be determined by the judex. For example, in case of the loan of a chattel (depositum) which the borrower has failed to return, the formula might read: "Let Lucius Titius be judex. Whereas Aulus Agerius deposited a silver table with N. Negidius, which is the ground of the action, whatever on that account N. Negidius ought in good faith to pay or to render to Aulus Agerius, do thou, judex, condemn N. Negidius to do, unless he makes restitution. If it be not proved, absolve him." Such a formula is said to be conceived

85. Gaius 4, 131.
86. Gaius 4, 131a.

in law.[87] On the other hand, a formula reading: "Let Lucius Titius be judex. If it is proved that Aulus Agerius deposited a silver table with Numerius Negidius, and that by the fraud of Numerius Negidius it has not been restored to Aulus Agerius, do thou, judex, condemn Numerius Negidius to pay to Aulus Agerius whatever the table is worth. If it be not proved, absolve him," is conceived in fact.[88] The first class of formulas gives rise to an issue of law, that is, the defendant's legal obligation. The second class raises an issue of fact, that is, whether the defendant did or did not do the thing charged. In deciding such issues of law, the judex in certain actions, known as actions bonae fidei,[89] was called upon to decide what was fair and equitable between the parties in connection with the transaction upon which the suit was brought. Again, if a patron was suing his freedman for summoning him before a magistrate (which thing a freedman could not legally do), the formula may have run: "Let so and so be recuperatores. If it be proved that such and such a patron was summoned to appear by so and so his freedman against the edict of the praetor, condemn the said freedman to pay the said patron 10,000 sesterces; if it be not proved, absolve him." Such an issue is clearly one of fact. On the other hand, an intentio claiming that a thing legally belongs to the plaintiff is manifestly an issue of law.[90] Some actions, as, for example, those based upon depositum and commodatum (deposit and loan) could be cast in either form, as illustrated above in connection with the "deposit" of the silver table.[91]

A formula in factum concepta should not be con-

87. Gaius 4, 47.
88. Ib.
89. Post.
90. Gaius 4, 46.
91. Gaius 4, 47.

fused with an action in factum with particular introductory words (praescriptis verbis). The latter was analogous to "an action on the case" in English Common Law procedure. The ordinary formulas were taken from the praetor's Album, an official set of formulas for regular use. When a cause of action did not come within such formulas, the praetor framed a formula to suit the facts of the case and stated in praescripta verba such facts in place of the usual demonstratio. Consequently, although the issue was in jus concepta, yet the action was in factum.[92]

Fictions: In framing formulas resort was at times made by the praetor to certain fictions in order to bring a case within the recognized procedure. By the use of fictions effect was also given to various equities; and in this way the praetor greatly extended and reformed the rigid rules of the jus civile by enforcing rights not recognized under that law. For example, one might be equitably entitled to a deceased person's estate and the praetor may have given to him the possession of the property (possessio bonorum). Such a person could not claim, however, to be the legal heir, the heir under the jus civile, and consequently could not sue as heir (haeres). In such a case, the praetor framed the formula by a fiction so that he could sue, as follows: "Let so and so be judex. If Aulus Agerius were the legal heir of so and so (fiction), and if as such heir it be proved that the land (in question) ought to be his by the jus civile, then award said land to Aulus Agerius," etc.[93] Again, an alien might sue or be sued for theft (furtum) or injury (injuria) by a fiction representing him as a Roman citizen.[94] Other illustrations are given by Gaius

92. Dig. 19, 5.
93. Gaius 4, 34.
94. Gaius 4, 37.

relating to usucapio and capitis deminutio.[95] The defendant was not permitted to question the fiction or to object on the ground that the supposed facts were not true. In this way the praetor was enabled by his power to grant or to deny actions to modify greatly the rigors of the old law.

The Proceedings in Judicio:

The formula being determined upon and reduced to writing, the next step was the hearing, or the trial, conducted by the appointed judex. The twofold proceedings in jure and in judicio had an analogy in early English Common Law procedure. The plaintiff went to the Chancellor, or Court of Chancery, to obtain an original writ, or, we may say, a formula, of the action he was entitled to bring. Such a writ had to conform to someone of the recognized writs on file in the Court of Chancery. Armed with this writ the plaintiff then repaired to the court of law to which his writ was directed, and there prepared his declaration which had to conform to the original writ. There were striking differences, however, in the Roman and the English procedure. The Roman praetor had no scruples in framing new actions. If the customary formulas on file in his records (the praetor's Album) did not fit a particular case, he did not hesitate to frame one that would. The characteristic conservative attitude of the English Court of Chancery and its unwillingness to grant new writs prevented English procedure, however, from developing normally and effectively so as to meet the requirements of litigation. Thus it was that, in England, courts of equity and courts of law remained separate and distinct for centuries, while, in Rome, instead of two systems of jurisprudence, law and equity, growing up side by side, the old jus civile and the jus gentium under the mould-

---

95. Gaius 4, 36, 38.

ing influence of the praetor became blended into one as in our modern "code" procedure.

The English original writ was the commission or warrant by which the plaintiff brought his suit in a court of law. In like manner the Roman formula was the official warrant for the judex's power to hear and adjudge the case. No new pleadings, however, were filed in the court of the judex. He tried the case invariably upon the original formula. It marked the complete limits of his jurisdiction.

The English original writ was taken to a court of law, to a judge or judges learned in the law. Not so the Roman formula. The judex was not a learned lawyer, not a juris consult, he was only a private citizen, a layman. He had no magisterial authority in himself. The judgment he declared in any case presented to him was not his judgment, it was the judgment of the praetor by virtue of the power delegated to the judex in the formula.

The proceedings in jure, or before the praetor, being completed, the parties returned on the thirtieth day for the appointment of a judex.[96] At least, such was the procedure under the old system of the legis actiones and the presumption is that the same practice was followed under the formula. Doubtless the formula had been framed in the interval and at this second appearance before the praetor the name of the judex, after consultation with the parties, was probably inserted. The judex was required to be a disinterested person,[97] and while it was desirable that the parties should agree upon a judex, yet it was not proper for the praetor to appoint anyone suggested by only one side.[98]

---

96. Gaius 4, 15, 18. Such was the practice, says Gaius, after the Lex Cinaria. The date of this statute is uncertain.
97. Dig. 5, 1, 17.
98. Dig. 5, 1, 47.

The judex being appointed the parties appeared before him two days later,[99] at some place in the Forum, and the judex appointed a day for the hearing. If the judex was so engrossed with other duties that a considerable time would elapse before the hearing could be held, the praetor appointed another judex.[100]

On the day appointed for the hearing the trial took place somewhere in the Forum. The hearing, however, could be postponed for proper cause, as, for example, where important witnesses were absent in the service of the State.[101]

The litigants were often assisted by patroni or advocati, and the judex could summon, and usually did, learned jurists (jurisconsults) to sit with him in order that they might advise him upon matters of law.[102] The proceedings were open to the public. A case was opened, regularly, by the parties, either in person or, more usually, by their patroni or advocati, stating to the judex its nature. These introductory speeches were very long, at times, but they afforded schools of oratory for hundreds of ambitious young men who crowded the places of the law hearings. After the opening addresses came the evidence which might consist of both oral testimony and documents,[103] and also of the written statements of absent witnesses.[104] The witnesses were sworn and were subject to cross-examination. The burden of proof was upon the plaintiff.[105]

After the evidence the arguments of the patroni or the advocati followed, summing up the case very much as in modern times. Again, these speeches were

99. Gaius 4, 15.
100. Dig. 5, 1, 18, pr.
101. Dig. 5, 1, 36, pr.
102. Cicero in Verr. 2, 29, 72; pro P. Quintio 10, 30.
103. Dig. 5, 1, 36, pr.; 22, 4; Cod. 4, 21.
104. Dig. 22, 5.
105. Dig. 50, 17, 125.

often prolonged. They sometimes occupied five or six hours, and even a whole day. A water-clock,[106] on the principle of a sand glass, was used to measure the time, and to give an advocate time was said "to give him water." Pliny said [107] that whenever he held court he gave the advocates "all the water they wanted." An advocate was often assisted by a brief prepared by some jurisconsult. While in court an advocate's professional costume consisted of a white toga. An advocate's services were considered above mere hire, consequently no action lay to recover his fees. Substantial gifts, as honoraria, were, however, bestowed upon advocates by their clients, and often the gratitude of clients was further shown by legacies in their wills. Some advocates became very rich. Cicero was a noted example in this respect.

The earliest age at which one could appear in court for another was seventeen years, and it is said that Nerva the Younger practiced as an advocate when he was of that age.[108] In Justinian's time a period of five years of study was required for admission to the bar,[109] and applicants had to be of good character.[110] Women were not allowed to practice.[111] For misconduct after his admission an advocate might be disbarred.[112]

The courts of Rome developed some very brilliant orators, but oratory reached its greatest height in the closing days of the Republic. The profession of the law was also the gateway, next to leadership in the army, to political preferment. It is remarkable, however, that so many of the distinguished advocates of

106. Clepsydra.
107. Epis. 6, 2.
108. Dig. 3, 1, 1, 3.
109. Dig. Const. Omnem.
110. Dig. 3, 1, 1, 5.
111. Dig. 3, 1, 1, 5.
112. Dig. 3, 1, 8.

Rome were also famous in literature. Cato the Elder, Crassus, Julius Caesar, Hortensius, Cicero, Catulus, Asinius Pollio, Quintilian, Tacitus, Suetonius, and Pliny were all advocates, yet were likewise men of letters, writers of history, philosophy, essays, letters, and poetry. Cicero stands forth as the most eminent of the Romans both as an orator and as a writer.

However, then as now, there were advocates and advocates. There was always "room at the top." The tendency of some advocates to wander from their objectives, and to indulge in many irrelevant digressions in connection with their orations before the court, brought forth from the Roman poet, Martial, a famous epigram which will, doubtless, have its appropriate application in every age: "O mister Advocate, my case has nothing to do with violence, murder, or poison. I merely accuse my neighbor of having stolen my three goats, and the court expects me to prove it. You, however, with all the strength of your voice and with a pounding of the table with your fist, only shout about the battle of Cannae, the war of Mithridates, the perfidy of the Carthaginians, and about Sylla, Marius, and Mucius. Say something, I beseech you, about my three goats." [113]

At the conclusion of the arguments the judex rendered judgment, either a "condemno" or an "absolvo" as directed by the formula. In case of a judgment of condemnation the plaintiff was always ordered to pay the defendant a certain sum even if no definite sum was named in the formula.[114] When, however, a certain sum was laid in the formula he was required, in case of condemnation, to assess that exact sum. A condemnation in a greater or a lesser sum rendered the judex liable to the injured party in

---

113. Martial 6, 19.
114. Gaius 4, 51.

a quasi delictual action.[115] It was disputed at one time whether a judex had power to absolve a defendant who satisfied the plaintiff before judgment but after the trial had begun.[116] The practice was to absolve, and Justinian confirmed this view.[117]

New Trials:

New trials as we understand the term, that is, granting for various grounds hearings de novo by the trial judge or court, were unknown to Roman procedure, but there were possible proceedings that more or less resembled them. Since a judex had no authority to enforce a judgment rendered by him, it was necessary for a plaintiff in whose favor a judgment had been rendered to go back to the praetor to obtain execution in case the defendant failed to pay. At such a time, if the judgment were null and void or defective or unjust, it was within the power of the praetor to issue a new formula and to appoint a new judex. A judgment was null and void in that it was based on an error of law appearing on its face;[118] or in that it was for a larger sum than authorized,[119] unless the parties agreed to such sum;[120] or in that it had been obtained by the wilful suppression of evidence, as the concealment of documents;[121] or if rendered in a party's absence due to illness or public business.[122]

Classes of Actions:

While there were particular names for specific actions, yet actions were variously classified by the Roman jurists. In some cases they were classed ac-

---

115. Gaius 4, 52; Inst. 4, 5, 1, pr.; Dig. 5, 1, 15, 1.
116. Gaius 4, 114.
117. Inst. 4, 12, 2.
118. Dig. 49, 1, 19; Cod. 1, 21, 3; Dig. 42, 1, 27; 49, 8, 1, 2.
119. Dig. 50, 17, 170.
120. Dig. 5, 1, 74, 1.
121. Cod. 2, 4, 19.
122. Dig. 5, 1, 75; 42, 1, 60; 42, 1, 9; 49, 8, 2, pr.

cording to the rights and duties of the parties, in others according to the origin of the actions, or the form in which they were framed, or the nature of the remedy sought. Justinian defines an action as the right to obtain by means of a judicial prosecution what is due to one.[123] Actions, says Gaius,[124] are of two classes, real (in rem) or personal (in personam), and in this statement he is followed by Justinian.[125] A real action is brought against one not because of any obligation on the defendant's part, but because the plaintiff claims to be the owner of some corporeal thing or of some particular right in a thing, as, for example, where a plaintiff claims to be the owner of land in the possession of the defendant, or a right to use a thing owned by another, or a right of way across another's land, or a right to conduct water over a neighbor's land.[126] Actions relating to praedial servitudes, such as a right to raise one's house above a certain height, or to have an unobstructed view, or to project one's house over a neighbor's land, or to use a neighboring house wall for the insertion of beams to support one's own building, are also real actions.[127] Actions relating to usufructus and servitudes may be positive or negative.[128] They are positive when the right is claimed, and negative when the right is denied and the action is brought against one who is alleged to be unlawfully exercising such a use or servitude.[129]

A real action was founded upon a jus in rem, that is, a property right, and included, as shown above, rights of ownership and rights in the property of an-

123. Inst. 4, 6, pr.
124. Gaius 4, 1.
125. Inst. 4, 6, 1; Dig. 44, 7, 25.
126. Gaius 4, 3; Inst. 4, 6, 1 and 2.
127. Gaius 4, 3; Inst. 4, 6, 2.
128. Gaius 4, 3; Inst. 4, 6, 2.
129. Ib.

other, jura in re aliena. It extended to both immovable and movable property, and thus differed from our English Common Law "real actions." The Roman real actions are often said to include disputes relating to the status of a person, that is, whether a man is free born, or a freedman, or whether he is the child of a reputed father. Justinian however, calls such actions prejudicial actions,[130] or questions preliminary to the determination of other questions. They seem to be real actions in that they are not based upon any defendant's obligation.

A personal action is an action brought against a person who is under an obligation by reason of his contract, quasi contract, delict, or quasi delict.[131]

A real action, that is, an action to recover property, was called vindicatio, and a personal action was called condictio.[132] Both of these terms were derived from the ancient legis actiones procedure, although not used in the ancient technical sense. Condictio meant "notice," the plaintiff formerly giving notice to the defendant to appear before the praetor. In the time of Gaius, the term was applied to personal actions although notice was no longer the practice.[133] Condictio, however, was applied to actions stricti juris and did not include actions bonae fidei.

Another division of actions consisted of civil and praetorian actions.[134] The former are derived from the civil law (jus civile) or from special statutes. The latter were actions granted by the praetor by virtue of his magisterial power.[135] Praetorian actions were otherwise called actiones honorariae. All actions fall

130. Inst. 4, 6, 13; Gaius 4, 44.
131. Gaius 4, 2; Inst. 4, 6, 1.
132. Gaius 4, 5; Inst. 4, 6, 15.
133. Gaius 4, 18.
134. Inst. 4, 6, 3.
135. Inst. 4, 6, 3; Gaius 4, 103.

into one or the other of these two classes.[136] For example, an action based upon a formal verbal contract (stipulatio) was a civil action, but an action allowed by the praetor upon an informal agreement, an agreement not recognized by the jus civile as creating an obligation, was a praetorian action. Praetorian actions could be brought, as a rule, only during the praetor's year of office, but civil actions could be brought at any time except as limited by special statute.[137]

A third important division of actions, especially during the formulary procedure, was that of actions stricti juris, actions bonae fidei, and actions arbitrariae, a classification of actions based upon the amount of discretion given to a judex in the trial of a case. Actions stricti juris were founded on unilateral contracts. The rights of the parties were governed by the literal terms of the agreement, and by the strict letter of the law, as in the case of an action condictio brought upon a stipulation. No discretion was given to a judex in such an action, since the parties were held to the exact statement of the formula. Actions bonae fidei, on the other hand, were based upon bilateral contracts and were actions of praetorian origin. In such actions a judex had ample powers to consider all the equities of the case, and to use his discretion in deciding how much was due the plaintiff, after considering what each owed to the other in the light of their mutual duty to exercise good faith in the transaction upon which the action was founded. Counterclaims of the defendant arising out of the same transactions could be considered by the judex,[138] as could also any acts of dolus malus although no "exceptio," or defense, on that ground had been inserted in the

---

136. Dig. 44, 7, 25.
137. Gaius 4, 104, 105.
138. Gaius 4, 61, 63; Dig. 21, 1, 31, 20; The C. B. Sanford, 22 Fed. Rep. 863.

formula.[139] Bonae fidei actions included actions of purchase and sale, letting and hiring, negotiorum gestio, mandate, depositum, fiducia (mortgage), partnership, guardianship, dotal property, commodatum, pledge, partition of an inheritance, partition of land, and actions on the case (praescriptis verbis) based on a commission to sell at a fixed price (de aestimato) or exchange (permutatio).[140] It will be noted that all these actions are personal actions, since a real action (vindicatio) was stricti juris, being based upon a single question, that is, the ownership of the property in issue. Justinian, however, placed the real action for the demand of an inheritance (petitio heredatis) among bonae fidei actions, thus making an exception to the general rule.[141] Actiones arbitrariae were actions for the production or the restitution of property. In these actions, called arbitrary because depending upon the order (arbitrium) of the judex,[142] if the defendant did not comply with the order to produce or to restore the thing demanded the judex could order him to pay the value of the property in question.[143] Of these actions some were real and some personal. They differed from a strict real action, however, since in a vindicatio rei the plaintiff had no alternative relief if the defendant was no longer in possession of the property.[144] Moreover, arbitrary actions were bonae fidei in their nature since the judex was authorized to consider the circumstances and equities of the case, and to decide what the plaintiff ought to receive.[145]

Actions were further divided into direct and con-

---

139. Dig. 30, 84, 5.
140. Gaius 4, 62; Inst. 4, 6, 28.
141. Inst. 4, 6, 28.
142. Inst. 4, 6, 31.
143. Inst. 4, 6, 31; Dig. 12, 3, 5.
144. Dig. 6, 1, 68; 12, 3, 1, 2.
145. Inst. 4, 6, 31.

[Roman Law]

trary (actiones directae and actiones contrariae), direct and noxal (actiones noxales), and direct and "serviceable" (actiones utiles). In these three divisions of actions the term "direct" was used in different senses. Direct and contrary actions were reciprocal or counter actions in connection with bilateral contracts where from the nature of the contract one of the parties was practically the only beneficiary, and where ordinarily an action would be brought only by the other party. For example, in the contract of commodatum or of depositum the action, if any, would ordinarily be brought by the party who had loaned or deposited a thing. This was called a direct action (actio directa). However, if the other party had any just ground for refusing to deliver, or had incurred expense or suffered damage in connection with the transaction, he, in turn, had a counter action. Such an action in case of commodatum was called an actio commodati contraria,[146] and in case of depositum, an actio depositi contraria.[147]

The terms "direct" and "noxal" were also used at times, in connection with actions, to distinguish one's liability for his own wrong (direct) from his vicarious liability for the wrong (noxia) done by one in his power, as a son or a slave.[148] Noxal actions were either statutory or praetorian. The Twelve Tables gave an action against a father or a master for a theft committed by a son or a slave, the Lex Aquilia gave a similar action for injury to property (damnum injuria datum), and the praetor for "insult" (injuria) and for rapine (vi bona rapta).[149] In the time of Justinian, noxal actions applied only to wrongs committed by

146. Dig. 13, 6, 17.
147. Dig. 16, 3, 5, pr.
148. Gaius 4, 75–80; Inst. 4, 8.
149. Gaius 4, 76; Inst. 4, 8, 4.

slaves.[150] A noxal action was also allowed for damage done by one's animals (pauperies).[151]

The term "direct action" was more frequently used, however, in contrast with an action "utilis." In this connection a direct action was one grounded directly upon the words of the statute creating it. An actio utilis was one created by the praetor. It was not based upon the direct words of a statute, but was an equitable extension of the statutory action whereby the praetor permitted an action to be brought under circumstances that were similar to those set forth in the statute yet not identical with them. It was in the granting of such actions to meet new but similar cases that the great constructive work of the Roman praetor was done. An existing statutory action was often not applicable to numerous cases that arose, but the praetor was able, by means of fictions (actiones fictitiae) or by means of a formula based upon the facts of the case (in factum concepta), to frame an action that was serviceable (utilis) for the purpose. The nature of the actio utilis was similar always to the original statutory action, and by the means mentioned above was brought within its spirit. The relation of an actio utilis to an actio directa was the same as the relation of writs in trespass on the case, framed more than a thousand years later, in England, by the clerks in Chancery, to the old writ of trespass.

An action in factum concepta is sometimes confused with an action in factum praescriptis verbis. They differed, however, in that the former action was based upon an existing statutory action, while the latter was not. When the praetor granted actions for contract which had no specific names in the jus civile, and for which, in consequence, no recognized statutory action existed, he framed a formula in which the words which

150. Inst. 4, 8, 7.
151. Inst. 4, 9, pr.; Dig. 9, 1.

gave rise to the contract (praescriptis verbis) were substituted for the demonstratio. Since this was a special form of an action based upon the facts of an innominate contract it was called an actio in factum praescriptis verbis, although it was similar to an action in jus concepta in the case of a nominate contract.[152]

In addition to the divisions of actions already mentioned, they were also divided into actions for the recovery of a thing, actions to enforce a penalty, and mixed actions.[153] Actions for the recovery of a thing were actions whereby the plaintiff seeks to recover what belongs to him whether specific property, a debt, or compensation for damage sustained. Such actions included all real actions and most of the personal actions arising from contract.[154] The action of theft (actio furti) was purely a penal action, that is, an action to recover a penalty,[155] since the owner of the property could recover it by a separate action.[156] Mixed actions were those where the object was to recover a thing and also a penalty. Actions arising from delict were either penal or mixed.[157] The action for theft, as already stated, was penal, but the action for goods taken by force (vi bona rapta) was mixed, because the value of the property could be recovered in addition to the penalty.[158]

The term "mixed actions" was also used in another sense, that of describing actions as being, from one point of view, real, and, from another, personal. For example, actions for the partition of an inheritance, the partition of property held in common, and for the

152. Dig. 19, 5.
153. Inst. 4, 6, 16.
154. Inst. 4, 6, 17.
155. Inst. 4, 6, 18.
156. Inst. 4, 6, 18.
157. Inst. 4, 6, 18.
158. Inst. 4, 6, 19.

determination of boundary lines were called mixed actions.[159]

Actions were again classified, according to the relative amount recoverable, as single (in simplum), double (in duplum), triple (in triplum), and quadruple (in quadruplum).[160] The action in simplum sought recovery only for the value of the subject matter, as in case of a sale.[161] The other actions were penal. Thus, in the actio furti nec manifesti double the value of the stolen article could be recovered;[162] a triple value when a plaintiff in a summons to a defendant claimed a sum greater than what was due;[163] and a quadruple value in an action for manifest theft (furti manifesti).[164]

Limitation of Actions:

With reference to the time in which actions could be brought they were said to be either perpetual (perpetuae) or temporal (temporales).[165] Under the jus civile all actions were originally perpetual, that is, they could be brought regardless of the lapse of time, but most praetorian actions were limited to a year from the time the action accrued.[166] Statutes, however, limited some civil actions to a five year period, and Theodosius II limited all others to thirty years,[167] which period was extended by Justinian to forty years in a few cases.[168]

159. Inst. 4, 6, 20.
160. Inst. 4, 6, 21.
161. Inst. 4, 6, 22.
162. Inst. 4, 6, 23.
163. Inst. 4, 6, 24.
164. Inst. 4, 6, 25.
165. Inst. 4, 12.
166. Gaius 4, 110; Inst. 4, 12, **pr.**
167. Cod. 7, 39, 3.
168. Cod. 7, 39, 71.

Interdicts:

In connection with remedies granted by the praetor there was a very important class known as interdicts. They were orders directing one to do or not to do a certain thing and were issued for the purpose of protecting property or rights in property from apprehended disturbance or injury.[169] They were, therefore, connected with rights in rem as distinguished from rights in personam. Praetorian rights in personam, or rights in personam created by the praetor were protected by actions also created by him, but new rights in rem created by his authority as magistrate were protected by interdicts.

Interdicts were classed as prohibitory, restoratory, and exhibitory. Prohibitory interdicts were orders forbidding the doing of certain things. Restoratory interdicts were orders directing the restoration of something to another person. Exhibitory interdicts were orders directing some person or thing to be brought before the court.[170]

Upon a complaint made to the praetor with a proper showing of facts, he would, in case of a prohibitory interdict, order the defendant to do, or refrain from doing, the thing upon which the complaint was based. If the defendant refused to obey, the question was then by means of a formula referred to a judex just as in case of an ordinary action. Each party, however, was usually required to furnish security, or to enter into an agreement by way of wager (cum poena), the loser of the suit to pay the amount of his security, or wager, as a forfeit. In some cases, however, the judex was directed to condemn the defendant to pay damages if he continued to refuse to obey the order. In connection with applications for restoratory and exhibitory interdicts, the reference to a judex cum poena might

---

169. Gaius 4, 138–170; Inst. 4, 15; Dig. 43, 1.
170. Gaius 4, 140; Inst. 4, 15, 1.

be avoided by either party asking for the appointment of an arbiter.[171]

The exhibitory interdict included the order to produce one who claimed to be unlawfully deprived of his liberty (de libero homine exhibendo).[172] This interdict was, therefore, like unto our writ of habeas corpus.

Interdicts were most frequently employed in questions relating to the possession of property. The interdict uti possidetis applied to lands and buildings, and the interdict utrubi applied to movables. These interdicts were given in connection with actions for ownership when the preliminary question of possession was raised by the parties,[173] and also when existing possession of property was disturbed by another.[174] Possession was temporarily awarded, pending the outcome of the action, to that litigant who offered the highest penal sum which would be forfeited in case he did not prove his ownership.[175]

The interdict unde vi [176] was granted in favor of one who had been ejected with force from the possession of lands or buildings.[177] Like the two preceding interdicts it was based merely on the fact of possession, not on title or the right of possession. It had two forms, interdictum unde vi in case one had been ejected merely by force, and interdictum unde vi armata when the ejection was made by force and arms. By the term "arms," says Gaius, we understand not only shields, swords, and helmets are meant, but also sticks

    171. Gaius 4, 141, 162, 165.
    172. Dig. 43, 29; Cod. 8, 8.
    173. Gaius 4, 148; Dig. 43, 17, 1, 3.
    174. Dig. 43, 17, 3, 2.
    175. Gaius 4, 166-169.
    176. Dig. 43, 16 and 24.
    177. Gaius 4, 154.

and stones.[178] These two forms were subsequently merged into one interdict.[179]

Interdicts are said by some writers to be the same thing as injunctions. This, however, is not a careful statement. Interdicts were, as already stated, remedies for the protection of praetorian property rights, and the procedure in connection with them followed substantially the course of an action. They were not mere interlocutory decrees, as the actiones praejudiciales in Roman Law, and they were not final decrees per se. Prohibitory interdicts did resemble our modern restraining orders, but this was not true of exhibitory interdicts or of restoratory interdicts. The exhibitory interdictum de libero homine was, as already pointed out, analogous to our writ of habeas corpus, and restoratory interdicts somewhat resembled, at times, decrees for specific performance, coupled with an action for damages.[180] Interdicts were so much like actions that under the extra ordinem system of procedure the name disappeared. There was no longer any necessity for them as under the formulary system. Judgments were given without any interlocutory interdicts, the same as if an action utilis had been granted.[181]

III. The Extraordinary or Libellary Procdure:

The third and last procedural system of Rome was known as the extraordinary or libellary procedure. It was called "extraordinary" because it was a procedure "outside of" the regular order of the formulary procedure, and was otherwise called "libellary" by reason of the notice of the suit (libellus conventionis) served upon a defendant.

This system of procedure did not come into exist-

178. Gaius 4, 154, 155.
179. Dig. 43, 16.
180. Colquhoun, Rom. Civil Law, III, 547.
181. Inst. 4, 15, 8.

ence by any one definite act of legislation, and there is no positive date that can be assigned for its adoption. Step by step the new procedure took the place of the formulary procedure until, in time, a complete transition was made. The fundamental character of the formulary system was the existence of two courts, one court presided over by the praetor, and another court conducted by the referee, or arbitrator, known as the judex. The first court, the praetor's court, settled the issue and the pleadings, the proceedings in jure, while the trial of the issue and the decision of the case, the proceedings in judicio, were referred to a judex, not a magistrate but a private citizen and a layman. These proceedings, the first in jure and the second in judicio, constituted the regular order of private lawsuits (ordo judiciorum privatorum).

However, even during the time of the formulary procedure, certain cases were heard and decided by the praetor alone, no reference being made to a judex. This the praetor had ample authority to do by virtue of his imperium, his plenary jurisdiction. Such hearings were called cognitiones, and included matters of interdicts, cases involving the construction and enforcement of legacies in the nature of trusts (fideicommissa),[182] orders giving creditors possession of the property of a bankrupt debtor (missio in possessionem),[183] granting to minors under twenty-five years of age the restoration of their goods (restitutio in integrum) when contracts made by them were to their disadvantage,[184] orders directing children in certain cases to provide for the support of their parents, or parents to provide for their children,[185] and questions

182. Gaius 2, 278.
183. Dig. 13, 7, 26; 42, 4, 7; 42, 5, 12, pr.
184. Dig. 4, 4.
185. Dig. 25, 3, 5.

of suitable honoraria for advocates, teachers, and physicians.[186] The consideration of such matters was called a cognitio extraordinaria, or an investigation outside of the regular order of procedure. Such hearings were also called judicia extraordinaria in contrast to the judicia ordinaria held by a judex.[187]

The convenient and more expeditious way of thus disposing of various matters had great influence in bringing to pass a more general practice of the same kind in other litigated questions. There was, however, a reason greater than this that was responsible for the gradual decline and disappearance of the formulary system. It was the waning power of the creator of the system, the praetor. When, by order of the emperor Hadrian, Julianus compiled and revised the accumulated praetorian edicts, and they were published in a consolidated form known as The Perpetual Edict,[188] and that Edict was given statutory force by the emperor, from which Edict even the praetor himself could not depart, then was the power of the praetor to frame new actions and to adopt old ones to new conditions practically ended. Consequently, in time, the procedure under the formula became almost as fixed and as technical as it had been under the ancient procedure of the legis actiones. It was probably for this reason that the new magistrates who were appointed in imperial times departed from the customary and fixed order of the praetorian procedure, and further expedited the business of their courts by hearing and deciding cases in person, thus dispensing with all proceedings in judicio. The office of city prefect was created by Augustus,[189] as was also that of the praetorian prefect. The city prefect in time took over

186. Dig. 5, 13, 1.
187. Inst. 3, 12, pr.
188. A. D. 131.
189. B. C. 25.

all the judicial duties of a praetor and became the chief magistrate of the city. The praetorian prefect, who was originally the commander of the imperial guard, was later given judicial authority, and became, ultimately, the highest magistrate, being inferior only to the emperor. In the courts many complaints, both civil and criminal, were heard and disposed of by the presiding official. For example, the city prefect entertained complaints of needy patrons against their freedmen who failed to help their former masters;[190] guardians and curators were brought before his court when they were charged with corrupt or fraudulent acts in connection with their duties;[191] and applications either by or against bankers, and in pecuniary matters generally, could be made to him.[192]

In all such cases the procedure was extra ordinem, that is, it did not follow the usual order, the formulary method, of the praetor's court. There was no judicium in the sense that the case was referred to a judex, and, consequently, no need of a formula, the office of which was to instruct the judex.

Due to the foregoing causes, the formulary procedure gradually became obsolete. Paulus, writing probably about 225 A. D., says:[193] "Whether an action is direct or utilis is no longer of importance, because in the extra ordinem suits where the framing of a formula is not observed this technicality is immaterial especially since both forms of action have the same force and effect." In 294 A. D., judicia, except in some special cases, were abolished in the provinces by Diocletian,[194] thus implying that they had disappeared in Rome. In 342 A. D., Constantius and Constans, the

190. Dig. 1, 12, 1, 2.
191. Dig. 1, 12, 1, 7.
192. Dig. 1, 12, 2.
193. Dig. 3, 5, 46 (47), **1.**
104. Cod. 3, 3, 2.

sons of Constantine, expressly abolished the use of formulae, together with all technicalities of pleadings associated with them.[195]

In Justinian's time, the formulary procedure was as ancient to him as were the legis actiones to Cicero. However, the terms of the formula remained. The Institutes repeatedly speak of the "intentio" and of the "exceptio" but they were merely terms of convenience.[196] The written formula was a thing of the past. The pleadings were oral and made in the presence of the clerks of the courts who recorded their substance for the use of the magistrate.[197] The method of procedure in all actions was now extraordinaria, all cases being heard and decided by the magistrate alone.[198]

In the extra ordinem procedure the defendant was no longer summoned by the plaintiff personally. The old vocatio in jus was replaced, first, by a notice given by the praetor (denuntiatio) either by being posted upon the praetor's tablet or delivered by a messenger.[199] Later, the summons took the form of a written statement of the cause of action coupled with a demand for the appearance of the defendant. This was served upon the defendant by an officer of the court. From the name of this summons, the libellus conventionis, the extra ordinem procedure is also called the libellary procedure. In Justinian's time, the defendant was given twenty days after the service of the summons to appear and make up the issue (litis contestatio).[200] All actions were regarded as bonae fidei,[201] and accordingly all proper counterclaims of

195. Cod. 2, 57 (58), 1.
196. In the Institutes the term exceptio means any defense made before the court. Inst. 4, 13, 4 and 5; 4, 13, 8-10.
197. Cod. 7, 62, 32, 2.
198. Inst. 4, 15, 8.
199. Dig. 42, 1, 53, 1.
200. Nov. 53, 3, 2.
201. Inst. 4, 6, 30.

the defendant were taken into consideration.[202] The issues being settled, the same order of trial followed as in the old judicia, the evidence was heard and then the advocates made their speeches to the court.

Appeals:

Appeals in civil cases, in the sense of an application to a higher court to retry or to review the proceedings of a lower court, were unknown to Roman Law before the times of the Empire. What is sometimes called an appeal was an application (appellatio) for an intercession (intercessio), that is, for a veto interposed by an official of high rank upon the act of some other official. Thus the college of the tribunes could veto the act of a magistrate, or a praetor could veto the judicial act of another praetor.[203] Such intercessions did not, however, operate as a reversal of the judgment but as a stay of execution. A notable illustration in Roman history was the case of Licius Scipio who was convicted of the misappropriation of public funds. He was sentenced to pay a heavy fine and also to be imprisoned. The tribune, however, interposed his veto against the prison clause of the sentence.

However, during the Empire, appeals became a regular part of the established procedure. An appeal could be taken from any magistrate in Rome to the city prefect,[204] thence to the praetorian prefect, and finally to the emperor.

Generally, appeals lay only from a final judgment.[205] Appeals, however, that were apparently vexatious and provocative of unreasonable delay were, as a rule, not allowed.[206] For a long period, an appeal was taken by notice given at the time of the rendition of the judg-

202. Inst. 4, 6, 39.
203. Dig. 5, 1, 58.
204. Cod. 7, 62, 17; 7, 62, 23.
205. Dig. 49, 5, 4.
206. Dig. 49, 5, 7, pr.; 49, 5, 7, 2.

ment,[207] but Justinian provided that an appeal might be taken within ten days from the judgment.[208] The record was sent to the court of appeal, and the case was there heard de novo, new evidence, if any, being admitted.[209]

Execution of Judgments:

A judex rendered judgment but he had no power to execute it. In case a judgment debtor did not pay, it was necessary to institute a new action upon the judgment before the praetor. Under the ancient actiones legis the action known as per manus injectionem was regularly employed to enforce a judgment. The judgment creditor took into custody his judgment debtor who was required, upon his failure to pay, to furnish a vindex to defend the suit for him, or otherwise the debtor could be taken to the creditor's house, and later reduced to slavery.[210] Under the formulary procedure by means of the actio judicati, a debtor was required to give security for the payment of the debt in case the decision should be against him.[211] The action proceeded as in an original action by formula with reference to a judex, and, according to Gaius, the judgment debtor if condemned was required to pay twice the amount of the former judgment.[212]

It was not until the Lex Julia, passed either in the time of Julius Caesar or of Augustus, that a judgment debtor who failed to pay could escape imprisonment by means of bankruptcy (cessio bonorum), either voluntary or involuntary.[213] The debtor's property was seized, sold, and distributed among his creditors, and if this was not sufficient to pay his debts in full his

207. Dig. 49, 1, 2.
208. Nov. 23, 1.
209. Cod. 7, 62, 24; 7, 62, 6, pr.; 7, 62, 6, 1.
210. Gaius 4, 21.
211. Gaius 4, 25.
212. Gaius 4, 171.
213. Gaius 3, 78; Dig. 42, 3; Cod. 7, 71, 1.

subsequently acquired property was also liable.[214] Later, in the reign of the emperor Antoninus Pius, execution directly against the property of the debtor was for the first time in Roman Law allowed.[215] Animals and other movables were first taken before lands,[216] but slaves, oxen, and farm implements were exempt.[217] In the time of Theodosius, a judgment debtor who did not pay a judgment within two months from the date of its rendition was liable to an action for interest at the rate of twenty-four per cent.[218] Justinian amended this law by providing that if a judgment was not satisfied within four months, the judgment creditor could recover twelve per cent.[219]

Checks Upon Litigation:

Reckless litigation was attended with severe consequences. The parties were sometimes restrained by pecuniary penalties, sometimes by an oath, and sometimes by fear of infamy.[220] In an action on a judgment, or on money paid, by a sponsor, or for injury (under the Aquilian Law), if the defendant denied his liability the damages were doubled in case the decision was against him.[221] An action known as calumnia, that is, an action based upon the charge of unfounded litigation, and corresponding to our action for malicious prosecution, lay against a plaintiff in all sorts of actions, the amount recoverable being one tenth of what he unjustifiably claimed.[222] A defendant could also demand that a plaintiff should be required to take

214. Inst. 4, 6, 40; Dig. 42, 3, 4.
215. Dig. 42, 1, 6, 2; 42, 1, 31.
216. Dig. 42, 1, 15, 8.
217. Cod. 8, 17, 7.
218. Cod. Theod. 4, 19, 1.
219. Cod. 7, 54, 2, 3.
220. Gaius 4, 171; Inst. 4, 16, pr.
221. Gaius 4, 171; Inst. 4, 16, 1.
222. Gaius 4, 175.

an oath as to his sincerity in bringing an action.[223] In the time of Justinian, the old action of calumnia was obsolete, and each party was required to take an oath as to his good faith, the plaintiff that the suit was not vexatious, the defendant that he believed his defense was good.[224] As a further restraint, the costs of a suit were thrown upon the losing party.[225] Under the former procedure costs were not taxed against one merely in consequence of a judgment against him, the successful party being left to his action of calumnia in case it appeared that the original action was instituted without probable cause.[226]

The American lawyer who reviews the history of procedure in the Roman courts cannot fail to be impressed with the marked similarity, in many respects, of that procedure to our own. The rigid formality of the ancient legis actiones may be compared, in some ways, to the like character of the early English actions at Common Law. The various parts of the formula were also like unto the successive steps of pleading under our Common Law procedure. In the application by the praetors of equitable principles to legal actions may be seen the prototype of the blending of law and equity in our modern code procedure. As said by the supreme court of California, "Our system of pleading is founded upon the model of the Civil Law, and one of its principal objects is to discourage protracted and vexatious litigation." [227] In fact, there is hardly a doctrine in the prevailing procedure of today that does not have its likeness in the Roman Law. Sir Frederick Pollock has truly said that "the history of the

---

223. Gaius 4, 176.
224. Inst. 4, 16, 1.
225. Cod. 3, 1, 13, 6.
226. See note appended by the Court to Hutson v. Jordan, 1 Ware (U. S. Dist. Ct. for Maine) 385.
227. Jones v. Steamship Cortes, 17 Cal. 487, 497.

Roman legis actiones may in a general way be compared with that of Common Law pleading in its earlier stages; and it may be found that the praetorian actions have not less in common with our actions on the case than with the remedies peculiar to courts of equity, which our text writers have habitually likened to them." [228] And Judge Story has said: [229] "The pleadings in equity were probably borrowed from the Civil Law, or from the Canon Law (which is a derivative from the Civil Law), or from both. The early chancellors were for the most part, if not altogether, ecclesiastics, and many of them were bred up in the jurisprudence of the Civil and Canon Law; and it was natural for them, in the administration of their judicial functions in the Court of Chancery, to transfer into that court the modes of proceeding with which they were most familiar. Hence, at almost every step, we may now trace coincidences between the pleadings and practice in chancery and the pleadings and practice in a Roman suit and in an ecclesiastical suit." Particularly do the courts of admiralty and maritime law owe the origin of their procedure to the Civil Law.[230] The general rules of practice in admiralty come to us directly from the Roman Law,[231] and the practice so far as it relates to the libel and answer, is in its forms identical with that of the Roman Law.[232] In some of the old sea laws, said Mr. Justice Curtis of the Supreme Court of the United States,[233] the rules governing liens for a ship's supplies and repairs are declared in ex-

---

228. Pollock on Torts, Webb's Ed., p. 645.
229. Equity Pleadings, 10th ed., sec. 14.
230. New England Mut. Mar. Ins. Co. v. Dunham, 11 Wall. (U. S.) 1; De Lovio v. Boit, 7 Fed. Cas. No. 3,776; The C. B. Sanford, 22 Fed. Rep. 863.
231. Hutson v. Jordan, 1 Ware (U. S. Dist. Ct. Maine) 385.
232. Judge Ware in note appended to Hutson v. Jordan, 1 Ware 385.
233. Thomas v. Osborn, 19 How. (U. S.) 22.

[Roman Law]

press terms as they were in the Roman Law. And in this case the Court followed the Roman Law action de exercitoria (Dig. 14, 1) which authorized a simple loan without confining the master of a ship to a loan on a bottomry bond. In the courts of equity and admiralty, again says Mr. Justice Story,[234] no jury intervenes. The judge is in general the sole arbiter of fact and law, and the mode of procedure is borrowed from the Civil Law. An appeal in these courts removes the whole proceedings.

The modern practice in Civil Law countries is founded upon the practice that was followed in the time of Justinian. An ordinary action is regularly begun by filing a written complaint stating the facts upon which the action is based. A copy of this complaint is served upon the defendant together with a citation to appear. Upon appearance the defendant may plead dilatory exceptions, which include our English pleas to the jurisdiction, pleas in abatement, and, to some extent, the demurrer. Dilatory exceptions being overruled, the defendant files his answer, which may include peremptory exceptions (such as res judicata, for example), and counterclaims. In some jurisdictions, the plaintiff may file a replication to the answer, followed by a rejoinder on the part of the defendant, a waiver of replication by the plaintiff depriving a defendant of his right of rejoinder. In this procedure all distinction between law and equity is unknown, and it was upon the general principles and forms of modern Civil Law procedure that the "code" procedure of a majority of our American states was modeled.

234. U. S. v. Wonson, Fed. Cas. No. 16,750.

CHAPTER XXIII

THE LAW OF PUBLIC WRONGS

The concept of crime in the sense of public wrong prosecuted and punished by the state, was one of slow development in the Roman Law even as it was in our own English Law.

The word "crimen" was used in two senses. Primarily it meant a charge or accusation. Later it came to mean a public wrong, an offense against the state.

The acts that were regarded as public wrongs varied in the different periods of Roman history. Nothing affords a clearer insight into the character and stage of the civilization of a people than the acts which its day and age regard as criminal, that is, acts adjudged as wrongs against the state itself or against the people in general. A catalogue of its crimes reveals not alone a state's view of what constitutes punishable conduct, but it also demonstrates its ideas of liberty and public welfare. By its laws is a nation known. They show what matters are deemed most important and, therefore, most in need of protection, and they also show whether a people is being governed with bigotry and persecution or with toleration and justice.

It seems to be the history of all peoples whose evolution in human government is recorded that their earliest notions of wrongs, in the sense of "crimes," were offenses against the gods and religion. Offenses against men and property were first regarded as private wrongs, wrongs not punishable by the state but left to personal remedies. The conception that such wrongs are offenses also against the state, that is, against the people generally, belongs not to primitive but to much later times. As civilization advances in intelligence and freedom, crimes against religion more and more disappear, and crimes against personal security and property rights become more and more developed.

The evolution of the law of crimes among the Romans went on in just such a way. Their earliest crimes were wrongs against the gods, and offenders were punished in propitiation of offended deity. Crimes, in the conception of the early Romans, were offenses that tended to provoke the gods to wrath against an entire people, that is, against the country of the offenders, and for that reason they were to be expiated by making the wrongdoers sacrificial victims. By such means it was hoped that the sacrilege could be atoned, and divine vengeance averted.

In the earliest days of Rome the kings were vested with the supreme power (imperium),[1] which applied not only to things secular but also to things connected with the worship of the gods, the state religion. This power gave the king jurisdiction to impose even sentences of death.[2] Probably only cases of grave and serious import were brought to the attention of the king, such as hostile acts against the state, its ruler, its institutions, or acts of assistance to a foreign foe. All such wrongs or crimes were included within the term perduellio.[3] It was also doubtless true that for a long period during the early development of the Roman State, the paterfamilias, by virtue of his paternal power (patria potestas), administered many cases of wrongs outside domestic affairs, and even in some cases inflicted the death penalty for great wrongs, or

1. Dig. 1, 2, 2, 14.
2. Walter, Ges. der Rom. R. Para. 790.
3. From per-duellis, a public enemy.

crimes, committed by persons under his power.[4] Another fact which retarded the development of criminal law among the Romans was that the notion of a delict (delictum) included a penalty as well as compensation for the actual damage suffered. The defendant, if adjudged guilty, was required to pay the plaintiff a sum twofold or, at times, even fourfold the amount of his real loss as a punishment for the wrong. In time, as stated in a previous chapter, the wrongdoer was also liable, in many cases of delict, to a public prosecution, but this was not true in the earliest days.

Offenses punishable by the state became known, in the later days of Roman Law, as crimina publica (public wrongs), while wrongs viewed as wrongs against the individual, corresponding to our notion of torts, were called, in distinction, crimina private (private wrongs).[5]

By the time of the Twelve Tables (450 B. C.), a number of public offenses had become recognized. Some of these were punishable with death, some with scourging, and some with the law of retaliation (lex talionis). Other offenses were subject to personal actions for the recovery of penal damages. Among the wrongs of that period were libels and insulting songs,[6] bodily injuries, damage to property, theft, burning the house or a stock of corn of another, breaches of trust, the giving of false testimony, murder, the use of wicked enchantments, and public disturbances.

One who in the nighttime stole the crops of another or furtively pastured his herds or flocks upon the land of another was punishable with death if an adult, or if

4. Livy 1, 26; 2, 41.
5. Dig. 21, 1, 17, 18.
6. The classical authorities are not agreed as to the meaning of "malum carmen" of the Twelve Tables. Cicero (Repub. 4, 10, 2) says it meant scandalous songs against an individual. Pliny (28, 2, 17) limits the term to wicked enchantments. Both of these authors were distinguished lawyers.

under the age of puberty was flogged. A slave taken in an act of theft was liable to the death penalty, and any nocturnal thief could be lawfully killed. Riotous disturbances in the nighttime were also punishable with death. A freeman taken in theft was scourged and he became the bondman of the person from whom he had stolen.[7] A false witness was hurled from the Tarpeian Rock. If one wilfully broke the limb of another the law of retaliation applied, and the limb of the criminal was likewise broken unless he was forgiven by the injured person. Libel was punished with flogging. In case of theft nec manifestum, the owner could exact a penalty double the value of the stolen property.[8] The malicious killing of a freeman was punished with death, as was also the giving of poison or the use of wicked enchantments. A breach of trust in case of a deposit, and embezzlement by a guardian of his ward's property were punished by double damages. Arson was punished with flogging and burning.

As the years passed, the number and character of public offenses increased, since different times and different conditions of living, together with the growth of population and wealth, gave rise to new views of public wrongs. From time to time statutes were passed providing punishments for various specific offenses, until the number of recognized crimes became large.

In all periods of Roman Law, the greatest public wrong known to the law was perduellio[9] or treason. In later days, such offenses were classed under the more comprehensive term crimen laesae majestatis, from which is derived the modern European term lèse majesty (wounded majesty). Perduellio included not only what are usually regarded as treasonable acts

7. Gaius 3, 189.
8. Gaius 3, 190.
9. Supra.

but also acts of sedition which tended to disturb public tranquillity.[10] In the reign of Tiberius, the slightest affront or disrespect to the emperor was included in this crime.[11]

Prior to the Republic, the imperium, or the highest judicial authority, was vested in the kings,[12] and the trial of offenses was conducted by the king either in person or by two commissioners (duumviri capitales) appointed by him for a particular case. The consuls upon the institution of the Republic, succeeded to the imperium, and they heard and decided cases as magistrates, with power to impose a sentence of death. However, even in the days of the kings an appeal lay in capital cases, first, to the comitia curiata, and after the establishment of the comitia centuriata in the reign of Servius Tullius, the sixth of the kings, similar appeals lay to that popular assembly. Soon after the beginning of the Republic, the power to pass judgment in a capital case was taken from the consuls by the Valerian Law,[13] which gave the comitia curiata exclusive jurisdiction in such cases. The Twelve Tables transferred this jurisdiction to the comitia centuriata, and this jurisdiction was continued by the Lex Sempronia[14] to the end of the Republic.[15] Cases were brought before the comitia centuriata by the consuls, or by one of them, the two consuls being the public prosecutors until the creation of the office of praetor.

The comitia tributa had, at first, jurisdiction as an appellate court to pass upon the legality of fines im-

10. Lex Apuleia, 102 B. C.; Lex Varia, 92 B. C.; Lex Cornelia, 81 B. C.; Lex Julia, 46 B. C.

11. Tac. Ann. 1, 73-74; 2, 50; 3, 38, 64; 6, 18; 14, 48; Suet. Tib. 58; Nero, 53; Domit. 10, 12; Dig. 48, 4, 4.

12. Dig. 1, 2, 2, 14.

13. 508 B. C.; Dig. 1, 2, 2, 16.

14. 123 B. C.

15. Dionys. 5, 19, 70; 7, 41, 52; Cicero de Repub. 2, 31; Livy 2, 7, 55.

posed by the tribunes of the people.[16] In the course of time, however, this comitia extended its jurisdiction to the hearing, in the first instance, of all cases involving the penalty only of a fine (multa). Accordingly if an offense was punishable only by a fine, the tribunes usually brought the charge before the comitia tributa which had authority to inflict a fine up to one half of a guilty defendant's property.[17]

When the comitia centuriata assembled for the purpose of passing upon the guilt or innocence of an accused person it was known as a judicium populi or a court of the people. Before this court a magistrate was the prosecutor. In later times when a criminal court consisted of a judge, either with or without a jury (consilium), it was known as a judicium publicum since a criminal charge might be prosecuted before it by any private person.[18]

Proceedings before the comitia centuriata in criminal trials were begun by an accusation made by a consul, or by a praetor after that office was created. A day being set for the hearing, the accused was thereupon admitted to bail or detained in custody. However, before the day of trial three contiones were held, each several days apart, for the purpose of investigating the case and informing the people of the nature of the crime. A contio was an assembly of the people, not as members of the comitia centuriata, but an informal assembly called by order of a magistrate for a conference.[19] They did not come together at such times to legislate or to vote, but only that they might be informed upon matters of public interest. It was a requirement of the law of those early days that the

16. The tribunes had authority to impose fines for political offenses, such as, for example, the mismanagement of a war by a Roman general, or the usurpation of public authority.
17. Cicero de Leg. 3, 19; de Repub. 2, 36.
18. Inst. 4, 18, 1.
19. Mommsen, Strafrecht, 164.

comitia could not pass upon the guilt or innocence of an accused person until after three contiones or investigating assemblies had been held. The accused was permitted to be present at these public meetings and to defend himself before the people. At the conclusion of the third contio the magistrate either withdrew the charge or decided against the accused, practically like a judge in a modern preliminary hearing holding the accused for trial.[20] In case the magistrate decided to present the case to the comitia he named a day for its meeting, thirty days, at least, after the third contio. The comitia being assembled, the magistrate renewed the charge and asked for the judgment of the people. The evidence already considered in the preliminary meetings was briefly submitted, the accused or his counsel was allowed to speak in defense, and the votes of the comitia were then taken by the constituent centuries. If a majority of the centuries voted in condemnation the penalty was immediately inflicted.[21]

Such was the usual procedure in criminal cases in the comitia centuriata. It was cumbersome and not adapted to a large population, or to the trial of numerous accused persons. Accordingly as the city increased, and criminal cases became more and more frequent, other means for disposing of them became necessary. Even in early days,[22] a special trial or investigation (quaestio) was conducted, now and then, by a magistrate alone, he being commissioned by some legislative body so to act. The Roman historian Livy speaks of such trials being authorized by decrees of

20. Ib., p. 165.
21. A sentence imposed by the people could, however, be set aside by their subsequent vote. This was known as restitutio. It was particularly applicable to cases restoring citizenship lost by the previous condemnation.
22. As early, at least, as 331 B. C., Livy 8, 18.

the senate,[23] and at other times we read that they were ordered by a vote of the plebs.[24] In 171 B. C., the senate appointed a commission for the trial of the governors of the Spanish provinces who had been accused of extortion,[25] and in the year 149 B. C., the Lex Calpurnia Repetundarum [26] created, for the duration of a year, a standing or permanent court (quaestio perpetua) for the trial of provincial officials in general who might be charged with extorting money from the people of their districts. The jurisdiction of this court was limited to this particular class of crimes and was exclusive. The punishment was also prescribed. This statute, the first of the standing commissions for the trial of crimes, was followed by other statutes creating other courts of justice for the trial of other particular crimes of the most common occurrence. Each one of these courts was independent of the others, and heard only such cases as were covered by its creating law. Each quaestio was established for a year, but was continued from year to year by the order of the comitia centuriata.

Among the additional statutes creating standing commissions were the Lex Maria de Ambitu (119 B. C.) having jurisdiction over bribery at elections; the Lex Cornelia de Falsis (81 B. C.), also called testamentaria (concerning wills), providing penalties for the forgery of a will or other document, slaves under this law being punishable with death, freemen with banishment;[27] the Lex Cornelia de Parricidiis (81 B.

23. Livy 40, 37, 4.

24. For example, the Lex Marcia, about 172 B. C., Mommsen, Strafrecht, 172; Cicero, de Finibus, 2, 16, 54.

25. Livy 43, 2.

26. Crimen repetundarum pecuniarum was the name given to the crime "of money to be restored," meaning the money unlawfully exacted by Roman officials in connection with provincial administration.

27. Inst. 4, 18, 7; Dig. 48, 10.

C.) for murder; the Lex Cornelia de Vi,[28] for forcible obstruction of public officials in connection with their duties; the Lex Cornelia de Incendio, for arson; and the Lex Cornelia de Sicariis et Veneficiis, for assassins and poisoners.[29] Among later important statutes for the punishment of crime were the Lex Pompeia de Parricidiis (55 B. C.) punishing the murder of blood relations;[30] and the laws of Julius Caesar and of Augustus, relating to treason (Lex Julia Majestatis);[31] adultery (Lex Julia Adulteriis);[32] public or private violence on the part of persons whether armed with a dangerous weapon or not (Lex Julia de Vi Publica seu Privata);[33] and the embezzlement of public funds (Lex Julia Peculatus).[34] There were also statutes punishing kidnapping (Lex Fabia de Plagiariis),[35] and unlawfully raising the price of food (Lex Julia de Annona).[36]

The foregoing list comprises many of the important criminal statutes of Rome but they are not exhaustive. Moreover, these statutes were amended from time to time or extended by judicial construction so that they covered most of the recognized offenses. Further, these cited statutes covered a much wider field of crimes than their titles would indicate. The actual text of none of these laws is extant, but from the various comments upon them in the Corpus Juris we know their general intent. For example, the Lex Julia Adulteriis covered practically all sexual offenses, adultery on the part of a wife (but not of a

---

28. These "Cornelian Laws" of which there were a number were passed during the consulship of Sulla, 81 B. C.
29. Inst. 4, 18, 5; Dig. 48, 8.
30. Inst. 4, 18, 6; Dig. 48, 9.
31. Inst. 4, 18, 3; Dig. 48, 4.
32. Inst. 4, 18, 4; Dig. 48, 5.
33. Inst. 4, 18, 8; Dig. 48, 6; 48, 7.
34. Inst. 4, 18, 9; Dig. 48, 13.
35. Inst. 4, 18, 10; Dig. 48, 15.
36. Inst. 4, 18, 11; Dig. 48, 12.

husband), fornication (stuprum), incest, bigamy, procuring, and crimes against nature. The Lex Julia de Vi Publica included rape, assaults upon ambassadors, and the scourging or execution by a public officer of a Roman citizen pending an appeal. The Lex Cornelia de Falsis, often cited as the crimen falsi, which term it also used in our own law in connection with infamous crimes, covered not only the forgery and suppression of wills, but also was later extended to the forgery of every sort of instrument.[37] It also included counterfeiting, false evidence, bribery of judges, false measures, and certain fraudulent contracts.

The Lex Julia de Annona punished with a heavy fine those who increased the price of corn or wheat by artificial means, a forerunner of the English crimes of forestalling and regrating.[38]

Offenses not covered by statutes creating quaestiones perpetuae for their trial were, in the days of the Republic, tried either by the people in their public assembly (comitia centuriata), or by a special commission (quaestio) appointed for the particular case. In the later Empire, such offenses were called extraordinaria crimina, that is, offenses not covered by the ordinary procedure. Among the crimes thus less formally prosecuted the Digest mentions attempts to disturb the marital relations of others, especially soliciting a married woman to leave her husband;[39] abortion;[40] raising the price of corn,[41] although it is not stated how this offense differs from the Lex Julia de Annona; scopelismus, from a Greek word meaning a rock, a name given to an offense peculiar to the province of Arabia, consisting in the erection of a pile of

37. Dig. 48, 10, 9, 3.
38. Dig. 48, 2, 2, pr.; 48, 12, 2, 2.
39. Dig. 47, 11, 1.
40. Dig. 47, 11, 4.
41. Dig. 47, 11, 6.

stones on the land of an enemy as a warning that if he cultivated his land he would meet with a terrible death at the hands of those who had placed there the stones;[42] vagabondage, or vagrants who travel from place to place giving snake exhibitions thereby causing fear to the people;[43] the violation of tombs and the bodies of the dead;[44] blackmailing (concussio), or the extortion of money or other property from another by means of threats;[45] cattle thieves (abigei), or the "drivers away" of another's cattle or horses or sheep or swine from their pastures or stables;[46] prevarication, or insincere prosecution, pretending to be an honest accuser when secretly aiding the defendant;[47] receivers of stolen goods;[48] various kinds of aggravated thieving, such as stealing the clothing of bathers in the public baths (balnearii), stealing at night, breaking into houses to steal, robbery of one's clothes from his person (expilatio), stealing by artifice or trick, pickpockets (saccularii), and sneak thieves (directarii), or those who secretly enter another's house for the purpose of stealing.[49]

In a trial conducted by a quaestio perpetua the presiding judge was known as the quaesitor. He might be either a praetor[50] or a special judge (judex quaestionis) appointed by the statute creating the commission. A magistrate did not prosecute as in trials before the comitia, and, in fact, there was no public prosecutor.

42. Dig. 47, 11, 9. It is interesting to note this early form of what in modern times is called "the black hand." The punishment of scopelismus was death.
43. Dig. 47, 11, 11.
44. Dig. 47, 12, 3.
45. Dig. 47, 13, 2.
46. Dig. 47, 14, 1, 1; 47, 14, 3.
47. Dig. 47, 15, 1; 48, 16, 1, 6.
48. Dig. 47, 16, 1.
49. Dig. 47, 11, 7; 47, 17 and 18.
50. In Sulla's time there were six praetors for criminal cases.

Any person, except women, infants, and those who were infames, could bring a charge. The first step in the procedure was known as the postulatio. This was the request made by a complainant to the praetor having jurisdiction of the particular crime, asking permission to charge a certain person with such a particular crime. For the consideration of such requests the praetor held regular sittings in the Forum, and if the complaint seemed well founded the request was granted. Thereupon, the praetor issued a summons (citatio) for the accused, known as the reus, to appear at a certain day.[51] Upon his appearance, the reus was, in the early procedure, before the trial by jury, subjected to a preliminary examination by the quaesitor.[52] This examination, known as the interrogatio, was rigid and searching, and was designed to obtain, if possible, a confession of guilt. If the reus declared his innocence, but there seemed to be reasonable ground for the accusation, the praetor or other presiding magistrate reduced the charge to writing (inscriptio) which was thereupon signed by the accuser, or accusers if there were more than one (subscriptores).

The details of the subsequent procedure varied from period to period of Roman history, the procedure of the middle Republic differing from that of the later Republic, and both differing from the later imperial times. The introduction of trials by jury, sometime in the later Republic, changed greatly the general character of criminal trials. It is not known when the employment of jurors in criminal cases became first established. The practice was undoubtedly slowly developed, and was introduced after the analogy of ju-

---

51. It was customary in ancient Rome for a person accused of crime (reus) to appear in public in the garb of mourning, beard and hair unkempt and every sign of rank removed. An accused person was forthwith deprived of some of his rights. He could not, for instance, be a candidate for office.

52. Whence the later medieval term "inquisitor."

rors (judices) in civil cases. It is known, however, that during the days of Cicero trial by jury in criminal cases was the regular procedure.

When jury trials became established the former inquisitorial procedure of the criminal courts, or commissions, was abandoned. The guilt or innocence of the accused (reus) was then to be determined by the jury and not by the quaesitor or praetor.

Upon the appearance of the accused, the court appointed a day for the trial (dictio diei) which was, in the time of the later Republic, not less than ten, and in no case more than one hundred, days later. The usual period was ten days, although if more time was necessary in order to insure the presence of witnesses, a longer period was granted. During this period it was incumbent upon the accuser to collect his evidence and to see that his witnesses were summoned. Witnesses for the prosecution could be compelled to appear by a denunciatio sub poena.[53]

On the day set for the trial, the accuser and the defendant (reus) were summoned to the court by a herald (praeco).[54] If the accuser did not appear the case was dismissed,[55] but if the defendant failed to appear he was adjudged guilty and his property was confiscated.[56] However, in later imperial days, the presence of the defendant was necessary, and if after being cited by an edict he failed to appear his property, after the interval of a year, was confiscated but he was not sentenced.[57] If both parties were in court on the appointed day, the praetor ordered jurors (judices) to be selected by lot from the official jury list.

The laws regulating the number and the qualifica-

53. Cicero in Verr. 2, 26.
54. Quint. Inst. Orat. 6, 4, 7.
55. Cicero in Verr. 2, 40.
56. Cicero in Verr. 2, 17, 38, 40.
57. Dig. 48, 17, 1, 5; 48, 19, 5, pr.; Cod. 9, 40, 1, 2; Nov. 134, 5.

tions of jurors varied in the different periods of Roman Law. Prior to 123 B. C., only Romans of senatorial rank were qualified for jury service. However, as the years passed it became more and more apparent that such jurors favored their own class, and that seldom did they convict one of their rank. In fact, it was, in time, openly charged by the people that the jurors often acquitted persons of their own rank despite the amount of evidence against them. In order to obtain more impartial jurors, Caius Gracchus, a champion of the popular party against the Optimates, succeeded, in 123 B. C., in getting a law enacted (Lex Sempronia) which excluded from the Album Judicum Selectorum (the official list of selected jurors) all Romans of senatorial rank, and provided that jurors hereafter should be selected only from the equites, or knights. The equites were originally a division of the Roman army, but the Ordo Equester created by this law was not a military body but a political division of the people, exclusive of those of senatorial rank, who possessed a certain amount of property, namely 400,000 sesterces, somewhere, approximately, between $15,000 and $18,000 in our money. It was thus a well-to-do class, although not a rich class. However, subsequent laws first restored to the jury list those of senatorial rank, and then, in turn, again excluded them. Still later laws added other groups of citizens to the list, the tribuni aerarii being appointed [58] to represent the plebeians. In the reign of Augustus, senators, knights (equites), tribunes of the treasury, and all other citizens possessing property to the value of 200,000 sesterces were qualified as jurors. Both in criminal and civil cases the jurors were selected from the same list.

58. In the early days the tribuni aerarii (Tribunes of the Treasury) were members of a wealthy class who were appointed to levy the war taxes. In later times they comprised a property class next below the equites.

The number of names on the jury list also varied in the various periods of Roman history. In the early days of exclusive senatorial eligibility, the number was three hundred. Under successive laws the number was increased to 360, 450, 850, and in the time of Augustus to about 4000. The list was made up annually by the praetor urbanus, who selected the names from the duly qualified classes.[59]

From this selected list inscribed on the Album Judicum the praetor, or other presiding judge, or the parties selected a jury (consilium) for the trial of a criminal case. The number varied from time to time, being often governed by the particular law under which the trial (quaestio) was held. It was, however, always large. At times there were 32, and at other times such numbers as 50, 65, or even as many as a hundred.[60] For example, under the Lex Acilia Repetundarum,[61] the accuser proposed 100 names out of the album of 450 provided by this law, and the accused proposed a like number, and then from each list fifty were selected by the parties, making a hundred jurors in all. The prevailing practice in most cases was for the praetor to select a number of jurors by lot, each side having certain rights to reject or to challenge undesired persons.[62]

The jury being selected and sworn, the trial was opened by an address of the accuser who usually set forth in detail the nature of the charge and also the substance of the evidence. There were often several accusers (subscriptores [63]), and in such cases each one spoke, if he wished. Then followed the addresses in behalf of the defense, that of the defendant in person,

---

59. Cicero, pro Cluent., 43.
60. Cicero, pro Cluent., 27, 74; in Pisonem, 40, 96; ad Att. 4, 15, 4.
61. Cicero, pro Plancio, 17, 41.
62. Cicero ad Att. 1, 16.
63. So called because they signed the indictment (inscriptio).

[Roman Law]

if he chose, and of his patronus [64] or patroni, since an accused person was permitted to be represented by counsel. These speeches were often very long, and in later times in order to put a limit upon the length of such addresses a water-clock [65] was brought into court and speakers were required by the judge to time their remarks by this means.

After the addresses, which were often of great oratorical effect, the evidence (probatio) was introduced. This included not only the oral testimony of witnesses but also documents,[66] great latitude being allowed in presenting any matters bearing directly or circumstantially upon the case. There were practically no rules of evidence, but the witnesses were sworn to tell the truth.[67] Character witnesses (laudatores) were often introduced, and letters from well-known persons testifying to the good character of the defendant were permitted to be read. Not infrequently, evidence was introduced during the accuser's address, a witness being called, or a letter or other document being read in order to substantiate what the accuser was saying. Also, after the opening speeches on both sides but before the introduction of the evidence, there was, sometimes, an altercatio between the accuser and the defendant (or his patronus), consisting of questions and answers concerning the charge and what was expected to be proved.[68] The attendance of duly cited witnesses was compulsory,[69] and the number of wit-

64. In the days of the Republic, a patronus causae was one who spoke in defense of an accused person. An advocatus was merely a friend who advised one in a lawsuit. In imperial days, advocatus was applied to counsel who spoke in court in behalf of a client.

65. A clepsydra. This was a vessel filled with water. There was a hole in the bottom which emptied the vessel in a definite time.

66. Cicero pro Cluent. 23, 60; in Verr. 2, 1, 31, 33; Quint. 5, 6, para. 1, 2, 25, 32.

67. Cod. 4, 40, 9, pr.

68. Quint. 6, 3, 4; Cic. ad Quint. fr. 6, 4.

69. Dig. 22, 5, 1.

nesses that should be called was discretionary with the court.[70] Persons who had been convicted of crime,[71] or who were less than twenty years old,[72] or officials guilty of embezzling public funds,[73] were not competent to testify. A patronus likewise was not a competent witness in a cause that he represented.[74] The emperor Justinian imposed a religious qualification. Jews, pagans, and heretics were not permitted to testify, only Christians.[75] In the time of Hadrian, slaves accused of crime, in case there was sufficient evidence to warrant a probability of their guilt, could be lawfully subjected to torture in order to make them confess.[76] Such a practice was followed, however, long before Hadrian made it legal.

It has been said that there was a presumption in the Roman Law in favor of the innocence of an accused person,[77] and Ulpian cites a rescript of the emperor Trajan declaring that no one in a criminal case should be condemned in his absence, and that it were better for a guilty man to go unpunished than for an innocent man to be condemned.[78] Also a constitutio of the emperors Valentinian and Theodosius said: "All accusers should know that no criminal charge should be brought unless it can be supported by competent witnesses, or established by the most convincing documents, or shown by circumstantial evidence clearer than daylight resulting in undoubted proof." [79] Gaius, Paulus, and Marcellus also said that in matters of

70. Dig. 22, 5, 2.
71. Dig. 22, 5, 3; 22, 5, 20.
72. Dig. 22, 5, 20.
73. Dig. 22, 5, 15, pr.
74. Dig. 22, 5, 25.
75. Cod. 1, 5, 21.
76. Dig. 48, 18, 1, 1.
77. Coffin v. United States, 156 U. S. 432; see, also, Howe's Studies in the Civil Law, 2d ed., p. 125.
78. Dig. 48, 18.
79. Cod. 4, 18, 25.

doubt it is always safer and more just to follow the more favorable (benignior) construction.[80] The Supreme Court of the United States, speaking by Mr. Chief Justice White, in the case of Coffin v. United States,[81] further quotes an anecdote of the emperor Julian, as follows:[82] "A provincial governor was the defendant in a criminal case which was being tried before the emperor. There was not sufficient proof to convict the accused who denied his guilt, and the accuser, seeing that the failure of the accusation was inevitable, could not restrain himself, and exclaimed, 'Oh, illustrious Caesar! if it is sufficient to deny, what hereafter will become of the guilty?' to which Julian replied, 'If it suffices to accuse, what will become of the innocent?'"

These quotations tend to show, however, the burden and the amount of proof that the Roman Law required in criminal cases, and the burden and the amount of proof constitute all there is in the doctrines of presumptions.[83] What we mean in English Law by the presumption of innocence in criminal cases is that the alleged criminal act must be proved beyond a reasonable doubt.[84]

On the other hand, it has been said by others that while English Law presumes an accused man's innocence, Roman Law presumes his guilt. There is no foundation, however, for such a comparison. There was no presumption either of guilt or of innocence in Roman Law. In that law, as is the rule in English Law, the burden of proof was upon the accuser, and the amount of proof required, judging from the authorities already cited, would seem to be as great as in

80. Dig. 50, 17, 56; 50, 17, 155, 2; 50, 17, 192, 1.
81. 156 U. S. 432, 455.
82. Reported in Rerum Gestarum, L. 18, c. 1.
83. Presumptions and the Law of Evidence, Thayer, 3 Harv. L. R. 148-166.
84. Steph. Dig. Ev., art. 94.

our own law. In fact, such an expression as "clearer than daylight" goes even beyond our familiar phrase "reasonable doubt." Our constitutional provisions of confronting one with the witnesses against him, and of immunity from self-incrimination were, however, unknown doctrines in Roman criminal procedure. The inquisitorial method employed in the trial of accused persons, especially in the days of the Empire, was in sharp contrast to our modern English accusatorial form of prosecution, and the fair or unfair treatment of a defendant both in the interrogatio and in the admission of evidence depended upon the sense of justice and the integrity of the presiding judge.

Upon the completion of the evidence the presiding officer of the quaestio asked the jurors if they were ready to vote. In some cases one or many members of the jury might respond that it was not clear (non liquet) what the decision ought to be, and would like to hear further evidence (ampliatio). Thereupon, in the discretion of the court, a continuance for the purpose of obtaining additional evidence might be granted.[85] In still other cases a comperendinatio, or a new trial, with the consent of the accuser and the defendant, might be agreed upon. If so, it was regularly held on the third day.

In case there was no delay the votes of the jury were collected immediately upon the conclusion of the evidence.[86] The jurors were judges both of law and of fact for they represented the Roman people, and had by the law creating the quaestio the delegated authority of the comitia centuriata. Consequently they were not instructed as to the law by the presiding judge. Each juror was given a small tablet, or card, having a waxed surface, and upon this tablet were written an "A" for absolvo, I acquit, and a "C" for condemno, I

---

[85]. Cicero, in Verr. 2, 65, 156.
[86]. Cicero, in Verr. 2, 30.

convict. The juror merely erased the letter he did not wish to vote, and in order to insure absolute fairness and secrecy of the ballot, each juror with outstretched naked arm (the toga being pulled back), and covering the letters on his tablet with his fingers, dropped his ballot in an urn in plain sight of all in open court. There was no retiring of the jury, no consulting among themselves, only a casting of their ballots when the evidence was all presented. After all had voted the praetor or the chairman of the jury drew the tablets one by one from the urn and announced each time the vote. Often among the "A" and "C" ballots would be found a tablet with both of these letters erased and the letters "N. L." (it is not clear) substituted. Sometimes the ballot was simply blank, the "A" and "C" being erased without explanation.

It required a majority to convict, a tie vote being an acquittal.[87] But whether a mere majority of one was sufficient to convict is not clear from the meagre extant writings upon the subject. The probability is that the number necessary to convict varied with the statutes creating the particular quaestiones. In order to prevent the casting of a blank ballot, the Lex Servilia provided that such a ballot should be counted as a vote of guilty.

The votes being counted by the praetor, or other presiding magistrate, he immediately announced the final result. If the accused were acquitted he could not be tried again, unless it was proved that the acquittal was due to collusion between the prosecutor and the accused (praevaricatio). In such a case a second trial might be obtained by another prosecutor.

In case there was a verdict of guilty sentence was immediately imposed. If the punishment was merely a fine, its amount was determined by the praetor in

---

87. Cicero, pro Cluent. 27.

consultation with the judices. In case the penalty was one involving infamia or exile (interdictio aquae et ignis), it was announced by the praetor. The death penalty was very rarely inflicted during the days of the Republic.

There was no right of appeal from the judgment of a quaestio since an appeal (provocatio) was made to the people as a court of last resort, and a quaestio was a commission representing the people.[88] However, the infamia resulting from a sentence could be taken away by a vote of the people, and one could by the same means be recalled from exile. This resulted from the pardoning power of the highest authority, the people themselves. A similar power was exercised by the emperors in later days.

During the long period in which the quaestiones perpetuae were maintained, the comitia centuriata had concurrent jurisdiction with such courts, and, moreover, despite the fact that a quaestio perpetua was in existence for the trial of a certain class of crimes, the comitia at times created a special quaestio for the trial of a particular case falling within such a class. For until the Roman emperors seized absolute power, the supreme judicial authority resided in the comitia centuriata. The Roman senate possessed no general jurisdiction in criminal cases, yet in matters of grave importance to the State, as in the case of the secession of colonies,[89] or in time of public danger when sedition or insurrection threatened the public peace,[90] the senate asserted jurisdiction and either tried such cases itself or appointed a special quaestio to do so. Thus, in the case of Clodius, and also in the

---

88. Cicero, Philip, 1, 9. In the later imperial days, the usual term for appeal was appellatio. See post.

89. Liv. 4, 30; 6, 12.

90. Liv. 8, 18; 9, 26; Cic. ad Att. 2, 24; Cic. in Cat. 1, 2; Sallust, Cat. 29, 50, 52, 55.

case of Milo[91] the senate appointed a special commission for their trials. It was by such an asserted jurisdiction of the senate that Cicero in his consulship prosecuted before that body the Catilinian conspirators, and they were condemned and executed. The political enemies of Cicero later brought about his temporary banishment on the ground that Roman citizens had been unlawfully put to death in that they were condemned by the senate rather than by the people in the comitia centuriata.

"Capital" punishment had a broader meaning in Roman Law than in our law. Capital punishment affected the caput, that is, the status of the condemned, and included penalties resulting in loss of citizenship, or of liberty, as well as of life. The death penalty was known as the summum supplicium. Other punishments were banishment (relegatio, deportatio) flogging, imprisonment, degradation from rank, and fines.

The Roman criminal courts known as quaestiones perpetuae continued till the third century of the present era. They were gradually superseded by courts of general criminal jurisdiction called judicia publica, presided over by regular magistrates. The office of praetor existed during the entire imperial period, and the praetors, whose number varied from time to time, were the judges of the trial courts. Augustus, however, created a new judicial office, that of prefect of the city (praefectus urbi). This official was a regular magistrate and had authority to take all necessary steps to maintain the peace and order of the city.[92] The prefect of the city had great power, both in ad-

91. Cic. pro Milone, 6, 14; ad. Att. 1, 15.

92. The office of prefect was revived in France in the eighth year of the Republic (1800), the title being bestowed on heads of the departments into which the country had been divided by the National Assembly in 1790. The office also exists in a number of other Civil Law countries, the prefect usually being the head of the police department. See Crespin v. United States, 168 U. S. 208, 18 Sup. Ct. 53.

ministrative and judicial matters. His magisterial jurisdiction embraced all criminal offenses committed within the city of Rome [93] and also anywhere within a radius of a hundred miles from the city.[94] He had power to impose sentences of banishment to any island the emperor might prescribe.[95] He could order any one to keep away from the city, or forbid one to carry on any business or profession, even that of practicing law, either temporarily or permanently.[96]

In the judicia publica trial by jury gradually became obsolete, the magistrate acting in the capacity of both judge and jury.[97] Otherwise, the procedure was substantially the same as in the former quaestiones perpetuae. These courts were designated publica since anyone could be an accuser,[98] there being no official prosecutor. The accuser gave notice to the person he was about to accuse to appear before the magistrate at a certain time, and compulsory process, if necessary, could be obtained for his appearance. When the accuser and the accused were before the court, the accuser took an oath as to the good faith of his accusation and stated what his charge was. If the accused denied the charge, it was reduced to writing (libellus, inscriptio) by the judge,[99] signed by the accuser, and a day was fixed for the trial (judicium). As in the quaestiones perpetuae, witnesses were either voluntary or could be compelled by the court to appear and testify. After the presentation of the testimony, the parties or their counsel (advocati) had the right to address the court. Upon the

93. Dig. 1, 12, 1, pr.; 1, 12, 1, 4.
94. Dig. 1, 12, 1, 4.
95. Dig. 1, 12, 1, 3.
96. Dig. 1, 12, 1, 13.
97. Dig. 48, 1, 8.
98. Inst. 4, 18, 1; Dig. 48, 2, 11.
99. A form of one of these informations is given by Paulus in Dig. 48, 2, 3.

conclusion of the trial, the magistrate at once gave judgment and pronounced sentence at once in case of a judgment of guilt. If the judgment were one of acquittal, and it appeared that the charge was unfounded and maliciously made, the accuser was liable to a conviction of calumny.[100] If convicted, he lost the right to appear again as a prosecutor, and in early times he was branded with a "K"[101] upon the forehead. Constantine substituted a similar brand upon the hands and calves of the legs.

Many of the old statutes concerning specific offenses and their respective punishments remained in force during the imperial days, and new statutes and new constitutions of the emperors were promulgated from time to time. In case of convictions under such laws the magistrates imposed the specified penalties. In case, however, of accusations covered by no particular statute (extraordinaria crimina), the punishment, upon conviction, was left to the discretion of the magistrate. The procedure in such cases was also customarily less formal, the written accusation (libellus, inscriptio) being often omitted.

In the Roman provinces, in imperial days, criminal procedure was not as formal as it was in Rome, since it was not restricted by the precedents and customs of the courts in the capital city. The provincial governors[102] had power of life and death (jus gladii) over their subjects, and were authorized to judge according to their own views of public policy, being answerable to the emperor only for an impolitic abuse of discretion. Their jurisdiction extended to all classes of people, both Roman citizens and aliens. The chief

---

100. Dig. 48, 16, 3, 1.
101. The initial of the old Latin Kalumnia.
102. A provincial governor was usually known as an imperial legate (legatus Caesaris). At times, remote districts of a province were governed by a procurator, as for example, in the case of Pontius Pilate, the procurator of Judaea.

provincial court, presided over by the governor, made its own rules and did not hesitate to change them in order to expedite business. The formal, written accusation (inscriptio) was often omitted, and power was vested in imperial legates to deal summarily, and in accord with their own discretion in cases involving any disturbance of the public tranquillity.[103] It was under such plenary powers that the early Christians were relentlessly put to death in various provinces in the periods of religious persecution.[104] Often in the case of certain high crimes no appeal was allowed, and there was no delay in the execution of the sentence even in the case of Roman citizens.

Letters still preserved in the writings of Pliny the Younger throw a very interesting light upon the criminal practice in provincial courts during the reign of Trajan. Pliny was sent by Trajan in 103 A. D. to Bithynia in Asia Minor, as propraetor, or governor, of that province. Pliny found there a number of Christians, and in connection with his duties as a provincial judge he wrote to Trajan a famous letter. A part of this letter reads as follows: "It is a rule, Sire, invariably observed by me to refer to you all my doubts. . . . Having never been present at any trials of those who profess Christianity, I am not acquainted with their crimes, or with the measure of their punishment. I also am in doubt how far it is proper to go in the conduct of an investigation concerning them. . . . The method I have followed in the cases brought before me is this: I have asked whether they were Christians; if they admitted it I repeated the question twice again, threatening them at the same time. If they still persisted I have ordered

---

103. Dig. 1, 18, 3, 12; 48, 3, 6, 1; 48, 13, 4, 2; 48, 18, 22; Tac. 5 Ann. 12, 54.

104. Act. S. Justin. 1, 5; S. Pionii, 3, 20; S. Cyprian, 1, 2, 3; S. Saturnin, 2; Phin. Ep. 10, 97, 98.

them to be put to death.[105] . . . Some others, however, who were found to be Roman citizens I ordered to be sent to Rome for trial. . . . An accusation was presented to me without any name subscribed. It contained a charge against several persons who, upon examination, denied that they were, or ever had been, Christians. They repeated after me an invocation to the gods, and made offerings with wine and frankincense before your statue . . . and even reviled the name of Christ. . . . I thought it proper, therefore, to discharge them. . . . On one occasion I endeavored to extort the truth (concerning their religious practices) by putting to the torture two female slaves who were accused of officiating in the ceremonies of the Christians, but I was able to discover nothing more than an absurd and excessive superstition. I thought it proper, therefore, to adjourn all further proceedings in order to consult with you."

To this letter of Pliny, the emperor Trajan replied as follows: "The method you have employed, my dear Pliny, against those Christians who were brought before you, is entirely proper, since it is not possible to lay down any fixed rule by which to act in all cases of this nature. . . . If they are brought before you, and the charge is proved, they must be punished, with the restriction, however, that when the accused denies he is a Christian, and shall make it evident that he is not by invoking our gods, he should be pardoned. Accusations without the accuser's name subscribed ought not to be received in prosecutions of any sort, since it introduces a very dangerous precedent. Such

---

[105]. I have translated Pliny's word "supplicium" as the death penalty which I think he meant. Summum supplicium is the technical phrase for the death penalty, but supplicium alone was often used in that sense.

a practice is by no means agreeable to my government."

The ordinary procedure in the provinces regularly began by an arrest made by the police (milites stationarii), who forthwith took the prisoner to an examining magistrate known as the irenarcha,[106] an officer corresponding to our justice of the peace. This magistrate interrogated the prisoner and decided whether there was probable cause for holding him for trial. If so, the prisoner was either detained and the irenarcha sent a written report of the case (notarium, elogium) to the governor (praeses) of the province, or the prisoner was sent directly to the governor together with the report. The actual trial was conducted in its entirety (ex integro audiendi)[107] by the praeses, or governor who travelled through his province holding court at various towns.[108] The local irenarcha appeared at these trials and prosecuted his cases, and if it appeared that his report was malicious he himself was liable to punishment.[109]

In order to elicit testimony, torture was frequently employed in all trials whether in the provinces or in Rome. This method of compulsory evidence was limited, legally, to slaves, and especially used in cases where their masters were accused of crime.[110] It was declared, however, that testimony of this nature was to be received with caution.[111]

Appeals were recognized in the criminal procedure

106. Dig. 48, 3, 6; 50, 4, 18.
107. Dig. 48, 3, 6.
108. Even in the days of the Republic the same practice was followed, as, for example, by Julius Caesar when he was pro-consul of Gaul. He held court in various places. De Bello Gal. 1, 54; 6, 44. Each province was divided into districts, and the pro-consul travelled from district to district.
109. Dig. 48, 3, 6.
110. Dig. 48, 18, 1, 1.
111. Dig. 48, 18, 1, 23.

of Rome, but the right to appeal did not exist in all cases. Our word "appeal" is derived from appellatio which was not originally used in the same sense. Appellatio was an application to a consul, or to a tribune of the people, in the days of the Republic, to obtain their intervention for the purpose of preventing an injustice that would result if the judgment of some other magistrate were executed. The two consuls, during the Republic, exercised the imperium independently. There was no "appeal" in its literal sense of a rehearing of a case, but each consul could interpose his veto (intercessio) to any judicial act of the other in both civil and criminal matters. The appellatio if granted and followed by a veto afforded no affirmative relief in the sense of reversing the judgment, it merely operated as a stay, and prevented the judgment from being carried into effect. In the same way after the creation of the office of tribune of the people, a tribune could veto the official acts of consuls and praetors.

The technical word for an appeal in our modern sense of the term was provocatio, especially during the days of the Kingdom and of the Republic. In the very early days of Rome we read [112] that Horatius, the sole survivor of the three Horatii who defended the city against the Curatii, and who murdered his sister, appealed from the sentence of death, imposed upon him by the two commissioners (duo viri) appointed by the king to try him, to the people. During the early Republic the Valerian Law [113] gave such a right of appeal (provocatio) to any Roman citizen condemned for a crime, the appeal being from the consul to the comitia centuriata. This was an appeal in its strict technical sense, not a review of alleged errors, but a

112. Livy, 1, 26.
113. From Valerius, one of the early consuls. This law, passed in 508 B. C., has been called "the Roman Habeas Corpus Act."

trial de novo, a rehearing upon the merits of the case with a new judgment. It applied only to criminal cases, for at that time in civil cases no appeal was allowed. After the institution of the quaestiones perpetuae which, as already stated, were commissions with the delegated power of the comitia centuriata, no appeal to the whole body of the comitia was allowed.

A later method of appeal, and like unto our modern practice, was developed during the Empire. From the time of Augustus, the comitia centuriata no longer had the imperium, the supreme judicial power. The emperor by virtue of his life office as tribune, and also by the doctrine that the power of the people was likewise vested in him, vetoed and set aside such magisterial acts and decrees as he disapproved. This prerogative was applied to both civil and criminal cases, and during this period of procedure the words appellatio and provocatio were practically synonymous in civil cases, although provocatio remained the technical term for criminal appeals.[114] Augustus planned a two-fold division of appeals between himself and the senate. Appeals from the imperial provinces were to be made to the emperor, while appeals from Rome, Italy, and the senatorial provinces were apportioned to the senate. Under this arrangement there was no appeal from the senate to the emperor, its jurisdiction being final.[115] However, as the imperial power became more and more absolute in the course of time, the appellate jurisdiction that Augustus had assigned to the senate was taken over by successive emperors so that as a result all appellate jurisdiction was centered in them. Later, however, judicial matters, including appeals, were left almost entirely to the magistrates, the emperor intervening only in special cases

---

114. Dig. 49, 1, de appellationibus, employs both terms for civil appeals.

115. Dig. 49, 2, 1, 2.

in which he was interested or which were brought to his attention by political influence.

The creation by Augustus of the office of prefect of the city of Rome has already been mentioned. When Constantinople became the capital of the Empire, a prefect of the city was also appointed for that city. This prefect was, within the territorial limits of his jurisdiction, the executive officer of the Emperor, and all other administrative officials were subject to his authority.[116] There was, moreover, another even more important office, and one that is often confused with that of the city prefect. It was the office of the pretorian prefect. Originally, as created by Augustus, the pretorian prefect was the commander of the praetorian guard, the personal bodyguard of the emperor.[117] Later, it became the most powerful political office in Rome, second only to the emperor himself. The pretorian prefect thus became like unto a prime minister, or a grand vizir, of the sovereign. He administered all departments of the government, the army, the finances, and the judiciary. He was also the representative of the emperor in appeals from the provinces. Among the distinguished incumbents of this great office were the eminent jurists Papinian, Paulus, and Ulpian. Not at all times, however, was the office filled by worthy men. In the reign of Tiberius, the pretorian prefect for many years was the notorious and monstrous Sejanus.

The authority of the pretorian prefect became so great in judicial matters that no appeal could be made from his decisions.[118] Such appeals were at first

---

116. Cod. 1, 28, 1.

117. The office of praefectus praetorio (prefect to the pretorium) is said to have been suggested by the ancient magister equitum, the military commander selected by a dictator armed with supreme authority. Dig. 1, 11, 1, pr.

118. Dig. 1, 11, 1, 1.

allowed, but subsequently this right of appeal was taken away, the emperor holding that they who were appointed to this exalted office ought to be men of such character and attainments that they would pronounce the same judgments as would the emperor himself.[119]

At times a special magistrate was appointed by the emperor with a provision that his judgment should be final.[120] In all other cases, however, the decision of an ordinary magistrate was appealable. In Rome, the practice was to appeal from the magistrate to the prefect of the city,[121] while in the province an appeal lay from the proconsul, or governor, to the pretorian prefect.[122]

The procedure upon appeal where the right existed was a petition presented to the magistrate who decided the case requesting that an appeal might be granted,[123] and a judge who unjustly refused to allow an appeal was subject to a fine.[124] In such a case, upon the judge's refusal, the appellant could carry his appeal directly to the higher magistrate.[125] The case was heard anew by the appellate judge who could admit new evidence, if desired, the case being an actual retrial of the cause just as if no previous trial had been held.[126] Such is the strict meaning of appeal in our own law, a trial de novo in distinction from a review of judicial errors.

Roman criminal procedure influenced the procedure in criminal cases in every country of conti-

119. Dig. 1, 11, 1, 1; Cod. 7, 62, 19.
120. Dig. 49, 2, 14.
121. Cod. 7, 62, 17 and 23.
122. Cod. 7, 62, 32, pr.
123. Dig. 49, 1, 1, 4.
124. Cod. 7, 62, 22.
125. Dig. 49, 5, 5, pr.
126. Cod. 7, 62, 6.

[Roman Law]

nental Europe, and a modern English or American visitor who has some knowledge of Roman Law can see in the criminal trials of these countries many evidences of the inquisitorial methods of the Roman days, a system in strange contrast to the accusatorial procedure of his own country. Even those countries which have in late years undergone great changes in political theories and legal doctrines still retain in their criminal procedure many customs which are centuries old. This is true of Italy, Germany, and even Russia, as the writer observed during several months recently spent in visiting their courts. With the exception of the employment of a jury in criminal cases which at the present time is used only in France, such mode of trial having been discarded by Italy and Germany in the past few years, the general plan of procedure is much the same. Particularly is this the fact in Italy and France.

To get a closer view of this procedure, let us visit a criminal trial in France. In a felony case the prosecution is divided into three stages, the preliminary examination; the formal accusation based upon a review of the evidence obtained in this examination; and the trial proper. The preliminary examination is secret, and according to the French Code of Criminal Procedure must take place within twenty-four hours after the arrest. It is conducted by a judge, known as a juge d'instruction, of whom there are over fifty in the city of Paris alone. This judge examines the prisoner and then either discharges him or holds him for the next court, the Court of Accusation. The examining judge informs the prisoner that he may refuse to be examined until he obtains counsel, and in such a case counsel is given another twenty-four hours' notice of the examination. The judge interrogates the defendant, calls the witnesses, decides what witnesses are material, and asks all the questions. The judge may also issue search warrants in order to get into the custody of the court any papers or anything else relating to the alleged crime. There is no immunity for witnesses, and they are never excused on the ground of self-incrimination. The purpose of the personal examination of the defendant is to obtain his confession if possible. The entire proceeding is a sort of judicial "third degree." The testimony is reduced to writing, and this record, known as the dossier, is sent to the Court of Accusation in case the prisoner is held for trial.

The Court of Accusation consists of five judges. If the prisoner is held for this court, the record transmitted to it by the juge d'instruction is carefully examined. The witnesses who testified in the preliminary examination can be again called, also the prisoner, and even the examining judge can be cited to appear as a witness. No new witnesses, however, are called. This court can also discharge the prisoner if it considers the evidence insufficient to convict. If, however, the court believes the prisoner guilty, a formal accusation is drawn, corresponding to our information or indictment although much more voluminous. This accusation, together with all the evidence reduced to writing is then transmitted to the trial court proper, the Court of Assize.

The trial itself is public and oral. There are three judges upon the bench, one of whom, the president of the court, takes full charge of the proceedings.

The first proceeding is the selection of the jury. Prior to the French Revolution there was no jury in France in any court, but since that time a jury of twelve has been used for the trial of the most serious offenses. The jury list is prepared annually by canton officials in each arrondissement. The arrondissement revises and submits its list to the Department. From this final departmental list a jury panel of 36 names is drawn for each quarterly session of the provincial assizes and as often as may be required for the Paris assizes. Just before the trial begins the jury is selected from this panel in the presence of the prisoner. The President draws the names of the jurors one by one and reads the name of each juryman as drawn. He asks if there is any objection which is indicated by the public prosecutor or by defendant's counsel by simply raising his toque (the small, black hat worn by advocates), no word being uttered. If no toque is raised there is no objection. The prosecutor and defendant are each entitled to twelve peremptory challenges and no more, not even for cause. Upon the acceptance of the twelfth name the regular jury is completed. Then two additional names may be drawn to provide substitutes in case of the illness or death of a regular juror. The drawing is quickly done, objections are very few, and there are no delays as with us. All the jurors are sworn to pronounce a just verdict and to declare, in case of a verdict of guilty, whether there are any extenuating circumstances. This is a very important part of a French verdict since a finding of extenuating circumstances materially affects the sentence, reducing, it may be, in a capital case, a sentence of death to one of comparatively brief imprisonment. Instead of returning a general verdict of guilty or not guilty, as in this country, the jury is told to bring in what we call a special verdict, that is, to answer a series of questions, such as, First, in a murder case, for example, did the defendant commit the act? Second, if he did, was the act done in self-defense? Third, if not done in self-defense, was the defendant mentally responsible? Fourth, if mentally responsible, were there extenuating circumstances? Upon the answers to these, or other questions, the judges will either discharge the accused or assess the penalty.

The two substitute jurors sit near the regular twelve, but take no part in their deliberations unless they may be substituted in case of a possible emergency.

The next step is the reading, by the clerk, of the arret en renvoi (the record) of the Court of Accusation and then he reads the long, rambling indictment. Thereupon, the President explains to the jury the nature of the case and the charge, reading from the dossier of the examining magistrate the substance of the evidence, and giving that magistrate's views concerning the guilt and character of the accused. Then he usually begins his own inquisitorial examination of the defendant. This examination is not obligatory but is discretionary with the court. It may, moreover, be made at this stage of the proceedings or at any time during the trial. It is a most strange and amazing practice to one familiar with criminal trials in this country or in England. It usually consists of an examination into the heredity, past life, habits, and reputation of the defendant, or, rather, these matters are usually stated by the judge from information collected by the police department. The demeanor of the presiding judge as he conducts this inquisition is sometimes very stern, like unto an indignant master who is accusing a disobedient servant. The judge with great skill often interrogates the accused concerning the most petty details of his life. Matter having no connection with the charge at bar is spread before the jury, the purpose appearing to be to confound the defendant, and to compel him to confess. It is the modern form of the Inquisition, a sort of mental torture derived from the physical torture of Rome and of the Middle Ages. However, even if the defendant should confess he is not necessarily found guilty by the jury, since the law requires that the prosecution must always establish the guilt of the accused. Nevertheless, a confession has great weight with the jury. It seems to be the intention that the jury shall be informed of all the evil that is known or even suspected in the life of the defendant in order that they may understand with what sort of a man they are dealing, and that they may more readily believe him guilty of the crime with which he is charged. Now and then, however, one whose past life has been free from serious fault is able to parry the insinuations and innuendoes of the court, but such cases are rare. Moreover, an accused person is seldom free from nervous excitement and apprehension, and, therefore, is usually at a great disadvantage in defending himself. On the other hand, a bold and resourceful criminal succeeds, at times, in baffling and outwitting his judicial tormentor.

The witness stand is between the dais and the advocates, and it is partly inclosed with a top railing. Here the witness stands while giving his testimony.

The witnesses are called from an adjoining room one by one, but after giving their testimony they are permitted to remain in the court room. When the witness comes in, he is sworn, unless, as is regularly done, the witnesses are sworn as a group and then excluded from the court room until individually called.

The French criminal code provides that a witness shall as far as possible give his testimony without being questioned by anyone. Often the witness's recital is prolix, irrelevant, and immaterial, a strange mixture of fact, opinion, and hearsay, including what the witness knows and what he suspects, often requiring an interruption by the President. The witness is, moreover, interrupted, at times, by one or many persons in the audience who express their approval or disapproval as the partisans of either side like or dislike what has been said. This may require the ringing by the President of the little bell upon his desk as an order for silence.

The code provides that a witness may refuse to answer any questions put to him either by the court or by counsel. However, if he is willing to answer questions, and he usually is, the President asks the procureur and counsel for the defense if they wish to ask questions. If so, they state what they wish to have brought out and, thereupon, the judge puts the questions himself. The judge, moreover, decides the materiality and relevancy of each question. When a witness in making his statement contradicts what a previous witness has said, the presiding judge may recall the previous witness and the two are made to "confront," as it is called, each other. Not infrequently they, thereupon, engage in a wordy and angry denunciation of each other's testimony.

Upon the completion of the evidence the procureur addresses the jury and he is followed by counsel for the defense,[127] the code providing that the defense shall have the closing argument. Thereupon the President of the court instructs the jury as to the form of their verdict. No instructions are given, however, upon the law of the case since instructions as understood in our procedure are forbidden by the code.

A unanimous verdict is not required. Seven votes, or a majority of the twelve, is sufficient to convict. If the jury is evenly divided, six to six, on the question of guilt, the accused is acquitted. Consequently there is never as in England and America, a "hung jury." The term "reasonable doubt" in criminal cases is

127. In France, a tort action based on a criminal act may be tried in connection with the criminal action, thus avoiding a separate trial. The plaintiff in such a case is called the "civil party," and counsel for this party may also address the jury who by their verdict may determine the civil liability of the accused as well as his criminal guilt.

unknown to French Law since the code expressly provides that the only test for a juror is whether he has "a sincere personal conviction" of the guilt of the accused. This instruction is printed upon a tablet posted conspicuously in the jury room.

While a trial in a French court of assize is sometimes long drawn out, even at times much longer than a similar case in an American court, yet no time is wasted, as is frequently and notoriously the fact in our courts, in selecting a jury, and many cases last only two or three hours. Moreover, there is not the scandalous delay after delay so common in our American practice in the proceedings after the trial. In France, punishment after conviction is usually sure and swift. There are no motions for new trials for a court of assize has no power to grant a new trial. The Court of Cassation may, upon appeal, grant a new trial for errors of law, but this is seldom done. In most cases a verdict of conviction by the trial jury is a finality.

The criminal procedure of the Civil Law is often compared with that of our law to the great disparagement of the former. It is said that the Civil Law does not protect the rights of accused persons as does our law, and that in this respect our law is far in advance of the Civil Law. Our law, it is said, provides greater safeguards for persons unjustly accused of crimes, and the inquisitorial methods of the Civil Laws are tyrannical and barbarous in comparison with the fairer and more humane accusatorial method of our law. Our presumption of innocence and our rules of evidence are bulwarks of personal security, it is asserted, against abuses of judicial authority. The Civil Law may be more scientific, more equitable, it is said, in its principles of private law, yet as far as procedure in criminal cases is concerned, our law is manifestly superior.

To the extent that such comparisons are confined to the modern procedure in English and American courts on the one hand and in Civil Law courts on the other, the matter is merely one of opinion. Many who are familiar with both the American and the French methods of procedure prefer the French since they believe it is more efficient. French jurists are also of the opinion that their method of examining the defendant in criminal cases is just as advantageous to the accused as to the government, since a skillful investigator can quickly determine whether there is any cause for detaining an accused person for trial, and an innocent person is, accordingly, promptly released. Each country prefers its own method.

In making comparisons, however, between these methods of criminal procedure, and extolling the Common Law at the expense of the Roman and Civil Law, many seem to forget that what we call, to-day, "Common Law procedure" is not the same procedure which was followed for centuries in the English criminal courts.

On the contrary, our present day criminal procedure is not ancient. It is not even the same procedure that was followed in England three hundred years ago, or even two hundred years ago and less. The "Common Law procedure" in criminal cases in Coke's day would be regarded today, as barbarous. Many of the doctrines that are familiar to us to-day in connection with the rights of accused persons are comparatively modern in their origin. Our constitutional rights in criminal cases were won only after centuries of injustice and cruelty practiced in the name of law.

Those who point in condemnation to the imperial Roman Law which permitted the torture of slaves, and to the inquisitorial, ecclesiastical law of the Middle Ages which practiced the torture of accused heretics, apparently forget that in England, long after the discovery of America, confessions were extorted by the torture of accused persons and the testimony thus obtained was admitted against them. In the reign of Henry VI, the rack was imported from the Continent, and in the reign of Henry VIII, "the Scavenger's Daughter" was invented by Skevington the Keeper of the Tower. The rack tore apart the joints of an accused person. The "Scavenger's Daughter," a hideous machine for compressing the body, crushed the legs into the thighs, and by means of iron bands forced the entire body into a human ball, many bones being often broken by the horrible instrument. In the reign of Elizabeth, torture continued to be practiced, and for a long period accused persons were thus compelled to incriminate themselves and others. Down to the times of the Commonwealth it was the usual practice to convict persons accused of treason on the written testimony of persons not before the court, and often this testimony was obtained by bribes or by compulsion.

In the reign of Henry VIII, Sir Thomas More, Ex-Chancellor of the realm, was accused falsely and maliciously of treason, tried by the judicial puppets of the King, and condemned without a shred of real evidence against him. After his execution, his head was placed upon a pole and exposed on London Bridge to the gaze of the multitudes. A modern Lord Chancellor [128] has said, "After the lapse of three centuries, considering the splendor of More's talents, the greatness of his acquirements, and the innocence of his life, we must still regard his murder as the blackest crime that ever has been perpetrated in England under the form of law."

In Throckmorton's case, tried in the reign of Mary, the depositions of two witnesses imprisoned in the

---

128. Lord Campbell, in his "Lives of the Lord Chancellors," 5th Ed., Vol. 2, p. 59.

Tower and forced to testify were read. The accused was not permitted to have counsel or even witnesses. It was an arbitrary, ex parte proceeding, a mockery of justice. The judges openly assumed the guilt of the prisoner, and made it very evident to the jury that they believed him guilty. Throckmorton complained of the injustice of his treatment, yet it was only the usual course of procedure at that time.

In Sir Walter Raleigh's trial, in 1603, in the reign of James I, the court was composed of eleven commissioners of oyer and terminer. Four were judges, and seven were laymen. Among the judges were Chief Justice Popham and Lord Cecil, the latter a bitter enemy of Raleigh. Coke, "the father of our Common Law," was attorney-general at the time and was, accordingly, the prosecutor. He subjected Raleigh to outrageous insult, calling him "a damnable atheist," "a spider of hell," "a viperous traitor," "an odious fellow, hateful to all the realm of England."[129] A modern English judge, an ultra conservative and inclined to defend the procedure of those intolerant and tyrannical days, has said that the rancorous ferocity of Coke was never imitated before or since in any English court of justice, except perhaps in those in which Jeffreys presided.[130] Raleigh was convicted upon the unsupported written testimony (a letter) of Lord Popham, an alleged accomplice, who had repudiated his letter but was not permitted to testify that his letter was not a truthful statement.

In the trial of the regicides in the reign of Charles II, forty-nine persons were indicted, and the same tactics of angry and brutal denunciation of the accused by the court and prosecutor were employed. Cromwell, Ireton, and Bradshaw were dead, but Parliament passed an act of attainder against their lifeless

---

129. 2 St. Trials, 1073.
130. Stephen, Hist. of the Cr. Law, I, 333.

bodies. They were taken from their graves at Westminster Abbey, their corpses hanged at Tyburn, and then buried again beneath the gallows. Twenty of the forty-nine who were indicted escaped from the country. They were, thereupon, declared outlaws, and some of them were captured and taken back to England and executed without a trial by virtue of the outlawry act of 1662.

The trial of Stephen College, in 1681, was another iniquity. He was a "Protestant joiner" and was accused of saying treasonable words at Oxford. He was permitted after his arrest to have pen, ink, and paper, but after he had made notes for his defense they were all taken from him and used against him by the prosecution. He was denied counsel, and despite contradiction after contradiction by witnesses for the Crown he was convicted and executed.

In 1683, Lord William Russell and Algernon Sidney were tried for treason. Both were unjustly convicted and beheaded. The brutal Jeffreys, who presided, acted more like a prosecutor than a judge. Again, in the trial of Lady Alice Lisle, who was illegally convicted and sentenced, in 1665, to be burnt alive for harboring two rebels (at the time of Monmouth's insurrection), the conduct of Judge Jeffreys was infamous. He swore and railed at the chief witness for the Crown, compelling him to say what the prosecution wished him to say. The jury, not satisfied with the evidence, brought her in "Not Guilty," but the execrable judge, in great fury, sent them out again, yet they brought in a verdict of "Not Guilty" the second time. Then Jeffreys flew into a transport of rage, and threatened the jury with attaint of treason. Overcome with fear, the jury the third time brought her in "Guilty." [131]

It was not until 1695 that persons indicted for treason were allowed to have a copy of the indictment, and to be assisted by counsel. It was in 1702 that in felony cases witnesses for the defense were first permitted to testify under oath. For many years after this period witnesses were allowed to tell their story in their own way. It was not until the middle of the eighteenth century that trials in England in criminal cases began to be similar in their procedure to what they are to-day, and it was not till 1849 that persons accused of crime had any legal right to know what evidence was to be brought against them, since the preliminary investigation was secret. In 1836, it was first provided that all persons on trial should have a right to inspect all depositions against them (6 & 7 Wm. IV, c. 114, s. 4), and in 1849 (11 & 12 Vict. c. 42, s. 27) it was enacted that an accused person should be permitted to have a copy of the depositions. In 1868 (30 & 31 Vict. c. 35), a statute was passed authorizing accused persons to call witnesses before the examining magistrate and to have them, if necessary, bound over to appear at the trial and to have their expenses allowed.

It should be evident from these facts relating to the old procedure in English courts, that there is no ground for the statement that the criminal procedure of our Common Law has more jealously preserved the rights of accused persons than has the Civil Law. Our modern procedure in criminal cases has had a very deplorable background, and only after generations of barbarity and misery has it arrived at its present excellence in England, which, in some respects, could be followed in this country for greater efficiency, promptness, and justice. In our own country we have gone to the other extreme. We have preserved so meticulously "the rights of the accused" that society has long suffered, and our inefficiency in the prosecution of criminals is a reproach. Unless we can

131. State Trials, Vol. 11, 372, Notes.

show that our method produces better results than does the Civil Law, both in the prevention of crime and in the protection of society, we are hardly justified in insisting upon the superiority of our procedure.

INDEX

A

	PAGE
Absolvo	694
Acceptilatio	515, 521, 537
Accessio	333, 336, 338
Accessio temporis	345
Accessory things	320
Accursius	175
Acilian Law	204
Acquisitio hereditatis	481
Acquisition of property	324

Actio—

Ad supplendam legitimam	609
Aestimatoria	446
Communi dividundo	480
Damni injuria dati	509
De pauperie	499
De recepto	482
Direct	446
Empti	446
Exercitoria	426
Familiae erciscundae	480
Finium regundorum	480
Furti	492, 509, 661
Furti oblati	491
Furti prohibiti	489, 490
Hypothecaria	381
In factum	509
In personam	301
In rem	301
Institoria	427
Legis Aquiliae	497
Locati	448
Mandati contraria	461
Mandati directa	461
Per condictionem	632
Pro socio	455
Publiciana	346
Quod metus causa	396
Recepticia	470
Redhibitoria	446
Rerum amotorum	492

Actio—continued PAGE
    Utilis 563
    Venditi 446
Actions, in general 626
    Classification of—
        Arbitrary 658
        Civil and praetorian 656
        Direct and contrary 659
        Direct and noxal 659
        Direct and utilis 660
        Fictitious 660
        In factum concepta 660
        In factum prescriptis verbis 660
        Mixed 661
        Real and personal 655
        Stricti juris and bonæ fidei 541, 542, 657
        To enforce penalties 661
        To recover property 661
    Limitation of 529, 662
Actor 639
Actus 362
Addictio 330, 331
Addictio bonorum libertatis causa 547
Aditio 603
Adjudicatio 332, 334, 640
Adjunctio 334, 340
Admiralty 55, 75
Adoption .... 246 et seq.
Adpromisor 418
Adstipulator 418
Advocates 651
Aediles 98, 128
Aelian Code 110
Aestimatum 466
Affinitas 214, 219
Agency 424, 459
Agnates 551, 553
Agnatic family 253
Agnatio 214
Agnitio 560
Agrarian laws 114
Agreement not to sue 534
Alaric, Breviary of 13, 14
Album judicum selectorum 689
Aliens (see Peregrini) 198
    Incompetent to make will 591
Alluvio 324, 339

[Roman Law]

INDEX 723

	PAGE
Altius tollendi	367
Amalfi	165
Ambitus	367
American Law's debt to Roman Law	4
Ampliatio	694
Animus furandi	487, 488
Antestatio	627
Antichresis	383
Apocha	523
Appeal—	
Civil	670
Criminal	680, 702–706
Appellatio	670
Aquaeductus	363
Aquaehaustus	363
Aquilian Law	495–498
Aquilian stipulation	523
Arrogatio	246, 247
Artificial persons	274
Ascendants	571
Assessors	506
Assignatio	332
Auctor	348
Auctoritas	264, 268, 269
Auctoritatis interpositio	265
Authentic act	352
Avulsio	339
Azo	72. 175

B

Bail	628, 630
Bailments	55
Banishment	206
Bankrupt debtors	666
Bankruptcy	671
Barter	444
Bartolus	176
Basilica Julia	637
Basilicas	637
Beneficium	65, 305
Inventari	604
Betrothal	220
Blackstone	35–37, 56, 57, 85
Bologna, Law School	18
Bona	300
Bona fides	328, 444
Bona materna	258

724 INDEX

	PAGE
Bonitary ownership	326
Bonitary title	561
Bonorum emptor	540
Bonorum possessio	556, 557
Contra tabulas	558, 585
Cum re	562
Secundum tabulas	558, 585
Sine re	562
Bracton	71
Breviarium Alarici	13
Bryce	32

C

California	47, 48
Calumnia	699
Canada	52, 53
Canon Law	57, 61, 62, 74, 75, 82, 172
Canuleian Law	100
Capitis deminutio	204
Maxima	205
Media	206
Minima	205
Capito Gaius Ateius	120, 121, 126
Caput	184
Catilinian conspirators	697
Causa	410, 411, 464
Causa mortis gifts	133, 430
Cautio	437
Caveat venditor	445
Censors	208, 256
Central American Law	55
Centumviri	635
Centuries or Hundreds	94
Checks upon litigation	672
China	29, 30
Chirographa	433, 435
Citations, Law of	146–149
Citizenship	198, 199, 201
City prefect	667
Cives	96, 198
Clients	93
Codes—	
Gregorian	143, 144, 149
Hermogenian	143, 144, 149
Laws of Oleron	76
Laws of Wisby	76

INDEX 725

Codes—continued. PAGE
Napoleon 11, 12, 41, 42
Theodosian 146-150
Visigothic 150
Codex Gregorianus 143, 144, 149
Codex Hermogenianus 143, 144, 149
Codex Justinianus (Code of Justinian) 155, 168
Codes Vetus 158, 169
Codex Theodosianus 146-150
Codicils 611, 613, 614
Codification—
  Roman Law 8, 9
  Modern Civil Law 9, 10
  English Law 9
  American Law 9, 10
  Chinese Law 29, 30
  Japanese Law 30, 31
  Ethelbert 62
  Wessex 62
  King Alfred 63
Coemptio 223
Cognates 555, 560, 565-568
Cognatio 214
Cognitiones 660
Cognitors 638
Collaterals—
  When entitled to inherit 571, 572
College of Pontiffs 101
Collegia .... 279 et seq.
Comitia—
  Centuriata 91, 94-98, 104, 106, 113, 117, 680, 696
  Curiata 94, 95, 680
  Tributa 94-96, 98, 106, 108, 680
Commentators 175
Commixtio 340
Commodatum 416, 438
Common Law—
  Influence of Roman Law .... Chapter III
  Influence of Church 57, 61, 62
  Influence of Lanfranc 65
  Influence of Henry II 68- 70
  Writings of Bracton 71, 72
  Maritime Law not part of 76
  In California 48
  In Louisiana 40, 41
Common Law marriage 227
Communio 476, 479, 484
Compensatio .... 539 et seq.

726 INDEX

	PAGE
Comperendinatio	694
Concubinage	230
Condemnatio	640
Condemno	694
Condictio	632
Conditions	407
Suspensive or resolutive	408
Impossible conditions	408
Confarreatio	222
Confusio	334, 340, 515, 530
Consensual contracts	442
Consideration and causa	410
Constantine	143
Constitutio	141
Constitutum	424
Constitutum debiti	469–471
Consuls	96, 119
Contio	681
Contracts—	
Parties	392
Consent	394
Effect of force and fear	395
Effect of fraud	397
Effect of mistake	399
Illegal agreements	403
Time of performance	404
Place of performance	407
Conditions	407
Real contracts (Re)	438
Verbal contracts (Verbis)	438, 441
Consensual contracts (Consensu)	438, 442
Contracts for work and labor	447
Innominate real contracts	462
Unilateral and bilateral	392
Contra tabulas	558
Contubernium	232
Convicium	501, 503
Corporate property	282
Corporations, in general	274
Influence of Roman Law on English	55
Corporations sole	292
Capacity to be made heirs	597
Corporeal things	310
Corpore corpori	498
Corpus	284
Corpus Juris Civilis	150, 154 et seq.
Correal creditors	418

INDEX 727

	PAGE
Correal debtors	418– 420
Correality	418, 421
Correus	418
Council of Trent	227
Crimen falsi	685
Criminal Law (see also Procedure, criminal)	
In general	Chapter XXIII
In Louisiana	42, 43
Cujas	11, 177
Culpa	414, 495, 498
Cura	263
Curators	268, 270, 271
Curia	289
Curiæ	92
Curtesy	574
Custom of Paris	38, 39, 46, 53

D

Damnum infectum	635
Damnum injuria datum	485, 495
Dare, facere, præstare	389
Datum corpori	496
Debtors under law of Twelve Tables	633
Decemvirs	99
Decretum	141
Decretum of Gratian	173
Dediticii	202
Degrees of blood-relationship	567
Dejectum effusumve aliquid	507
Delatio of inheritance	603
Delators	122
Delegatio	525
Delicts	485
Furtum	487
Rapina	487
Damnum	487
Injuria	487
Demonstratio	640
Denunciatio	381
Denuntiatio	669
Depositum	439
Derivative titles	347
Descendants—	
When entitled to inherit	571
Descent and distributions—	
Influence of Roman upon English Law	575
Dies (day of performing obligation)	404– 406

728 INDEX

	PAGE
Dies fasti and nefasti	637
Diffareatio	236
Digest 88, 94, 109, 115, 128–134, 155, 160–	163
How cited	164
Oldest manuscript	165
Diligentia	415
Disinheriting clause of will	605
Dissolution of obligations	515
By performance	515, 516
By formal release	515, 521
By novation	515, 524
By praescription	515, 528
By merger	515, 530
By impossibility of performance	515, 530
By agreement not to sue	515, 534
By litis contestatio	516, 538
By set-off	516, 539
Divine Law	306
Divisible things	315
Divorce	232
By diffarreatio	236
By remancipatio	236
By mutual consent	235
By repudium	237
Divortium	235, 237
Bona gratia	235
Mala gratia	235
Dolus	397, 414, 446
Dolus malus 414, 416, 487, 493, 495,	598
Domat	11
Domestic heirs	549
Dominium	325
Donatio	350, 351
Donatio ante nuptias	230
Donations	428
In vivos	428
Causa mortis	429, 430
Restrictions upon	429
Doneau	11
Dorotheus	160, 166
Dos	229, 430
Dower	574
Dowry (dos)	229, 430
Ductus aquae	355
Duplicatio	642
Duumviri capitales	680, 703
Dutch Law	50, 51

E

	PAGE
Easements (see Servitudes)	55
Ecclesiastical Law (see Canon Law)	66
Edicta repentina	127
Edictum	141
Edictum Perpetuum (see Perpetual Edict)	127, 141
Emancipation	260
Embezzlement	438
Emphyteusis	354, 375, 384
Emptio-venditio	442–444
England—	
Early settlement	60– 68
Roman Law influence	68– 74
Decline of Roman Law in	75– 78
Roman Law, in Courts of Equity	54, 79, 80
Epistula	141
Equites, or Knights	95
Equity	1, 3
Influenced by Roman Law	54, 79, 80
Error	399
Error in corpore	400
Error in materia or substantia	401
Euric, Laws of	13, 14
Ex bono et aequo	4, 561, 563
Exceptio	642, 643, 669
Exceptio doli mali	543
Execution of judgments	671
Exercitor	426
Existimatio	207
Expensilatio	433, 435
Expromissio	525
Extraneous heirs	549
Extraordinary Procedure	665

F

Falcidian Fourth	604
Falcidian Law	608
Familia	212
Familia pecuniaque	548
Familiae emptor	548, 584
Fasces	105
Ferae naturae	308
Feud	64, 65, 305
Feudal system	64, 65
Fictions in pleading	648
Fideicommissa	293, 598, 612, 613, 618, 619 et seq.
Fidejussio	422, 423

	PAGE
Fidepromissio	422
Fiducia	379
Filia familias	253
Filius familias	253
Fiscus	284, 293
Florida	49, 50
Forms of Wills	582
In calatis comitiis	582
In procinctu	582, 583
Per aes et libram	583
Praetorian	585
Testamentum militis	587
Formula	640
Demonstratio	640
Intentio	640
Adjudicatio	640
Condemnatio	640
Formula in factum concepta	646
Formula in jus concepta	646, 647
Formulary Procedure	636
Forum	637
Forum Judicum	14
Fraud	397
Freedmen	184, 185
Freemen	93
French Law—	
Customs	10, 11
Codification	10- 13
In Canada	53
In Louisiana	40, 41
In Missouri	43
In New Mexico	49
In Northwest Territory	46
Fructus	333, 336
Fuero de las Leyes	15
Fuero Real	15
Fungible things	316
Furtum	485- 487
Manifestum	488, 491
Nec Manifestum	488, 490
Conceptum	488, 489
Oblatum	488, 491
Future things	320

G

Gaius	129, 130, 135
Institutes of	130

INDEX 731

PAGE

Gens 92, 213, 551, 554
German Civil Code 21, 22, 23
German Law 19- 23
Gestio 264
Gibbon 1, 122, 141
Gifts 230, 351, 428–430, 473
Glossators 174
Gratian 173
Gregorian Code 143, 144, 149, 156, 158
Guardian and Ward 55, 262, 479
Guardianship of women 263
Guilds 278, 280

H

Habitatio 356, 360, 384
Hadrian 125
Hadrian's Edict 128
Half-blood 572
Heir 577
    Definition 581
    Who may be 595
    Must be certain 596
    Corporation 597
    The fiscus 597
    Churches 597
    Institution of 599
    Joint heirs 602
    Alternate heir 602
    Liability of heir 604
    Inventory by 604
    Falcidian Fourth 604
    Duties of an heir 622
Heirs, classes of 549
Hereditas 548, 581
Hereditas jacens 293
Hermogenian Code 143, 144, 149, 156, 158
History of Roman Law .... Chapters IV and V
Hotchpot 565
Husband and Wife 214, 560, 568, 573
Hypotheca 354, 381, 469, 472

I

Illegal promises 430
Immaginaria Solutio 521
Immovables 300–305, 314
Imperator 126
Imperium 557, 677, 680, 703, 704

732 INDEX

	PAGE
Impubes	262
Inaedificatio	334
Infamia	209, 461
Infants	262, 267, 393
Ingenui	184, 204
Inheritance	546
Succession to	548
Delatio	603
Aditio	603
Inheritance taxes	576
In jure cessio	331
Injuria	485, 501
Injuria atrox	503
In jus vocatio	636
Innkeepers	506, 509
Innominate real contracts	462, 464
Insane persons	216, 393, 591
Insinuatio	429
In solido, in solidum	417–420
Insolvent debtor	540
Institutes—	
Gaius	130
Justinian	129, 130, 150–155, **166** et seq.
Institution of an heir	599, 601
Insulae	368
Intentio	640, 669
Intercessio	670, 703
Interdicts	663
Prohibitory	663, 665
Restoratory	663
Exhibitory	663, 664
Quorum bonorum	561, 562
Unde vi	664
Uti possidetis	664
Utrubi	664
Interest	446
Intestate succession	546
Under the Twelve Tables	551
Praetorian succession	551, 556, 558 et seq.
Under Justinian's 118th Novel	570
Inventory by heir	604
Irnerius	174
Italian Law	18
Iter	362

J

Japanese Law	30

INDEX 733

	PAGE
Javolenus	60
Jettison	452
Rhodian Law	482
Joint-heirs	603
Joint-ownership	456
Judex	116, 630, 638, 650, 666
Judices	688–690
Judicia abolished	668
Judicia publica	697, 698
Judicium populi	681
Julian's Edict (Hadrian's Edict)	128
Jura in personam	386, 387
Jura in re aliena	354
Jura in rem	386
Jurisprudentes	120
Jurors (judices)	688–690

Jus—
    Definition 4, 180
    Civile 3, 87, 89, 96, 105
    Gentium 1, 3, 87, 89, 105, 140, 182
    Honorarium (Praetorian) 87, 183
    Naturale 182
    Commercii 203
    Connubii 199, 203
    Disponendi 325, 347
    Edicendi 104
    Eundi 362
    Honorum 199, 209
    Papirianum 91
    Pontificum 126
    Postliminii 205
    Suffragi 199, 209

Justa causa	324, 349, 410, 464
Justinian	152
His 118th Novel	570
Succession under	575
Justitia (justice)	4
Justus titulus	324

K

Kansas	43
Kent	6, 32
Kings of Rome	89 et seq.
Koran, The	28

L

Labeo, Marcus Antistius	120, 121, 123, 126

	PAGE
Laesae majestatis	679
Laesio enormis	447
Landlord and tenant (locatio-conductio rei)	448
Lanfranc	65
Larceny	488
Law (jus, definition)	4
Public and private	181
Law-courts	637
Law Merchant	76
Law of Citations	146–149, 157
Law of Nature	182
Law Schools	11, 18, 66, 67, 69, 150, 151
Laws of Oleron	76
Laws of Toro	15
Laws of Twelve Tables	88, 92, 100–102, 110
Lawyers	651 et seq.
Legacy	613, 614
Forms of	616, 618
Restrictions upon	619
Legatum	330, 333, 334
(See also Legacy)	
Leges Regiae	91
Legis Actiones	627
Per condictionem	627, 632
Per judicis postulationem	627, 631
Per manus injectionem	627, 632
Per pignoris capionem	627, 634
Sacramento	627–630
Abolished	635
Legitim	608
Legitimacy—	
By subsequent marriage	78, 242, 244
By curial membership	243
By imperial rescript	242
Legitimi, succession of	565
Leonine partnership	453
Letting and Hiring	442–450
Lex	180
Acilia Repetundarum	690
Aebutia	635, 636
Aquilia	495–498, 502
Calpurnia	632
Calpurnia Repetundarum	683
Cannuleia	217
Cincia	429
Cornelia	593
Cornelia de falsis	683, 685

INDEX 735

Lex—continued.   PAGE
  Cornelia de incendio 684
  Cornelia de parricidiis 683
  Cornelia de sicariis 499, 684
  Cornelia de vi 684
  Claudia 208
  Fabia de plagiariis 684
  Falcidia 608
  Junia 203
  Leges Juliae—
    Adulteriis 237, 684
    De anona 684
    De majestate 122, 684
    De vi 684, 685
    Peculatus 684
  Maria de ambitu 683
  Papia 598, 621
  Papia-Poppaea 217
  Plactoria 269
  Poetilia 634
  Pompeia de parricidiis 684
  Publilia 98, 108
  Rhodia de jactu 451
  Sempronia 689
  Servilia 695
  Silia 632
  Voconia 598
Lex Romana Burgundiorum 150
Lex Romana Visigothorum 13, 150
Liability for causing death 499
Liability of judex 506
Libel 503
Libellary procedure 665
Libellus 665
Liberi, succession of 564
Liber Judicum 14
Libripens 313
Libro de las leyes 15
Licinian Laws 103, 113
Licinian Rogations 103, 105, 113
Lictors 105
Limitation of actions 662
Literis 436, 437
Litis contestatio 516, 538, 645, 669
Loans for consumption 217
Locatio-Conductio 440, 442, 447
  Rei 447, 448
  Operarum 447, 450

Locatio-Conductio—continued. PAGE
  Operis 447, 450
  Merces 447
  Warranty of fitness 449
Louisiana 38– 43
Lucri causa 487
Lumina 369

M

Mancipatio 197, 313, 330, 432
Mancipative will 583
Mancipium 330
Mandatarius 427
Mandate (mandatum) .... 427, 442, 457 et seq.
Mandator 427
Mandatum qualificatum 424, 459
Manumission 192
Manus 221, 225
Marital fourth 573
Marriage .... 212, 215, 217 et seq.
  Cum manu 221
  Sine manu 221, 229
  By proxy 228
  By confarreatio 222
  By coemptio 223
  By usucapio, or usus 223, 224
  By jus gentium 224– 226
Married women—
  Contractual capacity 394
  Capacity to make will 592
Materfamilias 225
Merger 515, 530
Metus 395
Mexican Law—
  In California 47, 48
  In New Mexico 49
Minors (minores XXV annis) 216, 262
Missouri 43, 44
Mistake 399
Modalities 404
Modern Civil Law practice .... 673 et seq.
Modestinus 135
Mohammedan Law 27– 29
Mora 534
Moral turpitude 210
Mortgage 55, 354
  Fiducia 379
  Pignus 380

Mortgage—continued. PAGE
Hypotheca 381
Movables 300, 302, 303, 305, 314
Municipal corporations 279–281, 286
Municipia 280, 281
Mutuum 318, 433

N

Napoleon 12
Naturales liberi 231
Naturalization 202
Natural Law 182
Nazi Regime and German Law 22, 23
Necessary heirs 549
Negligence 414
Negotiorum gestio .... 476 et seq., 484
New Mexico 48, 49
New trials 654
New York 50, 51
Nexum 432, 517
Nomina 437
Non liquet 694
Nocturnal thief 492
Northwest Territory 45, 46
Nota censoria 208
Novation .... 515, 522, 524 et seq.
Novels .... 157, 170 et seq.
Novissima Recopilacion 17, 52
Noxal action 510
Nudum pactum 390, 410
Nueva Recopilacion 16

O

Oath (witness) 651
Obligations, in general .... 386 et seq.
    Arise how—
        Ex contractu 389, 431
        Quasi ex contractu 389, 474, 476
        Ex delicto 389
    Kinds of—
        Naturales and civiles 390
        Civil and praetorian 391
        Stricti juris and bonae fidei 391
    Plurality of parties 417
    Obligations in solidum 417
    Modalities 404
    Performance of 516

[Roman Law]—47

Obligations, in general—continued. PAGE
    Impossibility of performance 402, 532
    Dissolution 515
Obligations between guardian and ward 479
Obligatory rights 388
Occupatio 333, 334, 351
Old Code 158, 169
Oneris ferendi 367, 371
Operae servorum 356, 361
Oratory in Roman courts 652
Original ownership 333, 351
Ownership 326
    Restricted by law 379
Own heirs 549, 550

P

Pacts 462, 467
    Adjecta 468
    Vestita 468
    Praetorian 468, 469
    Legitima 468, 472
Pactum de dote 474
Pactum de non petendo 515, 534
Pactum de pecunia constituta 424
Pandects 155
Papinian (Aemilius Papinianus) 60, 86, 132–135, 161
Papinianistae 132
Papirian Law, the 91
Paraphernal property 230
Parent and child 241
Partidas 15, 52
Partnership (see Societas) 281, 442
Paterfamilias 212, 253
Patria potestas 214, 241, 253, 259, 677
Patricians and plebeians 98
Patrimony 306
Patroni 651
Paulus, Julius 60, 134, 135
Pauperies 499
Pauperistae 67
Payment 517, 518
Peculium 256, 257
Peculium adventitium 574
Peculium castrense 257
Peculium quasi-castrense 258
Pensio 376
Per aes et libram 313, 432

[Roman Law]

	PAGE
Per capita	571
Per condictionem	632
Perduellio	679
Peregrini	198, 394
Periculum rei	443
Per judicis postulationem	631
Per manus injectionem	632, 634
Permutatio	444, 465
Perpetual Edict	127, 128, 667
Per pignoris capionem	634
Person, meaning of	183, 276
Personal rights	386
Personal servitudes	355, 371
Usus	355
Usufructus	355
Persons, law of	180 et seq.
Natural and juristic	184
Sui juris and alieni juris	196
Per stirpes	571
Philippines	52
Piae causae	295
Instituted as heir	597
Pictura	334, 340
Pignus	354, 378, 380, 440
Plantatio	334, 340
Pleadings, civil actions—	
Proceedings, Legis Actiones	627
Formulary procedure—	
Demonstratio	640
Intentio	640
Adjudicatio	640
Condemnatio	640
Exceptio	642, 643
Praescriptio	645
Replicatio	642
Duplicatio	642
Triplicatio	642
Fictions	648
In jus concepta	646, 647
In factum concepta	646
Libellary Procedure	665
Oral	629, 639, 669
Plebeians	90, 98
Plebiscites	98, 183
Plebs	93, 97, 98
Pledge (see Pignus)	440
Pliny's letter to Trajan	700

	PAGE
Plurality of parties (Obligations)	417
Pontifex Maximus	101, 222
Porto Rico	52
Possession	327
Natural	327
Civil	328
Justa	328
Injusta	328
Bonae fidei	328, 337
Malae fidei	328, 337
Longi temporis	343
Posthumous children, succession of	552
Postliminy	593
Pothier	11, 177
Praedial servitudes	361, 364
Rural	356, 362
Urban	356, 367
Praedium	315
Praefactus urbi	697
Praescriptio	334, 343, 351, 515, 528 et seq.
In pleadings	645
Praescriptis verbis	660
Praetor	119, 639, 666
Peregrinus	109, 115
Urbanus	109
Fideicommissarius	621
Praetorian Law	87, 105, 183
Praetorian pacts	468, 469
Praetorian prefect	122, 667, 705
Praetorian succession	556
Liberi	564
Legitimi	565
Cognati	565
Vir et uxor	568
Praetorian will	585
Praetorship	102, 104, 106
Praevaricatio	695
Precarious benefice	305
Precarium	360, 466
Prefect of the City (see also City Prefect)	697, 705
Presumption of innocence	692, 693
Price	443
Principal and accessory things	320
Privata delicta	485
Private law	181
Probatio	691

INDEX 741

Procedure, civil— PAGE
    Under the jus civile, Legis Actiones 627
    Formulary procedure 636
    Extraordinary procedure 665
    In jure 630, 638, 650
    In judicio 630, 638, 649
    Law courts 637
    Summons 636
    Bail 628, 630
    Trial 651
    Witnesses 630
    Vindex 628
    Advocati 651
    Judgment 653
    New trials 654
    Appeals 670
    Execution of judgments 671
Procedure, criminal 687
    Postulatio 687
    Citatio 687
    Interrogatio 687
    Inscriptio 687
    Trial by jury 688-690
    Probatio 691
    Amount of proof 692, 693
    Verdict 694, 695
    Sentence 695
    Appeals 680, 702, 703, 706
    Punishments 697, 699
    Trials before comitia centuriata 681, 682
    Quaestiones 682, 685, 697
    Later judicia publica 698
    Provincial trials 699, 700
    Trials, modern France ...... 707 et seq.
    Civil Law compared with Common Law 713
Proculians 120, 121, 123
Procuration 428
Procurators 638
Projiciendi jus 367, 368
Promisor 418, 434
Proof, amount required 692, 693
Property, acquisition of 324
Property, definition of 579
Property, divisions of 298
Property, Law of ...... 298 et seq.
Property, "real and personal" in English Law 303
Property rights 325

742 INDEX

	PAGE
Proprietas	325
Prospectus	370
Provocatio	703
Proximi agnates	553
Proximi agnati	553
Prudentes	506
Puberes minores XXV annis	216, 262
Publica crimina	485
Public law	181
Public wrongs	485
Evolution slow	671-678
Kings vested with imperium	677, 680
Time of Twelve Tables	678
Appeals in early times	680
Trials before comitia centuriata	681
Contiones	681
Quaestiones	683, 685
Special statutes	684, 685
Various offenses	685, 686
Publilian Laws	106
Punishments	697, 699
Pupillus, pupilla	263

Q

Quaestio, quaestiones	682, 685, 697
Quasi contracts	462, 474
Quasi delicts	485, 504, 513
Unjust judgment	505
Dejectum aliquid	507
Suspensum	507
Wrongs by servants	509
Quasi torts and crimes	510
Quebec	53
Querela inofficiosi testamenti	607
Quiet possession	445
Quintus Mucius Scaevola	115, 116
Quiritary Law	89, 96
Quiritary owner	326
Quirites	96
Quorum bonorum	561, 562

R

Rapina	485, 487, 493
Real and personal actions	301
Real contracts	438
Real rights	386, 387
Real servitudes	370

INDEX

	PAGE
Receipt for payment	523
Receptum arbitrii	469, 472
Receptum nautarum, cauponum, stabulariorum	482
Recopilacion de las Indias	16, 40
Recording of gifts	429
Recuperatores	647
Rei promittendi	418
Rei stipulandi	418
Release	515, 521
Religious gifts	295
Rent	376, 448, 449
Replicatio	642
Representation	424
Repudium	237
Res, meaning of	299
Alicujus	308
Communes	307, 310
Corporales	307
Divini juris	310
Fungibiles	316, 319
Immobiles	305, 314, 321
Incorporales	310
Mancipi	312
Mobiles	305, 314, 321
Nec mancipi	312
Nullius	307, 308
Sacred	306, 309
Universitats	282, 308
Rescripta	141
Resolutive conditions	408
Responsa prudentium	120, 127
Restitutio in integrum	269, 666
Reus	418, 639, 687
Revocability of gifts	429
Right of Search	489
Roman Law—	
Historical outlines	Chapters IV and V
Influence on English Law	Chapter III
To what extent in United States and Canada	Chapter II
Reaction against in England	75, 77, 78
Reasons for study of	33, 34
Tributes to	5–7, 32, 33, 57, 58, 59, 61
World-wide extension of	Chapter I
Rome	2 et seq.
Fall of	147
Rural servitudes	356, 362, 363

	PAGE
Russia	23, 25
Revolution of 1917	24
Recent codes	25

S

Sabinians	121
Sabinus	121
Sacrae	309
Sacramentum	627–630, 636
Sacred Mount	97
Sale	442, 447
Absolute or conditional	447
Caveat venditor	446
Duty of seller to deliver	444
Good faith required	444
Nature of the contract	442
No implied warranty of title	350
Periculum rei	443
Price necessary	443
Sale of land terminates lease	449
Warranty of quality	445, 446
Warranty of quiet possession	445
Satio	334, 340
Savigny	178
Scaevola, Quintus Mucius	115, 116
Scopelismus	685
Scriptura	334, 340
Seals (wills)	585, 586, 589
Secundum tabulas	558
Sella curulis	637
Senate	88, 93, 690
Senatuo consulta	98
Senatus Consultum Claudianum	547
Senatus Consultum Orphitianum	569
Senatus Consultum Pegasianum	624
Senatus Consultum Tertullianum	569
Senatus Consultum Trebellianum	624, 625
Sententiae Receptae of Paulus	134
Servants, wrongs by	509
Servitudes	354 et seq.
How created and lost	372 et seq.
Personal	255, 371
Personal	355, 371
Rural	356, 362, 363
Urban	367
Negative and positive	371
Servius Tullius	90

	PAGE
Set-off	539
Singular succession	547
Slander	503
Slavery, origin	186
Slaves, in general	93, 186 et seq.
Vast numbers	188
Master's power over	189
Peculium	191
Manumission	192
Contubernium	232
As managers of master's business	426
Societas	281, 442, 452, 454
Good faith required	454
Universal	453
Rei unius	457
Leonina	453
Negotiationis alicujus	454
Duration	455
Sodales	280
Soldier's will	587
Solidarity	419, 421
Solidus	473
Solum	314
Solutio	515, 516
Imaginaria	521
Indebiti	476, 480, 484
South America	55
Spain	13– 17
Spanish Law	
In California	47
In Florida	50
In Louisiana	41
In Texas	45
In Philippines	52
Specificatio	334, 341
Spondes, spondeo, verbal contracts	434
Sponsalia	219
Sponsio	422
Spurii	231
Stable-keepers	506, 509
Status of persons	183
Stillicidii	367–369
Stipulatio	433–435, 441
Stipulator	418, 434
Stricti juris (actio)	657
Substitutions, see Fideicommissa	

INDEX

Succession	PAGE
Intestate	546
Under Twelve Tables	551
Praetorian	556
Justinian's 118th Novel	570
Testamentary	577
Singular and universal	547
Sui heredes	549, 550
Sui juris	196
Superficies	354, 367, 377
Suretyship	422, 459, 571
Surface water	364
Suspensum	507
Syndicus (Syndic)	284, 289
Syngraphae	433, 435

T

Tacking	345
Tenancy at will	361
Tenants	358, 360, 375, 449
Tender	520
Oblatio	520
Obsignatio	521
Deposito	521
Testamentary succession	577
Testamenti factio	591
Testamentum	549, 577
In comitiis calatis	582
In procinctu	582, 583
Per aes et libram	583
Praetorian	585–587
Injustum	599
Inofficiosum	607
Irritum	610
Ruptum	610
Militis	587
Texas	44, 45
Theodosian Code	146–150, 156, 158
Theophilus	160, 166
Things, Law of, see Res	298
In commercio	306
Extra commercium	306
Consumable and inconsumable	305, 316
Corporeal and incorporeal	307, 310
Divisible and indivisible	305, 315
Fungible and non-fungible	316, 319
Mancipi and nec mancipi	312

INDEX 747

Things, Law of—continued. PAGE
    Movable and immovable 314, 321
    Principal and accessory 305, 320
    Public and private 306
    Single and collective 320
Tigni immitendi 367, 368
Time of performance of contracts 405
Traditio 324, 347–352
Treasure-trove 335
Trial by jury 687–690
Trial of Sir Thomas More 715
Tribonian 159, 166
Tribunes 98, 119
Tripertita 110
Triplicatio 642
Trusts, see Fideicommissa
Turkey 25, 26
Turpis causa 413
Tutela 263
    Impuberum 263
    Mulierum 263, 268
    Tutors .... 264 et seq.
Twelve Tables 88, 100, 126, 489–492

U

Ulpian (Domitius Ulpianus) 60, 134, 135
Unde liberi, unde legitimi, unde cognati 560
Unde vi 664
Unduteous will 608
Unilateral contracts 392
Universal succession 547
Universitas 274, 282
Universitas rerum 547
Unjust enrichment 481
Unjust judgments 505
Urban servitudes 367
Usucapio 330, 342, 344, 351
Usufruct 288, 355, 356
Usufructuary 357, 358
Usus 355, 356, 358, 384
Uti possidetis 664
Utrubi 664

V

Vacarius 67, 86, 175
Vades 628
Valentinian Law of Citations 157
Valerian Horatian Laws 100

	PAGE
Valerian Laws	87, 97, 680
Venditio sub hasta	332
Verbal contracts	441
Verbis	434
Verdict, criminal cases	694
Via	355, 363
Vinculum juris	388, 411, 431, 515
Vindex	628
Vir et uxor, succession of	560, 568, 573
Vis	395
Visigothic Code	14
Vis major	482
Voconian Law (heirs)	598
Voluntary heirs	549

W

Ward, see Guardian and Ward, Tutela
Warranty—
  Against eviction 445
  Of fitness 449
  Of quality 445, 446
  Of title 445
Waste 357
Waters, surface 364
Will (see Testamentum) 549
  Definition of 577
  Purpose of 581, 588
  Forms 582, 583, 585
  Execution of 588, 589
  Essential part 588
  Capacity to make 590–593
  Witnesses 593
  Illustration of will 599
  Disinheriting clause 605
  Unduteous will 608
  Codicils 611
  Legacies 614
Witnesses—
  In mancipatio (per aes et libram) 313, 331
  In civil actions 630
  In criminal trials 691, 692, 698
  To a will 585–587, 589
      Qualifications 593
Written contracts .... 435 et seq., 443
Wrongs by servants 509

Z

Zeno's constitutio concerning emphyteusis 376

www.ingramcontent.com/pod-product-compliance
Lightning Source LLC
Chambersburg PA
CBHW031152020526
44117CB00042B/228